ML   Nite, Norm N.
105
.N47   Rock on

Cop. 2

14.95

DATE			

© THE BAKER & TAYLOR CO.

ROCK ON

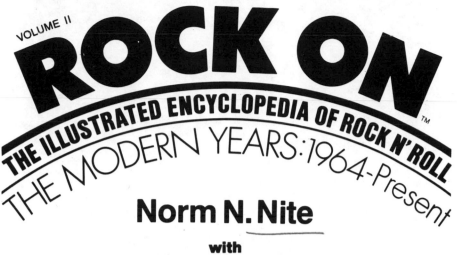

VOLUME II

ROCK ON

THE ILLUSTRATED ENCYCLOPEDIA OF ROCK N' ROLL
™

THE MODERN YEARS: 1964-Present

Norm N. Nite

with
Ralph M. Newman

Special Introduction by Wolfman Jack

Thomas Y. Crowell, Publishers

New York   Established 1834

Designed by Stephanie Tevonian

Library of Congress Cataloging in Publication
Data

Nite, Norm N
   Rock on: the illustrated encyclopedia of rock
n' roll, the modern years.
   Includes discographies.
   1. Rock music—Bio-bibliography. I. Title.
ML105.N47   784'.092'2   [B]   78-3312
ISBN 0-690-01196-2

   79 80 81 82 10 9 8 7 6 5 4 3 2

Dedication

This book is dedicated to both my mother, Jean, and, especially, to the memory of my late father, Jim, whose inspiration and guidance of me towards music, as a youngster, enabled this book to become a reality today.

Contents

Acknowledgments

The depth and complexity of the material covered in the modern years of rock made it necessary to interview many of the most knowledgeable people familiar with today's music market in order to compile the information for this volume. It would never have been completed had it not been for the dedication and comprehensive gathering of material by my researcher, Ralph M. Newman. Without his exhaustive research and efficient organization this book might still be in the writing stage. His research was aided by his wife, Suzanne, along with his good friends Alan Kaltman, of "American Top 40," musician Billy Vera, and Marcy Drexler of Arista Records.

I want to personally extend my deepest gratitude to some dear friends, all of whom gave of their time and knowledge to this project. Thanks to Dick Clark, Wolfman Jack, Don Kirshner, Lou O'Neill Jr., president of the Rock Wire Service, Jimmy "JP" Pullis, owner of JP's and Trax, Tony DeLauro, Dick Fox of the William Morris Agency, Jay Acton, Steve Popovich, Stan Snyder of Cleveland International Records, Micky Eichner of Columbia Records, Bruce Morrow of "Newscenter 4," New York, Kevin G. McCoy, Jack G. Thayer, president of NBC Radio, Michael Purcell, Tom Long, Michael Lynne, Donald Durma, Barbara and Rich Durma, Carolyn and Joe Lascko, Sanford Fisher, and Jeff Mazzei of WNEW Radio.

Heartfelt appreciation to Ron Alexenburg, Bob Sherwood of Columbia Records, Don Imus, Bob Guccione, Jr. of Omni Magazine, Chuck Collier of WGAR Radio, Richard Turk of Colony Records, Randy Hoffman of Champion Music, Brad Hammond and Don Kelly of the Don Kelly Organization, Steve Rubell of Studio 54, Bob Pittman of WNBC Radio, Suzy Phalin, Jerry Wexler, Joe Rock, Bob Schwartz of Laurie Records, Jim Pewter, Kari Clark, Lou LoFredo, Marc Wiener, Denny Greene, Donna Gould, Frank Lanziano, John Welch, Michel Landron, Peter DePietro, Charles Scimeca, Bryon N. Rowland, Phil Dunning, Bruce McKay, Andy Friendly, Rick Carson, Merlin David, Jeff Thompson, and John Zwart.

Special thanks to BMI, ASCAP, Billboard, Record World, Cash Box, Rolling Stone, Les Kippel and *Relix* magazine, Greg Shaw and *Bomp* magazine, Janis Schacht and John Gillespie of Sire Records, Gregg Turner, Robert Pruter, Tommy DiBella, Brandon L. Harris, Cliff White, Sal Passantino, Stan R. Krause, Bob Abramson of House of Oldies, Bill Schwartz, Clark Marcus, Marc Kaplan of Rock Bios Unlimited, Ann Martin, Marc and Natalie Dinkes, Sadie Hollander, Eva H. Newman, Steve and Arlene Coletti, Edward R. Engel, Harriet Wasser, Arthur

Acknowledgments

Berlowitz, Gary Knight and Gene Allen.

A very special thanks for the many sensational photos to Tommy Edwards of Tommy Edwards Record Heaven in Cleveland, Jim Bland of James J. Kriegsmann Copy Art, Sherry Jones of A & M Records, Dennis Fine of Arista Records, Donna Signorini of Atlantic Records, Josephine Mangiarcina of Columbia and Epic Records, Carolyn Glassheim of Big Tree Records, Lea Grammatica of MCA Records, Maureen O'Connor of Capitol Records, Tracy Gold of Casablanca Records, Laurie Kramer of Columbia Records, Don Paulsen of RCA Records, Sari Becker of RSO Records, Vivian Crissy of United Artists Records, Pam Osmundsen of Warner Brothers Records, Janice Azrak of Elektra and Asylum Records, Dot Lenhart and Peggy Parham of Epic Records, Annette Monaco of Capitol Records and Ted and Steve Petryszyn.

And finally to my editor, Buddy Skydell, whose efforts, patience, and dedication to this book made it a reality.

All of the above people gave limitlessly of their time and knowledge in making this the best book ever to deal with the subject matter of rock. We are all friends with one universal interest— a true love of rock 'n' roll and the artists who have made this the world's most exciting music.

Introduction
by Wolfman Jack

Hi, all you fantastic rock 'n' roll lovers out there in rock 'n' roll land! I see you definitely got your face in da right place!

If you've already got Norm N. Nite's first *Rock On* (and what fan doesn't?), then you probably thought you knew as much about the insides of rock 'n' roll as anybody around. Hey, 'til now I'd say you did.

When Norm took me out to lunch and told me he had another book, I couldn't believe it. I mean, how much rock 'n' roll can one guy come up with? (But I gotta hand it to ya, Norm . . . you beat me at it again. I don't mean the book, I'm talking about me gettin' stuck with the lunch tab.)

When he finally got around to asking me to write this introduction, I wasn't just flattered . . . I was relieved. In the old days Norm asked me only to do his laundry. (He kept telling me that was how Dick Clark got his start.)

I'll tell ya this much, nobody but nobody has a grasp on what's happened, what's happening, and what's gonna happen with rock music than this guy. I think Alice Cooper writes out his personal diary a month in advance and then gives it to Norm for approval.

And talk about a rock fan who won't give up. To this day Norm refuses to believe that The Beatles ever split up. He thinks they just changed their name to "The Ex-Beatles." And for all we know, Norm is probably right. (He's right about everything else.)

Rock On's not just a significant and meaningful history of modern rock, it's a hand-held supermarket of rock 'n' roll heroics. I doubt if there's a disc jockey anywhere that won't have Norm N. Nite's books next to him when that little red light goes on.

Norm isn't just a good buddy of mine an' everyone else who cares about music past and future, he's one of the best friends rock 'n' roll's ever had. And best of all, he cared enough to put it all down on paper.

An' since Norm has put it all down for ya . . . the thing to do now is just "Rock On." Like we say, rock 'n' roll forever. From Abba to Bill Medley to ZZ Top, they're all here. He picks up where the record liner notes leave off and puts it all between the grooves.

More than a wham-bam, vibratin' book *about* rock 'n' roll since '64, this *is* rock 'n' roll. The only person I figure missing is my Uncle Henry who made some very strange records down in his basement. In fact, if Norm *had* mentioned Uncle Henry's records, the book would probably just get raided by the Board of Health. (Sorry, Uncle Henry . . . you'll have to wait 'til my own book comes out.)

If you could put this book on your turntable, it'd be the greatest LP of 'em all. As it is, it still may be the first of its kind to go platinum. If ya flip the pages real fast, you can almost tap your feet to the inside beat. In fact, if you're in a library right now . . . don't even thumb through it unless you're in a demo booth.

Norm, you keep putting out more books like you're doing, you're gonna be the Guinness of rock 'n' roll. Your publisher's gonna be lookin' over your shoulder every chance they get, if they're not already.

(I'll take back all the kidding I've given ya, Norm, if YOU promise not to take back the free copy you sent me.)

Whatever ya do, man . . . keep up the good work, and don't ever lose your dedication. We don't just thank you . . . we need ya.

And talk about a dedicated rock 'n' roll buff. If Linda Ronstadt was singin' in the bathtub, Norm would definitely just put his *ear* to the keyhole.

Oh, yeah . . . one last message to the *Rock On* readers: From here on out, get yourself down close to the pages. It's all gonna be music to your eyes.

Author's Introduction

About eight years ago, I had an idea of putting together a thoroughly comprehensive book dealing with the recording stars that have made rock music the gigantic industry that it has become today. Little did I know at the time what a monumental task I had undertaken, for the gathering of information on literally thousands of artists was a job in itself. But to make sure this information was accurate and all inclusive was the real task at hand.

After several years on the project, I realized that all the information could not be put comfortably into one book, so I decided to divide it into two. The first was *Rock On: The Solid Gold Years,* which was published in 1974 and covered the years 1950 through 1963; the second, this volume, *Rock On: The Modern Years,* covers the period from 1964 until today.

When Volume 1 was published four years ago, many people wondered why certain performers such as The Beatles, The Temptations, Simon & Garfunkel, and so many others were not included. It was an oversight that in my introduction I did not explain the deliberately planned scope of the first book, nor inform the public that a second volume was forthcoming—which would include all the artists who had Top 100 records from January 1964 through December 1977. Any artist who had hit records during this period

had his/her discography brought up to date as of May 1978. Recording stars whose careers blossomed prior to 1964 are included *in toto* in Volume 1; others, who either made recording comebacks or who had hits consistently through the rock 'n' roll era—such as Paul Anka, Elvis Presley, and Neil Sedaka—were again included in Volume 2. "New" stars—with recording hits *post*-January 1978—will be included in subsequent editions of *Rock On.*

Most people would feel that the first volume of *Rock On* would be the more difficult to put together since it dealt with music of over twenty years ago. However, Volume 2 was the more arduous task, because so much has happened over the past fourteen years . . . with music branching off into so many different directions.

During the fifties there was either Pop music (e.g., Patti Page, Guy Mitchell, Nat "King" Cole, The Four Lads, Johnnie Ray, and Rosemary Clooney) or Rock 'n' Roll, consisting of "White" rock (Pat Boone, Frankie Avalon, Connie Francis, Bobby Darin, Elvis Presley, Dion, and Paul Anka) or Rhythm and Blues (The Drifters, Chuck Berry, Fats Domino, Little Richard, The Coasters, and Sam Cooke). The music was very basic, with simple lyrics about love and romance and a good, driving beat. The artists of the various singing groups remained in the background and rarely moved out on their own.

With The Beatles exploding on the scene in 1964, Pop music began to proliferate. We had the "English" invasion—The Beatles, The Rolling Stones, The Dave Clark Five, The Yardbirds, Herman's Hermits, The Hollies, The Animals, Gerry & The Pacemakers, and The Zombies, to name a few. The "Motown" sound swung into full force with The Supremes, The Four Tops, The Temptations, and Stevie Wonder. Bob Dylan surfaced and introduced a brand-new sound, with lyrics that conveyed deep meaning to millions of young people all over America. The "San Francisco" beat developed with The Byrds, Jefferson Airplane, The Grateful Dead, and Scott McKenzie. (All of these artists were joined by people like Janis Joplin, The Lovin' Spoonful, The Mamas and Papas, and The Turtles.) Then came the "Acid" rock sound of Jimi Hendrix, Cream, and Iron Butterfly. The sixties closed with the beginning of the nostalgia craze—the rock 'n' roll "oldies" shows.

Rock music was big not only on the radio, but on Broadway (with *Hair, Grease, Jesus Christ Superstar,* and *Godspell*), the silver screen (*Woodstock, American Graffiti, Saturday Night Fever,* and *Grease*) and TV ("Happy Days").

The seventies brought a tremendous diversification of rock due, in a large part, to the breakup of The Beatles. The term "rock 'n' roll" became known simply as "rock." And rock music evolved into a multitude of sounds like "Shock" rock with Alice Cooper, Elton John, and Kiss; "Folk/Soft/Ecology" rock with America, John Denver, Olivia Newton-John, and Harry Chapin; "Country" rock with The Eagles and

Linda Ronstadt; "Soul" rock with Earth, Wind & Fire, The Commodores, The Manhattans, and The O'Jays; "Disco" with Donna Summer, K.C. and The Sunshine Band, The Bee Gees, and The Village People; "Punk" rock with Patti Smith, The Dead Boys, Lou Reed, and the Sex Pistols; "Country Pop" with Dolly Parton, Ronnie Milsap, Kenny Rogers, Crystal Gayle, and Willie Nelson; "Jazz" rock with Chicago, Chuck Mangione, Chick Corea, and George Benson. Today, there is such a tremendous crossover of artists that the best way to describe rock is "a contemporary sound listened to by mostly the young or young at heart."

In Volume 1 the criterion for including artists was that if anyone had a chart record on the national charts he or she would be in the book. This would not work for Volume 2, for many of the artists never had chart singles, but instead sold millions of albums. Unlike the fifties, the sixties and seventies became the era of the album as big business. Many artists became very popular on FM radio stations, filled concert auditoriums to capacity crowds, and sold millions of albums while never having a pop single. Therefore, not only artists with hit singles, but those with hit albums had to be included in Volume 2.

Another important factor in deciding who was to be included was the knowledge of today's record buyers. During the fifties not that many people knew or even cared who was in a particular group. Today, not only do they know and care, but there is a tremendous interest in ascertaining the various birthdates and biographical data of each star. Because of the many more entries (a full one-third more) much more research had to go into compiling Volume 2. Consequently, I had many more people working with me researching information from all over the United States as well as the United Kingdom. Heading up the research was my good friend Ralph M. Newman, who was invaluable in compiling the information contained in this book. If there is information omitted, it is because we exhausted every possible avenue to acquire it and were unsuccessful.

Unfortunately, space did not allow me to include a separate entry for every artist who eventually made it on his/her own. What you will find is the artist under the group or groups under which he or she flourished. Only The Beatles and a few others warranted separate entries for each member in addition to their history under the group name.

To sum up, my goal in this huge endeavor was and is to present the most definitive books dealing with the very complex era of rock. I wanted to make sure that any music lover would have all the information possible— both in terms of entries and discographies—on any artists from 1950 until the present. I hope I have accomplished my task, with the aid of the hundreds of people who have given freely of themselves in making this project a reality. To them, along with the thousands of artists who have made rock music a supreme art form, I simply want to say thanks for the millions of people you have made happy, both with your music and help in allowing me to make this book a contribution to the history of rock 'n' roll.

—Norm N. Nite

July, 1978

ROCK ON

Abba

MEMBERS:

Agnetha "Anna" Faltskog Ulvaeus (vocals) /
born: Apr. 5, 1950

Bjorn Ulvaeus (guitar) / born: Apr. 25, 1945

Benny Andersson (piano) / born: Dec. 16, 1946

Annifrid "Frida" Lyngstad Andersson (vocals) /
born: Nov. 15, 1945

HOMETOWN: Stockholm, Sweden

Abba stands alongside Blue Swede as one of only two Swedish rock groups to achieve worldwide success. Their unusual name was formed by combining the first letters of the members' first names.

Although Abba first became a group during the seventies, each of the members had previously enjoyed success. Benny was in a sixties pop band called The Hep Stars while Bjorn sang with The Hootenanny Singers. Their paths crossed in 1966, and they have been musical collaborators ever since. Anna was one of Sweden's most popular female vocalists during the late sixties, and Frida was widely known through her role in the Swedish TV program "Hyland's Corner."

Abba's early efforts as a group brought them major success. Their song "Waterloo" competed against

Abba. Left to right: Benny Andersson, Annifrid Andersson, Agnetha Ulvaeus, and Bjorn Ulvaeus

seven thousand others in the 1974 Eurovision Song Festival and was the first rock song ever to win that contest. It became a multimillion seller throughout Europe, and later became a hit in the United States when Atlantic Records released an English-language version. They have since continued with a series of sixties-flavored hits.

Today Benny and Frida are married as are Bjorn and Anna.

June 74	*WATERLOO* / Atlantic	
Sept. 74	*HONEY HONEY* / Atlantic	
Aug. 75	*S.O.S.* / Atlantic	
Feb. 76	*I DO, I DO, I DO, I DO, I DO* / Atlantic	
May 76	*MAMMA MIA* / Atlantic	
Sept. 76	*FERNANDO* / Atlantic	
Dec. 76	*DANCING QUEEN* / Atlantic	
May 77	*KNOWING ME, KNOWING YOU* / Atlantic	
Oct. 77	*MONEY, MONEY, MONEY* / Atlantic	
Dec. 77	*NAME OF THE GAME* / Atlantic	
Apr. 78	*TAKE A CHANCE ON ME* / Atlantic	

Ace

MEMBERS:

Alan "Bam" King (rhythm guitar) / born: Sept. 18, 1946 / Kentish Town, London, England

Philip Harris (lead guitar) / born: July 18, 1948 / Muswell Hill, London, England

Paul Carrack (keyboards) / born: Apr. 22, 1951 / Sheffield, England

Terry "Tex" Comer (bass) / born: Feb. 23, 1949 / Burnley, Lancashire, England

Fran Byrne (drums, percussion) / born: Mar. 17, 1948 / Dublin, Ireland

This group began as a late sixties pub band called Clat Thyger, which had been formed by "Bam" King and Phil Harris. Through a number of personnel changes they evolved into Flash & The Dynamos and eventually into Ace.

In April 1973 Ace made their first professional appearance at Tally Ho, a club in Bam's native Kentish Town area of London. Although the group suffered badly in the beginning from mismanagement, they were able to survive through the kindness of friends who provided sound systems and much encouragement. After spending over a year on the pub circuit, the members of Ace were about to seek regular jobs to support their families when they were asked to join a British tour with Hawkwind. They were heard and offered a production deal by John Anthony, known for his work with the groups Queen, Genesis, and Lindisfarne. Anthony booked time at Rockfield Studios in Wales, and the material for their first album session included one of Paul Carrack's songs, titled "How Long." It was released as a single on the Anchor label and became an immediate hit in England early in 1975 and, via distribution by ABC Records, became a number one record in the States. The record's success established Ace as a major act on both sides of the Atlantic.

Mar. 75	*HOW LONG (HAS THIS BEEN GOING ON?)* / Anchor	
July 75	*ROCK & ROLL RUNAWAY* / Anchor	

Cannonball Adderley

REAL NAME: Julian Adderley
BORN: Sept. 15, 1928
DIED: Aug. 8, 1975
HOMETOWN: Tampa, Florida

Julian "Cannonball" Adderley was one of the world's leading alto saxophonists; his unusual nickname was a corruption of "cannibal," which he had been called because of his enormous appetite.

Cannonball grew up in Tampa and Tallahassee, Florida, later teaching

Aerosmith. Back row, left to right: Joe Perry, Brad Whitford, Tom Hamilton, Joey Kramer; front row: Steve Tyler

high school music in Ft. Lauderdale. During the mid-fifties he joined the Miles Davis Sextet and his reputation began to develop. In 1959 he formed his own Cannonball Adderley Quintet and became a leading attraction in the jazz world.

By the early sixties Cannonball was beginning to receive popular acclaim via his recordings for the Riverside label, and several of his records were minor chart successes. However, it was his 1967 recording of the Joe Zawinul classic "Mercy, Mercy, Mercy" that gave Cannonball Adderley a top ten record and mass recognition. His popularity from that point on was universal, and one of his last projects was a folk opera titled *Big Man (The Legend of John Henry),* which was released on the Fantasy label in July 1975.

During that same month he suffered a massive stroke which led to his death a month later.

Jan. 67	*MERCY, MERCY, MERCY /* **Capitol**
Apr. 67	*WHY (AM I TREATED SO BAD?) /* **Capitol**
Jan. 70	*COUNTRY PREACHER /* **Capitol**

Aerosmith

MEMBERS:
Steve Tyler (lead vocals) / born: Mar. 26, 1948
Joe Perry (lead guitar) / born: Sept. 10, 1950
Brad Whitford (rhythm guitar) / born: Feb. 23, 1952
Tom Hamilton (bass guitar) / born: Dec. 31, 1951
Joey Kramer (drums) / born: June 21, 1950
HOMETOWN: Boston, Massachusetts

These five young men got together in 1970 and played many local clubs in Boston and the New England area. In many cases they weren't even paid,

3

but they worked for the exposure. Their efforts were rewarded in 1972, when they were signed by Columbia Records. Soon they released their first LP, titled *Aerosmith.*

Since that time the group has blossomed into one of the premiere rock bands of the seventies. The vocalizing of lead singer Steve Tyler gives Aerosmith a unique sound that should keep them around for a long time to come.

Oct. 73 *DREAM ON* / Columbia
June 75 *SWEET EMOTION* / Columbia
Jan. 76 *DREAM ON (rereleased)* / Columbia
June 76 *LAST CHILD* / Columbia
Sept. 76 *HOME TONIGHT* / Columbia
Nov. 76 *WALK THIS WAY* / Columbia
Apr. 77 *BACK IN THE SADDLE* / Columbia
Oct. 77 *DRAW THE LINE* / Columbia
Mar. 78 *KINGS & QUEENS* / Columbia

Morris Albert

BORN: 1951
HOMETOWN: Rio de Janeiro, Brazil

Morris Albert became a musician at age five when he stole the key to the family piano from his mother and, much to her amazement, played the standard "I Wish You Love" entirely by ear. He was encouraged to pursue music and in 1965 formed a band in high school called The Thunders. They became popular, playing parties, school dances, and teen-age clubs with reworked hits of the day. Within two years Morris went solo and landed a job at Rio's top night spot, Canecão, where his reputation began to build.

In 1969 Morris came to the United States for several years and enrolled at Columbia University to study language phonology but returned to Brazil in the early seventies to resume his musical career. By 1975 he was selling out month-long engagements at Brazil's top spots and had been signed to a recording contract, which resulted in one of his own compositions, "Feelings," rising to the number one position not only in Brazil but throughout most of Central and South America as well. An English language version was released in the United States by RCA, remained on the charts for more than four months, and was followed by a best-selling album of original material.

Today Morris Albert makes his permanent home in São Paulo, Brazil.

June 75 *FEELINGS* / RCA
Feb. 76 *SWEET LOVING MAN* / RCA

Allman Brothers Band

MEMBERS:
Gregg Allman (Gregory Lenoir Allman) (organ, guitar, vocals) / born: Dec. 8, 1947 / Nashville, Tennessee
Duane Allman (Howard Duane Allman) (lead guitar) / born: Nov. 20, 1946 / Nashville, Tennessee / died: Oct. 29, 1971 / Macon, Georgia
Berry Oakley (Raymond Berry Oakley) (bass guitar) / born: Apr. 4, 1948 / Chicago, Illinois / died: Nov. 11, 1972 / Macon, Georgia
Dicky Betts (guitar) / born: Dec. 12, 1943 / West Palm Beach, Florida
Jai Johnny "Jaimoe" Johanson (drums) / born: July 8, 1944 / Ocean Springs, Mississippi
Butch Trucks (Claude Hudson Trucks) (drums) / Jacksonville, Florida
ADDED IN 1972:
Lamar Williams (bass guitar) / Hansboro, Mississippi
Chuck Leavell (piano) / Tuscaloosa, Alabama

During the late sixties Duane and Gregg left Nashville for Los Angeles, where they formed a band called Hourglass. After a few mediocre recordings for Liberty Records the brothers left for Florida where they began to do some studio work. While they were in Florida, Rick Hall, who ran Fame Studios near

Allman Brothers Band. Left to right: Dicky Betts, "Jaimoe" Johanson, Butch Trucks, Gregg Allman, Lamar Williams, Chuck Leavell

Muscle Shoals, Alabama, got in touch with Duane about guitar work on a session for Wilson Pickett. Duane went to Alabama, where he remained for several months, backing up such artists as King Curtis, Aretha Franklin, and Arthur Conley. Duane still wanted his own group and formed the Allman Brothers Band during the spring of 1969. A recording contract with Capricorn Records followed shortly. Later that year they had their first LP, titled *The Allman Brothers Band* and within a year became noted as one of the best bands in the rock and blues field.

Tragedy struck the group when Duane Allman and Berry Oakley died almost a year to the day apart, both on motorcycles in Macon, Georgia.

Today, the group no longer exists. Gregg Allman gets publicity because of his on-and-off-again marriage to Cher. Dicky Betts records as a solo on Arista Records while Jaimoe Johanson, Lamar Williams, and Chuck Leavell record with the group Sea Level.

Jan. 71	*REVIVAL (LOVE IS EVERYWHERE)* / Capricorn	
May 72	*AIN'T WASTIN' TIME NO MORE* / Capricorn	
Aug. 72	*MELISSA* / Capricorn	
Nov. 72	*ONE WAY OUT* / Capricorn	
Aug. 73	*RAMBLIN' MAN* / Capricorn	
Jan. 74	*JESSICA* / Capricorn	
Nov. 75	*NEVERTHELESS* / Capricoorn	

Gregg Allman

Dec. 73	*MIDNIGHT RIDER* / Capricorn

Herb Alpert

BORN: Mar. 31, 1935
HOMETOWN: Los Angeles, California

Herb, who cofounded A & M records with his good friend Jerry Moss in 1962, spent most of the sixties as leader of the famous Herb Alpert and the Tijuana Brass. Although the group

5

America. Left to right: Dewey Bunnell, Gerry Beckley, Dan Peek

was very successful, with many hit singles and albums, Alpert wanted to try his hand at more than his trumpet, so during the spring of 1968, he recorded a Burt Bacharach-Hal David composition titled "This Guy's in Love with You." Instead of just playing the trumpet, he sang the tune, a gamble that paid off, for the song became a number one national hit.

Today Alpert continues to run A & M records with Moss and records for the label as a solo performer.

May 68 *THIS GUY'S IN LOVE WITH YOU* / **A & M**
Sept. 68 *TO WAIT FOR LOVE* / **A & M**
June 69 *WITHOUT HER* / **A & M**

America

MEMBERS:

Gerry Beckley / born: Sept. 12, 1952 / Texas

Dewey Bunnell / born: Jan. 19, 1951 / Yorkshire, England

Daniel Peek / born: 1950 / Florida

Although this group first became popular with British audiences, all three members were raised in the United States and were sons of American servicemen. They first met in high school on an Air Force base in England where their fathers were stationed and decided to join forces as an acoustic rock group. In the beginning they played mostly on the base, but in 1971 they auditioned for Jeffrey Dexter and Ian Samwell, who became their agents and got them other work in the London area. By late in the year Samwell had gotten them a contract with Warner Brothers in England, and an album was released. A single from that album, a haunting song called "A Horse with No Name," became a number one record first in England and later in the United States.

By 1974 America had scored with several more hits, but none were nearly as big as the first. Feeling their career needed a boost, they approached producer George Martin of Beatles fame, who agreed to work with them. The first result of that association, a song titled "Tin Man," became a top five record, and they have since had an unbroken string of major hits.

Now, even though Dan Peek has left the group, they still are one of the most successful groups in the rock field, and appeal to many followers of the defunct Crosby, Stills, Nash & Young, whose sound they closely resemble.

Feb. 72	***A HORSE WITH NO NAME / Warner Bros.***
May 72	***I NEED YOU /Warner Bros.***
Oct. 72	***VENTURA HIGHWAY /Warner Bros.***
Jan. 73	***DON'T CROSS THE RIVER / Warner Bros.***
Apr. 73	***ONLY IN YOUR HEART / Warner Bros.***
Aug. 73	***MUSKRAT LOVE /Warner Bros.***
Aug. 74	***TIN MAN /Warner Bros.***
Dec. 74	***LONELY PEOPLE /Warner Bros.***
Apr. 75	***SISTER GOLDEN HAIR / Warner Bros.***
July 75	***DAISY JANE /Warner Bros.***
Nov. 75	***WOMAN TONIGHT /Warner Bros.***
May 76	***TODAY'S THE DAY /Warner Bros.***
Aug. 76	***AMBER CASCADES /Warner Bros.***

The American Breed

MEMBERS:
Al Ciner (rhythm guitar) /born: May 14, 1947
Gary Liozzo (lead guitar, lead vocals) /born: Aug. 16, 1945
Lee Graziano (drums) /born: Nov. 9, 1943
Charles Colbern (bass) /born: Aug. 30, 1944
HOMETOWN: Chicago, Illinois

Members of The American Breed first met in Chicago during the early sixties and decided to form a band to perform in the local teen-age clubs. By 1967 the group had developed an enormous regional following and had

attracted the attention of Bill Traut of the local Dunwich production company, who began producing their recordings for the West Coast Acta label. Their first few records became minor hits, but their fourth release, "Bend Me, Shape Me," brought them major success. They were asked to sing a tune called "A Quiet Place" in the film *No Way to Treat a Lady,* and they followed with several more hits.

By 1969 The American Breed had faded from popularity and the group decided to change its base of operations to Los Angeles. After numerous personnel changes, including the addition of a keyboard player named Kevin Murphey and a female lead singer, they evolved into a group called Ask Rufus (named after a newspaper column). They eventually became known as Rufus (see *RUFUS*), which, led by Chaka Khan, has become one of today's most popular "soul" groups.

June 67	***STEP OUT OF YOUR MIND / Acta***
Dec. 67	***BEND ME, SHAPE ME /Acta***
Feb. 68	***GREEN LIGHT /Acta***
May 68	***READY WILLING AND ABLE / Acta***
Aug. 68	***ANYWAY THAT YOU WANT ME /Acta***

Ed Ames

BORN: July 9, 1927
HOMETOWN: Malden, Massachusetts

Ed was one of the Ames Brothers (see *Rock On: The Solid Gold Years*) who were immensely popular during the fifties until they disbanded in 1959.

In 1960 Ed decided to pursue a career in theater and attended the Herbert Berghof School in New York to sharpen his acting skills. His first role was in an off-Broadway production of

Arthur Miller's *The Crucible,* which was followed by starring roles in *The Fantasticks, Carnival,* and *One Flew over the Cuckoo's Nest.* He then played the role of Mingo on the popular "Daniel Boone" TV series.

All of Ed's recording activity had ceased after he left the brother act; however, in 1964 he received an offer from his former label, RCA, to do an album of Broadway show songs. A single from the album, released in 1965, "Try to Remember," was the first of a string of hits that lasted nearly five years, the biggest of which was "My Cup Runneth Over."

At present Ed Ames lives with his wife and three children in Los Angeles and keeps up a busy schedule of nightclub and TV variety show appearances.

Jan. 65	*TRY TO REMEMBER* /RCA
Jan. 67	*MY CUP RUNNETH OVER* / RCA
May 67	*TIME, TIME* /RCA
Sept. 67	*WHEN THE SNOW IS ON THE ROSES* /RCA
Dec. 67	*WHO WILL ANSWER?* /RCA
May 68	*APOLOGIZE* /RCA
May 69	*SON OF A TRAVELING MAN* / RCA

Lynn Anderson

BORN: Sept. 26, 1947
HOMETOWN: Grand Forks, North Dakota

Lynn Anderson was raised in the San Francisco Bay area of California where her family moved shortly after her birth. Her mother, Liz, dabbled in singing and songwriting while her father, Casey, worked at several odd jobs. While working as a car salesman he met fellow salesman Jack McFadden, who was becoming important in the country music business. McFadden used his connections to get Liz

Anderson's career started and, by the mid-sixties, she was a star. Lynn, still a teen-ager, was beginning to show signs of doing the same.

Lynn first went to Nashville with her mother, who was receiving a BMI award, and auditioned for executives of Chart Records, who signed her to the label. She became popular in the country field and was offered a regular spot on Lawrence Welk's nationally syndicated TV show. Her big breakthrough, however, came in 1970, when she was signed by Columbia Records and recorded the Joe South tune "Rose Garden," which went to the top of both the country and pop charts. Since then she has been one of country music's major stars.

At present Lynn lives in Nashville with her husband, Glen Sutton, a leading writer-producer, and her young daughter, Lisa, while keeping an active schedule of recording and personal appearances. Liz Anderson continues to be as popular as ever, often appearing with her daughter, and Casey Anderson has become one of Nashville's leading music publishers.

Nov. 70	*ROSE GARDEN* /Columbia
May 71	*YOU'RE MY MAN* /Columbia
Aug. 71	*HOW CAN I UNLOVE YOU?* / Columbia
Jan. 72	*CRY* /Columbia
June 73	*TOP OF THE WORLD* / Columbia
Jan. 75	*WHAT A MAN MY MAN IS* / Columbia

The Animals

MEMBERS:
Eric Burdon (lead vocals) /born: May 11, 1941
Hilton Valentine (lead guitar) /born: May 21, 1943
Alan Price (keyboards) /born: Apr. 19, 1942/ replaced by Dave Rowberry /born: July 4, 1943

Bryan "Chas" Chandler (bass)/born: Dec. 18, 1938

John Steel (drums)/born: Feb. 4, 1941/ replaced by Barry Jenkins/born: Dec. 22, 1944

HOMETOWN: Newcastle-on-Tyne, England

This group began in 1958 as The Alan Price Combo. Their name change came about when their audiences began calling them "animals" because of their wild appearance.

During the early sixties The Animals came to the attention of Graham Bond, the noted London bandleader, who became the group's manager and got them work in the London area. By 1964, when Beatlemania was in full swing, The Animals were one of the most popular groups on the London club circuit and were signed by the British Columbia label. They began working with producer Mickie Most, and their first release, "Baby Let Me Take You Home," became a modest hit in England. Their second record was an Alan Price adaptation of the blues standard "House of the Rising Sun," simultaneously released in the United States on the MGM label. It became a number one record in America (the first British post-Beatle recording to do so) and throughout most of Europe. In mid-1965, after several more hits, a conflict developed between Eric Burdon and Alan Price. Price left to form his own group, The Alan Price Set, and The Animals continued as a quartet for the next year. However, more personality problems and personnel changes caused The Animals to disband by late 1966. In 1967 Eric Burdon moved to California and formed The New Animals, which produced hits through the end of 1968. At that point Burdon went solo and The Animals came to an official end.

Burdon later emerged with a group named War and had two hits before separating from them as well. War has become a leading contemporary soul group, and Eric Burdon went on to head his own band, consisting of Randy Rice (bass), Alvin Taylor (drums), and Aalon (lead guitar).

Bryan "Chas" Chandler, after leaving The Animals, was responsible for the discovery of Jimi Hendrix and the management of his career until Hendrix's death in 1970. Chandler currently handles Slade.

Alan Price spent several years in collaboration with English rock star Georgie Fame, with whom he cohosted a British TV show and recorded several albums. That partnership dissolved, and Price is now recording solo.

Hilton Valentine went into retirement for several years for health reasons and returned to recording as a solo act in 1969.

Aug. 64	*HOUSE OF THE RISING SUN /* MGM
Sept. 64	*GONNA SEND YOU BACK TO WALKER* /MGM
Sept. 64	*I'M CRYING* /MGM
Dec. 64	*BOOM BOOM* /MGM
Feb. 65	*DON'T LET ME BE MISUNDERSTOOD* /MGM
May 65	*BRING IT ON HOME TO ME /* MGM
Aug. 65	*WE GOTTA GET OUT OF THIS PLACE* /MGM
Nov. 65	*IT'S MY LIFE* /MGM
Feb. 66	*INSIDE LOOKING OUT* /MGM
May 66	*DON'T BRING ME DOWN /* MGM
Sept. 66	*SEE SEE RIDER* /MGM
Nov. 66	*HELP ME GIRL* /MGM
Apr. 67	*WHEN I WAS YOUNG* /MGM
Aug. 67	*SAN FRANCISCAN NIGHTS /* MGM
Dec. 67	*MONTEREY* /MGM
Apr. 68	*ANYTHING* /MGM
June 68	*SKY PILOT* /MGM
Nov. 68	*WHITE HOUSES* /MGM

Paul Anka
BORN: July 30, 1941
HOMETOWN: Ottawa, Ontario, Canada

Paul Anka made a recording come-back on United Artists Records when he began singing with female vocalist Odia Coates in 1974. (His early career and discography can be found in *Rock On: The Solid Gold Years*.)

July 74	*(YOU'RE) HAVING MY BABY* / United Artists
Oct. 74	*ONE MAN WOMAN/ ONE WOMAN MAN* / United Artists
Mar. 75	*I DON'T LIKE TO SLEEP ALONE* / United Artists
June 75	*(I BELIEVE) THERE'S NOTHING STRONGER THAN OUR LOVE* / United Artists
Nov. 75	*TIMES OF YOUR LIFE* / United Artists
Apr. 76	*ANYTIME (I'LL BE THERE)* / United Artists
Dec. 76	*HAPPIER* / United Artists
Apr. 77	*MY BEST FRIEND'S WIFE* / United Artists
July 77	*EVERYBODY OUGHT TO BE IN LOVE* / United Artists

Apollo 100

Apollo 100 was a studio group made up of the cream of England's session musicians, including Z. Jenkins, Vic Flick, Clem Cattini, Brian Odgers, Jim Lawless, and a full-session orchestra. The group was conceived and assembled by Tom Parker, one of England's leading arrangers.

Parker comes from Newcastle-on-Tyne and taught himself to play piano at the age of six. By the time he was a teen-ager, he was proficient with several instruments and began to perform in local jazz clubs. Soon he was working with various pop groups, including The Mark Leeman Five, Jimmy James & The Vagabonds, and Eric Burdon's Animals. In 1969 he became a full-time session musician and was offered several positions as musical director for TV programs.

Apollo 100 was formed in 1972, and their first recording, "Joy," Parker's adaptation of Bach's "Jesu, Joy of Man's Desiring," became a top ten record in England as well as in the United States. Parker's arrangements of other classical pieces have been successful as well.

At present Tom Parker continues to make recordings with Apollo 100 and is in demand as an arranger of pop recording sessions.

Jan. 72	*JOY* / Mega
Apr. 72	*MENDELSSOHN'S 4TH* / Mega

The Arbors
MEMBERS:
Edward Farran
Fred Farran
Scott Herrick
Thomas Herrick
HOMETOWN: Ann Arbor, Michigan

This vocal group was formed during the mid-sixties by two pairs of brothers (the Herrick brothers are twins) who were attending the University of Michigan. After adopting the name of their hometown, they established a local reputation with a vocal sound reminiscent of The Four Freshmen.

In 1966 The Arbors were signed by Columbia's subsidiary Date label and began a string of middle-of-the-road hits with "A Symphony for Susan." After their national popularity subsided during the early seventies, they moved their base of operations to Chicago, where they are active today in the field of radio and television commercials.

Oct. 66	*A SYMPHONY FOR SUSAN* / Date
June 67	*GRADUATION DAY* / Date

10

Feb. 69 *THE LETTER* / Date
May 69 *I CAN'T QUIT HER* / Date

Nov. 69 *JINGLE JANGLE* / Kirshner
Mar. 70 *WHO'S YOUR BABY?* / Kirshner
July 70 *SUNSHINE* / Kirshner

The Archies

Ron Dante
BORN: August 22, 1945
HOMETOWN: Staten Island, New York

The Archies were created by rock entrepreneur Don Kirshner after the success of an animated television program based on the comic-strip character Archie. The Archies' sound was aimed squarely at the pre-teen market and was one of the first examples of what was to become known as "bubblegum" music.

The Archies were a studio group whose personnel varied from record to record, with the exception of Ron Dante, who always sang lead. Ron has been the voice of several other studio groups as well and is best known for his recordings as The Detergents ("Leader of the Laundromat") and The Cuff Links ("Tracy").

Other participants in The Archies' many records were Toni Wine, Jeff Barry, Ellie Greenwich, Andy Kim, Tony Passalacqua (lead singer of the fifties group The Fascinators), and Ray Stevens, who reportedly joined in the prominent hand claps heard on the group's multimillion selling "Sugar Sugar."

Ron Dante continues to be a leading studio singer and is active in commercials. In 1975 he emerged as the producer of Barry Manilow's hits and released a recording of "Sugar Sugar" under his own name produced, in turn, by Barry Manilow!

Sept. 68 *BANG SHANG A LANG* / Calendar
Dec. 68 *FEELING SO GOOD* / Calendar
July 69 *SUGAR SUGAR* / Calendar

Argent

MEMBERS:
Russell Ballard (guitar) / born: Oct. 31, 1947 / Waltham Cross, Herts, England / replaced (1974) by John Verity and John Grimaldi
Rodney Terence Argent (keyboards) / born: June 14, 1945 / St. Albans, Herts, England
James Rodford (bass) / born: July 7, 1945 / St. Albans, Herts, England
Robert Henrit (drums) / born: May 2, 1946 / Broxbourne, Herts, England

One of the leading groups to emerge from the mid-sixties in England was The Zombies. By the summer of 1967 problems had begun to develop within the group and Rod Argent, their leader and principal songwriter, disbanded The Zombies in favor of a new band.

The new group, Argent, made its debut in early 1969, ironically at a time when an earlier Zombies recording, "Time of the Season," had been released and was at the top of the charts. During 1970 and 1971 Argent released two albums, *Argent* and *Ring of Hands,* which were successful. However, it was their 1972 single release, "Hold Your Head Up," that reached the top five and brought the group international recognition.

In mid-1974 Russ Ballard had left the group for a solo career and was replaced by two guitarists, John Verity and John Grimaldi. The expanded band continued to tour, and Russ Ballard released an album on the Epic label. He also became active as an independent record producer and songwriter.

June 72 *HOLD YOUR HEAD UP* / Epic

Ashford & Simpson

Ashford & Simpson

MEMBERS:
Nicholas Ashford /born: 1943/Willow Run, Michigan
Valerie Simpson /born: 1948/Bronx, New York

Nick Ashford and Valerie Simpson became a team during the early sixties, when they recorded briefly as Valerie & Nick for producer Henry Glover. However, real success came a few years later when they joined first Scepter Records and then the Motown organization, not as recording artists, but as songwriter-producers. In that ca-pacity they were represented on the charts with dozens of major hit songs, including "Ain't No Mountain High Enough," "Ain't Nothing Like the Real Thing," "California Soul," "Let's Go Get Stoned," "Reach out and Touch," "You're All I Need to Get By," and numerous others.

In 1974 they returned to recording and hit the charts with a song titled "Anywhere." However, they continued their activities as writers and produc-ers for Motown and in 1975 succeed-ed in launching a new act called The Dynamic Superiors for the label.

Jan. 74 *ANYWHERE* / Warner Bros.
Mar. 78 *DON'T COST YOU NOTHING* / Warner Bros.

The Association

MEMBERS:

Russ Giguere (guitar) / hometown: Portsmouth, New Hampshire / replaced by Richard Thompson / born: Oct. 18, 1945

Gary Alexander (guitars) / hometown: Chattanooga, Tennessee / replaced (1967) by Larry Ramos

Jim Yester (guitar, keyboards) / hometown: Birmingham, Alabama

Terry Kirkman (woodwinds, keyboards) / hometown: Salinas, Texas

Brian Cole (bass) / born: 1944 / Tacoma, Washington / died: Aug. 2, 1972

Ted Bluechel, Jr. (drums) / hometown: San Pedro, California

The Association was formed by Terry Kirkman (who also wrote most of their material) and Gary Alexander, a veteran of several rock groups. They auditioned members and rehearsed the group for its debut at The Ice House in Pasadena, California, in early 1965. Their popularity led to a contract with the local Davon record label, where their first release was "Along Comes Mary." The record was so popular that Davon sold it to a larger company, Valiant Records. Partially because of unclear lyrics, supposedly drug related, the record became an immediate top ten hit. The Association recorded several more hits for Valiant until, in 1967, the label was absorbed by Warner Brothers. They continued their pattern of hits, beginning with a number one record called "Windy."

During the following years, the group survived several personnel changes and the death (due to accidental drug poisoning) of one of their charter members, Brian Cole. They have never stopped touring and, in the spring of 1975, a group consisting of original members Ted Bluechel, Jim Yester, and Larry Ramos, and new members Maurice Miller, David Vaught, and Dwayne Smith signed with RCA Records and released a new record titled "One Sunday Morning."

June 66 *ALONG COMES MARY* / Valiant
Aug. 66 *CHERISH* / Valiant
Nov. 66 *PANDORA'S GOLDEN HEEBIE JEEBIES* / Valiant
Feb. 67 *NO FAIR AT ALL* / Valiant
May 67 *WINDY* / Warner Bros.
Aug. 67 *NEVER MY LOVE* / Warner Bros.
Sept. 67 *REQUIEM FOR THE MASSES* / Warner Bros.
Feb. 68 *EVERYTHING THAT TOUCHES YOU* / Warner Bros.
May 68 *TIME FOR LIVIN'* / Warner Bros.
Aug. 68 *SIX MAN BAND* / Warner Bros.
Mar. 69 *GOODBYE COLUMBUS* / Warner Bros.
Feb. 73 *NAMES, TAGS, NUMBERS & LABELS* / Mums

The Atlanta Rhythm Section

MEMBERS:

Ronnie Hammond (lead vocals)

Barry Bailey (lead guitar)

J. R. Cobb (rhythm guitar)

Dean Daughtry (keyboards)

Paul Goddard (bass)

Robert Nix (drums)

HOMETOWN: Doraville, Georgia

This group is a conglomeration of some of the most active musicians on the southern rock scene. Daughtry and Nix are former members of The Candymen, Roy Orbison's back-up group; J. R. Cobb was writer and producer of The Classics IV hits; and all the members have played behind the major

Atlanta Rhythm Section

acts who record in Atlanta, such as Billy Joe Royal, Tommy Roe, Joe South, and The Classics IV.

In 1970 these studio musicians got together to form a working unit. They signed with Polydor Records in 1974, and "Doraville" became the first of several national hits for them.

Oct. 74 *DORAVILLE*/Polydor
Feb. 75 *ANGEL*/Polydor
June 76 *JUKIN'*/Polydor
Jan. 77 *SO IN TO YOU*/Polydor
June 77 *NEON NITES*/Polydor
Sept. 77 *DOG DAYS*/Polydor
Oct. 77 *GEORGIA RHYTHM*/Polydor
Mar. 78 *IMAGINARY LOVER*/Polydor

The Average White Band

MEMBERS:

Onnie McIntire (guitar)/born: Sept. 25, 1945/ Lennox Town, Scotland

Michael Rosen (guitar)/replaced by Hamish Stuart/born: Oct. 8, 1949/Glasgow, Scotland

Alan Gorrie (bass)/born: July 19, 1946/Perth, Scotland

Malcolm "Mollie" Duncan (sax)/born: Aug. 24, 1945/Montrose, Scotland

Roger Ball (sax)/born: June 4, 1944/Dundee, Scotland

Robbie McIntosh (drums)/died: Sept. 23, 1974/ replaced by Steven Ferrone/born: Apr. 25, 1950/Brighton, England

This entire group originated in Scotland and was formed in 1971, almost by accident, by bass player Alan Gorrie. At that time he was part of a group called Forever More, but he booked time in a recording studio to experiment on his own with some songs he had written. He got several of his friends, all members of other bands, to play at the session. When it was over, they realized that they had created a jazz-oriented "soul" sound unique in the rock field. They were unable to form a working unit, however, since each member was still contracted to his current band.

By 1972 all were free of their obligations and The Average White Band was born. After extensive rehearsals, the group made its debut later that year at the Lincoln Festival in England. One appearance led to another, and, in 1973, they achieved a major breakthrough by being asked to appear at Eric Clapton's famed Rainbow concert

in London. Shortly thereafter, they produced their first album at an inexpensive "demo" studio and were able to sell it to MCA.

Early in 1974 the group was in Los Angeles after finishing an American tour and rented a studio to record their second album. Called simply *Average White Band,* it was originally intended for release on MCA but was purchased by Atlantic instead. The album was extremely successful and yielded one of the best-selling singles of 1974, "Pick up the Pieces." Before they were able to return to Scotland, tragedy struck the group when drummer Robbie McIntosh passed away due to accidental drug poisoning. He was immediately replaced by an old friend of the group's, Steve Ferrone.

Today, after a number of best-selling singles and albums, AWB (as they are now known) reign as Scotland's leading soul band.

The Average White Band. Left to right: Roger Ball, Alan Gorrie, Onnie McIntyre, Steve Ferrone, Malcolm Duncan, Hamish Stuart

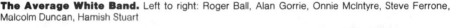

Hoyt Axton

Dec. 74 *PICK UP THE PIECES /*
          Atlantic
Apr. 75 *CUT THE CAKE /* **Atlantic**
Aug. 75 *IF I EVER LOSE THIS HEAVEN /*
          Atlantic
Nov. 75 *SCHOOL BOY CRUSH /*
          Atlantic
Sept. 76 *QUEEN OF MY SOUL /* **Atlantic**

Hoyt Axton

BORN: Mar. 25, 1938
HOMETOWN: Duncan, Oklahoma

Although born in Oklahoma, Hoyt grew up in various parts of the country, including Florida, Michigan, California, and Texas. His father was a blues singer and his mother, Mae Axton, gained fame as a songwriter after composing "Heartbreak Hotel" for Elvis Presley.

Hoyt's big break came when the Kingston Trio recorded his song "Greenback Dollar" in the early sixties. Since then his songs have been recorded by countless artists—"Joy to the World" and "Never Been to Spain" by Three Dog Night, "The Pusher" by Steppenwolf, and "The No No Song" by Ringo Starr.

At present Hoyt Axton has diversified into several areas. In 1974 he signed a contract with A & M to record his own songs. His first outside production project was an album during the summer of 1975 with Commander Cody & His Lost Planet Airmen. Also, his TV show titled "Country Western Rock & Roll Boogie Woogie Gospel Hour" is currently being shown in syndication throughout the country.

June 74 *WHEN THE MORNING COMES /*
          A & M

The Babys

MEMBERS:

John Waite (lead vocals, bass guitar)/born: July 4, 1955

Wally Stocker (lead guitar)/born: Mar. 27, 1954

Mike Corby (rhythm guitar)/born: July 3, 1955

Tony Brock (drums)/born: Mar. 31, 1954

HOMETOWN: London, England

This quartet started out by recording a few tunes that they eventually put on videotape. They then took the tape around to various record companies so that the latter could not only hear the group but see what they would look like on stage. This resulted in a recording contract with Chrysalis Records.

Their first album for the label was called *The Babys,* from which came the hit single "If You've Got the Time." Next came the album *Broken Heart* and their biggest single, "Isn't It Time."

Mar. 77 *IF YOU'VE GOT THE TIME /* **Chrysalis**

Oct. 77 *ISN'T IT TIME /* **Chrysalis**

Feb. 78 *SILVER DREAMS /* **Chrysalis**

The Bachelors

MEMBERS:

Con Cluskey

Declan Stokes

John Stokes

HOMETOWN: Dublin, Ireland

The Babys. Left to right: Tony Brock, John Waite, Mike Corby, Wally Stocker

Con Cluskey and brothers John and Dec Stokes first met as Dublin schoolmates during the late fifties. They formed a three-harmonica instrumental band called The Harmonichords and became quite well known in Ireland, appearing often on radio and television. In 1959 they made their first tour of England with Irish singing star Patrick O'Hagan, who convinced them to add singing to their act. As a result, they had to change their name and soon settled on The Bachelors.

Although they continued to be popular, the turning point in their career came in the summer of 1962, when they were appearing at Arbroath, a small seaside town in Scotland. Their agent, Dorothy Solomon, invited the A & R director of British Decca, Dick Rowe, to see their performance. Rowe offered the Bachelors a trip to London and an audition; the song they sang, "Charmaine," got them a recording contract and became their first release. It was a major hit in England, and an arrangement was made for London Records to release their recordings in America. They soon had a top ten hit on both sides of the Atlantic called "Diane."

The Bachelors continued to record international hits well into the late sixties. Today their popularity is primarily centered in their native Ireland.

Apr. 64 *DIANE*/London
June 64 *I BELIEVE*/London
Sept. 64 *I WOULDN'T TRADE YOU FOR THE WORLD*/London
Dec. 64 *NO ARMS CAN EVER HOLD YOU*/London
June 65 *MARIE*/London
Oct. 65 *CHAPEL IN THE MOONLIGHT*/London
Apr. 66 *LOVE ME WITH ALL YOUR HEART*/London
July 66 *CAN I TRUST YOU?*/London

Jan. 67 *WALK WITH FAITH IN YOUR HEART*/London

Bachman-Turner Overdrive (BTO)

MEMBERS:
Randy Bachman (lead guitar)/born: Sept. 27, 1943/replaced by Jim Clench
Robin Bachman (drums)/born: Feb. 18, 1953
Fred "C. F." Turner (bass)/born: Oct. 16, 1943/(replaced Chad Allen)
Timothy Bachman (rhythm guitar)/replaced (1975) by Blair Thornton/born: July 23, 1950
HOMETOWN: Winnipeg, Canada

This group evolved from an early-sixties Canadian rock band named Chad Allen & The Expressions, of which Randy Bachman was a charter member. When Allen left the group during the early sixties, Bachman reorganized it as The Guess Who, which became Canada's most important rock band. They also placed a long string of hits, mostly cowritten by Bachman, high on the American charts.

In 1970 Randy Bachman left The Guess Who to record a solo album. Shortly afterward he formed a new group named Brave Belt which consisted of his brothers Robby and Tim, his old collaborator Chad Allen, and himself. Brave Belt recorded two unsuccessful albums for Warner Brothers, and in 1971 Chad Allen was replaced by C. F. Turner. By 1972 they had decided to shift musical directions and adopted the name of the truckers' trade publication *Overdrive*. The new group was signed by Mercury Records and by 1974 had recorded several hits. Their biggest success came during the fall of that year, when their recording of "You Ain't Seen Nothing Yet" went to number one, and the al-

Bachman-Turner Overdrive (BTO). Left to right: Randy Bachman, Blair Thornton, Robbie Bachman, Fred Turner

bum from which it was taken, *Not Fragile,* became similarly successful.

Although The Guess Who continued for several years after Randy Bachman's departure, they disbanded during 1975, leaving Bachman-Turner Overdrive the most successful Canadian rock group. Tim Bachman left the group in 1975 to become a record producer and Randy Bachman has left to pursue a solo career.

See *THE GUESS WHO.*

Dec. 73	*BLUE COLLAR* /Mercury
Feb. 74	*LET IT RIDE* /Mercury
May 74	*TAKING CARE OF BUSINESS* /Mercury
Sept. 74	*YOU AIN'T SEEN NOTHING YET* /Mercury
Jan. 75	*ROLL ON DOWN THE HIGHWAY* /Mercury
May 75	*HEY YOU* /Mercury
Dec. 75	*DOWN THE LINE* /Mercury
Feb. 76	*TAKE IT LIKE A MAN* /Mercury
Apr. 76	*LOOKING OUT FOR NUMBER ONE* /Mercury
Sept. 76	*GIMME YOUR MONEY PLEASE* /Mercury

Bad Company

MEMBERS:

Paul Rodgers (lead vocals)/born: Dec. 12, 1949/Middlesborough, Yorkshire, England

Michael Jeffrey Ralphs (guitar)/born: Mar. 31, 1948/Herefordshire, England

Simon Frederick St. George Kirke (drums)/born: July 28, 1949/Shropshire, England

Raymond "Boz" Burrell (bass)/born: 1946/Lincolnshire, England

Bad Company was formed late in 1973 by former members of several important British rock groups.

Simon Kirke and Paul Rodgers were the nucleus of the group Free (best known for their top five record in 1970 of "All Right Now"), and Rodgers was the principal writer of the group's material. When Free disbanded permanently in 1973, Kirke and Rodgers decided to start a new band. They formed an association with Mick Ralphs, one of the founding members of Mott The Hoople, and Boz Burrell, formerly with King Crimson.

Naming themselves Bad Company after one of Kirke and Rodgers's songs, and handled by Led Zeppelin's manager, Pete Grant, they were signed to a recording contract in 1974 and debuted in the United States on Led Zeppelin's new Swan Song label. A single titled "Can't Get Enough of Your Love" became a top five hit. They followed with several more hit singles and albums and by mid-1975 had become one of the top-grossing groups on the concert circuit.

Aug. 74	*CAN'T GET ENOUGH (OF YOUR LOVE)* / Swan Song
Jan. 75	*MOVIN' ON* / Swan Song
Apr. 75	*GOOD LOVIN' GONE BAD* / Swan Song
July 75	*FEEL LIKE MAKING LOVE* / Swan Song
Mar. 76	*YOUNG BLOOD* / Swan Song
July 76	*HONEY CHILD* / Swan Song
May 77	*BURNIN' SKY* / Swan Song

Badfinger

MEMBERS:

Peter Ham (lead guitar, keyboards) / born: Apr. 26, 1947 / Swansea, Wales / died: Apr. 23, 1975

Michael Gibbons (drums) / hometown: Swansea, Wales

Thomas Evans (bass) / hometown: Liverpool, England

Ronald Griffiths (rhythm guitar) / hometown: Liverpool, England / replaced by Joseph Molland / born: June 21, 1948 / Liverpool, England

Badfinger began as a band called The Iveys and was one of many struggling for recognition in the Liverpool area during the late sixties. In 1968 they were heard by noted English bandleader Bill Collins. He agreed to become their manager and sent a tape of the group to his friend Mal Evans at Apple Records. Evans turned the tape over to producer Derek Taylor, who arranged for it to be heard by Paul McCartney. The group was immediate-

ly signed and a record titled "Maybe Tomorrow" was released in early 1969. It became a hit, but, more importantly, McCartney decided to use the group to record the soundtrack for a new film starring Ringo Starr called *The Magic Christian*. During these sessions, guitarist Ron Griffiths left the group and was replaced by Joey Molland. Apple executive Neil Aspinall suggested the group's name be changed to Badfinger.

Early 1970 saw the release of the film, the soundtrack album, and a single taken from it called "Come and Get It," which became a top ten record. Badfinger took part in the famed Bangladesh concert with George Harrison in the summer of 1971, and other artists successfully recorded their songs, most notably Nilsson, who took "Without You" to number one. Badfinger released several successful singles and albums of their own until 1972, when contractual difficulties caused a two-year hiatus in their recording activities.

In 1974, the group signed with Warner Brothers and their *Badfinger* album, released that year, sold very well and proved them as popular as ever. However, in April 1975, apparently despondent about a difficult American tour, Pete Ham took his own life and brought the group's career to an abrupt end.

Feb. 70	*COME AND GET IT* / Apple
Oct. 70	*NO MATTER WHAT* / Apple
Dec. 71	*DAY AFTER DAY* / Apple
Mar. 72	*BABY BLUE* / Apple

Joan Baez

BORN: Jan. 9, 1941
HOMETOWN: Staten Island, New York

Joan Baez is known as "the queen of protest" as a result of the many underdog causes with which she identified herself during the sixties and early seventies.

Although born in New York City, she was raised primarily in the Redlands area of southern California. The daughter of a Mexican doctor and an Irish drama teacher, she was exposed at an early age to the discrimination Mexican-Americans tended to suffer in that area and took up the ukulele as a schoolgirl to gain acceptance in a generally hostile environment. Joan began singing in local choirs and involved herself in the folk movement of the late fifties. Her appearance at the 1959 Newport Folk Festival brought her national recognition and a recording contract with Vanguard Records. The many albums of her folk songs have been continual best sellers since then, and several of her occasional single releases have become hits as well. The first of these was her 1963 recording of the civil rights anthem "We Shall Overcome." Her biggest hit was the 1971 release of a Robbie Robertson song titled "The Night They Drove Old Dixie Down."

In 1972, after twelve years with Vanguard, Joan Baez switched her affiliation to Herb Alpert's A & M label. She continues to tour extensively and was an integral part of Bob Dylan's Rolling Thunder Review.

Joan Baez

The George Baker Selection

MEMBERS:
George Baker (Johannes Bouwens)
Jan Hop
Jacobus Anthonius Greuter
Jan Gerbrand Visser
George The

The George Baker Selection originated in northern Holland and were part of the brief so-called Dutch invasion of early 1970. This was largely the result of producer Jerry Ross's campaign of obtaining master recordings of the period's leading Dutch rock groups for release in the United States on his Colossus label.

In pattern with The Tee Set and The Shocking Blue (the other two major principals in the "invasion"), The George Baker Selection placed two substantial hits on the United States charts and disappeared from the American music scene. However, they remained active in their homeland

Nov. 63	**WE SHALL OVERCOME/** **Vanguard**
Sept. 65	**THERE BUT FOR FORTUNE/** **Vanguard**
Apr. 69	**LOVE IS JUST A FOUR LETTER** **WORD/Vanguard**
Aug. 71	**THE NIGHT THEY DROVE OLD** **DIXIE DOWN/Vanguard**
Nov. 71	**LET IT BE/Vanguard**
July 72	**IN THE QUIET MORNING/** **A & M**
Sept. 75	**DIAMONDS & RUST/A & M**

through the mid-seventies, when a renewed interest in the group developed both in England and the United States. They achieved their first chart entry in many years during 1975 with their recording of "Una Paloma Blanca."

Mar. 70 *LITTLE GREEN BAG /*
Colossus
June 70 *DEAR ANN /* Colossus
Nov. 75 *UNA PALOMA BLANCA /*
Warner Bros.

Ginger Baker

REAL NAME: Peter Baker
BORN: Aug. 19, 1939
HOMETOWN: Lewisham, London, England

Ginger Baker is universally acknowledged to be the leading British drummer and percussionist to come out of the sixties and seventies rock period.

He was raised in a tough, working-class area of London and early developed an intense interest in jazz drumming. As a teen-ager, he played in several English jazz bands, most notably Terry Lightfoot's and Acker Bilk's, and by the early sixties was playing in such blues-oriented rock bands as Alexis Korner's and The Graham Bond Organization. He remained with Bond for three years and, in 1966, he and the group's bass player, Jack Bruce, joined forces with guitarist Eric Clapton to form Cream. Generally considered to be the most important and influential of the sixties "supergroups," Cream disbanded after two years because of personality problems. Clapton and Baker joined Rick Grech on bass and Steve Winwood playing keyboards to form Blind Faith. This too was an extremely important, though short-lived, group. In 1970, Ginger Baker briefly formed his own band, Air Force.

During the mid-seventies Baker divided his time between his own recording studio in Lagos, Nigeria, and touring with a new group, The Baker-Gurvitz Army.

Ginger Baker's Air Force
May 70 *A MAN OF CONSTANT*
SORROW / Atco

The Band

MEMBERS:

Jaime "Robbie" Robertson (lead guitar) / born: July 5, 1944 / Toronto, Canada

Richard Manuel (keyboards) / born: Apr. 3, 1944 / Ontario, Canada

Rick Danko (bass) / born: Dec. 9, 1943 / Ontario, Canada

Garth Hudson (keyboards) / born: Aug. 2, 1942 / Ontario, Canada

Levon Helm (drums) / born: May 26, 1943 / Marvell, Arkansas

The group was formed in 1960 when American country rock 'n' roll star Ronnie Hawkins moved to Canada and assembled a back-up band of local musicians who were fans of American country music. Levon Helm was an old friend of Hawkins from their native Arkansas, and he too moved to Canada to become the group's drummer. Calling themselves Levon & The Hawks, they spent several years backing Ronnie Hawkins and touring on their own.

One night in 1965, while appearing in Atlantic City, New Jersey, the group got a call from Bob Dylan, who told them that he was planning to become more rock oriented and offered them a job as his back-up band. As a result they toured the world with Dylan during the mid-sixties until he was injured in a motorcycle accident and retired to Woodstock, New York, to recuperate. The group moved there to be near him and began recording as The Band in a now-legendary pink house in Woodstock. In the fall of 1968 an album featuring some of those recordings was

The Band. Left to right: Garth Hudson, Robbie Robertson, Rick Danko, Richard Manuel, Levon Helm

released. Called *Music from the Big Pink,* it instantly established the group's success. A record from the album, "The Weight," became their first single hit.

The Band developed a considerable reputation in their own right as a concert attraction, later headlining such events as the Watkins Glen Festival in 1973. However, when Bob Dylan recovered fully from his injuries and resumed his career, the group recorded and appeared with him as well. Dylan and The Band played together at the Isle of Wight concert in 1969 and went on an extensive American tour in 1974.

During the summer of 1975 an album called *The Basement Tapes* was released. A collection of recordings— rumored for years to exist—of Dylan and The Band during the sixties Woodstock period, it went almost immediately to the top of the charts.

The Band played their last concert on Thanksgiving, 1976, at San Francisco's Winterland before a star-studded audience of some five thousand fans.

Aug. 68	***THE WEIGHT* / Capitol**
Nov. 69	***UP ON CRIPPLE CREEK* / Capitol**
Feb. 70	***RAG MAMA RAG* / Capitol**
Oct. 70	***TIME TO KILL* / Capitol**
Oct. 71	***LIFE IS A CARNIVAL* / Capitol**
Sept. 72	***DON'T DO IT* / Capitol**
Mar. 76	***OPHELIA* / Capitol**

The Bar-Kays

ORIGINAL MEMBERS:
James King (guitar) / died: Dec. 10, 1967
Ronald Caldwell (keyboards) / died: Dec. 10, 1967
Phalon Jones (sax) / died: Dec. 10, 1967
Benjamin Cauley (trumpet)
James Alexander (trumpet)
Carl Cunningham (drums) / died: Dec. 10, 1967
HOMETOWN: Memphis, Tennessee

The story of The Bar-Kays is among the sadder ones in the music business.

The group was originally made up of six young men, all in their mid-teens, who grew up in Memphis and whose interest in music drew them naturally to the city's famous Stax-Volt Studios. They worked as session musicians and were eventually assembled as a group and began to release records as The Bar Kays. Their first single was called "Soulfinger" and reached the top twenty in the summer of 1967. By October they had scored with two more hits and were recording extensively with Otis Redding. The Bar-Kays were to be the back-up band for Redding's upcoming winter tour but on December 10, 1967, a charter plane carrying Redding and the group crashed into a lake near Madison, Wisconsin, killing all but Ben Cauley. Jim Alexander was on a different plane. In 1968 he and Cauley went about the task of forming a new group.

The reorganized Bar-Kays consisted of Cauley and Alexander both playing trumpet, Harvey Henderson (tenor sax), Barry Wilkins (guitar), Willie Hall (drums), Winston Stewart (organ), and Larry Dotson singing lead.

In 1971 Ben Cauley left the group to become a member of The Isaac Hayes Movement and was replaced by trumpeter Charles Allen. Two years later Donnelle Hagan on trumpet and Vernon Burch on guitar were added.

The "new" Bar-Kays are considered to be among the leading studio musicians in Memphis.

May 67 *SOULFINGER* / **Volt**
Sept. 67 *KNUCKLEHEAD* / **Volt**
Oct. 67 *GIVE EVERYBODY SOME* / **Volt**
Dec. 71 *SON OF SHAFT* / **Volt**
Oct. 76 *SHAKE YOUR RUMP TO THE FUNK* / **Mercury**

Feb. 77 *TOO HOT TO STOP (PART I)* / **Mercury**

Len Barry

REAL NAME: Leonard Borisoff
BORN: June 12, 1942
HOMETOWN: Philadelphia, Pennsylvania

Len Barry was born and raised in Philadelphia. As a child he favored sports over music and had hoped to become a professional baseball player when he graduated from school.

His first serious involvement with music came during the late fifties when he joined the army and occasionally sang with military bands. The response to his singing was so enthusiastic that he thought about making it his career when he returned to civilian life.

Len Barry came home in 1960 and, with some old friends with whom he had sung in school, formed The Dovells (see THE DOVELLS, Rock On: The Solid Gold Years). After a string of hits with that group, he left in 1965, and his first solo recording, "Lip Sync," became a hit. But his second release, "1-2-3," brought him major success by going to the top of the charts.

Today Len Barry makes occasional appearances at oldies shows and continues to record in search of a new hit.

May 65 *LIP SYNC* / **Decca**
Sept. 65 *1-2-3* / **Decca**
Jan. 66 *LIKE A BABY* / **Decca**
Mar. 66 *SOMEWHERE* / **Decca**
June 66 *IT'S THAT TIME OF YEAR* / **Decca**
Sept. 66 *I STRUCK IT RICH* / **Decca**

Fontella Bass

BORN: July 3, 1949
HOMETOWN: St. Louis, Missouri

With the help of her mother, a member of the famed Clara Ward gospel

Len Barry

singers, Fontella Bass launched her career by playing piano and singing in a St. Louis church choir at the age of five. By the time she graduated from college, she was director of the choir as well as its pianist-organist. Blues artist Little Milton heard her in church in 1960 and asked her to join his band as pianist. After several years she became the vocalist.

In 1964 Milton took Fontella to Checker Records, the label for which he was recording. There she was teamed up with Bobby McClure, and in early 1965 they released their first joint recording, a hit titled "Don't Mess up a Good Thing." After a follow-up hit with McClure, she recorded "Rescue Me" on her own, which established her as an R & B star when it reached the top five on the national charts.

Although she had several more R & B hits, Fontella became more jazz oriented in later years. She is now mar-

ried to jazz trumpeter Lester Bowie and records for Epic Records.

Feb. 65	***DON'T MESS UP A GOOD THING (with Bobby McClure) / Checker***
May 65	***YOU'LL MISS ME (with Bobby McClure) / Checker***
Oct. 65	***RESCUE ME / Checker***
Dec. 65	***RECOVERY / Checker***
Mar. 66	***I SURRENDER / Checker***
Aug. 66	***SAFE AND SOUND / Checker***

Shirley Bassey

BORN: Jan. 8, 1937
HOMETOWN: Tiger Bay, Cardiff, Wales

Shirley Bassey began singing at parties and small local affairs as a child. Her first professional job was during the early fifties in the chorus line of a touring English show called "Memories of Al Jolson." After several parts in other stage productions, she was signed to a recording contract by Phillips Records in England. In 1956 Shirley had her first hit with "The Banana Boat Song" at about the same time that The Tarriers and Harry Belafonte were scoring a hit with the same song in America. In the early sixties, after several other hits, Shirley changed affiliation to the British Columbia label and achieved major success with such Broadway show tunes as "Climb Every Mountain" from *The Sound of Music* and "As Long as He Needs Me" from *Oliver*.

Shirley's big break came in 1964 when the producers of the film *Goldfinger* decided to use her to sing the title song. Although she was by then a well-known nightclub entertainer, this exposure brought her international success and her first American hit. Since then, her many LPs, released in the United States by United Artists, have been major best sellers, and Shir-

Shirley Bassey

ley Bassey is considered among the top club attractions in the business.

Jan. 65 *GOLDFINGER*/**United Artists**
Sept. 70 *SOMETHING*/**United Artists**
Jan. 72 *DIAMONDS ARE FOREVER*/
United Artists

Bay City Rollers

MEMBERS:
Eric Faulkner (guitar)/born: Oct. 21, 1954/
Edinburgh, Scotland
Leslie McKeown (vocals)/born: Nov. 12, 1955/
Edinburgh, Scotland
Stuart Wood (guitar)/born: Feb. 25, 1957/
Edinburgh, Scotland
Ian Mitchell (bass guitar)/born: Aug. 22, 1958/
Downpatrick, County Down, Northern Ireland

Derek Longmuir (drums)/born: Mar. 19, 1952/
Edinburgh, Scotland

The group first formed in the late sixties with Derek Longmuir and his brother Alan as The Longmuir Brothers, who then became The Saxons. They were a very big act throughout Scotland and England and eventually came to the attention of Dick Leahy at Bell Records. The group chose a new name by simply pointing at random to a spot on a map of the United States. The spot happened to be Bay City, Michigan; ergo The Bay City Rollers.

They eventually signed with Arista Records in the United States and hit the charts in the fall of 1975 with "Sat-

Bay City Rollers. Left to right: Eric Faulkner, Derek Longmuir, Stuart "Woody" Wood, Les McKeown

urday Night." In 1976 Alan Longmuir left the group and was replaced by Ian Mitchell.

Although the press tried to set them up as the new Beatles, they have not come close to the popularity of the Liverpool four. However, The Rollers have created their own following and have created "Rollermania" with millions of teen-age girls throughout the world.

Oct. 75	*SATURDAY NIGHT* / Arista
Feb. 76	*MONEY HONEY* / Arista
May 76	*ROCK AND ROLL LOVE LETTER* / Arista
Sept. 76	*I ONLY WANT TO BE WITH YOU* / Arista
Dec. 76	*YESTERDAY'S HERO* / Arista
Feb. 77	*DEDICATION* / Arista
June 77	*YOU MADE ME BELIEVE IN MAGIC* / Arista
Oct. 77	*THE WAY I FEEL TONIGHT* / Arista

The Beatles

MEMBERS:

John Winston Lennon (guitar) / born: Oct. 9, 1940

James Paul McCartney (bass) / born: June 18, 1942

George Harrison (lead guitar) / born: Feb. 25, 1943

Peter Best (drums) / replaced (1962) by Ringo Starr (Richard Starkey) born: July 7, 1940

Stuart Sutcliffe (guitar) / died: April 1962

HOMETOWN: Liverpool, England

The Beatles' contribution to pop music and their influence on the culture of the sixties and seventies are beyond estimation. Rivaled only by Elvis Presley, the foursome from England stand as the biggest phenomenon ever to emerge from the world of modern music. Within the narrower context of pop and rock, the history of the music is

The Beatles (1964). Left to right: Paul McCartney, John Lennon, George Harrison, Ringo Starr

popularly divided into two main categories: pre-Beatles and all that which followed. This is the primary reason this book starts its coverage with 1964, the year of The Beatles and the beginning of rock music's second generation.

The group's story began in Liverpool during the late fifties, when school friends John Lennon and Paul McCartney formed a band to play "skiffle" music in local clubs. At first calling themselves The Quarrymen, they had several names—including Johnny & The Moon Dogs, The Moonshiners, Long John & The Silver Beatles—before settling on The Beatles. By 1960

the group was composed of John, Paul, George Harrison, Stu Sutcliffe, and Pete Best and ranked as one of the top bands in Liverpool playing "beat" music. In 1960 and 1961 they made two extended trips to Hamburg, Germany, between which they continued to advance their reputation by playing at such clubs as The Casbah and the legendary Cavern. It was during the Hamburg period that they developed their unique sound. Upon their return home from the second trip, several big changes occurred.

First, Stu Sutcliffe left the group to settle in Hamburg with a local girl; he was to die less than one year later of a brain hemorrhage. Next, John, Paul, and George decided to release drummer Pete Best in favor of a fellow named Ringo Starr whom they had met playing in Hamburg with Rory Storm & The Hurricanes. Finally, they found when they returned that their reputation had preceded them and that they were the rage of the entire Merseyside area. The excitement attracted the attention of Brian Epstein, whose family owned a Liverpool retail record operation, and he went one night to The Cavern to hear them. Epstein became The Beatles' manager, and his direction was an important factor in their rise to fame.

Epstein worked with the group to create a more clean-cut image. Late in the summer of 1962, after several companies had turned them down, he got The Beatles a recording contract with Parlophone. Epstein subsequently died on August 27, 1967. Their first record, "Love Me Do," was issued in October 1962 and became a hit throughout England. It was followed by

"Please Please Me," which went to number one, and such others as "From Me to You," "She Loves You," and "Thank You Girl," all of which became major hits and enabled the group to tour England as stars throughout 1963. Although these records were leased to various American record companies for distribution, none caught on. It was "I Want to Hold Your Hand," released in late 1963, that took the world by storm and started the phenomenon known as Beatlemania. All their earlier recordings were released in the United States, and by April 1964, The Beatles had placed an incredible fifteen records on the American charts. The immediate aftereffect became known as the "English invasion" as the American market was flooded with material by other English artists. Much of it was successful and eclipsed many established American acts.

The Beatles themselves went on to have one of the most extraordinary careers in the annals of show business.

The Beatles (circa 1970). Left to right: Ringo Starr, Paul McCartney, George Harrison, John Lennon

During the next six years they managed to place well over three dozen additional singles on the charts, their LPs sold in the millions, and Beatle songs became overnight standards. The group was seen in three feature films, *Hard Day's Night, Help,* and *Let It Be,* and they were the subject of a full-length animated film incorporating their music titled *Yellow Submarine.* Their *Sergeant Pepper* album of 1967 was so influential as to change substantially the direction of rock music production techniques, and in 1968 they formed their own Apple record company, which launched the careers of James Taylor, Billy Preston, Mary Hopkin, and Badfinger.

In 1971 The Beatles officially confirmed a rumor that had been circulating for some time; because of severe differences arising out of the management of their vast business interests, John, Paul, George, and Ringo were separating permanently to pursue individual careers.

During 1976 amidst rampant rumors that the group might re-form, a vast new wave of interest in them began to develop. More than a dozen of their earlier recordings appeared on the British best-seller lists and prompted the American release of an album titled *Rock & Roll Music.* This was a random repackaging of vintage material, and it reached the top of the album charts. It also generated a top five single, "Got to Get You into My Life," and placed The Beatles back on the pop charts nearly five years after their separation! After that came the albums *The Beatles Live at the Hollywood Bowl* and *Love Songs* in 1977.

See *John LENNON; Paul McCARTNEY; George HARRISON;* and *Ringo STARR.*

Jan. 64	*I WANT TO HOLD YOUR HAND* / Capitol
Jan. 64	*SHE LOVES YOU* / Swan
Feb. 64	*PLEASE PLEASE ME* / Vee Jay
Feb. 64	*I SAW HER STANDING THERE* / Capitol
Feb. 64	*MY BONNIE (with Tony Sheridan)* / MGM
Mar. 64	*FROM ME TO YOU* / Vee Jay
Mar. 64	*TWIST AND SHOUT* / Tollie
Mar. 64	*ROLL OVER BEETHOVEN* / Capitol/Canada
Mar. 64	*ALL MY LOVING* / Capitol
Mar. 64	*CAN'T BUY ME LOVE* / Capitol
Mar. 64	*DO YOU WANT TO KNOW A SECRET* / Vee Jay
Apr. 64	*THANK YOU GIRL* / Vee Jay
Apr. 64	*LOVE ME DO* / Tollie
Apr. 64	*THERE'S A PLACE* / Tollie
Apr. 64	*WHY (with Tony Sheridan)* / MGM
May 64	*P.S. I LOVE YOU* / Tollie
July 64	*AIN'T SHE SWEET* / Atco
July 64	*A HARD DAY'S NIGHT* / Capitol
July 64	*I SHOULD HAVE KNOWN BETTER* / Capitol
July 64	*AND I LOVE HER* / Capitol
Aug. 64	*IF I FELL* / Capitol
Aug. 64	*I'LL CRY INSTEAD* / Capitol
Aug. 64	*I'M HAPPY JUST TO DANCE WITH YOU* / Capitol
Sept. 64	*MATCHBOX* / Capitol
Sept. 64	*SLOW DOWN* / Capitol
Dec. 64	*I FEEL FINE* / Capitol
Dec. 64	*SHE'S A WOMAN* / Capitol
Feb. 65	*8 DAYS A WEEK* / Capitol
Feb. 65	*I DON'T WANT TO SPOIL THE PARTY* / Capitol
Apr. 65	*TICKET TO RIDE* / Capitol
May 65	*YES IT IS* / Capitol
Aug. 65	*HELP* / Capitol
Sept. 65	*YESTERDAY* / Capitol
Sept. 65	*ACT NATURALLY* / Capitol
Dec. 65	*WE CAN WORK IT OUT* / Capitol
Dec. 65	*DAY TRIPPER* / Capitol
Mar. 66	*NOWHERE MAN* / Capitol
Mar. 66	*WHAT GOES ON* / Capitol
June 66	*PAPERBACK WRITER* / Capitol
June 66	*RAIN* / Capitol
Aug. 66	*YELLOW SUBMARINE* / Capitol

Aug. 66 *ELEANOR RIGBY* / Capitol
Feb. 67 *PENNY LANE* / Capitol
Feb. 67 *STRAWBERRY FIELDS FOREVER* / Capitol
July 67 *ALL YOU NEED IS LOVE* / Capitol
July 67 *BABY, YOU'RE A RICH MAN* / Capitol
Dec. 67 *HELLO, GOODBYE* / Capitol
Dec. 67 *I AM THE WALRUS* / Capitol
Mar. 68 *LADY MADONNA* / Capitol
Mar. 68 *INNER LIGHT* / Capitol
Sept. 68 *HEY JUDE* / Apple
Sept. 68 *REVOLUTION* / Apple
May 69 *GET BACK (with Billy Preston)* / Apple
May 69 *DON'T LET ME DOWN (with Billy Preston)* / Apple
June 69 *BALLAD OF JOHN & YOKO* / Apple
Oct. 69 *COME TOGETHER* / Apple
Oct. 69 *SOMETHING* / Apple
Mar. 70 *LET IT BE* / Apple
May 70 *LONG AND WINDING ROAD* / Apple
May 70 *FOR YOU BLUE* / Apple
June 76 *GOT TO GET YOU INTO MY LIFE* / Capitol

The Beau Brummels

MEMBERS:

Ronald Charles Elliott (lead guitar) / born: Oct. 21, 1943 / Healdsburgh, California

Ronald Meagher (bass) / born: Oct. 2, 1941 / Oakland, California

John Louis Peterson (drums) / born: Jan. 8, 1942 / Rudyard, Michigan

Sal Valentino (Salvatore Willard Spanpinato) (lead vocals) / born: Sept. 8, 1942 / San Francisco, California

Declan Mulligan (guitar) / County Tipperary, Ireland

Sal Valentino's childhood ambition was to be a singer. By 1964 he had been a member of several San Francisco Bay area groups and had appeared often on local television shows. In the summer of that year he joined with school friend Ron Elliott and formed The Beau Brummels to sing in Bay area clubs. The group was heard during one of these performances by disc jockey Tom Donahue, who was in the process of starting the Autumn record label. He signed them immediately and, along with Sylvester Stewart (later to become Sly of The Family Stone), he produced their first recording, "Laugh, Laugh," which became a major national hit in early 1965.

Although The Beau Brummels were originally a five-man group, Dec Mulligan left after their first recording session because of legal difficulties, and the remaining four went on to enjoy a string of hits as one of the first American alternatives to the "English invasion." The group continued to release records well into the late sixties and then went into limbo for several years.

In 1975 a re-formed group emerged with original members Sal Valentino, John Peterson, and Dec Mulligan and a new guitarist named Daniel Levitt. They signed with Warner Brothers and released an LP and a single, both of which placed on the charts.

Jan. 65 *LAUGH, LAUGH* / Autumn
Apr. 65 *JUST A LITTLE* / Autumn
July 65 *YOU TELL ME WHY* / Autumn
Oct. 65 *DON'T TALK TO STRANGERS* / Autumn
Dec. 65 *GOOD TIME MUSIC* / Autumn
June 66 *ONE TOO MANY MORNINGS* / Warner Bros.

The Bee Gees

MEMBERS

Barry Gibb (guitar, vocals) / born: Sept. 1, 1946
Robin Gibb (lead vocals) / born: Dec. 22, 1949
Maurice Gibb (guitar, vocals) / born: Dec. 22, 1949

HOMETOWN: Douglas, Isle of Man

The group, consisting of three brothers (two of them twins) began performing during the mid-fifties. Calling themselves The Blue Cats, they

The Bee Gees. Left to right: Barry Gibb, Maurice Gibb, Robin Gibb

performed at amateur shows in their native Manchester.

In 1958 the family relocated in Brisbane, Australia, where the boys continued performing in local clubs. They named themselves The Bee Gees (taken from the Brothers Gibb) and became extremely popular. By the mid-sixties, they had their own weekly TV show and several Australian hits and decided to return to England to expand their career. In 1967 they signed a management agreement with Robert Stigwood, then an executive with The Beatles' NEMS Enterprises, and their first recording, "Spicks and Specks," was released. It became a minor hit, but their second record, "New York Mining Disaster, 1941," issued simultaneously in the United States by Atco Records, became a top ten record and established their success internationally.

Since then The Bee Gees have rarely been absent from the charts. In 1973 Robert Stigwood formed his own record company, RSO, for which the group now records. In 1975, backed by their new band—Blue Weaver (keyboards), Olan Kendall (guitar), and Dennis Bryon (drums)—The Bee Gees had their first number one record in several years with a rhythm-rock single called "Jive Talkin'."

In late 1977, they released the album *Saturday Night Fever,* containing the music from the motion picture. Since that time, the album has grossed more money and sold more albums (15 million) than any other album in the history of the music business. This success has made The Bee Gees the hottest recording act in the business today.

May 67	***NEW YORK MINING DISASTER, 1941***/Atco
July 67	***TO LOVE SOMEBODY***/Atco
Sept. 67	***HOLIDAY***/Atco
Nov. 67	***MASSACHUSETTS***/Atco
Jan. 68	***WORDS***/Atco

Apr. 68	*JUMBO* / Atco
Aug. 68	*I'VE GOT TO GET A MESSAGE TO YOU* / Atco
Dec. 68	*I STARTED A JOKE* / Atco
Mar. 69	*THE FIRST OF MAY* / Atco
May 69	*TOMORROW, TOMORROW* / Atco
Sept. 69	*DON'T FORGET TO REMEMBER* / Atco
Mar. 70	*IF ONLY I HAD MY MIND ON SOMETHING ELSE* / Atco
July 70	*I.O.I.O.* / Atco
Dec. 70	*LONELY DAYS* / Atco
June 71	*HOW CAN YOU MEND A BROKEN HEART* / Atco
Oct. 71	*DON'T WANNA LIVE INSIDE MYSELF* / Atco
Jan. 72	*MY WORLD* / Atco
July 72	*RUN TO ME* / Atco
Nov. 72	*ALIVE* / Atco
Mar. 73	*SAW A NEW MORNING* / RSO
Mar. 74	*MR. NATURAL* / RSO
May 75	*JIVE TALKIN'* / RSO
Oct. 75	*NIGHTS ON BROADWAY* / RSO
Dec. 75	*FANNY (BE TENDER WITH MY LOVE)* / RSO
June 76	*YOU SHOULD BE DANCING* / RSO
Sept. 76	*LOVE SO RIGHT* / RSO
Jan. 77	*BOOGIE CHILD* / RSO
July 77	*EDGE OF THE UNIVERSE* / RSO
Sept. 77	*HOW DEEP IS YOUR LOVE* / RSO
Dec. 77	*STAYIN' ALIVE* / RSO
Feb. 78	*NIGHT FEVER* / RSO

Archie Bell & The Drells

MEMBERS:
Archie Bell (lead vocals) / born: Sept. 1, 1944 / Henderson, Texas

James Wise / born: May 1, 1948 / Houston, Texas

Willie Pernell / born: Apr. 12, 1945 / Houston, Texas

Lee Bell / born: Jan. 14, 1946 / Houston, Texas (added in 1969)

Archie Bell first met the members of his back-up group at Houston's Phyllis Wheatley High School during the mid-sixties. They entered various talent shows in the area and in 1966 were signed to the small East-West label and had a minor regional hit called "She's My Woman."

In 1967 the group entered the Skipper Lee Talent Show and won first prize. The show's sponsor, Skipper Lee Jackson, signed them to a management contract and took them to Atlantic Records. There they recorded a dance hit called "Tighten Up" which climbed to number one nationally in early 1968. During the next three years they had several more hits, mostly, dance related.

Today Archie Bell & The Drells record for Gamble and Huff's Philadelphia International label and are a major discotheque attraction.

Mar. 68	*TIGHTEN UP* / Atlantic
July 68	*I CAN'T STOP DANCING* / Atlantic
Sept. 68	*DO THE CHOO CHOO* / Atlantic
Dec. 68	*THERE'S GONNA BE A SHOWDOWN* / Atlantic
Mar. 69	*I LOVE MY BABY* / Atlantic
June 69	*GIRL, YOU'RE TOO YOUNG* / Atlantic
Sept. 69	*MY BALLOON'S GOING UP* / Atlantic
Dec. 69	*WORLD WITHOUT MUSIC* / Atlantic
Apr. 70	*DON'T LET THE MUSIC SLIP AWAY* / Atlantic
Dec. 70	*WRAP IT UP* / Atlantic

William Bell

BORN: July 16, 1939
HOMETOWN: Memphis, Tennessee

William Bell was born and raised in Memphis, where he began pursuing music at Booker T. Washington High School.

In the early sixties Bell was attracted to the city's Stax-Volt Studios and was signed to a contract. He had several hits during the next few years, the biggest of which was "I Forgot to Be Your Lover" in 1969. He became a popular concert attraction and was featured in the WattStax '72 Festival, which played to more than one hundred thousand people.

Today William Bell lives in Atlanta, Georgia, where he and his manager operate a firm called Bel-Wyn Management. They also have a record label, Peachtree, and devote their time to finding and developing new talent.

Apr. 62	**YOU DON'T MISS YOUR WATER** / Stax
Mar. 67	**EVERYBODY LOVES A WINNER** / Stax
Apr. 68	**TRIBUTE TO A KING** / Stax
Jan. 69	**I FORGOT TO BE YOUR LOVER** / Stax
Feb. 77	**TRYING TO LOVE TWO** / Mercury

Bellamy Brothers

MEMBERS:
Howard Bellamy (organ)

David Bellamy (guitar)

David began writing poems at the age of eight and a year later began taking lessons on the accordion. Brother Howard began playing the guitar and after a few years of practice they began performing as a duo. By 1965 Howard switched from the accordion to the organ and did some back-up work for Percy Sledge. Three years later they played in a band called Jericho and worked high-school proms and local clubs. A year later they went into a recording studio in Atlanta to do their first recording, which, unfortunately, failed miserably. They decided to focus on recording technique and for the next few years worked as studio musicians throughout the South.

In 1973 David wrote a tune called

"Spiders and Snakes" which he sent to producer Phil Gernhard, who at the time was recording Jim Stafford. The song was eventually recorded by Stafford and became one of his biggest hits. After that the brothers left for Los Angeles to work with Gernhard on their own album. In early 1976 they recorded a tune called "Let Your Love Flow" and the Bellamy Brothers were on their way.

Jan. 76	**LET YOUR LOVE FLOW** / Warner/Curb
July 76	**HELL CAT** /Warner/Curb
Sept. 76	**SATIN SHEETS** /Warner/Curb

The Bells

MEMBERS:
Jacki Ralph (lead vocals)/hometown: Surrey, England

Cliff Edwards (lead vocals)/hometown: Montreal, Canada

Douglas Gravelle (drums)/hometown: Montreal, Canada

Charles Clarke (guitar)/hometown: St. John, New Brunswick, Canada

Michael Waye (bass)/hometown: St. John, New Brunswick, Canada

Dennis Will (keyboards)/hometown: Lake of Two Mountains, Quebec, Canada

Doug Gravelle started playing drums as a child and by the late sixties was one of the drummers most in demand in the Montreal area. At one of his performances he met Cliff Edwards, who asked him to join the group he was forming. Edwards also auditioned and hired the rest of the members at this time. The primary lead singer was a young woman named Jacki Ralph, who had been born in England and had moved to Canada as a youngster.

In 1971 The Bells were signed by Polydor in Canada and in January had a minor hit with "Fly Little White Dove, Fly." However, their second release, "Stay Awhile," became a number one record in Canada and a top ten hit in the United States. They placed another record on the American charts later in the year, after which their popularity became centered in their native Canada.

Jan. 71 *FLY LITTLE WHITE DOVE, FLY* / Polydor
Mar. 71 *STAY AWHILE* / Polydor
June 71 *I LOVE YOU, LADY DAWN* / Polydor

George Benson

BORN: Mar. 2, 1943
HOMETOWN: Pittsburgh, Pennsylvania

George Benson has been a jazz/blues guitarist for over twenty years and has played with some of the best musicians of the era.

During the mid-sixties he left Jack McDuff's group to pursue a solo career. Over the past decade he has built a reputation as one of the best jazz guitarists in the business.

In early 1976 Benson signed with Warner Brothers Records and teamed up with producer Tommy LiPuma to create his hit debut LP, *Breezin'*. A tune from the album, "This Masquerade," written by rock star Leon Russell, became a top ten hit.

June 76 *THIS MASQUERADE* / Warner Bros.
Oct. 76 *BREEZIN'* / Warner Bros.
July 77 *GONNA LOVE YOU MORE* / Warner Bros.
July 77 *THE GREATEST LOVE OF ALL* / Arista
Mar. 78 *ON BROADWAY* / Warner Bros.

Biddu Orchestra

HOMETOWN: Bangalore, Southern India

Biddu became interested in music as a youngster but left his native coun-

try before finding success. During the early sixties, after hearing The Beatles, he went to England to learn more about this music.

In England he met a Jamaican singer named Carl Douglas who had written a tune called "Kung Fu Fighting." Carl wanted Biddu to produce the tune, as he eventually did, and the song went on to become a big international hit during late 1974.

In early 1975 Biddu signed with Epic Records and, using studio musicians, came up with the hit single "Summer of 42," a disco version of the movie theme.

Oct. 75 *SUMMER OF 42* / Epic
Jan. 76 *I COULD HAVE DANCED ALL NIGHT* / Epic

Big Brother & The Holding Company

MEMBERS:
Janis Joplin (lead vocals) / born: Jan. 14, 1943 / Port Arthur, Texas / died: Oct. 3, 1970
Peter Albin (bass) / born: June 6, 1944 / San Francisco, California
Sam Andrew (guitar) / born: Dec. 18, 1941 / Taft, California
James Gurley (guitar) / born: 1941 / Detroit, Michigan
David Getz (drums) / born: 1938 / Brooklyn, New York

Big Brother & The Holding Company were a major part of the San Francisco music explosion of the mid-sixties.

They began as a four-man band and were associated with Chet Helms, a Haight-Ashbury musician and manager. The leading "spiritual adviser" to the area's music community, Helms suggested that they follow The Jefferson Airplane's recent example and hire a female lead singer. He introduced a young woman from his home state of Texas named Janis Joplin to the group and soon Big Brother & The Holding Company, featuring Janis, were the rage of San Francisco. They were signed to Mainstream Records and recorded an album from which two singles were released. All the recordings sold well in the Bay area. However, it was Big Brother's now-legendary appearance at the 1967 Monterey Pop Festival that brought the group international attention and a contract with Columbia Records. Their *Cheap Thrills* album became one of the biggest sellers of 1968, and a single from it called "Piece of My Heart" reached the top ten. Also, as a result of their immense popularity, some of their earlier Mainstream recordings appeared on the charts as well.

In 1969 differences began to develop, and Janis Joplin left the group to form one of her own. She was joined by guitarist Sam Andrew, and although Big Brother continued for a while with replacements, they never really recovered from the loss and soon disbanded.

Janis's new group never took real shape either, and she spent what was to be the last year of her life as a solo act and rock music's leading female personality. She died in October 1970 at the height of her superstardom, after an accidental overdose of drugs. See *Janis JOPLIN.*

Aug. 68 *DOWN ON ME /* **Mainstream**
Aug. 68 *PIECE OF MY HEART /* **Columbia**
Nov. 68 *COO COO /* **Columbia**

Elvin Bishop

BORN: Oct. 21, 1942
HOMETOWN: Tulsa, Oklahoma

Elvin Bishop moved north in 1960 to attend the University of Chicago and to pursue his favorite form of music, the blues. Already an accomplished blues guitarist, he played during his off hours with such leading Chicago blues figures as Junior Wells and Hound Dog Taylor.

In 1965 Bishop joined his college friend, Paul Butterfield, in forming the Butterfield Blues Band. He spent three years as their lead guitarist and the next several years touring with his own band, consisting of himself, Applejack Walroth (harmonica), Art Starvo (bass), and John Chambers (drums).

During the early seventies Bishop was affiliated with Phil Walden's Capricorn label and began to record actively. A number of his albums and singles appeared on the charts, but his major breakthrough came in 1976 when he achieved a top ten hit with "Fooled Around and Fell in Love." His back-up band during the mid-seventies included John Verazza, Michael Brooks, Donald Baldwin, and Phil Aaberg.

Oct. 74 *TRAVELIN' SHOES /* **Capricorn**
June 75 *SURE FEELS GOOD /* **Capricorn**
Mar. 76 *FOOLED AROUND AND FELL IN LOVE /* Capricorn
July 76 *STRUTTIN' MY STUFF /* **Capricorn**
Dec. 76 *SPEND SOME TIME /* **Capricorn**

Stephen Bishop

BORN: 1951
HOMETOWN: San Diego, California

After being involved with music throughout his youth, young Bishop's big break came in 1975 when he met top performers while doing session work for Art Garfunkel's LP *Breakaway*. Bob Ellis became his manager and got him a contract with ABC Records.

His debut LP for the label, called *Careless,* produced the hit "Save It for a Rainy Day," a tune Bishop wrote. The interesting thing about the song is that Bishop used Eric Clapton for some guitar work and singer Chaka Kahn of Rufus for some background vocalizing.

Dec. 76 *SAVE IT FOR A RAINY DAY /*
ABC
May 77 *ON AND ON / ABC*

Stephen Bishop

Cilla Black

REAL NAME: Priscilla White
BORN: May 27, 1943
HOMETOWN: Liverpool, England

Cilla Black grew up in the same neighborhood as The Beatles, The Pacemakers, and The Dakotas. Although she knew them well, she gave no thought to music as a career and left school as a teen-ager to take a daytime secretarial job. At night, she visited her friends in the local clubs.

In 1962 Cilla was offered a part-time hatcheck job at the legendary Cavern. Appearing there at the time was a group named Rory Storm & The Hurricanes, whose drummer and leader was an unknown Ringo Starr. One night Storm invited her onstage to help him sing the song "Fever." So enthusiastic was the response that she developed a reputation and was asked by other groups to sit in when they appeared at the club. Cilla White became Cilla Black when a local newspaper, *Mersey Beat,* printed her name incorrectly in an article about her success at The Cavern. Before long she attracted the attention of The Beatles' manager Brian Epstein, who became her manager as well and got her a contract with Parlophone. In August 1963 her first record, "Love of the Loved," was released and became a hit. Her next recording, "Anyone Who Had a Heart," hit number one in England and the follow-up, "You're My World," scored on both sides of the Atlantic.

Although Cilla had only two more American hits, she went on to become one of England's most popular entertainers of the sixties and seventies.

Today Cilla lives in semiretirement with her husband, Bob Willis, and their young child. Although her personal appearance schedule is limited, she continues to record, and her material is now released in the United States on the Private Stock label.

July 64 *YOU'RE MY WORLD /* Capitol
Sept. 64 *IT'S FOR YOU /* Capitol
Aug. 66 *ALFIE /* Capitol

Black Oak Arkansas

MEMBERS:

Jim "Dandy" Mangrum (lead vocals) / born: Mar. 30, 1948 / Black Oak, Arkansas

Harvey Jett (guitar) / Marion, Arkansas

Stanley Knight (guitar) / born: Feb. 12, 1949 / Jonesboro, Arkansas

Rick Reynolds (guitar) / born: Oct. 28, 1948 / Black Oak, Arkansas

Pat Daugherty (bass) / born: Nov. 11. 1947 / Jonesboro, Arkansas

Thomas Aldrich (drums) / born: Aug. 15, 1950 / Jackson, Mississippi

James Henderson (lead guitar) / born: May 20, 1954 / Jackson, Mississippi

This group is an informal collective of musicians from various places in Arkansas and nearby Mississippi. As teen-agers in the late sixties several of the members got together and rented a sixteen-room house outside the town of Black Oak and named themselves after the town. The remaining members joined the group during the next few years.

In 1970 the group was signed to Atco Records, and their first album, *Black Oak Arkansas,* was released. Over the next five years, seven more LPs followed, all of which were successful, and the group became one of the top "live" concert attractions in the country. They have not directed their efforts primarily toward selling single records and only two have appeared on the charts.

At present the members of Black Oak Arkansas still occupy that original house when not touring and have become active doing benefits for charitable causes. In July 1975 the group changed their label affiliation to MCA Records.

Dec. 73 *JIM DANDY* / Atco
Jan. 76 *STRONG ENOUGH TO BE GENTLE* / MCA

Black Sabbath

MEMBERS:

Anthony Iommi (guitar) / born: Feb. 19, 1948

John "Ozzie" Osbourne (vocals) / born: Dec. 3, 1948

William Ward (drums) / born: May 5, 1948

Terry "Geezer" Butler (bass) / born: July 17, 1949

HOMETOWN: Birmingham, England

All four members of this group had played in several local bands before they joined in 1969 to form a band called Earth. For most of that year they toured the Continent and built a strong reputation. By the end of the year much of their original material was mystical, and they changed their name to Black Sabbath.

The newly named group was signed to the British Vertigo label and their first LP, *Black Sabbath,* was released in early 1970. The album was released in the United States on Warner Brothers, as was their second album, *Paranoid,* which yielded a hit single of the same name later in the year.

Black Sabbath has not been a singles-oriented group, but their albums have been continual best sellers. They keep an extremely active tour schedule, especially in Europe, where they are most popular.

Nov. 70 *PARANOID* / Warner Bros.
Jan. 72 *IRON MAN* / Warner Bros.

The Blackbyrds

MEMBERS:

Allan Curtis Barnes (flute, sax) / born: 1949 / Detroit, Michigan

Barney Perry (guitar) / born: 1953 / Buffalo, New York

Kevin Kraig Toney (keyboards) / born: 1953 / Detroit, Michigan

Joseph Hall III (bass) / born: 1954 / Washington, D.C.

Pericles Jacobs, Jr. (percussion)/born: 1951/Washington, D.C.

Keith Killgo (drums)/born: 1954/Baltimore, Maryland

The Blackbyrds were organized at Howard University in Washington, D.C., by veteran jazz musician Donald Byrd, who spent several years as chairman of the university's black music department. Byrd encouraged the members of the group to continue their studies while pursuing their musical career, which he boosted by getting them signed to Fantasy Records.

In 1974 Byrd produced the group's first album, *The Blackbyrds,* from which a single, "Do It, Fluid," was released. Both sold moderately well and established the group, paving the way for a major hit single in early 1975 called "Walking in Rhythm." Later in the year a major film called *Cornbread, Earl and Me* featured a soundtrack composed by Byrd and played by The Blackbyrds. As a result of their success Donald Byrd left his position at Howard University to manage their interests.

Sept. 74 *DO IT, FLUID* /Fantasy
Feb. 75 *WALKING IN RHYTHM* /Fantasy
Aug. 75 *FLYIN' HIGH* /Fantasy
Mar. 76 *HAPPY MUSIC* /Fantasy
July 76 *ROCK CREEK PARK* /Fantasy
Mar. 77 *TIME IS MOVIN'* /Fantasy

Blood, Sweat & Tears

ORIGINAL MEMBERS:

David Clayton-Thomas (lead vocals)/born: Sept. 13, 1941/Surrey, England/replaced Al Kooper (lead vocals, keyboards)/born: Feb. 5, 1944/Brooklyn, New York

Robert Colomby (drums)/born: Dec. 20, 1944/Manhattan, New York

James Thomas Fielder (bass)/born: Oct. 4, 1947/Denton, Texas

Steven Katz (guitar, harmonica)/born: May 9, 1945/Brooklyn, New York

Richard Halligan (keyboards, flute, trombone)/born: Aug. 29, 1943/Troy, New York

Fred Lipsius (piano, sax)/born: Nov. 19, 1944/Manhattan, New York

Lewis Soloff (fluegelhorn, trumpet)/born: Feb. 20, 1944/Brooklyn, New York

Charles Winfield (fluegelhorn, trumpet)/born: Feb. 5, 1943/Monessen, Pennsylvania

Jerry Hyman (trombone, recorder)/born: May 19, 1947/Brooklyn, New York

This large group was formed in New York City in the late sixties by Al Kooper, a veteran member of the fifties Royal Teens ("Short Shorts") and The Blues Project, and a leading New York session musician famous for his organ solos on Bob Dylan's albums. During his years with The Blues Project, he often spoke of forming a blues and jazz-oriented rock band featuring a large horn section, and late in 1967 he and guitarist Steve Katz left to do just that. Called Blood, Sweat & Tears, the new group was signed by Columbia Records, and an album titled *The Child Is Father to the Man* was released in February 1968. After the appearance of this one album, considered a milestone in the field of rock music, Al Kooper left to pursue a solo career as a performer and record producer, and the future of the group seemed to be in jeopardy.

In 1969 Kooper was replaced by David Clayton-Thomas, a leading figure on the Canadian rock scene, and work was immediately begun on a new album. Called simply *Blood, Sweat & Tears,* it became one of the year's top sellers and generated three consecutive singles which went to the top of the charts. The first of these was an old Brenda Holloway song called "You've Made Me So Very Happy."

Although the group went on to re-

Blood, Sweat & Tears

cord several additional hit singles and albums, they underwent dozens of personnel changes during the following years, most notably David Clayton-Thomas, who separated from the group late in 1971. Several different lead singers were tried, but none remained.

In November 1974 it was announced that Clayton-Thomas would head a completely re-formed group who are currently performing all over the country while recording for ABC records.

On January 30, 1978, Gregory Herbert, a sax player for Blood, Sweat & Tears died of a drug overdose in Amsterdam at the age of thirty-one.

Mar. 69	*YOU'VE MADE ME SO VERY HAPPY* / **Columbia**
May 69	*SPINNING WHEEL* / **Columbia**
Oct. 69	*AND WHEN I DIE* / **Columbia**
Aug. 70	*HI DE HO* / **Columbia**
Oct. 70	*LUCRETIA MAC EVIL* / **Columbia**
July 71	*GO DOWN GAMBLING* / **Columbia**
Oct. 71	*LISA LISTEN TO ME* / **Columbia**
Sept. 72	*SO LONG DIXIE* / **Columbia**
June 74	*TELL ME THAT I'M WRONG* / **Columbia**
June 75	*GOT TO GET YOU INTO MY LIFE* / **Columbia**

Bloodstone

MEMBERS:
Willis Draffen (lead guitar, vocals)
Charles Love (rhythm guitar, vocals)
Charles McCormick (bass, vocals)
Harry Williams (percussion, vocals)
Roger Lee Durham (percussion) / died: Oct. 1973 / replaced by Harry Wilkins
Edward Summers (drums) / replaced by Melvin Webb / replaced by Daryl Clifton
HOMETOWN: Kansas City, Missouri

Bloodstone began during the early sixties on the streets of Kansas City as an a capella group called The Sinceres. As they learned to play instruments, they started appearing in local clubs and established an act.

They gravitated toward the West Coast, performing in many cities on the way, and wound up spending a year in Las Vegas. From there they moved to Los Angeles, where they built a substantial reputation and were able to sell out their performances without benefit of a record release.

In the summer of 1972 they formed

an association with record producer Mike Vernon (John Mayall, Ten Years After, and Savoy Brown) and were signed to a contract by London Records. In 1973 an album was released called *Natural High,* from which a top ten single of the same name was taken.

In 1975 Bloodstone scored and appeared in a full-length feature film titled *Night Train.*

Apr. 73 *NATURAL HIGH* /London
Sept. 73 *NEVER LET YOU GO* /London
Feb. 74 *OUTSIDE WOMAN* /London
July. 74 *THAT'S NOT HOW IT GOES* /London
Mar. 75 *MY LITTLE LADY* /London

Bobby Bloom

DIED: Feb. 28, 1974

Bobby Bloom began his singing career as a teen-age member of a group called The Imaginations. They recorded during the early sixties for the Music Makers label. During the mid-sixties he formed a partnership with John Linde and became active as a songwriter and record producer. In addition he worked as a studio singer and sang background on many hits of the period.

In 1970 Bloom, who was friendly with producers Joey Levine and Artie Resnick, was asked to record for their new L & R label. One of his first releases, a song he cowrote with top songwriter Jeff Barry, was called "Montego Bay," and became a top ten hit. He followed during the next year with several more hits. The Staple Singers had a top twenty record with one of his songs, "Heavy Makes You Happy."

Bobby Bloom's career was abruptly cut short in 1974 when he died as the result of an accidental shooting.

Sept. 70 *MONTEGO BAY* /L & R (MGM)
Jan. 71 *WHERE ARE WE GOING* /Roulette
Jan. 71 *MAKE ME HAPPY* /MGM
June 71 *WE'RE ALL GOING HOME* /MGM

Blue Cheer

MEMBERS:
Leigh Stephens (guitar) / replaced by Randy Holden
Richard Peterson (bass)
Paul Whaley (drums)
HOMETOWN: Boston, Massachusetts

Blue Cheer was a pioneer group in the musical form that came to be known as "heavy-metal" rock.

The group was formed in Boston in 1967 and built a strong local following in the area's clubs with their unusual act. They played extended riffs in unison at an extremely high volume, surrounded by a stage full of amplifiers.

In 1968 Blue Cheer was signed by Mercury's subsidiary Philips label and during the summer of that year had a top twenty hit with Eddie Cochran's classic "Summertime Blues." The next year they followed with another single hit and three successful albums; *Vincebus Eruptum, Outside Inside,* and *Improved Blue Cheer.*

By 1970, after influencing many other groups and contributing to the changing sound of rock, Blue Cheer vanished from the charts. They continue to perform, but without original member Leigh Stephens, who has affiliated with Motown Records as part of a new group called Foxtrot.

Mar. 68 *SUMMERTIME BLUES* /Philips
July 68 *JUST A LITTLE BIT* /Philips

Blue Magic

MEMBERS:

Theodore Mills (lead tenor) / hometown: Philadelphia, Pennsylvania

Vernon Sawyer (second tenor) / hometown: Bronx, New York

Wendell Sawyer (baritone) / hometown: Philadelphia, Pennsylvania

Keith Beaton (tenor) / hometown: Philadelphia, Pennsylvania

Richard Pratt (bass) / hometown: Philadelphia, Pennsylvania

Blue Magic is a vocal group whose singing style is deeply rooted in the fifties harmony sound.

The group first got together and began practicing in 1973 in north Philadelphia, all the while holding regular jobs. Without having made a single personal appearance they began approaching record companies to audition and were signed in early 1974 by Atlantic Records.

In February 1974 their first release, "Stop to Start," became a moderate hit. However, it was their next record, "Side Show," that established the group by reaching to top ten of the pop charts and going to the top of the soul lists.

At present the group is a popular concert attraction. When not touring, lead singer Ted Mills attends Temple University in Philadelphia.

Feb. 74 *STOP TO START* / Atco
May 74 *SIDE SHOW* / Atco
Oct. 74 *THREE RING CIRCUS* / Atlantic

Blue Swede

MEMBERS:

Björn Skifs (lead vocals)

Bosse Liljedahl (bass guitar)

Anders Berglund (keyboard, vocals)

Hinke Ekestubbe (saxophone)

Jan Guldback (drums)

Michael Areklew (guitar)

Thomas Berglund (trumpet, vocals)

HOMETOWN: Stockholm, Sweden

This unusual group originated in Holland and Sweden. They gained fame in Sweden as Björn Skifs & Blabus, but when it was decided to release their recordings in America, their name was simplified for English-speaking audiences. As Blue Swede, they were the first Swedish rock act to place a hit on the American charts. They did so with a number one record—a shouting version of the 1968 B. J. Thomas hit "Hooked on a Feeling," backed by the continual tribal chant of the phrase "ooga chaga, ooga ooga chaga!" Amidst widespread speculation as to the origin of that unusual arrangement, English rock entrepreneur Jonathan King took the credit. An almost identical version of the song had appeared on one of his earlier albums.

Blue Swede followed with the release of an original song, "Silly Milly," and late in 1974 returned to recording old rock hits featuring similarly unusual arrangements.

Feb. 74 *HOOKED ON A FEELING* / EMI
June 74 *SILLY MILLY* / EMI
Aug. 74 *NEVER MY LOVE* / EMI
Feb. 75 *HUSH* / EMI

The Blues Image

MEMBERS:

Michael Pinera (guitar, lead vocals) / born: 1949 / Tampa, Florida

Frank "Skip" Konte (keyboards) / Canyon City, Oklahoma

Manuel Bertematti (percussion) / born: 1946 / Tampa, Florida

Malcolm Jones (bass) / Cardiff, Wales

Joseph Lala (drums) / Tampa, Florida

This group began as a trio in Tampa, Florida, during the mid-sixties.

High school friends Mike Pinera, Manuel Bertematti, and Joe Lala first got together to play at local functions, and in 1966 they were joined by Malcolm Jones, who had played bass in various British blues bands before moving to Florida. Calling themselves The Blues Image, the group toured the United States and England for the next two years, during which time they added a fifth member, Skip Konte, formerly with a band called The Blue Chip Stock. In 1968 they moved to New York City and renovated an old bowling alley into a club called The Image. They were able to book acts like The Mothers of Invention, Cream, and The Lovin' Spoonful and put together enough money to travel to Los Angeles in search of a record deal.

In 1969 The Blues Image were signed to Atco Records, and late in the year their first album, *Blues Image,* was released. In 1970 a second album, *Open,* was issued followed by a top five single hit called "Ride Captain Ride." Ironically, immediately after the record became a million seller, the group disbanded. Another single and album taken from previously recorded material, were later released.

After the break-up Skip Konte began to work as a studio musician with Three Dog Night, which he joined in 1974. Several of The Blues Image's other members re-formed as a group called Manna and signed with Columbia Records.

May 70 *RIDE CAPTAIN RIDE* / Atco
Sept. 70 *GAS LAMPS AND CLAY* / Atco

The Blues Magoos

ORIGINAL MEMBERS:
Ronald Gilbert (bass) / born: 1946 / New York City

Ralph Scala (keyboards) / born: 1947 / New York City

Emil "Peppy" Thielhelm (rhythm guitar) / born: 1950 / New York City

Michael Esposito (lead guitar) / born: 1943 / Delaware

Jeffrey Daking (drums) / born: 1947 / Delaware

The Bloos Magoos, as they were originally known, formed during the mid-sixties in the Bronx in New York City. They developed a reputation by playing in such Greenwich Village clubs as The Nite Owl and the Cafe Wha, where they were discovered and signed in 1966 by manager Art Polhemus. He changed the "Bloos" to the literal spelling and got them a contract with Mercury Records. Their first album, *Psychedelic Lollipop,* was released at the end of the year. It became an immediate best seller and generated a single called "We Ain't Got Nothing Yet," which reached the top five. They recorded several more hit singles and albums during the next three years, after which the group drifted apart.

During the early seventies a new Blues Magoos group, headed by original lead singer and guitarist Peppy Thielhelm, emerged and was signed by ABC Records. The other personnel included current American Flyer member Eric-Justin Kaz (keyboards, horns), John Liello (percussion), Roger Eaton (bass), Herb Lovelle (drums), Dean Evanson (flute), and Richard Dickson (percussion).

Dec. 66 *WE AIN'T GOT NOTHING YET* / Mercury
Mar. 67 *PIPE DREAM* / Mercury
Apr. 67 *THERE'S A CHANCE WE CAN MAKE IT* / Mercury
June 67 *ONE BY ONE* / Mercury

The Blues Magoos

Debby Boone

BORN: Sept. 22, 1956
HOMETOWN: Los Angeles, California

Debby, the third of four girls born to singer Pat Boone and his wife, Shirley, was born in Hackensack, New Jersey, but was relocated to Los Angeles as a child.

As a teen-ager she became interested in singing, partly due to the fact that both her parents were deeply involved in the business. Her big break came in 1969 when her father was headlining a show in Japan and asked the girls if they would like to accompany him in a song. They agreed and that was the beginning of The Boone Sisters. A few years ago the sisters broke up their act and producer Mike Curb asked Debby if she would consider going out as a solo. She agreed and Curb decided to have her record the song "You Light up My Life" which was the title song from the motion picture of the same name. The song was released in the fall of 1977 and quickly shot up to the number one position on the charts, remaining there for the longest period of time for a female artist, and won an Oscar as the best song for a motion picture in 1977. Debby is a performer who will be around for a long time to come.

Debby Boone

Sept. 77 *YOU LIGHT UP MY LIFE /* **Warner/Curb**
Feb. 78 *CALIFORNIA /* Warner/Curb
May 78 *GOD KNOWS/BABY I'M YOURS /* Warner/Curb

Daniel Boone

REAL NAME: Peter Lee Stirling
HOMETOWN: Birmingham, England

Daniel Boone's interest in music began with piano lessons at the age of seven; at thirteen he became proficient on the guitar during an illness. Three years later he was appearing regularly around the London area as a member of a group called The Beachcombers, and by the early sixties he had switched to another group called The Bruisers, which had a minor hit in England called "Blue Girl."

In 1965 Boone became associated with songwriter Les Reed, who asked him to participate in the recording session that resulted in Tom Jones's first hit, "It's Not Unusual." Afterwards, he worked on several more of Jones's sessions, and the songwriters he met urged him to start writing himself. As a result he scored with several hits by The Merseybeats and with Kathy Kirby's Eurovision Song Festival winner, "I Believe."

Daniel Boone made his breakthrough as an artist during the early seventies after a demo session on which he played all the instruments and sang the vocal part for "Daddy Don't You Walk So Fast." The song became a major hit in the United States for Wayne Newton, but the demo was acquired by English record producer Larry Page, who added an orchestra to the basic track and released it under Boone's name. It became his first hit single in England and was followed shortly by "Beautiful Sunday," which placed high on the charts on both sides of the Atlantic.

Since then he has had several more hits as "Daniel Boone," but in England he has begun recording under his own name.

June 72 *BEAUTIFUL SUNDAY /* **Mercury**
Nov. 72 *ANNABELLE /* Mercury
May 75 *RUN, TELL THE PEOPLE /* Pye

Boston

MEMBERS:
Brad Delp (lead vocals)/born: June 12, 1951
Tom Scholz (guitar)/born: Mar. 10, 1947
Barry Goudreau (guitar)/born: Nov. 29, 1951
Fran Sheehan (bass guitar)/born: Mar. 26, 1949
Sib Hashian (drums)/born: Aug. 17, 1949
HOMETOWN: Boston, Massachusetts

Tom Scholz, an MIT graduate with a master's degree in mechanical engineering, wanted to put together a rock band. In 1971 he began to experiment in his basement studio making demo tapes using only singer Brad Delp and a drummer. Dozens of tapes were sent to record companies, and all were eventually returned with rejection slips. Then, late in 1975, one of the tapes wound up at Epic Records; eventually an audition was arranged for the group and a recording contract was signed. Their first LP, called *Boston,* produced a top ten national hit called "More Than a Feeling," written by Scholz. *Boston* proved to be the largest grossing debut album in the history of the music business, selling more than six million copies, and establishing Boston as a group that should be around for a long time to come.

Sept. 76 *MORE THAN A FEELING /* **Epic**
Jan. 77 *LONG TIME /* Epic
May 77 *PEACE OF MIND /* Epic

Boston. Left to right: Sib Hashian, Fran Sheehan, Barry Goudreau, Tom Scholz, Brad Delp

David Bowie

REAL NAME: David Robert Hayward-Jones
BORN: Jan. 8, 1947
HOMETOWN: Brixton, London, England

David Bowie is one of the leading figures in the "glitter rock" form that emerged during the early seventies.

He got his first musical experience while attending Bromley Technical School in London and heading a group called George & The Dragons. He later attended art school but dropped out to take a job as a commercial artist at an advertising agency. At the same time he was playing in such groups as The Conrads and David Jones & The Lower Third.

By the mid-sixties David Bowie had changed his name from Jones to avoid confusion with David Jones of The Monkees, and in 1967 he was signed to a contract by Deram Records. Two albums were released, *David Bowie & the Buss* and *Lindsay Kemp Mime Troupe,* neither of which was especial-

ly successful. After two minor singles for the Pye label, he signed with British Philips in 1969 and recorded the album *David Bowie.* A single titled "Space Oddity" was released to coincide with the first Apollo moon flight that year. It became Bowie's first single hit in England. After touring the country with Humble Pie, he temporarily retired from music to operate an art lab in Beckenham.

In 1971 Bowie resumed his musical career with an album called *The Man Who Sold the World*, which was simultaneously released in the United States by RCA Records and gave him his first taste of American success. It was the release of his next album, *Ziggy Stardust and the Spiders from Mars,* that set his career in motion by becoming a best seller both in England and the United States.

In 1972 RCA began issuing his earlier singles in America, and they became increasingly more successful until "Space Oddity" reached the top fifteen early in 1973. This prompted the repackaging of his earlier *David Bowie* album and, renamed after the hit single, it too went to the top of the charts.

Once a major success as a recording artist, David Bowie began incorporating high theater into his stage act and became one of the most visual attractions in rock. Although he announced his retirement in 1973, he continued to record and make personal appearances on a somewhat limited basis. He presently lives in London with his wife, Angie, and their young son, Zowie.

Apr. 72	*CHANGES* /RCA	
July 72	*STARMAN* /RCA	
Nov. 72	*THE JEAN GENIE* /RCA	
Jan. 73	*SPACE ODDITY* /RCA	
June 74	*REBEL REBEL* /RCA	
Dec. 74	*CHANGES* (rereleased)/RCA	
Mar. 75	*THE YOUNG AMERICANS* /RCA	
June 75	*FAME* /RCA	
Dec. 75	*GOLDEN YEARS* /RCA	
May 76	*TVC 15* /RCA	
Apr. 77	*SOUND AND VISION* /RCA	

David Bowie

The Box Tops

MEMBERS:

Alex Chilton (lead vocals)/born: Dec. 28, 1950/Memphis, Tennessee

Gary Talley (lead guitar)/born: Aug. 17, 1947/ Memphis, Tennessee

William Cunningham (bass)/born: Jan. 23, 1950/Memphis, Tennessee/replaced (1969) by Swain Scharter

Daniel Smythe (drums)/replaced (1967) by Thomas Boggs/born: July 16, 1947/Wynn, Arkansas

John Evans (keyboards)/replaced (1967) by Rick Allen/born: Jan. 28, 1946/Little Rock, Arkansas/replaced (1969) by Harold Cloud

The Box Tops were formed by several high school friends in the Memphis area in the mid-sixties. All had had previous experience in local bands; Rick Allen had played organ for The Gentrys of "Keep on Dancing" fame, and

Tom Boggs's former group, Flash & The Board of Directors, often toured with Paul Revere & The Raiders.

In 1967 The Box Tops came to the attention of independent record producer Dan Penn, who took them to American Recording Studios in Memphis and produced a record called "The Letter." Released by the Mala label, a subsidiary of Bell Records, it became a number one hit in the summer of that year. After another major hit, "Neon Rainbow," two of the group's members left to resume their studies, and replacements were immediately made (see above). The reorganized group had the majority of The Box Tops' hits during the next two years.

During the early seventies the group

faded from popularity and several members began working individually as session musicians in the Memphis area.

During the mid-seventies former lead singer Alex Chilton emerged with a new group called Big Star.

Aug. 67	*THE LETTER* / Mala	
Nov. 67	*NEON RAINBOW* / Mala	
Mar. 68	*CRY LIKE A BABY* / Mala	
June 68	*CHOO CHOO TRAIN* / Mala	
Sept. 68	*I MET HER IN CHURCH* / Mala	
Dec. 68	*SWEET CREAM LADIES FORWARD MARCH* / Mala	
Apr. 69	*I SHALL BE RELEASED* / Mala	
July 69	*SOUL DEEP* / Mala	
Oct. 69	*TURN ON A DREAM* / Mala	
Mar. 70	*YOU KEEP TIGHTENING UP ON ME* / Bell	

Tommy Boyce

BORN: Sept. 29, 1944
HOMETOWN: Charlottesville, Virginia

At the age of twelve Tommy Boyce and his family moved from Virginia to Hollywood, California where he soon became involved in the music business. Although he had a minor hit on RCA in 1962, his real success was to be as a songwriter. He formed a partnership with Bobby Hart, and by the mid-sixties, their writing credits included "Pretty Little Angel Eyes" by Curtis Lee, "Peaches and Cream" by The Ikettes, "Come a Little Bit Closer" by Jay & The Americans, the theme for the TV show "Where the Action Is," and much of The Monkees' material.

In 1967 Boyce and Hart were signed as performers to Herb Alpert's A & M label, and their first release, "Out and About," became a hit. Their second record was the title song from a Dean Martin film called *The Ambushers,* backed with "I Wonder What She's Doing Tonight." The latter side be-

came their biggest hit and reached the top ten late in 1967. They followed with two more hits and returned for the next several years to their writing and production work.

In 1975 Tommy Boyce and Bobby Hart teamed up with two of the original Monkees, billing themselves as "The Guys That Wrote 'Em and the Guys Who Sung 'Em." Later in the year the re-formed Monkees signed with Capitol Records and began recording.

Oct. 62	*I'LL REMEMBER CAROL* / RCA	
Dec. 67	*OUT AND ABOUT* (with Bobby Hart) / A&M	
Dec. 67	*I WONDER WHAT SHE'S DOING TONIGHT* (with Bobby Hart) / A&M	
Apr. 68	*GOOD BYE BABY* (with Bobby Hart) / A&M	
July 68	*ALICE LONG (YOU'RE STILL MY FAVORITE GIRLFRIEND)* (with Bobby Hart) / A&M	

Brass Construction

MEMBERS:
Randy Muller (vocals)
Wade Williamston (bass guitar)
Joseph Arthur Wong (guitar)
Morris Price (trumpet)
Wayne Parris (trumpet)
Jesse Ward (tenor sax)
Mickey Grudge (sax)
Sandy Billups (percussion)
Larry Payton (drums)
HOMETOWN: Brooklyn, New York

The group first formed in high school and began by working school functions and parties. Jeff Lane, producer of albums for the B. T. Express, worked with this new group for several years, eventually getting them a contract with United Artists Records. With the popularity of the disco scene in New York City, their release "Movin" quickly moved up the pop charts and

Bread. Back row: Larry Knechtel; front row, left to right: James Griffin, David Gates, Mike Botts

established the group on a national level.

Apr. 76 *MOVIN*/United Artists
Dec. 76 *HA CHA CHA*/United Artists

Bread

MEMBERS:

David Gates (lead vocals, guitar)/born: Dec. 11, 1940/Tulsa, Oklahoma

James Griffin (guitar)/Memphis, Tennessee

Robb Royer (guitar, bass)/Los Angeles, California/replaced (1971) by Larry Knechtel/Bell, California

James Gordon (drums)/replaced by Michael Botts/Sacramento, California

This group began in Hollywood as a trio called Pleasure Faire whose members, Robb Royer, Jim Griffin, and David Gates, all had had prior experience as studio musicians. Gates had also done some solo recording and had been active as a writer-producer on hit records like "Popsicles and Icicles" by The Murmaids and "My One and Only Jimmy Boy" by The Girlfriends. Royer and Griffin were responsible for writing most of Pleasure Faire's material. In 1969, under the pseudonyms Robb Wilson and Arthur James, they created the Academy Award-winning song "For All We Know," heard in the film *For Lovers and Other Strangers.*

Late in 1969 the group added a fourth member, drummer James Gordon, and changed their name to Bread. They were signed by Elektra Records and their first album, *Bread,* was released. Soon afterward Mike Botts replaced Gordon in the group, and a second album, called *On the Water,* was issued. By the summer of 1970 their first single, a David Gates song titled "Make It with You," reached number one and became the first of a long string of major hits.

In 1971 Robb Royer left the group to become a scriptwriter and was replaced by Larry Knechtel, a West Coast session musician who is practically a legend for his work with Duane Eddy, The Byrds, and Phil Spector. Bread continued producing hit singles and albums until they disbanded in 1973. David Gates continued to record solo for Elektra, Jim Griffin signed with Polydor, and Larry Knechtel returned to studio work. However, in the summer of 1976 the group officially reformed and began recording once again as Bread.

In March 1978 James Griffin left the group to pursue a career as a solo performer. The group is now known as David Gates & Bread.

June 70	*MAKE IT WITH YOU* / **Elektra**
Sept. 70	*IT DON'T MATTER TO ME* / **Elektra**
Jan. 71	*LET YOUR LOVE GO* / **Elektra**
Mar. 71	*IF* / **Elektra**
July 71	*MOTHER FREEDOM* / **Elektra**
Oct. 71	*BABY I'M A WANT YOU* / **Elektra**
Jan. 72	*EVERYTHING I OWN* / **Elektra**
Apr. 72	*DIARY* / **Elektra**
July 72	*GUITAR MAN* / **Elektra**
Nov. 72	*SWEET SURRENDER* / **Elektra**
Feb. 73	*AUBREY* / **Elektra**
Nov. 76	*LOST WITHOUT YOUR LOVE* / **Elektra**
Apr. 77	*HOOKED ON YOU* / **Elektra**

Brenda & The Tabulations

HOMETOWN: Philadelphia, Pennsylvania

Brenda & The Tabulations formed during the mid-sixties in the Philadelphia area, developing their act in the local clubs. Late in 1966 they signed with the local Dionn label, which was nationally distributed by one of the city's top record companies at the time, Jamie-Guyden. Working closely with producer Bob Finiz, the group recorded a string of releases which became national hits and best sellers in the R & B market.

In 1970 Brenda & The Tabulations switched to the Top & Bottom label, another Jamie-Guyden affiliate, and began working with writer, arranger, and producer Van McCoy. Under McCoy's direction the group continued their success well into the seventies.

Feb. 67	*DRY YOUR EYES* / **Dionn**
May 67	*STAY TOGETHER, YOUNG LOVERS* / **Dionn**
June 67	*WHO'S LOVING YOU* / **Dionn**
Aug. 67	*JUST ONCE IN A LIFETIME* / **Dionn**
Nov. 67	*WHEN YOU'RE GONE* / **Dionn**
Mar. 68	*BABY, YOU'RE SO RIGHT FOR ME* / **Dionn**
Jan. 70	*THE TOUCH OF YOU* / **Top & Bottom**
May 70	*AND MY HEART SANG* / **Top & Bottom**
Aug. 70	*DON'T MAKE ME OVER* / **Top & Bottom**
Apr. 71	*RIGHT ON THE TIP OF MY TONGUE* / **Top & Bottom**
Aug. 71	*PART OF YOU* / **Top & Bottom**

Brewer & Shipley

MEMBERS:
Michael Brewer (acoustic guitar, vocals) / born: 1944 / Oklahoma City, Oklahoma
Thomas Shipley (acoustic guitar, vocals) / born: 1942 / Mineral Ridge, Ohio

Mike Brewer and Tom Shipley were both heavily influenced during their childhood by country and folk music.

By the mid-sixties they had pursued individual careers as performers and were active on the national coffeehouse and college circuit. Their paths crossed at a coffeehouse in Los Angeles and Mike, who had a songwriting contract with A & M Records' Irving-Almo publishing division, asked Tom to collaborate with him. In 1968 the label released an album called *Brewer & Shipley,* a collection of demo sessions. The album became somewhat successful and brought them to the attention of Kama Sutra Records, who offered them a contract. During the next two years they released two albums on that label, *Weeds* and *Tarkio,* the latter yielding a top ten single called "One Toke over the Line."

Brewer and Shipley continued to record successfully through 1972, when they temporarily separated to pursue individual careers. However, they have reunited and today jointly own and live on a farm outside Kansas City, Missouri.

Feb. 71 *ONE TOKE OVER THE LINE /* **Kama Sutra**
May 71 *TARKIO ROAD /* **Kama Sutra**
Feb. 72 *SHAKE OFF THE DEMON /* **Kama Sutra**

Brick

MEMBERS:
Eddie Irons (drums)
Regi Hargis (lead guitar, vocals)
Jimmy "Lord" Brown (lead vocals, sax, trumpet)
Ray Ransom (vocals, brass piano)
Donald Nevins (sax, flute)
HOMETOWN: Atlanta, Georgia

Ray Ransom formed the group about 1972; soon they were working as studio musicians in Atlanta behind many top singers. After perfecting their sound they signed with Bang Records in early 1976 and recorded a song called "Dazz," a tune that Eddie, Regi, and Ray had written. The song, which became a top ten national hit, set the tone for their "disco-jazz"-oriented sound.

Oct. 76 *DAZZ /* **Bang**
Sept. 77 *DUSIC /* **Bang**
Jan. 78 *AIN'T GONNA HURT NOBODY /* **Bang**

Johnny Bristol

HOMETOWN: Morganton, North Carolina

Johnny Bristol launched his career while serving in the air force in Detroit during the late fifties. There he met Jackie Beavers, and the two began appearing in local clubs as Johnny & Jackie. They were heard by Gwen Gordy (sister of Motown head Berry Gordy and wife of Harvey Fuqua, former lead singer of The Moonglows) and were signed to the Tri-Phi label. They recorded a number of regional Detroit hits before the label was absorbed into the Motown organization in 1960.

At that point Jackie Beavers left to pursue a solo career, and Bristol joined Harvey Fuqua in the A & R department at Motown. During the next ten years he became one of the label's most successful writers and producers. Two of his Johnny & Jackie recordings from the Tri-Phi days, "Someday We'll Be Together" and "Do You See My Love for You Growing," were reworked into hits for The Supremes and Junior Walker. He was also responsible for records such as "My Whole World Ended" by David Ruffin, "Twenty-Five Miles" by Edwin Starr, "Yester-Me, Yester-You, Yesterday" by Stevie Wonder, and countless others.

In 1973 Bristol left Motown and signed a production contract with Columbia Records. After achieving success as a writer and producer, he tried his hand at recording, and signed with MGM Records in 1974. His very first release, "Hang on in There Baby," became a top seller.

Today Bristol concentrates on his independent production activities, working with such artists as Johnny Mathis, Al Wilson, Buddy Miles, Boz Scaggs, Jerry Butler, and The Jackson Sisters.

June 74 *HANG ON IN THERE BABY /*
MGM
Nov. 74 *YOU AND I /MGM*
Nov. 76 *DO IT TO MY MIND /* Atlantic

The Brooklyn Bridge

ORIGINAL MEMBERS:
Johnny Maestro (lead vocals) / born: May 7, 1939
Fred Ferrara (background vocals) / born: 1945
Mike Gregorio (background vocals) / born: 1947
Les Cauchi (background vocals) / born: 1945
Tom Sullivan (arranger, bandleader) / born: 1946
Carolyn Woods (organ) / born: 1947
Jim Rosica (bass) / born: 1947
Jim Macioce (guitar) / born: 1947
Artie Cantanzarita (drums) / born: 1949
Shelly Davis (trumpet, keyboards) / born: 1950
Joe Ruvio (sax) / born: 1947
HOMETOWN: New York City

The Brooklyn Bridge was formed during the mid-sixties as an eleven-member group, made up of musicians from three earlier groups.

Their lead singer was Johnny Maestro, former lead of The Crests. After separating from that group in 1960 he performed for several years as a solo act. Later he began working with a new back-up group called The Del-Satins, two of whose members, Les Cauchi and Fred Ferrara, had been with the group since the days when The Del-

Satins backed Dion DiMucci's recordings.

In 1968 Johnny Maestro and The Del-Satins entered a talent contest at The Cloud Nine in the Long Island suburbs of New York City. Another of the entries was a seven-member band named The Rhythm Method, which had been formed by Tom Sullivan and featured the lead voice of his wife, Carolyn Woods.

After the contest the two groups decided to join forces and arrived at their new name when someone told them that they had as much chance of succeeding as an eleven-member group as selling the Brooklyn Bridge!

Later that year they did become successful and, through the efforts of producer Wes Farrell were signed by Buddah Records. Their first hit was a Jim Webb song (recorded earlier by The Fifth Dimension) called "The Worst That Could Happen." It reached the top three and was followed by a long string of hits through 1970.

Over the years the group has undergone numerous personnel changes. The current Brooklyn Bridge is a five-man group, containing original members Maestro and Cauchi. They make occasional appearances at oldies shows and, in 1975, were signed to a new recording contract by Private Stock Records.

Dec. 68 *THE WORST THAT COULD HAPPEN /* Buddah
Mar. 69 *BLESSED IS THE RAIN /* Buddah
May 69 *WELCOME ME LOVE /* Buddah
July 69 *YOUR HUSBAND, MY WIFE /* Buddah
Oct. 69 *YOU'LL NEVER WALK ALONE /* Buddah
July 70 *DOWN BY THE RIVER /* Buddah
Oct. 70 *DAY IS DONE /* Buddah

The Brooklyn Bridge. Center: Johnny Maestro

The Brothers Johnson

MEMBERS:

George Johnson (guitar)/born: May 17, 1953

Louis Johnson (bass guitar)/born: Apr. 13, 1955

HOMETOWN: Los Angeles, California

The two brothers began playing around Los Angeles while in their teens and eventually wound up with Billy Preston and his band. After a few years of touring they returned to Los Angeles and became studio musicians. In 1974 they met Quincy Jones, who spotted something unique about the duo. He worked with them, eventually getting them a contract with A & M Records. His faith in them led to several hit singles and a platinum LP.

May 76	*I'LL BE GOOD TO YOU* /A & M	
Aug. 76	*GET THE FUNK OUT MA FACE* /A & M	
July 77	*STRAWBERRY LETTER 23* /A & M	

Polly Brown

Polly Brown first became known during the late sixties as lead singer of the

53

The Brothers Johnson. Left to right: Louis and George

British group Pickettywitch. When they disbanded in 1972, she joined a new group called Sweat Dreams, in which she used the stage name of Sarah Leone and made personal appearances in blackface makeup and a wig.

Early in 1975 Polly began recording as a solo artist and achieved her first hit single with "Up in a Puff of Smoke."

Jan. 75 *UP IN A PUFF OF SMOKE /* **GTO**

Jackson Browne

BORN: Oct. 9, 1950
HOMETOWN: Heidelberg, Germany

Jackson Browne grew up primarily in Los Angeles, where his parents had moved during his early childhood. He was proficient on several instruments, active as a songwriter, and a member of the fledgling Nitty Gritty Dirt Band while still in high school. In 1967, at the age of seventeen, he moved to New York City to seek his fortune.

After a year of performing his own material on the city's folk-rock circuit, he returned to Los Angeles during the late sixties to find that his reputation as a songwriter had preceded him and that many major West Coast artists were performing his songs.

In 1971 his growing reputation attracted the attention of rock entrepreneur David Geffen, who was in the process of starting the Asylum record company. Browne was signed to the label and late in the year his first album, *Jackson Browne,* was released. A single taken from the LP, "Doctor, My Eyes," became a top ten national hit early in 1972 and established Browne as a performer. Later that year another new act called The Eagles was signed to Asylum, and they launched their career with a major hit recording of a Jackson Browne song, "Take It Easy."

At present Jackson Browne continues to record for Asylum and his material is also widely recorded by other artists.

Mar. 72 *DOCTOR, MY EYES /* **Asylum**
Aug. 72 *ROCK ME ON THE WATER /* **Asylum**
Sept. 73 *REDNECK FRIEND /* **Asylum**
Jan. 77 *HERE COME THOSE TEARS AGAIN /* **Asylum**
May 77 *THE PRETENDER /* **Asylum**
Feb. 78 *RUNNIN' ON EMPTY /* **Asylum**

Brownsville Station

MEMBERS:
Michael John "Cub" Koda (guitar, lead vocals) / born: Oct. 1, 1948 / Detroit, Michigan
Michael "Sam" Lutz (bass) / born: June 15, 1949 / Ann Arbor, Michigan
T. J. Cronley (drums) / replaced (1971) by David Lynn (Henry) Weck / born: July 27, 1949 / Van Wert, Ohio
Anthony Driggins (bass) / (left 1973; not replaced)

Jackson Browne

Bruce Nazarian (guitar) / (added in 1975)
HOMETOWN: Ann Arbor, Michigan

In early 1969 the four original members of Brownsville Station were introduced in an Ann Arbor record shop by its owner, Al Nalli. He had known them individually and suggested that they form a group under his management.

Calling themselves The Station, they began touring in 1970 and one of their stops, Brownsville, Texas, prompted the expansion of their name to Brownsville Station. After recording for several local Michigan labels, they were signed in 1971 by Warner Brothers, and an album *No B.S.,* was released. It was successful enough to send them on their first major national tour, and late in the year they were offered a contract by Big Tree Records.

Their new label began releasing singles late in 1972, and their first, "Red Back Spider," barely dented the charts. At this point the group's bass player left to pursue other interests, and they continued as a trio with guitarist Mike Lutz switching to bass. In February 1973 a second single was issued and this, a Jimmy Cliff tune titled "Let Your Yeah Be Yeah," became much more successful. However, it was their next release, "Smokin' in the Boys' Room," that proved to be the group's breakthrough and took them into the top three.

Today Brownsville Station is a leading exponent of contemporary punk rock. During the summer of 1975 they became a quartet once more with the addition of noted session guitarist Bruce Nazarian.

They now record for Private Stock Records.

Dec. 72	*RED BACK SPIDER* / Big Tree	
Mar. 73	*LET YOUR YEAH BE YEAH* / Big Tree	
Oct. 73	*SMOKIN' IN THE BOYS' ROOM* / Big Tree	
May 74	*I'M THE LEADER OF THE GANG* / Big Tree	
Aug. 74	*THE KINGS OF THE PARTY* / Big Tree	
June 77	*LADY (PUT THE LIGHT ON ME)* / Private Stock	
Aug. 77	*MARTIAN BOOGIE* / Private Stock	

The B. T. Express

MEMBERS:

William Risbrook (tenor sax, flute) / born: Jan. 14, 1951 / Brooklyn, New York

Louis Risbrook (bass guitar) / born: June 27, 1953 / Brooklyn, New York

Richard Thompson (guitar) / born: Jan. 6, 1951 / Fairfax, South Carolina

Barbara Joyce Lomas (lead vocals) / born: May 19, 1952 / Bessemer, Alabama

Olando "Terrell" Woods (drums) / Barnesville, Georgia / replaced by Leslie Ming / born: Nov. 17, 1951 / Brooklyn, New York

Carlos Ward (alto sax) / born: May 1, 1947 / Panama, Central America

Dennis Rowe (percussion) / born: Oct. 23, 1949 / St. Louis, Missouri

Michael Jones (organ) / born: Dec. 26, 1950 / New York City

The B. T. Express is one of the leading exponents of the big-band disco sound prevalent in the seventies.

The seven members were brought together by their manager, King Davis, though they all had had prior professional experience. Bill Risbrook and Rich Thompson were part of a band Davis had managed earlier called The King Davis House Rockers. Barbara Joyce Lomas had sung extensively in Alabama church choirs and had recorded with a singing group called The Uptights. Carlos Ward, who is proficient on several instruments, had played with such leading jazz artists as John Coltrane, McCoy Tyner, Don Cherry, and Pharaoh Sanders, while the other members had played in various bands around the Brooklyn area.

Under Davis's management, the group became popular on the club circuit and underwent several name changes—from The Madison Express to The Brothers Trucking to the B. T. Express. Record producer Fred Frank caught their act and signed them to a production contract. Their records were released on the Roadshow label (nationally distributed by Scepter), and late in 1974 they scored with their first hit, a number one record titled "Do It (Till You're Satisfied)." After several more hits they switched affiliations in 1976 to Columbia Records.

B. T. Express. Back row, left to right: Louis Risbrook, Leslie Ming, Dennis Rowe; center: Michael Jones; front row, left to right: Richard Thompson, Carlos Ward, Bill Risbrook

Sept. 74	***DO IT (TILL YOU'RE SATISFIED)* / Scepter-Roadshow**
Jan. 75	***EXPRESS* / Scepter-Roadshow**
Aug. 75	***GIVE IT WHAT YOU'VE GOT* / Roadshow**
Sept. 75	***PEACE PIPE* / Roadshow**
Jan. 76	***CLOSE TO YOU* / Roadshow**
June 76	***CAN'T STOP GROOVING NOW* / Columbia**

Bubble Puppy

MEMBERS:

Rod Prince (lead and rhythm guitar)

Todd Potter (lead and rhythm guitar)

Roy Cox (bass)

M. Taylor (drums, percussion) / replaced by David Fore

HOMETOWN: Austin, Texas

Bubble Puppy was a psychedelic punk-rock band. After building a local reputation in Austin, the group was signed in 1968 by the Texas-based International Artists label and an album, *Gathering Promises,* was released. It yielded a single called "Hot Smoke and Sassafrass," but, in spite of the record's having reached the national top twenty, International Artists ceased operations shortly thereafter.

In 1971, after replacing the original drummer with David Fore, the group reemerged as Demian and recorded an album of the same name for ABC Records. They toured Texas and the Los Angeles area to help promote the

The Buckinghams. Left to right: Denny Tufano, Dennis Miccoli, Jon Paulos, Carl Giamarese, Nick Fortune

album, but poor sales caused the group to disband.

Feb. 69 *HOT SMOKE AND SASSAFRASS* **/International Artists**

The Buckinghams

MEMBERS:
Dennis Tufano (lead vocals)/born: Sept. 11, 1948
Dennis Miccoli (keyboards)/born: Sept. 2, 1947/replaced by Martin Grebb
Nicholas Fortune (bass)/born: May 4, 1946
Carl Giamarese (guitar)/born: Aug. 21, 1947
Jon Jon Paulos (drums)/born: Mar. 31, 1948
HOMETOWN: Chicago, Illinois

The Buckinghams began playing in the clubs in the Chicago area during the mid-sixties and soon built a strong reputation. In 1966 they were signed by the small USA record company and an early release, "Kind of a Drag," did

the nearly impossible by going to number one on the national charts. They followed with another hit, Lloyd Price's "Lawdy Miss Clawdy," but the company had distribution problems, and early in 1969 the group accepted an offer to switch to the Columbia label.

At Columbia they were united with writer-producer James William Guercio, a former member of Frank Zappa's Mothers Of Invention. Under his direction The Buckinghams produced a string of hit singles and albums through the late sixties, when Guercio began turning his attention to a new group named Chicago.

Early in 1975 The Buckinghams emerged once again with an album of their earlier hits mixed with new material, produced by Jim Guercio, who today operates the famed Caribou Ranch recording studios in Colorado.

Dec. 66 *KIND OF A DRAG* **/USA**

Mar. 67 *LAWDY MISS CLAWDY* / **USA**
Mar. 67 *DON'T YOU CARE* / **Columbia**
June 67 *MERCY, MERCY, MERCY* / **Columbia**
Sept. 67 *HEY BABY, THEY'RE PLAYING OUR SONG* / **Columbia**
Dec. 67 *SUSAN* / **Columbia**
June 68 *BACK IN LOVE AGAIN* / **Columbia**

Buffalo Springfield

MEMBERS:

Stephen Arthur Stills (guitar) / born: Jan. 3, 1945 / Dallas, Texas

Neil Young (lead guitar) / born: Nov. 12, 1945 / Toronto, Ontario, Canada

Richard Furay (rhythm guitar) / born: May 9, 1944 / Dayton, Ohio

Dewey Martin (drums) / born: Sept. 30, 1952 / Chesterville, Ontario, Canada

Bruce Palmer (bass) / Ontario, Canada / replaced by James Messina / born: Dec. 5, 1947 / Maywood, California

This group of rock superstars was formed during the spring of 1966 when Steve Stills and Richie Furay were in a Los Angeles traffic jam and noticed a hearse in front of their car bearing an Ontario license plate. Furay discovered that it belonged to a friend of his, Neil Young. Traveling with Young was Bruce Palmer, and the four decided to form a group. After recruiting drummer Dewey Martin, they called themselves The Herd until they noticed the name "Buffalo Springfield" on a parked steamroller. Soon after the group's formation Bruce Palmer left to pursue other interests and was replaced by bassist Jim Messina.

Late in 1966 the group was signed by Atlantic Records, and their first release, "For What It's Worth," became a top ten hit. After another hit single and an extremely successful album, Buffalo Springfield was heralded as one of the most important new forces in rock. Then they suddenly disbanded during the summer of 1967. Stunned by the loss of a major act, Atlantic attempted to persuade them to re-form, but found the group's decision irrevocable. Drawing upon previously recorded material, the company continued to release Buffalo Springfield records through the end of 1968.

Less than two years later Steve Stills and Neil Young were back on Atlantic as half of Crosby, Stills, Nash & Young, one of the most successful and highly acclaimed rock acts of the sixties and seventies. Jim Messina and Richie Furay in the meantime had formed Poco, one of that era's best-selling and most influential country-rock bands.

At present Stills and Young are successful solo performers. Messina eventually became half of the recently separated rock duo Loggins & Messina, and Richie Furay played in the now defunct Souther-Hillman-Furay Band.

See *CROSBY, STILLS, NASH & YOUNG; POCO; LOGGINS & MESSINA;* and *SOUTHER-HILLMAN-FURAY BAND.*

Jan. 67 *FOR WHAT IT'S WORTH* / **Atco**
July 67 *BLUEBIRD* / **Atco**
Sept. 67 *ROCK & ROLL WOMAN* / **Atco**
Jan. 68 *EXPECTING TO FLY* / **Atco**
Oct. 68 *ON THE WAY HOME* / **Atco**

Jimmy Buffett

BORN: Dec. 25, 1946
HOMETOWN: Pascagoula, Mississippi

After earning a degree in journalism from Auburn University, Buffett moved to Nashville where he did one country album that was only moderately successful. From there he ventured to Florida and began recording new material. In 1973 he recorded an LP called

Jimmy Buffett

A White Sports Coat and a Pink Crustacean, which was one of the first to show his special brand of humor.

In 1976, Buffett went back to Nashville to record the album *Changes in Latitudes, Changes in Attitudes* from which came his biggest hit single "Margaritaville." Today he, along with his Coral Reefer Band, travels all over the country entertaining millions.

May 74	*COME MONDAY* / ABC	
Apr. 77	*MARGARITAVILLE* / ABC	
Sept. 77	*CHANGES IN LATITUDES, CHANGES IN ATTITUDES* / ABC	
Apr. 78	*CHEESEBURGER IN PARADISE* / ABC	

The Byrds

ORIGINAL MEMBERS:

James Joseph "Roger" McGuinn III (guitar, lead vocals) / born: July 13, 1942 / Chicago, Illinois

David Van Cortland Crosby (guitar) / born: Aug. 14, 1941 / Los Angeles, California

Eugene Clarke (guitar) / born: Nov. 17, 1944 / Tipton, Missouri

Christopher Hillman (bass) / born: Dec. 4, 1942 / Los Angeles, California

Michael Clark (drums) / born: June 3, 1944 / New York City

The Byrds emerged in 1965 as the first group to play electronically amplified folk music and created an entirely new direction in popular music known as folk rock. When the group first became popular they were considered a serious threat to The Beatles.

Each of The Byrds' members came to the group with a good deal of prior experience. Roger McGuinn had toured for two years with The Chad Mitchell Trio and for a year with Bobby Darin; David Crosby had been a popular folk singer since the early sixties; Gene Clarke was an alumnus of The New Christy Minstrels; Chris Hillman had led his own group called The Hillmen; and Mike Clark was one of the West Coast's most sought-after jazz drummers.

With the help of a California man in the folk field named James Dickson, The Byrds got together during the summer of 1964 and spent the next several months rehearsing. They quickly recorded one album for Elektra, and, early in 1965 Dickson took the group to the head of A & R at Columbia Records, Terry Melcher. They were signed to the label, and their first release was a Bob Dylan song called "Mr. Tambourine Man," which went straight to number one. Drawing again on Dylan, they followed with "All I Really Want to Do," followed in turn by a Pete Seeger adaptation of a passage from the book of Ecclesiastes called "Turn Turn Turn." After scoring success with outside material, The Byrds continued with a five-year string of hits consisting almost entirely of Roger McGuinn's original songs before disbanding permanently during the early seventies.

The Byrds. Clockwise from top left: Roger McGuinn, Gene Clarke, Chris Hillman, Mike Clark, Dave Crosby

During the group's seven-year history, they sustained numerous personnel changes in which some of rock music's leading figures came and went. The first to leave was Gene Clarke who joined one of the original Dillards to form Dillard & Clarke. By 1968 drummer Mike Clark was gone, and David Crosby had left to become a part of Crosby, Stills & Nash. They were replaced with Kevin Kelley and Gram Parsons, but The Byrds were dealt another severe blow when Parsons and Chris Hillman separated from the group to form The Flying Burrito Brothers in 1969. At this point they were joined by Clyde "Skip" Battin, a former member of the fifties Skip & Flip group, who remained with Roger McGuinn until the end in 1973.

Most of The Byrds' original members continue to be active today. Roger McGuinn, who spent several years recording solo, recently joined former members of Commander Cody to form a new band called Thunderbyrd. David Crosby often appears in various combinations with members of Crosby, Stills, Nash & Young. Chris Hillman, after a stint with Souther-Hillman-Furay, recently went solo and formed his own Chris Hillman Band.

May 65	*MR. TAMBOURINE MAN* / Columbia
July 65	*ALL I REALLY WANT TO DO* / Columbia
Oct. 65	*TURN TURN TURN* / Columbia
Feb. 66	*IT WON'T BE WRONG* / Columbia
Feb. 66	*SET YOU FREE THIS TIME* / Columbia
Apr. 66	*EIGHT MILES HIGH* / Columbia
July 66	*5 D (FIFTH DIMENSION)* / Columbia
Sept. 66	*MR. SPACEMAN* / Columbia
Jan. 67	*SO YOU WANT TO BE A ROCK & ROLL STAR* / Columbia
Apr. 67	*MY BACK PAGES* / Columbia
June 67	*HAVE YOU SEEN HER FACE* / Columbia
Aug. 67	*LADY FRIEND* / Columbia
Nov. 67	*GOING BACK* / Columbia
May 68	*YOU AIN'T GOING NOWHERE* / Columbia
Nov. 69	*BALLAD OF EASY RIDER* / Columbia
Feb. 70	*JESUS IS JUST ALRIGHT* / Columbia

Canned Heat

ORIGINAL MEMBERS:
Robert Hite (lead vocals)/born: Feb. 26, 1945/
Torrance, California

Henry Vestine (lead guitar)/born: Dec. 25,
1944/Washington, D.C.

Alan Wilson (guitar)/born: July 4, 1943/Boston,
Massachusetts/died: Sept. 3, 1970

ADDED IN 1968:
Lawrence Taylor (bass)/born: June 26, 1942/
New York City

Adolfo De La Parra (drums)/born: Feb. 8,
1946/Mexico City, Mexico

Canned Heat

This Los Angeles blues band, formed in 1967 as a trio, built a strong reputation playing in the area's clubs. They were seen during a performance by executives of Liberty Records who signed them to a contract, and late in the year their first album, *Canned Heat,* was released. In 1968 the group added a bass player and drummer, and a second LP was issued called *Boogie with Canned Heat,* followed by a top twenty single, "On the Road Again." After another hit single, "Going up the Country," bassist Larry Taylor left the group to join John Mayall's Blues Band, marking the beginning of numerous personnel changes over the following years. A one-time member was Harvey Mandel, who also spent some time with John Mayall and is now considered one of the premiere solo guitarists in rock.

The group in its various forms has continued to produce successful albums and occasional singles. Their most recent line-up consists of original members Bob Hite, Henry Vestine (who left the group for several years and returned), and Adolfo De La Parra, along with new members James Shane (guitar and bass), Richard Hite (guitar and bass), and Edward Beyer (keyboards). Original member Alan Wilson remained with Canned Heat until 1970; on September 3 of that year he died of accidental drug poisoning.

Aug. 68	***ON THE ROAD AGAIN*/Liberty**
Dec. 68	***GOING UP THE COUNTRY*/Liberty**
Mar. 69	***TIME WAS*/Liberty**
Oct. 70	***LET'S WORK TOGETHER*/Liberty**
Mar. 72	***ROCKING WITH THE KING*/United Artists**

Cannibal & The Headhunters

MEMBERS:
Frankie "Cannibal" Garcia
Robert "Rabbit" Jaramillo
Joe "Yo-Yo" Jaramillo
Richard "Scar" Lopez
HOMETOWN: Los Angeles, California

This was one of several Latin-rock groups which became popular in the Los Angeles area during the mid-sixties and helped pave the way for the success of Santana a few years later.

In 1965 Cannibal & The Headhunters made an appearance at a club called The Rhythm Room, where a "live" recording was made of a 1963 hit by Chris Kenner called "Land of 1,000 Dances." Released on the Rampart label, it became a top thirty record and made the group popular enough to continue with several regional California hits.

During the late sixties the master of "Land of 1,000 Dances" was obtained by Date Records, a subsidiary of Columbia, and the recording was moderately popular a second time.

Feb. 65 *LAND OF 1,000 DANCES /* **Rampart**

Jim Capaldi

BORN: Aug. 24, 1944
HOMETOWN: Evesham, Worcestershire, England

Jim Capaldi was involved with music early, since his father was a music teacher and his mother had been a professional singer. While planning a career in engineering during his teens, he formed his own group and developed a strong reputation as a drummer. He was asked to join Traffic when they formed in 1967, and he remained with them for nearly four years before leaving for a solo career (see *TRAFFIC*). He continued to record for Island Records, the British label with which the group was affiliated.

During the early seventies Island expanded operations to the United States and their stateside releases included records by Jim Capaldi. He achieved an American hit in 1972 with "Eve," followed in 1975 by two chart entries, "It's Alright" and "Love Hurts." The latter, an early-sixties tune by Felice and Beauleaux Bryant, was overshadowed by a top ten recording of the same song by another British act, Nazareth.

Apr. 72 *EVE* / **Island**
Jan. 75 *IT'S ALRIGHT* / **Island**
Dec. 75 *LOVE HURTS* / **Island**

The Capitols

MEMBERS:
Donald Norman (guitar)
Richard Mitchell (piano organ)
Samuel George (drums)
HOMETOWN: Detroit, Michigan

Each member of this group had sung in various high school groups before, forming The Capitols in January 1966. During one of their first performances at a local club, they met Detroit record producer Ollie McLaughlin, who agreed to audition them for his new Karen record label. The Capitols were signed to a contract, and McLaughlin produced a recording of "Hello Stranger," formerly a top three hit for another of his artists, Barbara Lewis. On the flip side, McLaughlin released one of the group's original songs, written by Don Norman under the name Don Storball, about a dance step called the "Cool Jerk." The dance side became the hit

The Captain & Tennille

and reached the top ten on the national charts.

The Capitols were able to follow with two additional hits, after which their popularity was limited to their native Detroit.

Apr. 66	***COOL JERK***/**Karen**
Aug. 66	***I GOT TO HANDLE IT***/**Karen**
Nov. 66	***WE GOT A THING THAT'S IN THE GROOVE***/**Karen**

The Captain & Tennille

MEMBERS:

Daryl Dragon (keyboards)/born: Aug. 27, 1942/Studio City, California

Toni Tennille (keyboards, vocals)/born: May 8, 1943/Montgomery, Alabama

Daryl Dragon is the son of Carmen Dragon, the famed symphony orchestra conductor. His childhood friendship with The Beach Boys' Brian Wilson led to a six-year stint as that group's arranger. Toni Tennille was born into a musical family in Alabama and moved to California with her parents during her college years. She became active as a studio background singer and was best known for her work on the Elton John *Caribou* album. During the early seventies she wrote the music for and appeared in a short-lived Broadway stage production called *Mother Earth*.

Dragon and Tennille met when Toni began organizing a Los Angeles company for *Mother Earth* and Dragon was recommended to her as a keyboard player. Before taking the job he asked for a tape of some of the show's material, fell in love with her voice, and immediately accepted. The production was not successful, but The Captain (a name he picked up because of the captain's hat he wore during his appearances with The Beach Boys) & Tennille have been together ever since.

At first Toni joined Daryl and The Beach Boys as a keyboard player and toured with the group as their only "beach girl." Later they separated from the group and performed in numerous small clubs around the Los Angeles area as The Dragons.

In 1973 Toni wrote a song called "The Way I Want to Touch You." Using some studio time they were owed by a friend, they cut the song with Daryl playing all the instruments and Toni singing all the vocal parts. They pressed five hundred copies on their own Butterscotch Castle label (named after their apartment house!) and sent them to various local radio stations. Much to their amazement, the song received a great deal of airplay and attracted the attention of Joyce Records, a small company that distributed it throughout the Los Angeles area. After the record became a regional top ten hit, it was later released for national distribution and became a best seller. The Captain & Tennille received numerous offers from large companies and signed with A & M. While in the process of recording their first album, they went to The Troubador for Neil

Sedaka's comeback appearance, and one of the songs he performed was his own "Love Will Keep Us Together." They liked the song so much that they included it in the album. When it was released as their first single, it went to number one nationally and became 1975's largest-selling single record.

The Captain & Tennille, who were married on Valentine's Day, 1974, presently live in the Chatsworth area of the San Fernando Valley.

Apr. 75	*LOVE WILL KEEP US TOGETHER* / A & M
Aug. 75	*POR AMOR VIVEREMOS (SPANISH-LANGUAGE VERSION OF LOVE WILL KEEP US TOGETHER)* / A & M
Sept. 75	*THE WAY I WANT TO TOUCH YOU* / A & M
Jan. 76	*LONELY NIGHT (ANGEL FACE)* / A & M
June 76	*SHOP AROUND* / A & M
Sept. 76	*MUSKRAT LOVE* / A & M
Mar. 77	*CAN'T STOP DANCING* / A & M
June 77	*COME IN FROM THE RAIN* / A & M
Apr. 78	*I'M ON MY WAY* / A & M

Henson Cargill

BORN: Feb. 5, 1941
HOMETOWN: Oklahoma City, Oklahoma

Although Henson Cargill played guitar and sang as a child, he gave no thought to music as a career and went to college to study commercial farm management. After graduation he returned home to establish his own ranch and took a second job as a deputy sheriff. In that capacity Cargill met Harold Gay, lead singer of the famed Kimberleys, who convinced him to accompany the group on a tour. When he returned Cargill traveled to Nashville in search of a recording contract and succeeded at Monument Records. Late in 1967 his first release, "Skip a

Rope," went to the top twenty-five nationally and launched his career as a country artist.

Since then Cargill has recorded for Mega and Atlantic Records and has continued to be active in the country field. When not performing he lives with his wife and family on his ranch near Oklahoma City.

Dec. 67 *SKIP A ROPE*/Monument

Carl Carlton

HOMETOWN: Detroit, Michigan

Carl Carlton grew up in Detroit where one of his childhood friends was Stevie Wonder. He became proficient in music as a child and was signed as a young teen-ager to the local Lando label. His records there did not become successful, and in 1967 he was signed as "Little" Carl Carlton (borrowed from "Little" Stevie Wonder) to Don Robey's Backbeat label, where he recorded two national hits.

During the early seventies Backbeat became part of the ABC family of labels. In 1974 Carlton began working with producer Bobby Russell, who produced a recording of a song, "Everlasting Love," which he had written and produced as a top ten hit for Robert Knight seven years earlier. Aimed squarely at the discotheque market, this new version rose to the top of the charts and revived Carlton's career.

He followed early in 1975 with another hit and became a popular discotheque attraction. Today he records for Mercury Records.

June 68 *COMPETITION AIN'T NOTHING* (as "Little" Carl Carlton)/ Backbeat
July 70 *DROP BY MY PLACE*/ Backbeat

Sept. 74 *EVERLASTING LOVE*/ABC
Feb. 75 *SMOKIN' ROOM*/ABC

Eric Carmen

FULL NAME: Eric Howard Carmen
BORN: Aug. 11, 1949
HOMETOWN: Cleveland, Ohio

About 1970 Eric, along with friends Wally Bryson, Dave Smalley, and Jim Bonfanti, formed a group called the Raspberries and began playing the Cleveland area. A few years later they were signed by Capitol Records and turned out a few national hits including "Go All the Way" and "I Wanna Be with You."

By 1974 Carmen had left the group to pursue a solo career and was eventually signed by Arista Records. His first release for the label was a tune he wrote called "All by Myself." It became a top ten national hit, and today Carmen is one of the hottest musical talents in the business.

Eric Carmen

Dec. 75	ALL BY MYSELF / Arista
May 76	NEVER GONNA FALL IN LOVE AGAIN / Arista
Aug. 76	SUNRISE / Arista
Aug. 77	SHE IT / Arista
Dec. 77	BOATS AGAINST THE CURRENT / Arista

The Carpenters

MEMBERS:
Richard Carpenter / born: Oct. 15, 1946
Karen Carpenter / born: Mar. 2, 1950
HOMETOWN: New Haven, Connecticut

This brother and sister duo emerged during the early seventies to become one of the leading pop acts of their time.

Although both Karen and Richard were born in Connecticut, where Richard had played keyboards in a high school band, the family moved to California where they both attended California State College. Karen took up the drums and joined forces with her brother and bassist Wes Jacobs to form The Carpenters Trio. They entered a "battle of the bands" contest in Hollywood and won, receiving as first prize a contract with RCA Records. Although two singles were recorded, they were never released. In 1968 the bass player left the group to play tuba with an opera company, and The Carpenters formed a rock sextet called Spectrum. After a few personal appearances that group disbanded in 1968.

During the following year Karen and Richard Carpenter began working in the garage studio of musician friend Joe Osborne, who experimented with their voices in multitrack recording. After enough material was completed for an album, Osborne made the rounds to various record companies and, after several rejections, found interest in the tape at Herb Alpert's A & M label. The group was signed, and the album, called *Offerings,* was released late in 1969. A single released from the LP, a reworking of The Beatles' "Ticket to Ride," became a moderate hit, but it was their next release, a song recorded earlier by Dionne Warwicke called "Close to You," that established the group by going to number one on the charts.

Since then The Carpenters have never been absent from the singles and album charts and have been a leading concert attraction.

Feb. 70	TICKET TO RIDE / A & M
June 70	CLOSE TO YOU / A & M
Sept. 70	WE'VE ONLY JUST BEGUN / A & M
Feb. 71	FOR ALL WE KNOW / A & M
May 71	RAINY DAYS & MONDAYS / A & M
Sept. 71	SUPERSTAR / A & M
Dec. 71	BLESS THE BEASTS AND CHILDREN / A & M
Jan. 72	HURTING EACH OTHER / A & M
Apr. 72	IT'S GOING TO TAKE SOME TIME / A & M
July 72	GOODBYE TO LOVE / A & M
Feb. 73	SING / A & M
June 73	YESTERDAY ONCE MORE / A & M
Oct. 73	TOP OF THE WORLD / A & M
Apr. 74	I WON'T LAST A DAY WITHOUT YOU / A & M
Nov. 74	PLEASE, MR. POSTMAN / A & M
Mar. 75	ONLY YESTERDAY / A & M
Aug. 75	SOLITAIRE / A & M
Feb. 76	THERE'S A KIND OF HUSH / A & M
June 76	I NEED TO BE IN LOVE / A & M
Sept. 76	GOOFUS / A & M
May 77	ALL YOU GET FROM LOVE IS A LOVE SONG / A & M
Oct. 77	CALLING OCCUPANTS OF INTERPLANETARY CRAFT / A & M
Feb. 78	SWEET, SWEET SMILE / A & M

The Carpenters

Vikki Carr

REAL NAME: Florencia Bisenta de Casillas
Martinez Cardona
BORN: July 19, 1941
HOMETOWN: El Paso, Texas

Vikki Carr grew up in the San Gabriel
Valley outside Los Angeles, where her
engineer father had moved just after
her birth. While attending Rosemead
High School she began singing on
weekends with local bands and upon
graduation was offered the soloist's
job with The Pepe Callahan Mexican-
Irish Band. After a tour with the band to
Reno, Las Vegas, Lake Tahoe, and

Hawaii, she returned home and began circulating demo records in the hope of getting a recording contract.

During the mid-sixties she was signed by the Liberty label, and her records were distributed worldwide. Although at first not successful in the United States, her records began selling well in Australia and she was asked to tour that country. Upon her return home Vikki was signed for the Ray Anthony television show on which she appeared as a featured vocalist. By this time her popularity had spread from Australia to England and one of her records, "It Must Be Him," placed high on the English charts. The success of this record eventually spread to America as well, and it reached the top three in the fall of 1967.

Since that time Vikki Carr has scored with several additional hit singles, and her albums are continual best sellers. Now considered one of the top club attractions in the business, she lives with her husband, Dann Moss, in Coldwater Canyon, California.

Sept. 67 *IT MUST BE HIM* /Liberty
Dec. 67 *THE LESSON* /Liberty
Mar. 68 *YOUR HEART IS FREE, JUST LIKE THE WIND* /Liberty
Mar. 68 *SHE'LL BE THERE* /Liberty
May 69 *WITH PEN IN HAND* /Liberty
Oct. 69 *ETERNITY* /Liberty
Jan. 71 *I'LL BE HOME* /Columbia

Keith Carradine

BORN: 1950
HOMETOWN: Los Angeles, California

Keith, son of actor John Carradine and brother of David, comes from a highly talented family of actors, which made most people feel that acting would be his forte. Contrary to this, his main interest has been playing his guitar and singing.

His big break came in 1975 when he was chosen to appear in the Robert Altman film *Nashville,* playing a hippie-type drifting singer. For his role in the film he was asked to compose a song; the tune, "I'm Easy," went on to win an Oscar in 1976 as best song written for a motion picture. It also became a smash national hit single for his label, Asylum Records, and established him as a major talent.

May 76 *I'M EASY* /Asylum

Clarence Carter

BORN: Jan. 1936
HOMETOWN: Montgomery, Alabama

Clarence Carter taught himself the guitar. He sang for a time in a gospel choir and, although totally blind since childhood, earned a degree in music from a college in his native Alabama.

Carter's first experience in the recording field was with his friend Calvin Thomas in their group called Clarence & Calvin. The two booked time at Rick Hall's Fame Studios in Muscle Shoals, Alabama, and produced a master that was purchased by Atlantic but was not a commercial success.

Shortly thereafter Calvin Thomas was injured in an automobile accident and could no longer perform. Clarence Carter returned to Muscle Shoals where Rick Hall agreed to produce him as a solo act. Beginning in 1967, their collaboration resulted in a long string of hits, the biggest of which was "Patches," which went to the top five in the summer of 1970.

At present Clarence Carter continues to work with Rick Hall in Muscle Shoals. He writes all his own arrangements in braille and has them transcribed to regular lead sheets for the musicians.

June 67	*THREAD THE NEEDLE* / Fame	
Jan. 68	*LOOKING FOR A FOX* / **Atlantic**	
June 68	*FUNKY FEVER* / Atlantic	
July 68	*SLIP AWAY* / Atlantic	
Nov. 68	*TOO WEAK TO FIGHT* / **Atlantic**	
Mar. 69	*SNATCHING IT BACK* / **Atlantic**	
June 69	*THE FEELING IS RIGHT* / **Atlantic**	
Sept. 69	*DOING OUR THING* / Atlantic	
Feb. 70	*TAKE IT OFF HIM AND PUT IT ON ME* / Atlantic	
Apr. 70	*I CAN'T LEAVE YOUR LOVE ALONE* / Atlantic	
July 70	*PATCHES* / Atlantic	
Nov. 70	*IT'S ALL IN YOUR MIND* / **Atlantic**	
May 71	*THE COURT ROOM* / Atlantic	
Aug. 71	*SLIPPED, TRIPPED AND FELL IN LOVE* / Atlantic	
June 73	*60 MINUTE MAN/MOTHER IN LAW* / Fame	

Alvin Cash & The Crawlers

MEMBERS:
Alvin Cash
Robert Cash
George Cash
HOMETOWN: St. Louis, Missouri

Alvin Cash & The Crawlers (later known as The Registers) were not a vocal group but a dance team of three brothers.

The group emerged during the mid-sixties on One-Der-Ful's subsidiary Mar-V-Lus label with a series of funky, instrumental dance recordings. Featuring occasional dance calls shouted by Alvin Cash over the music and a studio back-up band led by "Monk" Higgins, a number of these records placed on the charts well into the late sixties. The biggest of these was "Twine Time," which became a top fifteen hit early in

1965 and was widely banned because of its allegedly suggestive lyrics.

Jan. 65	*TWINE TIME* / Mar-V-Lus	
Mar. 65	*THE BARRACUDA* / Mar-V-Lus	
July 66	*THE PHILLY FREEZE* / **Mar-V-Lus**	
Nov. 66	*ALVIN'S BOOGALOO* / **Mar-V-Lus**	
Nov. 68	*KEEP ON DANCING* / **Toddlin' Town**	

Cashman & West

Terry Cashman, Gene Pistilli, and Tommy West comprise a team of record producers and songwriters who occasionally perform as recording artists.

Pistilli and West recorded during the sixties as Gene & Tommy, and the three in various combinations have been the studio voices of such groups as The Buchanan Brothers and The Morning Mist. As a producer Tommy West became best known for his work with the late Jim Croce.

Late in 1972 Terry Cashman and Tommy West placed two hits on the charts as Cashman & West. They have continued to be active in the areas of writing and production and have established their own Lifesong record label.

Sept. 72	*AMERICAN CITY SUITE* / **Dunhill**	
Dec. 72	*SONG MAN* / Dunhill	

Casinos

MEMBERS:
Gene Hughes (lead vocals)
Glen Hughes
Ray White
Pete Boulton
Joe Patterson
Mickey Denton
Bob Armstrong

Tom Matthews
Bill Hawkins
HOMETOWN: Cincinnati, Ohio

The group was formed by Gene with his brother Glen and friends Ray, Pete, and Joe in the early sixties while the members were still in their teens. After a period of performing in the local area they were signed by Harry Carlson to his Cincinnati-based Fraternity Records.

The group was looking for a hit song, when one night Gene heard Johnny Nash do a John D. Loudermilk tune called "Then You Can Tell Me Goodbye," which he felt would be perfect for the group. They recorded the song, and by early 1967 it was a national top ten hit.

Jan. 67   ***THEN YOU CAN TELL ME GOODBYE* /Fraternity**
May 67   ***IT'S ALL OVER NOW* / Fraternity**

David Cassidy

BORN: Apr. 12, 1950
HOMETOWN: New York City

David Cassidy is the son of the late singer-actor Jack Cassidy and actress

David Cassidy

Evelyn Ward. During his early childhood the family moved to West Orange, New Jersey, where he lived until the age of ten. At that point his parents separated, and he moved with his mother to Los Angeles, where he attended high school and college.

Although he majored in psychology, acting was in David's blood, and his first professional role was in a California stage production called *And So to Bed.* From there he went to New York and a Broadway show written by Allan Sherman called *The Fig Leaves Are Falling.* Afterward he returned home and began auditioning for television roles. He was seen in episodes of shows such as "Mod Squad," "Ironside," "Marcus Welby, M.D.," and "Bonanza" and eventually in a permanent role as Keith in "The Partridge Family." His costar was Shirley Jones, who became his real-life stepmother when she married Jack Cassidy, and the show was a major success. Late in 1970 Shirley Jones and David Cassidy began releasing records as The Partridge Family (see *THE PARTRIDGE FAMILY*) and a year later Cassidy began a solo career with a string of hits.

David Cassidy continues to live in Los Angeles with his actress-wife, Kay Lenz, where he has been recording for RCA in association with producer Bruce Johnston.

Nov. 71   ***CHERISH* /Bell**
Feb. 72   ***COULD IT BE FOREVER* /Bell**
May 72   ***HOW CAN I BE SURE* /Bell**
Sept. 72 ***ROCK ME BABY* /Bell**

Shaun Cassidy

BORN: Sept. 27, 1959
HOMETOWN: Los Angeles, California

Shaun certainly has been no stranger to show business, for even before

Shaun Cassidy

he began his singing career he was consistently surrounded by talented people like his mother, Shirley Jones, his dad, the late Jack Cassidy, and his half-brother, David Cassidy, himself a big teen idol a few years back.

Shaun's big break came when he was chosen to co-star in the TV series "The Hardy Boys" and he sang a song in one of the episodes that was a big hit for a group called The Crystals in 1963. The song, "Da Doo Ron Ron," was released during the spring of 1977 and went on to become a major smash for Cassidy. Today he is "hotter" than any other singer his age and on the verge of a very big career.

May 77	***DA DOO RON RON /*** Warner/Curb
July 77	***THAT'S ROCK 'N' ROLL /*** Warner/Curb
Nov. 77	***HEY DEANIE /*** Warner/Curb
Mar. 78	***DO YOU BELIEVE IN MAGIC /*** Warner/Curb

The Castaways

MEMBERS:
Richard Robey (lead vocals, bass) / born: 1947
Robert Folschow (lead guitar) / born: 1947

Roy Hensley (rhythm guitar) / born: 1946
James Donna (keyboards) / born: 1945
Dennis Craswell (drums) / born: 1947
HOMETOWN: Minneapolis, Minnesota

The members of The Castaways met while attending the University of Minnesota and formed the group in 1965 to play at school functions. During the summer of 1965 they decided to give recording a try and using their own money cut a song organ player Jim Donna had written, called "Liar Liar." They were able to sell the master to the local Soma label, and the song became a top ten hit. Their follow-up was less successful, but The Castaways continued to tour through 1966 when the draft broke up the group.

At present Roy Hensley is a folk singer, Jim Donna has a desk job for a construction company and occasionally moonlights as a rock singer, and Bob Folschow and Denny Craswell operate a recording studio in Minneapolis.

Aug. 65 *LIAR LIAR /* **Soma**

Jimmy Castor
HOMETOWN: New York City

Jimmy Castor, who began his career as a child performer, formed a group named Jimmy Castor & The Juniors during his early teens. In 1956 the group recorded one of Castor's songs, "I Promise to Remember," for the Wing subsidiary of Mercury Records. It became a minor local hit but was immediately covered by Frankie Lymon & The Teenagers, whose version became a million seller. From that point on Castor was often asked to substitute for Lymon on tour with the group.

Castor attended Music & Art high school but later enrolled at Manhattan's City College as an accounting major. After working for a while in that field, his musical inclinations got the best of him, and he formed a group called The Jimmy Castor Bunch, consisting of Gerry Thomas (keyboards), Douglas Gibson (bass), Harry Jensen (guitar), Leonard Fridie, Jr. (percussion), and Robert Manigault (drums). Led by Castor's vocals and sax, the group had several pop and soul hits for various labels over the years.

The Jimmy Castor Bunch has most recently recorded for Atlantic Records and is a popular concert attraction.

Dec. 66 *HEY LEROY* / **Smash**
May 72 *TROGLODYTE* / **RCA**
Feb. 75 *THE BERTHA BUTT BOOGIE* / **Atlantic**
Oct. 75 *KING KONG (PT. 1)* / **Atlantic**

Cat Mother & The All Night Newsboys

MEMBERS:
Roy Michaels (bass, guitar)
Michael Equine (drums, guitar)
Lawrence Packer (lead guitar, strings)
Robert Smith (keyboards)
Charles Chin (rhythm guitar, banjo)

This group began during the mid-sixties as a jug band in New York City's Greenwich Village and evolved gradually into rock. In 1969, while playing in Woodstock, they were discovered and signed to a contract by Jimi Hendrix, who became their manager and producer. He collaborated with the group on an album called *The Street Giveth and the Street Taketh Away,* which was sold to Polydor and released during the summer of 1969. The LP became successful, and a single was released from it which became a top

twenty hit. Called "Good Old Rock & Roll," it was a medley of six R & R standards: "Sweet Little Sixteen," "Long Tall Sally," "Chantilly Lace," "Whole Lotta Shakin' Goin' On," "Blue Suede Shoes," and "Party Doll."

Cat Mother & The All Night Newsboys recorded three more albums and continued to tour well into 1973, after which they faded from popularity.

June 69 *GOOD OLD ROCK & ROLL* / **Polydor**

Chad & Jeremy

MEMBERS:
Chad Stuart / born: Dec. 10, 1943 / Durham, England
Jeremy Clyde / born: Mar. 22, 1944 / Buckinghamshire, England

Chad and Jeremy first met while attending drama school in the early sixties and teamed up to play in local folk clubs. They were noticed at one of these performances by executives of British Ember Records, who signed them to a contract. Arrangements were made with an American company, World Artists, to distribute them, and their first record titled "Yesterday's Gone," was released early in 1964. This reached the top twenty on the American charts but was not successful in England. The duo continued with a string of United States hits that lasted for nearly three years without ever achieving hit status in their own country.

Chad and Jeremy separated in 1967. Jeremy Clyde went on to become a successful actor in the theater. Chad Stuart and his wife, Jill, recorded for a brief time as a duet before he too left singing to compose for musical comedy.

May 64 *YESTERDAY'S GONE* / **World Artists**

Aug. 64	*SUMMER SONG*/World Artists
Nov. 64	*WILLOW WEEP FOR ME*/World Artists
Feb. 65	*IF I LOVED YOU*/World Artists
Apr. 65	*WHAT DO YOU WANT WITH ME*/World Artists
May 65	*BEFORE AND AFTER*/Columbia
July 65	*FROM A WINDOW*/World Artists
Aug. 65	*I DON'T WANT TO LOSE YOU BABY*/Columbia
Oct. 65	*I HAVE DREAMED*/Columbia
July 66	*DISTANT SHORES*/Columbia
Oct. 66	*YOU ARE SHE*/Columbia

The Chairmen of the Board

MEMBERS:
Norman "General" Johnson (lead vocals)
Edward Curtis (back-up vocals)
Daniel Woods (back-up vocals)
Harrison Kennedy (back-up vocals)
HOMETOWN: Detroit, Michigan

When the Holland-Dozier-Holland team left Motown in 1969 to form their own recording and production companies, one of their first projects was to find a group similar to The Four Tops, with whom they had been so successful. Their search led to the formation of The Chairmen of the Board. Featuring the unique, gravelly voice of General Johnson (former lead singer of The Showmen), The Chairmen scored with a series of pop and soul hits that extended well into the seventies.

Charter member Eddie Curtis left the group in 1971 to pursue other interests, and The Chairmen continued as a trio. At present Harrison Kennedy pursues a side career as a folk-oriented singer; General Johnson has been signed as a solo act to the Arista label.

Jan. 70	*GIVE ME JUST A LITTLE MORE TIME*/Invictus

May 70	*DANGLING ON A STRING*/Invictus
Aug. 70	*EVERYTHING'S TUESDAY*/Invictus
Nov. 70	*PAY TO THE PIPER*/Invictus
Feb. 71	*CHAIRMEN OF THE BOARD*/Invictus
June 73	*FINDERS KEEPERS*/Invictus

The Chambers Brothers

MEMBERS:
George Chambers (bass)/born: Sept. 22, 1931/Flora, Mississippi
Willie Chambers (guitar)/born: Mar. 2, 1938/Flora, Mississippi
Joe Chambers (guitar)/born: Aug. 22, 1942/Scott County, Mississippi
Lester Chambers (percussion)/born: Apr. 13, 1940/Flora, Mississippi
Brian Keenan (drums)/born: Jan. 28, 1944/Yorkshire, England

The four Chambers brothers were farmers until their family moved to Los Angeles during the early sixties. They sang in local church choirs and eventually recorded a gospel song called "I Trust in God" for the local Proverb label. By the mid-sixties they had chosen recording as a career and signed with the Vault label, where they recorded a mixed bag of songs, including gospel, blues, and rock. They established a stage act by playing at New York City discotheques, and at one of these performances, they met drummer Brian Keenan, who was added to the group.

By 1968 The Chambers Brothers had built a strong reputation and were offered a contract by Columbia Records. An album called *The Time Has Come* was released; the title track was issued as a single and became a top ten hit. They followed with the Otis Redding song "I Can't Turn You Loose" and a number of singles and albums in the afro-rock vein.

After four successful years The Chambers Brothers temporarily disbanded as a working group in 1972. They resumed touring in 1976 and have signed with Chelsea Records.

Aug. 68	*TIME HAS COME TODAY /* **Columbia**
Nov. 68	*I CAN'T TURN YOU LOOSE /* **Columbia**
Dec. 68	*SHOUT /* **Vault**
July 69	*WAKE UP /* **Columbia**
Feb. 70	*LOVE, PEACE & HAPPINESS /* **Columbia**

Harry Chapin

BORN: Dec. 7, 1942
HOMETOWN: New York City

Harry Chapin

During the late fifties Harry Chapin and his brothers, Tom and Steve, formed a folk group in the Brooklyn Heights section of New York. When one of the brothers dropped out, he was replaced by their father (Jim Chapin, a noted jazz drummer) and they continued as a family act. Shortly thereafter the group disbanded when the other brother left to pursue his studies.

During the late sixties Harry enrolled at Cornell University to study film, and in 1969 he produced and directed a collage of old boxing films titled *The Legendary Champions,* which received an Oscar nomination. Another documentary, *Blue Water, White Death,* featured some of Harry's original songs and led to Harry's determination to succeed in the world of music.

He assembled a new group and, using his own money, rented the Village Gate after each evening's performance of *Jacques Brel* and played to small audiences in the hope of being "discovered."

The big break came early in 1972 in a most unexpected way. *The New York Times* cover story of a skyjacking at Kennedy Airport was continued on an inside page. Directly under that continuation was an otherwise inconspicuous piece captioned "Chapin sings gorgeous ballads," a rave review of Harry's act! One night he was seen by Ann Putril, an executive of Elektra Records, and she convinced the label's owner, Jac Holzman, to sign Harry. The first record released, "Taxi," became an instant best seller and established Harry as a major act.

During 1974 Harry and his music were featured in the Broadway stage production of *The Night That Made America Famous,* which included his number one hit, "The Cat's in the Cradle." Harry is also the composer of all the original music in the popular children's TV show "Make a Wish," which is hosted by his brother Tom.

At present Harry is touring extensively, and three out of every four of his performances are benefits for charity!

Mar. 72	*TAXI /* **Elektra**
Oct. 72	*SUNDAY MORNING SUNSHINE /* **Elektra**

Jan. 74 *W.O.L.D.* /Elektra
Oct. 74 *THE CAT'S IN THE CRADLE* /
Elektra
Feb. 75 *I WANNA LEARN A LOVE
SONG* /Elektra
June 76 *A BETTER PLACE TO BE* /
Elektra

The Checkmates, Ltd.

MEMBERS:
Sonny Charles (lead vocals)
Robert Stevens (vocals)
William Van Buskirk (bass)
Harvey Trees (guitar)
Marvin Smith (drums)
HOMETOWN: Fort Wayne, Indiana

This group was comprised of several friends who grew up together in Indiana. They began performing there, worked their way through the Midwest, and eventually wound up in Las Vegas. There they were discovered by singer Nancy Wilson at a club called The Pussy Cat A Go-Go. Under her direction the group became the top lounge act in Las Vegas and Nancy took them to Capitol Records, the label to which she was signed. The Checkmates were offered a contract by Capitol and a moderately successful album titled *Live at Las Vegas* was released.

In 1969 The Checkmates were signed by A & M Records, where they worked in association with producer Phil Spector. A single called "Love Is All I Have to Give" became a modest hit, but their next record, "Black Pearl," took them to the top ten. After two more hit singles and an album the group announced in 1970 that they were separating. Sonny Charles became a record producer, and the rest of the group currently records for Fantasy Records.

Late in 1974 Sonny Charles and The Checkmates announced that they would be working together once again as a singing group and as business partners. They formed their own entertainment complex, including the Rustic record label (for which they now record), the Charisme public relations firm, and a television production company called Associated Video. They continue to appear regularly in Las Vegas and to make occasional tours.

Apr. 69 *LOVE IS ALL I HAVE TO GIVE* /
A & M
May 69 *BLACK PEARL* /A & M
Oct. 69 *PROUD MARY* /A & M

Cheech & Chong

MEMBERS:
Cheech (Richard Marin) /born: 1947 /Los
Angeles, California
Chong (Thomas Chong) /born: May 24, 1940 /
Edmonton, Alberta, Canada

Cheech and Chong are the leading team in the field of "rock comedy."

Both started early with music. Chong, who is part Chinese, played in several Canadian rock groups, the most successful of which was Bobby Taylor & The Vancouvers (who achieved several American hits during 1968 on the Gordy label). Cheech, a Mexican-American, was a member of various groups in the Watts section of Los Angeles where he grew up. He first met Chong in Canada when he lived there to escape the draft. The two originally got together to form a rock group, but their audiences' reaction to the comedy routines they did before performances prompted them to stick with humor. They formed a comedy troupe called City Lights, but eventually settled into performing as a duet.

Cheech & Chong played for a while in Canada, and later moved to Los Angeles, where they eventually got a job at The Troubador. They were seen by Lou Adler, president of Ode Records,

Cheech & Chong

and signed to a contract. Their first album, *Cheech & Chong,* became a best seller in the summer of 1971 and was followed the next year by *Big Bambu.* Since then their LPs have been continual best sellers, and they make occasional singles, which are successful as well.

Sept. 73	***BASKETBALL JONES*** / Ode
Nov. 73	***SISTER MARY ELEPHANT*** / Ode
Aug. 74	***EARACHE, MY EYE*** / Ode
Nov. 74	***BLACK LASSIE*** / Ode
Oct. 75	***HOW I SPENT MY SUMMER VACATION*** / Ode
June 76	***FRAMED*** / Ode
Nov. 77	***BLOAT ON*** / Ode

Chic

MEMBERS:
Norma Jean (vocalist)
Claire Bethe (vocalist)
Nile Rodgers (guitar)
Bernard Edwards (bass guitar)
Kenny Lehman (woodwinds)
Andy Schwartz (keyboards)
Tony Thompson (drums)
HOMETOWN: New York City

During the summer of 1977 the group was working in New York as studio musicians when they had the idea to record some original material. Under the direction of Marc Kreiner and his MK Productions, the group recorded a tune that Nile, Bernard, and Kenny had written called "Dance, Dance, Dance (Yowsah, Yowsah, Yowsah)," which was then released as a twelve-inch disco song. When the recording began to get air time, Atlantic Records signed the group and had them record the album *Chic,* on which Nile and Bernard wrote all the tunes along with arranging and producing the entire album with group member Lehman. The catchy tune put Chic on the national charts and made them a big hit at all the discos.

Oct. 77 *DANCE, DANCE, DANCE (YOWSAH, YOWSAH, YOWSAH)* / **Atlantic**
Apr. 78 *EVERYBODY DANCE* / **Atlantic**

Chicago

MEMBERS:

Robert Lamm (keyboards) / born: Oct. 13, 1944
Peter Cetera (bass) / born: Sept. 13, 1944
Terry Kath (guitar) / born: Jan. 31, 1946 / died: Jan. 23, 1978 / replaced by Donnie Dacus
Lee Loughnane (trumpet) / born: Oct. 21, 1946
Walter Parazaider (woodwinds) / born: Mar. 14, 1945
James Pankow (trombone) / born: Aug. 20, 1947
Daniel Seraphine (drums) / born: Aug. 28, 1948
Laudir De Oliveira (percussion)
HOMETOWN: Chicago, Illinois

Chicago, the most successful of the jazz-oriented rock groups, was formed in 1967 by several school friends and was originally known as The Big Thing. After playing for a time in various Midwest clubs, they joined forces with James William Guercio, another school friend who had since moved to Los Angeles and become a leading record producer. Guercio was associated with Columbia Records as a result of his work with two of their acts, The Buckinghams and Blood, Sweat & Tears. After working with the group for a while and helping them develop their sound, he was able to get them a contract with Columbia also. At Guercio's suggestion the group changed its name to Chicago Transit Authority, and their first album appeared in 1968. It was not immediately successful, as was true of their first single, ''Ques-

Chicago. Back row, left to right: James Pankow, Terry Kath, Laudir de Oliveira, Walter Parazaider, Peter Cetera, Danny Seraphine; front row, left to right: Lee Loughnane, and Robert Lamm

tions 67 & 68." However, their next single release, "Make Me Smile," went to the top ten and firmly established the group. Their first album then began to sell and became one of the top LPs of 1970. By the time their second album was issued the group's name had been shortened to simply Chicago.

Since that time the group has never been absent from the singles and album charts, and they presently continue to tour with their original personnel. In October 1977 James William Guercio left the group as their manager.

In April 1978 Donnie Dacus was chosen to replace the deceased Terry Kath, who had accidentally shot himself earlier in the year.

Aug. 69	*QUESTIONS 67 & 68 /* Columbia
Apr. 70	*MAKE ME SMILE /* Columbia
July 70	*25 OR 6 TO 4 /* Columbia
Nov. 70	*DOES ANYBODY REALLY KNOW WHAT TIME IT IS? /* Columbia
Feb. 71	*FREE /* Columbia
May 71	*LOWDOWN /* Columbia
June 71	*BEGINNINGS /* Columbia
June 71	*COLOR MY WORLD /* Columbia
Oct. 71	*QUESTIONS 67 & 68 (rereleased) /* Columbia
Oct. 71	*I'M A MAN /* Columbia
Aug. 72	*SATURDAY IN THE PARK /* Columbia
Oct. 72	*DIALOGUE /* Columbia
June 73	*FEELING STRONGER EVERY DAY /* Columbia
Sept. 73	*JUST YOU & ME /* Columbia
Mar. 74	*SEARCHIN' SO LONG /* Columbia
June 74	*CALL ON ME /* Columbia
Oct. 74	*WISHING YOU WERE HERE /* Columbia
Feb. 75	*HARRY TRUMAN /* Columbia
Apr. 75	*OLD DAYS /* Columbia
Sept. 75	*A BRAND NEW LOVE AFFAIR /* Columbia
June 76	*ANOTHER RAINY DAY IN NEW YORK CITY /* Columbia
Aug. 76	*IF YOU LEAVE ME NOW /* Columbia

Apr. 77	*YOU ARE ON MY MIND /* Columbia
Sept. 77	*BABY, WHAT A BIG SURPRISE /* Columbia
Feb. 78	*LITTLE ONE /* Columbia
May 78	*TAKE ME BACK TO CHICAGO /* Columbia

The Chi-Lites

MEMBERS:
Eugene Record (lead vocals)
Marshall Thompson (background)
Robert Lester (background)
Creadel Jones (background)
HOMETOWN: Chicago, Illinois

This group was formed in Chicago in 1961 as a trio called Marshall & The Chi-Lites. They performed in local clubs and made several records for small labels in the area, the most successful of which was a regional hit on the Daran label called "Love Bandit."

During the mid-sixties two things were instrumental to the group's success. First, a Chicago cab driver named Eugene Record auditioned for the group and became their lead singer. Second, the Chi-Lites got their "big break" by meeting noted record producer Carl Davis. Davis was a vice-president of Brunswick Records and got the group signed to the label where their first record was released early in 1969. Titled "Give It Away," it was the first of several records which became moderate soul hits and barely crept onto the pop charts, but "Have You Seen Her?" (1971) changed that by going to the top of both charts. Since then The Chi-Lites have continued with a big string of major hits.

Today the group still records for Brunswick, but Eugene Record is a solo performer on Warner Brothers.

Mar. 69	*GIVE IT AWAY /* Brunswick
Aug. 69	*LET ME BE THE MAN MY DADDY WAS /* Brunswick

The Chi-Lites. Clockwise from top left: Robert Lester, Eugene Record, Creadel Jones, Marshall Thompson

Aug. 70	*I LIKE YOUR LOVING /* **Brunswick**
Dec. 70	*ARE YOU MY WOMAN? /* **Brunswick**
Apr. 71	*GIVE MORE POWER TO THE PEOPLE /* **Brunswick**
July 71	*WE ARE NEIGHBORS /* **Brunswick**
Oct. 71	*HAVE YOU SEEN HER? /* **Brunswick**
Nov. 71	*I WANT TO PAY YOU BACK /* **Brunswick**
Apr. 72	*OH GIRL /* **Brunswick**
July 72	*THE COLDEST DAYS OF MY LIFE /* **Brunswick**
Sept. 72	*A LONELY MAN /* **Brunswick**
Dec. 72	*WE NEED ORDER /* **Brunswick**
Feb. 73	*A LETTER TO MYSELF /* **Brunswick**
June 73	*MY HEART JUST KEEPS ON BREAKING /* **Brunswick**
Aug. 73	*STONED OUT OF MY MIND /* **Brunswick**
Nov. 73	*I FOUND SUNSHINE /* **Brunswick**
Feb. 74	*HOMELY GIRL /* **Brunswick**
June 74	*THERE WILL NEVER BE ANY PEACE /* **Brunswick**
Aug. 74	*YOU GOT TO BE THE ONE /* **Brunswick**
Mar. 75	*TOBY /* **Brunswick**
Nov. 75	*IT'S TIME FOR LOVE /* **Brunswick**

The Choir

MEMBERS:

Wally Bryson (lead guitar)

David Smalley (rhythm guitar)

James Skeen (bass)

James Bonfanti (drums)
HOMETOWN: Cleveland, Ohio

The Choir was formed in 1965 as The Mods but changed their name to avoid confusion when another local group shortened their name from The Modanaires to The Mods. After achieving a local reputation, The Choir traveled to Chicago to cut a record called "It's Cold Outside," which was released on the Canadian-American label. When it became a large regional seller, the master was purchased by Roulette Records for distribution. The record rose to number one in Cleveland and became a sizable national hit. A follow-up was released early in 1968 called "No One to Play With," but it sold primarily in the Cleveland area.

Shortly thereafter the group added lead singer Eric Carmen and, as The Raspberries, rose to national prominence on the Capitol label during the early seventies.

See *THE RASPBERRIES.*

June 67 *IT'S COLD OUTSIDE* **/Roulette**

Christie
MEMBERS:
Jeff Christie (lead vocals, bass guitar)
Vic Elms (lead guitar)
Mike Blakey (drums)
HOMETOWN: London, England

This trio became very popular in many of the London clubs and eventually came to the attention of a few record producers. They recorded a tune called "Yellow River" that began to get much attention throughout Europe. The single was sold to Epic Records in the United States and in the summer of 1970 Christie became a big American favorite.

July 70 *YELLOW RIVER* **/Epic**
Feb. 71 *SAN BERNARDINO* **/Epic**

Eric Clapton
REAL NAME: Eric Patrick Clapp
BORN: Mar. 30, 1945
HOMETOWN: Ripley, Surrey, England

Eric Clapton rose from a working-class background to become one of the premiere guitarists in all of rock.

The son of a bricklayer, Clapton at first studied stained-glass-window design but was spending most of his time playing guitar before he was seventeen. Shortly thereafter, he formed a band called Eric Clapton's Power House, which among other members contained future rock stars Jack Bruce and Steve Winwood. During the early sixties Clapton was a founding member of the legendary Yardbirds, but was replaced in that group by Jeff Beck when he left to join John Mayall's Bluesbreakers. After a one-year stint with the Mayall band Clapton was known as the top guitarist in British rock, but his first real commercial success came in 1966 when he joined Jack Bruce and Ginger Baker to form the first of the "supergroups," Cream (see *CREAM*). After three years and a number of chart hits, the group disbanded in 1969 and Clapton and Baker joined with Steve Winwood and Rick Grech to form a second "supergroup" called Blind Faith. Although a very important group, Blind Faith was short-lived, and Clapton spent the early seventies as part of the Delaney & Bonnie revue before joining with three musicians from that band to form Derek & The Dominoes (see *DEREK & THE DOMINOES*). After a period of chart success with this group, Clapton went into semiretirement for nearly a year and half because of personal diffi- culties. During this period Pete Town- shend of The Who was able to per- suade him to do the famed Rainbow concert. With the exception of a "live" album of that event released during 1973, Clapton did no recording after his separation from Derek & The Domi- noes until he emerged in 1974 with an album called *461 Ocean Boulevard,* named for the house in Florida where he was staying while recording it. He was also seen in the role of the preacher in the film version of the rock opera *Tommy.*

At present Clapton heads a new band, which records for Robert Stig- wood's RSO label, and is actively touring.

Oct. 70	*AFTER MIDNIGHT* / Atco	
Sept. 72	*LET IT RAIN* / Polydor	
Feb. 73	*BELL BOTTOM BLUES* / Polydor	
July 74	*I SHOT THE SHERIFF* / RSO	
Nov. 74	*WILLIE & THE HAND JIVE* / RSO	
Oct. 76	*HELLO OLD FRIEND* / RSO	
Jan. 78	*LAY DOWN SALLY* / RSO	
May 78	*WONDERFUL TONIGHT* / RSO	

The Dave Clark Five

MEMBERS:
Dave Clark (drums) / born: Dec. 15, 1942 / Tottenham, London, England

Lenny Davidson (guitar) / born: May 30, 1944 / Enfield, Middlesex, England

Rick Huxley (bass) / born: Aug. 5, 1942 / Dartford, Kent, England

Denis Payton (tenor sax) / born: Aug. 11, 1943 / Walthamstow, London, England

Michael Smith (lead vocals, keyboards) / born: Dec. 6, 1943 / Edmonton, London, England

The Dave Clark Five rose to fame in the wake of Beatlemania and became one of the most popular British groups in America.

Although Dave Clark's primary inter- est was in sports, he developed a side interest in the drums. When his football team required funds for traveling ex- penses, Clark assembled a group of friends to play local clubs and raise the money. After building a strong reputa- tion as a result of these performances, the group was offered a recording contract. Early in 1964 their first re- lease, "Glad All Over," was threaten- ing the Beatles' number one position on the British charts. It was released in the United States on the Epic label and became a top ten chart entry and the first of nearly two dozen hits.

During the mid-sixties the group was seen in two feature films, *Get Yourself a College Girl* and *Having a Wild Weekend* (originally titled *Catch Us If You Can*).

Dave Clark currently tours the Eng- lish cabaret circuit with a group called Dave Clark & Friends and is active in television and film.

Feb. 64	*GLAD ALL OVER* / Epic	
Apr. 64	*BITS & PIECES* / Epic	
Apr. 64	*I KNEW IT ALL THE TIME* / Congress	
May 64	*DO YOU LOVE ME* / Epic	
June 64	*CAN'T YOU SEE THAT SHE'S MINE?* / Epic	
Aug. 64	*BECAUSE* / Epic	
Oct. 64	*EVERYBODY KNOWS* / Epic	
Nov. 64	*ANYWAY YOU WANT IT* / Epic	
Feb. 65	*COME HOME* / Epic	
Apr. 65	*REELING & ROCKING* / Epic	
June 65	*I LIKE IT LIKE THAT* / Epic	
Aug. 65	*CATCH US IF YOU CAN* / Epic	
Nov. 65	*OVER & OVER* / Epic	
Feb. 66	*AT THE SCENE* / Epic	
Apr. 66	*TRY TOO HARD* / Epic	
June 66	*PLEASE TELL ME WHY* / Epic	
Aug. 66	*SATISFIED WITH YOU* / Epic	
Oct. 66	*19 DAYS* / Epic	
Jan. 67	*I'VE GOT TO HAVE A REASON* / Epic	
Apr. 67	*YOU'VE GOT WHAT IT TAKES* / Epic	
June 67	*YOU MUST HAVE BEEN A BEAUTIFUL BABY* / Epic	

The Dave Clark Five. Clockwise from top left: Len Davidson, Dave Clark, Denny Payton, Mike Smith, Rick Huxley

Aug. 67 *A LITTLE BIT NOW*/Epic
Nov. 67 *RED & BLUE*/Epic
Dec. 67 *EVERYBODY KNOWS* (rereleased)/Epic

Petula Clark

BORN: Nov. 15, 1933
HOMETOWN: Epsom, Surrey, England

One of the world's leading female performers, "Pet" Clark launched her career at the age of eight by auditioning for a BBC radio show in 1941. A German air raid began during the audition, and she was asked to continue singing in order to prevent panic in the studio. As the result of her perform-

ance she was given her own show called "Pet's Parlor," which turned her into a radio star. She also achieved fame as a child actress by appearing in over two dozen films beginning in the mid-forties and continuing for more than ten years, and during the early fifties she began her career as a recording artist. Several of her records became popular in England and on the Continent, but she was particularly popular in France.

During the early sixties Pet moved to France and one of her records, "The Ya-Ya Twist," became a major European hit. In 1963 she formed an association with songwriter-arranger Tony

Hatch, whose composition of "Downtown" became a hit throughout Europe and in America late in 1964. For the next several years Hatch provided virtually all her material, and she was almost never absent from the charts.

After being firmly established as a recording artist, Pet Clark resumed her acting work in 1968 with featured appearances in *Finian's Rainbow* and *Goodbye Mr. Chips.*

Today Pet has become active in television commercials and industrial films. Married to a Frenchman, she lives in Geneva, Switzerland, with their two young daughters, Barbara-Michele and Catherine.

Dec. 64	*DOWNTOWN* /Warner Bros.
Mar. 65	*I KNOW A PLACE* /Warner Bros.
July 65	*YOU'D BETTER COME HOME* /Warner Bros.
Oct. 65	*ROUND EVERY CORNER* /Warner Bros.
Dec. 65	*MY LOVE* /Warner Bros.
Mar. 66	*SIGN OF THE TIMES* /Warner Bros.
July 66	*I COULDN'T LIVE WITHOUT YOUR LOVE* /Warner Bros.
Oct. 66	*WHO AM I* /Warner Bros.
Dec. 66	*COLOR MY WORLD* /Warner Bros.
Mar. 67	*THIS IS MY SONG* /Warner Bros.
June 67	*DON'T SLEEP IN THE SUBWAY* /Warner Bros.
Sept. 67	*CAT IN THE WINDOW* /Warner Bros.
Dec. 67	*THE OTHER MAN'S GRASS IS ALWAYS GREENER* /Warner Bros.
Feb. 68	*KISS ME GOODBYE* /Warner Bros.
July 68	*DON'T GIVE UP* /Warner Bros.
Nov. 68	*AMERICAN BOYS* /Warner Bros.
Apr. 69	*HAPPY HEART* /Warner Bros.
Aug. 69	*LOOK AT MINE* /Warner Bros.
Nov. 69	*NO ONE BETTER THAN YOU* /Warner Bros.
June 72	*MY GUY* /MGM
Oct. 72	*THE WEDDING SONG* /MGM

Roy Clark

BORN: Mar. 15, 1933
HOMETOWN: Meaherrin, Virginia

Roy Clark began his career as a teen-age banjo player. With the help of his father he learned to play well enough to win the national country banjo championship. Part of the first prize was an appearance at the Grand Ole Opry, which earned him enough of a reputation to keep him working in the Baltimore-Washington area for several years.

During the late forties Clark began incorporating humor into his act. This eventually led to a starring role in the network version of "Hee Haw" in 1969. During that same year Roy Clark was signed to a contract by the Dot label, and his first release, "Yesterday When I Was Young," became a top country and western hit and reached the top twenty on the pop charts. Since then his records have continued to be best sellers in the country field and many of his releases have become national hits as well.

Today Clark lives with his wife, Barbara, in Davidsonville, Maryland. He also has several side interests, including real estate, cattle ranching, and broadcasting.

June 69	*YESTERDAY WHEN I WAS YOUNG* /Dot
Jan. 70	*THEN SHE'S A LOVER* /Dot
Oct. 70	*THANK GOD & GREYHOUND* /Dot
May 73	*COME LIVE WITH ME* /Dot
Dec. 73	*SOMEWHERE BETWEEN LOVE AND TOMORROW* /Dot

Jimmy Cliff

REAL NAME: James Chambers
BORN: 1948
HOMETOWN: St. Catherine, Jamaica, West Indies

Jimmy Cliff was one of the first singer-composers to popularize the Jamaican musical form known as reggae.

His interest in music led him to Kingston during the early sixties in search of a career. After making a few inconsequential recordings for local labels in the sixties, he became one of the first artists to be signed to Chris Blackwell's Island Records. Island's distribution in England made him widely known to audiences there and he had a number of British hits during the late sixties. Several of these, most notably "Wonderful World, Beautiful People," were released in the United States by A & M Records and gained American recognition as well. However, he greatly advanced his own popularity and the influence of reggae on pop music via his appearance in the 1972 film *The Harder They Come.* Featuring Cliff's music, the film portrayed the conditions in Jamaica out of which reggae music evolved.

Since the film Cliff has been represented in the United States with two albums, *Unlimited* and *Struggling Man,* and his songs are widely recorded by leading rock artists. He continues to make his home in Kingston, Jamaica, and tours extensively with his back-up band, Dansak.

Dec. 69   *WONDERFUL WORLD, BEAUTIFUL PEOPLE* / A & M
Mar. 70   *COME INTO MY LIFE* / A & M

Climax

MEMBERS:
Sonny Geraci (lead vocals)
Walter Nims (guitar)
Steven York (bass)
Virgil Weber (keyboards) / replaced by Rick Lipp
Robert Neilson (drums)
HOMETOWN: Los Angeles, California

During the mid-sixties Sonny Geraci was an original member of a Cleveland group called The Outsiders, which rose to prominence on the Capitol label. After the group disbanded Geraci moved to Los Angeles and was joined by Walt Nims, who had played with The Outsiders toward the end of that group's existence.

The two formed Climax in 1971, and the group came to the attention of Marc Gordon, manager of The Fifth Dimension, and Al Wilson. Gordon signed the group to his new Rocky Road label, and their first release, a song written by Walt Nims titled "Precious and Few," became a top ten hit.

Climax was able to follow with one more hit, after which they vanished from the charts.

See *THE OUTSIDERS.*

Jan. 72   *PRECIOUS AND FEW* / Rocky Road
May 72   *LIFE AND BREATH* / Rocky Road

Climax Blues Band

MEMBERS:
Peter Haycock (guitar, vocals)
Colin Cooper (sax, vocals)
Derek Holt (bass guitar, vocals)
Richard Jones (keyboard, vocals)
John Cuffley (drums)
HOMETOWN: Middlesex, England

In 1969 Peter, Colin, and Derek, along with two other friends, formed the Climax Blues Band and started playing the various small clubs around London. In a short time they received a recording contract with Sire records.

In 1975 Richard and John entered the group and they started having some hit records throughout England.

In early 1977 the group had their first

Joe Cocker

hit in this country with a song called "Couldn't Get It Right."

Feb. 77 *COULDN'T GET IT RIGHT* / Sire

Joe Cocker

FULL NAME: John Robert Cocker
BORN: May 20, 1944
HOMETOWN: Sheffield, England

Joe Cocker was born into a working-class environment and studied plumbing at the Sheffield Central technical trade school. As a teen-ager he was influenced by Ray Charles's music and played harmonica in a group called The Cavaliers. When the group was later reorganized as Vance Arnold & The Avengers, Cocker became lead singer. During the mid-sixties he was offered a recording contract as a solo artist by British Decca and obtained a leave of absence from his plumber's job. However, that did not prove successful and he returned to his profession while organizing a back-up group called The Grease Band. Consisting of Chris Stainton (keyboards), Henry McCullough (guitar), Alan Spenner (bass), Bruce Rowlands (drums), and Cocker singing lead, the group played around the Sheffield area and attracted the attention of record producer Denny Cordell. Their first release, "Marjorine," was a moderate success, but their next record, a slowed-down reworking of The Beatles' "With a Little Help from My Friends," went to number one in England and became a sizable American hit when released on the A & M label. An album of the same name followed, and another single, "Feeling Alright."

In 1969 while on his first American tour Cocker met Leon Russell, then a keyboard player for Delanie & Bonnie, and the two became good friends. Russell provided Cocker's next hit, "Delta Lady," and was responsible for organizing the mammoth, forty-day collective American tour known as "Mad Dogs and Englishmen," which was later made into a successful feature film. The tour proved to be a major factor in advancing Leon Russell's career, but did exactly the opposite for its star, Joe Cocker. He returned to England physically and mentally shaken and went into semiretirement.

Beginning in 1971 Cocker underwent a period of contractual and legal problems, personnel problems within his musical organization, and failing health. Although he did manage to release an occasional record, there was much speculation as to the future of his career. However, he reemerged in 1975, apparently recovered from his troubles, and topped the charts with an uncharacteristic ballad called "You Are So Beautiful."

Nov. 68	*WITH A LITTLE HELP FROM MY FRIENDS* / A & M
June 69	*FEELING ALRIGHT* / A & M
Oct. 69	*DELTA LADY* / A & M
Dec. 69	*SHE CAME IN THROUGH THE BATHROOM WINDOW* / A & M
Apr. 70	*THE LETTER* / A & M
Oct. 70	*CRY ME A RIVER* / A & M

May 71	*HIGH TIME WE WENT* / A & M
Jan. 72	*FEELING ALRIGHT (rereleased)* / A & M
Sept. 72	*MIDNIGHT RIDER* / A & M
Dec. 72	*WOMAN TO WOMAN* / A & M
Feb. 73	*PARDON ME SIR* / A & M
Jan. 75	*YOU ARE SO BEAUTIFUL* / A & M

Natalie Cole
BORN: February 6, 1950
HOMETOWN: Los Angeles, California

Natalie began her show-business career as a child singing with her father, Nat "King" Cole, in a black version of *Gigi* in Los Angeles. It was then she knew she wanted to be a singer.

After college, in the early seventies, she began appearing in New York clubs and wound up in 1974 in Chicago, where she was awarded a recording contract with her late father's label, Capitol Records. Her first album, *Inseparable* produced the Grammy-winning top ten hit "This Will Be," which launched Ms. Cole's star in the recording business.

Today she is married to her producer, Marvin Yancy, and is one of the hottest female properties around and plays to capacity crowds everywhere.

Aug. 75	*THIS WILL BE* / Capitol
Dec. 75	*INSEPARABLE* / Capitol
May 76	*SOPHISTICATED LADY* / Capitol
Sept. 76	*MR. MELODY* / Capitol
Jan. 77	*I'VE GOT LOVE ON MY MIND* / Capitol
July 77	*PARTY LIGHTS* / Capitol
Jan. 78	*OUR LOVE* / Capitol

Judy Collins
BORN: May 1, 1939
HOMETOWN: Seattle, Washington

Although born in the state of Washington, Judy Collins grew up primarily in Denver, Colorado, where her father, Chuck Collins, was a radio personality.

Early in life, she began studying to be a classical pianist and played for a time in The Denver Businessmen's Symphony Orchestra. But while attending the University of Colorado she became increasingly attracted to folk music. After building a strong reputation on the Midwest folk circuit, Judy was signed by Elektra Records in 1961, and her first album, *A Maid of Constant Sorrow,* was an immediate success. Throughout the sixties and early seventies she continued to release at least one successful album per year, and in 1967 her records began selling in the singles market as well. Over the years she helped to advance the careers of unknown songwriters like Joni Mitchell, Randy Newman, and Leonard Cohen by singing their material.

Judy Collins's popularity has continued into the mid-seventies.

Jan. 67	**HARD LOVING LOSER /** **Elektra**
Nov. 68	**BOTH SIDES NOW (CLOUDS) /** **Elektra**
Feb. 69	**SOMEDAY SOON / Elektra**
Aug. 69	**CHELSEA MORNING / Elektra**
Nov. 69	**TURN TURN TURN / Elektra**
Dec. 70	**AMAZING GRACE / Elektra**
Dec. 71	**OPEN THE DOOR (SONG FOR** **JUDITH) / Elektra**
Feb. 73	**COOK WITH HONEY / Elektra**
June 75	**SEND IN THE CLOWNS /** **Elektra**
Sept. 77	**SEND IN THE CLOWNS** **(rereleased) / Elektra**

Jessi Colter

REAL NAME: Miriam Johnson Jennings
BORN: May 25, 1947
HOMETOWN: Phoenix, Arizona

Jessi Colter began her music career at the age of eleven as a church pianist and accordion player. During her teens

Judy Collins

she began writing songs and performing in clubs. She eventually met and married rock 'n' roll guitarist Duane Eddy.

Jessi began recording during the sixties under the name Miriam Eddy and her songs were used by such artists as Dottie West, Don Gibson, and Nancy Sinatra. In 1970 she took the stage name of Jessi Colter (after her great-great grandfather, Jesse Colter, a friend of the legendary Jesse James) and concentrated her activities in Nashville.

Jessi eventually separated from Duane Eddy and married country star Waylon Jennings. She was signed by Capitol Records and in 1975 had her first major country and pop hit with her own composition of "I'm Not Lisa," which Jennings produced.

Waylon and Jessi Jennings currently live in Nashville with their children, Terry, Julie, Buddy, and Jennifer. The couple often tour together, each performing solo.

Apr. 75 *I'M NOT LISA* **/ Capitol**
Sept. 75 *WHAT'S HAPPENED TO BLUE EYES* **/ Capitol**

Chi Coltrane

BORN: Nov. 16, 1948
HOMETOWN: Racine, Wisconsin

Chi (her real name, pronounced "shy") Coltrane is no relation to legendary jazz artist John Coltrane. She began studying classical piano at the age of eight and was soon singing in local church choirs. By the time she graduated from high school she was taking voice lessons and singing professionally in her hometown.

During the late sixties Chi moved to Chicago and formed a small band to play coffeehouses and clubs. After nearly three years she graduated to major rooms like The Playboy Club, and the strong reputation she built led to a contract from Columbia Records.

In May 1972 her first album, *Chi Coltrane,* was released and a few months later yielded a top twenty single, "Thunder & Lightning." She has since continued as a popular "album" artist.

Sept. 72 *THUNDER & LIGHTNING* **/ Columbia**

Commander Cody & His Lost Planet Airmen

MEMBERS:
Commander Cody (George Fayne) (keyboards, vocals) / Boise, Idaho
William C. Farlow (harp, lead vocals) / Decatur, Alabama

William Kirchen (lead guitar, trombone) / Ann Arbor, Michigan
John Tichy (rhythm guitar) / St. Louis, Missouri
Robert Black (guitar) / replaced by Ernest Hager (Dec. 1974 / May 1975)
Bruce Barlow (bass) / Oxnard, California
Andrew Stein (sax, fiddle) / New York City
Lance Dickerson (drums) / Livonia, Michigan

This was an extremely popular and influential country-rock concert act whose nucleus was George Fayne. Raised in the Brooklyn / Long Island area of New York City, Fayne's primary interest was in the fine arts, and he entered the University of Michigan in 1962 to study sculpture and painting. He pursued music as a side interest and joined groups called The Amblers and The Fantastic Surfing Beavers to play at local functions. Also during this period he worked as a summer lifeguard at Jones Beach, where he performed for several years with an all-lifeguard group called Lorenzo Lightfoot.

In 1967 after finishing college, Fayne formed a group in the Detroit area with the unusual name of Commander Cody & His Lost Planet Airmen. (His "Cody" indentity was taken from a forties serial called "Commando Cody" and the group's name is a line from *The Ancient Mariner.*) During the following years, while Fayne studied for his master's degree and taught fine arts at Oshkosh College in Wisconsin, the group underwent numerous personnel changes and eventually evolved into the above line-up. In 1968 they relocated in San Francisco and built a substantial reputation during the late sixties and early seventies.

Mass recognition came for Cody in 1971, when the group was signed by Paramount and had a top ten single with a rockabilly standard called "Hot

Rod Lincoln.'' Although they released occasional singles that placed on the charts, the group's popularity was reflected primarily in their concert appearances and album sales.

In 1976 Commander Cody & His Airmen disbanded. George Fayne performs as a solo act and has been exhibiting his paintings and sculptures. Many of the group's other members have occupied themselves as session musicians and two, Lance Dickerson and Bruce Barlow, have become members of Roger McGuinn's new group, Thunderbyrd.

Mar. 72	*HOT ROD LINCOLN /* **Paramount**
July 72	*BEAT ME DADDY, 8 TO THE BAR /* **Paramount**
July 73	*SMOKE, SMOKE, SMOKE /* **Paramount**
Feb. 75	*DON'T LET GO /* **Warner Bros.**

The Commodores

MEMBERS:
Walter "Clyde" Orange (drums) / born: 1947
Thomas McClary (lead guitar) / born: 1950
Ronald LaPread (bass, trumpet) / born: 1950
Lionel Richie (horns, lead vocals) / born: 1950
William King (trumpet) / born: 1949
Milan Williams (drums) / born: 1949
HOMETOWN: Tuskegee, Alabama

The six members of The Commodores met while attending Tuskegee Institute in Alabama where they developed a stage act known as the Jays.

In 1971 the group became The Commodores and signed with Motown Records. They recorded a few unsuccessful singles and toured as an opening act for The Jackson Five. Their luck turned during the summer of 1974 when Milan Williams's composition

The Commodores. Left to right: Thomas McClary, Milan Williams, Ronald LaPread, Walt Orange, Lionel Richie, William King

"Machine Gun," a big-band discotheque instrumental, became a major hit and reached the national top twenty.

Since then The Commodores have recorded several vocal hit singles and are a popular concert attraction.

June 74	*MACHINE GUN* / Motown
Nov. 74	*I FEEL SATISFIED* / Motown
May 75	*SLIPPERY WHEN WET* / Motown
Dec. 75	*SWEET LOVE* / Motown
Sept. 76	*JUST TO BE CLOSE TO YOU* / Motown
Jan. 77	*FANCY DANCER* / Motown
June 77	*EASY* / Motown
Aug. 77	*BRICKHOUSE* / Motown
Dec. 77	*TOO HOT TO TROT* / Motown

Arthur Conley

BORN: Jan. 4, 1946
HOMETOWN: Atlanta, Georgia

Arthur Conley was active on the southern club circuit by the time he was a teen-ager. In 1965 he was discovered in Baltimore by Otis Redding, who signed him to a production contract and took him to Rick Hall's Fame Studios in Muscle Shoals, Alabama. His first release, "I'm a Lonely Stranger," appeared on Redding's own Jotis label. After this became a minor regional success Conley recorded three similar songs. In early 1967 he scored with a chart-topping hit released by Atlantic Records, the same label that distributed Redding's work. The song, "Sweet Soul Music," was a tribute to the soul stars of the sixties.

Conley followed with a string of hits during the next two years, after which he faded from national popularity.

Mar. 67	*SWEET SOUL MUSIC* / Atco
June 67	*SHAKE, RATTLE & ROLL* / Atco
Nov. 67	*WHOLE LOTTA WOMAN* / Atco
Mar. 68	*FUNKY STREET* / Atco
June 68	*PEOPLE SURE ACT FUNNY* / Atco
Oct. 68	*AUNT DORA'S LOVE SOUL SHACK* / Atco
Jan. 69	*OB LA DI, OB LA DA* / Atco

Norman Connors

BORN: Mar. 1, 1948
HOMETOWN: Philadelphia, Pennsylvania

Connors began his career as a jazz drummer and played with greats like Pharaoh Sanders, Sun Ra, Marion Brown, Leon Thomas, and Billy Paul. In 1972 he began recording as a solo performer for Cobblestone Records, which is distributed by Buddah.

In 1976 Connors recorded the album *You Are My Starship,* which produced a top-selling single of the same name and established him as a new talent to watch.

Jan. 76	*VALENTINE LOVE* / Buddah
Aug. 76	*YOU ARE MY STARSHIP* / Buddah

Consumer Rapport

HOMETOWN: Detroit, Michigan

Before *The Wiz* opened on Broadway in 1974, one of the show's songs, "Ease on Down the Road," was used in radio and television promotion. The song generated so much interest that Harold Wheeler, the show's orchestrater and arranger, decided to record a full-length 45 rpm version. The vocals were added by Frank Floyd, a member of the show's cast, and three studio singers from his native Detroit. Released on Wheeler and producer Stever Scheaffer's own Wing and a Prayer label, the record became so popular in the New York area discotheques that it was picked up by Atlantic Records for general distribution.

When the record became a national hit, Frank Floyd formed Consumer Rapport with back-up singers Yolanda McCullough, Krystal Ann Davis, and Janet Wright, and the group became a popular discotheque attraction.

Apr. 75 *EASE ON DOWN THE ROAD /* **Wing And A Prayer**

Bill Conti

BORN: 1940
HOMETOWN: Providence, Rhode Island

At the age of seven, Bill began taking lessons on the piano from his father, who was an accomplished pianist. At the age of twelve his family moved to Miami where, a few years later, Bill organized a rock band to play at high-school functions. In 1960 he entered Louisiana State University majoring in composition with piano as a minor. From L.S.U. he went to Juilliard in New York, getting a master's degree in composition.

In 1966 he moved to Rome, returning to Los Angeles in 1972 to work as a composer on films like *Harry and Tonto.*

In 1977 his version of the movie theme *Rocky* climbed up the charts to become one of the biggest hits of the year.

Apr. 77 *GONNA FLY NOW* **(THEME FROM** *ROCKY***)/United Artists**

Rita Coolidge

BORN: May 1, 1945
HOMETOWN: Nashville, Tennessee

Rita Coolidge, the daughter of a Nashville preacher, began singing in church choirs as a child. However, she first sang seriously in college, where she formed a group called R. C. & The Moonpies.

Rita Coolidge

By the late sixties her sister Priscilla, had married Booker T. Jones (of Booker T. & the M. G.'s) and Rita followed her to Memphis. She recorded radio commercials and eventually met Delanie & Bonnie, who invited her to California to join their group, Friends. After Friends disbanded she remained with Delanie & Bonnie and became part of the famed "Mad Dogs & Englishmen" tour in 1970. Rita was featured singing "Superstar" at the opening of the subsequent feature film.

Rita's recording career began in earnest in 1970, when she was signed by Herb Alpert's A & M label. Her first album, *Rita Coolidge,* was released in

1971 and was an immediate best seller. Since then she has had a hit single and nearly half a dozen best-selling albums.

At present Rita tours with husband Kris Kristofferson and Billy Swan. She is also active as a studio singer and works with such artists as Eric Clapton and Steve Stills.

May 69 TURN AROUND AND LOVE/
Pepper
Dec. 72 FEVER/A & M
May 77 HIGHER AND HIGHER/A & M
Sept. 77 WE'RE ALL ALONE/A & M
Jan. 78 THE WAY YOU DO THE
THINGS YOU DO/A & M

Alice Cooper

MEMBERS:
Alice Cooper (Vincent Furnier) (lead vocals, harmonica)/born: Feb. 4, 1948/Detroit, Michigan

ORIGINAL MEMBERS:
Michael Bruce (rhythm guitar, keyboards)/born: Mar. 16, 1948
Glen Vuxton (lead guitar)/born: Nov. 10, 1947/ Akron, Ohio
Neal Smith (drums)/born: Sept. 23, 1947/ Akron, Ohio
Dennis Dunaway (bass)/born: Dec. 9, 1948/ Cottage Grove, Oregon

MEMBERS (1975):
Jozeff Chirowski (keyboards)/born: Mar. 2, 1947/Germany
Richard Wagner (guitar)/born: 1946/Oelwein, Iowa
Steven Hunter (lead guitar)/born: 1948/ Decatur, Illinois
Pentti Olan (drums)/born: July 8, 1946/Finland
Prakash John (bass)/born: 1947/Bombay, India

The Alice Cooper group emerged during the early seventies as the leading exponent of theatrical "shock-rock." Their central figure is Vincent Furnier, the son of a conservative Protestant minister. When Vincent was eleven years old the family moved to Phoenix, Arizona, where he met the group's original members on the high school track team. They formed a group called The Spiders and became successful as a local club band. By 1965 the group had been billed as The Husky Babies and The Nazz (no relation to Todd Rundgren's group) and had had a number one record in Phoenix called "Don't Blow Your Mind."

Early in 1966 Vincent Furnier changed his name to Alice Cooper; he claimed to have dreamed that he was a reincarnation of a sixteenth-century woman of that name who was burned at the stake for witchcraft. The Nazz moved to Los Angeles, where they built a considerable reputation with the S & M stage antics they began to adopt. One of their performances was seen by Frank Zappa and Shep Gordon, and the group was signed by Zappa to his Straight record label and by Gordon to a management contract. However, due to the popularity of another group named Nazz, they collectively adopted the stage name of Alice Cooper. After two albums were released by Straight, the group became discouraged by a lack of personal attention and promotion and asked to be switched to Straight's parent Warner Brothers label.

A 1969 incident was the turning point in the group's career. Impressed by the angry, street-fighting atmosphere that dominated the Detroit rock scene, they had decided to settle there. One night they ended a performance at the local Eastown Ballroom by throwing several live chickens from the stage; these were ripped to pieces by the frenzied crowd, and the result was a national scandal and widespread publicity for Alice Cooper.

During the following year Shep Gor-

Alice Cooper

don arranged for the Canadian production team of Jack Richardson and Bob Ezrin to work with the group. Their initial effort was a single titled "Love It to Death (I'm Eighteen)" first released in Canada. Thought to be by a Canadian group, the song reached number one on a major station there, and its popularity spread across the border to

Detroit and other northcentral American cities. As a result, the record, retitled simply "Eighteen," was issued on Warner Brothers and became a top twenty hit in February 1971.

During the next four years the group scored with nearly a dozen hit singles. They are best known for their albums, such as *Killer, School's Out, Billion Dol-*

lar Babies, and Welcome to My Nightmare, which are based on their highly theatrical stage shows.

In 1975, just before the famed "Nightmare" tour, the entire original back-up band retired and Cooper assembled a new band (see above).

Feb. 71	EIGHTEEN / Warner Bros.	
June 71	CAUGHT IN A DREAM / Warner Bros.	
Dec. 71	UNDER MY WHEELS / Warner Bros.	
Mar. 72	BE MY LOVER / Warner Bros.	
June 72	SCHOOL'S OUT / Warner Bros.	
Oct. 72	ELECTED / Warner Bros.	
Feb. 73	HELLO MURRAY / Warner Bros.	
Apr. 73	NO MORE MR. NICE GUY / Warner Bros.	
Aug. 73	BILLION DOLLAR BABIES / Warner Bros.	
Dec. 73	TEENAGE LAMENT '74 / Warner Bros.	
Apr. 75	ONLY WOMEN BLEED / Warner Bros.	
Aug. 75	DEPARTMENT OF YOUTH / Atlantic	
Oct. 75	WELCOME TO MY NIGHTMARE / Atlantic	
July 76	I NEVER CRY / Warner Bros.	
Apr. 77	YOU AND ME / Warner Bros.	

The Cornelius Brothers & Sister Rose

MEMBERS:
Edward Cornelius / born: 1943
Carter Cornelius / born: 1948
Billie Jo Cornelius / born: 1946 (added in 1973)
Rose Cornelius / born: 1947
HOMETOWN: Dania, Florida

This vocal group is part of a large family—five sisters and ten brothers—each of whom sings or plays a musical instrument. The group, started by Eddie and Carter, played small local clubs in the late sixties.

In 1970 they came to the attention of Bob Archibald, producer-engineer at Miami's Music Factory studio. He became their manager and in early 1971 produced their "Treat Her Like a Lady," releasing it on his own Platinum label. It became a major regional hit, was picked up by United Artists for national distribution, and became the first of a string of major hits.

The Cornelius Brothers & Sister Rose currently tour with a back-up band made up entirely of their brothers and sisters.

Apr. 71	TREAT HER LIKE A LADY / United Artists
May 72	TOO LATE TO TURN BACK NOW / United Artists
Sept. 72	DON'T EVER BE LONELY / United Artists
Dec. 72	I'M NEVER GONNA BE ALONE ANYMORE / United Artists
Apr. 73	LET ME DOWN EASY / United Artists

The Count Five

MEMBERS:
Kenn Ellner (lead vocals) / born: 1948 / Brooklyn, New York
John Michalski (lead guitar) / born: 1948 / Cleveland, Ohio
Sean Byrne (rhythm guitar) / born: 1947 / Dublin, Ireland
Roy Chaney (bass) / born: 1948 / Indianapolis, Indiana

A psychedelic punk-rock group that emerged during the mid-sixties in San Jose, California, The Count Five began by playing in the area's clubs and were often seen with The Syndicate of Sound ("Little Girl") and The Golliwogs, who later became Creedence Clearwater Revival.

In 1966 The Count Five signed with Double Shot Records in Los Angeles and scored with a top five hit called "Psychotic Reaction." Although several follow-up records were released, their popularity remained regional and the group disbanded.

Sept. 66 *PSYCHOTIC REACTION /*
Double Shot

Country Joe & The Fish

MEMBERS:
Joseph McDonald (lead vocals, rhythm guitar) / born: Jan. 1, 1942 / El Monte, California
Barry "The Fish" Melton (lead guitar) / born: 1949 / Brooklyn, New York
Bruce Barthol (bass) / born: 1949 / Berkeley, California
David Cohen (lead guitar, keyboards) / born: 1944 / New York City
Chicken Hirsch (drums) / born: 1942

Country Joe & The Fish were the best known of the political rock groups to emerge from the mid-sixties, San Francisco scene. The nucleus of the group was Joe McDonald, the son of leftist parents who named him after Joseph Stalin. He began his musical career in high school and developed a reputation after moving to Berkeley, California. There, he actively wrote and performed protest songs while publishing a magazine called *Et Tu Brute.*

In 1965 McDonald met Barry Melton on the local folk circuit. With the addition of three friends, the act became Country Mao & The Fish (after a Mao Tse-tung quotation). They were a fixture at the Berkeley student demonstrations and gained fame with their "Fixin' to Die Rag" and "Fish Cheer"—two anthems of student protest. Late in 1966 (after a name change to Country Joe & The Fish), the group was signed by Vanguard, one of the leading labels in the folk field.

Country Joe & The Fish was the first band to 1) bring a psychedelic light show to New York City, 2) do a stereo radio broadcast (live on KSAN in San Francisco), 3) lead an audience in the chanting of obscenities (the F-U-C-K cheer), 4) be convicted by the Commonwealth of Massachusetts for leading an audience in the chanting of same and 5) be paid $10,000 by Ed Sullivan not to appear on his show.

The group became well known through their many albums of protest songs, the first of which, *Electric Music for the Mind and Body,* was released during the summer of 1967. They achieved the height of their popularity via their appearance at the Woodstock Festival in 1969 and in the subsequent film.

Country Joe McDonald and Barry "the Fish" Melton have reformed the band and have signed with Fantasy Records.

Aug. 67 *NOT SO SWEET MARTHA LORRAINE* / Vanguard

Coven

MEMBERS:
Jinx Dawson (lead vocals)
John Hopps
Chris Nelson
Steven Ross

Coven built their recording career around an unusual song titled "One Tin Soldier." It was written by veteran pop songwriters Dennis Lambert and Brian Potter, who produced the first recorded version in 1969 with a group called The Original Caste.

In 1971 John Laughlin, star and producer of the film *Billy Jack,* selected the song as the film's theme and had Coven record it. It was released by Warner Brothers in conjunction with the film, and, although the film did not do well initially, the record became a top twenty hit. *Billy Jack* was rere-

The Cowsills

leased in 1973 and became one of that year's most successful films. In the meantime Coven had switched affiliation to the MGM label, and they recorded a new version of "One Tin Soldier" to capitalize on the film's popularity. This new version became a chart hit during the summer of 1973, but Warner Brothers, not to be outdone, reissued the original soundtrack version, which became a hit again as well.

Sept. 71 *ONE TIN SOLDIER (THE LEGEND OF BILLY JACK)/* Warner Bros.
July 73 *ONE TIN SOLDIER (THE LEGEND OF BILLY JACK)/* MGM
Dec. 73 *ONE TIN SOLDIER (THE LEGEND OF BILLY JACK)/* Warner Bros.

The Cowsills

MEMBERS:
John Cowsill (vocals, drums)/born: May 20, 1960
Robert Cowsill (vocals, guitar)/born: Aug. 26, 1950
Barry Cowsill (vocals, bass)/born: Sept. 14, 1955
William Cowsill (vocals, guitar)/born: Jan. 9, 1948
Paul Cowsill (vocals, keyboards)/born: Nov. 11, 1952
Richard Cowsill (vocals)/born: Aug. 26, 1950/replaced (1967) by Susan Cowsill (vocals)/born: May 20, 1960
Barbara Cowsill (vocals)/born: 1929
HOMETOWN: Newport, Rhode Island

This was a family act consisting originally of six brothers, who were organized as a singing group by their father and manager, Bud Cowsill.

After a brief stay at Johnny Nash's Joda label, where they made one record called "All I Really Wanna Be Is Me," the group received an offer from MGM and began recording for that company in 1967. Their first release,

"The Rain, the Park and Other Things," went straight to number one and was followed by a long string of hits during the next two years. The boys' sister, Susan, and mother, Barbara, joined the group before it faded from popularity during the early seventies.

Sept. 67 *THE RAIN, THE PARK AND OTHER THINGS/* MGM
Jan. 68 *WE CAN FLY/* MGM
Mar. 68 *IN NEED OF A FRIEND/* MGM
June 68 *INDIAN LAKE/* MGM
Sept. 68 *POOR BABY/* MGM
Mar. 69 *HAIR/* MGM
June 69 *THE PROPHECY OF DANIEL & JOHN THE DIVINE/* MGM
Oct. 69 *SILVER THREADS AND GOLDEN NEEDLES/* MGM

The Crazy World of Arthur Brown

MEMBERS:
Arthur Brown (Arthur Wilton) (lead vocals)/born: June 24, 1944/Whitby, Yorkshire, England
Vincent Crane (keyboards)
Sean Nicholas (bass)
Drachian Theaker (drums)

Arthur Brown showed little interest in music during his early years, although he was fascinated by comedy from childhood. It was while doing graduate work in law that he first took an interest in music and began playing with friends at local affairs.

After graduation he formed a band called The Crazy World of Arthur Brown, which combined rock music with decades-old vaudeville routines. As he customarily appeared onstage with burning hair and illuminated clothes, Brown quickly developed a reputation. He came to the attention of The Who's Peter Townshend who got Brown a contract with his manager's label, Track Records. By the fall of

98

1968 Brown's recording of "Fire," produced by Townshend, was a number one hit in both the United States and England. Although that was the extent of his American activity, he continued successfully in England with such material as Screamin' Jay Hawkins's classic "I Put a Spell on You."

During the summer of 1975 Brown returned to the American recording scene with an album called *Dance* on the Gull label.

Sept. 68 *FIRE* / Track

Cream

MEMBERS:

Ginger Baker (Peter Baker) (drums) / born: Aug. 19, 1939 / Lewisham, London, England

Jack Bruce (bass) / born: May 14, 1943 / Glasgow, Scotland

Eric Clapton (Eric Patrick Clapp) (guitar) / born: Mar. 30, 1945 / Ripley, Surrey, England

Cream was formed in 1967 by former members of other leading rock bands and was the first of the "super-groups" to emerge during the late sixties. Ginger Baker and Jack Bruce came to the group from The Graham Bond Organization and Clapton from John Mayall's Bluesbreakers (see *Ginger BAKER* and *Eric CLAPTON*).

After the release of Cream's first album, *Fresh Cream,* early in 1967, they were generally regarded as one of the most important and influential groups in rock. They occupied that position for two years, following with the albums *Disraeli Gears* and *Wheels of Fire* as well as a number of hit singles. By the end of 1968 the strain of having three dominant musical personalities in the same group had proven to be too much, and Cream dissolved. They did one last concert which was recorded as the *Goodbye* album early in 1969.

Ginger Baker and Eric Clapton went on to form Blind Faith later in 1969, and Jack Bruce, after playing briefly with various bands, achieved wide popularity as a member of West, Bruce, and Laing.

Jan. 68 *SUNSHINE OF YOUR LOVE* / Atco

May 68 *ANYONE FOR TENNIS* / Atco

July 68 *SUNSHINE OF YOUR LOVE (rereleased)* / Atco

Oct. 68 *WHITE ROOM* / Atco

Jan. 69 *CROSSROADS* / Atco

Apr. 69 *BADGE* / Atco

Creedence Clearwater Revival

MEMBERS:

John Fogerty (lead guitar, lead vocals) / born: May 28, 1945 / Berkeley, California

Thomas Fogerty (rhythm guitar) / born: Nov. 9, 1941 / Berkeley, California

Stuart Cook (bass) / born: Apr. 24, 1945 / Oakland, California

Douglas Ray Clifford (drums) / born: Apr. 24, 1945 / Palo Alto, California

Creedence Clearwater Revival was the leading American rock 'n' roll band of the late sixties. They began as The Blue Velvets when brothers John and Tom Fogerty joined the other two members in high school. They entertained at school functions and made one recording for the small Orchestra label. During the early sixties the group used several different names and built a substantial following in the San Francisco Bay area. As The Golliwogs they auditioned in 1964 for the Fantasy label and were signed to a contract. After several unsuccessful releases the label lost interest in the group, and they recorded briefly for Scorpio Records.

By 1968 Fantasy had been purchased by one of its former employees, Saul Zaentz. He had liked the

Golliwogs' work and invited them back for another attempt. He also suggested that they use a more contemporary name and they chose Creedence Clearwater Revival (based on a friend's name and a line from a beer commercial). After two moderate hits with rock 'n' roll standards, the group broke through with a number one recording of John Fogerty's composition "Proud Mary." Once established they followed with more than a dozen hit recordings of Fogerty's original material.

In 1971 Tom Fogerty left the group for a solo career; his departure began a series of problems which caused Creedence to disband before year's end. Tom began recording solo in 1973 and spent much of 1975 touring with Jerry Garcia's Legion of Mary. John Fogerty began work on his Blue Ridge Rangers project and later emerged during the mid-seventies as a solo artist on Elektra Records. Stu Cook and Doug Clifford became founding members of a new group called The Don Harrison Band.

In 1976, after Creedence Clearwater Revival had been defunct for nearly five years, Fantasy issued "I Heard It through the Grapevine" from one of the group's early albums, and it became their last chart entry.

Sept. 68	*SUZIE-Q* / Fantasy	
Nov. 68	*I PUT A SPELL ON YOU* / Fantasy	
Jan. 69	*PROUD MARY* / Fantasy	
May 69	*BAD MOON RISING* / Fantasy	
May 69	*LODI* / Fantasy	
Aug. 69	*GREEN RIVER* / Fantasy	
Aug. 69	*COMMOTION* / Fantasy	
Jan. 70	*TRAVELING BAND* / Fantasy	
Jan. 70	*WHO'LL STOP THE RAIN* / Fantasy	
Apr. 70	*UP AROUND THE BEND* / Fantasy	

Apr. 70	*RUN THROUGH THE JUNGLE* / Fantasy	
Aug. 70	*LOOKING OUT MY BACK DOOR* / Fantasy	
Aug. 70	*LONG AS I CAN SEE THE LIGHT* / Fantasy	
Jan. 71	*HAVE YOU EVER SEEN THE RAIN* / Fantasy	
Jan. 71	*HEY TONIGHT* / Fantasy	
July 71	*SWEET HITCH HIKER* / Fantasy	
May 72	*SOMEDAY NEVER COMES* / Fantasy	
Jan. 76	*I HEARD IT THROUGH THE GRAPEVINE* / Fantasy	

The Bob Crewe Generation

This was a large studio orchestra assembled by writer-producer Bob Crewe. Crewe was one of the leading producers of the sixties, known for his work with The Four Seasons, Mitch Ryder & The Detroit Wheels, Diane Renay, and numerous others.

Late in 1966 The Bob Crewe Generation scored with a major instrumental hit, "Music to Watch Girls By," which was based on a popular diet soft drink commercial. They followed a year later with an original tune called "The Birds of Britain." Both were on Crewe's own Dyno-Voice label.

In 1975 Bob Crewe reemerged as one of the most important forces in popular music. He wrote and produced major chart hits for Frankie Valli, LaBelle, Disco Tex & The Sexolettes, and The Eleventh Hour. He also reactivated The Bob Crewe Generation name for the purpose of recording disco records which, in keeping with the times, was shortened to BCG.

Dec. 66	*MUSIC TO WATCH GIRLS BY* / Dyno-Voice	
Oct. 67	*THE BIRDS OF BRITAIN* / Dyno-Voice	
Mar. 76	*STREET TALK* / 20th Century	

The Critters

MEMBERS:

James Ryan (lead guitar)/born: 1947/ Plainfield, New Jersey

Don Ciccone (rhythm guitar, lead vocals)/born: 1947/Plainfield, New Jersey

Kenneth Gorka (bass)/born: 1947/East Orange, New Jersey

Christopher Darway (organ)/born: 1947/ Brooklyn, New York

Jack Decker (drums)/born: 1947/Newark, New Jersey

The Critters were a "soft-rock" group very much in the vein of The Lovin' Spoonful. In fact, they began a string of hits during the mid-sixties with "A Younger Girl," a song that had been recorded by The Spoonful and was written by its leader, John Sebastian. The Critters' biggest hit came during the summer of 1966 and was an original called "Mr. Dieingly Sad."

After four single hits and several albums, The Critters faded from popularity during the late sixties when hard rock became more prevalent. Today Don Ciccone plays as one of The Four Seasons.

May 66	***A YOUNGER GIRL*** /Kapp
Aug. 66	***MR. DIEINGLY SAD*** /Kapp
Dec. 66	***BAD MISUNDERSTANDING*** / Kapp
July 67	***DON'T LET THE RAIN FALL DOWN ON ME*** /Kapp

Jim Croce

BORN: Jan. 10, 1943

DIED: Sept. 20, 1973— *Natchitoches, Louisiana*

HOMETOWN: Philadelphia, Pennsylvania

While a student at Villanova college, Croce formed several bands to play at fraternity functions and performed with one of these in Africa as part of a foreign exchange program.

After returning home to Pennsylvania, Croce found it difficult making a living as a band member and augmented his income with various odd jobs. In 1968 he and his wife, Ingrid, moved to New York City and began performing in Greenwich Village coffeehouses as a folk duo. At this point, Villanova college-friend-turned-producer, Tommy West, introduced them to his partner, Gene Pistilli, who produced an album for Capitol called *Jim & Ingrid.* Croce also recorded a solo album titled *Approaching.* When both failed to generate any sales, Croce and his wife became discouraged and returned to Pennsylvania.

In 1971, after much prodding by Pistilli and West, Croce returned to New York and recorded another album. Titled *You Don't Mess Around with Jim,* the album was released by ABC Records in 1972 and yielded a top ten single of the same name. After two more sizable hit singles, a second LP was issued; *Life and Times,* providing Croce with his first number one single, "Bad, Bad Leroy Brown."

In September 1973, after an appearance at Louisiana State University, Jim Croce was killed in a plane crash that also took the lives of four members of his band and the pilot. Unfortunately his recordings achieved their greatest popularity after his death and sold in the millions. His earlier material began to sell extensively, and new recordings were released from material "in the can."

Today Jim Croce's widow, Ingrid, lives in New York with their young son, Adrian James.

July 72	***YOU DON'T MESS AROUND WITH JIM*** /ABC
Oct. 72	***OPERATOR*** /ABC
Feb. 73	***ONE LESS SET OF FOOTSTEPS*** /ABC
Apr. 73	***BAD, BAD LEROY BROWN*** / ABC

Jim Croce

Oct. 73	*I GOT A NAME* / **ABC**
Nov. 73	*TIME IN A BOTTLE* / **ABC**
Dec. 73	*IT DOESN'T HAVE TO BE THAT WAY* / **ABC**
Mar. 74	*I'LL HAVE TO SAY I LOVE YOU IN A SONG* / **ABC**
June 74	*WORKIN' AT THE CARWASH BLUES* / **ABC**
Jan. 76	*CHAIN GANG MEDLEY* / **Lifesong**

Crosby, Stills, Nash & Young

MEMBERS:

David Van Cortland Crosby (guitar) / born: Aug. 14, 1941 / Los Angeles, California

Stephen Arthur Stills (guitar, bass) / born: Jan. 3, 1945 / Dallas, Texas

Graham Nash (guitar) / born: Feb. 2, 1942 / Blackpool, Lancashire, England

Neil Young (guitar) / born: Nov. 12, 1945 / Toronto, Ontario, Canada

Crosby, Stills, Nash & Young was an informal group made up of former members of some of the leading groups in rock. Stills and Young came from Buffalo Springfield, Graham Nash from The Hollies, and David Crosby from The Byrds.

The group began in 1969 as Crosby, Stills & Nash and released an album by that name in 1969. Two singles from the album, "Marrakesh Express" and "Judy Blue Eyes" (written by the group for Judy Collins), became major hits later in the year. In 1970 the group was joined by Neil Young and their first album, *Deja Vu,* became one of the year's best sellers, in addition to yielding several hit singles.

Since then each of the members has gone on to record solo, although they continue, in various combinations, to make personal appearances and record together.

See *THE BYRDS; THE HOLLIES; BUFFALO SPRINGFIELD.*

Crosby, Stills, & Nash
July 69 *MARRAKESH EXPRESS /* **Atlantic**
Oct. 69 *SUITE: JUDY BLUE EYES /* **Atlantic**
May 77 *JUST A SONG BEFORE I GO /* **Atlantic**
Oct. 77 *FAIR GAME /* **Atlantic**

Crosby, Stills, Nash & Young
Mar. 70 *WOODSTOCK /* **Atlantic**
June 70 *TEACH YOUR CHILDREN /* **Atlantic**
June 70 *OHIO /* **Atlantic**
Sept. 70 *OUR HOUSE /* **Atlantic**

David Crosby
May 71 *MUSIC IS LOVE /* **Atlantic**

Stephen Stills
Dec. 70 *LOVE THE ONE YOU'RE WITH /* **Atlantic**
Mar. 71 *SIT YOURSELF DOWN /* **Atlantic**
June 71 *CHANGE PARTNERS /* **Atlantic**
Aug. 71 *MARIANNE /* **Atlantic**
May 72 *IT DOESN'T MATTER /* **Atlantic**
July 72 *ROCK & ROLL CRAZIES /* **Atlantic**
Apr. 73 *ISN'T IT ABOUT TIME? /* **Atlantic**

Graham Nash
June 71 *CHICAGO /* **Atlantic**
Sept. 71 *MILITARY MADNESS /* **Atlantic**

Neil Young
June 70 *CINNAMON GIRL /* **Reprise**
Oct. 70 *ONLY LOVE CAN BREAK YOUR HEART /* **Reprise**
Apr. 71 *WHEN YOU DANCE /* **Reprise**

Feb. 72 *HEART OF GOLD /* **Reprise**
Apr. 72 *OLD MAN /* **Reprise**
July 74 *WALK ON /* **Reprise**

Neil Young & Graham Nash
July 72 *THE WAR SONG /* **Reprise**

Graham Nash & David Crosby
May 72 *IMMIGRATION MAN /* **Atlantic**
Aug. 72 *SOUTHBOUND TRAIN /* **Atlantic**
Nov. 75 *CARRY ME /* **ABC**

The Crusaders

MEMBERS:
Wilton Felder (tenor sax, bass)
Wayne Henderson (trombone)
Nesbert "Stix" Hooper (percussion)
Joseph Sample (keyboards)
HOMETOWN: Houston, Texas

This jazz-oriented group was formed during the mid-fifties and toured the South under various names (The Chitterling Circuit, The Swingsters, and The Nite-Hawks).

During the early sixties the group was signed to World Pacific as The Jazz Crusaders and gained fame with their many albums. In 1966 a single from one of these ("Uptight") became a hit. In 1972, after a brief stay with Hugh Masekela's Chisa label, the group signed with Blue Thumb Records and dropped the "jazz" prefix from their name in order not to be limited to that sound. The Crusaders, now considered a "jazz-rock" band, continue to be a popular concert attraction.

The Jazz Crusaders
Apr. 66 *UPTIGHT (EVERYTHING'S ALRIGHT) /* **Pacific Jazz**
Dec. 70 *WAY BACK HOME /* **Chisa**

The Crusaders
July 72 *PUT IT WHERE YOU WANT IT /* **Blue Thumb**
Apr. 74 *SCRATCH /* **Blue Thumb**

The Cryan' Shames

MEMBERS:
Thomas Doody (lead vocals)
David Purple (guitar)
Lenny Kerley (guitar, bass)
Isaac Guillory (guitar, bass, keyboards)
James Hooke (percussion)
Dennis Conroy (drums)
HOMETOWN: Chicago, Illinois

This group was formed during the mid-sixties and developed a strong following in local clubs. They were signed by the Destination label, and their first release, a remake of The Searchers' "Sugar and Spice," became a big regional hit that eventually reached the top fifty on the national charts.

Based on this success, The Cryan' Shames were offered a contract by Columbia Records late in 1966. But although several singles and an album were released, none were quite as successful as their first record.

After many personnel changes, The Cryan' Shames continue to perform in the Chicago area. Two of their original members, Lenny Kerley and Dennis Conroy, joined a group called Possum River, which recorded for Ovation Records.

July 66 *SUGAR AND SPICE /* **Destination**
Nov. 66 *I WANT TO MEET YOU /* **Columbia**
Aug. 67 *IT COULD BE WE'RE IN LOVE /* **Columbia**
Apr. 68 *UP ON THE ROOF /* **Columbia**
June 68 *YOUNG BIRDS FLY /* **Columbia**

The Cuff Links

Ron Dante
BORN: August 22, 1945
HOMETOWN: Staten Island, New York

The Cuff Links was a name given to the collective overdubbed voices of studio singer Ron Dante, and the "group" managed to place three records on the national charts during the late sixties and early seventies. The biggest of these was "Tracy," which reached the top ten.

Ron Dante is also known as the studio voice of The Archies and The Detergents ("Leader of the Laundromat") and for many years has been active in radio and television commercials. He emerged during 1975 as the producer of Barry Manilow's hits and as a recording artist under his own name with a remake of The Archies' multimillion seller, "Sugar Sugar."

Sept. 69 *TRACY /* **Decca**
Dec. 69 *WHEN JULIE COMES AROUND /* **Decca**
Mar. 70 *RUN SALLY RUN /* **Decca**

Burton Cummings

BORN: December 31, 1947
HOMETOWN: Winnipeg, Canada

During the mid-sixties Burton, along with Randy Bachman, Mike Kale, and Garry Peterson, formed a group called The Guess Who, who signed with RCA and had countless hit singles throughout the sixties.

During the mid-seventies Burton left the group and signed with Columbia Records as a solo performer. In fact, Columbia wanted him to launch their new subsidiary Portrait label. And launch it he did with "Stand Tall," a top ten national hit he wrote and recorded which also launched him on a new career.

Oct. 76 *STAND TALL /* **Portrait**
Feb. 77 *I'M SCARED /* **Portrait**
Sept. 77 *MY OWN WAY TO ROCK /* **Portrait**

The Cyrkle

MEMBERS:

Donald Dannemann (lead guitar)/born: May 9, 1944/Brooklyn, New York

Thomas Webster Dawes (bass)/born: July 25, 1943/Albany, New York

Martin Leslie Fried (guitar, drums)/born: Jan. 28, 1944/Neptune, New Jersey

Earl Pickens (guitar added in 1966) replaced (1966) by Michael Losekamp/born: 1947/Dayton, Ohio

Tom Dawes, Don Dannemann, and Marty Fried formed a group called The Rondells (no relation to the later Rhondells) while attending Lafayette College in Pennsylvania during the early sixties. After performing locally for a few years, they were booked in 1966 at Trude Heller's famed discotheque in New York City. There The Beatles' manager Brian Epstein heard them and signed them as the first American group he would handle.

Epstein suggested the name change to The Cyrkle and obtained a recording contract with Columbia. Their first release, a Paul Simon song titled "Red Rubber Ball," became an immediate best seller, and the group was asked to join The Beatles on their 1966 American tour. At that point guitarist Earl Pickens was recruited only to be replaced almost immediately by Mike Losekamp.

The death of Brian Epstein in 1967 left The Cyrkle with no direction, and the group disbanded soon thereafter. Don Dannemann and Tom Dawes became independent record producers during the seventies.

May 66	*RED RUBBER BALL* / Columbia	
Aug. 66	*TURN DOWN DAY* / Columbia	
Dec. 66	*PLEASE DON'T EVER LEAVE ME* / Columbia	
Feb. 67	*I WISH YOU COULD BE HERE* / Columbia	
May 67	*WE HAD A GOOD THING GOING* / Columbia	
Sept. 67	*PENNY ARCADE* / Columbia	

Charlie Daniels

BORN: Oct. 28, 1936
HOMETOWN: Wilmington, North Carolina

At fifteen Charlie Daniels taught himself guitar and spent the next years playing in various bluegrass bands.

While visiting a friend in Texas in the sixties, Daniels was introduced to a little-known producer named Bob Johnston from Nashville. Daniels moved there to work with Johnston, and as Johnston grew to be one of the city's most important producers, Daniels got increasingly more work as a session guitarist. He is heard on records by Bob Dylan, Ringo Starr, Leonard Cohen, Pete Seeger, Flatt & Scruggs, and numerous others.

During the early seventies Daniels became associated with Don Rubin, (a veteran of the Koppelman-Rubin production and publishing company) who produced a single titled "Uneasy Rider." Released on the Kama Sutra label, it became a top ten hit during the summer of 1973 and was followed by a successful album, *Honey in the Rock.*

Since then Charlie Daniels has formed his own band and continues to live in Nashville when not touring.

June 73 *UNEASY RIDER* / **Kama Sutra**
Feb. 75 *THE SOUTH IS GONNA DO IT* / **Kama Sutra**
May 75 *LONG HAIRED COUNTRY BOY* / **Kama Sutra**
Feb. 76 *TEXAS* / **Kama Sutra**

David & Jonathan

MEMBERS:
David: Roger Greenway / born: Aug. 23, 1942
Jonathan: Roger Cook / born: Aug. 19, 1940
HOMETOWN: Bristol, England

David and Jonathan met in 1965 and collaborated as songwriters. By the end of the year, they were responsible for nearly a dozen hits by such artists as The Fortunes, Freddie & The Dreamers, and Petula Clark. One of their demonstration records was heard by The Beatles' producer George Martin, who signed the duo as artists and produced a recording of The Beatles' "Michele." This became a major hit in both England and America and was followed by several successful albums. They continued to write for other artists and in 1968 retired as performers to become record producers under their real names.

Individually and as a team Cook and Greenway have become two of the most important and successful forces in the production of pop music. Their songwriting credits include "You've Got Your Troubles" (The Fortunes), "Softly Whispering I Love You" (The English Congregation), "Love Grows" (Edison Lighthouse), "Doctor's Orders" (Carol Douglas), and "I'd Like to Teach the World to Sing," the popular song originally written as a leading soft drink commercial. Roger Cook also achieved success during the seventies as the leader of a vocal group, Blue Mink.

Jan. 66 *MICHELE* / Capitol

Mac Davis

BORN: Jan. 21, 1942
HOMETOWN: Lubbock, Texas

Mac Davis

After graduating from high school, Mac Davis settled in Atlanta, where he worked for the Georgia State Board of Probation and attended the State University at night, all the while playing part time with a band he had formed called The Zotz.

During the early sixties Davis toured the south but made little money as a performer. He accepted a job in Atlanta as regional manager, first for the Vee Jay record company and later for Liberty. He was meanwhile writing original material and presenting it to various performers; he gained recognition in 1968 when Lou Rawls recorded his composition of "You're Good for Me" and Glen Campbell cut "Within My Memory." Late in the year Mac Davis was asked by the Elvis Presley organization for original material, and Elvis later scored with four hit recordings of Davis's songs: "A Little Less Conversation," "Memories," "In the Ghetto," and "Don't Cry Daddy." His reputation as a songwriter was firmly established, and Davis's songs were successfully recorded by many other artists, including The First Edition ("Something's Burning"), Bobby Goldsboro ("Watching Scotty Grow"), and O. C. Smith ("Daddy's Little Man" and "Friend, Lover, Woman, Wife").

In 1970 Mac Davis was signed as an artist to Columbia Records. He cut two moderately successful singles and the widely acclaimed *Songpainter* album during the following year. However, his major breakthrough came in 1972, when he reached number one with his release of "Baby, Don't Get Hooked on Me."

During the mid-seventies, he began hosting his own network television show.

May 70 *WHOEVER FINDS THIS, I LOVE YOU* / Columbia
Feb. 71 *BEGINNING TO FEEL THE PAIN* / Columbia
July 72 *BABY DON'T GET HOOKED ON ME* / Columbia
Nov. 72 *EVERYBODY LOVES A LOVE SONG* / Columbia
Feb. 73 *DREAM ME HOME* / Columbia
May 73 *YOUR SIDE OF THE BED* / Columbia
Mar. 74 *ONE HELL OF A WOMAN* / Columbia
Aug. 74 *STOP AND SMELL THE ROSES* / Columbia

Dec. 74	***ROCK & ROLL (I GAVE YOU THE BEST YEARS OF MY LIFE)*** / **Columbia**
Apr. 75	***ALL THE LOVE IN THE WORLD*** / **Columbia**
May 75	***BURNING THING*** / **Columbia**
Apr. 76	***FOREVER LOVERS*** / **Columbia**

Paul Davis

BORN: Apr. 21, 1948
HOMETOWN: Meridian, Mississippi

Paul Davis spent part of his childhood in Nashville, where he was heavily influenced by country music. Later he returned to Mississippi for high school and formed his own country-rock band.

After developing a reputation as a "live" performer, Davis was signed in 1970 by Bang Records, where Bert Berns, the label's owner, produced his recording of "A Little Bit of Soap," which had been a hit for The Jarmels many years before. It was successful for Davis as well, and was the first of his several hits.

His biggest release, "I Go Crazy," broke the record (39 *consecutive* weeks set by Johnny Mathis with his hit tune "Wonderful! Wonderful!" in 1957) for the longest *consecutive* ride on the charts (40 weeks).

Apr. 70	***A LITTLE BIT OF SOAP*** / **Bang**
Sept. 70	***I JUST WANT TO KEEP IT TOGETHER*** / **Bang**
Dec. 72	***BOOGIE WOOGIE MAN*** / **Bang**
Oct. 74	***RIDE 'EM COWBOY*** / **Bang**
July 75	***KEEP OUR LOVE ALIVE*** / **Bang**
Apr. 76	***THINKING OF YOU*** / **Bang**
Aug. 76	***SUPERSTAR*** / **Bang**
Aug. 77	***I GO CRAZY*** / **Bang**
May 78	***DARLIN*** / **Bang**

The Spencer Davis Group

ORIGINAL MEMBERS:
Spencer Davis (guitar) / born: July 17, 1942
Steven Winwood (lead vocals, guitar, keyboards) / born May 12, 1948
Mervyn "Muff" Winwood (bass) / born: June 14, 1943
Peter York (drums) / born: Aug. 15, 1942
HOMETOWN: Birmingham, England

In the early 1960s Spencer Davis, a German teacher at the University of Birmingham, decided to launch a career in music by singing in local folk clubs. One night he heard a group that impressed him and proposed to its leader, Muff Winwood, that they all join forces.

During the next few years The Spencer Davis Group developed a reputation as one of the best bands on the English rock-club circuit, first in Birmingham and later in London. During the mid-sixties, the group was signed by Island Records, and their first release, "Keep on Running," became a hit in England and a minor success in America. However, the release of "Gimme Some Lovin' " late in 1966 established the group on both sides of the Atlantic by rising to the top of the charts. After several additional hits, Steve Winwood announced in 1967 that he was leaving to join Traffic, and The Spencer Davis Group soon disbanded.

After a brief hiatus Davis formed a new group consisting of original member York, Eddie Hardin (keyboards), and Phil Sawyer (lead guitar), who was replaced almost immediately by Roy Fenwick. After recording one album Hardin and York left to form their own group, and Dee Murray and Nigel Olsson (who later rose to fame as the nucleus of Elton John's band) replaced them. This band lasted until 1969, when Davis formed an acoustic duo, first with Alun Davies (now with Cat Stevens) and then with Peter Jameson. After recording two albums Davis went into semiretirement for several years for personal and health reasons.

During the mid-seventies, Spencer Davis emerged with yet another group, made up of Hardin, York, Fenwick, and a new bassist named Charlie McCracken. With the exception of the original line-up, Spencer Davis's several groups have been known primarily for their success as "album" artists. Today Spencer Davis is an A & R man with Island Records in New York.

Mar. 66	**KEEP ON RUNNING** / Atco
Dec. 66	**GIMME SOME LOVIN'** / United Artists
Mar. 67	**I'M A MAN** / United Artists
June 67	**SOMEBODY HELP ME** / United Artists
June 67	**TIME SELLER** / United Artists

Tyrone Davis

BORN: 1938
HOMETOWN: Greenville, Mississippi

In 1957 Davis moved to Chicago, where he got a job as driver and valet for noted blues singer Freddie King. As a result he met Bobby Bland, Little Milton, and Otis Clay, who helped and encouraged him with his singing career. During the early sixties he formed an association with Chicago producer-songwriter Harold Burrage. While Davis held a daytime job at a steel mill, Burrage helped him get club dates and a contract with a small local label. Burrage also wrote and produced several records, none of which were successful, and just after Davis left his job to concentrate on his singing career, Bur-

Tyrone Davis

rage died and left him without direction.

In 1968 Davis made the rounds of Chicago record companies with demo records and was eventually signed by the Dakar label. A record release titled "A Woman Needs to Be Loved" did not sell in spite of a fair amount of airplay, and Davis was discouraged enough to almost give up singing when suddenly he got his proverbial "break." A disc jockey in Houston began playing the other side, "Can I Change My Mind?," which became a regional hit and eventually reached the top five nationally. After that lucky turn Tyrone Davis had a virtually unbroken string of soul and pop hits.

Dec. 68	**CAN I CHANGE MY MIND?** / Dakar
Mar. 69	**IS IT SOMETHING YOU'VE GOT?** / Dakar
Mar. 70	**TURN BACK THE HANDS OF TIME** / Dakar
June 70	**I'LL BE RIGHT HERE** / Dakar
Oct. 70	**LET ME BACK IN** / Dakar
Mar. 71	**COULD I FORGET YOU?** / Dakar

July 71 *ONE WAY TICKET* /Dakar
Nov. 71 *YOU KEEP ME HOLDING ON* / Dakar
Mar. 72 *I HAD IT ALL THE TIME* /Dakar
Apr. 73 *WITHOUT YOU IN MY LIFE* / Dakar
July 73 *THERE IT IS* /Dakar
Feb. 74 *I WISH IT WAS ME* /Dakar
July 74 *WHAT GOES UP* /Dakar
Sept. 76 *GIVE IT UP (TURN IT LOOSE)* / Columbia

Dawn

MEMBERS:

Tony Orlando (Michael Anthony Orlando Cassevitis) (lead vocals) /born: Apr. 3, 1944/ New York City

Telma Louise Hopkins (background vocals) / born: Oct. 28, 1948/Louisville, Kentucky

Joyce Elaine Vincent Wilson (background vocals) /born: Dec. 14, 1946/Detroit, Michigan

The nucleus of this group is Tony Orlando, who originally became known as a recording artist during the early sixties (see *Tony ORLANDO, Rock On: The Solid Gold Years*).

After Orlando's recording career subsided, he busied himself for several years as professional manager at April-Blackwood Music, Columbia Records' publishing company, and with occasional studio singing jobs. His responsibilities at the publishing company included promoting the material of such people as Laura Nyro, James Taylor, and Van McCoy.

In 1970 Orlando was contacted by Hank Medress (an ex-member of The Tokens turned record producer), who asked him to record as lead voice on a single called "Candida." The voices had been recorded by a studio group, and Medress was not satisfied with the sound of the lead singer. Orlando agreed, the master was purchased by Bell Records, and the single was released a few weeks later. "Candida" became a top three hit and Orlando,

considering it a fluke, continued at his publishing job. Toward the end of the year the producers called him back to provide the voice for a follow-up recording. Titled "Knock Three Times," this record went to number one and Tony Orlando was finally persuaded to leave his job and become the lead singer of Dawn.

All that was needed now was a permanent back-up group, and Telma Hopkins and Joyce Vincent were selected. Both had been popular background singers at recording sessions for many years, and were heard on hits by Johnnie Taylor, Freda Payne, Edwin Starr, Frijid Pink, and numerous others. (In addition, Telma was a long-time member of Isaac Hayes's back-up group, Hot Buttered Soul, and hers was the sultry voice behind Hayes on the *Shaft* theme.) Dawn made their debut appearance at Carnegie Hall in September 1971 and continued to produce major hit recordings. Their release of "Tie a Yellow Ribbon" in 1973 became the largest-selling record of that year and one of the biggest sellers in history.

In 1977 Tony Orlando retired from show business, but is now back performing solo.

July 70 *CANDIDA* /Bell
Nov. 70 *KNOCK THREE TIMES* /Bell
Mar. 71 *I PLAY AND SING* /Bell
June 71 *SUMMER SAND* /Bell
Oct. 71 *WHAT ARE YOU DOING SUNDAY?* /Bell
Jan. 72 *RUNAWAY* /Bell
June 72 *VAYA CON DIOS* /Bell
Nov. 72 *YOU'RE A LADY* /Bell
Feb. 73 *TIE A YELLOW RIBBON (ROUND THE OLD OAK TREE)* / Bell
July 73 *SAY, HAS ANYBODY SEEN MY SWEET GYPSY ROSE?* /Bell
Nov. 73 *WHO'S IN THE STRAWBERRY PATCH WITH SALLY?* /Bell

Dawn. Left to right: Joyce Wilson, Tony Orlando, and Telma Hopkins

Mar. 74 *IT ONLY HURTS WHEN I TRY TO SMILE* / Bell

Aug. 74 *STEPPIN' OUT* / Bell

Dec. 74 *LOOK IN MY EYES PRETTY WOMAN* / Bell

Mar. 75 *HE DON'T LOVE YOU* / Elektra

June 75 *MORNIN' BEAUTIFUL* / Elektra

Aug. 75 *YOU'RE ALL I NEED TO GET BY* / Elektra

Nov. 75 *SKYBIRD* / Arista

Feb. 76 *CUPID* / Elektra

Apr. 77 *SING* / Elektra

Bill Deal & The Rhondells

MEMBERS:

William Deal (lead vocal, keyboards)

Ammon Tharp (alternate lead vocals, drums)

Michael Kerwin (trumpet)

Jeffrey Pollard (trumpet)

Kenneth Dawson (trumpet)

Donald Queinsenburry (bass)

Ronald Rosenbaum (trombone)

Robert Fisher (guitar)

HOMETOWN: New York City

Although this large and heavily instrumental group achieved popularity in 1969, their name and sound were a throwback to the late fifties and early sixties vocal group style.

The group was signed by producer Jerry Ross to his Heritage label and they had a string of hits which lasted into early 1970.

Jan. 69	*MAY I* / Heritage
Apr. 69	*I'VE BEEN HURT* / Heritage
Aug. 69	*WHAT KIND OF FOOL (DO YOU THINK I AM?)* / Heritage
Nov. 69	*SWINGING TIGHT* / Heritage
Mar. 70	*NOTHING SUCCEEDS LIKE SUCCESS* / Heritage

Kiki Dee

REAL NAME: Pauline Matthews

BORN: Mar. 6, 1947

HOMETOWN: Bradford, Yorkshire, England

Pauline Matthews launched her career during the early sixties singing with various dance bands around northern England. Eventually she reached London cabarets and was spotted by songwriter-producer Mitch Murray. He suggested the name change to Kiki Dee and, after getting her a contract with British Philips, wrote and produced her first single, "Early Night." This was followed by an album, *Hi, I'm Kiki Dee,* and nearly a dozen singles

over the next five years, none of which achieved any substantial success. However, the general "Motown sound" of her recordings led to an offer from that label in 1969; she recorded one album there called *Great Expectations.*

This album too was unsuccessful (one single on the subsidiary Rare Earth label made a brief United States chart appearance), but her association with Motown ultimately became important. There she had befriended a young Scotsman named John Reid, who emerged four years later as a key member of Elton John's organization. Reid arranged for Elton to hear Kiki, and she was signed to his new Rocket label. An album titled *Loving and Free* was released and yielded two hit singles in England, "Lonnie & Josie" and "Amoureuse." This was followed in 1974 by another LP, *I've Got the Music in Me,* and the title track became a top ten hit both in England and America.

During the mid-seventies Kiki Dee formed her own band, consisting of Roger Pope (drums), Jo Partridge (lead guitar), Bias Boshell (keyboards), and Phil Curtis (bass). In 1976 she teamed up with Elton John on his first number-one single in England, "Don't Go Breaking My Heart."

Mar. 71	*LOVE MAKES THE WORLD GO ROUND* / Rare Earth
Sept. 74	*I'VE GOT THE MUSIC IN ME* / Rocket
May 75	*HOW GLAD I AM* / Rocket
Mar. 76	*ONCE A FOOL* / Rocket

Deep Purple

MEMBERS:

Jon Lord (keyboards) / born: June 9, 1941 / Leicester, England

Ian Paice (drums) / born: June 29, 1948 / Nottingham, England

Deep Purple

Ritchie Blackmore (lead guitar)/born: Apr. 14, 1945/Weston, Super Mare, England/replaced (1975) by Thomas Bolin/died: Dec. 4, 1976

Rod Evans (lead vocals)/born: Jan. 19, 1945/Edinburgh, Scotland/replaced (1969) by Ian Gillan/replaced (1973) by David Coverdale

Nicholas Simper (bass)/born: Nov. 3, 1946/Norwood Green, Middlesex, England/replaced (1969) by Roger Glover/replaced (1973) by Glenn Hughs

Success came rather quickly for this British group when they were signed by Parlophone Records almost immediately after their formation in 1968.

By the middle of the year they had released an album called *Shades of Deep Purple,* which was leased for American distribution to Tetragrammaton Records, a label partially owned by comedian Bill Cosby and marketed by Warner Brothers. This yielded a single titled "Hush," a remake of the Joe South song that had been a hit for Billy Joe Royal in 1967. After this reached the top five in the U.S., the group followed with another version of a previous hit, Neil Diamond's "Kentucky Woman," and the classic "River Deep-Mountain High." By the summer of 1969 Tetragrammaton was having operating difficulty and Deep Purple took the opportunity to reorganize. Rod Evans and Nic Semper left to be replaced by Ian Gillan and Roger Glover (both formerly of Episode Six), and the new group featured a completely new sound that relied almost entirely on original material. One of their first projects was the *Concerto for Group and Orchestra,* a rock symphony which they composed and performed with a full symphony orchestra in September 1969 at the famed Albert Hall. A "live" recording of this event was released as an album and Deep Purple went on to become an extremely popular "heavy-metal" concert and album act. In addition they returned to the singles charts during the mid-seventies with several hits, the biggest of which was "Smoke on the Water."

After undergoing numerous personnel changes, the group became an informal arrangement that allowed its members to pursue parallel careers. Former member Ritchie Blackmore went on to form Rainbow; Rod Evans formed Captain Beyond; Roger Glover became a producer for Nazareth; and Ian Gillan became known for his title role in *Jesus Christ Superstar.* Tommy Bolin died on December 4, 1976 in North Miami, Florida, at the age of twenty-five. The cause of death was drug overdose.

Aug. 68	**HUSH**/Tetragrammaton
Nov. 68	**KENTUCKY WOMAN**/ Tetragrammaton
Jan. 69	**RIVER DEEP-MOUNTAIN HIGH**/Tetragrammaton
Dec. 70	**BLACK NIGHT**/ Warner Bros.
Apr. 73	**WOMAN FROM TOKYO**/ Warner Bros.
May 73	**SMOKE ON THE WATER**/ Warner Bros.
Mar. 74	**JUST MIGHT TAKE YOUR LIFE**/ Warner Bros.

Rick Dees & His Cast of Idiots

REAL NAME: Rigdon Osmond Dees III
BORN: 1950
HOMETOWN: Memphis, Tennessee

Rick, while working as a morning disc jockey and program director at WMPS in Memphis, had an idea for a disco novelty song. A man of many voices, Dees recorded the tune he wrote, called "Disco Duck," for Memphis-based Fretone Records, and it was shortly a big local hit. The master was leased to RSO Records, and within a few months the song was a number one national hit.

Although his popularity as a performer caused him to leave WMPS, Dees is now employed at WHBQ in Memphis and is developing new material to record.

Aug. 76	**DISCO DUCK (Pt. 1)**/RSO
Jan. 77	**DIS-GORILLA (Pt. 1)**/RSO

The De Franco Family

MEMBERS:
Anthony De Franco (lead vocals)/born: Aug. 31, 1959
Benjamin De Franco/born: July 11, 1954
Nino De Franco/born: Oct. 19, 1956
Marisa De Franco/born: July 23, 1955
Merlina De Franco/born: July 20, 1957
HOMETOWN: Port Colborne, Ontario, Canada

The five De Franco children were raised by musically inclined parents and gradually evolved into a popular band in the Ontario region. Their pictures appeared regularly in local newspapers, and a friend of the group's sent clippings to several teen magazines in an attempt to get them publicity. One of these was seen by Charles Laufer at *Tiger Beat* magazine, who noticed a resemblance between Tony De Franco and teen star Donny Osmond. He invited the De Francos to Hollywood for a picture story, and the overwhelming mail response prompted him to contact his friend Russ Regan at 20th Century Records and arrange a recording session.

The De Francos' first release, "Heartbeat—It's a Lovebeat," exceeded everyone's expectations and sold more than two million copies, firmly establishing the group as a top teen attraction.

Sept. 73	*HEARTBEAT—IT'S A LOVEBEAT* / 20th Century
Dec. 73	*ABRA CADABRA* / 20th Century
May 74	*SAVE THE LAST DANCE FOR ME* / 20th Century

Desmond Dekker

REAL NAME: Desmond Dacres
BORN: 1942
HOMETOWN: Jamaica, West Indies

Desmond Dekker, one of the leading reggae singers, has placed more than three dozen of his own songs high on the Jamaican charts since the early sixties. During the mid-sixties his popularity spread to England, where he scored with numerous hits. First "007 (Shanty Town)" went to number twelve; their "The Israelites" became a top ten record in America as well and was followed by an album of the same name.

| May 69 | *THE ISRAELITES* / Uni |

Delaney & Bonnie

Delaney Bramlett / born: July 1, 1939 / Pontotoc, Mississippi

Bonnie Lynn Bramlett / born: Nov. 8, 1944 / Granite City, Illinois

This husband and wife team rose to fame during the early seventies with a unique, old-time-revival form of gospel rock.

Delaney took up the guitar before he reached his teens and first played with his brother at local church and school affairs. During the early sixties he entered the service and played with various country and rock bands which passed through the area where he was based. After his discharge Delaney moved to Los Angeles where he played in local clubs and got a regular job on the L.A.-based "Shindig" television show.

Bonnie Lynn's career began in her native Illinois, where she sang in small clubs while attending high school. During the early sixties she moved to Memphis and became active as a session singer at the Stax-Volt Studios, after which she traveled with the Ike & Tina Turner Revue and eventually settled in Los Angeles.

Delaney met Bonnie in 1967 when he was in the audience of one of her performances at a Los Angeles club. They were married only a few days later. After establishiing an act by playing local nightspots, they recorded an album, *Home,* for Stax, but it was not released until they later achieved fame. Next Delaney & Bonnie assembled an informal back-up group known as Friends, which consisted of musicians with whom Delaney had played on "Shindig:" Leon Russell (keyboards and guitar), Jerry McGee (guitar), Bobby Whitlock (keyboards), Carl Radle (bass), Bobby Keltner (drums), Bobby Keyes (sax), Jim Price (horns), and Rita Coolidge, a friend of Bonnie's from Memphis (vocals).

The Friends were signed by Elektra (the contract was eventually assigned to Atlantic) and an album titled *Accept No Substitute* was recorded. They became one of the top touring attractions in rock and at various times included Dave Mason, Eric Clapton, and George Harrison. Their albums, such as *Original Delaney & Bonnie, To Bonnie from Delaney,* and *Motel Shot* were best sellers, and they were represented with numerous hit singles. The biggest was "Never Ending Song of

Love," which reached the top ten in 1971. Many of the group's members were also part of John and Yoko's original Plastic Ono Band.

In 1972 Delaney & Bonnie switched affiliation to the Columbia label, and shortly afterward they separated. Delaney became a member of Mobius and Bonnie headed the Bonnie Bramlett Band. Aside from their contribution to music, the most important aspect of the Delaney & Bonnie period is that it was a breeding-ground for many of today's leading rock figures. Bobby Keyes and Jim Price went on to The Rolling Stones band; Eric Clapton, Jim Gordon, Carl Radle, and Bobby Whitlock became Derek & The Dominoes and are currently premiere studio musicians, as are Bobby Keltner and Jerry McGee. Rita Coolidge is a leading solo singer and also performs with Kris Kristofferson, her husband.

See *Leon RUSSELL; Rita COOLIDGE; DEREK & The DOMINOES; Eric CLAPTON.*

Feb. 70	*COMING HOME* / Atco	
May 70	*FREE THE PEOPLE* / Atco	
Aug. 70	*SOUL SHAKE* / Atco	
May 71	*NEVER ENDING SONG OF LOVE* / Atco	
Sept. 71	*ONLY YOU KNOW AND I KNOW* / Atco	
Jan. 72	*MOVE 'EM OUT* / Atco	
Apr. 72	*WHERE THERE'S A WILL, THERE'S A WAY* / Atco	

The Delfonics

MEMBERS:

William Hart / born: Jan. 17, 1945

Wilbert Hart / born: Oct. 19, 1947

Randy Cain / born: May 2, 1946 / replaced (1971) by Major Harris

HOMETOWN: Philadelphia, Pennsylvania

The Delfonics were one of the earliest vocal groups featuring what is now known as the "Philadelphia sound." Brothers Bill and Wilbert Hart joined Randy Cain in the fifties to sing at high school and other local affairs. During the early sixties, the group began to sing seriously and obtained a contract with Philadelphia's Cameo-Parkway label. This resulted in several regional hits, one of which was rereleased on the subsidiary Moonshot label after the group's later national success.

One of the key factors of their success was The Delfonics' association with Thom Bell, a writer-arranger who was to become a cornerstone of the "Philadelphia sound." The group was signed to the Philly Groove label in 1968 and recording songs arranged by Bell and cowritten with Bill Hart, they scored a 5-year string of soul and pop hits.

In 1971 original member Randy Cain left The Delfonics and was replaced by another old school friend, Major Harris. Harris, in turn, also left to pursue a solo career and achieved success in 1975.

See *Major HARRIS.*

Feb. 68	*LA LA MEANS I LOVE YOU* / Philly Groove	
Apr. 68	*I'M SORRY* / Philly Groove	
May 68	*HE DON'T REALLY LOVE YOU* / Moonshot	
Aug. 68	*BREAK YOUR PROMISE* / Philly Groove	
Dec. 68	*READY OR NOT, HERE I COME* / Philly Groove	
Feb. 69	*SOMEBODY LOVES YOU* / Philly Groove	
June 69	*FUNNY FEELING* / Philly Groove	
Aug. 69	*YOU GET YOURS AND I'LL GET MINE* / Philly Groove	
Jan. 70	*DIDN'T I* / Philly Groove	
June 70	*TRYING TO MAKE A FOOL OF ME* / Philly Groove	
Sept. 70	*WHEN YOU GET RIGHT DOWN TO IT* / Philly Groove	
June 71	*HEY, LOVE* / Philly Groove	
Oct. 71	*WALK RIGHT UP TO THE SUN* / Philly Groove	

John Denver

John Denver

REAL NAME: Henry John Deutchendorf, Jr.
BORN: Dec. 31, 1943
HOMETOWN: Roswell, New Mexico

John Denver is the son of an air force pilot who holds three world records in military aviation. In high school, John was influenced by Elvis Presley and learned to play the guitar on his grandmother's 1910 Gibson. Later, while studying architecture at Texas Tech, he became caught up in the folk music boom of the early sixties and migrated to Los Angeles to break into the business. After playing in a number of small clubs, he was hired by Randy Sparks for an extended stay at Leadbetters. Afterward, for nearly four years, he replaced Chad Mitchell in the trio bearing his name.

In 1969 Denver went solo and was signed by RCA Records. His first album, *Rhymes and Reasons,* was released shortly thereafter and provided Peter, Paul & Mary with the number one song "Leaving on a Jet Plane," their last hit before disbanding. Denver followed with three albums during the next two years, *Take Me to Tomorrow, Whose Garden Was This,* and *Poems, Prayers & Promises,* the last of which yielded his first hit single, a million seller called "Take Me Home, Country Roads."

Since then his singles and albums have been among the best sellers in all of pop music. He is active in television, hosting his own specials and appearing in occasional dramatic roles.

In 1975 he scored and acted in his first film, a remake of the thirties movie *Mr. Smith Goes to Washington.* In 1976 he established his own Windsong record label. Denver lives with his wife, Ann (subject of his 1974 hit, "Annie's Song"), in Aspen, Colorado.

Apr. 71	***TAKE ME HOME, COUNTRY ROADS*** /RCA
Nov. 71	***FRIENDS WITH YOU*** /RCA
Mar. 72	***EVERYDAY*** /RCA
July 72	***GOODBYE AGAIN*** /RCA
Nov. 72	***ROCKY MOUNTAIN HIGH*** /RCA
May 73	***I'D RATHER BE A COWBOY*** /RCA
Sept. 73	***FAREWELL ANDROMEDA*** /RCA
Dec. 73	***PLEASE, DADDY*** /RCA
Jan. 74	***SUNSHINE ON MY SHOULDER*** /RCA
June 74	***ANNIE'S SONG*** /RCA
Sept. 74	***BACK HOME AGAIN*** /RCA
Dec. 74	***SWEET SURRENDER*** /RCA
Mar. 75	***THANK GOD I'M A COUNTRY BOY*** /RCA
Aug. 75	***I'M SORRY*** /RCA
Aug. 75	***CALYPSO*** /RCA
Dec. 75	***FLY AWAY*** /RCA
Dec. 75	***CHRISTMAS FOR COWBOYS*** /RCA
Mar. 76	***LOOKING FOR SPACE*** /RCA
May 76	***IT MAKES ME GIGGLE*** /RCA
Sept. 76	***LIKE A SAD SONG*** /RCA
Dec. 76	***BABY, YOU LOOK GOOD TO ME TONIGHT*** /RCA
Mar. 77	***MY SWEET LADY*** /RCA
Nov. 77	***HOW CAN I LEAVE YOU AGAIN*** /RCA
Mar. 78	***IT AMAZES ME*** /RCA
Apr. 78	***I WANT TO LIVE*** /RCA

Deodato

FULL NAME: Eumir Deodato
HOMETOWN: Rio De Janeiro, Brazil

Eumir Deodato, who was playing classical music (piano) in his teens, became interested in jazz as he grew older and assimilated the styles of John Coltrane and Miles Davis. While attending an engineering college, he played as part of a small rock band in and around Rio.

In 1967 he decided on a career in music and migrated to New York City. One of his first jobs was as an arranger for fellow Brazilian Astrud Gilberto ("The Girl from Ipanema"), which led to his arranging three of the cuts on Wes Montgomery's *Down Here on the Ground* album. His work on this LP established his reputation and, for the next several years, he was kept busy arranging for such artists as Aretha Franklin, Bette Midler, Roberta Flack, and Frank Sinatra.

In 1972 Deodato was signed by jazz producer Creed Taylor to his CTI label and, early the following year, he scored with an arrangement of "Also Sprach Zarathustra (2001)." In 1975 Deodato switched affiliation to MCA Records

Feb. 73	***ALSO SPRACH ZARATHUSTRA (2001)*** /CTI

Aug. 73 *RHAPSODY IN BLUE* /CTI
Oct. 76 *PETER GUNN* /MCA

Derek

REAL NAME: Johnny Cymbal
HOMETOWN: Cleveland, Ohio

"Derek" was the name under which Johnny Cymbal made recordings during the late sixties, the biggest of which was a top ten hit titled "Cinnamon." Cymbal, best known for his 1963 hit "Mr. Bass Man," which he wrote and recorded, is currently a West Coast record producer.

Oct. 68 *CINNAMON* /Bang
Feb. 69 *BACK DOOR MAN* /Bang

Derek & The Dominoes

MEMBERS:
Eric Clapton (guitar)/born: Mar. 30, 1945/ Ripley, Surrey, England
Robert Whitlock (keyboards)/born: 1948/ Memphis, Tennessee
Carl Radle (bass)/born: 1942/Oklahoma City, Oklahoma
James Gordon (drums)/born: 1945/Los Angeles, California

This short-lived but important group was a spinoff from Delaney & Bonnie and Friends. Bobby Whitlock, Carl Radle, and Jim Gordon had been brought into The Friends by Delaney Bramlett as a result of their association on the "Shindig" TV show; Eric Clapton had toured for awhile with The Friends after Blind Faith disbanded.

When The Friends separated in late 1970, these four musicians recorded an album entitled *Layla* (nickname for George Harrison's wife; Harrison had also played for a brief time with The Friends). Halfway through the sessions they were joined by Duane Allman of the Allman Brothers Band, whose guitar playing on this recording is considered a milestone in rock. Two singles, "Bell Bottom Blues" and the album's title track, were released early in 1971 and were chart entries. However, "Layla" was reissued a year later and became a top ten hit. Derek & The Dominoes did a "farewell" concert at New York's Fillmore East late in 1972, after which the group disbanded. A "live" album of this event, called *In Concert,* was released early the following year.

See *Eric CLAPTON; DELANEY & BONNIE.*

Feb. 71 *BELL BOTTOM BLUES* /Atco
Mar. 71 *LAYLA* /Atco
May 72 *LAYLA (rereleased)* /Atco

Rick Derringer

REAL NAME: Richard Zehringer
BORN: Aug. 4, 1947
HOMETOWN: Celina, Ohio

Rick Derringer spent the middle and late sixties as Ricky Zehringer, lead singer and guitarist of the McCoys (see *THE McCOYS).* After the group's popularity subsided as a recording act, they became the house band at Steve Paul's famed Scene (in New York City), where they were often joined onstage by such musicians as Buddy Miles, Jimi Hendrix, and Eric Clapton. In 1969 Steve Paul, who already handled Johnny Winter, took over management of The McCoys and they became Winter's back-up band. Their first album together, called *Johnny Winter And . . . ,* was produced by Derringer, who also wrote most of the songs. When Johnny Winter temporarily retired during the early seventies Derringer joined Edgar Winter's White Trash group and produced their recordings. Upon Johnny Winter's return, Derringer became active in both groups.

In 1974 Rick Derringer emerged as a solo artist on Steve Paul's Blue Sky label; his first hit was a song which he had written for the *Johnny Winter And . . .* LP, titled "Rock & Roll Hoochie Koo." This was followed by several other hits as well as two successful albums, *All American Boy* and *Spring Fever.*

Jan. 74	*ROCK & ROLL HOOCHIE KOO / Blue Sky*
Apr. 74	*TEENAGE LOVE AFFAIR / Blue Sky*
Apr. 75	*HANG ON SLOOPY / Blue Sky*
Aug. 76	*LET ME IN /Blue Sky*

The Detergents

Ron Dante
BORN: Aug. 22, 1945
HOMETOWN: Staten Island, New York

This was a studio "group," all of whose voices were sung and overdubbed by singer Ron Dante. The Detergents placed two records on the charts during the mid-sixties, most notably "Leader of the Laundromat," a top twenty hit and a satire of the Shangri-Las' "Leader of the Pack."

Ron Dante is also known as the studio voice of The Cuff Links and The Archies and emerged in 1975 as the producer of Barry Manilow's many hits. He also recorded a new version, under his own name, of The Archies' multimillion-selling "Sugar Sugar," which was produced by Manilow.

Dec. 64	*LEADER OF THE LAUNDROMAT /Roulette*
Mar. 65	*DOUBLE O SEVEN / Roulette*

The Detroit Emeralds

MEMBERS:
Abraham Tilmon (lead vocals)/born: Jan. 12, 1949/hometown: Little Rock, Arkansas
Ivory Tilmon (baritone)/born: Oct. 14, 1948/hometown: Little Rock, Arkansas
James Mitchell (tenor)/born: May 27, 1949/hometown: Perry, Florida

During the mid-sixties, Abe and Ivy Tilmon joined childhood friend James Mitchell to form The Emeralds. In 1966 they appeared regularly in a Detroit club called The Angel and decided to add "Detroit" to the group's name.

Through their cousin "Sweet James," who was leading a group called The Fantastic Four, Ivy and Abe were signed to the Ric Tic label in 1968 and had one hit before the label was purchased by Motown. The group then elected to sign with another of the area's record companies, Westbound. They formed an association with Memphis producer Willie Mitchell (famed for his work with Al Green) and began appearing regularly on the charts.

The Detroit Emeralds continue to tour and record while operating their own Detroit nightclub called The Emerald Lounge. Abe showcases new talent in the club and produces his discoveries for Westbound.

Mar. 68	*SHOW TIME /Ric Tic*
Feb. 71	*DO ME RIGHT /Westbound*
Aug. 71	*WEAR THIS RING /Westbound*
Jan. 72	*YOU WANT IT, YOU GOT IT / Westbound*
May 72	*BABY LET ME TAKE YOU IN MY ARMS /Westbound*

William De Vaughn

BORN: 1948
HOMETOWN: Washington, D.C.

De Vaughn was designing water and drainage facilities for the government when his interest in music led him to answer an ad placed in *Billboard* magazine by Omega Sounds, a Philadelphia-based production company seeking new talent. He auditioned with "Be Thankful for What You Got," which the company recorded as a master and sold to Roxbury, a subsidiary of producer Wes Farrell's Chelsea label. The record became a top five hit nationally and was followed later in the year by "Blood Is Thicker Than Water."

May 74 *BE THANKFUL FOR WHAT YOU GOT*/**Roxbury**
Sept. 74 *BLOOD IS THICKER THAN WATER*/**Roxbury**

Barry DeVorzon & Perry Botkin, Jr.

Barry DeVorzon
Perry Botkin, Jr. /born: April 16, 1933/Los Angeles, California

Both Barry and Perry have worked as writers, producers and arrangers with some of the biggest artists in the business and have turned out many hit singles.

In 1971 they cowrote a tune called "Cotton's Dream," which was part of the soundtrack to Stanley Kramer's film *Bless the Beasts and the Children.* A few years later the same tune was used as the theme song for CBS-TV's soap opera "The Young and the Restless."

Then, during the 1976 Olympics, ABC used the music during playbacks of the gymnastic feats of fourteen-year-old Nadia Comaneci of Romania. The music became so popular during the Olympics from Montreal that A & M records released DeVorzon and Botkin's tune as "Nadia's Theme" and donated a portion of the sales proceeds to the United States Olympic Committee.

Aug. 76 *NADIA'S THEME (THE YOUNG AND THE RESTLESS)*/**A & M**
Jan. 77 *BLESS THE BEASTS AND CHILDREN*/**A & M**

The Devotions

MEMBERS:
Frank Pardo
Joseph Pardo
Robert Hovorka
Andrew Sanchez /replaced (1961) by Robert Weisbrod
Raymond Herrera /(left in 1961)
William Crache /(left in 1961)/replaced by Raymond Sanchez
HOMETOWN: New York City

The Devotions began as a six-man group in 1960 in the Astoria, Queens, section of New York. After several local appearances and personnel changes, they were heard by Joe Petralia, a former promotion man for Tony Bennett. He brought them to Bernie Zimming at Delta Records where they made "For Sentimental Reasons," backed with their own composition, "Rip Van Winkle." A few weeks later, The Cleftones' version of "Sentimental Reasons" became a substantial hit and Delta began promoting "Rip" instead. Delta later sold the master to Roulette Records, who did nothing with it until 1964, when they released it as a cut on an "oldies" album. After the song began to receive airplay in the Pittsburgh area, Roulette released a single, and much to their amazement, it sold more than ten thousand copies in a week. "Rip Van Winkle" eventually placed high on the national charts and today is considered a classic of the urban "streetcorner" style.

Feb. 64 *RIP VAN WINKLE*/**Roulette**

Daddy Dewdrop

REAL NAME: Richard Monda
HOMETOWN: Cleveland, Ohio

At nineteen Richard Monda became interested in music and recording and got a job in the early seventies as songwriter and producer for the Saturday morning cartoon show "Sabrina & the Groovy Goolies." Under the name of Daddy Dewdrop he recorded a song from the score called "Chick-A-Boom," and it became a national top ten hit.

Mar. 71   CHICK-A-BOOM / Sunflower

Neil Diamond

BORN: Jan. 24, 1941
HOMETOWN: Brooklyn, New York

During high school and college Neil Leslie Diamond spent virtually all his spare time learning to play guitar and write songs. Before he finished his pre-med studies, a music publisher offered him a staff songwriter's contract at fifty dollars a week. During the next several years he worked for numerous publishers without success. In 1963 he recorded an unsuccessful single titled "Clown Town" for Columbia Records. Determined to make a breakthrough, he rented a tiny office over Broadway's famed Birdland club, bought a used upright piano for thirty-five dollars, and sent the songs he wrote to various performers. To raise money and to give his songs exposure he did one-night stands at Greenwich Village coffeehouses.

Diamond's luck began to turn late in 1965, when Jay & The Americans recorded one of his songs, "Sunday & Me," and made it into a top twenty hit. In 1966 he was seen at one of his Village performances by the produc-tion team of Jeff Barry and Ellie Greenwich, who arranged for him to be signed to the late Bert Berns's Bang label. His first release, in 1966, "Solitary Man," became a sizable hit, but it was his next record, "Cherry, Cherry," that established him by going to the top ten. While still working with Barry and Greenwich he produced a string of hits on Bang through the summer of 1968 and wrote two major hits for The Monkees, "I'm a Believer" and "A Little Bit Me, a Little Bit You."

In 1969 Diamond was signed by the Uni label (a division of MCA), where he continued his pattern of hit singles but also established himself as an "album" artist with such LPs as *Velvet Gloves and Spit, Brother Love's Travelling Salvation Show,* and *Touching Me, Touching You.* In addition Bang reissued some of his older material, and many of these records placed on the charts as well.

In the early seventies Diamond scored the film *Jonathan Livingston Seagull* and recorded a soundtrack album for Columbia Records, which became the largest-selling original soundtrack in LP history. Neil Diamond was signed to Columbia (the label that had released the unsuccessful "Clown Town" more than ten years earlier!) as the result of one of the largest deals in the company's history.

May 66   SOLITARY MAN / Bang
Aug. 66   CHERRY, CHERRY / Bang
Nov. 66   I GOT THE FEELING / Bang
Jan. 67   YOU GOT TO ME / Bang
Apr. 67   GIRL, YOU'LL BE A WOMAN SOON / Bang
July 67   THANK THE LORD FOR THE NIGHT TIME / Bang
Oct. 67   KENTUCKY WOMAN / Bang
Jan. 68   NEW ORLEANS / Bang
Apr. 68   RED RED WINE / Bang
May 68   BROOKLYN ROADS / Uni

Neil Diamond

July 68	*TWO BIT MANCHILD* / Uni
Oct. 68	*SUNDAY SUN* / Uni
Feb. 69	*BROTHER LOVE'S TRAVELLING SALVATION SHOW* / Uni
June 69	*SWEET CAROLINE* / Uni
Nov. 69	*HOLLY HOLY* / Uni
Feb. 70	*SHILO* / Bang
Feb. 70	*UNTIL IT'S TIME FOR YOU TO GO* / Uni
May 70	*SOOLAIMON* / Uni
July 70	*SOLITARY MAN* / Bang
Aug. 70	*CRACKLING ROSIE* / Uni
Nov. 70	*DO IT* / Bang
Nov. 70	*HE AIN'T HEAVY, HE'S MY BROTHER* / Uni
Mar. 71	*I AM, I SAID* / Uni
June 71	*DONE TOO SOON* / Uni
June 71	*I'M A BELIEVER* / Bang
Nov. 71	*STONES* / Uni
May 72	*SONG SUNG BLUE* / Uni
Aug. 72	*PLAY ME* / Uni
Nov. 72	*WALK ON WATER* / Uni
Mar. 73	*CHERRY, CHERRY (rerecorded live)* / MCA
Aug. 73	*THE LONG WAY HOME* / Bang
Aug. 73	*THE LAST THING ON MY MIND* / Uni
Oct. 73	*BE* / Columbia
Mar. 74	*SKYBIRD* / Columbia
Oct. 74	*LONGFELLOW SERENADE* / Columbia

Feb. 75 *I'VE BEEN THIS WAY BEFORE* / Columbia

June 76 *IF YOU KNOW WHAT I MEAN* / Columbia

Sept. 76 *DON'T THINK . . . FEEL* / Columbia

Dec. 77 *DESIREE* / Columbia

"Little" Jimmy Dickens

BORN: Dec. 19, 1925
HOMETOWN: Bolt, West Virginia

"Little" Jimmy Dickens (he is only 4'11" tall) rose to fame during the late forties and early fifties with his country novelty songs.

In the sixties he recorded occasional country hits for the Columbia label, and one of these, "May the Bird of Paradise Fly up Your Nose," became a top fifteen national hit late in 1965. He followed with a major country hit, "Where Were You When the Ship Hit the Sand," and has since faded from the recording scene. His songs, however, continue to be standards with "live" bluegrass bands today.

Oct. 65 *MAY THE BIRD OF PARADISE FLY UP YOUR NOSE* / Columbia

Dino, Desi & Billy

FULL NAMES:

Dean Paul Anthony Martin, Jr. / born: Nov. 12, 1951 / Los Angeles, California

Desiderio Alberto Arnaz IV / born: Jan. 19, 1953 / Los Angeles, California

William Ernest Joseph Hinsche / born: Jun. 29, 1951 / Manila, Philippines

This trio was made up of Dean Martin's son, Lucille Ball and Desi Arnaz's son, and their schoolmate. The boys met in 1965 at a Beverly Hills Little League baseball game.

While practicing one day at Dean Martin's house, the group was heard by Frank Sinatra, who signed them to his Reprise label. Dino, Desi & Billy had a string of hits that lasted over three years before they separated to pursue individual interests.

Dino and Desi are currently members of The Beverly Hills Blues Band and are being produced by Bruce Johnston and Terry Melcher. Billy is a West Coast session musician who occasionally tours as a keyboard player with The Beach Boys.

June 65 *I'M A FOOL* / Reprise

Sept. 65 *NOT THE LOVING KIND* / Reprise

Dec. 65 *PLEASE DON'T FIGHT IT* / Reprise

Mar. 66 *SUPERMAN* / Reprise

June 67 *2 IN THE AFTERNOON* / Reprise

Aug. 68 *TELL SOMEONE YOU LOVE THEM* / Reprise

Disco-Tex & The Sex-O-Lettes

Monti Rock III

REAL NAME / Joseph Moses Aponte Montanez, Jr. (lead vocals) / born: May 29, 1942 / Bronx, New York

Disco-Tex & The Sex-O-Lettes was the name given to a studio group assembled by producer Bob Crewe featuring the lead voice of Monti Rock III, who was owner of a chain of hairdressing shops known as Mr. Monti's Salons. They became an integral part of the discotheque craze in late 1974 with a top ten record called "Get Dancing." The record was recorded "live" in California's Village Sound Studios with more than a hundred people. Crewe then sold the master to Wes Farrell's Chelsea label. The follow-up, "I Wanna Dance Wit' Choo," became a hit early in 1975. Monti was also featured as the disco disc jockey in the hit film Saturday Night Fever.

The Dixie Cups. Left to right: Rosa Lee Hawkins, Joan Johnson, Barbara Hawkins

Nov. 74 *GET DANCING* / **Chelsea**
Apr. 75 *I WANNA DANCE WIT' CHOO* / **Chelsea**
Aug. 75 *JAM BAND* / **Chelsea**
July 76 *DANCIN' KID* / **Chelsea**

The Dixie Cups

MEMBERS:
Barbara Ann Hawkins / born: 1943
Joan Marie Johnson / born: 1945
Rosa Lee Hawkins / born: 1946
HOMETOWN: New Orleans, Louisiana

The Dixie Cups were one of the key contributors to the "girl-group sound" of the early sixties.

After they had been together for about a year, The Dixie Cups were seen in 1964 by New Orleans record producer Joe Jones (famed as an artist for "You Talk Too Much"), who assumed their management. Jones learned that Leiber & Stroller were establishing a new record label, Red Bird, and took the group for an audition. The Dixie Cups were signed, and their first release, "Chapel of Love," became a number one hit in the summer of 1964. After several follow-up hits, Red Bird

Records suddenly ceased operations and the group was signed by ABC-Paramount. None of their later recordings, however, achieved more than regional success.

May 64	*CHAPEL OF LOVE* / Red Bird	
July 64	*PEOPLE SAY* / Red Bird	
Oct. 64	*YOU SHOULD HAVE SEEN THE WAY HE LOOKED AT ME* / Red Bird	
Dec. 64	*LITTLE BELL* / Red Bird	
Apr. 65	*IKO IKO* / Red Bird	

Dr. Buzzard's Original Savannah Band

MEMBERS:

Cory Daye (lead vocals) / born: Apr. 25, 1952 / Bronx, New York

Stony Browder, Jr. (guitar, piano) / born: Feb. 7, 1949 / Bronx, New York

Mickey Sevilla (percussion) / born: 1953 / Puerto Rico

Andy Hernandez (vibes) / born: 1951 / New York City

August Darnell (bass guitar) / born: Aug. 12, 1950 / Montreal, Canada
HOMETOWN: New York City

These five got together in New York to create a fresh new sound and a new visual act. They dress in the style of the thirties with the guys wearing double-breasted pinstriped suits and Cory wearing bright red lipstick and loud print dresses.

Their sound is a combination of soul, big band, and disco and has created a sensation in discos around the country.

Their manager, Tommy Mottola (who also manages Hall & Oates and is the person they sing about in their hit "Cherchez La Femme"), got them a recording contract with RCA that produced a hit LP and single.

Sept. 76	*I'LL PLAY THE FOOL* / RCA
Nov. 76	*WHISPERING / CHERCHEZ LA FEMME / SE SI BON* / RCA

Dr. Buzzard's Original Savannah Band. Left to right: August Darnell, Mickey Sevilla, Andy Hernandez, Stony Browder, Jr., Cory Daye

Dr. Hook. Left to right: Jance Garfat, Bill Francis, Rik Elswit, John Wolters, Ray Sawyer, Bob Henke, Dennis Locorriere

Dr. Hook & The Medicine Show

MEMBERS:

Ray "Dr. Hook" Sawyer (lead vocals)/born: Feb. 1, 1937/Chicksaw, Alabama

Dennis La Corriere (guitar)/born: June 13, 1949/New Jersey

George Cummings (Hawaiian steel guitar)/born: July 28, 1938

William Francis (keyboards)/born: Jan. 16, 1942/Los Angeles, California

Jay David (drums)/born: Aug. 8, 1942/New Jersey

Rik Elswit (guitar)/born: July 6, 1945/New York City (added in 1972)

Jance Garfat (bass)/born: Mar. 3, 1944/California/(added in 1972)

This group was formed during the early seventies by five musicians who met on the New Jersey folk and rock circuit. The lead singer was dubbed "The Hook" because of the patch he wears due to the loss of his right eye in an automobile accident.

The group came to the attention of Shel Silverstein, the famed cartoonist turned writer-producer, who was known for such songs as "The Unicorn" and "A Boy Named Sue." Dr. Hook and company were selected to perform the songs Silverstein had written for the film *Who Is Harry Kellerman,* which led to a contract with Columbia Records.

In 1972 Silverstein wrote all the material for their first album, "Dr. Hook," which yielded a top five single called "Sylvia's Mother." To solidify their stage act, the group added Rik Elswit and Jance Garfat and followed during the next year with several hit singles. However, they became best known for their albums *Sloppy Seconds, Belly Up,* and *Ballad of Lucy Jordan.*

In 1975 Dr. Hook & The Medicine Show began recording for Capitol Records.

Apr. 72   *SYLVIA'S MOTHER* / Columbia
Sept. 72 *CARRY ME CARRIE* / Columbia

Dec. 72	*THE COVER OF "ROLLING STONE"* / Columbia
July 73	*ROLAND THE ROADIE AND GERTRUDE THE GROUPIE* / Columbia
Sept. 73	*LIFE AIN'T EASY* / Columbia
Aug. 75	*THE MILLIONAIRE* / Capitol
Jan. 76	*ONLY SIXTEEN* / Capitol
June 76	*A LITTLE BIT MORE* / Capitol
Nov. 76	*IF NOT YOU* / Capitol
June 77	*WALK RIGHT IN* / Capitol

Dr. John

REAL NAME: Malcolm John Michael Creaux Rebennac, Jr.
BORN: Nov. 21, 1940
HOMETOWN: New Orleans, Louisiana

Mac Rebennac is one of the most influential rock figures to emerge from the musically rich New Orleans area. He entered show business at the age of one as the famed Ivory Snow baby and was exposed to the music business as a child, when he accompanied his father to repair PA systems in local clubs; Rebennac got to meet and hear the top musicians of the day.

During his teens he became friendly with Walter "Papoose" Nelson of the Fats Domino band, under whose guidance he became a proficient guitarist at the age of fourteen. He worked as a sideman on local recording sessions and was asked to join the house band at Lincoln Beach, an establishment that featured all the leading blues acts that toured the area. As a result, he got to back his idol, Professor Longhair (Ron Byrd), on the legendary 1957 recording of "Mardi Gras In New Orleans."

During the 1960s Rebennac toured with several local bands and recorded a number of regional hits. After a stint as a junior A & R man at Ace Records, he wound up on the West Coast as a session musician and worked with Phil Spector and Sonny & Cher. Under the name of Dr. John, The Night Tripper ("Dr. John" patterned after "Professor Longhair" and "The Night Tripper," an answer to The Beatles' "Day Tripper"), Rebennac began recording as a solo artist. He soon shortened his name to Dr. John and achieved major commercial success in 1972.

Signed by Atlantic he began working with leading New Orleans writer-producer Allen Toussaint. His first single chart entry was a reworking of the popular New Orleans street chant, "Iko Iko." During the next years he followed with several additional hits, the biggest of which was the top ten recording of "Right Place, Wrong Time." However, he has become best known for his many albums in collaboration with the leading figures in blues and rock.

Apr. 72	*IKO IKO* / Atco
Apr. 73	*RIGHT PLACE, WRONG TIME* / Atco
Sept. 73	*SUCH A NIGHT* / Atco
May 74	*RITE AWAY* / Atco

Bo Donaldson & The Heywoods

MEMBERS:
Robert Donaldson (keyboards, trumpet) / born: June 13, 1954
David Krock (background vocals) / born: Oct. 13, 1953
Gary Coveyou (sax) / born: Nov. 25, 1958
Michael Gibbons (lead vocals, trumpet) / born: Dec. 29, 1953
Richard Joswick (lead vocals) / born: Aug. 7, 1952
Scott Baker (guitar) / born: 1951
Richard Brunetti (drums) / born: 1953
HOMETOWN: Cincinnati, Ohio

This group was formed in Cincinnati during the mid-sixties and built a strong regional reputation. In 1966 they were

Bo Donaldson & The Heywoods. Left to right: Scott Baker, Rick Joswick, Gary Coveyou, Bo Donaldson, David Krock, Mike Gibbons, Richard Brunetti

signed by Dick Clark Productions and spent the sixties and early seventies touring as the opening act for such groups as The Rascals, Herman's Hermits, The Raiders, and The Osmonds.

In 1973 The Heywoods were signed to Artie Ripp's Family label, where they recorded their first album, *Special Someone*. They were asked by Dick Clark to score a TV special, "The Real World of Make Believe," in 1973 and became regulars on Clark's "Action '73" show. However, their breakthrough came in 1974 when they were signed by ABC Records; their first release, "Billy, Don't Be a Hero," went to number one, establishing the group as a top teen attraction. Today the group records for Playboy Records.

Apr. 74 *BILLY, DON'T BE A HERO /*
          ABC

July 74 *WHO DO YOU THINK YOU*
          ARE? / ABC
Nov. 74 *THE HEARTBREAK KID / ABC*
July 75 *OUR LAST SONG TOGETHER /*
          ABC

Donovan

FULL NAME: Donovan Phillip Leitch
BORN: May 10, 1946
HOMETOWN: Maryhill, Glasgow, Scotland

At the age of ten Donovan moved to Hatfield, England, with his family. He left school during his early teens to become a laborer and at fifteen picked up an old guitar and taught himself to play. By the time he reached seventeen he had befriended Gypsy Dave, and the two spent the early sixties rambling around England singing and passing hats. Early in 1965 Donovan

Donovan

returned to Hatfield and settled into playing the area's clubs.

Peter Eden saw Donovan at one of these performances and introduced him to his friend Geoff Stephens at Southern Music. They became his managers and brought him to the attention of Terry Kennedy, A & R man for Pye Records, who signed him to the label. An appearance on the BBC-TV program "Ready Steady Go," in conjunction with his first release, the Dylanish "Catch the Wind," instantly established his fame in England, and his records were leased to the American Hickory label for United States distribution.

In 1966 Donovan began working

with producer Mickie Most and completely changed his musical direction to the "flower-power" sound. His next records appeared in the United States on the Epic label, and the first of these, "Sunshine Superman," went to number one. A long string of hits lasted well into the late sixties.

During the early seventies Donovan worked on the film soundtracks of *If It's Tuesday, This Must Be Belgium* and *Brother Sun, Sister Moon.* He also appeared in the title role of the TV show *The Pied Piper of Hamlin,* for which he composed the original music. In 1972 he was signed directly to the Epic label and revived his recording career with such albums as *Cosmic Wheels* and *Essence To Essence* (produced by Andy Oldham of Rolling Stones fame), and a hit single, "I Like You."

Today Donovan lives near London with his wife, Linda Lawrence (formerly married to the late Brian Jones of The Rolling Stones), and their daughter, Astrella Celeste. Donovan now records for Arista Records.

May 65	*CATCH THE WIND*/Hickory	
Aug. 65	*COLOURS*/Hickory	
Sept. 65	*UNIVERSAL SOLDIER*/Hickory	
July 66	*SUNSHINE SUPERMAN*/Epic	
Nov. 66	*MELLOW YELLOW*/Epic	
Feb. 67	*EPISTLE TO DIPPY*/Epic	
Aug. 67	*THERE IS A MOUNTAIN*/Epic	
Nov. 67	*WEAR YOUR LOVE LIKE HEAVEN*/Epic	
Mar. 68	*JENNIFER JUNIPER*/Epic	
June 68	*HURDY GURDY MAN*/Epic	
Oct. 68	*LALENA*/Epic	
Feb. 69	*TO SUSAN ON THE WEST COAST WAITING*/Epic	
Apr. 69	*ATLANTIS*/Epic	
Aug. 69	*GOO GOO BARABAJAGAL (LOVE IS HOT)*(with The Jeff Beck Group)/Epic	
Aug. 70	*RIKI TIKI TAVI*/Epic	
Feb. 71	*CELIA OF THE SEALS*/Epic	
Apr. 73	*I LIKE YOU*/Epic	

The Doobie Brothers

ORIGINAL MEMBERS:

Thomas Johnston (lead vocals, guitar, keyboards)/Visalia, California

Patrick R. Simmons (guitar)/Aberdeen, Washington

"Little" John Hartman (lead drums, percussion)/Falls Church, Virginia

David Shogren (bass)/San Francisco, California (replaced Gregg Murphy)/replaced by Tiran Porter/Los Angeles, California

Michael Hossack (drums)/Paterson, New Jersey/(added in 1973)/replaced by Keith Knudson

Jeffrey Allen Baxter (steel guitar)/Washington, D.C. (added in 1974)

This group, none of whose members are related, was formed in northern California during the early seventies.

Tom Johnston, the nucleus of the group, left his studies at San Jose State College to become a full-time guitarist on the local club circuit. He and Little John (so known because of his great size) joined Gregg Murphy to form a trio. Murphy was soon replaced by Dave Shogren and, backed by an informal band, the group made appearances at various area clubs. At one of these, The Gaslighter Theatre, they shared the bill with Pat Simmons, and the four joined forces to become The Doobie Brothers. Beginning as a gospel-oriented group, they became a resident band at a club in the Santa Cruz mountains called The Chateau, where they gradually evolved into rock.

In 1972 The Doobies sent a demonstration tape to producers Lenny Waronker and Ted Templeman at Warner Brothers records, and were signed to the label. Their first album, *The Doobie Brothers,* was not successful (although it did yield a hit single, "Nobody," almost two years later), and after a similarly unsuccessful debut tour, bassist

The Doobie Brothers. Back row, left to right: Keith Knudsen, Tiran Porter, Michael McDonald; front row, left to right: Jeff Baxter, John Hartman, Patrick Simmons

Dave Shogren became discouraged and left the group. The Doobies replaced him with Tiran Porter and at the same time added a second drummer, Mike Hossack (later replaced by Keith Knudson). Their second album, *Toulouse Street,* provided a top ten single called "Listen to the Music" and launched the group's career.

In 1974 The Doobie Brothers expanded to six with the addition of steel guitarist "Skunk" Baxter, originally from Ultimate Spinach and later the founding member of Steely Dan. In late 1977 Tom Johnston left the group to record for Warner Bros. as a solo performer.

Sept. 72	*LISTEN TO THE MUSIC* / Warner Bros.
Dec. 72	*JESUS IS JUST ALRIGHT* / Warner Bros.
Apr. 73	*LONG TRAIN RUNNING* / Warner Bros.
Aug. 73	*CHINA GROVE* / Warner Bros.

Apr. 74	*ANOTHER PARK, ANOTHER SUNDAY* / Warner Bros.
July 74	*EYES OF SILVER* / Warner Bros.
Nov. 74	*NOBODY* / Warner Bros.
Dec. 74	*BLACK WATER* / Warner Bros.
May 75	*TAKE ME IN YOUR ARMS* / Warner Bros.
Aug. 75	*SWEET MAXINE* / Warner Bros.
Dec. 75	*I CHEATED THE HANGMAN* / Warner Bros.
Apr. 76	*TAKIN' IT TO THE STREETS* / Warner Bros.
Aug. 76	*WHEELS OF FORTUNE* / Warner Bros.
Nov. 76	*IT KEEPS YOU RUNNIN'* / Warner Bros.
July 77	*LITTLE DARLING (I NEED YOU)* / Warner Bros.
Oct. 77	*ECHOES OF LOVE* / Warner Bros.

The Doors

MEMBERS:

James Douglas Morrison (lead vocals) / born: Dec. 8, 1943 / Melbourne, Florida / died: July 3, 1971 / Paris, France

The Doors. Left to right: Jim Morrison, John Densmore, Bobby Krieger, Ray Manzarek

Robert Krieger (guitar)/born: Jan. 8, 1946/Los Angeles, California

Raymond Manzarek (bass, keyboards)/born: Feb. 12, 1943/Chicago, Illinois

John Densmore (drums, keyboards)/born: Dec. 1, 1945/Los Angeles, California

The Doors, led by the volatile and controversial Jim Morrison, began their career during the mid-sixties at U.C.L.A. Morrison was studying film when he met fellow student Ray Manzarek, a keyboard player in a local band. They became acquainted with Robbie Krieger and John Densmore at a Maharishi Yogi meditation class, and the four decided to form a group. Morrison suggested the group's name from a William Blake quote that appeared on the flyleaf of Aldous Huxley's *Doors of Perception:* "There are things that are known and things that are unknown; in between are the doors."

The Doors first played small clubs on Sunset Strip, usually as a warm-up group. One night Jac Holzman, president of Elektra Records, went to the Whiskey A Go Go to catch a performance by Love and happened to see The Doors as the opening act. Although he did not like the group at first, he went back several times and eventually signed them to a contract late in 1966. Their first album, *The Doors,* was released early in 1967 along with a single, "Break on Through." However, when the seven-minute cut of "Light My Fire" began receiving the most airplay, it was edited and issued as a single, which went straight to number one along with the album. During the next two years The Doors achieved several additional hit singles and a number of successful LPs, including *Strange Days, Waiting for the Sun, Morrison Hotel, Soft Parade,* and *L.A. Woman.* By the time this last album was released (and had yielded the single "Love Her Madly"), Jim Morrison had developed extreme personal difficulties. Friction began developing within the group, and when Morrison traveled to Paris in mid-1971 to rest and write, the remainder of the group practiced (and reportedly began recording) without him. On July 3, 1971, Jim Morrison died and was buried in the Poets' Corner of the Père Lachaise Cemetery in Paris.

Although the remaining members recorded two additional albums, *Weird Scenes inside the Goldmine* and *Full Circle,* they disbanded early in 1973. Ray Manzarek went solo, while Robbie Krieger and John Densmore joined former Bronco vocalist Jess Roden, Roy Davies (keyboards), and Phillip Chen (bass) to form The Butts Band.

June 67	*LIGHT MY FIRE* / Elektra
Sept. 67	*PEOPLE ARE STRANGE* / Elektra
Dec. 67	*LOVE ME TWO TIMES* / Elektra
Mar. 68	*THE UNKNOWN SOLDIER* / Elektra
July 68	*HELLO, I LOVE YOU* / Elektra
Aug. 68	*LIGHT MY FIRE* (rereleased)/Elektra
Dec. 68	*TOUCH ME* / Elektra
Mar. 69	*WISHFUL SINFUL* / Elektra
June 69	*TELL ALL THE PEOPLE* / Elektra
Sept. 69	*RUNNING BLUE* / Elektra
Apr. 70	*YOU MAKE ME REAL* / Elektra
Apr. 71	*LOVE HER MADLY* / Elektra
July 71	*RIDERS ON THE STORM* / Elektra
Nov. 71	*TIGHTROPE RIDE* / Elektra
Sept. 72	*THE MOSQUITO* / Elektra

Carl Douglas

Carl Douglas

HOMETOWN: Jamaica, West Indies

Carl Douglas received part of his education in America before studying engineering in England. While still in school, however, he was bitten by the "music bug" and began playing in various semipro bands. In 1964 he went solo and had a British hit titled "Crazy Feeling."

Ten years later Douglas combined his fascination with the body rhythms of the martial arts (he had studied Kung Fu extensively) with his reggae background and recorded his own composition of "Kung Fu Fighting." Released by the Pye label in England, the record went to number one and touched off a "Kung Fu" dance craze in the British discotheques. Later in the year, 20th Century obtained the master for United States distribution and the song went to number one in America as well.

Oct. 74 **KUNG FU FIGHTING** / 20th Century
Feb. 75 **DANCE THE KUNG FU** / 20th Century

Carol Douglas

BORN: Apr. 7, 1948
HOMETOWN: Brooklyn, New York

During her teens, Carol Douglas sang professionally on television commercials and played small roles in several TV shows and movies. She also appeared in the off-Broadway production of *Moon on a Rainbow Shawl,* the show that launched the careers of James Earl Jones and Cicely Tyson.

During the early seventies, Carol spent a year on the "oldies revival" circuit as a member of The Chantels and later appeared in the Do Your Own Thing revue. In 1974 she broke out as a solo artist and was signed by Bob Reno's Midland International label. Her first release, "Doctors Orders," became an instant discotheque hit and eventually rose high on the national charts.

Nov. 74 **DOCTORS ORDERS** / Midland International
Apr. 75 **A HURRICANE IS COMING TONIGHT** / Midland International

Mike Douglas

REAL NAME: Michael Dowd
BORN: August 11, 1925
HOMETOWN: Chicago, Illinois

Douglas, who sang with Kay Kyser's band during the forties, received a major break in 1961, when he was chosen to host a local TV show in Cleveland. Within a few years the show was a highly successful syndicated program.

Mike Douglas, 1965

In August 1965 it moved to Philadelphia where it is today.

In late 1965 Douglas recorded "The Men in My Little Girl's Life" for Epic Records. It became his only pop single, though today Douglas is as popular as ever as a TV talk-show host.

Dec. 65 **THE MEN IN MY LITTLE GIRL'S LIFE** / Epic

Ronnie Dove

BORN: Sept. 7, 1940
HOMETOWN: Baltimore, Maryland

Although he was born in Virginia, Ronnie Dove grew up in Baltimore. He began his singing career in a high school group but eventually broke away as a solo act.

In 1964 Dove was signed by Phil Kahl's Diamond label (which also launched Bobby Vinton). Beginning with "Say You," he achieved a five-year string of national hits with country-oriented pop songs. His biggest single was "One Kiss for Old Times' Sake."

135

Today Dove is affiliated with the country division of Motown Records and often appears on the country charts. He most recently scored with a revival of one of his earliest hits, "Right or Wrong."

July 64	**SAY YOU** / Diamond
Oct. 64	**RIGHT OR WRONG** / Diamond
Jan. 65	**HELLO, PRETTY GIRL** / Diamond
Mar. 65	**ONE KISS FOR OLD TIMES' SAKE** / Diamond
June 65	**A LITTLE BIT OF HEAVEN** / Diamond
Aug. 65	**I'LL MAKE ALL YOUR DREAMS COME TRUE** / Diamond
Nov. 65	**KISS AWAY** / Diamond
Jan. 66	**WHEN LIKING TURNS TO LOVING** / Diamond
Apr. 66	**LET'S START ALL OVER AGAIN** / Diamond
June 66	**HAPPY SUMMER DAYS** / Diamond
Sept. 66	**I REALLY DON'T WANT TO KNOW** / Diamond
Nov. 66	**CRY** / Diamond
Feb. 67	**ONE MORE MOUNTAIN TO CLIMB** / Diamond
Apr. 67	**MY BABE** / Diamond
Aug. 67	**I WANT TO LOVE YOU FOR WHAT YOU ARE** / Diamond
Dec. 67	**DANCING OUT OF MY HEART** / Diamond
Mar. 68	**IN SOME TIME** / Diamond
June 68	**MOUNTAIN OF LOVE** / Diamond
Sept. 68	**TOM BOY** / Diamond
May 69	**I NEED YOU NOW** / Diamond

The Dramatics

MEMBERS:

Ronald Banks (lead vocals) / born: May 10, 1951 / Detroit, Michigan

Willie Lee Ford, Jr. / born: July 10, 1950 / Detroit, Michigan

Lawrence Demps / born: Feb. 23, 1949 / Detroit, Michigan

William Franklin Howard / born: July 13, 1950 / Detroit, Michigan / replaced by L. J. Reynolds

Elbert Vernell Wilkins / born: May 1, 1947 / Monroe, Louisiana / replaced by Leonard Mays

The Dramatics first got together in 1964 to compete in a Detroit high school talent show and decided afterward to sing professionally. They developed enough of a reputation on the Detroit club circuit to be offered a contract by Stax-Volt Records.

In 1971 an album titled *Whatcha See Is Whatcha Get* was released; several singles from the LP became major hits —most notably the title track and "In the Rain." After several more singles and albums on Stax-Volt, the group made one album on Cadet: "The Dramatics vs. The Dells," which yielded the hit single, "The Door to Your Heart." The Dramatics are now with ABC.

July 71	**WHATCHA SEE IS WHATCHA GET** / Volt
Dec. 71	**GET UP & GET DOWN** / Volt
Feb. 72	**IN THE RAIN** / Volt
Aug. 72	**TOAST TO THE FOOL** / Volt
May 73	**HEY YOU, GET OFF MY MOUNTAIN** / Volt
Oct. 73	**FELL FOR YOU** / Volt
Aug. 74	**THE DOOR TO YOUR HEART** / Cadet
May 75	**ME & MRS. JONES** / ABC
Nov. 75	**THE STARS IN YOUR EYES** / ABC
Jan. 76	**YOU'RE FOOLING YOU** / ABC
Dec. 76	**BE MY GIRL** / ABC
Oct. 77	**SHAKE IT WELL** / ABC

Patty Duke

FULL NAME: Anna Maria Patricia Duke Astin
BORN: Dec. 14, 1947
HOMETOWN: New York City

Patty Duke first became known as one of the youngest actresses ever to win an Academy Award—for her performance as the young Helen Keller in *The Miracle Worker*. She later went on to roles in TV situation comedy and in other films.

During the mid-sixties she had a

brief career as a recording artist and placed several hits on the charts, the biggest of which was a top ten record titled "Don't Just Stand There."

Today she lives in Los Angeles with her husband, John Astin.

June 65 *DON'T JUST STAND THERE /* United Artists
Sept. 65 *FUNNY LITTLE BUTTERFLIES /* United Artists
Oct. 65 *SAY SOMETHING FUNNY /* United Artists
Feb. 66 *WHENEVER SHE HOLDS YOU /* United Artists

Dusk

Late in 1970 a group called Dawn was rapidly becoming popular. Although Tony Orlando was singing the lead vocals, this was not widely known, and Dawn was considered just another studio group. (See *DAWN*.)

Early in 1971 Dawn's producers, Hank Medress and Dave Appell, created a "sister" studio group called Dusk. The lead was sung by Peggy Santiglia, former lead singer of The Angels, and Dusk placed two records on the charts in 1971.

Feb. 71 *ANGEL BABY /* Bell
June 71 *I HEAR THOSE CHURCH BELLS RINGING /* Bell

Dyke & The Blazers

Led by Lester (Dyke) Christian, this group emerged during the late sixties on the Los Angeles-based Original Sound label. Their funky soul sound was a major influence on other soul acts of the era. The Blazers were the first to record the Lester Christian composition "Funky Broadway," later made into a top ten hit by Wilson Pickett and today considered a rock standard.

The career of Dyke & The Blazers ended abruptly in the early seventies, after Lester Christian was fatally shot during a performance.

Apr. 67 *FUNKY BROADWAY /* Original Sound
Apr. 68 *FUNKY WALK /* Original Sound
May 69 *WE GOT MORE SOUL /* Original Sound
Sept. 69 *LET A WOMAN BE A WOMAN /* Original Sound

Bob Dylan

REAL NAME: Robert Allen Zimmerman
BORN: May 24, 1941
HOMETOWN: Duluth, Minnesota

Dylan first emerged during the folk music explosion of the early sixties and went on to become one of rock music's all-time superstars. His protest songs became the anthems of social change during the sixties and his later material was the root of what became known as folk rock. His influence on other musicians, most notably The Beatles, has been inestimable.

At six Dylan moved with his family to the Canadian border town of Hibbing, Minnesota. He began playing guitar at twelve and left home periodically during his early teens to perform. During high school and his brief stay at the University of Minnesota he performed with various folk groups in coffeehouses and took his stage name from one of his favorite poets, Dylan Thomas.

Late in 1959 Dylan moved to New York's Greenwich Village and became a fixture in the area's coffeehouse scene. Shabby and poor, he often rode the subways to sleep and keep warm. His "break" came in September 1961, when *The New York Times* reviewed his performance at Gerde's

Bob Dylan

Folk City. This attracted the attention of Columbia Records executive John Hammond, who saw and signed him on the spot. His first album, *Bob Dylan,* consisting mainly of traditional folk material, was released in 1962 and was moderately successful.

On April 12, 1963, Bob Dylan made his debut at New York's Town Hall, and the rave reviews instantly established him as a star. Columbia followed two weeks later with *Freewheelin' Bob Dylan,* an album containing many of the songs that would become the litany of the civil rights movement. A single released from the LP, "Blowin' in the Wind" with "Don't Think Twice," generated top ten "cover" recordings of both songs by Peter, Paul & Mary. Dylan closed out 1963 as costar with Joan Baez of the Monterey Folk Festival. For the next two years he reigned as the undisputed leader of the world-wide folk movement.

In 1965 Dylan began to turn toward rock and was subjected to bitter criticism by his former fans. The first inkling came in March with the release of the *Bringing It All Back Home* album, which for the first time featured electric instrumentation and musicians like Al Kooper and Paul Butterfield. Next came The Byrds' rock versions of "Mr. Tambourine Man" and "All I Really Want To Do" and Dylan's summer appearance at the Newport Festival with electric guitar in hand. He was nearly booed off the stage, but responded just one month later with a total commitment to rock: the release of *Highway 61 Revisited* with his own rock back-up group, The Band. (See *THE BAND*.) The summer of 1966 marked his most "commercial" year, in which he placed several hits high on the national charts. On July 30, 1966, Dylan was injured in a motorcycle accident and retired for nearly a year and a half.

While recuperating, Dylan lived in Woodstock New York, where The Band also settled to work with him. The legendary "basement tapes" (finally released as an album in 1975) were produced during this period, but Dylan did not consider them appropriate material with which to resume his career. Instead he flew to Nashville to record the *John Wesley Harding* LP, and it was released in January 1968 to coincide with his return appearance at a New York tribute to Woody Guthrie.

Dylan's superstar career has been marked by numerous "events": the publication of his *Tarantula* book in the early seventies, his appearances at the Isle of Wight and Bangladesh concerts, his starring role in *Pat Garrett & Billy the Kid,* his nationwide 1974 tour with The Band, the extended Rolling Thunder review of 1975–1976, and his featured performance in the film *The Last Waltz.*

Apr. 65	***SUBTERRANEAN HOMESICK BLUES*** / **Columbia**
July 65	***LIKE A ROLLING STONE*** / **Columbia**
Oct. 65	***POSITIVELY 4TH STREET*** / **Columbia**
Jan. 66	***CAN YOU PLEASE CRAWL OUT YOUR WINDOW*** / **Columbia**
Apr. 66	***RAINY DAY WOMEN #12 & 35*** / **Columbia**
July 66	***I WANT YOU*** / **Columbia**
Sept. 66	***JUST LIKE A WOMAN*** / **Columbia**
May 67	***LEOPARD SKIN PILL BOX HAT*** / **Columbia**
May 69	***I THREW IT ALL AWAY*** / **Columbia**
July 69	***LAY LADY LAY*** / **Columbia**
Nov. 69	***TONIGHT, I'LL BE STAYING HERE WITH YOU*** / **Columbia**
July 70	***WIGWAM*** / **Columbia**
June 71	***WATCHING THE RIVER FLOW*** / **Columbia**
Dec. 71	***GEORGE JACKSON*** / **Columbia**
Sept. 73	***KNOCKING ON HEAVEN'S DOOR*** / **Columbia**
Dec. 73	***A FOOL SUCH AS I*** / **Columbia**
Feb. 74	***ON A NIGHT LIKE THIS*** / **Asylum**
Aug. 74	***MOST LIKELY YOU GO YOUR WAY*** / **Asylum**
Mar. 75	***TANGLED UP IN BLUE*** / **Columbia**
Nov. 75	***HURRICANE*** / **Columbia**
Mar. 76	***MOZAMBIQUE*** / **Columbia**

Ronnie Dyson

BORN: June 5, 1950
HOMETOWN: Washington, D. C.

Ronnie Dyson grew up in Brooklyn, where his parents had relocated during his infancy. His singing career began with gospels at the age of three. At five he entered a talent show at the Brooklyn Academy Of Music with his rendition of Frankie Lymon's "Why Do Fools Fall in Love."

Dyson's break in show business came in an unexpected way while he was in high school with plans for a career in medicine. His mother was working as an operator at a telephone-answering service. When one of the service's clients received a casting call for the upcoming Broadway production of *Hair*, she returned the call herself and made an appointment for her son to audition! Dyson got a lead part in the show and stayed with the production for nearly two years, after which he was offered a role in the film *Putney Swope.*

In 1970 Dyson was signed by Columbia Records, and his first release was taken from an off-Broadway show called *Salvation.* Called "Why Can't I Touch You," the record reached the top ten and launched his career as a recording artist.

June 70	*(IF YOU LET ME MAKE LOVE TO YOU, THEN) WHY CAN'T I TOUCH YOU* / Columbia
Oct. 70	*I DON'T WANNA CRY* / Columbia
July 71	*WHEN YOU GET RIGHT DOWN TO IT* / Columbia
Feb. 73	*THE ONE MAN BAND* / Columbia
Aug. 73	*I JUST DON'T WANT TO BE LONELY* / Columbia
July 76	*THE MORE YOU DO IT (THE MORE I LIKE IT DONE TO ME)* / Columbia

The Eagles

MEMBERS:

Randy Meisner (bass)/born: Mar. 8, 1946/
Scottsbluff, Nebraska/replaced by Timothy B.
Schmidt/born: Oct. 30, 1947/Oakland,
California

Bernard Leadon (guitar)/born: July 19, 1947/
Minneapolis, Minnesota/replaced (Jan. 1976)
by Joe Walsh/born: Nov. 20, 1947

Glenn Frey (guitar)/born: Nov. 6, 1948/Detroit
Michigan

Donald Henley (drums)/born: July 22, 1947/
Linden, Texas

Donald Felder (guitar)/born: Sept. 21, 1947/
Topanga, California/(added in 1975)

The Eagles were organized in 1971 by Glenn Frey and Don Henley and emerged shortly thereafter as one of the leading exponents of country rock.

Frey and Henley first met as members of Linda Ronstadt's band and decided almost immediately to form their own group. They recruited Randy Meisner, formerly with Poco and at that time a member of Rick Nelson's Stone Canyon Band, and Bernie Leadon, a charter member of The Flying Burrito Brothers. Through the efforts of singer-songwriter Jackson Browne, a friend of Glenn Frey's, the group was brought to the attention of David Geffen, head of the Asylum label for which Browne was recording. Geffen signed The Eagles, and Browne was the co-writer with Frey of "Take It Easy," the group's first release and a top ten hit in the summer of 1972.

Later that year The Eagles followed

The Eagles. Left to right: Bernie Leadon, Don Henley, Glenn Frey, Don Felder, Randy Meisner

with an album, *Eagle,* which became a best seller and yielded two hit singles, "Witchy Woman" and "Peaceful, Easy Feeling." Since then, the group has continued with an unbroken string of hits, the biggest of which was the number one recording of "Best of My Love." They have also become established as an "album" act with their releases of *Desperado, On the Border,* and *One of These Nights.*

In 1975 The Eagles became a five-man group with the addition of guitarist Don Felder. In late 1977 Randy Meisner left the group replaced by Timothy B. Schmidt of Poco.

June 72	*TAKE IT EASY* / **Asylum**	
Sept. 72	*WITCHY WOMAN* / **Asylum**	
Dec. 72	*PEACEFUL, EASY FEELING* / **Asylum**	
June 73	*TEQUILA SUNRISE* / **Asylum**	
Sept. 73	*OUT LAW MAN* / **Asylum**	
May 74	*ALREADY GONE* / **Asylum**	
Sept. 74	*JAMES DEAN* / **Asylum**	
Nov. 74	*THE BEST OF MY LOVE* / **Asylum**	
May 75	*ONE OF THESE NIGHTS* / **Asylum**	
Sept. 75	*LYIN' EYES* / **Asylum**	
Dec. 75	*TAKE IT TO THE LIMIT* / **Asylum**	
Dec. 76	*NEW KID IN TOWN* / **Asylum**	
Mar. 77	*HOTEL CALIFORNIA* / **Asylum**	
May 77	*LIFE IN THE FAST LANE* / **Asylum**	

Earth, Wind & Fire

MEMBERS:

Maurice White (lead vocals, percussion) / born: Dec. 19, 1941

Verdine White (bass, percussion) / born: July 25, 1951

Phillip Bailey (lead vocals, percussion) / born: May 8, 1951

Larry Dunn (Lawrence Dunhill) (keyboards) / born: June 19, 1953

Alan McKay (guitar, sitar, percussion) / born: Feb 2, 1948

Ralph Johnson (drums, percussion) / born: July 4, 1951

John Graham (guitar, percussion) / born: Aug. 3, 1951

Andrew Woolfolk (soprano sax, flute). born: Oct. 11, 1950

Jessica Cleaves (drums, percussion) / born: 1948 / replaced (1973) by Fred White / born Jan. 13, 1955

HOMETOWN: Chicago, Illinois

This group emerged during the early seventies with a unique sound that fused jazz, rhythm & blues, and rock.

The nucleus of Earth, Wind & Fire is Maurice White, who began his musical career by singing gospels at the age of six. He continued this into his teens, and, as a high school student, played his first professional job as part of a school band led by Booker T. Jones of The MGs. Later he attended the Chicago Conservatory and played in local clubs on the side. In addition he worked extensively as a session drummer for many of the leading Motown acts and for Chicago artists like The Impressions, Billy Stewart, Sugar Pie DeSanto, and Muddy Waters. This eventually led to a three-year stint with The Ramsey Lewis Trio. He decided during the late sixties to form his own group, one large enough to avoid having to supplement stage shows with local musicians.

After the group was assembled White selected earth, wind, and fire— three of the four elements—as their name. (Water is the fourth element, but there are no water signs in White's astrological chart.) They were signed to Warner Brothers Records and during the early seventies placed a minor hit on the singles charts and recorded three albums: *Earth, Wind & Fire, The Need of Love,* and the soundtrack L P for Melvin Van Peebles's *Sweet Sweetback's Baadassss Song.*

Earth, Wind & Fire. Clockwise from far left: Al McKay, Philip Bailey, Maurice White, Andrew Woolfolk, Ralph Johnson, Larry Dunn, Johnny Graham, Verdine White

By 1973 difficulties had developed between the group and their label, and they switched to Columbia Records. During this period Maurice White reorganized them into the above line-up. The new members included Phil Bailey from the Stoval Sisters' Band, Johnny Graham from The Nite-Liters, Al McKay from The Watts 103rd St. Rhythm Band, and Jessica Cleaves from The Friends of Distinction (soon replaced by Maurice's younger brother Fred). The group has had a continual string of hit singles and has had successful albums such as *Last Days & Time* and *Head to the Sky.*

Earth, Wind & Fire's biggest success came in 1975 with their appearance in the film *That's the Way of the World.* The soundtrack album featuring their music reached the top ten and yielded a number one single called "Shining Star."

July 71	*LOVE IS LIFE* / **Warner Bros.**
Aug. 73	*EVIL* / **Columbia**
Nov. 73	*KEEP YOUR HEAD TO THE SKY* / **Columbia**
Mar. 74	*MIGHTY MIGHTY* / **Columbia**
July 74	*KALIMBA STORY* / **Columbia**
Sept. 74	*DEVOTION* / **Columbia**
Feb. 75	*SHINING STAR* / **Columbia**
July 75	*THAT'S THE WAY OF THE WORLD* / **Columbia**
Nov. 75	*SING A SONG* / **Columbia**
Mar. 76	*CAN'T HIDE LOVE* / **Columbia**
July 76	*GETAWAY* / **Columbia**
Nov. 76	*SATURDAY NITE* / **Columbia**
Oct. 77	*SERPENTINE FIRE* / **Columbia**
Mar. 78	*FANTASY* / **Columbia**

The Easybeats

ORIGINAL MEMBERS:

"Little Stevie" Wright (lead vocals)

Harry Vanda (Harry Wandan) (lead guitar)
born: Mar. 22, 1947/Holland

George Young (rhythm guitar)/born: Nov. 6, 1947

Richard Diamonde (bass)/born: Dec. 28, 1947/Australia

Gordon "Snowy" Fleet (drums)/born: Aug. 16, 1945/Australia

Although all the group's members were born in England, The Easybeats began their career in Australia, where they developed an enormous following during the early sixties. By 1965 they were the country's leading group and were represented with numerous top ten singles and LPs, and an album titled *Easy*. Early in 1966 the group returned to their native Britain and signed a worldwide recording contract with United Artists.

In association with producer Shel Talmy (famed for his work with The Who and The Kinks), The Easybeats recorded "Make You Feel Alright (Woman)," which became a major hit in Australia and was moderately successful in England. However, it was their next release, "Friday on My Mind," which established the group by doing well in both countries and by placing high on the American charts as well. The subsequent album of the same name, comprised mainly of original material by Harry Vanda and George Young, was also successful.

Several additional recordings were produced under The Easybeats' name, and although each of these included Vanda and Young, the personnel varied from record to record as did the size of the group. Only one more single appeared on the American

charts, in 1969. The group officially disbanded in 1970.

During the early seventies Vanda and Young continued to write songs and started producing records. Under the name Happy's Whiskey Sour, the two scored with an English hit called "Shot in the Head," and, as The Marcus Hook Roll Band, placed high on the British charts with "Natural Man."

At present Harry Vanda and George Young are once again based in Australia, where they operate a production company. Steve Wright has also returned to Australia and has topped the charts there with an album titled *Hard Road,* produced by Vanda and Young.

Mar. 67	***FRIDAY ON MY MIND*** /United Artists
Nov. 69	***ST. LOUIS*** /Rare Earth

Ecstasy, Passion & Pain

MEMBERS:

Barbara Roy (vocals)

William Gardner (keyboards)

Joseph Williams, Jr. (bass)

Alan Tiza (percussion)

Althea Smith (drums)

HOMETOWN: New York City

This group was originally formed in 1972 and spent nearly two years perfecting their act on the New York City discotheque circuit before being signed to a contract by Roulette Records.

Their first release, "Good Things Don't Last Forever," barely dented the charts, but the group followed with two sizable hits and a successful album.

At present, Ecstasy, Passion & Pain tour as a popular disco attraction.

July 74	***GOOD THINGS DON'T LAST FOREVER*** /Roulette
Oct. 74	***ASK ME*** /Roulette

Mar. 75 *ONE BEAUTIFUL DAY /*
Roulette
June 76 *TOUCH & GO /* **Roulette**

Edison Lighthouse

This was not a permanent working group, but rather one of several English studio groups featuring the voices of songwriter-producers Tony Burrows and Tony MacAuley.

The group's masters were leased to Bell Records for American distribution, and early in 1970 they placed a top five hit, "Love Grows," on the United States charts. Another hit followed, and essentially the same personnel recorded numerous additional hits under names like The Pipkins and White Plains.

Feb. 70 *LOVE GROWS (WHERE MY*
ROSEMARY GOES) / **Bell**
Jan. 71 *IT'S UP TO YOU, PETULA /* **Bell**

Dave Edmunds

BORN: Apr. 15, 1944
HOMETOWN: Cardiff, Wales

Dave Edmunds began playing the guitar as a child; by the mid-sixties he was playing with the group Love Sculpture. He became widely known for his guitar work on the group's 1967 rock version of "Sabre Dance," which hit number one on the English charts.

After Love Sculpture disbanded, shortly after their hit, Edmunds founded his own Rockfield Recording Studios and learned record production. In 1970 he produced his own recording of Smiley Lewis's 1955 classic, "I Hear You Knocking." Released on Tom Jones's MAM label, the record reached the top five and was followed in 1971 by another hit titled "I'm Coming Home."

At present Edmunds continues to operate the studio and is active as a record producer while recording for Swan Song Records.

Dec. 70 *I HEAR YOU KNOCKING /* MAM
May 71 *I'M COMING HOME /* MAM

Edward Bear

MEMBERS:
Paul Weldon (bass, keyboards) / hometown: Toronto, Canada / replaced by Robert Kendall (organ)
Daniel Marks (guitar, vocals) / replaced (1971) by Roger Ellis / hometown: London, England / (left band in 1974)
Lawrence Evoy (drums, vocals) / hometown: Toronto, Canada

Edward Bear began during 1968 in Toronto and borrowed their unusual name from the character in A. A. Milne's classic children's book, *Winnie the Pooh*. At first, the group underwent a number of rapid personnel changes, and at various times had four or five members, but they eventually settled in as a trio.

Work was difficult to find in Toronto, and the group's first job was on a ferry playing for a private party of oil executives. By 1969 they had obtained a recording contract in Canada, and several of their releases had become moderate hits. One of these, "You, Me & Mexico," crossed the border and placed on the United States charts as well. However, their real breakthrough came in 1972, when their recording of "The Last Song" reached the top of both the Canadian and American bestseller lists.

Since early 1973 Edward Bear's success has been concentrated in their native Canada. In 1974 Roger Ellis moved to Los Angeles to form a new group; Edward Bear continues as a duo.

May 70 *YOU, ME & MEXICO* / Capitol
Dec. 72 *THE LAST SONG* / Capitol
Apr. 73 *CLOSE YOUR EYES* / Capitol

Jonathan Edwards

BORN: July 28, 1946

Jonathan Edwards was born in Minnesota but moved to Virginia at six, when his father got a government job there. Edwards got involved with the local bluegrass music scene and persuaded some of the musicians in the area to teach him the guitar.

In the early sixties he formed his own group, called The Rivermen (at various times also known as The St. James Doorknob and Headstone Circus), and spent the next several years touring the national one-nighter bluegrass circuit with limited success. In 1965 the group was "discovered" by manager Peter Casperson, who changed their name to Sugar Creek and helped them build a strong reputation as a concert act. In addition they recorded an album of original material but it did not sell well.

In 1970 Edwards separated from the group and was signed as a solo artist to Phil Walden's Capricorn label. Work was begun on his first album, *Jonathan Edwards* which was released during the following year and yielded the top five single "Sunshine."

Since then Jonathan Edwards's primary success has been as an album artist; and he currently records for the Warner Brothers label.

Nov. 71 *SUNSHINE* / Capricorn

The Eighth Day

HOMETOWN: Detroit, Michigan

The Eighth Day was a group of Detroit session musicians assembled by the Holland-Dozier-Holland production team for their Invictus label and featured the lead voice and guitar of Bruce Nazarian. The group placed several hits on the charts during the early seventies, the biggest of which was a top ten record called "She's Not Just Another Woman."

Bruce Nazarian spent the next years as a leading studio musician and, during the summer of 1975, became a permanent member of Brownsville Station.

May 71 *SHE'S NOT JUST ANOTHER WOMAN* / Invictus
Sept. 71 *YOU'VE GOT TO CRAWL* / Invictus
Jan. 72 *IF I COULD SEE THE LIGHT* / Invictus

El Chicano

MEMBERS:

Jerry Salas (lead vocals, guitar) / Oxnard, California

Michael "Mickey" Lespron (lead guitar) / Los Angeles, California

Robert Espinosa (keyboards) / Los Angeles, California

Fred Sanchez (bass) / replaced by Brian Magness / Los Angeles, California

Andre Baeza (percussion)

Hector "Rudy" Regaldo (percussion) / Caracas, Venezuela

John DeLuna (drums, percussion) / replaced by Edward Rodriguez / New York City

El Chicano began in east Los Angeles during the mid-sixties as a group called The VIP's and launched their career by playing at weddings, proms, and community dances. Over the years they underwent many personnel changes and gradually evolved into the above group, whose core members included Sanchez (later replaced), Espinosa, Baeza, and Lespron.

In 1970 El Chicano signed with the Kapp label (a division of MCA) and

The Electric Light Orchestra. Left to right: Melvyn Gale, Hugh MacDowell, Bev Bevan, Jeff Lynne, Rich Tandy, Kelly Groucutt, Mik Kaminski

scored with their first hit, a Latin-jazz instrumental titled "Viva Tirado." During the next years they followed with several other hit singles and albums.

Apr. 70	*VIVA TIRADO* /Kapp
June 72	*BROWN EYED GIRL* /Kapp
Nov. 73	*TELL HER SHE'S LOVELY* / MCA

The Electric Light Orchestra

MEMBERS:

Jeff Lynne (guitar, Moog synthesizer, lead vocals)/born: Dec. 30, 1947

Richard Tandy (guitar, keyboards)/born: Mar. 26, 1948

Michael Edwards (cello)/replaced by Mik Kaminski/born: Sept. 2, 1951

Colin Walker (cello)/replaced by Hugh Mac–Dowell/born: July 31, 1953

Wilf Gibson (violin)/replaced by Kelly Groucutt/born: Sept. 8, 1945

Michael Alberquerque (bass)/replaced by Melvyn Gale/born: Jan. 15, 1952

Bev Bevan (drums)/born: Nov 25, 1946

HOMETOWN: Birmingham, England

The Electric Light Orchestra was a spinoff from an extremely popular English rock group called The Move. In 1970 Move members Roy Wood, Bev Bevan, and Jeff Lynne formed ELO as a more traditional "pop" orchestra. They continued as active members of The Move while working on the first ELO album, *No Answer.* It was released in 1972 and featured guest soloists from The London Symphony Orchestra. After a subsequent tour of England, Roy Wood left the group to form a rock 'n' roll band called Wizzard, and Jeff Lynne became ELO's acknowledged leader. He made several personnel changes, and the above group made its debut at the famed Reading Festival. In 1973 their single release of "Roll Over Beethoven" placed at the top of the English charts for several weeks and became their first American hit. Although they followed with several more hits, including a top ten record called "Can't Get It out of My Head," they are best known for their albums: *ELO 2, On the Third Day, Showdown,* and *Eldorado.*

Apr. 73	***ROLL OVER BEETHOVEN /*** **United Artists**
Dec. 73	***SHOWDOWN* /United Artists**
May 74	***DAYBREAKER* /United Artists**
Dec. 74	***CAN'T GET IT OUT OF MY HEAD* /United Artists**
Nov. 75	***EVIL WOMAN* /United Artists**
Mar. 76	***STRANGE MAGIC* /United Artists**
Aug. 76	***SHOWDOWN* /United Artists**
Oct. 76	***LIVIN' THING* /United Artists**
Jan. 77	***DO YA* /United Artists**
June 77	***TELEPHONE LINE* /United Artists**
Nov. 77	***TURN TO STONE* /United Artists**
Feb. 78	***SWEET TALKING WOMAN* / United Artists**

The Electric Prunes

ORIGINAL MEMBERS:
James Lowe (lead vocals, autoharp, rhythm guitar)
Kenneth Williams (lead guitar)
Mark Tulin (bass, keyboards)
Preston Ritter (drums, percussion)
HOMETOWN: Seattle, Washington
MEMBERS (1967):
Mark Kincaid (guitar)
Ronald Morgan (guitar)
Richard Whetstone (lead vocals, drums)
Brett Wade (bass)
John Herren (piano)

The Electric Prunes were formed in the mid-sixties, and, after developing a strong regional following in the Northwest, were signed in 1966 by Reprise Records. Their first release, "I Had Too Much to Dream Last Night," be-

came a top ten hit and was followed successfully by "Get Me to the World on Time." However, in 1967, after recording two albums, *The Electric Prunes* and *Underground,* the original members retired from recording and an entirely different group emerged under The Electric Prunes' name. This "new" group recorded a "religious-rock" album titled *Mass in F Minor* and a few singles, but none ever duplicated the success of the original Prunes.

Dec. 66	***I HAD TOO MUCH TO DREAM LAST NIGHT* /Reprise**
Apr. 67	***GET ME TO THE WORLD ON TIME* /Reprise**

The Elephant's Memory

MEMBERS:
Stanley Bronstein (sax, woodwinds) /born: July 17, 1938
Richard "Rick" Frank (drums) /born: Feb. 12, 1942
Richard Sussman (keyboards) /born: Feb. 28, 1946 /replaced (1971) by Adam Ippolito / (left in 1973)
John Ward (bass) /born: Feb. 12, 1949 / replaced (1971) by Gary Van Scyoc /(left in 1973)
Myron Yules (electric bass trombone) /born: Mar. 6, 1935 (left in 1970)
Michael Shapiro (vocals) /born: Apr. 20, 1949 /(left in 1970)
Wayne "Tex" Gabriel (guitar) / (added in 1971) /replaced (1975) by David Jiminez
HOMETOWN: New York City

This group originated during the late sixties in the East Village section of New York, where they gained a substantial following with their free concerts in parks. They also became widely known as the house band for the benefit concerts organized by WBAI, a listener-sponsored underground radio station.

The Elephant's Memory began making records in 1968 when their first single, "Keep Free," was released. They followed in 1969 with an album, *Elephant's Memory,* but first gained national prominence in 1970 with the hit single "Mongoose." That year also marked the beginning of a number of personnel changes, and in 1971 the group became friendly with Yoko Ono, who was active in New York's avant garde underground. Through Yoko, they cut an album, *Elephant's Memory,* for Apple Records in 1972 and were featured on the John & Yoko *New York City* album. They also backed Yoko Ono on several of her solo recordings.

In 1975 Elephant's Memory, reduced to three men, affiliated with Atlantic Records. Stan Bronstein has begun a side career as a solo act.

Aug. 70 *MONGOOSE* / **Metromedia**

Yvonne Elliman

BORN: 1953

Of Hawaiian origin, Yvonne Elliman became widely known during the early seventies via her stage, film, and studio portrayals of Mary Magdalene in the rock opera *Jesus Christ Superstar.* She spent four years in the production and in 1971 had a major hit with one of the show's songs, "I Don't Know How to Love Him." In 1974 Yvonne accompanied Eric Clapton on his famed comeback tour and was featured as a vocalist on two of his albums, *461 Ocean Boulevard* and *E. C. Was Here.*

In 1975 Elliman recorded a solo album titled *Rising Sun* for Robert Stigwood's RSO label.

Apr. 71 *I DON'T KNOW HOW TO LOVE HIM* / **Decca**
Sept. 71 *EVERYTHING'S ALRIGHT* / **Decca**
Oct. 76 *LOVE ME* / **RSO**

Yvonne Elliman

Mar. 77 *HELLO STRANGER* / **RSO**
Jan. 78 *IF I CAN'T HAVE YOU* / **RSO**

Cass Elliott

See *THE MAMAS & PAPAS.*

Emerson, Lake & Palmer

MEMBERS:
Keith Emerson (keyboards, Moog synthesizer) / born: Nov. 2, 1944
Gregory Lake (bass) / born: Nov. 10, 1948
Carl Palmer (drums, percussion) / born: Mar. 20, 1947
HOMETOWN: Bournemouth, England

Made up of members of several important English rock groups, Emerson, Lake & Palmer was formed during the late sixties and became a leading

Emerson, Lake & Palmer

force in classically oriented electronic rock.

In 1969 Emerson was with The Nice and Lake with King Crimson; the two met at San Francisco's Fillmore West where both their respective groups were booked. Upon their return home to England they recruited Carl Palmer, formerly with The Crazy World of Arthur Brown, then with Atomic Rooster. After rehearsing for several months, the group made their debut at the famed Isle Of Wight concert in 1970. Shortly afterward they were signed by Island Records in England and their first album, *Emerson, Lake & Palmer*, was released early in 1971. It brought the group immediate success and became similarly successful when released in the United States on Atlantic's Cotillion label. The group also scored with a number of hit singles during the next two years.

Since then Emerson, Lake & Palmer have been known primarily for their LPs, including *Tarkus, Pictures at an Exhibition, Trilogy, Brain Salad Surgery, Welcome Back My Friends,* and *ELP.* In 1973 they formed their own Manticore label, for which they presently record.

Mar. 71	**LUCKY MAN** / Cotillion
Mar. 72	**NUTROCKER** / Cotillion
Aug. 72	**FROM THE BEGINNING** / Cotillion
Dec. 72	**LUCKY MAN** (rereleased) / Cotillion

Greg Lake

Sept. 77	**C'EST LA VIE** / Atlantic

The Emotions

MEMBERS:

Sheila Hutchinson

Wanda Hutchinson

Jeanette Hutchinson / replaced by Theresa Davis / replaced by Pamela Hutchinson

HOMETOWN: Chicago, Illinois

Not to be confused with the group of the same name, who recorded "Echo" in 1962, The Emotions began as a sister act and were managed by their father, Joe Hutchinson. Sheila, Wanda, and Jeanette began singing together

The Emotions. Left to right: Pamela Hutchinson, Sheila Hutchinson, Wanda Hutchinson

as children on the local Jerry Van Dyke "Children's Gospel" TV show. They were eventually signed by the Stax-Volt organization and had their first hit, "So I Can Love You," in the summer of 1969.

One year later Jeanette left the group to be married and was replaced by her cousin, Theresa Davis, who was then replaced by Pamela Hutchinson. In 1975 Maurice White, leader of Earth, Wind & Fire, arranged for them to be signed to Columbia with himself as producer.

May 69	*SO I CAN LOVE YOU* /Volt
Nov. 71	*SHOW ME HOW* /Volt
July 72	*I COULD NEVER BE HAPPY WITHOUT YOU* /Volt
Mar. 74	*PUT A LITTLE LOVE AWAY* /Volt
Oct. 76	*FLOWERS* /Columbia
Nov. 76	*I DON'T WANNA LOSE YOUR LOVE* /Columbia
June 77	*BEST OF MY LOVE* /Columbia
Oct. 77	*DON'T ASK MY NEIGHBORS* /Columbia

Enchantment

MEMBERS:

David Banks
Emanuel Johnson
Edgar Clanton
Bobbi Green
Joe Thomas

HOMETOWN: Detroit, Michigan

The members met while attending music classes at Pershing High School on the northeast side of Detroit in early 1966. After much practice, they got a break during the summer of 1969 when they entered a local talent contest sponsored by a radio station and won first prize, which led to numerous bookings at local night clubs.

After a while Dick Scott began working with the group to get them to polish up their act. In a short while, they were working on stage with The Four Tops and Eddie Kendricks, to name a few.

Enchantment

In 1977 they hit it big with the ballad "Gloria."

Jan. 77 *GLORIA* / **United Artists**
Aug. 77 *SUNSHINE* / **Roadshow**
Feb. 78 *IT'S YOU THAT I NEED* / **Roadshow**

England Dan & John Ford Coley

Danny Seals / born: Feb. 8, 1950
John Edward Coley / born: Oct. 13, 1951
HOMETOWN: Austin, Texas

Danny, the brother of Jimmy Seals of Seals & Crofts, teamed up with fellow Texan John Coley to tour the Southwest. After a successful debut at the Ice House in Pasadena, they were asked to tour England with Elton John. Hence the name England Dan.

After the tour with Elton they began a United States tour as opening act for performers like Carole King, Chicago, and Three Dog Night. In a short while they were signed to Big Tree Records and debuted in the summer of 1976 with the top ten smash "I'd Really Love to See You Tonight" which established them as stars with a future.

June 76 *I'D REALLY LOVE TO SEE YOU TONIGHT* / **Big Tree**
Oct. 76 *NIGHTS ARE FOREVER WITHOUT YOU* / **Big Tree**
May 77 *IT'S SAD TO BELONG* / **Big Tree**
Oct. 77 *GONE TOO FAR* / **Big Tree**
Feb. 78 *NEVER HAVE TO SAY GOODBYE* / **Big Tree**

David Essex

REAL NAME: David Cook
BORN: July 23, 1947
HOMETOWN: Plaistow, London, England

David Cook had a strong childhood interest in jazz drumming. At fourteen

England Dan & John Ford Coley

he was playing with a blues band in local pubs and was seen by Derek Bowman, a show-business journalist. Bowman became his manager, convinced him to go solo, and suggested he change his name to Essex (where David was living at the time). He also arranged for voice training and dance lessons.

During the mid-sixties Essex made several moderately successful British pop records, numerous appearances on British TV and broke into the theater with the leading role in a touring company of *The Fantasticks*. He understudied Tommy Steele in the 1969 pantomime production of *Dick Whit-*tington and in 1970 made his film debut in *Assault*. In 1971 he followed with an appearance in *All Coppers Are* and later that year was chosen for the role of Christ in the London production of *Godspell*. The reviews elevated him to stardom, and in 1973 he took a leave of absence to costar with Ringo Starr in the award-winning film, *That'll Be the Day*. He also recorded "Rock On" in association with producer Jeff Wayne; the record went to number one in England and became a major success in the United States as well. It was followed in 1974 by "Lamplight."

In 1975 David Essex appeared in a sequel to *That'll Be The Day*. The film,

David Essex

titled *Stardust,* was set in the sixties and featured a soundtrack of period hits.

Today David lives just outside London with his wife and young daughter. His large home also contains a recording studio.

Nov. 73 *ROCK ON* / Columbia
June 74 *LAMPLIGHT* / Columbia

Betty Everett

BORN: Nov. 23, 1939
HOMETOWN: Greenwood, Mississippi

Betty Everett began singing and playing piano at the age of eight in a local church choir.

In the late fifties she moved to Chicago and began her recording career on such small local labels as Cobra, C. J., and One-Derful. This eventually led to a contract with Vee Jay Records during the early sixties, and her first release, "You're No Good," became a

hit in 1963 (the same song provided a number one record for Linda Ronstadt in 1975). Betty followed with her biggest all-time hit, "The Shoop Shoop Song," which reached the top five, and she went on to have numerous hits throughout the sixties on various labels. During her years with Vee Jay she teamed up with another of the label's artists, Jerry Butler, to place two major hits on the charts.

At present, Betty Everett records for Fantasy Records and has occasional hits on the soul charts.

Nov. 63 *YOU'RE NO GOOD* / Vee Jay
Feb. 64 *THE SHOOP SHOOP SONG (IT'S IN HIS KISS)* / Vee Jay
June 64 *I CAN'T HEAR YOU* / Vee Jay
Nov. 64 *GETTING MIGHTY CROWDED* / Vee Jay
Jan. 69 *THERE'LL COME A TIME* / Uni
Apr. 69 *I CAN'T SAY NO TO YOU* / Uni
Dec. 69 *IT'S BEEN A LONG TIME* / Uni
Dec. 70 *I GOT TO TELL SOMEBODY* / Fantasy
Betty Everett & Jerry Butler
Sept. 64 *LET IT BE ME* / Vee Jay
Dec. 64 *SMILE* / Vee Jay

Every Mother's Son

MEMBERS:

Lary Larden (lead vocals, rhythm guitar) / born: Aug. 10, 1945 / Brooklyn, New York

Dennis Larden (lead vocals, lead guitar) / born: Nov. 22, 1948 / Kansas

Bruce J. Milner (keyboards) / born: May 9, 1943 / Brooklyn, New York

Christopher Augustine (drums, percussion) / born: Apr. 25, 1941 / New York City

Schuyler Larden (bass) / born: Feb. 19, 1947 / New York City / replaced by Donald Kerr

The nucleus of this group was the folksinging team of brothers Lary and Dennis Larden, who spent the early sixties performing at parties and small Greenwich Village clubs. In 1966, while performing at one of these, they met organist Bruce Milner, and the three decided to form a rock group. They recruited Chris Augustine and Schuyler Larden (later replaced) and began rehearsing as Every Mother's Son.

The Larden brothers contacted a manager they knew from their folk days, Peter Leeds. Leeds brought them to the attention of producer Wes Farrell, who signed them to a recording contract and produced their first album, *Every Mother's Son.* It was sold to MGM Records, released early in 1967 and yielded the group's first hit single, "Come on down to My Boat,"

which reached the top ten. After several more hit singles and another album, *Every Mother's Son's Back,* the group faded from popularity as the sound of rock music hardened during the late sixties.

May 67	*COME ON DOWN TO MY BOAT*/MGM
Aug. 67	*PUT YOUR MIND AT EASE*/MGM
Nov. 67	*PONY WITH THE GOLDEN MANE*/MGM
Jan. 68	*NO ONE KNOWS*/MGM

Faces

MEMBERS:

Roderick David Stewart (lead vocals)/born: Jan. 10, 1945/North London, England

Ronald Wood (guitar)/born: June 1, 1947/London, England/replaced (1969) by Steven Marriott/born: Jan. 30, 1947

Ronald Lane (bass)/born: Apr. 1, 1948/replaced (July 1973) by Tetsu Yamauchi/born: Oct. 21, 1947

Ian McLagen (keyboards)/born: May 12, 1946

Kenneth Jones (drums)/born: Sept. 16, 1949

This group was the direct descendant of The Small Faces, famed for their mid-sixties hit "Itchycoo Park," and was the breeding-ground for some of the mid-seventies' most important rock musicians.

Lead singer and guitarist Steve Marriott left The Small Faces during the late sixties to join Humble Pie. He was replaced by Ron Wood and Rod Stewart (who had come from the disintegrating Jeff Beck Group) and the "Small" prefix was dropped from their name. Signed by Warner Brothers in 1970, The Faces rose to prominence with their albums *First Step, Long Prayer, A Nod's As Good As a Wink* and *Ooh La La.* They also had two hit singles during the early seventies.

Rod Stewart began a parallel solo career in 1971 and scored immediately with his number one record "Maggie May." In 1973 founding member Ronnie Lane separated from The Faces to go solo and was replaced by Free's former bassist, Tetsu Yamauchi. Like Rod Stewart, Ron Wood no longer records as a member of The Faces, but instead Wood records with the Rolling Stones.

See *THE SMALL FACES; Rod STEWART.*

Jan. 72 **STAY WITH ME** /Warner Bros.
Mar. 73 **CINDY INCIDENTALLY** /
Warner Bros.

Faith, Hope & Charity

REAL NAMES:

Faith: Brenda Hillard

Hope: Albert Bailey

Charity: Zulema/replaced (1974) by Diane Destry

This group first gained prominence in 1970 under Van McCoy, the writer-producer who became widely known as an artist with his number one recording "The Hustle" in 1975. In association with Joe Cobb, McCoy wrote and produced a number of recordings for Bob Crewe's Maxwell label, of which several placed on the R & B charts, and two, "So Much Love" and "Baby Don't Take Your Love," became national pop hits.

During the summer of 1975 Faith, Hope & Charity reemerged and were signed by RCA Records, where they have successfully resumed recording under Van McCoy's direction.

May 70 **SO MUCH LOVE** /Maxwell

Faces. Left to right: Ian McLagen, Rod Stewart, Ron Wood, Ken Jones, Tetsu Yamauchi

Sept. 70 *BABY DON'T TAKE YOUR LOVE*/**Maxwell**
Aug. 75 *TO EACH HIS OWN*/**RCA**

Marianne Faithfull

BORN: 1948
HOMETOWN: Hampstead, North London, England

Marianne Faithfull is the daughter of Dr. Robert Glynn Faithfull, a professor at the University of London, and Ava Sacher-Masoch, Baroness Erisso. At the age of eight she entered St. Joseph's Convent School at Reading and gave no thought to music as a career. However, a stroke of fate during her 1964 summer vacation changed her life entirely and she never returned to school. One day she and a friend accompanied Peter Asher (who was soon to become famous as half of Peter & Gordon) to a show-business party. One of the other guests was Andrew Loog Oldham, manager of The Rolling Stones. Oldham was so taken with Marianne's name and appearance that he signed her immediately without even asking if she could sing! Fortunately she could, and Rolling Stones Mick Jagger and Keith Richard reworked an old English madrigal into the song that would become her first release, "As Tears Go By." The record became an immediate success, and before she could return to school in the fall, Marianne was booked on a tour. Later released in the United States on the London label, the record reached the American top twenty.

Although Marianne had several additional international hits, she remained in the public eye for a variety of reasons. In 1967 she was chosen for the role of Irina in the London production of Chekhov's *Three Sisters*. Later in the year she began filming *Girl on a Motorbike,* in which she costarred with Alain Delon, and shortly thereafter returned to the stage as Ophelia in a production of *Hamlet*. In 1969, with Jagger, she made another film titled

Ned Kelly, and she was regularly seen on British television. However, it was for her continual personal difficulties that she was best known well into the early seventies.

After nearly two years in retirement Marianne Faithfull reemerged in 1973 to resume her stage career.

Nov. 64	*AS TEARS GO BY* / London	
Feb. 65	*COME AND STAY WITH ME* / London	
June 65	*THIS LITTLE BIRD* / London	
Aug. 65	*SUMMER NIGHTS* / London	
Dec. 65	*GO AWAY FROM MY WORLD* / London	

Georgie Fame

REAL NAME: Clive Powell
BORN: June 26, 1943
HOMETOWN: Leigh, Lancashire, England

Clive Powell's first exposure to music came through his father, a one-time piano and accordion player in a semiprofessional dance band. At fifteen, while away at summer camp in North Wales, Clive got the chance to sing with Rory Blackwell's band and was immediately offered a job. Soon Blackwell was sidelined by an auto wreck, and Powell was asked to join Larry Parnes's celebrated stable of artists, including Billy Fury, Dicky Pride, Johnny Gentle, and Gerry Dorsey (later to become Engelbert Humperdinck). Powell took the stage name of Georgie Fame and became part of a new back-up group for Billy Fury called The Blue Flames. Consisting of Fame (lead vocals and keyboards), Colin Green (guitar), Tex Makins (bass), Michael Ewe (sax), and Red Reece (drums), the group eventually separated from Fury and became a resident band at Rick Gunnell's legendary Flamingo R & B Club in London. They played there for almost three years beginning in 1962

and under Gunnell's management developed a strong reputation.

In 1964 Rick Gunnell negotiated a contract for the group with British Columbia Records, and their first release, a "live" album titled *R & B at the Flamingo,* became an immediate success. The following year they had a number one single in England with a vocal version of Mongo Santamaria's "Yeh Yeh." It was released in the United States on the Imperial label and established Fame with American audiences as well. In 1966 Fame left The Blue Flames to fulfill a long-standing ambition to sing with big bands like those of Count Basie and Harry South; in 1968 he had a worldwide best seller as a solo artist with "The Ballad of Bonnie & Clyde." During the early seventies he joined former Animal Alan Price to record, appear on television, tour, and make a film. They separated in 1974, and Georgie Fame has formed a new Blue Flames group and records for Island Records.

Feb. 65	*YEH, YEH* / Imperial
May 65	*IN THE MEANTIME* / Imperial
Aug. 66	*GET AWAY* / Imperial
Feb. 68	*THE BALLAD OF BONNIE & CLYDE* / Epic

Fancy

MEMBERS:
Helen "Fancy" Court (lead vocals) / replaced by Anne Kavanagh
"Marlon" (lead guitar)
Mo Foster (bass)
Les Binks (drums)

This group was formed in England during the early seventies and developed a reputation with their contemporary reworkings of rock "oldies." Their first recording, an update of The Troggs' mid-sixties hit "Wild Thing," remained on the English charts for nearly three months during the summer of 1974 and, when released in the United States on the Big Tree label, became a top twenty hit.

June 74 *WILD THING*/**Big Tree**
Oct. 74 *TOUCH ME*/**Big Tree**

Don Fardon

REAL NAME: Donald Maughn

Don Maughn first became known during the mid-sixties as lead singer of The Sorrows, the English group famed for their recording of "Take a Heart." The song was written by Miki Dallon, later to become a leading British producer and record-company executive.

In 1967 Maughn left The Sorrows and, after assuming the stage name Don Fardon, became the premiere artist on Dallon's newly formed Young Blood label. After several minor hits, Fardon scored with an old John D. Loudermilk song called "Indian Reservation" (later a number one record by The Raiders) which became a major success in England. Leased to the GNP Crescendo label for United States distribution, it became a top twenty American hit as well.

Fardon continues his association with Miki Dallon and Young Blood Records, but only one other record, "Delta Queen" released in the United States on Wes Farrell's Chelsea label, ever became widely known to American audiences.

Aug. 68 *INDIAN RESERVATION*/**GNP Crescendo**
Mar. 73 *DELTA QUEEN*/**Chelsea**

Donna Fargo

REAL NAME: Yvonne Vaughan
BORN: Nov. 10, 1949
HOMETOWN: Mount Airy, North Carolina

Although Donna was interested in singing as a child, she did not pursue it as a career until she had become firmly established in Los Angeles as a teacher.

In her spare time Donna began using her own money to make recordings. Several were released by such companies as Challenge and Ramco and became northwestern regional hits. In 1972 she was signed by the Dot label, where her first release was her own composition of "The Happiest Girl in the Whole USA." Donna continued to teach English until this record was well on its way to becoming a hit; it eventually reached the top of the country charts. It also became a top ten national pop hit and was followed by another original, "Funny Face," which reached the top five. Since then Donna's records, mostly her own songs, have been major hits on both the country and pop charts.

Today, Donna Fargo lives in Nashville with her husband and manager, Stan Silver.

May 72 *THE HAPPIEST GIRL IN THE WHOLE USA*/**Dot**
Sept. 72 *FUNNY FACE*/**Dot**
Feb. 73 *SUPERMAN*/**Dot**
June 73 *YOU WERE ALWAYS THERE*/**Dot**
Oct. 73 *LITTLE GIRL GONE*/**Dot**
June 74 *YOU CAN'T BE A BEACON*/**Dot**
Nov. 74 *THE U.S. OF A.*/**Dot**
Mar. 75 *IT DO FEEL GOOD*/**Dot**

José Feliciano

BORN: Sept. 8, 1945
HOMETOWN: Lorez, Puerto Rico

Blind from birth, José Feliciano moved at the age of five to New York City with his parents and seven brothers. He was given a guitar as a young-

José Feliciano

ster and spent several hours a day teaching himself to play.

At nine Feliciano made his first public appearance at El Teatro Puerto Rico in New York's Spanish Harlem and by the early sixties was well known on the Greenwich Village folk circuit. He was discovered at Gerde's Folk City in 1963 when an A & R man from RCA came to hear another act but signed Feliciano instead. During the next five years, he made recordings primarily for the Latin market, but his breakthrough to pop came in 1968 with the release of an album called *Feliciano*. It became a best seller and yielded the number one single "Light My Fire." Later in the year he received international publicity as the result of his controversial rendering of "The Star Spangled Banner" before the fifth game of the 1968 World Series in Detroit.

Since then José Feliciano has achieved a long string of chart singles and more than a dozen best-selling albums. He has also become active in film; composed the soundtracks for *MacKenna's Gold* and *Aaron Loves Angela* and is presently heard singing the theme song on the weekly TV series "Chico and the Man."

Today Feliciano is affiliated with the Private Stock label, and he and his wife, Janna, make their home in California.

July 68	*LIGHT MY FIRE* /RCA
Oct. 68	*HI HEEL SNEAKERS* /RCA
Oct. 68	*HITCHCOCK RAILWAY* /RCA
Nov. 68	*THE STAR SPANGLED BANNER* /RCA
Jan. 69	*HEY BABY* /RCA
Feb. 69	*MY WORLD IS EMPTY WITHOUT YOU* /RCA
May 69	*MARLEY PURT DRIVE* /RCA
Aug. 69	*RAIN* /RCA
July 70	*DESTINY* /RCA
Jan. 75	*CHICO AND THE MAN* /RCA

Freddy Fender

REAL NAME: Baldermar Huerta
BORN: June 4, 1937
HOMETOWN: San Benito, Texas

Freddy Fender, the leading exponent of the contemporary "Tex-Mex" sound, spent his early years in the South and Midwest as a migrant farmworker. He was first exposed to music at the parties that were customarily held after a day's work. By eleven he had learned the guitar and was imitating the country singers he heard on the radio. Soon he was playing local dances, and during the mid-fifties he joined the marines, where he continued his playing, with the USO. He returned home in 1956 and formed a small band to play local Texas "beer joints."

During the late fifties Fender began his recording career singing background for a friend's recording session. The owner of the label, Falcon Records, liked him and signed him as a solo artist. He had several regional hits, including a Spanish version of "Don't Be Cruel," "Crazy Crazy Baby," and "Wasted Days and Wasted Nights." (The last song was leased to the Imperial label, and became Fender's biggest hit of that period; the same song became a major national hit in 1975.) After several more years on the Texas bar circuit, Fender's career took a sharp upward turn in 1971 when he met record producer Huey Meaux and began recording for Meaux's Crazy Cajun label. In 1975 a single titled "Before the Next Teardrop Falls" was leased to ABC/Dot for national distribution and became a major country and pop hit. During the following months Fender placed a number of records high on the charts, sometimes several at the same time.

Today Freddy Fender makes his home in Corpus Christie, Texas.

Feb. 75	*BEFORE THE NEXT TEARDROP FALLS* / ABC/Dot
June 75	*WASTED DAYS AND WASTED NIGHTS* /ABC/Dot
Oct. 75	*SECRET LOVE* /ABC/Dot
Oct. 75	*SINCE I MET YOU BABY* /GRT
Feb. 76	*YOU'LL LOSE A GOOD THING* /ABC/Dot
May 76	*VAYA CON DIOS* /ABC/Dot
Oct. 76	*LIVING IT DOWN* /ABC/Dot

Freddy Fender

The Fifth Dimension

MEMBERS:

Marilyn McCoo / born: Sept. 30, 1943 / Jersey City, New Jersey / replaced (1976) by Marjorie Barnes / replaced by Terri Bryant

Florence LaRue Gordon / born: Feb. 4, 1944 / Glenside, Pennsylvania

William Davis Jr. / born: June 26, 1940 / St. Louis, Missouri / replaced (1976) by Daniel Beard

Ronald Townson / born: Jan. 20, 1941 / St. Louis, Missouri / replaced by Michael Bell

Lamonte McLemore / born: Sept. 17, 1940 / St. Louis, Missouri

This group was formed in Los Angeles in the mid-sixties by Marilyn McCoo, who had moved to California as a child, and Lamonte McLemore, who was a photographer for a Los Angeles fashion magazine. Marilyn had won a number of beauty contests and was working as a model. She and Lamonte met during one of his assignments and decided to draw upon their individual gospel-singing experiences and form a group. After recruiting Floyd Butler and Harry Elston, they briefly recorded and toured as The Hi-Fi's, but Elston and Butler left to eventually form The Friends of Distinction. They were replaced by three new members, Florence LaRue, Ron Townson, and Billy Davis, Lamonte's cousin, and the group's name was changed to The Versatiles. They auditioned for Marc Gordon, a Los Angeles record executive turned manager, and he agreed to handle their career. He obtained a contract with Johnny Rivers's Soul City label, where they achieved a minor regional hit called "I'll Be Loving You Forever" and changed their name to The Fifth Dimension.

Their first national success came early in 1967 with a cover version of The Mamas & Papas' "Go Where You Wanna Go," followed by "Another Day, Another Heartache." However, their breakthrough was their recording of "Up, Up and Away," which also launched the career of songwriter Jim Webb. After several additional hits with Webb's songs, The Fifth Dimension went on to establish another unknown writer, Laura Nyro, by recording major hit versions of a number of her songs: "Stoned Soul Picnic," "Sweet Blindness," "Wedding Bell Blues," "Blowing Away," and "Save the Country."

The Fifth Dimension continued with a string of more than two dozen hit singles and today are a leading nightclub and television attraction. In 1970 they switched to the Bell label and in 1975 were signed by ABC Records.

Marc Gordon and Florence LaRue are presently married as are Billy Davis and Marilyn McCoo. Early in 1976, charter members Davis and McCoo left the group for solo careers and were immediately replaced by Danny Beard and Marjorie Barnes.

Jan. 67	*GO WHERE YOU WANNA GO / Soul City*
Apr. 67	*ANOTHER DAY, ANOTHER HEARTACHE / Soul City*
June 67	*UP, UP AND AWAY / Soul City*
Nov. 67	*PAPER CUP / Soul City*
Feb. 68	*CARPET MAN / Soul City*
June 68	*STONED SOUL PICNIC / Soul City*
Sept. 68	*SWEET BLINDNESS / Soul City*
Dec. 68	*CALIFORNIA SOUL / Soul City*
Mar. 69	*AQUARIUS / LET THE SUNSHINE IN / Soul City*
July 69	*WORKING ON A GROOVY THING / Soul City*
July 69	*WEDDING BELL BLUES / Soul City*
Jan. 70	*BLOWING AWAY / Soul City*
Feb. 70	*A CHANGE IS GONNA COME / PEOPLE GOTTA BE FREE / Bell*
Apr. 70	*THE GIRLS' SONG / Soul City*
Apr. 70	*PUPPET MAN / Bell*
June 70	*SAVE THE COUNTRY / Bell*
Aug. 70	*ON THE BEACH / Bell*
Oct. 70	*ONE LESS BELL TO ANSWER / Bell*
Feb. 71	*LOVE'S LINES, ANGLES & RHYMES / Bell*
May 71	*LIGHT SINGS / Bell*
Sept. 71	*NEVER MY LOVE / Bell*
Jan. 72	*TOGETHER, LET'S FIND LOVE / Bell*
Apr. 72	*LAST NIGHT, I DIDN'T GET TO SLEEP AT ALL / Bell*
Sept. 72	*IF I COULD REACH YOU / Bell*
Jan. 73	*LIVING TOGETHER, GROWING TOGETHER / Bell*
Apr. 73	*EVERYTHING'S BEEN CHANGED / Bell*
Aug. 73	*ASHES TO ASHES / Bell*
Dec. 73	*FLASHBACK / Bell*
Apr. 76	*LOVE HANGOVER / ABC*

The Fifth Estate

MEMBERS:

Rick Engler (vocals, kazoo, electric clarinet, violin, bass)

Dick Ferrar (vocals, guitar, bass)

"Wads" Wadhams (keyboards)

William Shute (mandolin, guitar)
Furvus Evans (drums, percussion)

This was a group of studio musicians and vocalists assembled by independent record producers Steve and Bill Jerome. In 1967 they recorded a classic song from "The Wizard of Oz" titled "Ding Dong! The Witch is Dead." The master was sold to Jubilee Records and became a top ten hit during the summer of that year. The Fifth Estate followed with an album featuring the hit as the title track, and although several additional singles were issued, they never returned to the charts.

May 67 *DING DONG! THE WITCH IS DEAD* / Jubilee

Firefall

MEMBERS:
Rick Roberts (vocals, guitar)
Larry Burnett (vocals, guitar)
Jock Bartley (vocals, lead guitar)
Mark Andes (vocals, bass guitar)
Michael Clarke (drums)
HOMETOWN: Denver, Colorado

The five members of Firefall got together in 1975 and began playing in the Denver-Boulder area of the Rockies. Leader Rick Roberts took his country-rock group to New York later that year to appear at the Other End club, where they were spotted by an A & R man from Atlantic Records who was impressed enough to offer them a recording contract. In 1976 the group recorded a tune that Rick wrote called "You Are the Woman," which quickly became a top ten hit.

June 76 *LIVIN' AIN'T LIVIN'* / Atlantic
Aug. 76 *YOU ARE THE WOMAN* / Atlantic
Mar. 77 *CINDERELLA* / Atlantic

Aug. 77 *JUST REMEMBER I LOVE YOU* / Atlantic
Jan. 78 *SO LONG* / Atlantic

The First Choice

MEMBERS:
Rochelle Flemming (lead vocals)
Annette Guest (back-up vocals)
Joyce Jones (back-up vocals)
HOMETOWN: Philadelphia, Pennsylvania

The nucleus of this vocal trio is Rochelle Flemming, who sang as a child in the Philadelphia Baptist Church. She met the other members in high school, and the three formed The First Choice in 1971.

They developed their act with many personal appearances in Philadelphia's local clubs and eventually attracted the attention of Scepter Records. After the release of a moderately successful regional hit titled "The House Where Love Died," the group was introduced by Philadelphia disc jockey Georgie Woods to Stan Watson, head of Philly Groove Records. Beginning in 1973 The First Choice made several recordings that began as discotheque hits and went on to national chart success.

Mar. 73 *ARMED AND EXTREMELY DANGEROUS* / Philly Groove
Nov. 73 *SMARTY PANTS* / Philly Groove
Mar. 74 *NEWSY NEIGHBORS* / Philly Groove
Sept. 74 *THE PLAYER* / Philly Groove
Sept. 77 *DR. LOVE* / Gold Mind

First Class

MEMBERS:
Chas Mills (vocals)
Tony Burrows (vocals)
John Carter (vocals)
Del John (vocals)
Spencer James (vocals, lead guitar)

Edward Richards (vocals, drums)
Robin Shaw (vocals, bass)
Clive Barrett (vocals, keyboards)

This is a group of England's leading studio musicians and vocalists who, in various combinations, have made dozens of pop hits under names like Edison Lighthouse, White Plains, and The Brotherhood of Man.

During the summer of 1974 they made a record for Jonathan King's UK label titled "Beach Baby," a rousing tribute to the sixties style of The Beach Boys. It reached the top five and remained on the charts through November. By the summer of 1975 First Class had followed with two more hits.

Although they continue to occasionally record as First Class, all the members are active with other studio work.

July 74	***BEACH BABY*** /UK
Nov. 74	***DREAMS ARE TEN A PENNY*** /UK
May 75	***FUNNY HOW LOVE CAN BE*** /UK

The Five Americans

MEMBERS:
Michael Rabon (lead vocals, lead and rhythm guitar)
Leonard Goldsmith (lead vocals, keyboards)
Robert Rambo (lead and rhythm guitar)
James Grant (bass)
James Wright (drums)
HOMETOWN: Dallas, Texas

The Five Americans began by playing local clubs and developed enough of a reputation to be signed by HBR Records, a division of the Hanna-Barbera Company. After two moderate hits the group switched to the Abnak label, where they were produced by Dale Hawkins (famed as an artist for his fifties hit "Suzie Q"). They recorded a series of hits, the biggest of which was a top five record titled "Western Union." They later faded from national popularity.

Jan. 66	***I SEE THE LIGHT*** /HBR
Apr. 66	***EVOL—NOT LOVE*** /HBR
Mar. 67	***WESTERN UNION*** /Abnak
May 67	***THE SOUND OF LOVE*** /Abnak
Aug. 67	***ZIP CODE*** /Abnak
Jan. 68	***7:30 GUIDED TOUR*** /Abnak

The Five Man Electrical Band

MEMBERS:
Les Emmerson (lead vocals, guitar)
Theodore Gorow (keyboards, sax)
Brian Rading (bass)
Michael Belanger (percussion)
Richard Belanger (drums)
HOMETOWN: Ottawa, Ontario, Canada

This group was formed in the early sixties and spent several years building a following in Ontario. Originally known as The Staccatos, they were signed during the mid-sixties by Capitol of Canada and recorded over a dozen minor hits, the biggest of which was "Half Past Midnight."

In 1969 the group traveled to California to appear at the Whiskey A Go-Go and The Troubador and while in the area recorded an album at Capitol's Los Angeles studio. Named after one of the cuts, "The Five Man Electrical Band," the album was not successful but it gave the group a new name. They also formed an association with Los Angeles-based record producer Dallas Smith; he circulated demo tapes of the group to various record companies to find them a new label. They received a contract from Lionel Records, a division of MGM, and scored during the summer of 1971 with a chart-topping hit called "Signs" (recorded earlier, but unsuccessfully, for

Capitol. After a string of hits for this company (whose name was later shortened to Lion), the group switched affiliation to the Polydor label.

May 71 *SIGNS* /Lionel (MGM)
Oct. 71 *ABSOLUTELY RIGHT* /Lionel (MGM)
Sept. 72 *MONEY BACK GUARANTEE* / Lion
Apr. 73 *I'M A STRANGER HERE* /Lion
Mar. 74 *WEREWOLF* /Polydor

The Five Stairsteps

MEMBERS:
Aloha Burke /born: 1949
Clarence Burke, Jr. /born: 1950
James Burke /born: 1951
Dennis Burke /born: 1953
Kenneth Michael Burke /born: 1954
Cubie Burke /born: 1966/ (added in 1968)
HOMETOWN: Chicago, Illinois

The Five Stairsteps were one of the first "family groups" and the forerunners of such acts as The Jackson Five, The Robinson Family Plan, The Sylvers, and Brotherly Love. Although they began as a group of five, they brought their younger brother, Cubie, into the act when he was barely two years old!

Managed by their father, The Stairsteps began their career by entering a talent contest at Chicago's Regal Theatre. They won first prize and were seen by Curtis Mayfield, lead singer of The Impressions and a leading Chicago record producer, who was in the audience scouting talent. He took the group to the local Windy C label and produced their sessions which resulted in a number of hits on both the R & B and pop charts. In 1967 Mayfield became associated with Buddah Records, where he continued to produce hits for The Stairsteps (several ap-

peared on his own Curtom label, which Buddah distributed).

In 1970 the group began working with producer Stan Vincent under whose direction they recorded their biggest hit, "Ooh Child."

May 66 *YOU WAITED TOO LONG* / Windy C
Aug. 66 *THE WORLD OF FANTASY* / Windy C
Nov. 66 *COME BACK* /Windy C
Jan. 67 *DANGER! SHE'S A STRANGER* / Windy C
Apr. 67 *AIN'T GONNA REST* / Windy C
May 67 *OOH, BABY BABY* / Windy C
Dec. 67 *SOMETHING'S MISSING* / Buddah
Jan. 68 *A MILLION TO ONE* / Buddah
Apr. 68 *THE SHADOW OF YOUR LOVE* / Buddah
Aug. 68 *DON'T CHANGE YOUR LOVE* / Curtom
Dec. 68 *STAY CLOSE TO ME* /Curtom
Oct. 69 *WE MUST BE IN LOVE* / Curtom
Mar. 70 *DEAR PRUDENCE* /Buddah
Mar. 70 *OOH CHILD* /Buddah
Oct. 70 *AMERICA* /Buddah
Feb. 71 *DIDN'T IT LOOK SO EASY* / Buddah

Roberta Flack

BORN: Feb. 10, 1940
HOMETOWN: Asheville, North Carolina

Roberta Flack grew up in Arlington, Virginia, where her mother played church organ and her father piano. She began formal training on the piano at the age of nine. During her teens she won second prize in a state-wide piano contest and eventually won a full scholarship to Howard University in Washington, D.C., where she majored in music education. After graduation she took a teaching job in Washington and worked part-time accompanying op-

Roberta Flack

era singers at the Tivoli restaurant in the Georgetown section.

In May 1967, after three years with the Washington school system, Roberta decided on music as a full-time career and began an extended singing engagement at Mr. Henry's Pub. She developed a cult following over the years and well-known entertainers often went to catch her act. One of these was famed jazz musician Les McCann, who brought Roberta to his label, Atlantic Records, for an audition. She was signed and, in late 1969, her debut album *First Take,* was released. It became an excellent seller and was followed in 1970 by two best-selling LPs, *Chapter Two* and *Quiet Fire.* In

1971 Roberta teamed up with fellow Atlantic artist Donny Hathaway, with whom she recorded two hit singles, James Taylor's "You've Got a Friend" and the classic "You've Lost That Loving Feeling."; early in 1972 she had her first solo hit, "Will You Love Me Tomorrow." Her major breakthrough came shortly thereafter when a cut from *First Takes,* "The First Time Ever I Saw Your Face," was used in the film *Play Misty for Me.* The song was released as a single and went to number one on the charts while reactivating sales of the album. A year later Roberta followed with another number one record, "Killing Me Softly with His Song," a tune she had heard when Lori Leiberman recorded it.

Since then Roberta Flack has continued with a number of best-selling recordings and is today a leading concert attraction.

Roberta Flack
Jan. 72 *WILL YOU LOVE ME TOMORROW* / Atlantic
Mar. 72 *THE FIRST TIME EVER I SAW YOUR FACE* / Atlantic
Jan. 73 *KILLING ME SOFTLY WITH HIS SONG* / Atlantic
Sept. 73 *JESSE* / Atlantic
June 74 *FEEL LIKE MAKIN' LOVE* / Atlantic
June 75 *FEELIN' THAT GLOW* / Atlantic
Feb. 78 *THE CLOSER I GET TO YOU* / Atlantic
May 78 *IF EVER I SEE YOU AGAIN* / Atlantic
Roberta Flack & Donny Hathaway
June 71 *YOU'VE GOT A FRIEND* / Atlantic
Oct. 71 *YOU'VE LOST THAT LOVING FEELING* / Atlantic
June 72 *WHERE IS THE LOVE* / Atlantic

The Flaming Ember

MEMBERS:
Joseph Sladich (lead guitar)
William Ellis (keyboards)
James Bugnel (bass)

Jerry Plunk (drums)
HOMETOWN: Detroit, Michigan

This group began as The Flaming Embers and launched their recording career by signing with the small Detroit-based Ric-Tic label. The label was eventually absorbed by Motown Records, but Motown released no new recordings by the group.

During the late sixties the Holland-Dozier-Holland team separated from Motown and formed their own Hot Wax label. One of the first groups to be signed was The Flaming Ember (the "s" was dropped from their name in an effort to sound more contemporary). They placed several hits high on both the R & B and pop charts during the early seventies; the biggest of these was "Westbound #9."

Sept. 69 *MIND, BODY & SOUL* / Hot Wax
Jan. 70 *SHADES OF GREEN* / Hot Wax
May 70 *WESTBOUND #9* / Hot Wax
Oct. 70 *I'M NOT MY BROTHER'S KEEPER* / Hot Wax

Flash Cadillac & The Continental Kids

MEMBERS:
"Flash" Samuel McFadden (lead vocals, guitar / born: Mar, 30, 1952 / Colorado
"Spike" Lin Phillips (vocals, guitar) / born: Aug. 1, 1947 / Pennsylvania
"Butch" Warren Knight (vocals, bass) / born: Dec. 31, 1948 / Colorado
"Spider" Dwight Bement (sax) born: Dec. 28, 1940 / California
"Angelo" Chris Moe (lead vocals, keyboards) born: Dec. 26, 1949 / Colorado
"Wally" Jeff Stuart (vocals, drums) / born: July 31, 1952 / Colorado / replaced (1975) by *"Wheaty" Paul Wheatbread* / born: Feb. 8, 1946

Flash Cadillac & The Continental Kids are among the best known of several groups that emerged in the sixties and seventies to spoof the vocal and instrumental styles of the fifties.

The group was formed in 1970 by six students at the University of Colorado in Boulder, and their first job was at a fraternity party on campus. After a period of local bookings they drove to Los Angeles and landed an appearance at the famed Troubador club. As a result, they received enough bookings to quit the university and pursue music full-time. They developed a strong reputation on the college circuit as an opening act for various leading rock groups and in 1972 were signed by Epic Records. After the release of their first album, *Flash Cadillac & the Continental Kids,* they got a big break when they were asked to appear as the prom band in the film *American Graffiti.* They followed in 1974 with a second album, *There's No Face Like Chrome,* which yielded their first hit single, "Dancin' (On Saturday Night)."

In 1975 Flash & The Kids began recording for Larry Uttal's Private Stock label, where they recorded an album titled *Sons of the Beaches* and scored with their second hit single, "Good Times, Rock & Roll." They now live communally in their own house in Los Angeles.

May 74 *DANCIN' (ON A SATURDAY NIGHT)* / **Epic**
Feb. 75 *GOOD TIMES, ROCK & ROLL* / **Private Stock**
Aug. 76 *DID YOU BOOGIE (WITH YOUR BABY)* / **Private Stock**

Fleetwood Mac

MEMBERS:

Peter Green (lead guitar) / born: Oct. 29, 1946 replaced (1969) by Christine Perfect McVie / (keyboards) / born: July 12, 1943

John McVie (bass) / born: Nov. 26, 1945

Jeremy Spencer (lead guitar) / born: July 4, 1948 / replaced (1971) by Robert Welch / born: July 31, 1946 / replaced (1975) by Lindsay Buckingham / born: Oct. 3, 1947

Mick Fleetwood (drums, percussion) / born: June 24, 1942

Daniel Kirwan (lead guitar) / (added in 1968) / replaced (1973) by Robert Weston / (left in 1974)

Stevie Nicks (vocals) / born: May 26, 1948 / (added in 1975)

This British blues band began in 1967 when Peter Green left John Mayall's Bluesbreakers (where he had replaced Eric Clapton) to form his own group. The new band, known at first as Peter Green's Fleetwood Mac, was built around Mick Fleetwood, with whom Green had played in various groups during the early sixties, and John McVie, another former member of the Mayall band. They also featured Jeremy Spencer, a noted British blues guitarist.

In 1968 Fleetwood Mac made their debut appearance at the seventh National Jazz & Blues Festival in England and were offered a contract by Blue Horizon Records almost immediately. After the release of their first album, *Fleetwood Mac,* the group added a third guitarist, Danny Kirwan. It was with this line-up that late in 1968 they achieved their first British hit single, "Albatross."

In 1969 a series of personnel changes substantially changed the group's sound. Peter Green retired, and his replacement was Christine McVie (wife of John McVie and previously known to British audiences as Christine Perfect, lead singer of Chicken Shack) playing keyboards. Jeremy Spencer departed to become a member of a religious cult and recorded a solo album titled *Jeremy & Children.* Spencer eventually emerged with his own band, Albatross, named after Fleetwood Mac's hit.

Fleetwood Mac (1971). Left to right: Christine McVie, Dave Walker, Bob Welch, Mick Fleetwood, Bob Weston, John McVie

Fleetwood Mac (1975). Left to right: Lindsey Buckingham, Christine McVie, Mick Fleetwood, Stevie Nicks, John McVie

In spite of more changes, Fleetwood Mac continued as a major concert attraction with several best-selling albums, including *English Rose, Blues Jam, Then Play On, Kiln House, Future Games, Bare Trees, Penguin, Mystery to Me,* and *Heroes Are Hard to Find.* Although originally not known as a "singles" group (only one placed on the American charts before 1975), Fleetwood Mac became widely known to pop audiences in the mid-seventies with three substantial hits. Their 1977 album release, *Rumours,* has already sold over eight million units, making it the second largest selling album ever (after The Bee Gees' *Saturday Night Fever).*

Jan. 70	*OH WELL* /Reprise
Nov. 75	*OVER MY HEAD* /Warner Bros.
Mar. 76	*RHIANNON (WILL YOU EVER WIN)* /Warner Bros.
July 76	*SAY YOU LOVE ME* /Warner Bros.
Dec. 76	*GO YOUR OWN WAY* /Warner Bros.
Apr. 77	*DREAMS* /Warner Bros.
July 77	*DON'T STOP* /Warner Bros.
Oct. 77	*YOU MAKE LOVIN' FUN* /Warner Bros.

The Floaters

MEMBERS:
Ralph Mitchell (lead singer)
Charles Clark (first tenor)
Larry Cunningham (second tenor)
Paul Mitchell (baritone)
HOMETOWN: Detroit, Michigan

The group met in Detroit and began singing at local clubs and eventually touring with the Detroit Emeralds. In a short while they came to the attention of ABC Records and were signed to a recording contract. Working with Detroit Emeralds members James Mitchell, Jr., Marvin Willis, and Brimstone

Ingram—who wrote, produced, and arranged the material for their debut album—along with famed guitarist Dennis Coffey—who worked on a few of the arrangements—they produced the album *The Floaters.* From that LP came the group's debut single, "Float On," which placed them on the national charts.

July 77 *FLOAT ON* /ABC

Eddie Floyd

BORN: June 25, 1935
HOMETOWN: Montgomery, Alabama

Eddie Floyd began his professional singing career in the mid-fifties as lead singer for The Falcons, best known for their 1959 hit "You're So Fine." Managed by Floyd's uncle, they relocated in Detroit, where Joe Stubbs (brother of The Four Tops' lead singer, Levi) joined the group. During the early sixties Floyd left The Falcons for a solo career, and an unknown singer named Wilson Pickett assumed the lead spot.

During the mid-sixties Floyd's first solo release appeared on the Lupine and Safice labels. After a brief stint with Atlantic, he was signed by Stax, where his first release was "Things Get Better." It was the follow-up, however, the rock and soul classic "Knock on Wood," that established him by becoming a top thirty hit and the first of a long string of hit singles that extended into the early seventies. In addition to writing most of his own material, Floyd actively wrote for other leading Stax artists including Carla Thomas and Otis Redding. He was also responsible for one of Wilson Pickett's biggest hits, "634-5789."

At present Eddie Floyd continues to record for Stax. Although he has not

The Floaters. Left to right: Charles Clark, Ralph Mitchell, Larry Cunningham, Jonathan Murray Clark, Paul Mitchell

been active in the singles market, he has released approximately one successful album a year since 1970.

Sept. 66	*KNOCK ON WOOD*	/Stax
Feb. 67	*RAISE YOUR HAND*	/Stax
July 67	*DON'T ROCK THE BOAT*	/Stax
Aug. 67	*LOVE IS A DOGGONE THING* / Stax	
Oct. 67	*ON SATURDAY NIGHT*	/Stax
July 68	*I'VE NEVER FOUND A GIRL* / Stax	
Oct. 68	*BRING IT ON HOME TO ME* / Stax	

June 69	*DON'T TELL YOUR MAMA* / Stax	
Nov. 69	*WHY IS THE WINE SWEETER?* / Stax	
Feb. 70	*CALIFORNIA GIRL*	/Stax

King Floyd

BORN: Feb. 13, 1945
HOMETOWN: New Orleans, Louisiana

King Floyd began singing at high school talent shows and later went on to perform for troops in the service.

In 1963 while he was singing at a New Orleans club, Floyd was spotted by James Brown, who signed him to the Try Me label. Nothing was released, however, and Floyd spent the rest of the sixties recording for Capitol and Mercury-Pulsar. His breakthrough came in the early seventies, when he started recording for Chimneyville. His first release, "Groove Me," reached the national top five, and he followed with two more hits.

Today King Floyd records for Atlantic and, after a time in Los Angeles, once again makes New Orleans his home. He is also busy with session work at the famed Malaco Studios in Jackson, Mississippi.

Oct. 70 *GROOVE ME* / Chimneyville
Mar. 71 *BABY, LET ME KISS YOU* / Chimneyville
Sept. 72 *WOMAN, DON'T GO ASTRAY* / Chimneyville

The Flying Machine

Late in 1969 an English group named The Flying Machine (not to be confused with James Taylor's American group) placed a hit called "Smile a Little Smile for Me" in the American top five. The voices heard on this recording were largely those of a studio group led by producer Tony MacAuley, who also cowrote the song. However, entirely different people went on the road to tour. This group had previously been known as Pinkerton's Assorted Colours and consisted of Samuel Pinkerton Kempe, Barry Bernard, Thomas Long, and Anthony Newman. They had recorded a number of singles under their old identity during the mid-sixties and one, "Mirror, Mirror," had been a British chart hit in 1969. Later in the

year they "became" The Flying Machine.

The studio group achieved a lesser follow-up hit early in 1970, after which they vanished from the charts. The road group, although presently unaffiliated with a record company, continues to appear in England.

Oct. 69 *SMILE A LITTLE SMILE FOR ME* / Congress
Feb. 70 *BABY, MAKE IT SOON* / Congress

Focus

MEMBERS (1969–1970):
Thijs Van Leer (organ, flute)
Martin Dresden (bass)
Hans Cleuver (drums)
Jan Akkerman (guitar) / (added in 1970)

MEMBERS (post–1970):
Thijs Van Leer (organ, flute) / born: Mar. 31, 1948
Jan Akkerman (guitar, lute) / born: Dec. 24, 1946
Cyril Havermans (bass) / replaced (1971) by Bert Ruiter / born: Nov. 26, 1946
Pierre Van Der Linden (drums) / born: Feb. 19, 1946 / replaced (1973) by Colin Allen / replaced (1975) by David Kemper
HOMETOWN: Amsterdam, Holland

Focus began in 1969 as a trio formed by Thijs Van Leer, an alumnus of the Amsterdam Conservatorium. After establishing a reputation in local cabarets, they became the back-up band in the Dutch production of *Hair* and were offered a recording contract by Polydor Records. Early in 1970 the group began work on their first album, *In and out of Focus,* and were joined during these sessions by guitarist Jan Akkerman. After the album was released Akkerman re-formed his association with Pierre Van Der Linden, a drummer with whom he had played in such well known Dutch rock groups as

Dan Fogelberg

Johnny & The Cellar Rockets, The Hunters, and Brainbox. The two formed a new band and asked Thijs Van Leer to join; with that the original Focus was brought to an end. However, the new group took up the name and, after recruiting Cyril Havermans on bass, they recorded a second Focus album called *Moving Waves.* It was released simultaneously in the United States on Sire Records and was moderately successful.

In 1971 Cyril Havermans was replaced by Bert Ruiter, and it was with this line-up that the group established international success in 1973 with their hit singles of "Hocus Pocus" and "Sylvia." Focus has since undergone two more personnel changes, with charter member Pierre Van Der Linden being replaced by former Stone The Crows drummer Colin Allen; he in turn was replaced by a native Californian, David Kemper. Since 1973 Focus has not been considered a singles-oriented group; they are best known for their albums, including *Focus 3, Live at the Rainbow, Hamburger Concerto,* and *Mother Focus.* The latter two appeared in the United States on the Atlantic label.

Cyril Havermans went on to record as a solo act for the MGM label and debuted in 1973 with an album titled *Cyril.* Although he continued with Focus, Thijs Van Leer also recorded a solo LP called *Introspection;* Jan Akkerman recorded *Profile* and *Tabernakel.*

Mar. 73   *HOCUS POCUS* / Sire
July 73   *SYLVIA* / Sire

Dan Fogelberg

BORN: August 13, 1951
HOMETOWN: Peoria, Illinois

Dan Fogelberg sang with various local folk groups during high school. Although he entered the University of Illinois as an art major, he soon gave up his studies to tour the Midwest bar circuit as a solo act.

During the early 1970s Fogelberg moved to Los Angeles in search of a producer and a recording contract but found neither. Next he tried Nashville, where he became established as a session guitarist and met producer Norbert Putnam. In association with Putnam, Fogelberg recorded his first album, *Home Free,* which was released by Columbia Records and became modestly successful.

In 1974 he switched to Columbia's subsidiary Epic label and began working with rock musician and producer Joe Walsh. This association resulted in the album *Souvenirs,* which yielded Fogelberg's first hit single, "A Part of the Plan" in 1975.

Today Dan Fogelberg still lives in Nashville and tours with a back-up band called Fool's Gold.

Feb. 75 *A PART OF THE PLAN* /Epic

Foghat

MEMBERS:

Rod Price (lead guitar) / Berkshire, England

Lonesome Dave (David Peverett) (guitar) / Willisden, England

Anthony Stevens (bass) / Willisden, England, replaced (1975) by Nick Jameson / replaced (1976) by Craig MacGregor

Roger Earl (drums) / Berkshire, England

Foghat was formed in 1971 when Roger Earl, Lonesome Dave, and Tony Stevens separated from The Savoy Brown Blues Band. They auditioned for a lead guitarist and one of the first to try out, Rod Price, was hired. The group's unusual name was suggested by Lonesome Dave, who had created that word as a child during a Scrabble game and never had forgotten it.

After a rehearsal period Foghat contacted manager Tony Oteeta, whom they had met during their Savoy Brown days. Oteeta agreed to handle them and invited his friend Albert Grossman, who happened to be in London at the time, to hear them. Grossman signed them to his American Bearsville label where their first album, *Foghat,* was released during the summer of 1972. Although they followed with several chart singles, they became best known as a concert attraction and for their subsequent albums, including *Rock & Roll, Energized, Rock and Roll Outlaws,* and *Fool for the City.*

In 1975 the group settled permanently in New York. At the same time,

Tony Stevens retired and was replaced by Missouri-born Nick Jameson. Only one year later Jameson was replaced by another native American, Craig MacGregor.

Oct. 72 *I JUST WANT TO MAKE LOVE TO YOU* /Bearsville

Apr. 73 *WHAT A SHAME* /Bearsville

Dec. 75 *SLOW RIDE* /Bearsville

June 76 *FOOL FOR THE CITY* / Bearsville

Nov. 76 *DRIVIN' WHEEL* /Bearsville

Mar. 77 *I'LL BE STANDING BY* / Bearsville

Sept. 77 *I JUST WANT TO MAKE LOVE TO YOU* /Bearsville

May 78 *STONE BLUE* /Bearsville

Wayne Fontana & The Mindbenders

ORIGINAL MEMBERS:

Wayne Fontana (Glyn Geoffry Ellis) (lead vocals) / born: Oct. 28, 1945 / Manchester, England

Michael Eric Stewart, Jr (lead guitar) / born: Jan. 20, 1945 / Manchester, England

Robert F. Lang (bass) / born: Jan. 10, 1946 / Manchester, England

Ric Rothwell (drums) / born: Mar. 11, 1944 / Stockport, Cheshire, England

This group was formed in 1963 in Manchester, England, somewhat by accident.

Glyn Ellis began singing as a child and made his debut at five with a local skiffle group. By the age of eight he had his own group and played free concerts at local old-age homes. He left school at fifteen to become an apprentice telephone engineer by day and formed a group called The Jets to play small semipro club jobs at night. During the summer of 1963 Ellis learned of an audition being held by Fontana Records at the local Oasis Club and he arranged for his group to appear. Only one other member, Bob

Lang, was present and Ellis convinced two other musicians who were there, Eric Stewart and Ric Rothwell, to join him for the audition. Much to their amazement, they were signed. The company had Ellis change his name to Wayne Fontana, after the label. The name "Mindbenders" was taken from a film of that name being shown in Manchester at the time and the group's first release, Fats Domino's "My Girl Josephine," appeared late in 1963. After moderate hits with such material as Bo Diddley's "Road Runner" and Major Lance's "Um Um Um Um Um Um," Wayne Fontana & The Mindbenders scored international success with their number one recording of "Game of Love."

After one more American hit, Wayne Fontana left the group for a solo career, and the remaining members continued as The Mindbenders. They scored in 1966 with a chart-topping record called "A Groovy Kind of Love"; after one more hit they vanished from the United States charts. The group's final line-up before they disbanded in the late sixties was Eric Stewart, James O'Neil, Paul Hancox, and Graham Gouldman.

Wayne Fontana went on to become a pop singer, debuting in 1967 with an MGM album bearing his name. Eric Stewart became a member of Hotlegs, which, with the addition of Graham Gouldman, became the group now known as 10 cc. Stewart and Gouldman also operate England's famed Strawberry Studio.

See HOTLEGS; 10 cc.

Wayne Fontana & The Mindbenders

Mar. 65 *THE GAME OF LOVE*/Fontana
June 65 *IT'S JUST A LITTLE BIT TOO LATE*/Fontana

The Mindbenders

Apr. 66 *A GROOVY KIND OF LOVE*/Fontana
Aug. 66 *ASHES TO ASHES*/Fontana

Foreigner

MEMBERS:
Lou Gramm (lead vocals)/born: May 2, 1950/Rochester, New York
Mick Jones (lead guitar)/born: Dec. 27, 1944/London, England
Ian McDonald (rhythm guitar)/born: June 25, 1946/London, England
Ed Gagliardi (bass guitar)/born: Feb. 13, 1952/New York City
Al Greenwood (keyboards, synthesizer)/born: Oct. 20, 1951/New York City
Dennis Elliott (drums)/born: Aug. 18, 1950/London, England

During the early part of 1976, Mick Jones (ex-Spooky Tooth member) and Ian McDonald (ex-King Crimson member) were both living in New York and working as back-up musicians. It was while at a recording session for Ian Lloyd (ex-Stories member) that they decided to form their own group. When all the members got together they had a perfect combination of three Americans and three Englishmen, combining a new sound with two countries.

They chose the name Foreigner and began practicing to get their sound to one cohesive unit. Jerry Greenberg of Atlantic Records signed them to a recording contract. By November of 1976 they recorded the label's debut album, *Foreigner,* from which came their hit single, "Feels Like the First Time."

Mar. 77 *FEELS LIKE THE FIRST TIME*/Atlantic
July 77 *COLD AS ICE*/Atlantic
Dec. 77 *LONG, LONG WAY FROM HOME*/Atlantic

Foreigner. Left to right: Ian McDonald, Mick Jones, Lou Gramm, Al Greenwood, Ed Gagliardi, Dennis Elliott

The Fortunes

MEMBERS:

Barry Pritchard (lead guitar) / born: Aprl 3, 1944 / Birmingham, England

Glen Dale (Glenn Garforth) (rhythm guitar) / born: Apr. 2, 1943 / Deal, Kent, England

Rod Allen (Rod Bainbridge) (bass) / (born: Mar. 31, 1944 / Leicester, England

David Carr (keyboards) / born: Aug. 4, 1943 / Leyton, Essex, England

Andrew Brown (drums) / born: Jan. 7, 1946 / Birmingham, England

The Fortunes were formed during the early sixties, largely through the efforts of Reg Calvert, owner of a string of dance halls in northern England.

Barry Pritchard and Rod Allen attended school together in Birmingham, where they formed a duo to play local clubs. After three years of moderate success they auditioned for Calvert and began appearing regularly at his halls. Calvert teamed them with Glen Dale, a solo singer whom he had under contract, and the trio gained experience as a back-up group for other acts.

Late in 1963 they traveled to London to begin their recording career. They added Andy Brown, a friend of the group's, and Dave Carr, who was brought to their attention by Brian Poole of Tremeloes fame, and recorded their first successful single, "Caroline." The song was used by British Radio Caroline as a station signature and brought the group a great deal of attention, paving the way for the major success of their next release, "You've Got Your Troubles." In addition to being an international hit for The Fortunes, it was the first substantial success for the songwriting team of Roger Cook and Roger Greenaway (see *DAVID & JONATHAN*).

After another major hit with "Here It

177

Comes Again'' and a moderately successful follow-up, ''This Golden Ring,'' the group faded from popularity for a number of years. However, they scored again during the early seventies with another Cook-Greenaway song, ''Here Comes That Rainy Day Feeling Again.''

Aug. 65	*YOU'VE GOT YOUR TROUBLES* / Press
Nov. 65	*HERE IT COMES AGAIN* / Press
Feb. 66	*THIS GOLDEN RING* / Press
May 70	*THAT SAME OLD FEELING* / World Pacific
May 71	*HERE COMES THAT RAINY DAY FEELING AGAIN* / Capitol
Oct. 71	*FREEDOM COMES, FREEDOM GOES* / Capitol

The Foundations

MEMBERS:

Clem Curtis (lead vocals) / born: Nov. 28, 1940, replaced by Colin Young / born: Sept. 12, 1944 / Barbados, West Indies

Allan Warner (lead guitar) / born: Apr. 21, 1947 / London, England

Eric Allendale (trombone) / born: Mar. 4, 1936 / Dominican Republic

Peter Macbeth (bass) / born: Feb. 2, 1943 / London, England

Pat Burke (sax, flute) / born: Oct. 9, 1937 / Kingston, Jamaica

Anthony Gomez (keyboards) / born: Dec. 13, 1948 / Colombo, Ceylon

Tim Harris (drums) / born: Jan. 14, 1948 / Paddington, England

Michael Elliott (sax) / (left in 1969)

The members of this group were born in various parts of the world and migrated individually to England. After each had gained experience in other groups they came together as The Foundations during the mid-to-late sixties and, with a style reminiscent of the American ''Motown sound,'' became a major British entry on the soul market.

The group was signed in 1967 by the British Pye label and, in association with producers Tony MacAuley and John Macleod, recorded a two-year string of hits beginning with ''Baby, Now That I've Found You.'' Their records were released in the United States on the Uni label and most became sizable American hits as well.

Dec. 67	*BABY, NOW THAT I'VE FOUND YOU* / Uni
Mar. 68	*BACK ON MY FEET AGAIN* / Uni
Jan. 69	*BUILD ME UP, BUTTERCUP* / Uni
Apr. 69	*IN THE BAD OLD DAYS* / Uni
July 69	*MY LITTLE CHICKADEE* / Uni

Four Jacks & a Jill

MEMBERS:

Jill (Glenys Lynne) (lead vocals)

Bruce Bark (lead guitar, harmonica, sax)

Till Hannamann (rhythm guitar, trumpet, keyboards)

Clive Harding (bass)

Anthony Hughes (drums)

This group originated in South Africa and began in 1964 as a four-man band called The Nevadas. After a relative lack of success they patterned themselves after The Beatles by growing their hair and changing their name to The Zombies (no relation to the Rod Argent group from England), and their bookings began to increase rapidly. At one of their appearances they met Glenys Lynne, who joined the group and prompted them to change their name to Four Jacks & a Jill.

By 1967 they had become well known in South Africa and were signed to a recording contract. One of their first releases, ''Timothy,'' reached the top of the charts in South Africa and was followed by ''Master Jack,'' which was released in the United States on the RCA label and placed high on the American charts. After another Ameri-

The Four Seasons. Left to right: Gerry Polci, Don Ciccone, Lee Shapiro, John Paiva

can hit, "Mr. Nico," the group's popularity was confined mainly to their home country.

| Mar. 68 | *MASTER JACK* /RCA |
| Aug. 68 | *MISTER NICO* /RCA |

The Four Seasons

MEMBERS:

Frankie Valli (lead vocals) / born: May 3, 1937 / Newark, New Jersey

John Paiva (guitar)

Don Ciccone (bass guitar) / born: 1947 / Plainfield, New Jersey

Bob Gaudio (keyboards) / born: Nov. 17, 1942 / Newark, New Jersey

Lee Shapiro (keyboards)

Gerry Polci (vocals, drums)

After singing with the original Four Seasons from 1962 to 1969 (see *Rock On: The Solid Gold Years*), Frankie Valli formed an entirely new group. Using Bob Gaudio, an original member, for studio work only, they recorded new material and sold it to Warner / Curb Records in 1975. Their first LP for the label, called *Who Loves You,* produced their first hit in years—a disco number that Gaudio wrote and the title song of the album. It was followed by "December, 1963 (Oh, What a Night)," another Gaudio tune that became a number one national hit, the group's first since "Rag Doll" in 1964. In October 1977 Frankie Valli left the group to perform solo.

Aug. 75	*WHO LOVES YOU /* Warner/Curb
Dec. 75	*DECEMBER, 1963 (OH, WHAT A NIGHT)* /Warner/Curb
May 76	*SILVER STAR* /Warner/Curb
July 77	*DOWN THE HALL /* Warner/Curb

The Four Tops

MEMBERS:
Levi Stubbs (lead vocals)
Abdul "Duke" Fakir (back-up vocals)
Renaldo "Obie" Benson (back-up vocals)
Lawrence Payton (back-up vocals)
HOMETOWN: Detroit, Michigan

The Four Tops met at a high-school party in Detroit in 1954. All had had previous experience singing in neighborhood groups, and when they began harmonizing at the party the reaction was so good that they decided to officially join forces. Known as The Four Aims, they began to work small clubs around Detroit and Cleveland.

In 1956 they were signed by Chess Records, and their first release, "Kiss Me Baby," under their new name, was a minor regional success. They spent the following years switching labels, recording for Red Top, Singular, Riverside, and Columbia, but with no success (one of their Columbia recordings, "Ain't That Love," was rereleased after their later success and briefly made the charts). Their turning point came in 1963, when they were asked by an old friend from Detroit, Berry Gordy, to join his Motown label. Their first release was a jazz-oriented album, *Breaking Through,* on the subsidiary Workshop label, and they spent a year on national tour with Billy Eckstine to promote the jazz image. However, when they returned to Detroit it was decided to switch the group to the parent label and to establish them as a pop act.

In 1964 The Four Tops began working with the team of Holland, Dozier, and Holland, who had become established with Mary Wells, The Supremes, and other Motown acts. Their initial release was "Baby, I need Your Loving,"

which reached the top ten and was the first of more than two dozen hits the group recorded for Motown.

In 1972 The Four Tops signed with the ABC/Dunhill label, where they have continued to make hits.

Aug. 64	*BABY, I NEED YOUR LOVING*/Motown
Nov. 64	*WITHOUT THE ONE YOU LOVE*/Motown
Feb. 65	*ASK THE LONELY*/Motown
May 65	*I CAN'T HELP MYSELF*/Motown
July 65	*IT'S THE SAME OLD SONG*/Motown
July 65	*AIN'T THAT LOVE*/Columbia
Nov. 65	*SOMETHING ABOUT YOU*/Motown
Feb. 66	*SHAKE ME, WAKE ME*/Motown
May 66	*LOVING YOU IS SWEETER THAN EVER*/Motown
Sept. 66	*REACH OUT, I'LL BE THERE*/Motown
Dec. 66	*STANDING IN THE SHADOWS OF LOVE*/Motown
Mar. 67	*BERNADETTE*/Motown
May 67	*SEVEN ROOMS OF GLOOM*/Motown
July 67	*I'LL TURN TO STONE*/Motown
Sept. 67	*YOU KEEP RUNNING AWAY*/Motown
Feb. 68	*WALK AWAY RENEE*/Motown
Apr. 68	*IF I WERE A CARPENTER*/Motown
July 68	*YESTERDAY'S DREAMS*/Motown
Oct. 68	*I'M IN A DIFFERENT WORLD*/Motown
May 69	*WHAT IS A MAN*/Motown
Dec. 69	*DON'T LET HIM TAKE YOUR LOVE FROM ME*/Motown
Apr. 70	*IT'S ALL IN THE GAME*/Motown
Aug. 70	*STILL WATER*/Motown
Jan. 71	*JUST SEVEN NUMBERS*/Motown
July 71	*IN THESE CHANGING TIMES*/Motown
Sept. 71	*McARTHUR PARK*/Motown
Feb. 72	*A SIMPLE GAME*/Motown
Sept. 72	*IT'S THE WAY NATURE PLANNED IT*/Motown

The Four Tops. Left to right: Duke Fakir, Lawrence Payton, Levi Stubbs, Obie Benson

Nov. 72	*KEEPER OF THE CASTLE /* Dunhill	**May 75**	*SEVEN LONELY NIGHTS /* Dunhill
Feb. 73	*AIN'T NO WOMAN LIKE THE ONE I GOT /* Dunhill	**Dec. 75**	*WE ALL GOTTA STICK TOGETHER /* ABC/Dunhill
June 73	*ARE YOU MAN ENOUGH? /* Dunhill	**Oct. 76**	*CATFISH /* ABC
Oct. 73	*SWEET UNDERSTANDING LOVE /* Dunhill		
Jan. 74	*I JUST CAN'T GET YOU OUT OF MY MIND /* Dunhill		
May 74	*ONE CHAIN DON'T MAKE NO PRISON /* Dunhill		
Aug. 74	*MIDNIGHT FLOWER /* Dunhill		

Peter Frampton

BORN: Apr. 22, 1950
HOMETOWN: Beckenham, Kent, England

Frampton began his career during the late sixties as part of two different

Peter Frampton

English rock bands—The Herd and Humble Pie.

By 1971 he had decided to solo and made several worthwhile LPs. In 1975 he recorded an album for A & M records called *Frampton,* which made a major impact in the United States. Frampton and his United States manager, Dee Anthony, then negotiated a better contract with the record company. Next came the smash LP *Frampton Comes Alive* from which the hit single "Show Me the Way" was taken. The album not only sold over seven million copies but gave Frampton superstar status. With the hit records and the lead role of Billy Shears in the movie version of *Sgt. Pepper's Lonely Hearts Club Band,* he is well on his way to becoming one of rock's major forces.

Feb. 76 *SHOW ME THE WAY* / **A & M**
June 76 *BABY I LOVE YOUR WAY* / **A & M**

Sept. 76 *DO YOU FEEL* / A & M
May 77 *I'M IN YOU* / A & M
Aug. 77 *SIGNED, SEALED AND DELIVERED* / A & M
Dec. 77 *TRIED TO LOVE* / A & M

Nov. 67 *JUDY IN DISGUISE (WITH GLASSES)* / Paula
Mar. 68 *HEY HEY BUNNY* / Paula

John Fred & His Playboy Band

MEMBERS:
John Fred (lead vocals, harmonica) / born: May 8, 1941
Andrew Bernard (sax)
Ronald Goodson (trumpet)
Charles Spinosa (trumpet)
James O'Rourke (guitar)
Harold Cowart (bass)
Thomas De Generes (keyboards)
Joseph Miceli (drums, percussion)
HOMETOWN: Baton Rouge, Louisiana

Originally known as John Fred & His Playboys, this group was formed during the late fifties and was one of the first southern rock bands to achieve national popularity. They scored in 1959 with a minor hit called "Shirley" on the Montel label. Their popularity for the next several years centered in their native Louisiana.

In 1967 the group was signed by the Shreveport-based Paula label and recorded an album, *John Fred & His Playboys.* After changing their name to include the "Playboy Band," they released a second album, *Agnes English,* which yielded a single called "Judy in Disguise (With Glasses)." This parody of The Beatles' "Lucy in the Sky With Diamonds" was a bubblegum rocker that reached number one and remained on the national charts for nearly four months. After another hit single, "Hey Hey Bunny," and an album, *Permanently Stated,* the group's following remained primarily in the South, where they continue to be active today.

Freddie & The Dreamers

MEMBERS:
Fred Garrity (lead vocals) / born: Nov. 14, 1940
Derek Quinn (lead guitar) / born: May 24, 1942
Roy Crewdson (rhythm guitar) / born: May 29, 1941
Peter Birrell (bass) / born: May 9, 1941
Bernard Dwyer (drums) / born: Sept. 11, 1940
HOMETOWN: Manchester, England

This group was formed in 1961 by Fred Garrity, a milkman who had played in a skiffle band as a teen-ager in the late fifties and had had musical aspirations ever since. He organized a group of his friends from other local bands, and they established a reputation by playing the area's clubs on evenings and weekends. The group auditioned for an appearance on "Let's Go," a BBC television program in 1961, and the resulting exposure led to a contract from the British Columbia label in 1962.

In 1963 Freddie & The Dreamers became a resident band at the Top Ten Club in Hamburg, Germany, where many important English groups, including The Beatles, were also launching their careers. During that year they scored with three top ten English chart entries, including James Ray's hit "If You Gotta Make a Fool of Somebody," "I'm Telling You Now," and "You Were Made for Me." They continued in 1964 with "Over You," "I Love You Baby," and "I Understand," but their biggest success came the next year when, following the American success of The Beatles, both the

Freddie & The Dreamers

Tower and the Mercury labels obtained United States distribution rights to these records, and several placed high on the American charts. The group also scored with "Do the Freddie," a dance record especially created to promote Fred Garrity's unique stage antics.

Although they did not appear on the United States singles charts after the summer of 1965, the group continued selling in the album market with *Freddie & The Dreamers, Do the Freddie, Frantic Freddie, Fun Lovin' Freddie,* and *Seaside Swingers,* (a soundtrack LP for a feature film in which they appeared in 1966). The group was later seen in a second film called *Cuckoo Patrol.*

During the late sixties and early seventies Freddie & The Dreamers remained active with personal appearances on the British resort circuit, and a number of moderately successful recordings were released in England. At present Fred Garrity is seen regularly on British children's television programs.

Mar. 65	**I'M TELLING YOU NOW /**	
	Tower	
Mar. 65	**I UNDERSTAND / Mercury**	
Apr. 65	**DO THE FREDDIE / Mercury**	
May 65	**YOU WERE MADE FOR ME /**	
	Tower	
July 65	**A LITTLE YOU / Mercury**	

Free

ORIGINAL MEMBERS:

Paul Rodgers (lead vocals) / born: Dec. 17, 1949 / Middlesborough, Yorkshire, England

Paul Kossoff (guitar) / born: Sept. 14, 1950 / Hempstead, England

Andrew Fraser (bass) / hometown: London, England

Simon Frederick Kirke (drums) / born: July 28, 1949 / Shropshire, England

This group was formed in the late sixties by Paul Rodgers and Paul Kossoff, who became acquainted on the London blues-club circuit. They recruited drummer Simon Kirke and bassist Andy Fraser (a former member of John Mayall's Bluesbreakers) and began rehearsing the new band late in 1967. Veteran bandleader Alexis Korner worked with them, suggested the name Free, and arranged for their debut in 1968. After a number of major bookings and a period of residency at London's famed Marquee Club, the group was signed by Chris Blackwell's Island label, and arrangements were made with A & M Records for the American distribution of their records.

In 1969 Free recorded two albums, *Tons of Sobs* and *Free*, which sold moderately well, but it was their third album, *Fire and Water,* which brought them international attention the following year. They also scored in 1970 with two hit singles, "All Right Now" and "Stealer," and closed the year with the release of another LP called *Highway.* After recording the *Live Free* album in 1971, personality differences developed and the group disbanded before year's end. Rodgers and Fraser each formed their own bands while Kirke and Kossoff made an album with two musician friends, Tetsu Yamauchi and John "Rabbit" Bundrick.

After their individual projects failed, the four members regrouped briefly to record an album called *Free at Last.* Then Andy Fraser left in 1972 to join Sharks and was replaced by the group's former two associates, Yamauchi and Bundrick. Next to quit was Paul Kossoff, and Free recorded a final album, *Heartbreaker,* largely without him. He was briefly replaced by guitarist Wendell Richardson (formerly with Osibisa). The departure of Tetsu Yamauchi, who joined Faces, proved to be the final blow.

Free formally disbanded late in 1973, and Paul Rodgers and Simon Kirke went on to form the highly successful group Bad Company.

See *BAD COMPANY.*

Aug. 70	**ALL RIGHT NOW / A & M**	
Nov. 70	**STEALER / A & M**	

The Free Movement

MEMBERS:

Godoy Colbert / born: 1939

Claude Jefferson

Adrian Jefferson / born: 1939

Cheryl Conley / born: 1939

Jennifer Gates

Josephine Brown

HOMETOWN: Los Angeles, California

This vocal sextet was formed in 1970 in the Los Angeles area. They met when several of the group's members, who came from various parts of the country, were all in California seeking musical careers.

In 1971 they circulated demo tapes of their material to various record companies, and as a result were asked to record for Decca. There, in association with producer Joe Porter, they recorded "I've Found Someone of My Own," which reached the top five during the fall of 1971. After their initial success they switched to the Columbia label, where they scored with a lesser hit later in the year.

May 71 *I'VE FOUND SOMEONE OF MY OWN*/**Decca**
Dec. 71 *THE HARDER I TRY*/**Columbia**

Friend & Lover

REAL NAMES: James and Cathy Post

Friend & Lover became a team during the summer of 1964, when they married—one month after meeting at a state fair in Edmonton, Alberta, Canada. Both had had some prior musical experience; Cathy had sung and danced in a chorus line, and Jimmie had been the lead singer with a group called The Rum Runners.

The duo made their debut at the Playboy Club in Atlanta, Georgia, then toured nationally with The Buckinghams. They soon went out on their own, however, and were introduced to MGM's Jerry Schoenbaum while performing at The Earl of Old Town in Chicago. Their first release, "Reach out of the Darkness," on Verve Records (a division of MGM) became a top ten record during the summer of 1968. They followed with a lesser hit several

months later, then faded from national popularity.

May 68 *REACH OUT OF THE DARKNESS*/**Verve/Forecast**
Aug. 68 *IF LOVE IS IN YOUR HEART*/**Verve/Forecast**

The Friends of Distinction

MEMBERS:
Floyd Lawrence Butler/born: June 5, 1941/San Diego, California
Harry James Elston/born: Nov. 4, 1938/Dallas, Texas
Jessica Cleaves/born: Dec. 10, 1948/Los Angeles, California
Barbara Jean Love/born: July 24, 1941/(left group in 1971) Los Angeles, California

The Friends of Distinction were formed in Los Angeles during the late sixties by Floyd Butler and Harry Elston, two vocalists who had met at San Diego City College. Following a stint in the armed forces, they joined a group called The Hi Fi's, which also included Marilyn McCoo and LaMonte McLemore. This group disbanded after some inconsequential recordings and a tour with the Ray Charles revue, and McCoo and McLemore went on to reform the group as The Fifth Dimension (see *THE FIFTH DIMENSION*). Butler and Elston were determined to form another group and recruited Jessica Cleaves and Barbara Love, two friends also seeking musical careers.

After a rehearsal period, The Friends of Distinction came to the attention of Jim Brown, the former football star, who was representing an organization seeking investments in up-and-coming new talent. With this assistance, they recorded demonstration tapes of their material and sent them to various record-company executives. The group was signed by RCA Records late in 1968 and soon began recording a string of hits which lasted into the early 70s.

In 1971 Barbara Love retired, and the group continued for a time as a trio. However, they eventually disbanded and Jessica Cleaves went on to join Earth, Wind & Fire.

Apr. 69	***GRAZING IN THE GRASS* / RCA**
July 69	***LET YOURSELF GO* / RCA**
Aug. 69	***GOING IN CIRCLES* / RCA**
Mar. 70	***LOVE OR LET ME BE LONELY* / RCA**
Oct. 70	***TIME WAITS FOR NO ONE* / RCA**
Jan. 71	***I NEED YOU* / RCA**

Frijid Pink

MEMBERS:

Thomas Beaudry (lead vocals) / Wyandotte, Michigan / replaced by Jon Wearing

Gary Ray Thompson (lead guitar) / Wyandotte, Michigan / replaced by Craig Webb

Lawrence Zelanka (keyboards)

Thomas Earl Harris (bass) / Florence, Alabama

Richard Stevers (drums) / Detroit, Michigan

Frijid Pink was organized during the late sixties by Tom Beaudry and Gary Thompson, two Michigan high school friends. The remainder of the group was recruited from local musicians (Tom Harris had moved from Alabama to nearby Melvindale, Michigan).

They emerged in 1970 on the Parrot label with a raucous, heavy-metal sound, saturated in echo. Their first and biggest hit, a remake of The Animals' "House of the Rising Sun," reached the top ten early in the year and was followed by two lesser hits. Their debut album, *Frijid Pink,* was also released that year and sold well.

In 1972, after a period of inactivity, the group reemerged on MGM's subsidiary Lion label. They have since been better known for their albums, including *Earth Omen* and *All Pink Inside.*

Feb. 70	***THE HOUSE OF THE RISING SUN* / Parrot**
July 70	***SING A SONG FOR FREEDOM* / Parrot**
Dec. 70	***HEARTBREAK HOTEL* / Parrot**

Lefty Frizzell

REAL NAME: William Orville Frizzell
BORN: Mar. 31, 1928
DIED: July 19, 1975, Nashville, Tennessee
HOMETOWN: Corsicana, Texas

William "Lefty" Frizzell was the son of an itinerant Texas oil driller. His nickname was derived from his abilities as a backroom boxer in Texas beer halls, where he was exposed to the "honky tonk" style of country music. He began singing as a teen-ager and by the forties had developed enough of a reputation to be offered a contract by Columbia Records.

During the early and mid-fifties Frizzell developed into a leading country artist and songwriter with a number of major hits in both capacities. His popularity continued well into the sixties, and in 1964 his recording of "Saginaw, Michigan" climbed to the top of the country charts and crossed over as a pop hit as well.

In 1974, after a period of relative inactivity, Frizzell was signed by ABC Records and began recording in association with producer Don Gant. However, he passed away the following year, at forty-seven, as the result of a stroke.

Jan. 64	***SAGINAW, MICHIGAN* / Columbia**

The Bobby Fuller Four

MEMBERS:

Robert Fuller (lead vocals, guitar)/born: Oct. 22, 1943/Baytown, Texas/died: July 18, 1966/Los Angeles, California

Randy Fuller (rhythm guitar)

DeWayne Quirico (bass)/replaced by Dalton Powell

James Reese (drums)

HOMETOWN: El Paso, Texas

Bobby Fuller was raised in the same general area of Texas that yielded the famed "Tex-Mex" sound of Buddy Holly & The Crickets. His parents later moved to El Paso, where Fuller formed his own group (which included his younger brother Randy) in the early sixties. They spent nearly three years as one of El Paso's leading teen-age dance bands but eventually relocated to Los Angeles in search of a recording contract. They established a reputation in the area's clubs with a sound reminiscent of The Crickets and made a few inconsequential recordings on small labels before being signed by disc jockey Bob Keene to his Mustang label.

The group's first release, "Let Her Dance," established them by becoming a southwestern regional best seller. However, it was their next recording, "I Fought the Law" (written by Sonny Curtis, a former member of The Crickets) that brought them national success by reaching the top ten. After an album of the same name, featuring mostly original material, the group followed with Buddy Holly's composition "Love's Made a Fool of You," which was another major hit. Soon Bobby Fuller made his film debut as the costar of *Bikini Party in a Haunted House,* and the group seemed destined for big success. However, Fuller's career came to an abrupt end when he was found asphyxiated in his car at his Hollywood home, having reportedly taken his own life. The group attempted to continue as The Randy Fuller Four, but with no success.

Randy Fuller eventually returned to Texas, where he plays in a country-rock band called Predictions.

Jan. 66 *I FOUGHT THE LAW*/Mustang
Apr. 66 *LOVE'S MADE A FOOL OF YOU*/Mustang

Funkadelic

MEMBERS:

Edward Hazel (lead guitar, vocals)

Lucas Tunia "Tawl" Ross (guitar)

Bernard Worrell (guitar)

Mickey Atkins (keyboards)

William Nelson, Jr. (bass, vocals)/replaced (1972) by Prakash John

Ramon "Tiki" Fulwood (drums, vocals)/replaced (1972) by Tyrone Lampkin

Funkadelic evolved in 1969 from an earlier group called The Parliaments. During the late sixties and early seventies they worked under the direction of George Clinton, a founding member of The Parliaments, and recorded a string of hits for the Detroit-based Westbound label. At the same time the identical personnel recorded for Holland-Dozier's Invictus label as Parliament and also made an occasional record as Parliament Thang.

After deciding on Parliament as their principal identity, the group changed affiliation to Casablanca Records and achieved a string of hits during the mid-seventies.

See *THE PARLIAMENTS.*

Funkadelic
Oct. 69 *I'LL BET YOU*/Westbound
Mar. 70 *I GOT A THANG*/Westbound
Aug. 70 *I WANNA KNOW IF IT'S GOOD TO YOU*/Westbound

Funkadelic

Apr. 71 **YOU AND YOUR FOLKS /**
Westbound
Sept. 71 **CAN YOU GET TO THAT? /**
Westbound
Nov. 75 **BETTER BY THE POUND /**
Westbound

Parliament

Aug. 74 **UP FOR THE DOWN STROKE /**
Casablanca
June 75 **CHOCOLATE CITY / Casablanca**
May 76 **TEAR THE ROOF OFF THE**
SUCKER / Casablanca

Gallery

MEMBERS:
Jim Gold (lead vocals, guitar)
Dennis Kovaricky (bass guitar, vocals)
Fred DiCenso (guitar, vocals)
Carl Freeman (steel guitar)
Danny Brucato (drums)
HOMETOWN: Detroit, Michigan

In the early seventies, Jim Gold was working in Detroit as a welder in the daytime and in the evening playing with a trio in a cocktail lounge. One evening Dennis Coffey and Mike Theodore, a couple of veterans of the music industry, came into the club and heard Gold's trio. They liked Gold's voice and decided to sign him. They went into a studio and recorded a tune called "Nice to Be with You," which was then released on Sussex Records. The song went on to become a national hit.

Gold was then asked to assemble a group, since the musicians used on the recording were only studio musicians. Gold got his friend Dennis, who was the only one used in the original session, along with three other Detroit musicians and formed Gallery.

Feb. 72   ***NICE TO BE WITH YOU /***
       Sussex

Aug. 72   ***I BELIEVE IN MUSIC /***
       Sussex

Jan. 73   ***BIG CITY MISS RUTH ANN /***
       Sussex

Art Garfunkel

BORN: Oct. 13, 1942
HOMETOWN: New York City

Art Garfunkel achieved fame during the late sixties as half of Simon & Garfunkel.

After their separation early in 1971 Paul Simon continued as a solo act while Garfunkel concentrated instead on an acting career. He appeared in *Catch 22* and *Carnal Knowledge,* both directed by Mike Nichols (Simon & Garfunkel had earlier scored Nichols's *The Graduate).*

In 1973 Garfunkel recorded his first solo album, *Angel Clare.* He also achieved a series of hit singles, all composed by other leading popwriters; "All I Know" was provided by Jim Webb, "I Shall Sing" by Van Morrison, and "Second Avenue" by Tim Moore. (Garfunkel was never a songwriter, and, with the exception of "Scarborough Fair," all of Simon & Garfunkel's original material was credited to Simon.)

Late in 1975 Simon and Garfunkel announced an arrangement by which each would continue his solo career while occasionally recording together. They began by collaborating on their first hit recording in nearly five years, titled "My Little Town." Garfunkel's recording of "Wonderful World" utilized the voices of James Taylor and Paul Simon.

Art Garfunkel

See *SIMON & GARFUNKEL.*

Sept. 73	*ALL I KNOW* / Columbia
Dec. 73	*I SHALL SING* / Columbia
Sept. 74	*SECOND AVENUE* / Columbia
Dec. 75	*BREAK AWAY* / Columbia
Jan. 78	*WONDERFUL WORLD* / Columbia

Gale Garnett

Gale Garnett entered show business in the early sixties as a television actress and was best known for her regular appearances on ''Bonanza.''

After a period of unemployment Gale began supporting herself by reciting poetry and singing in Los Angeles-area coffeehouses. She also developed a local reputation as a singer with a group known as The Gentle Reign.

In 1964 Gale came to the attention of executives at RCA Records, who invited her to audition in Las Vegas. She was signed and debuted with a top five single called "We'll Sing in the Sunshine." After recording a successful follow-up single and a number of albums, Gale faded from the national charts and returned to acting.

Aug. 64 *WE'LL SING IN THE SUNSHINE /RCA*
Dec. 64 *LOVING PLACE /RCA*

Leif Garrett

BORN: Nov. 8, 1961
HOMETOWN: Hollywood, California

Leif began his career as an actor at age five and has recently appeared in the three *Walking Tall* films and *Macon County Line,* along with many TV appearances, including "Gunsmoke," "Cannon," "Family Affair" and "Three for the Road."

In early 1977 he decided to pursue a singing career and signed with Atlantic Records, becoming their youngest artist. He got together with producer Michael Lloyd, who chose the songs, and recorded an album filled with oldies and a few original tunes.

Aug. 77 *SURFIN' USA /Atlantic*
Nov. 77 *RUNAROUND SUE /Atlantic*
Mar. 78 *PUT YOUR HEAD ON MY SHOULDER /Atlantic*
Apr. 78 *THE WANDERER /Atlantic*

David Gates

BORN: Dec. 11, 1940
HOMETOWN: Tulsa, Oklahoma

David Gates began studying violin at age four, the piano at five, and the ukulele at ten. He became proficient on the guitar during his early teens.

In 1961 he moved to Los Angeles to break into the record business as a session musician. He often played alongside such future rock luminaries as Glen Campbell and Leon Russell and gained arranging experience while working with The Ventures, Duane Eddy, Bobby Darin, Buck Owens, and Merle Haggard. He also wrote lead sheets and cut demo records for Metric Music (Liberty Records' publishing company) by day and played guitar in local clubs at night.

By 1963 Gates had expanded into songwriting and record production and had achieved commercial success with recordings by The Girlfriends ("My One and Only Jimmy Boy") and The Murmaids ("Popsicle & Icicles"). His production activities also brought him together with a group called Pleasure Faire, which he eventually joined. In 1969 this group evolved into Bread, one of the largest-selling recording acts of the late sixties and early seventies. After the temporary dispersal of Bread, beginning in 1973, Gates embarked on a solo career and achieved a number of successful singles and albums. Bread officially reunited as a group during the summer of 1976.

See *BREAD.*

July 73 *CLOUDS /Elektra*
Oct. 73 *SAIL AROUND THE WORLD / Elektra*
Jan. 75 *NEVER LET HER GO /Elektra*
Dec. 77 *GOODBYE GIRL /Elektra*

Crystal Gayle

HOMETOWN: Wabash, Indiana

Crystal's musical interests were originally in the "country" field be-

Crystal Gayle

cause of her older sister, the popular Loretta Lynn. In fact, Crystal along with Loretta and sister Peggy Sue performed as the Loretta Lynn Sisters. After a while Crystal started leaning toward the pop music scene, eventually leaving the trio to go on her own. Older sister Loretta wrote a song for her called "I Cried the Blue Right Out of My Eyes," which went on to become her first hit.

In 1973, Crystal signed with United Artists Records and started turning out the kinds of songs that got her all kinds of national exposure and the title "The Most Promising Country Female Vocalist of 1975."

In 1977 she recorded the album *We Must Believe in Magic,* from which came her biggest pop single ever, "Don't It Make My Brown Eyes Blue."

July 76	***I'LL GET OVER YOU*/United Artists**
Aug. 77	***DON'T IT MAKE MY BROWN EYES BLUE*/United Artists**
Feb. 78	***READY FOR THE TIMES TO GET BETTER*/ United Artists**

Gloria Gaynor

BORN: Sept. 7, 1949
HOMETOWN: Newark, New Jersey

Gloria Gaynor began her professional singing career at the Cadillac club around the corner from her Newark home. She sang along with the group onstage, Soul Satisfied, when they broke into Nancy Wilson's "Save Your Love for Me." The audience reaction was so favorable that the group hired her as featured vocalist. They spent the next year and a half playing New York area discotheques and supper clubs.

Gloria retired briefly after the death of her mother but eventually began singing again and joined a group known as The Soul Messengers. Soon she was heard by manager Jay Ellis, who got her a contract with Columbia Records. He also collaborated with producer Paul Leka on her first recording, "Honey Bee," which became a major discotheque hit but failed to make a showing on the national charts.

In 1974, after a change of affiliation to MGM, Gloria achieved her first major success with her disco treatment of The Jackson Five's "Never Can Say Goodbye" (written by Clifton Davis, star of TV and theater). After a string of similar hits Gloria became known as "the queen of the discotheques" and continues to tour on the disco circuit.

Nov. 74 *NEVER CAN SAY GOODBYE/MGM*
Mar. 75 *REACH OUT, I'LL BE THERE/MGM*
June 75 *WALK ON BY/MGM*
Oct. 75 *DO IT YOURSELF/MGM*
Nov. 75 *HOW HIGH THE MOON/MGM*

David Geddes

HOMETOWN: Michigan

At the age of sixteen, David put together a band known as Rock Garden with some of his neighborhood friends and remained as their drummer for about five years. After a few moderately popular singles for Capitol Records the group broke up, with David going off to college. After a while he tried a comeback by recording one song for Buddah as a solo performer, but returned to Wayne State in the fall of 1973.

In early 1975 he made one more attempt to record with "Run Joey Run," a song that quickly raced up the pop charts to become a top-ten hit.

Aug. 75 *RUN JOEY RUN/Big Tree*
Nov. 75 *THE LAST GAME OF THE SEASON/Big Tree*

J. Geils Band

MEMBERS:
Peter Wolf (vocals)/born: Mar. 7, 1946
J. Geils (guitar)/born: Feb. 20, 1946
Seth Justman (keyboards)
Magic Dick (mouth harp)/born: May 13, 1945
Daniel Klein (bass)
Stephen Jo Bladd (drums, percussion)
HOMETOWN: Boston, Massachusetts

This group was formed in the late sixties, originally as The J. Geils Blues Band. The members came from various cities along the East Coast and met on the Boston club circuit where they began working together. (Peter Wolf and Steve Bladd had worked together earlier in a band called Hallucinations.)

Almost all of J. Geils's members collected vintage R & B blues, and rock 'n' roll records, and the group soon

Geils. Left to right: J. Geils, Magic Dick, Seth Justman, Peter Wolf, Stephen Jo Bladd, Danny Klein

developed a strong reputation in New England with a sound fusing all these styles. Although Wolf and Justman provided some original material, much of their early repertoire was drawn from artists like Sam Cooke, Little Richard, Muddy Waters, and B. B. King.

In 1971 The J. Geils Band was spotted by executives of Atlantic Records while performing with Dr. John. They were signed and their first album, *J. Geils Band,* was soon released. Although they have achieved occasional hit singles, the first of which was a reworking of The Valentinos' "Looking for a Love," the group's reputation stems largely from their many concert appearances and best-selling albums, including *The Morning After, Live Full House, Bloodshot, Ladies Invited,* and *Nightmares and Other Takes from the Vinyl Jungle.*

Today the group is simply known as Geils. Lead vocalist Peter Wolf is married to actress Faye Dunaway.

Dec. 71	*LOOKING FOR A LOVE /* Atlantic
Mar. 73	*GIVE IT TO ME /* Atlantic
Sept. 73	*MAKE UP YOUR MIND /* Atlantic
Nov. 74	*MUST OF GOT LOST /* Atlantic
April 76	*WHERE DID OUR LOVE GO /* Atlantic
Aug. 77	*YOU'RE THE ONLY ONE /* Atlantic

Genesis

MEMBERS:

Peter Gabriel (lead vocals) / born: May 13, 1950 / (left group in 1975)

Tony Banks (keyboard)

Mike Rutherford (bass guitar) / born: Oct. 2, 1950

Steve Hackett (guitar) / born: Feb. 12, 1950 / (left group, June 1977)

Phil Collins (drums and vocals) / born: Jan. 31, 1951

HOMETOWN: London, England

In 1969 Tony and Mike formed Genesis, adding Steve, Mike, and Peter some five years later. In late 1972 the band made its American concert debut and a year later released their first album in America called *Selling England by the Pound*. Their first four American releases became hits, establishing their "classical rock" beat. In 1975 Gabriel left the group and was replaced by Phil Collins as lead vocalist. Today the group is a trio consisting of Collins, Rutherford, and Banks.

Mar. 77   *YOUR OWN SPECIAL WAY /* Atco
Apr. 78   *FOLLOW YOU, FOLLOW ME /* Atlantic

Bobbie Gentry

REAL NAME: Bobbie Lee Street
BORN: July 27, 1944
HOMETOWN: Chickasaw County, Mississippi

Bobbie Gentry spent her early years in Greenwood, Mississippi. She began performing at eleven as guitar accompanist for a local singer, and her memories of this period became the basis for many of her later hit songs. By the time Bobbie reached college age, her parents had moved to Palm Springs, California, and she entered UCLA to study philosophy. She also took courses at the Los Angeles Conservatory of Music.

In 1967 Bobbie took her material to Capitol Records' Hollywood office. One of the company's A & R men, Kelly Gordon, scheduled a recording session for Bobbie to cut the songs herself. Within a few months one of these, "Ode to Billy Joe" was a nationwide number one hit and had everybody guessing about the mystery of the Tallahatchie Bridge. (In 1976, almost ten years later, a paperback book based

on the song became a best seller and a feature film *Ode to Billy Joe* was released. Capitol reissued the original recording, and it made a second appearance on the national charts.)

Bobbie Gentry continued with a series of chart singles and albums. Today she is a popular nightclub and television variety-show performer.

Aug. 67   *ODE TO BILLY JOE /* Capitol
Nov. 67   *OKOLONA RIVER BOTTOM BAND /* Capitol
Apr. 68   *LOUISIANA MAN /* Capitol
Nov. 69   *FANCY /* Capitol
Apr. 70   *HE MADE A WOMAN OUT OF ME /* Capitol
July 70   *APARTMENT 21 /* Capitol
June 76   *ODE TO BILLY JOE (rereleased) /* Capitol

The Gentrys

ORIGINAL MEMBERS:
James Hart (vocals)
Bruce Bowles (vocals)
Lawrence Raspberry (guitar, lead vocals)
Robert Fisher (tenor sax, electric piano)
James Johnson (trumpet, organ)
Pat Neal (bass)
Lawrence Wall (drums)
HOMETOWN: Memphis, Tennessee
MEMBERS (post-1970):
James Hart (lead vocals)
James Tarbutton (lead guitar)
David Beaver (keyboards)
Stephen Speer (bass)
Michael Gardner (drums)

The original Gentrys were organized in Memphis in 1963 as a rock 'n' roll band to play local high school dances. Their reception by audiences encouraged them to enter the Mid-South Fair Talent Competition, in which they won third place. Next they auditioned for the "Ted Mack Amateur Hour" and made their debut on national television.

In 1965 The Gentrys were signed by a small local recording company and achieved a minor regional hit called "Sometimes." This brought them to the attention of MGM's A & R director in Nashville, Jim Vienneau, who had the group signed to the label. During the mid-sixties they succeeded in placing a string of hits on the charts, the biggest of which was their top five recording of "Keep on Dancing." However, the group soon disbanded.

Nearly four years later original member Jimmy Hart assembled a new group of "Gentrys," who were signed to the legendary Memphis-based Sun label. The new group scored with a series of hits but had faded from national popularity by 1971.

During the mid-seventies the "new" Gentrys became associated with producer Knox Phillips to attempt a comeback.

Sept. 65 *KEEP ON DANCING / MGM*
Jan. 66 *SPREAD IT ON THICK / MGM*
May 66 *EVERY DAY I HAVE TO CRY / MGM*
Feb. 70 *WHY SHOULD I CRY? / Sun*
Apr. 70 *CINNAMON GIRL / Sun*
Feb. 71 *WILD WORLD / Sun*

Gerry & The Pacemakers

MEMBERS:

Gerrard Marsden (lead vocals, guitar) / born Sept. 24, 1942

Leslie Maguire (keyboards) / born: Dec. 27, 1941

Leslie Chadwick (bass) / born: May 11, 1943

Fred Marsden (drums) / born: Oct. 23, 1940

HOMETOWN: Liverpool, England

Gerry & The Pacemakers were a leading example of the "Liverpool sound" that took hold in the early sixties. They were one of several groups that rose to fame in the United States in the wake of Beatlemania.

Gerry Marsden, the nucleus of the group, worked for British Railways after completing school and took a part-time job playing guitar in a skiffle group. In the late fifties Gerry played in various local rock 'n' roll bands, often with his older brother Freddie, and eventually formed his own group called The Mars Bars. This group disbanded after only a few months and, in 1959, the Marsden brothers joined with Les Chadwick to form The Pacemakers. After building a strong reputation in Liverpool, they followed The Beatles and many others of the area's groups to Hamburg, Germany, where they became a resident band at the famed Top Ten Club. When they returned to Liverpool they resumed their club appearances and added a pianist, Les Maguire, to the group.

In 1962 Brian Epstein (the Beatles' manager) signed Gerry & The Pacemakers and brought them to the attention of George Martin at Parlophone Records. Martin selected them to record a Mitch Murray tune called "How Do You Do It," which he had first offered to The Beatles but which they had refused to record. The Pacemakers' version reached number one on the British charts early in 1963 and was followed by three additional chart-topping hits: "I Like It," "You'll Never Walk Alone," and "I'm the One." By the time their fourth release, "Don't Let the Sun Catch You Crying," appeared in 1964, the "British invasion" was going strong in the United States, and this record was given to the American Laurie label for distribution. It reached the top five on both sides of the Atlantic, and Laurie began issuing the group's earlier British hits in America. They also released the soundtrack album and theme from *Ferry Cross the Mersey,* a major feature film of 1965 in which the group appeared.

Gerry & The Pacemakers continued with a series of international best-selling singles and albums through the end of 1966, when the group disbanded. Gerry Marsden continued for awhile as a solo performer and attempted to establish himself on the cabaret circuit.

Today Gerry works both as a performer and behind the scenes on children's television shows. The other group members have retired.

May 64	*DON'T LET THE SUN CATCH YOU CRYING* /Laurie
July 64	*HOW DO YOU DO IT?* /Laurie
July 64	*I'M THE ONE* /Laurie
Sept. 64	*I LIKE IT* /Laurie
Dec. 64	*I'LL BE THERE* /Laurie
Feb. 65	*FERRY CROSS THE MERSEY* / Laurie
Apr. 65	*IT'S GONNA BE ALRIGHT* / Laurie
June 65	*YOU'LL NEVER WALK ALONE* /Laurie
Aug. 65	*GIVE ALL YOUR LOVE TO ME* / Laurie
Apr. 66	*LA LA LA* /Laurie
Sept. 66	*GIRL ON A SWING* /Laurie

Andy Gibb

BORN: Mar. 5, 1958
HOMETOWN: Brisbane, Australia

Andy, the younger brother of Barry, Robin, and Maurice—the trio known as The Bee Gees—began his career while a youngster by playing a guitar around the local clubs in his hometown. After gaining some local success, his older brothers guided him toward their good friend and manager Robert Stigwood who immediately signed Andy to his label, RSO Records.

In early 1977 Andy, along with his brother Barry, went to Miami, Florida,

Andy Gibb

to work on material for his debut album. After months of hard work they emerged with the album *Flowing Rivers,* from which came the number-one hit tune "I Just Want to Be Your Everything." And now there is another Gibb on his way to new recording heights.

Apr. 77	*I JUST WANT TO BE YOUR EVERYTHING* /RSO
Nov. 77	*LOVE IS THICKER THAN WATER* /RSO
Apr. 78	*SHADOW DANCING* /RSO

Gary Glitter

REAL NAME: Paul Gadd
BORN: May 8, 1944
HOMETOWN: Banbury, Oxfordshire, England

Paul Gadd began his profession career in his early teens when he and two friends, under the name of Paul Raven & The Twilights, were booked as a guitar trio into London's Safari Club. During the late fifties Paul toured with such British stars as Cliff Richard and Tommy Steele, which led to his first single for British Decca. In 1961 he switched to Parlophone and had minor hits with popular American songs of the period such as "Walk on By" and "Tower of Strength."

Paul spent part of the sixties in Hamburg, Germany, the "proving ground" for many British acts; there he enjoyed an extended period of residency at the famed Top Ten Club. Between his German engagements he returned to England to assist in the production of the BBC's "Ready Steady Go," to produce recordings by other acts, and to sing the voices of two priests on the original-cast recording of *Jesus Christ Superstar.* He also recorded several singles himself, one under the pseudonym Paul Monday, and met producer Mike Leander, who was to be instrumental in his later success.

In the early seventies Paul changed his name to Gary Glitter and signed with Bell Records. In association with Leander, he produced a string of British hits, including "Rock & Roll, Pt. II," "I Didn't Know I Loved You (Till I Saw You Rock 'n' Roll)," "Do You Wanna Touch Me," "Leader of the Gang," and a number of others. The first two were hits in America as well.

Today Gary continues as a major concert attraction in England in the area of "glitter rock." His recordings are released in the United States on the Arista label.

| July 72 | **ROCK & ROLL, PT. II** / **Bell** |
| Nov. 72 | **I DIDN'T KNOW I LOVED YOU** / **Bell** |

Andrew Gold

BORN: Aug. 2, 1951
HOMETOWN: Burbank, California

Born of famous parents, Ernest Gold, a veteran composer, and Marni Nixon, an off-screen singing voice for many of filmdom's female leads, Andrew became influenced by music as a child. He quickly learned to play the piano, guitar, and bass and by the late sixties had formed a band of his own, Bryndle. Gold soon left to join Linda Ronstadt's band as a pianist and remained as the key man in her group. The association with Ronstadt led to a recording contract with Asylum Records and the debut LP, *Andrew Gold.*

He is going to be a major talent during the rest of the seventies.

Jan 76	**THAT'S WHY I LOVE YOU** / **Asylum**
Mar. 77	**LONELY BOY** / **Asylum**
Feb. 78	**THANK YOU FOR BEING A FRIEND** / **Asylum**

Golden Earring

MEMBERS:
Barry Hay (vocals)/born: Aug. 16, 1948/ Saizabad, Netherlands
George Kooymans (guitar)/born: Mar. 11, 1948/The Hague, Netherlands
Marinus Gerritsen (bass)/born: Aug. 9, 1946/ The Hague, Netherlands
Cesar Zuiderwijk (drums)/born: July 18, 1950/ The Hague, Netherlands

Golden Earring became known to British and American audiences as part of the second wave of the "Dutch invasion" that followed the success of Focus in 1973.

The group was formed in Holland during the mid-sixties by guitarist George Kooymans. For nearly eight years they struggled to survive by getting bookings wherever they could on the Continent. During the early seventies one of their performances was seen by The Who, who encouraged them to come to England. They were so well received that Peter Rudge (who was managing The Who and The Rolling Stones) agreed to handle them too. He got them wide exposure by booking them on tours with such acts as The Who, Joe Cocker, and Led Zeppelin and got them a recording contract with MCA's affiliated Track label.

In 1974 Golden Earring achieved two hit singles, but they have become best known for their concert appearances and albums. They continue to be most popular in their home country, where they have accumulated nearly twenty hit singles.

May 74   *RADAR LOVE*/MCA/Track
Oct. 74 *CANDY'S GOING BAD*/MCA/Track

Graham Central Station

MEMBERS:
Lawrence Graham (bass)/born: Aug. 14, 1946/Beaumont, Texas
Patryce "Chocolate" Banks (vocals)/replaced by Gail "Baby Face" Muldrow
Hershall "Happiness" Kennedy (keyboards, trumpet)
Robert "Butch" Sam (keyboards)
David "Dynamite" Vega (lead and rhythm guitar)
Manuel "Deacon" Kellough (drums)/replaced by Gaylord "Flash" Birch

The central figure in this group, Larry Graham, began his career in the early sixties by singing and playing guitar with his mother in lounges and nightclubs. Sylvester Stewart saw the duo in 1966 and recruited Graham as the bass player for his new group, Sly & The Family Stone. Graham remained with Sly for six years. After he left he

worked briefly as a studio musician and began working with a band called Patryce Banks & Hot Chocolate (no relation to Hot Chocolate, the British soul group). Patryce, who had first met Graham in 1969 when she and her band opened a Stone show, invited him to join her group. He restructured the group, and it emerged in 1973 as Graham Central Station. They were signed almost immediately by Warner Brothers Records.

Although Graham Central Station achieved a number of hit singles, their success has stemmed largely from their energetic concert performances and their albums, including *Graham Central Station, Release Yourself,* and *Ain't No Bout-A-Doubt It.*

May 74   *CAN YOU HANDLE IT?*/Warner Bros.
Aug. 75 *YOUR LOVE*/Warner Bros.
Nov. 75 *IT'S ALL RIGHT*/Warner Bros.
Feb. 76 *THE JAM*/Warner Bros.

Grand Funk

MEMBERS:
Mark Farner (lead vocals, guitar)/born: Sept. 29, 1948/Flint, Michigan
Mel Schacher (bass)/born: Apr. 8, 1951/Owosso, Michigan
Donald Brewer (drums)/born: Sept. 3, 1948/Flint, Michigan
Craig Frost (keyboards)/born: Apr. 20, 1948/Flint, Michigan (added in 1973)

Grand Funk was the most commercially successful American rock group of the sixties and early seventies.

They evolved in Michigan during the mid-sixties from a band led by Don Brewer called The Jazz Masters. The group eventually included Mark Farner, Mel Schacher, and disc jockey Terry Knight, who renamed them The Pack. In 1966 Terry Knight & The Pack were signed by the small Lucky Eleven label

Graham Central Station

and achieved a Top 40 national best seller with the standard "I (Who Have Nothing)." It was their only hit single, and the group disintegrated after recording two unsuccessful albums. Knight continued as a solo artist and became a record producer.

During the late sixties Farner, Schacher, and Brewer made another attempt at success and formed a new association with Terry Knight. This time he did not perform with the group but took over management of their career. He named them Grand Funk Railroad (after the turn-of-the-century Grand Trunk Railroad; they later shortened the name to Grand Funk) and began getting them bookings in upstate New

York. Their break came in 1969 when they appeared at the Atlanta Pop Festival and were so well received that they were asked to headline the final performances. Citing this success, Knight was able to get the group a contract with Capitol Records, and they debuted late in 1969 with the album *On Time* and a single, "Time Machine." In spite of universally poor reviews by critics and limited airplay, both records sold moderately well.

The group went on to receive some of the severest criticism in the annals of rock journalism and increasing resistance from radio stations. Terry Knight responded by renting the world's largest billboard in New York City's Times Square (the first time this device was ever used to advertise a rock act) and by staging other similar promotional stunts. The publicity caused such an increase in the group's following that they began selling out sports arenas across the country and in 1971 outdrew The Beatles at New York's Shea Stadium! They were represented on the singles charts with several hits every year and their albums, whose sales totaled in the millions, included *Grand Funk, Closer to Home, Live, Survival, E Pluribus Funk, Mark, Don & Mel,* and *Phoenix.*

In 1973 Grand Funk and Terry Knight separated in a celebrated series of lawsuits, and the group began working with producer Todd Rundgren. They also added a keyboard player, a long-time friend of the group's named Craig Frost. In association with Rundgren the four-man Grand Funk continued their series of best-selling albums (in spite of a change in sound) with *We're an American Band, Shinin' On,* and *All the Girls in the World Beware.* In mid-1976 their career took yet another turn when they changed affiliation to MCA Records and formed an association with legendary rock producer Frank Zappa.

Sept. 69	*TIME MACHINE* / Capitol
Dec. 69	*MR. LIMOUSINE DRIVER* / Capitol
Feb. 70	*HEARTBREAKER* / Capitol
Aug. 70	*CLOSER TO HOME* / Capitol
Dec. 70	*MEAN MISTREATER* / Capitol
May 71	*FEELING ALRIGHT* / Capitol
Aug. 71	*GIMME SHELTER* / Capitol
Jan. 72	*FOOTSTOMPING MUSIC* / Capitol
Apr. 72	*UPSETTER* / Capitol
Sept. 72	*ROCK & ROLL SOUL* / Capitol
July 73	*WE'RE AN AMERICAN BAND* / Capitol
Nov. 73	*WALK LIKE A MAN* / Capitol
Mar. 74	*THE LOCOMOTION* / Capitol
July 74	*SHININ' ON* / Capitol
Dec. 74	*SOME KIND OF WONDERFUL* / Capitol
Apr. 75	*BAD TIME* / Capitol
Jan. 76	*TAKE ME* / Capitol
Mar. 76	*SALLY* / Capitol
Aug. 76	*CAN YOU DO IT* / MCA

The Grass Roots

ORIGINAL MEMBERS:
Creed Bratton (lead guitar) / born: Feb. 8, 1943 / Sacramento, California / replaced by Dennis Provisor (keyboards)

Warren Entner (rhythm guitar) / born: July 7, 1944 / Los Angeles, California

Robert Grill (bass) / born: Nov. 30, 1944 / Los Angeles, California

Rick Coonce (drums) / born: Aug. 1, 1947 / Los Angeles, California

Re-formed group (mid-seventies):
Reed Kailing (lead guitar)

Warren Entner (rhythm guitar)

Virgil Weber (keyboards)

Robert Grill (bass)

Joel Larson (drums)

The Grass Roots emerged from Los Angeles during the mid-sixties as the most successful West Coast pop group of their time.

Warren Entner and Creed Bratton met in Europe in 1965 (although both were born in Los Angeles); both were traveling across the Continent playing wherever they could get paid. They joined forces and continued their travels through Europe and the Mideast before returning home.

In 1966 they formed their own group and recruited Rob Grill and Rick Coonce to the line-up. Under the name The Thirteenth Floor (not to be confused with the The Thirteenth Floor Elevators), they began performing in local clubs and circulated demonstration tapes to record companies. One of these came to the attention of writer-producers P. F. Sloan and Steve Barri at Dunhill Records. Sloan and Barri had just had a local hit with a version of Bob Dylan's "Ballad of a Thin Man," which they had produced with session musicians and released under the name of The Grassroots. Anxious to release a follow-up, they invited The Thirteenth Floor to take over the identity of The Grassroots (the name was later made two words) and offered them a contract.

In association with Sloan and Barri, The Grass Roots achieved nearly two dozen hits before eventually fading from the charts in the early seventies. They survived a number of major personnel changes and reemerged in 1975 on Lambert & Potter's Haven label.

June 66 *WHERE WERE YOU WHEN I NEEDED YOU* /Dunhill
Sept. 66 *ONLY WHEN YOU'RE LONELY* /Dunhill
May 67 *LET'S LIVE FOR TODAY* /Dunhill
Aug. 67 *THE THINGS I SHOULD HAVE SAID* /Dunhill
Oct. 67 *WAKE UP, WAKE UP* /Dunhill
Aug. 68 *MIDNIGHT CONFESSIONS* /Dunhill

Nov. 68 *BELLA LINDA* /Dunhill
Feb. 69 *LOVING THINGS* /Dunhill
Apr. 69 *THE RIVER IS WIDE* /Dunhill
July 69 *I'D WAIT A MIILLION YEARS* /Dunhill
Nov. 69 *HEAVEN KNOWS* /Dunhill
Feb. 70 *WALKING THROUGH THE COUNTRY* /Dunhill
May 70 *BABY HOLD ON* /Dunhill
Sept. 70 *COME ON AND SAY IT* /Dunhill
Dec. 70 *TEMPTATION EYES* /Dunhill
June 71 *SOONER OR LATER* /Dunhill
Oct. 71 *TWO DIVIDED BY LOVE* /Dunhill
Feb. 72 *GLORY BOUND* /Dunhill
June 72 *THE RUNAWAY* /Dunhill
Jan. 73 *LOVE IS WHAT YOU MAKE IT* /Dunhill
Aug. 75 *MAMACITA* /Haven

The Grateful Dead

MEMBERS:

Jerry Garcia (guitar)/born: Aug. 1, 1942/San Francisco, California

Robert Hall Weir (rhythm guitar)/born: Oct. 16, 1947/San Francisco, California

Phil Lesh (bass guitar)/born: Mar. 15, 1940/Berkeley, California

Bill Kreutzmann (drums)/born: June 7, 1946/Palo Alto, California

Ron "Pig-Pen" McKernan /born: Sept. 8, 1946/San Bruno, California/died: Mar. 8, 1973

Added in 1974:

Keith Godchaux (piano)/born: July 19, 1948/San Francisco, California

Donna Godchaux (vocals)/born: Aug. 22, 1947/San Francisco, California

Mickey Hart (percussion)/New York City

The Grateful Dead and The Jefferson Airplane became the two most popular rock bands ever to emerge from the San Francisco Bay Area.

During the early sixties lead guitarist Jerry Garcia met Bob Weir, Ron McKernan, and Bill Kreutzmann. McKernan and Kreutzmann formed a band called The Zodiacs while Garcia, along with friend Robert Hunter, formed a folk-blues band called The

The Grateful Dead. Left to right: Mickey Hart, Phil Lesh, Donna Godchaux, Jerry Garcia, Bob Weir, Bill Kreutzmann; center: Keith Godchaux

Wildwood Boys. Later Garcia, McKernan, and Kreutzmann formed Mother McCree's Uptown Jug Champions.

After trying several other names they chose The Grateful Dead in 1966 while under the influence of drugs. Acid was legal in California at this time and many of the group members were experimenting with it.

In 1967 they signed with Warner Brothers and released their first LP,

The Grateful Dead, and immediately became one of the most influential rock groups of San Francisco's "flower-power" period. Ron "Pig-Pen" McKernan died of a liver ailment in 1973.

Today the group records for Arista Records and is an institution of the heavy-rock/drug scene of the sixties.

Aug. 70 *UNCLE JOHN'S BAND /* **Warner Bros.**

Nov. 71 *TRUCKIN'*/Warner Bros.
Feb. 73 *SUGAR MAGNOLIA*/Warner Bros.
Oct. 75 *THE MUSIC NEVER STOPPED*/Grateful Dead

Jerry Garcia
Apr. 72 *SUGAREE*/Warner Bros.

Dobie Gray

REAL NAME: Leonard Victor Ainsworth, Jr.
BORN: July 26, 1942
HOMETOWN: Brookshire, Texas

Dobie Gray spent much of his early life in Houston, Texas, but moved to California in the early sixties in search of a recording career. He was briefly affiliated with the small Cor Dak label and recorded two regional hits, "I Can Hardly Wait" and "Look at Me" (which also dented the national charts). Later he auditioned for Sonny Bono, who was an A & R man at the time; he got Gray signed to Charger Records in 1964. Gray achieved the top ten with "The In Crowd" and recorded a moderately successful follow-up before fading temporarily from national popularity.

During the following years Gray toured the club circuit with an "oldie" act featuring his earlier hits and sang with a number of Las Vegas lounge bands. He spent two years in the Los Angeles production of *Hair* and in 1971 became a member of a group called Pollution. They had a regional R & B hit on the Prophesy label. Called "Do You Really Have a Heart," the song was written by Paul Williams and Roger Nichols. Gray became acquainted with Williams's brother Mentor, who helped write and produce a solo album by Gray titled *Drift Away.*

In 1973 Mentor sold the package to MCA Records, and the title cut became a top five national hit when it was released as a single. After a follow-up

hit for MCA, Dobie Gray affiliated with Phil Walden's Capricorn label in 1975.

Jan. 63 *LOOK AT ME*/Cor Dak
Jan. 65 *THE IN CROWD*/Charger
Apr. 65 *SEE YOU AT THE GO GO*/Charger
Feb. 73 *DRIFT AWAY*/MCA
Aug. 73 *LOVING ARMS*/MCA
Feb. 76 *IF LOVE MUST GO*/Capricorn
Oct. 76 *FIND 'EM, FOOL 'EM, FORGET 'EM*/Capricorn

R. B. Greaves

FULL NAME: Robert Bertram Aloysius Greaves III
BORN: Nov. 28, 1944
BIRTHPLACE: United States Air Force Base, Atkinson, Georgetown, British Guiana

R. B. Greaves emerged in the late sixties with a sound often compared to soul singers Sam Cooke and Otis Redding.

He spent much of his childhood on a ranch adjacent to the Seminole Indian Reservation at Hot Springs, Nevada (Greaves is half Seminole), and it was there that he learned to play guitar and developed his interest in singing.

In 1969 Greaves was signed by Atlantic's subsidiary Atco label. He achieved a string of pop and soul hits before fading from the charts in the early seventies.

Oct. 69 *TAKE A LETTER, MARIA*/Atco
Jan. 70 *ALWAYS SOMETHING THERE TO REMIND ME*/Atco
Apr. 70 *FIRE & RAIN*/Atco
Sept. 70 *GEORGIA TOOK HER BACK*/Atco
Dec. 70 *A WHITER SHADE OF PALE*/Atco

Al Green

BORN: Apr. 13, 1946
HOMETOWN: Forrest City, Arkansas

Al Green moved with his family to Grand Rapids, Michigan, at the age of nine. He began his singing career there at fifteen by joining his older brothers Robert, William, and Walter in the Green Brothers gospel group.

In 1964 Green helped form a pop-soul group called The Creations. They toured the southern "chittlin' circuit" for nearly three years. Several of The Creations joined Junior Walker's All Stars and two of the remaining members, Curtis Rogers and Palmer James, formed a record company in Grand Rapids called Hot Line Music Journal. Backed by a new group called The Soul Mates (including Al's brother Robert and a friend, Lee Virgins) Green signed with the new label, and his first release, "Back Up Train," made the national top forty. In spite of two follow-up recordings that were moderate soul hits ("Lovers' Hide-away" and "Don't Hurt Me No More"), Hot Line went out of business. (Two other Hot Line masters were released by Bell Records, the label's national distributor, after Green's later success; both appeared on the charts.)

In 1969 when Green was playing an engagement in Midland, Texas, he was seen by Hi Records' A & R director Willie Mitchell. Mitchell encouraged him to sign with Hi, and their first collaboration produced a hit recording of The Temptations' "I Can't Get Next to You." After two more releases that became minor soul hits ("You Say It" and "Driving Wheel"), Green achieved a multi-million seller with his own composition of "Tired of Being Alone." Green evolved into the leading soul star of the early seventies.

Today he makes his home in Memphis, Tennessee.

Al Greene & The Soul Mates
Dec. 67 *BACK UP TRAIN* /Hot Line Music Journal

Al Green
**Nov. 70 *I CAN'T GET NEXT TO YOU* /Hi
July 71 *TIRED OF BEING ALONE* /Hi
Dec. 71 *LET'S STAY TOGETHER* /Hi
Apr. 72 *LOOK WHAT YOU DONE FOR ME* /Hi
July 72 *I'M STILL IN LOVE WITH YOU* /Hi
Sept. 72 *GUILTY* /Bell
Oct. 72 *YOU OUGHT TO BE WITH ME* /Hi
Jan. 73 *HOT WIRE* /Bell
Feb. 73 *CALL ME* /Hi
July 73 *HERE I AM* /Hi
Dec. 73 *LIVING FOR YOU* /Hi
Mar. 74 *LET'S GET MARRIED* /Hi
Sept. 74 *SHA LA LA* /Hi
Mar. 75 *L-O-V-E* /Hi
July 75 *OH ME, OH MY* /Hi
Nov. 75 *FULL OF FIRE* /Hi
Oct. 76 *KEEP ME CRYIN'* /Hi
Jan. 78 *BELLE* /Hi**

Norman Greenbaum
BORN: Nov. 20, 1942
HOMETOWN: Malden, Massachusetts

During the late sixties Greenbaum played many of the clubs in the New England area hoping one day to "make it" as an artist. Then in late 1969 he recorded a song he wrote called "Spirit in the Sky" that eventually led to a recording contract with Reprise Records. The song was released in early 1970 and in a short time both Greenbaum and his song were nationally known.

**Feb. 70 *SPIRIT IN THE SKY* /Reprise
June 70 *CANNED HAM* /Reprise
May 71 *CALIFORNIA EARTHQUAKE* /Reprise**

Lorne Greene
BORN: 1915
HOMETOWN: Ottawa, Canada

Lorne Greene is, of course, known primarily as an actor. He rose to fame in the early sixties with his leading role in the "Bonanza" television series.

During the mid-sixties Greene enjoyed a brief parallel career as a recording artist with his recitation-style country songs. His biggest success was "Ringo," which reached number one on the national charts in 1964.

Oct. 64 RINGO/RCA
Jan. 65 THE MAN/RCA

Henry Gross
BORN: 1950
HOMETOWN: Brooklyn, New York

Henry Gross began his professional career as the lead guitarist with Sha Na Na, the rock 'n' roll satire group.

During the early seventies Gross separated from the group to pursue a solo career. He formed an association with Terry Cashman and Tommy West, who produced his album titled "Plug Me into Something." It was released by A & M and yielded a modest hit single, "One More Tomorrow."

Late in 1975 Cashman and West established their own Lifesong record company, and Henry Gross was signed to the label. He debuted with an album called *Release* and early in 1976 achieved a top five single with his Beach Boys-like composition, "Shannon."

**Apr. 75 ONE MORE TOMORROW/
A & M**
Feb. 76 SHANNON/Lifesong
July 76 SPRINGTIME MAMA/Lifesong
Oct. 76 SOMEDAY/Lifesong

The Guess Who
MEMBERS:

Randall Charles Bachman (lead guitar)/born: Sept. 27, 1943/replaced (1970) by Kurt Winter/born: Apr. 2, 1946, and Gregory Leskiw/born: Aug. 5, 1947/replaced (1972) by Donald McDougall/born: Nov. 5, 1947/replaced (1974) by Domenic Troiano

Burton Cummings (lead vocals, keyboards)/born: Dec. 31, 1947
Michael James Kale (bass)/born: Aug. 11, 1943/replaced (1972) by William Wallace/born: May 18, 1949
Garry Peterson (drums)/born: May 26, 1945
HOMETOWN: Winnipeg, Manitoba, Canada

This group began in 1960 as Chad Allen & The Expressions. When Allen separated from the group in 1961, it was reorganized by one of the founding members, Randy Bachman, as The Guess Who.

During the early sixties, The Guess Who developed a reputation as Winnipeg's leading rock band and appeared on their own weekly CBC-TV program called "Where It's At." Many of the original songs they introduced on this show were released as singles in the Canadian market, and several were distributed in the United States on the Scepter label. One of these, "Shakin' All Over," reached the American top twenty.

By 1968 The Guess Who were working with Jack Richardson of the Nimbus Nine Production Company, who jointly produced the group's biggest hit to date, "These Eyes." Drawing on this success, Richardson was able to get them a contract with RCA, and "These Eyes" was released in the United States. It became a top five hit and was the first of a long string of best-selling singles for the group. They also had a series of best-selling albums, including *Wheatfield Soul, Canned Wheat, American Woman, So Long Bannatyne, Rockin, Live at the Paramount, Number Ten,* and *Road Food.*

Randy Bachman departed in 1970 (see *BACHMAN-TURNER OVERDRIVE*), and, after many other personnel changes, the group disbanded in 1976. Burton Cummings signed a solo

The Guess Who. Left to right: Randy Bachman, James Kale, Domenic Troiano, Garry Peterson; center: Burton Cummings

contract with Portrait Records, and all the remaining members, except Dom Troiano, formed a new band called Delphia.

May 65	*SHAKIN' ALL OVER* / Scepter
Apr. 69	*THESE EYES* / RCA
July 69	*LAUGHING* / RCA
Oct. 69	*UNDUN* / RCA
Dec. 69	*NO TIME* / RCA
Mar. 70	*AMERICAN WOMAN* / RCA
July 70	*HAND ME DOWN WORLD* / RCA
Oct. 70	*SHARE THE LAND* / RCA
Jan. 71	*HANG ON TO YOUR LIFE* / RCA
Apr. 71	*ALBERT FLASHER* / RCA
Aug. 71	*RAIN DANCE* / RCA
Nov. 71	*SOUR SUITE* / RCA
Mar. 72	*HEARTBROKEN BOPPER* / RCA
May 72	*GUNS GUNS GUNS* / RCA
Oct. 72	*RUNNING BACK TO SASKATOON* / RCA
Feb. 73	*FOLLOW YOUR DAUGHTER HOME* / RCA
Feb. 74	*STAR BABY* / RCA
July 74	*CLAP FOR THE WOLFMAN* / RCA
Nov. 74	*DANCIN' FOOL* / RCA

Arlo Guthrie

BORN: July 10, 1947
HOMETOWN: Coney Island (Brooklyn), New York

Arlo is the son of legendary folk-singer Woody Guthrie and was exposed to music all his life.

He began his professional career in the mid-sixties by playing the Northeast folk circuit and then accompanying Judy Collins on a tour of Japan. In 1967 he wrote an autobiographical song called "Alice's Restaurant," based on his experiences of the previous two years with the army and with the police in Stockbridge, Massachusetts. When a New York underground radio station played a tape of the song, they were deluged with requests and began playing it every night. "Alice's Restaurant" was the hit of the 1967 Newport Folk Festival when Arlo performed it there and was also the title of his first album. It became a worldwide anthem for the antidraft movement of the late sixties and was the title of a 1970 feature film in which Arlo starred.

Although two of his singles have appeared on the national charts, Arlo Guthrie's real success has been with his personal appearances and albums, including *Arlo, Running down the Road, Hoboes' Lullabye, Last of the Brooklyn Cowboys,* and *Arlo Guthrie.*

Dec. 69	***ALICE'S ROCK & ROLL RESTAURANT* / Reprise**
July 72	***THE CITY OF NEW ORLEANS* / Reprise**

Merle Haggard

BORN: Mar. 6, 1937
HOMETOWN: Bakersfield, California

Merle Haggard was introduced to music by his father, who had been an Oklahoma country fiddler. At the age of nine he was forced by his father's death to support himself and spent much of his spare time listening to music in Bakersfield's many country saloons. During his teens he ran afoul of the law and in November of 1957 began serving a sentence of nearly three years at San Quentin State Prison. While there he heard country singer Johnny Cash, who would later serve as a major source of inspiration to him.

After his release in 1960 Haggard began playing lead guitar at a Bakersfield country music club. In 1962 he went to Las Vegas as a back-up guitarist for Wynn Stewart and in 1963 he was offered a recording contract by the Tally label. His first release sold only two hundred copies, but his subsequent singles, "Sing Me a Sad Song" and "Strangers," sold well and brought him to the attention of Capitol Records' producer Ken Nelson. Signed to Capitol, Haggard formed his own back-up group, The Strangers (named after the earlier hit), and achieved a string of country hits, including "Swinging Doors," "The Bottle Let Me Down," "Branded Man," "Sing Me Back Home," and "Mama Tried."

His major national breakthrough, however, came in 1969 with his controversial recording of "Okie from Muskogee."

Today "Hag" continues to make his home in Bakersfield. His wife is country star Bonnie Owens, whom he met and recorded with at Tally Records.

Nov. 69	*OKIE FROM MUSKOGEE* / Capitol
Feb. 70	*THE FIGHTING SIDE OF ME* / Capitol
Mar. 71	*A SOLDIER'S LAST LETTER* / Capitol
Dec. 71	*CAROLYN* / Capitol
Sept. 73	*EVERYBODY'S HAD THE BLUES* / Capitol
Nov. 73	*IF WE MAKE IT THROUGH DECEMBER* / Capitol
Oct. 77	*FROM GRACELAND TO THE PROMISED LAND* / MCA

Hall & Oates

MEMBERS:
Daryl Hall (electric organ) / born: Oct. 11, 1948 / Philadelphia, Pennsylvania
John Oates (guitar) / born: Apr. 7, 1949 / New York City

Both Daryl Hall and John Oates were established professional musicians before they met at Philadelphia's Temple University in the mid-sixties. Hall was with a vocal group called The Temptones (named after the college); Oates was a member of a band known as The Masters. The two began writing songs together and, for a brief period, Oates joined The Masters as their gui-

Hall & Oates

tarist. After this Hall worked for a time at Philly's fabled Sigma Sound Studios before joining a folk band named Gulliver. This group (with which Oates also played briefly) made one unsuccessful album for Elektra before disbanding.

During the early seventies Hall & Oates were signed as songwriters with the Chappell music publishing company. This eventually led to a recording contract with Atlantic and their debut album, *Whole Oates*. Their second album, *Abandoned Lucheonette*, yielded a single called "She's Gone," which, although only moderately successful,

generated a number of cover recordings by artists like Lou Rawls, Tavares, and Ujima (the same track was rereleased in the summer of 1976 and became a top ten hit). After a third and final album for Atlantic, *War Babies* (produced by Todd Rundgren), Hall & Oates switched in 1975 to the RCA label. Their first LP for that company, *Daryl Hall & John Oates*, was a best seller and generated the single, "Sara Smile," that established their career. The inspiration for the tune was Sandy "Sara" Allen, a friend of the band.

Today Daryl Hall and John Oates

are a leading concert attraction and have settled permanently in New York City.

Feb. 74	*SHE'S GONE*/Atlantic
Jan. 76	*SARA SMILE*/RCA
July 76	*SHE'S GONE*(rereleased)/Atlantic
Oct. 76	*DO WHAT YOU WANT, BE WHAT YOU ARE*/RCA
Jan. 77	*RICH GIRL*/RCA
May 77	*BACK TOGETHER AGAIN*/RCA
July 77	*IT'S UNCANNY*/Atlantic
Oct. 77	*WHY DO LOVERS BREAK EACH OTHERS HEARTS*/RCA

Tom T. Hall

BORN: May 25, 1936
HOMETOWN: Olive Hill, Kentucky

Born in the foothills of the Appalachian Mountains, Tom T. Hall began playing guitar and writing songs before he reached ten. His storylike songs were greatly influenced by Ernest Hemmingway and by the style of an innovative Olive Hill guitarist named Clayton Delaney.

During the fifties Hall entered Roanoke College as a journalism major and began sending some of his compositions to Nashville publishing companies. His first taste of success came when one of his tunes, "DJ for a Day," was recorded by country singer Jimmy Newman. Newman also signed him to a contract with his New Keys publishing firm, and for nearly a decade Hall wrote songs that were recorded by many of Nashville's leading artists. Ironically, however, Hall achieved major recognition only when an unknown secretary, Jeannie C. Riley, recorded his "Harper Valley P.T.A." and turned it into a worldwide number one hit (according to Hall, writing this song was like finding $90,000 in the street!). After this success Hall's songs were widely recorded and he was signed as an artist by Mercury Records. Since then he has scored with a long string of country hits, several of which have "crossed over" to the national pop charts.

Today Hall and his wife, singer-songwriter Dixie Dean, live in Brentwood, Tennessee, and raise cattle and Bassett hounds in their spare time.

Aug. 71	*THE YEAR THAT CLAYTON DELANEY DIED*/Mercury
May 72	*ME & JESUS*/Mercury
Dec. 73	*I LOVE*/Mercury
June 74	*THAT SONG IS DRIVING ME CRAZY*/Mercury
Mar. 75	*SNEAKY SNAKE*/Mercury

Hamilton, Joe Frank & Reynolds

MEMBERS:
Dan Hamilton/Los Angeles, California
Joe Frank Carollo/Mississippi
Tom Reynolds/replaced(1972) by Alan Dennison/Ohio

The nucleus of this group is Danny Hamilton, who came to Los Angeles as a teen-ager to break into the music business. By fifteen he was an established session musician and worked on recordings by The Ventures, Jerry Lee Lewis, Johnny Rivers, Chad & Jeremy, and The Marketts. He became a singer for the "Shindig" TV show and later assembled a loose conglomeration of musicians known as The T-Bones ("No Matter What Shape Your Stomach's In," etc.). Joe Frank Carollo and Tommy Reynolds were two musicians recruited for this group, and the three played together until The T-Bones disbanded in the late sixties.

In 1971 the trio regrouped as Hamilton, Joe Frank & Reynolds and emerged on the Dunhill label. They scored almost immediately with a top five single, "Don't Pull Your Love," and followed with two more hits before fading from popularity. Their biggest success, however, was yet to come. In 1975 H, JF & R resurfaced on the Playboy label with a number one recording of the ballad "Fallin' in Love," followed by a number of best-selling singles and albums.

Tom Reynolds left the group in 1972 to pursue other interests; today they are known as Hamilton, Joe Frank & Dennison.

May 71	**DON'T PULL YOUR LOVE/** Dunhill
Aug. 71	**ANNABELLA/Dunhill**
Dec. 71	**DAISY MAE/Dunhill**
June 75	**FALLIN' IN LOVE/Playboy**
Nov. 75	**WINNERS & LOSERS/Playboy**
Apr. 76	**EVERYDAY WITHOUT YOU/** Playboy

Hamilton, Joe Frank & Dennison

July 76	**LIGHT UP THE WORLD WITH SUNSHINE/Playboy**
Oct. 76	**DON'T FIGHT THE HANDS (THAT NEED YOU)/Playboy**

Marvin Hamlisch

BORN: 1945
HOMETOWN: New York City

Marvin Hamlisch, who has played piano since childhood, was at seven the youngest student ever accepted at the Juilliard School of Music.

By the time he was seventeen, Hamlisch had entered the world of pop music as author of two hits for Lesley Gore: "Sunshine, Lollipops & Roses" and "California Nights." He also began writing special material for Liza Minnelli, and this association led to his composing scores and title songs for several major films: *Kotch, Take the Money and Run, Bananas, The Way We Were,* and *Save the Tiger.*

In 1973 Hamlisch adapted Scott Joplin's ragtime classic, "The Entertainer," for use in another film, *The Sting.* The following year Hamlisch's own recording of the work was released as a single and reached the top of the charts.

Today Marvin Hamlisch continues to live in New York and is currently represented on Broadway by *A Chorus Line,* for which he composed the music.

Mar. 74 *THE ENTERTAINER/MCA*

Albert Hammond

BORN: May 18, 1942
HOMETOWN: London, England

Although born in England, Albert Hammond was raised in Gibraltar, on the southern tip of Spain. He had made his first recording, "New Orleans," by the time he was fifteen, and at sixteen he formed a group called The Diamond Boys with his brother. The band became Spain's first true rock 'n' roll ensemble and eventually landed a contract with RCA in Spain.

At eighteen Hammond left the group and relocated in England. He was joined by another former Diamond Boy, Richard Cartwright, and under the name Albert & Richard they toured Europe, made several records, appeared in a few Beatle-type films, and joined a vaudeville repertory company in London. From there Hammond went to another band called Los Cuico Ricardos, through which he met the man who was to become his partner in success, Mike Hazelwood.

Hammond and Hazelwood wrote several hits, including "The Train (Colours of Love)", "Good Morning Freedom (Blue Mink)", and "Make Me an Island" and were asked to score a children's TV program called "Oliver &

the Underworld.'' Two songs from the show were recorded by other artists and became international million sellers: ''Gimmie Dat Ding'' by The Pipkins and ''Little Arrows'' by Leapy Lee. Next Hammond and Hazelwood sang in two groups, The Family Dogg and Magic Lantern, and scored with the latter via a major hit, ''Shame Shame.''

In the early 1970s Hammond went to Los Angeles in search of a solo performing career. One of his demos was heard by Barry Gross and Marty Kupps, who were in the process of forming the Mums label, and Hammond was one of the first artists signed. He achieved a string of hits, the biggest of which was ''It Never Rains in Southern California.''

Today Albert Hammond lives in Los Angeles and continues to write with Mike Hazelwood.

July 72	*DOWN BY THE RIVER* /Mums
Oct. 72	*IT NEVER RAINS IN SOUTHERN CALIFORNIA* / Mums
Mar. 73	*IF YOU GOTTA BREAK ANOTHER HEART* /Mums
Apr. 73	*THE FREE ELECTRIC BAND* / Mums
Sept. 73	*THE PEACEMAKER* /Mums
Dec. 73	*HALF A MILLION MILES FROM HOME* /Mums
Mar. 74	*I'M A TRAIN* /Mums
June.74	*AIR DISASTER* /Mums
Apr. 75	*99 MILES FROM L.A.* /Mums

The Happenings

MEMBERS:

Robert Miranda (lead vocals, guitar, organ)

Ralph De Vito (guitar, vocals) / replaced by Bernard La Porta (lead guitar, rhythm guitar, vocals)

David Libert (bass, keyboards, vocals)

Thomas Giuliano (percussion, vocals)

HOMETOWN: Paterson, New Jersey

All natives of New Jersey, the four members of this group met and began singing together in the service at Ft. Dix, New Jersey. After they returned home they formed a group called The Four Graduates.

The Four Graduates broke into the recording field in the early sixties by singing backgrounds at recording sessions. Through the studio work they met producer Bob Crewe, who occasionally used them to back The Four Seasons. They also got to know Ernie Maresca of Laurie Records and The Tokens, who were producing for Laurie. The Tokens produced two records by The Four Graduates, ''What a Lovely Way to Spend an Evening'' and ''Candy Queen,'' which were released on Laurie's subsidiary Rust label; neither was successful.

In 1965 The Tokens established their own B. T. Puppy label. The Four Graduates joined the label's roster and changed their name to The Happenings. Their first release, ''On the Go,'' made little impact, but their second, a reworking of The Tempos' ''See You in September,'' reached the top of the charts. They continued well into the late sixties with a series of best-selling recordings of earlier hits. Their last chart entry, ''Where Do I Go'' (from the Broadway production *Hair*), was leased by The Tokens to the Jubilee label.

Today The Happenings, whose only original members are Bob Miranda and Tom Giuliano, continue to perform on the northeastern club circuit and record for Midland International.

July 66	*SEE YOU IN SEPTEMBER* / B. T. Puppy
Oct. 66	*GO AWAY LITTLE GIRL* /B. T. Puppy
Dec. 66	*GOODNIGHT, MY LOVE* /B. T. Puppy
Apr. 67	*I GOT RHYTHM* /B. T. Puppy

July 67 *MY MAMMY* /B. T. Puppy
Sept. 67 *WHY DO FOOLS FALL IN LOVE* /B. T. Puppy
Feb. 68 *MUSIC, MUSIC, MUSIC* /B. T. Puppy
July 68 *BREAKING UP IS HARD TO DO* /B. T. Puppy
July 69 *WHERE DO I GO* /*BE IN* /*HARE KRISHNA* /Jubilee

Harper's Bizarre

MEMBERS:

Theodore Templeman (lead vocals, trumpet, drums)/born: Oct. 24, 1944/Santa Cruz, California

Richard Scoppettone (guitar)/born: July 5, 1945/Santa Cruz, California

Edward James (guitar)/Santa Cruz, California

Richard Yount (guitar, bass, drums)/born: Jan. 9, 1943/Santa Cruz, California

John Peterson (drums)/born: Jan. 8, 1945/San Francisco, California

Harper's Bizzare emerged in Santa Cruz, California, in 1963, on the threshold of the "love generation" that was about to take root in the San Francisco area.

They performed around San Francisco as The Tikis, and developed a substantial local reputation that eventually brought them to the attention of Warner Brothers' producer Lenny Warnoker. They were signed to the label and, after changing their name to Harper's Bizarre, debuted with Paul Simon's lilting "59th Street Bridge Song (Feelin' Groovy)." The song reached the top ten and was followed by Van Dyke Parks's "Come to the Sunshine" and a string of standards reworked in the group's "sunshine" style. They also achieved many best-selling albums including *Feelin' Groovy, Anything Goes, Secret Life* and *Harper's Bizarre 4,* before the progressively hardening sound of rock caused the group's popularity to wane.

Feb. 67 *THE 59TH ST. BRIDGE SONG (FEELIN' GROOVY)* /Warner Bros.
May 67 *COME TO THE SUNSHINE* /Warner Bros.
Aug. 67 *ANYTHING GOES* /Warner Bros.
Nov. 67 *CHATTANOOGA CHOO CHOO* /Warner Bros.
Sept. 68 *THE BATTLE OF NEW ORLEANS* /Warner Bros.

Major Harris

HOMETOWN: Richmond, Virginia

Major Harris's grandparents had been vaudevillians, his father a professional guitarist, and his mother the leader of the local church choir. He naturally began singing in church and, during the fifties, occasionally backed up Frankie Lymon & The Teenagers when they appeared in his area. During the early sixties he sang with The Jarmels, also natives of Richmond (see *THE JARMELS, Rock On: The Solid Gold Years*).

In 1969 Harris moved to Philadelphia to break into the city's burgeoning soul scene. He became the featured vocalist with a group called Nat Turner's Rebellion, signed to the Philly Groove label. One of the label's other acts were the highly successful Delfonics. When one of their members, Randy Cain, left the group because of ill health in 1971, Major Harris replaced him but eventually left in search of a solo career.

His search ended in 1975, when he was signed by Atlantic and achieved a top five hit with "Love Won't Let Me Wait." Today Harris appears with his own Boogie Blues Band, with Dennis Dozier (lead guitar), Alfred Pollard (keyboards), George Howard (sax), Sylvester Bryant (trumpet), Eric Bodner (violin), Tyrone Hall (clarinet and trombone), Michael Foreman (bass), and vocalists Allison Hobbs, Phyllis Newman, and Karen Dempsey.

Mar. 75 *LOVE WON'T LET ME WAIT* / Atlantic
Apr. 76 *JEALOUSY* / Atlantic
Nov. 76 *LAID BACK LOVE* / Atlantic

Richard Harris

BORN: Oct. 1, 1933
HOMETOWN: Limerick, Ireland

Not really best known as a singer, Richard Harris first achieved fame as a poet and later as an actor on television and in films like *99 44/100 Per Cent Dead, Camelot, Major Dundee, This Sporting Life, The Snow Goose,* and *A Man Called Horse.*

However, he did enjoy a brief recording career during the late sixties in association with songwriter-producer Jim Webb. Webb, best known for his work with The Fifth Dimension and Glen Campbell, produced an album with Harris titled *A Tramp Shining.* It yielded a single, "McArthur Park," which, in spite of its extreme length—over seven minutes—managed to get to the top of the charts. After two more releases from the album, and a brief comeback with "My Boy" in 1971, Harris continued to concentrate on his acting.

May 68 *MC ARTHUR PARK* / Dunhill
Nov. 68 *THE YARD WENT ON FOREVER* / Dunhill
June 69 *DIDN'T WE* / Dunhill
Nov. 71 *MY BOY* / Dunhill

George Harrison

BORN: Feb. 25, 1943
HOMETOWN: Wavertree, Liverpool, England

Although George rose to the heights of superstardom with The Beatles, he

George Harrison

was for most of the group's history a background figure. John and Paul dominated the creation of The Beatles' music, and only occasionally ("Something," "Here Comes the Sun," etc.) did George contribute in that area. Ringo received constant attention for his comedic personality, but George remained something of a mystery. His single largest influence seems to have been the Eastern spiritualism which was laced through the group's music during the latter part of their existence.

In the two-year period before the official break-up of The Beatles, George composed the soundtrack for the film *Wonderwall* and produced an unusual album called *Electronic Sounds.* However, these were not regarded as indications of his real potential, and after the group disbanded in 1970 he was watched, probably the closest of all the members, to see how he would fare. His creativity surfaced and he has now clearly succeeded on his own.

George's first major solo project was the triple album called *All Things Must Pass,* which became an immediate best seller and yielded the number one single "My Sweet Lord." In the summer of 1971 he organized the legendary Bangladesh benefit concert at New York's Madison Square Garden, which generated both a hit album and a single. Through the mid-seventies he continued with a number of additional singles and albums such as *Living in the Material World, George Harrison, Dark Horse, Extra Textures,* and *33⅓.*

Today, although he continues to maintain a residence in England, George spends most of his time in California. He operates his own Dark Horse record label, whose roster includes Ravi Shankar, Splinters, and Jiva.

See *THE BEATLES.*

Nov. 70	*MY SWEET LORD* / **Apple**
Feb. 71	*WHAT IS LIFE* / **Apple**
Aug. 71	*BANGLA DESH* / **Apple**
May 73	*GIVE ME LOVE* / **Apple**
Nov. 74	*DARK HORSE* / **Apple**
Jan. 75	*DING DONG, DING DONG* / **Apple**
Sept. 75	*YOU* / **Apple**
Nov. 76	*THIS SONG* / **Dark Horse**
Jan. 77	*CRACKERBOX PALACE* / **Dark Horse**

Donny Hathaway

BORN: Oct. 1, 1945
HOMETOWN: Chicago, Illinois

Donny Hathaway grew up in St. Louis, Missouri, raised by Martha Crumwell, his grandmother and a noted gospel singer who introduced him to music. At the age of three he was billed as "Donny Pitts, The Nation's

Donny Hathaway

Youngest Gospel Singer," and he accompanied himself on the ukulele!

In 1964 Hathaway entered Howard University in Washington, D.C. and joined The Ric Powell Trio to raise money for his education. The exposure eventually led to arranging and production work with The Impressions, Carla Thomas, Jerry Butler, The Staple Singers, and Roberta Flack (with whom he would later record a number of hit duets; see *Roberta FLACK*). With help from King Curtis, Hathaway was signed by Atlantic Records, and his first first album, *Everything is Everything,* was released in 1970. This generated a moderately successful single, "The Ghetto," and was followed by many best-selling albums, including *Donny Hathaway, Live, Roberta Flack & Donny Hathaway* and *Extensions of a Man.* Aside from his singles with Roberta Flack, he made several hit solo singles and teamed up briefly with June Conquest on Curtis Mayfield's Curtom label.

Today Hathaway keeps a busy schedule of club appearances and remains active as a producer-arranger.

Donny Hathaway
Jan. 70 *THE GHETTO* / Atco
May 72 *GIVING UP* / Atco
Oct. 72 *I LOVE YOU MORE* / Atco
July 73 *LOVE LOVE LOVE* / Atco

Donny Hathaway & June Conquest
May 72 *I THANK YOU* / Curtom

Richie Havens

BORN: Jan. 21, 1941
HOMETOWN: Brooklyn, New York

Richie Havens was born into a musical family; his father had been a pianist and his mother a church singer. After singing in church during his childhood, Richie organized streetcorner gospel groups in the Bedford-Stuyvesant area of Brooklyn. The most successful of these was called the McCrea Gospel Singers.

During the late fifties Havens left

Richie Havens

home and began a series of odd jobs. As the folk boom of the early sixties approached he was drawn to Greenwich village and performed on the coffeehouse circuit. After building a substantial reputation and recording two inconsequential albums for small labels, he was signed during the mid-sixties by the Verve-Forecast label. His first album, *Mixed Bag,* firmly established him with "underground radio" audiences, and he became one of the most popular folk-rock artists of the late sixties as subsequent albums were issued (*Something Else Again, Richard P. Havens,* and *Stonehenge*). By this time, about 1970, Havens had established his own Stormy Forest label and continued his string of best-selling LPs: *Alarm Clock, State of Mind, Great Blind Degree, Live on Stage,* and *Portfolio.*

Primarily an album and a concert act, Richie Havens has not concentrated on single records. Only one, in fact, has placed on the charts, a version of George Harrison's "Here Comes the Sun," which reached the top twenty.

**Mar. 71 *HERE COMES THE SUN* /
Stormy Forest**

The Edwin Hawkins Singers

HOMETOWN: Oakland, California

This gospel group was formed in the late sixties by Oakland residents' Betty Watson and Edwin Hawkins as The Northern California State Youth Choir.

They toured the national gospel circuit and met with such enthusiastic response that they raised funds and recorded an album. It was originally intended simply to be sold at their concerts, but the LP got widespread airplay wherever they appeared—particularly a cut called "Oh Happy Day" was also released as a single and sped to the top of the national charts. In 1970 Buddah employed the group to back one of their leading artists, Melanie, and they were represented in the top ten once again with "Lay Down (Candles in the Rain)."

In 1969 Dorothy Morrison, the young woman who had sung lead on "Oh Happy Day," began a solo recording career by placing two singles on the national charts. The Edwin Hawkins Singers continued with a number of popular album releases including *More Happy Days, Children Get Together,* and *I'd Like to Teach the World to Sing.*

Apr. 69 *OH HAPPY DAY* / **Pavillion**

Isaac Hayes

BORN: Aug. 20, 1942
HOMETOWN: Covington, Tennessee

An orphan, Isaac Hayes was raised by his grandparents on a sharecropper's farm, near Memphis. They often took him to church, where he began singing at the age of five.

In his teens Hayes moved with his family to Memphis. While working at a series of odd jobs, he played in groups such as The Teen Tones, The Morning Stars, The Ambassadors, and Sir Isaac & The Doo-Dads and took occasional club dates at which he sang solo and accompanied himself on the piano. Hayes was one of the first musicians to get involved with the Stax-Volt complex that sprang up in Memphis in the early sixties. He became the resident session piano player and began writing songs with David Porter, whom he met at Stax-Volt. Together they provided hits for almost everyone on the com-

pany's roster, most notably Sam & Dave, for whom they wrote more than a dozen best sellers.

During the late sixties Stax established a new label, Enterprise, to showcase Hayes as a vocalist. His first album release, *Presenting Isaac Hayes,* was only moderately successful, but it paved the way for the success of the next album, *Hot Buttered Soul.* This LP brought Hayes national attention and yielded several hit singles, but his biggest breakthrough was yet to come. In 1971 he was scored the film *Shaft,* and the theme became a number one single. The innovative music he provided for the film also began to change the sound of pop-soul music and is generally regarded as the forerunner of the modern "disco" sound. The *Shaft* score brought Hayes an Oscar, and he subsequently scored several more films, including *Tough Guys* and *Truck Turner.*

In January 1977 Hayes filed bankruptcy. Today he records for Polydor Records and is one of the most visual concert attractions in popular music, often appearing barechested and draped in chains.

Isaac Hayes

Aug. 69 *WALK ON BY* / **Enterprise**
Aug. 69 *BY THE TIME I GET TO PHOENIX* / **Enterprise**
Aug. 70 *I STAND ACCUSED* / **Enterprise**
Feb. 71 *THE LOOK OF LOVE* / **Enterprise**
May 71 *NEVER CAN SAY GOODBYE* / **Enterprise**
Oct. 71 *THEME FROM "SHAFT"* / **Enterprise**
Feb. 72 *DO YOUR THING* / **Enterprise**
Apr. 72 *LET'S STAY TOGETHER* / **Enterprise**
Oct. 72 *THEME FROM "THE MEN"* / **Enterprise**
Dec. 73 *JOY, PT. 1* / **Enterprise**
May 74 *WONDERFUL* / **Enterprise**

Aug. 75 *CHOCOLATE CHIP /*
ABC/Hot Buttered Soul

Isaac Hayes & David Porter
May 72 *AIN'T THAT LOVING YOU /*
Enterprise

Roy Head

BORN: Sept. 1, 1941
HOMETOWN: Three Rivers, Texas

Roy Head became involved with music early in life, since both his parents were country fiddlers. During his teens he joined a country band and scored with a southwestern regional hit called "One More Time."

During the mid-sixties, in an effort to gain wider acceptance, Head began leaning toward a rock 'n' roll sound. His reputation in Texas was strong enough to get him a contract with the Houston-based Backbeat label, and he scored almost immediately with a number two national hit, "Treat Her Right." Backbeat issued several more best-selling records, and Scepter, a label for which he had recorded unsuccessfully before the hit, began to release his records as well.

In 1971 Head's sound began a turn back toward country with a record called "Puff of Smoke." Today he records for ABC/Dot Records and is an active country artist. He lives in Houston, Texas, where he is the resident performer at the Club Savaggio when he is not on the road.

Sept. 65 *TREAT HER RIGHT /*Backbeat
Oct. 65 *JUST A LITTLE BIT /*
Scepter
Nov. 65 *APPLE OF MY EYE /*
Backbeat
Jan. 66 *GET BACK /*Scepter
Mar. 66 *MY BABE /*Backbeat
Sept. 66 *TO MAKE A BIG MAN CRY /*
Backbeat
June 71 *PUFF OF SMOKE /*TMI

Heart

MEMBERS:
Ann Wilson (lead vocals)
Nancy Wilson (guitar)
Roger Fisher (guitar)
Steve Fossen (bass guitar)
Howard Leese (keyboard)
Mike Derosier (drums)
HOMETOWN: Vancouver, British Columbia, Canada

Ann and her sister Nancy began performing in folk clubs in the Seattle area during the late sixties. Soon they moved to Vancouver, where they met the other members of the group that eventually became Heart.

After gaining success in the Vancouver area, Heart was signed to the Canadian Mushroom label and began working on new material that Ann and Nancy had written. The result was the debut LP *Dreamboat Annie* early in 1976, which produced the top ten smash "Magic Man."

Today Heart is an international supergroup and will no doubt be around for a long time to come.

Apr. 76 *CRAZY ON YOU /*Mushroom
July 76 *MAGIC MAN /*Mushroom
Dec. 76 *DREAMBOAT ANNIE /*
Mushroom
May 77 *BARRACUDA /*Portrait
Sept. 77 *LITTLE QUEEN /*Portrait
Nov. 77 *KICK IT OUT /*Portrait
Jan. 78 *CRAZY ON YOU /*Mushroom
Apr. 78 *HEARTLESS /*Mushroom

Heatwave

MEMBERS:
Keith Wilder (lead vocals)/Dayton, Ohio
Johnnie Wilder (vocals, percussion)/Dayton, Ohio
Rod Temperton (keyboards)/London, England
Eric Johns (guitar)/replaced by Roy Carter/London, England

Heart. Left to right: Michael Derosier, Steven Fossen, Nancy Wilson, Ann Wilson, Roger Fisher, Howard Leese

Mario Mantese (bass guitar) / Spain

Ernest "Bilbo" Berger (drums) / Czechoslovakia

Even though the disco scene is big in America, some consider it to be even bigger in France, Germany, and England. In fact, some of the disco tunes that have become popular in America were hits first in Europe. A few years ago a group of American and English musicians got together in England to make up their own disco group. The result was Heatwave. With producer Barry Blue they recorded an album called *Too Hot to Handle.* From that debut LP for Epic records came a song Rod Temperton wrote called "Boogie Nights," a song that took this country by storm and launched the sound of Heatwave.

July 77 *BOOGIE NIGHTS* / Epic
Jan. 78 *ALWAYS & FOREVER* / Epic
May 78 *THE GROOVE LINE* / Epic

Bobby Hebb

BORN: 1939

Bobby Hebb grew up in the South and learned to play the guitar from his parents. Later he was one of the first black performers ever to sing with the Grand Ole Opry.

In the fall of 1963 two tragic events—the assassination of President Kennedy and, just one day later, Hebb's own brother's death in a mugging incident—moved him to write a song called "Sunny." (According to Hebb, the song is dedicated to the Creator and not to a woman, as was commonly supposed.) He attempted to sell the song to various publishers but received no offers. Nearly three years later, in 1966, when Hebb was recording an album in association with producer Jerry Ross, he recorded "Sunny" simply to use up time at the end of the session. As a single release from the album it went to the top of the charts and became an instant contemporary standard! Before the year ended, Hebb had two more hits and a tour with The Beatles under his belt.

During the following years Hebb concentrated on songwriting, winning a Grammy in 1971 for the Lou Rawls recording of his composition "A Natural Man." Today he makes occasional club appearances and lives in a colonial mansion in Salem, Massachusetts.

June 66 *SUNNY*/**Philips**
Oct. 66 *A SATISFIED MIND*/**Philips**
Dec. 66 *LOVE ME*/**Philips**

The Jimi Hendrix Experience

MEMBERS:
James Marshall "Jimi" Hendrix (guitar)/born: Nov. 27, 1942/Seattle, Washington/died: Sept. 18, 1970/London, England
Noel Redding (bass)/born: Dec. 25, 1945/Folkestone, Kent, England
John "Mitch" Mitchell (drums)/born: July 9, 1946/London, England

A legendary superstar, Jimi Hendrix is acknowledged to have changed the entire face of rock music, almost singlehandedly, with his innovative guitar work.

Jimi got his first guitar, a present from his father, at eleven. Within a year he had graduated to the electric guitar and was soon playing in local teen-age rock 'n' roll bands. In 1964 after a fourteen-month stint with the army, Jimi began playing as a sideman for leading acts like Chuck Jackson, Little Richard, Wilson Pickett, Ike & Tina Turner, Joey Dee, and The Isley Brothers. He traveled to New York to record with the Isleys, as well as with Lonnie Youngblood and Curtis Knight, and remained to form his own band, Jimmy James &

Jimi Hendrix

The Blue Flames. The group appeared regularly on the Greenwich Village club circuit, and one of their performances, at the Cafe Wha, was seen by veteran rock musician Chas Chandler. Chandler, the bass player for the original Animals, had turned producer-manager and decided to represent Hendrix.

In September 1966 Chandler brought Jimi to England and helped establish a rhythm section for him consisting of Mitch Mitchell and Noel Redding. The new group, called The Experience, began by recording the classic "Hey Joe," which was sold to Polydor Records. After an appearance by the group on the "Ready Steady Go" TV show, the record became a major British hit. Their subsequent recordings, beginning with "Purple Haze," appeared on Kit Lambert's Track label, and the group was well on its way to success.

The summer of 1967 brought the Monterey Pop Festival, an event that would have a profound effect on rock music by introducing such future superstars as Janis Joplin, Otis Redding, and, above all, Jimi Hendrix. That performance sent Jimi on his way to becoming rock's reigning guitarist, and Warner Brothers-Reprise began issuing his British tracks in America. His albums, including *Are You Experienced, Axis Bold As Love,* and *Electric Ladyland* became instant best sellers.

By 1969 personality problems had developed within The Experience, and Jimi thought it best to disband the group. He formed a new ensemble, Band of Gypsies, consisting of an old army buddy, Billy Cox (bass), and Buddy Miles (drums). The new band continued with a series of best selling LPs, including *Band of Gypsies* and *Rainbow Bridge.* Their final album was to be *Isle of Wight,* recorded at the famed Isle Of Wight concert in 1970. Only ten days later, Jimi Hendrix was dead, of an accidental barbiturate overdose.

Durning the following years several companies issued packages of previously recorded material, some never before released. Two singles made brief chart appearances in 1971.

Aug. 67 *PURPLE HAZE/* **Reprise**
Dec. 67 *FOXY LADY/* **Reprise**
Mar. 68 *UP FROM THE SKIES/* **Reprise**
Sept. 68 *ALL ALONG THE WATCH-TOWER/* **Reprise**
Nov. 68 *CROSSTOWN TRAFFIC/* **Reprise**
Apr. 71 *FREEDOM/* **Reprise**
Oct. 71 *DOLLY DAGGER/* **Reprise**

Herman's Hermits

MEMBERS:
Herman (Peter Blair Denis Bernard Noone) (lead vocals, piano, guitar)/born: Nov. 5, 1947/Manchester, England

Karl Anthony Greene (guitar, harmonica)/born: July 31, 1947/Salford, England
Keith Hopwood (guitar)/born: Oct. 26, 1946/Manchester, England
Derek "Lek" Leckenby (guitar)/born: May 14, 1945/Leeds, England
Barry Whitham (drums)/born: July 21, 1946/Manchester, England

A major component of the mid-sixties "British invasion," Herman's Hermits achieved the height of popularity in the United States without ever making any real impact in their own country.

The group began in 1963, when child actor Peter Noone attended a Manchester youth-club performance of a group known as The Heartbeats. The group needed someone to fill in that day and Noone, who had had some voice training, offered to help. The audience reaction was so overwhelming that they decided to form a permanent group. This evolved into Herman's Hermits, featuring the above line-up. Their name was chosen because Noone was thought to resemble Sherman in the TV cartoon "Rocky & His Friends"; the nickname eventually became "Herman."

After establishing a strong reputation in Manchester, the group came to the attention of producer Mickie Most and began recording in 1964. Their first success came later that year with a cover version of the Earl-Jean hit, "I'm into Something Good." They continued with a long string of hits that lasted nearly four years and appeared in the film *When the Boys Meet the Girls.* They eventually disbanded in 1970.

Today Peter Noone records as a solo singer and occasionally works as an actor. The Hermits, featuring a new lead singer, have regrouped and signed with the Buddah label.

Oct. 64	*I'M INTO SOMETHING GOOD/* MGM
Jan. 65	*CAN'T YOU HEAR MY HEARTBEAT/*MGM
Apr. 65	*SILHOUETTES/*MGM
Apr. 65	*MRS. BROWN, YOU'VE GOT A LOVELY DAUGHTER/*MGM
May 65	*WONDERFUL WORLD/*MGM
July 65	*I'M HENRY THE EIGHTH, I AM/*MGM
Sept. 65	*JUST A LITTLE BIT BETTER/* MGM
Dec. 65	*A MUST TO AVOID/*MGM
Feb. 66	*LISTEN PEOPLE/*MGM
Apr. 66	*LEANING ON THE LAMP POST/*MGM
July 66	*THIS DOOR SWINGS BOTH WAYS/*MGM
Oct. 66	*DANDY/*MGM
Dec. 66	*EAST WEST/*MGM
Feb. 67	*THERE'S A KIND OF HUSH/* MGM
Feb. 67	*NO MILK TODAY/*MGM
June 67	*DON'T GO OUT INTO THE RAIN/*MGM
Aug. 67	*MUSEUM/*MGM
Jan. 68	*I CAN TAKE OR LEAVE YOUR LOVING/*MGM
May 68	*SLEEPY JOE/*MGM

Dan Hill

BORN: June 3, 1954
HOMETOWN: Toronto, Canada

As a teen-ager Hill began writing songs and playing at local coffee houses. After a few years he went to America and traveled for about a year playing at small clubs, after which he returned to Canada.

When he got back to his hometown he worked very diligently at sharpening up his style and stage act. After a rave appearance at Toronto's Riverboat club and a successful tour, he received the Juno award as Canada's best new singer.

His first LP *Dan Hill* established his gentle sound, but his most recent album, *Longer Fuse,* made him a nation-al star because of a tune he wrote, along with hitmaker Barry Mann, called "Sometimes When We Touch."

Nov. 77	*SOMETIMES WHEN WE TOUCH/*20th Century

Al Hirt

FULL NAME: Alois Maxwell Hirt
BORN: Nov. 7, 1922
HOMETOWN: New Orleans, Louisiana

Well known in traditional jazz circles since the late forties, Al Hirt rose to nationwide popularity in the sixties with a series of rousing, New Orleans-style trumpet instrumentals.

He began his career in The Sons of the Police Department Junior Police Band and eventually entered the Cincinnati Conservatory to study music. In the late forties he traveled with various name bands, worked in a pit band, and began an eight-year period of residency with a New Orleans radio station ensemble.

By the mid-fifties Hirt had formed his own combo (which included clarinetist Pete Fountain) and was recording for the small, independent Audio Fidelity label (several of these recordings were later reissued by the larger Coral label). In 1960 Hirt was offered a contract by RCA and scored with a series of popular albums, including *Greatest Horn, He's the King, Bourbon Street, Horn a Plenty, At the Mardi Gras, Trumpet & Strings,* and *Honey in the Horn.* In 1964 he broke through with his top ten single recording of "Java," originally an R & B instrumental by Allen Toussaint; a string of additional hits followed.

Today Al Hirt continues to live in New Orleans and to produce best-selling albums.

Dan Hill

Jan. 64	*JAVA* /RCA
Apr. 64	*COTTON CANDY* /RCA
July 64	*SUGAR LIPS* /RCA
Oct. 64	*UP ABOVE MY HEAD* /RCA
Jan. 65	*FANCY PANTS* /RCA
Apr. 65	*AL'S PLACE* /RCA
Sept. 65	*THE SILENCE* /RCA
Jan. 68	*KEEP THE BALL ROLLING* / RCA

The Hollies

MEMBERS:

Allan Clarke (lead vocals) /born: Apr. 5, 1942/ Salford, Lancashire, England/replaced (1971- 1973) by Mikael Rickfors/birthplace: Sweden

Anthony Hicks (lead guitar) /born: Dec. 16, 1945/Nelson, Lancashire, England

Graham Nash (rhythm guitar) /born: Feb. 2, 1942/Blackpool, Lancashire, England/ replaced (1968) by Terry Sylvester/ born: Jan. 8, 1947/Liverpool, England

Eric Haydock (bass) /birthplace: England/ replaced (1966) by Bernard Calver/born: Sept. 16, 1942/Burnley, Lancashire, England

Donald Rathbone (drums) /birthplace: England/ replaced (1963) by Robert Elliott/born: Dec. 8, 1942/Burnley, Lancashire, England

This group began as The Deltas in 1962 and rose to prominence during the British "beat" era. Through a series of changes in personnel and sound they have been one of the only such groups to continue successfully into the seventies.

The Hollies. Left to right: Allan Clarke, Robert Elliott, Graham Nash, Bernard Calver, Tony Hicks

The group was started by Allan Clarke and Graham Nash, who had played together previously in several groups and who had teamed up briefly as Ricky & Dane. After making their debut in Manchester's famed Oasis Club, The Hollies secured a contract with Parlophone Records and launched their recording career with a remake of The Coasters' "Ain't That Just Like Me." They followed with another Coasters standard, "Searchin'," and Maurice Williams's "Stay." Continuing the pattern of recording American R & B hits, they released Doris Troy's "Just One Look" early in 1964. This crossed the Atlantic on the coat-tails of Beatlemania and became the first of The Hollies' nearly two dozen American hits.

The Hollies were able to survive the type of personnel changes that normally bring groups to an end. Drummer Don Rathbone left almost at the outset to be replaced by Bobby Elliott from The Fentones. Next Bernie Calvert took Eric Haydock's place, Eric having left to form his own group, Haydock's Rockhouse. Graham Nash split to team up with David Crosby and Steve Stills (see *CROSBY, STILLS, NASH & YOUNG*) and was replaced by Terry Sylvester, a veteran of The Swingin' Blue Jeans and The Escorts. Finally Allan Clarke separated from The Hollies for nearly two years to attempt a solo career but eventually returned. His replacement was Mikael Rickfors, formerly with a Swedish rock group called Bamboo.

Today The Hollies retain their 1973 line-up. In 1974 Terry Sylvester recorded a solo album, *For the Peace of All Mankind.*

May 64	*JUST ONE LOOK* /Imperial
Nov. 65	*LOOK THROUGH ANY WINDOW* /Imperial
Mar. 66	*I CAN'T LET GO* /Imperial

July 66	*BUS STOP*/Imperial
Oct. 66	*STOP, STOP, STOP*/Imperial
Mar. 67	*ON A CAROUSEL*/Imperial
June 67	*PAY YOU BACK WITH INTEREST*/Imperial
June 67	*CARRIE ANN*/Epic
Sept. 67	*JUST ONE LOOK (rereleased)*/Imperial
Oct. 67	*KING MIDAS IN REVERSE*/Epic
Dec. 67	*DEAR ELOISE*/Epic
Mar. 68	*JENNIFER ECCLES*/Epic
Sept. 68	*DO THE BEST YOU CAN*/Epic
Apr. 69	*SORRY, SUZANNE*/Epic
Dec. 69	*HE AIN'T HEAVY, HE'S MY BROTHER*/Epic
May 70	*I CAN'T TELL THE BOTTOM FROM THE TOP*/Epic
June 72	*LONG COOL WOMAN*/Epic
Nov. 72	*LONG DARK ROAD*/Epic
Feb. 73	*MAGIC WOMAN TOUCH*/Epic
Apr. 74	*THE AIR THAT I BREATHE*/Epic
Apr. 75	*SANDY*/Epic
June 75	*ANOTHER NIGHT*/Epic

Brenda Holloway

BORN: June 21, 1946
HOMETOWN: Atascadero, California

Ever since she was a child, all Brenda ever wanted to do was to be a singer. She used to constantly listen to the radio to hear various singing styles with the hope of being able to develop her own style.

In early 1964, when she was only seventeen, Tamla Records signed her to a recording contract. Shortly thereafter she made her debut on the charts with the tune "Every Little Bit Hurts," a song that was to be her biggest hit.

Mar. 64	*EVERY LITTLE BIT HURTS*/Tamla
Aug. 64	*I'LL ALWAYS LOVE YOU*/Tamla
Mar. 65	*WHEN I'M GONE*/Tamla
June 65	*OPERATOR*/Tamla
Apr. 67	*JUST LOOK WHAT YOU'VE DONE*/Tamla

Sept. 67	*YOU'VE MADE ME SO VERY HAPPY*/Tamla

Eddie Holman

BORN: 1946
HOMETOWN: Norfolk, Virginia

Eddie Holman attended the Victoria School of Music and Art in New York City and later studied music at Cheyney State College in Philadelphia.

In the early sixties he signed with Philadelphia's Cameo label and debuted in 1963 with "Crossroads." In 1965 he scored on Cameo's sister label, Parkway, with a national hit, "This Can't Be True." He followed with the regional hit "Don't Stop Now" and continued to record for the company through 1967.

After a brief affiliation with Bell Records, Holman signed with ABC in 1969. After scoring an R & B hit with his first release, "I Love You," he reached the top of the national charts with a reworked version of Ruby & The Romantics' "Hey There Lonely Girl (Boy)." Today Holman records for Salsoul Records.

Jan. 66	*THIS CAN'T BE TRUE*/Parkway
Dec. 69	*HEY THERE LONELY GIRL*/ABC
Apr. 70	*DON'T STOP NOW*/ABC
June 77	*THIS WILL BE A NIGHT TO REMEMBER*/Salsoul

Clint Holmes

BORN: May 9, 1946
HOMETOWN: Bournemouth, England

Clint Holmes grew up in Buffalo, New York, where his parents moved when he was a young child. He showed an early interest in singing, and his mother, a former British opera singer, served as his first vocal coach. Later he formed a band in high school and attended Fredonia Stage College as a trombone major.

In the mid-sixties Holmes found himself stationed in Washington, D.C., as part of the Army Chorus. After his discharge he stayed in the area and built a reputation as a singer in local clubs. By the early seventies, he was appearing regularly at Shepheard's in New York and in major clubs in Bermuda and The Bahamas. One of his performances was seen by Dionne Warwicke, who took him on tour as her "protégé."

Holmes formed an association with producer Paul Vance in 1972 and recorded a song called "Playground in My Mind" (the small child heard on the record was Vance's son Philip). Sold to Epic Records, the song became a regional hit and was in release more than a year before it started selling on a national level. It eventually reached the top of the charts and established Holmes as a star.

A major club attraction today, Clint Holmes began recording for Atlantic Records in the mid-seventies.

Mar. 73 *PLAYGROUND IN MY MIND /*
      Epic

Hombres

MEMBERS:
Gary Wayne McEwen (lead guitar)
Jerry Lee Masters (bass guitar)
B. B. Cunningham (organ)
John William Hunter (drums)
HOMETOWN: Memphis, Tennessee

Memphis has long been one of the country's most important music markets with just about everyone living in the town having dreams of someday recording a hit record.

The dream came true for four local boys, who in 1967 recorded a novel tune called "Let It Out (Let It All Hang Out")." They took the song to various companies with no success, finally settling with Verve/Forecast. The song went on to become a national hit. Unfortunately, it was the only one they ever had.

Sept. 67 *LET IT OUT (LET IT ALL HANG*
        OUT) / Verve / Forecast

The Hondells

Richard Burns
BORN: May 4, 1941/Buffalo, New York

The Hondells began as a studio group assembled by West Coast producer Mike Curb to record a commercial for Honda motorbikes. The central member of the group was Richie Burns, who had gained his experience playing in high school and college bands.

Burns traveled to California and broke into the burgeoning "surf-rock" scene in 1962. After the success of the commercial "You Meet the Nicest People on a Honda," The Hondells became a permanent working unit and signed with Mercury Records. They began with a hit single, "Little Honda," written by Brian Wilson of The Beach Boys, and recorded an album in association with leading "surf-rock" figures Gary Usher, Roger Christian, and Nick Venet. The Hondells achieved two more hit singles before the surf and car craze began to subside in the mid-sixties.

Sept. 64 *LITTLE HONDA /*
         Mercury
Dec. 64 *MY BUDDY SEAT /*
        Mercury
May 66 *A YOUNGER GIRL /*
        Mercury

The Hondells

The Honeycombs

MEMBERS:

Denis D'Ell (Denis Dalziell) (vocals, harmonica)/born: Oct. 10, 1943/London, England

Martin Murray (lead guitar)/born: Oct. 7, 1941/London, England/replaced (1964) by Peter Pye

Alan Ward (rhythm guitar)/born: Dec. 12, 1945/Nottingham, England

John Lantree (bass)/born: Aug. 20, 1940/Newbury, England

Ann "Honey" Lantree (drums)/born: Aug. 28, 1943/Middlesex, England

This group began in 1963 in North London as The Sherabons and quickly gained a reputation, since they had rock music's only female drummer. The group was organized by Martin Murray and Ann Lantree. Their present name is a combination of Ann's nickname, "Honey," and "Combs" (Ann had been a hairdresser at the time of the group's formation).

In 1964 The Honeycombs began recording for Pye Records and achieved immediate success with their first release, "Have I the Right." In view of The Beatles' impact on America, Pye leased the record to Vee Jay Records for United States distribution. Issued on

229

Vee Jay's Interphon subsidiary, established specifically for the release of the British product, the record became a top five American hit. Although The Honeycombs had only one more United States chart entry, they continued to record successfully in Britain through the end of 1966. At that point their producer, Joe Meek, died, leaving them without musical direction; they never had another hit.

Sept. 64 *HAVE I THE RIGHT* /Interphon
Dec. 64 *I CAN'T STOP* /Interphon

Honey Cone

MEMBERS:
Edna Wright /born: 1944/Los Angeles, California
Shellie Clark /born: 1943/Brooklyn, New York
Carolyn Willis born: 1947/Los Angeles, California/replaced by Denise Mills

This group was formed in the late sixties by three veteran "background" vocalists. In addition to the West Coast session work they had all done, Edna had sung with The Raelettes, Carolyn with The Girlfriends and Bob B. Soxx & The Blue Jeans, and Shellie with Ike & Tina Turner and Little Richard.

In 1969 the three young women were assembled to back up Burt Bacharach on an Andy Williams TV special. Edna, who was friendly with Eddie Holland (of the Holland-Dozier-Holland team), suggested that he watch the show; he was so enthused that he signed them to his new Hot Wax label. After naming them The Honey Cone, he produced a string of pop and soul hits for them which lasted more than three years.

Honey Cone eventually disbanded, and the members returned to their studio work. In the mid-seventies Carolyn Willis emerged as a featured vocalist

with Seals & Crofts, with a prominent role on their hit "Get Closer."

June 69 *WHILE YOU'RE OUT LOOKING FOR SUGAR* /Hot Wax
Nov. 69 *GIRLS, IT AIN'T EASY* /Hot Wax
Apr. 71 *WANT ADS* /Hot Wax
Aug. 71 *STICK UP* /Hot Wax
Nov. 71 *ONE MONKEY DON'T STOP NO SHOW* /Hot Wax
Feb. 72 *THE DAY I FOUND MYSELF* /Hot Wax
July 72 *SITTING ON A TIME BOMB* /Hot Wax

Mary Hopkin

BORN: May 3, 1950
HOMETOWN: Ystradgynlais, South Wales

Mary Hopkin began singing as a child at her mother's encouragement. At fifteen she received a guitar and began performing in neighborhood clubs. She also appeared on several Welsh television programs.

In 1968 Mary was preparing to enter the Cardiff School of Music when she auditioned for a TV talent show called "Opportunity Knocks." She won the chance to appear for several weeks, and one of her performances was seen by Twiggy. She recommended Mary to Paul McCartney, who called her to audition for The Beatles' new Apple label. She was signed immediately, and her first release, "Those Were the Days," was an international number one hit. She followed with a Lennon-McCartney composition, "Goodbye," and a string of best sellers that lasted well into the early seventies.

Today Mary is a popular club attraction in England and records for RCA Records.

Sept. 68 *THOSE WERE THE DAYS* /Apple

Hot. Left to right: Juanita Curiel, Gwen Owens, Cathy Carson

Apr. 69	**GOODBYE** / Apple
Feb. 70	**TEMMA HARBOUR** / Apple
July 70	**QUE SERA, SERA** / Apple
Nov. 70	**THINK ABOUT YOUR CHILDREN** / Apple
Dec. 72	**KNOCK KNOCK, WHO'S THERE** / Apple

Hot

MEMBERS:

Gwen Owens / born: June 19, 1953
Cathy Carson / born: Oct. 7, 1953
Juanita Curiel / born: Feb. 25, 1953

Cathy and Gwen met while audition-ing for the Wolfman Jack show in Los Angeles where they were selected to tour with Wolfman Jack's Shock & Rock Review. At this time they called themselves Sugar & Spice. By late 1976 they got to do some national television including an appearance on the Bill Cosby show. It was at this time that the two girls met Juanita and de-cided to perform as a trio calling them-selves Hot.

They were signed to Big Tree Rec-ords and went to Muscle Shoals, Ala-bama, where they recorded their debut album called *Hot* from which came their first hit single, "Angel in Your Arms."

Feb. 77 *ANGEL IN YOUR ARMS* / Big Tree
Aug. 77 *THE RIGHT FEELING AT THE WRONG TIME* / Big Tree
Feb. 78 *YOU BROUGHT THE WOMAN OUT OF ME* / Big Tree

Hot Chocolate

MEMBERS:

Errol Brown (vocals) / birthplace: Jamaica, West Indies

Harvey Hinsley (guitar) / hometown: Northhampton, England

Larry Ferguson (keyboards) / birthplace: Bahamas

Patrick Olive (guitar, percussion) / birthplace: Grenada, West Indies

Tony Wilson (bass) / birthplace: Trinidad, West Indies

Ian King (drums) / replaced (1973) by Tony Connor / hometown: Romford, England

HOMETOWN: Brixton, England

A major entry into the British soul market, Hot Chocolate was organized by Ian King in 1970. The six members, from various parts of the West Indies and England, got to know each other over a period of years by playing together in different combinations.

Errol Brown and Tony Wilson approached producer Mickie Most about having some of their songs recorded by Herman's Hermits. Most not only took one of their songs, "Bet Your Life I Do," which The Hermits turned into a hit, but he arranged for other artists, such as Mary Hopkin and Julie Felix, to record their material. He also took an interest in Hot Chocolate, signing the group to his newly formed RAK label and assuming the production of their records.

During the early seventies the group achieved several British hits, including "Brother Louie" (covered in the United

States by Stories), "Rumors," "Love Is Life" and "Emma." After 1975 their records were released in the United States on the Big Tree label, and they have scored with several major American hits.

Feb. 75 *EMMA* / Big Tree
May 75 *DISCO QUEEN* / Big Tree
Nov. 75 *YOU SEXY THING* / Big Tree
Apr. 76 *DON'T STOP IT NOW* / Big Tree
July 77 *SO YOU WIN AGAIN* / Big Tree

Thelma Houston

HOMETOWN: Long Beach, California

As a youngster, Thelma began singing gospel music at the various churches in her area. A few years later she, along with her family, left Mississippi for California where she began a more serious approach to singing.

She began working weekends in various clubs in Los Angeles towards the late sixties, when she met Marc Gordon, the manager of The Fifth Dimension. Marc liked her so much that he got her a recording contract with ABC-Dunhill Records.

After a few moderate hits she recorded in 1976 the album *Anyway You Like It,* on which was the Kenny Gamble-Leon Huff tune "Don't Leave Me This Way"—her ticket to national stardom.

Jan. 70 *SAVE THE COUNTRY* / Dunhill
Dec. 76 *DON'T LEAVE ME THIS WAY* / Tamla
June 77 *IF IT'S THE LAST THING I DO* / Tamla

The Hudson Brothers

MEMBERS:

William Louis Hudson II (guitar) / born: Oct. 17, 1949

Mark Jeffrey Anthony Hudson (keyboards) / born: Aug. 23, 1951

Brett Stuart Patrick Hudson (bass)/born: Jan. 18, 1953

All three Hudson brothers showed an early interest in music. Their mother, who was a singer, encouraged and coached them.

During the early sixties Mark and Bill launched individual careers by joining different high school bands, but by the mid-sixties the three brothers had their own band and were performing under the name of My Sirs. After winning a number of local "battle of the bands" contests, the group was asked by the Chrysler company to do a promotional tour. Since they were required to change their name to that of one of the company's cars, they began appearing as The New Yorkers. After the tour they traveled to Seattle, Washington, to rent a studio and record one of their songs, "When I'm Gone." The record was released by Scepter and became a regional northwestern hit. Next they signed with Decca and released an unsuccessful version of Nilsson's "I Guess the Lord Must Be in New York City." After that they changed their name to Everyday Hudson, then Hudson, and finally to The Hudson Brothers.

During the early seventies the group recorded for Playboy and Casablanca, but with only moderate success. They eventually came to the attention of Bernie Taupin, Elton John's cowriter, who arranged for them to be signed to Elton's Rocket record company. Their records became best sellers, and in 1975 they became the hosts of their own weekly TV show, "The Razzle Dazzle Comedy Hour."

Today The Hudson Brothers are a top teen attraction, traveling with a back-up band consisting of Barry Pullman (Moog synthesizer), Phil Reed (guitar), Mike Parker (keyboards), and Craig Krapf (drums and percussion).

Sept. 74 *SO YOU ARE A STAR* / **Casablanca**

June 75 *RENDEZVOUS* / **Rocket**

Nov. 75 *LONELY SCHOOL YEAR* / **Rocket**

Nov. 76 *HELP WANTED* / **Arista**

The Hues Corporation

MEMBERS:

Hubert Ann Kelly (soprano)/born: Apr. 24, 1947/Fairchild, Alabama

Bernard St. Clair Lee Calhoun Henderson (baritone)/born: Apr. 24, 1944/San Francisco, California

Fleming Williams /Flint, Michigan/replaced by Tom Brown/Birmingham, Alabama/replaced by Karl Russell/(second tenor)/born: Apr. 10, 1947/Columbus, Ohio

The Hues Corporation was formed in 1969 and took their name from billionaire recluse Howard Hughes. All three members had had singing experience in various church and semipro groups.

During the next four years The Hues Corporation perfected their act by playing various Los Angeles area clubs and an extended run as a Las Vegas lounge act. They were affiliated briefly with the Liberty label, for which they recorded one unsuccessful single.

In 1973 the group was offered a contract by RCA, and they achieved a hit single called "Freedom for the Stallion." After an album of the same name was released, Fleming Williams left to pursue other interests and was replaced by a childhood friend of H. Ann Kelly's, Tommy Brown. Brown came to the group from a Los Angeles ensemble known as Just Us and sang lead on The Hues' next single, a number one hit titled "Rock the Boat." After two more hits Brown left the group for a

The Hues Corporation. Left to right: Karl Russell, H. Ann Kelly, St. Clair Lee

solo career and was replaced by Karl Russell.

Today The Hues Corporation is a leading club attraction, and records for Warner Brothers.

Aug. 73	*FREEDOM FOR THE STALLION*/RCA
May 74	*ROCK THE BOAT*/RCA
Oct. 74	*ROCKIN' SOUL*/RCA
Feb. 75	*LOVE CORPORATION*/RCA
Apr. 77	*I CAUGHT YOUR ACT*/Warner Bros.

Jimmy Hughes

HOMETOWN: Florence, Alabama

Jimmy Hughes began singing in church as a child, and was the lead singer in his choir by the time he was eight. As a teen-ager he decided on a career as a spiritual singer and sang with several gospel groups.

In 1963 Hughes came to the attention of Rick Hall, head of Fame Records in nearby Muscle Shoals, Alabama. Signed to the label, he debuted with a regional blues hit called "I'm Qualified," a big seller in the South. However, it was his next release, "Steal Away," that established him by reaching the national top twenty.

Jimmy Hughes scored with several more chart entries before fading from popularity in the late sixties.

June 64	*STEAL AWAY*/Fame
Sept. 64	*TRY ME*/Fame
June 66	*NEIGHBOR NEIGHBOR*/Fame
Mar. 67	*WHY NOT TONIGHT*/Fame

Humble Pie

MEMBERS:

Steve Marriott (guitar)/born: Jan. 30, 1947

Peter Frampton (guitar)/born: Apr. 22, 1950/ replaced (1971) by David "Clem" Clempson/ born: Sept. 5, 1949

Gregory Ridley (bass)/born: Oct. 23, 1947

Jerry Shirley (drums)/born: Feb. 4, 1952

HOMETOWN: Essex, England

When Humble Pie was formed in late 1968, most of the members had already performed with other major rock bands. Peter Frampton had been with The Herd, Steve Marriott with Faces, and Greg Ridley with Spooky Tooth. Jerry Shirley, who had played with several bands around Essex, was a friend of Frampton's who was chosen to round out the line-up.

After several months of rehearsal Humble Pie had no difficulty getting a recording contract and debuted on the Immediate label with an album called *As Safe As Yesterday.* They followed in 1969 with another album, *Town & Country.* Soon, however, Immediate went out of business and left the group with no label affiliation. Their manager, Dee Anthony, obtained a contract with the American A & M label, and they continued their string of LPs with *Humble Pie, Rock On,* and *Live at the Fillmore.*

In 1971, just after the *Fillmore* LP, Frampton left Humble Pie to form his own group, Camel. His replacement, "Clem" Clempson, was recruited from Colosseum, and the group continued well into the seventies with best-selling albums such as *Smokin, Eat It,* and *Thunderbox.* Primarily an "album" group, Humble Pie placed only two singles on the charts.

Humble Pie disbanded at the height of their success, late in 1975. Steve Marriott began recording solo; "Clem" Clempson and Greg Ridley joined with a third musician, Cozy Powell, to form Strange Brew. Former "Pie" member Peter Frampton emerged in 1976 as one of rock music's leading stars.

Sept. 71 *I DON'T NEED NO DOCTOR / A & M*

May 72 *HOT & NASTY /* A & M

Engelbert Humperdinck

REAL NAME: Arnold George Dorsey
BORN: May 3, 1936
HOMETOWN: Madras, India

Arnold George Dorsey was raised in Leicester, England, where his parents had moved during his childhood. He developed an interest in singing during his late teens and occasionally entertained at local pubs.

After a two-year stint with the royal army, Dorsey returned home during the mid-fifties to work at a series of odd jobs and to launch a singing career. In 1966 Dorsey contacted Gor-

Engelbert Humperdinck

don Mills, an old friend who had become successful as Tom Jones's manager. Mills agreed to handle Dorsey's career too, and first suggested he change his name to Engelbert Humperdinck, after the nineteenth-century German opera composer best known for *Hansel and Gretel*. Eventually Mills obtained a recording contract with the British Decca label, but Humperdinck soon switched to the Parrot label, with which Tom Jones was affiliated, and began recording in Jones's "country" style. He scored immediately with the standard "Release Me," which became an international, chart-topping hit and the first of a series of best sellers that was to last well into the seventies.

During the early seventies Engelbert Humperdinck became a leading nightclub attraction, hosted an American network television show, and sold albums in the millions. Today he lives in Surrey, England, with his wife, Pat, and their daughter and two sons.

Apr. 67	*RELEASE ME* / Parrot
July 67	*THERE GOES MY EVERYTHING* / Parrot
Sept. 67	*THE LAST WALTZ* / Parrot
Dec. 67	*AM I THAT EASY TO FORGET?* / Parrot
May 68	*A MAN WITHOUT LOVE* / Parrot
Oct. 68	*LES BICYCLETTES DE BELSIZE* / Parrot
Mar. 69	*THE WAY IT USED TO BE* / Parrot
Aug. 69	*I'M A BETTER MAN* / Parrot
Dec. 69	*A WINTER WORLD OF LOVE* / Parrot
June 70	*MY MARIE* / Parrot
Sept. 70	*SWEETHEART* / Parrot
Mar. 71	*WHEN THERE'S NO YOU* / Parrot
Aug. 71	*ANOTHER TIME, ANOTHER PLACE* / Parrot
Apr. 72	*TOO BEAUTIFUL TO LAST* / Parrot
Aug. 72	*IN TIME* / Parrot
Dec. 72	*I NEVER SAID GOODBYE* / Parrot
June 73	*I'M LEAVING YOU* / Parrot
Sept. 73	*LOVE IS ALL* / Parrot
Oct. 76	*AFTER THE LOVING* / Epic
July 77	*GOODBYE MY FRIEND* / Epic

Janis Ian

REAL NAME: Janis Fink
BORN: Apr. 7, 1951
HOMETOWN: New York City

Although born in New York, Janis grew up in New Jersey, where her family relocated to several different cities during her childhood. She attended a variety of schools, eventually entering New York City's Music and Art High School to study music.

At the age of fifteen, while still a high school student, Janis began singing and playing acoustic guitar in local clubs and coffeehouses. This eventu-ally led to a contract offer from Verve Forecast Records, and she debuted in 1966 with her recording of "Society's Child." A highly controversial song that dealt with interracial love, the record was banned by most radio stations and sold very poorly. However, in 1967 conductor Leonard Bernstein featured Janis and her song on one of his TV specials, providing a great deal of pub-licity and sending the record into the national top twenty. Janis followed with two moderately successful LP's, *Janis Ian* and *For All Seasons,* before fading from popularity during the late sixties. Her last album for Verve, *The Secret*

Janis Ian

Life of J. Eddy Fink was released in 1968. During the early seventies, Janis made an unsuccessful comeback attempt by signing with Capitol Records. She later signed with Columbia, recording an album called *Stars,* which drew a great deal of attention to her songwriting ability. One of the cuts, "Jesse," was made into a top 30 hit by Roberta Flack, which encouraged Janis to make a second album entitled *Between the Lines.* This became an immediate best seller, generating a chart-topping single and Grammy Award winner titled "At Seventeen."

A bigger star than ever, Janis Ian today makes her permanent home in New York City.

May 67 *SOCIETY'S CHILD* /Verve/ Forecast
June 75 *AT SEVENTEEN* /Columbia

The Ides of March

MEMBERS:
James Peterik (lead vocals, guitar, keyboards)
Ray Herr (alternate lead vocals, guitar, bass)
Lawrence Millas (guitar, organ)
Robert Bergland (bass, sax)
John Larson (horns)
Chuck Somar (horns)
Michael Borch (drums)
HOMETOWN: Chicago, Illinois

The Ides of March, formed during the mid-sixties, took their name from a line in Shakespeare's *Julius Caesar.* All seven members had been classmates since grammar school and decided, during their high-school years, to organize a group.

After gaining a strong reputation for their club work, the group was signed by the Parrot label and was able to achieve two moderate hits in 1966. However, their major breakthrough came in 1970, when they were signed by Warner Brothers and topped the national charts with James Peterik's composition "Vehicle." After two additional chart entries, they began to fade from popularity and eventually disbanded.

During the mid-seventies The Ides of March regrouped in the hope of making a comeback.

June 66 *YOU WOULDN'T LISTEN* / Parrot
Sept. 66 *ROLLER COASTER* /Parrot
Mar. 70 *VEHICLE* /Warner Bros.
July 70 *SUPERMAN* /Warner Bros.
Mar. 71 *L.A. GOODBYE* /Warner Bros.

Luther Ingram

HOMETOWN: Jackson, Tennessee

Luther Ingram is one of seven children, all of whom began singing in church as youngsters. After graduating from high school, he launched his career by forming a spirituals vocal group with three of his brothers and several friends.

During the early sixties Ingram traveled to New York to enter the recording business as a studio singer. He became acquainted with Johnny Baylor, who became his manager and established the KoKo label to release his recordings. Through the late sixties, several of his releases became best sellers in the Soul market, including "I Spy for the FBI," "Missing You," "My Honey & Me," "Ain't That Loving You," and "Respect for the Other Man."

In 1970 Ingram's records began appearing on the national pop charts as well, and he also began writing for other artists, including The Staple Singers ("Respect Yourself") and Isaac Hayes ("Help Me Love").

Today Luther Ingram makes his home in Alton, Illinois.

Jan. 70	*MY HONEY AND ME* / KoKo
May 70	*AIN'T THAT LOVING YOU* / KoKo
May 71	*BE GOOD TO ME BABY* / KoKo
Apr. 72	*YOU WERE MADE FOR ME* / KoKo
June 72	*I DON'T WANT TO BE RIGHT* / KoKo
Dec. 72	*I'LL BE YOUR SHELTER* / KoKo
Apr. 73	*ALWAYS* / KoKo

The Innocence

MEMBERS:
Pete Anders (Peter Andreoli) / born: Apr. 28, 1941
Vincent Poncia, Jr. / born: Apr. 29, 1942
HOMETOWN: Providence, Rhode Island

This was a studio group made up of Pete Anders and Vinnie Poncia.

Anders and Poncia began their career in 1960, achieving a modest hit, "Mr. Lonely," with a group called The Videls. They became known later in the sixties for their work with The Critters, The Tradewinds, and numerous other groups. Beginning in 1966 they placed two singles on the charts as The Innocence.

Today Anders and Poncia are pursuing separate careers as songwriters and independent record producers. Poncia achieved major success during the mid-seventies as the producer of Melissa Manchester.

Dec. 66	*THERE'S GOT TO BE A WORD* / Kama Sutra
Mar. 67	*MAIRZY DOATS* / Kama Sutra

The Intruders

MEMBERS:
Phil Terry
Robert "Big Sonny" Edwards
Samuel "Little Sonny" Brown
Eugene "Bird" Daughtry

HOMETOWN: Philadelphia, Pennsylvania

This vocal quartet was organized during the early sixties at the height of the "group harmony" era. They recorded for a number of small labels and achieved a sizable regional hit in 1965 with their release of "Gonna Be Strong" on Excel.

In 1966 The Intruders became the first act to be signed to Philadelphia's burgeoning Gamble-Huff production company. The group provided Gamble-Huff with its first chart hit, "United," and with the company's first million seller, "Cowboys to Girls." They have continued into the seventies with a long series of Pop and Soul hits.

July 66	*UNITED* / Gamble
Apr. 67	*TOGETHER* / Gamble
Sept. 67	*BABY I'M LONELY* / Gamble
Dec. 67	*A LOVE THAT'S REAL* / Gamble
Mar. 68	*COWBOYS TO GIRLS* / Gamble
July 68	*BASEBALL GAME* / Gamble
Nov. 68	*SLOW DRAG* / Gamble
Aug. 69	*SAD GIRL* / Gamble
June 70	*WHEN WE GET MARRIED* / Gamble
Nov. 70	*THIS IS MY LOVE SONG* / Gamble
Mar. 71	*I'M GIRL SCOUTING* / Gamble
Oct. 71	*I BET HE DON'T LOVE YOU* / Gamble
June 73	*I'LL ALWAYS LOVE MY MAMA* / Gamble
Oct. 73	*I WANNA KNOW YOUR NAME* / Gamble

Iron Butterfly

MEMBERS:
Erik Keith Braunn (lead guitar) / born: Aug. 11, 1950 / Boston, Massachusetts / replaced (1969) by Michael Pinera and Lawrence Reinhardt
Doug Ingle (lead vocals, keyboards) / born: Sept. 9, 1946 / Omaha, Nebraska
Lee Dorman (bass) / born: Sept. 15, 1945 / St. Louis, Missouri
Ronald Bushy (drums) / born: Dec. 23, 1945 / Washington, D.C.

One of the first and most successful of the "heavy metal" rock bands, Iron Butterfly was organized in 1966 by Doug Ingle. He had moved with his family to San Diego, California, and there recruited a group of musicians from the local club circuit. After a number of personnel changes, the group evolved into Iron Butterfly (with the above line-up), a name provided by Ingle.

In 1967 the group traveled to Los Angeles to audition for clubs along Sunset Strip. They eventually landed an appearance at The Whiskey A Go Go, where the audience response was so enthusiastic that they were asked to remain for three weeks. They followed with a three-month period of residency at The Galaxy, where they were spotted by executives of Atlantic Records and signed to the subsidiary Atco label.

Iron Butterfly debuted in 1968 with an album titled *Heavy,* which was followed within a few months by a second LP, *In a Gadda Da Vida.* The latter became Atlantic's largest-selling rock album of all time, and generated the first of the group's several hit singles. After the release of two more LP's, *Ball* and *Live,* Eric Braunn left the group. He was replaced by two guitarists, Mike Pinera from The Blues Image and Larry Reinhardt, a veteran of the early Allman Brothers Band. This group recorded one more album, *Metamorphosis,* before internal difficulties caused them to disband early in 1972.

In 1975 a re-formed Iron Butterfly group emerged and began recording for MCA Records. Their membership included two originals, Erik Braunn and Ron Bushy, and two new additions, Howard Reitzes and Phil Kramer.

Aug. 68	*IN A GADDA DA VIDA* / Atco
May 69	*IN A GADDA DA VIDA (rereleased)* / Atco
Feb. 69	*SOUL EXPERIENCE* / Atco
July 69	*IN THE TIME OF OUR LIVES* / Atco
Oct. 70	*EASY RIDER* / Atco

J

Terry Jacks

HOMETOWN: Winnipeg, Manitoba, Canada

See also *POPPY FAMILY*.

Jan. 74 *SEASONS IN THE SUN* / Bell
June 74 *IF YOU GO AWAY* / Bell
Dec. 74 *ROCK 'N' ROLL (I GAVE YOU THE BEST YEARS OF MY LIFE)* / Bell

Deon Jackson

BORN: 1945
HOMETOWN: Ann Arbor, Michigan

Determined from childhood to become a musician, Deon Jackson studied clarinet and drums in grammar school. He launched his singing career in 1960, forming a group with several high-school friends.

In 1962 one of Jackson's high-school performances was seen by producer and music publisher Ollie McGlaughlin. McGlaughlin became his manager and produced two recordings, "You Said You Love Me" and "Come Back Home," which became regional Detroit hits. By the mid-sixties McGlaughlin had established his own Carla label and signed Deon Jackson's biggest hit, reaching the national top ten. He was able to achieve two additional best sellers, after which his popularity centered mainly in his home area of Detroit.

Jan. 66 *LOVE MAKES THE WORLD GO ROUND* / Carla
Apr. 66 *LOVE TAKES A LONG TIME GROWING* / Carla
Nov. 67 *OOH BABY* / Carla

Millie Jackson

BORN: 1944
HOMETOWN: Thomson, Georgia

At the age of fifteen, Millie Jackson moved with her family to Newark, New Jersey. They relocated again nearly two years later, this time settling in Brooklyn, New York. Millie began working in a garment factory and by the mid-sixties had become a noted fashion model. She occasionally sang, but only for personal enjoyment.

In 1964 Millie launched her professional career—quite by accident. One night a friend who was performing at a Harlem nightclub dared her to join him on stage and sing! Hesitant at first, she eventually did perform and was encouraged to begin a singing career. She became popular on the New York-New Jersey club circuit and in 1969 was offered a contract by MGM Records. After one recording, "A Little Bit of Something," she continued with her club work for the next two years.

During the early seventies, Millie became acquainted with Joe Simon, a veteran R & B recording artist and part-owner of Spring Records. Simon arranged for her to be signed, and in

1972 she began releasing a series of Pop and Soul hits.

Today Millie Jackson makes her home on a New Jersey estate.

Mar. 72	**ASK ME WHAT YOU WANT / Spring**
Aug. 72	**MY MAN'S A SWEET MAN / Spring**
Dec. 72	**I MISS YOU BABY / Spring**
Sept. 73	**HURTS SO GOOD / Spring**
June 74	**HOW DO YOU FEEL / Spring**
Jan. 75	**I DON'T WANT TO BE RIGHT / Spring**
Sept. 75	**LEFT OVERS / Spring**
Nov. 77	**IF WE'RE NOT BACK IN LOVE BY MONDAY / Spring**

The Jackson Five

MEMBERS:

Michael Joe Jackson / born Aug. 29, 1958

Marlon David Jackson / born: Mar. 12, 1957

Jermaine LaJaune Jackson / born: Dec. 11, 1954 / (left group in 1975)

Toriano Adaryll (Tito) Jackson / born: Oct. 15, 1953

Sigmund Esco (Jackie) Jackson / born: May 4, 1951

Randy Jackson / born: Oct. 29, 1961 / (added to group in 1975)

LaToya Jackson / born: 1956 / (added to group in 1975)

Maureen Jackson Brown / (added to group in 1975)

HOMETOWN: Gary, Indiana

The Jacksons emerged during the early seventies as one of the most successful families in popular music history.

The musical influence came from their father, Joe Jackson (who today functions as their manager), a one-time guitar player for a group called The Falcons. During the early sixties, Jackie, Tito, and Jermaine began performing at school and other local functions. With the later addition of brothers Michael and Marlon, the group became known as The Jackson Five and became one of Gary, Indiana's most popular local attractions. During the late sixties, they made one unsuccessful record, "Big Boy," for the Steeltown label.

In 1969 Gary's mayor, Richard Hatcher, brought The Jackson Five to the attention of Diana Ross, who was visiting the city to give a concert. She was so impressed with the group that she contacted Motown president Berry Gordy, Jr., and arranged for them to be signed. Debuting with four consecutive number one singles, The Jackson Five went on to become the largest record sellers in the label's history. In addition, both Michael and Jermaine began recording solo and achieved several best-selling singles and LP's.

Late in 1975, as the group's contract with Motown was about to expire, a decision was reached to change affiliation to Columbia Records' affiliated Epic label. Jermaine, who had since married Berry Gordy's daughter Hazel, chose to remain with Motown and left the group. At that point, the Jacksons were joined by their youngest brother, Randy, and by their two sisters, LaToya and Maureen.

Today known as The Jacksons, the group continues to play to sellout audiences wherever they appear.

Nov. 69	**I WANT YOU BACK / Motown**
Mar. 70	**ABC / Motown**
May 70	**THE LOVE YOU SAVE / Motown**
Sept. 70	**I'LL BE THERE / Motown**
Apr. 71	**NEVER CAN SAY GOODBYE / Motown**
July 71	**MAYBE TOMORROW / Motown**
Dec. 71	**SUGAR DADDY / Motown**
Apr. 72	**LITTLE BITTY PRETTY ONE / Motown**
July 72	**LOOKING THROUGH THE WINDOWS / Motown**
Oct. 72	**CORNER OF THE SKY / Motown**

The Jackson Five. Left to right: Randy, Michael, Jackie, Tito, Marlon

Mar. 73	*HALLELUJAH DAY* /Motown	
Sept. 73	*GET IT TOGETHER* /Motown	
Mar. 74	*DANCING MACHINE* /Motown	
Oct. 74	*WHATEVER YOU GOT, I WANT* /Motown	
Jan. 75	*I AM LOVE* /Motown	
July 75	*FOREVER CAME TODAY* / Motown	
Nov. 76	*ENJOY YOURSELF* /Epic	
Apr. 77	*SHOW YOU THE WAY TO GO* / Epic	
Oct. 77	*GOING PLACES* /Epic	

Jermaine Jackson

Sept. 72 *THAT'S HOW LOVE GOES* / Motown
Dec. 72 *DADDY'S HOME* /Motown
Oct. 73 *YOU'RE IN GOOD HANDS* / Motown
Sept. 76 *LET'S BE YOUNG TONIGHT* / Motown

Michael Jackson

Oct. 71 *GOT TO BE THERE* /Motown
Mar. 72 *ROCKING ROBIN* /Motown
May 72 *I WANNA BE WHERE YOU ARE* /Motown
Aug. 72 *BEN* /Motown
May 73 *WITH A CHILD'S HEART* / Motown
Jan. 75 *WE'RE ALMOST THERE* / Motown

June 75 *JUST A LITTLE BIT OF YOU* / Motown

The Jaggerz

MEMBERS:
Ben Faiella (guitar, bass)
Donald Iris (guitar) / replaced (1969) by Domenic Terrace (guitar, bass, trumpet)
Thom Davis (keyboards, trumpet)
James Ross (trombone, bass)
William Maybray (bass, drums)
James Pugliano (drums)
HOMETOWN: Pittsburgh, Pennsylvania

This group was formed during the mid-sixties by members of several semipro bands. Benny Faiella had been with The Silvertones, Don Iris with Donnie & The Donnells, and Thom Davis with The Starliners. Jim Ross and Jim Pugliano had played in an R & B group together while both were attending the Danna School Of Music in Youngstown, Ohio.

The Jaggerz were managed by Joe Rock, who had guided another Pitts-

243

burgh group, The Skyliners, to fame during the late fifties. In 1969 he obtained a recording contract for The Jaggerz with Gamble Records, and they debuted with an album titled *Introducing the Jaggerz*. After almost no success with Gamble, the group switched to Kama Sutra, releasing an LP called *We Went to Different Schools Together*. This yielded a single, "The Rapper," which became a number one best seller and was followed by two additional hits.

The Jaggerz, although undergoing a number of personnel changes, continued to be a sizable club attraction well into the seventies. In 1976 Jimmy Ross emerged as part of a reorganized Skyliners group.

Jan. 70 *THE RAPPER* / Kama Sutra
May 70 *I CALL MY BABY CANDY* / Kama Sutra
Aug. 70 *WHAT A BUMMER* / Kama Sutra

Tommy James & The Shondells

MEMBERS:

Tommy James (Thomas Gregory Jackson) (lead vocals) / born: Apr. 29, 1947 / Dayton, Ohio

Joseph Kessler (lead guitar) / replaced by Edward Gray

Ronald Rosman (keyboards)

Michael Vale (bass)

Vincent Pietropaoli (drums) / replaced by Peter Lucia

George Magura (sax, bass, organ) / (left group in 1967)

After receiving several hits of the day as a gift from his mother, Tommy James began developing an acute interest in popular music during the mid-fifties. During his early teens, he formed a band called The Shondells, which played at dances and school af-

fairs and eventually made a recording of an earlier Raindrops song, "Hanky Panky," at a local radio station. The song was released by the small Snap label and became a modest regional hit.

Several years later a Pittsburgh record-shop owner was looking for "oldies" masters to issue on his own label. He came across The Shondells' record, and, although it was not an "oldie," it sounded like one and he acquired the master for a few hundred dollars. After promoting the record at local record hops to encourage sales, he was amazed to receive heavy airplay on radio stations and orders in the tens of thousands! Tommy James was located, flown to Pittsburgh, and put on tour in the area to promote the record even further.

By the summer of 1966, sales of "Hanky Panky" had approached 100,000 copies, and national distribution was taken over by Roulette Records. Auditions were held to form a permanent group, and Tommy James & The Shondells (with the above line-up) were signed to the label. This group continued with a long string of best sellers through mid-1970, after which personal difficulties caused them to disband.

In August, 1970, Tom James re-emerged as a solo artist and placed a number of records on the charts. Early the following year, the remaining "Shondells" began recording under the name of Hog Heaven.

Today Tommy James, with a new group of Shondells, is a leading attraction on the revival circuit. He is currently signed to the Fantasy label.

Tommy James & The Shondells
June 66 *HANKY PANKY* / Roulette
Aug. 66 *SAY I AM* / Roulette

Nov. 66	*IT'S ONLY LOVE* / Roulette
Feb. 67	*I THINK WE'RE ALONE NOW* / Roulette
Apr. 67	*MIRAGE* / Roulette
July 67	*I LIKE THE WAY* / Roulette
Aug. 67	*GETTIN' TOGETHER* / Roulette
Oct. 67	*OUT OF THE BLUE* / Roulette
Jan 68	*GET OUT NOW* / Roulette
Apr. 68	*MONY, MONY* / Roulette
July 68	*SOMEBODY CARES* / Roulette
Oct. 68	*DO SOMETHING TO ME* / Roulette
Dec. 68	*CRIMSON & CLOVER* / Roulette
Mar. 69	*SWEET CHERRY WINE* / Roulette
June 69	*CRYSTAL BLUE PERSUASION* / Roulette
Oct. 69	*BALL OF FIRE* / Roulette
Dec. 69	*SHE* / Roulette
Feb. 70	*GOTTA GET BACK TO YOU* / Roulette
May 70	*COME TO ME* / Roulette

Tommy James

Aug. 70	*BALL & CHAIN* / Roulette
Dec. 70	*CHURCH ST. SOUL REVIVAL* / Roulette
Mar. 71	*ADRIENNE* / Roulette
June 71	*DRAGGING THE LINE* / Roulette
Sept. 71	*I'M COMING HOME* / Roulette
Nov. 71	*NOTHING TO HIDE* / Roulette
Feb. 72	*TELL 'EM WILLIE BOY'S A'COMIN'* / Roulette
June 72	*THE CAT'S EYE IN THE WINDOW* / Roulette
Aug. 72	*LOVE SONG* / Roulette
Nov. 72	*CELEBRATION* / Roulette
Feb. 73	*BOO BOO, DONCHA BE BLUE* / Roulette

Hog Heaven

Apr. 71	*HAPPY* / Roulette

The James Gang

MEMBERS:

James Fox (guitar, keyboards)

Dale Peters (bass)

Joseph Fidler Walsh (guitar) / replaced by Dom Troiano / replaced by Tom Bolin / replaced by Richard Shack / replaced by Bob Webb

Roy Kenner (vocals) / replaced by Bubba Keith / replaced by Phil Giallombardo (keyboards)

HOMETOWN: Cleveland, Ohio

This group was founded in 1966 by Jim Fox and Dale Peters, who took the group's name from the legendary band of outlaws.

After building a substantial reputation on the midwestern club circuit, the group was signed in 1969 by ABC/Dunhill. They debuted with a best-selling LP, *Yer Album,* which was followed by a string of successful album releases including *Rides Again, Thirds, Live at Carnegie Hall,* and *Straight Shooter.* They also achieved a number of hit singles, beginning with "Funk #49" in 1970. During the early seventies, The James Gang began having contractual difficulties with ABC, eventually leaving the label and signing with Atco.

The James Gang has survived a number of major personnel changes over the years. Of particular note is Joe Walsh, who originally left to form his own group, Barnstorm, in late 1971 and has gone on to become one of the premier guitarists with the rock group The Eagles.

Aug. 70	*FUNK #49* / ABC
May 71	*WALK AWAY* / ABC
Oct. 71	*MIDNIGHT MAN* / ABC
Feb. 74	*MUST BE LOVE* / Atco

Jay & The Techniques

MEMBERS:

Jay Proctor (lead vocals)

Karl Landis

Ronald Goodly

John Walsh

George Lloyd

Charles Crowl

Dante Dancho

HOMETOWN: Allentown, Pennsylvania

Formed during the mid-sixties in Pennsylvania, Jay & The Techniques

Jay & The Techniques

spent several years building a reputation in northeastern clubs and resorts. In 1967 they formed an association with producer Jerry Ross and recorded for Mercury's subsidiary Smash label, rendering a series of hits based on children's games. Their biggest was "Keep the Ball Rolling," which reached the top five.

After a period of inactivity, the group re-emerged during the seventies and is now recording for Polydor Records.

July 67	***APPLES, PEACHES, PUMPKIN PIE* / Smash**
Oct. 67	***KEEP THE BALL ROLLING* / Smash**
Jan. 68	***STRAWBERRY SHORTCAKE* / Smash**
Apr. 68	***BABY, MAKE YOUR OWN SWEET MUSIC* / Smash**

Jerry Jaye

HOMETOWN: Manila, Arkansas

In 1967, Jerry went to Memphis to record a song that Fats Domino had recorded in 1960 called "My Girl Josephine." Jerry paid $12 for the recording session—$10 for an hour of studio time and $2 for a box of tape—and wound up with one of the biggest songs of the year. Although he sounded a lot like Fats Domino he was still able to put his own style in the song. After a few country singles, "Poor Side of Town" and "It's All in the Game," in 1974 and 1975, he concentrated on working in clubs throughout the South and Midwest. During the summer of 1976 he returned to his original label, Hi Records, and recorded the country tune "Honky Tonk Women Love Redneck Men."

Apr. 67	***MY GIRL JOSEPHINE* / Hi**

Jefferson Airplane

MEMBERS:

Grace Slick (vocals) / born: Oct. 30, 1943 / Chicago, Illinois

Marty Balin (Martin Buchwald) (vocals) / born: Jan. 30, 1943 / Cincinnati, Ohio

Jefferson Starship. Back row, left to right: Paul Kantner, Marty Balin; middle row, left to right: Pete Sears, Craig Chaquico, David Freiberg; front row: Grace Slick, John Barbata

Paul Kantner (vocals, guitar) / born: Mar. 12, 1942 / San Francisco, California

Jorma Kaukonen (lead guitar) / born: Dec. 23, 1940 / Washington, D.C.

Jack Casady (bass guitar) / born: Apr. 13, 1944 / Washington, D.C.

Spencer Dryden (drums) / born: Apr. 7, 1943 / New York City

Jefferson Starship

MEMBERS:
Grace Slick
Marty Balin

Paul Kantner

David Freiberg (bass guitar) / born: Aug. 24, 1938 / Boston, Massachusetts

Pete Sears (rhythm guitar)

Craig Chaquico (lead guitar) / Sept. 1954

John Barbata (drums)

Marty Balin, along with Paul Kantner, formed the Airplane in 1965 in San Francisco with vocalist Signe Anderson, Kaukonen, Casady, and drummer Skip Spence, and they began to play in the club Matrix. Shortly after the group began playing at the club, Signe left the group and was replaced by an ex-model named Grace Slick.

It was about this time that the group was spotted by some A & R men from RCA and quickly signed to a contract, after which came their debut LP, *Jefferson Airplane Takes Off.*

In early 1967 came the group's first chart single, a top-ten tune written by Grace called "Somebody to Love."

In 1971 Marty Balin left the group, but he resumed writing with Kantner a few years later. In 1974 Balin, Slick, Kantner, and Freiberg formed a new group called The Jefferson Starship. Their first LP for Grunt Records, an RCA-distrubuted label, was *Dragon Fly,* after which came the highly successful *Red Octopus.*

The Jefferson Starship and The Grateful Dead were the most important groups to emerge from the San Francisco area during the sixties.

Over the years David Crosby, Jerry Garcia, and Papa John Creach have played on some of the group's recordings. Jack Casady and Jorma Kaukonen are working with their new band, Hot Tuna. Slick, Balin, Kantner, Chaquico, Freiberg, Sears, and Barbata have continued to make hit records for Grunt, while appearing in front of capacity crowds everywhere.

Jefferson Airplane

Apr. 67 *SOMEBODY TO LOVE* / RCA Victor
June 67 *WHITE RABBIT* / RCA Victor
Sept. 67 *BALLAD OF YOU & ME & POONEIL* / RCA Victor
Dec. 67 *WATCH HER RIDE* / RCA Victor
Apr. 68 *GREASY HEART* / RCA Victor
Nov. 68 *CROWN OF CREATION* / RCA Victor
Nov. 69 *VOLUNTEERS* / RCA Victor
Nov. 71 *PRETTY AS YOU FEEL* / Grunt

Jefferson Starship

Nov. 74 *RIDE THE TIGER* / Grunt
Aug. 75 *MIRACLES* / Grunt
Dec. 75 *PLAY ON LOVE* / Grunt
July 76 *WITH YOUR LOVE* / Grunt
Dec. 76 *ST. CHARLES* / Grunt
Mar. 78 *COUNT ON ME* / Grunt
May 78 *RUNAWAY* / Grunt

Waylon Jennings

BORN: June 15, 1937
HOMETOWN: Littlefield, Texas

At the age of twelve, Waylon Jennings became one of radio's youngest deejays by spinning records in his hometown of Littlefield. Within a few years, he was hosting his own Sunday afternoon show on KDAV in nearby Lubbock, Texas, and occasionally dabbling on the guitar. During this period, he became acquainted with another celebrated Lubbock resident, Buddy Holly.

In 1959 Jennings was recruited as the bass player for Holly's back-up group, The Crickets, accompanying them on the tour that ended with the infamous plane crash of February 3, 1959. Jennings, who was to have been a passenger on that plane, chose at the last minute to travel by car and relinquished his seat to The Big Bopper (who was, of course, killed along with Holly and Richie Valens). After the crash Jennings returned to Lubbock and resumed his work as a broadcast personality.

During the early sixties, Jennings formed a back-up group of his own, The Waylors, and began building a reputation in southwestern clubs. In 1965 he came to the attention of Chet Atkins, Nashville's A & R director for RCA, who signed him to the label. Since then he was achieved a long string of best-selling Country singles and albums, several of which have placed on the Pop charts as well. He has also gained a following among rock audiences, having toured with such bands as The Grateful Dead and Commander Cody.

Today Waylon Jennings is among the group of country musicians known as "the outlaws," who also include Willie Nelson, Jerry Jeff Walker, Tom T. Hall, and others. He lives in Hickory, Tennessee (near Nashville), with his wife, country star Jessi Colter, and their three children. (See *Jessi COLTER.*)

Sept. 69 *MC ARTHUR PARK* /RCA
Oct. 70 *THE TAKER* /RCA
Sept. 74 *I'M A RAMBLIN' MAN* /RCA
Sept. 75 *ARE YOU SURE HANK DONE IT THIS WAY?* /RCA
Oct. 76 *CAN'T YOU SEE* /RCA
May 77 *LUCKENBACH, TEXAS (BACK TO THE BASICS OF LOVE)* / RCA

Waylon & Willie
Feb. 78 *MOMMAS, DON'T LET YOUR BABIES GROW UP TO BE COWBOYS* /RCA

Jethro Tull

MEMBERS:
Ian Anderson (guitar, keyboards) / born: Aug. 10, 1947
Mick Abrahams (lead guitar) / born: Apr. 7, 1943 / replaced by Martin Barre
Glenn Cornick (bass) / born: Apr. 24, 1947 / replaced by Jeffrey Hammond-Hammond
Clive Bunker (drums) / replaced by Barriemore Barlowe / born: Sept. 10, 1949
John Evan (keyboards) / born: Mar. 28, 1948 / (added to group in 1970)
HOMETOWN: Blackpool, England

Formed in 1968 as a spinoff from the Blackpool-based John Evans Band, this group took its name from a legendary eighteenth-century British agriculturist.

Waylon Jennings

After gaining a reputation on the London-area club circuit, the group came to the attention of managers Chris White and Terry Ellis, who almost immediately were able to obtain a contract with Chris Blackwell's Island label. They debuted with a best-selling album, *This Was,* which also gained success when released in the United States on Reprise. After following with *Stand Up,* the group later switched to the Chrysalis label, where their album releases included *Benefit, Aqualung, Thick as a Brick, Living in the Past, A Passion Play,* and *War Child.* They also achieved a number of hit singles, the biggest of which was their top ten American chart entry, "Living in the Past."

Today only Ian Anderson remains from the original Jethro Tull group. Mick Abrahams went on to wide acclaim with a new group, Blodwyn Pig, as did Glenn Cornick with a band known as Wild Turkey.

Aug. 71 *HYMN 43* / Reprise
Nov. 72 *LIVING IN THE PAST* / Chrysalis
May 73 *A PASSION PLAY* / Chrysalis
Nov. 74 *BUNGLE IN THE JUNGLE* / Chrysalis
Oct. 75 *MINSTREL IN THE GALLERY* / Chrysalis
Feb. 76 *LOCOMOTIVE BREATH* / Chrysalis
Apr. 77 *THE WHISTLER* / Chrysalis

Jigsaw

MEMBERS:
Des Deyer (lead vocals, percussion)
Clive Scott (keyboards, vocals)
Tony Campbell (lead guitar)
Barrie Bernard (bass guitar)
HOMETOWN: Brisbane, Australia

Australia is a country that, as of late, has been turning out many top pop performers like Helen Reddy, Olivia Newton-John, The Bee Gees, and Andy Gibb, to name a few.

During the mid-seventies, Des and Clive started writing a lot of new material, hoping that they would be signed by a recording company. Their dream came true when they were signed by Chelsea Records. Des and Clive wrote all the tunes for an album and found the magic formula for one of the songs called "Sky High," and that's exactly what happened to the song, for it went right up the charts, launching the group on an international basis.

Aug. 75 *SKY HIGH* / Chelsea
Feb. 76 *LOVE FIRE* / Chelsea
Aug. 76 *BRAND NEW LOVE AFFAIR* / Chelsea
Aug. 77 *IF I HAVE TO GO AWAY* / 20th Century

Billy Joel

BORN: May 9, 1949
HOMETOWN: Hicksville, Long Island, New York

Billy Joel began his musical career by studying piano at age four. During his mid-teens he joined a well-known Long Island group called The Hassles, which performed hits by The Beatles, Rolling Stones, Zombies, and other mid-sixties bands. He also took work as a session musician, playing on hits by such artists as The Shangri Las and Chubby Checker. After The Hassles disbanded he appeared in a duo with the group's former drummer, but with no success.

In 1971 Joel entered into an association with producer Artie Ripp, who had formed his own Family record company. Signed to the label, he debuted with an album titled *Cold Spring Harbor,* which was a moderate success at best. The two years following the album were difficult for Joel, and he spent much of that period appearing in West Coast bars under the name of Bill Martin.

Joel's luck turned late in 1973, when Columbia Records acquired his Family contract and had him record a new album, *Piano Man.* The title cut, an autobiographical account of his past experiences, became a top twenty record when released as a single. He was able to follow with four additional hits, and since has been a popular "album" and concert artist. His smash album *The Stranger* has produced three hit singles.

Feb. 74 *PIANO MAN* / Columbia
June 74 *WORSE COMES TO WORST* / Columbia
Aug. 74 *TRAVELIN' PRAYER* / Columbia
Nov. 74 *THE ENTERTAINER* / Columbia
Nov. 77 *JUST THE WAY YOU ARE* / Columbia
Mar. 78 *MOVIN' OUT* / Columbia
May 78 *ONLY THE GOOD DIE YOUNG* / Columbia

Billy Joel

Elton John

REAL NAME: Reginald Kenneth Dwight
BORN: Mar. 25, 1947
HOMETOWN: Pinner, Middlesex, England

Universally acknowledged to be the leading superstar to emerge from the world of seventies pop and rock music, Elton John began his climb to the top at a very early age. By the time he was four, he was playing the classics on the piano and was eventually to gain a full scholarship to The Royal Academy of Music. However, as American rock 'n' roll began to make an impact on British audiences during the late fifties, he began to change his style by imitating the records of Little Richard, Bill Haley, and Elvis Presley.

During the early sixties, Elton broke into the music business by working at the Mills Music Publishing Company. As the sixties progressed, he began playing keyboards in a variety of

Elton John

groups, often backing American stars when they appeared in England. He eventually became the resident organ player for John Baldry's Bluesology, during which time he formulated his stage name by combining the first names of Elton Dean, the group's sax player, and Baldry.

In 1968 Elton developed an interest in songwriting and answered an advertisement for writers placed by Liberty Records. Responding to the same ad was lyricist Bernie Taupin, and the company teamed them up to provide material for the label. This led to a publishing contract from Dick James Music (the first company to publish a Beatles song) and an opportunity to record for their affiliated label, DJM. Thus, in 1969 Elton John debuted with an album titled *Empty Sky,* which was followed early in 1970 by *Elton John.* The latter LP, which was distributed in the United States by Universal, became an international best seller and yielded the single that would begin his string of hits—"Your Song." Since then he has never been absent from the charts; his albums, several of which accrued millions of orders prior to their release, have included *Tumbleweed Connection, Madman across the Water, Honkey Chateau, Don't Shoot Me, I'm Only the Piano Player, Goodbye Yellow Brick Road, Caribou,* and *Captain Fantastic.*

Today Elton John is one of the most visual performers in all of rock music. I lis stage antics and style of dress (not to mention his performance as the Pinball Wizard in the movie *Tommy*) have had a profound effect and he is universally imitated. In addition, he operates his own Rocket Record Company, which has launched the careers of such acts as The Hudson Brothers and Kiki Dee while rekindling the popularity of vintage R & R figures Neil Sedaka and Cliff Richard.

Aug. 70	***THE BORDER SONG / Universal***
Nov. 70	***YOUR SONG /Universal***
Mar. 71	***FRIENDS /Universal***
Dec. 71	***LEVON /Universal***
Mar. 72	***TINY DANCER /Universal***
May 72	***ROCKET MAN /Universal***
Aug. 72	***HONKY CAT /Universal***
Dec. 72	***CROCODILE ROCK /MCA***
Aug. 73	***SATURDAY NIGHT'S ALRIGHT FOR FIGHTING /MCA***
Oct. 73	***GOODBYE YELLOW BRICK ROAD /MCA***
Feb. 74	***BENNIE & THE JETS /MCA***
June 74	***DON'T LET THE SUN GO DOWN ON ME /MCA***
Sept. 74	***THE BITCH IS BACK /MCA***
Nov. 74	***LUCY IN THE SKY WITH DIAMONDS /MCA***
Mar. 75	***PHILADELPHIA FREEDOM / MCA***
July 75	***SOMEONE SAVED MY LIFE TONIGHT /MCA***
Oct. 75	***ISLAND GIRL /MCA***
Jan. 76	***GROW SOME FUNK OF YOUR OWN /MCA***
Jan. 76	***I FEEL LIKE A BULLET /MCA***
June 76	***DON'T GO BREAKING MY HEART* (with Kiki Dee)/ Rocket**
Nov. 76	***SORRY SEEMS TO BE THE HARDEST WORD / MCA/Rocket***
Feb. 77	***BITE YOUR LIP (GET UP AND DANCE) /MCA/Rocket***
Apr. 78	***EGO /MCA***

Robert John

REAL NAME: Robert Pedrick, Jr.
HOMETOWN: Brooklyn, New York

Robert John began his career during the late fifties in typical fashion—as a member of a streetcorner-type vocal group. As lead singer of Bobby & The Consoles, he achieved regional success in the New York City area with the release of "My Jelly Bean" on the Diamond label. He also made a number of recordings under his real name for the Big Top and Verve labels.

After occupying himself during the sixties as a magazine publisher, John came to the attention of music publishers Stan Catron and Lou Stallman in 1968. They were friendly with Dave Rubinson, a producer for Columbia Records, and arranged for the unusual, high-tenor-lead recording of "If You Don't Want My Love," to be released by the label. It became a Top 40 national hit and identified Robert John with that style. Following a brief stay at the A & M label, and a minor chart entry, John emerged on Atlantic in 1972 under the production auspices of The Tokens. Taking advantage of

John's unusual sound, they recreated their own 1961 hit of "The Lion Sleeps Tonight," a record that climbed to the top of the charts. John followed with "Hushabye," another "oldie," before he and his sound temporarily faded from national popularity. (Robert John's "sound" was recreated almost exactly, in 1976, in Leo Sayer's major hit recording of "You Make Me Feel like Dancing.")

Today, Robert John continues to call Brooklyn his home, living there with his wife and two sons.

Apr. 68	**IF YOU DON'T WANT MY LOVE/ Columbia**
Nov. 70	**WHEN THE PARTY IS OVER / A & M**
Jan. 72	**THE LION SLEEPS TONIGHT / Atlantic**
June 72	**HUSHABYE / Atlantic**

Sammy Johns

BORN: Feb. 7, 1946
HOMETOWN: Charlotte, North Carolina

A devotee of Elvis Presley since he was ten, Sammy Johns acquired his first guitar at that age and began performing in Presley's style. During his teen years, he joined a band called The Devilles, a group that was to have a local hit on the Dixie label with their release of "Makin' Tracks."

After nearly a decade with The Devilles, Johns embarked on a solo career and performed mostly around his home town of Charlotte. He was spotted during one of his performances by executives of the Atlanta-based General Recording Corporation, who signed him to their label. After the release of two unsuccessful singles, he scored in 1974 with a hit single titled "Early Morning Love" and with an album of the same name. However, his major breakthrough was to come dur-

ing the following year, when he achieved a top five hit with "Chevy Van."

Today, Sammy Johns and his wife, Vicki, make their permanent home in Atlanta, Georgia.

Oct. 74	**EARLY MORNING LOVE / GRC**
Feb. 75	**CHEVY VAN / GRC**
May 75	**RAG DOLL / GRC**

Jo Jo Gunne

MEMBERS:
Jay Ferguson (lead vocals, guitar)
Matt Andes (guitar) / replaced (1974) by Star Donaldson
Mark Andes (bass) / replaced (1973) by James Randall
Curley Smith (drums)
HOMETOWN: Los Angeles, California

A leading exponent of seventies punk rock, this group was formed in 1971 by several members of other successful bands. Jay Ferguson and Mark Andes came to the group from Spirit, which had achieved a major hit in 1969. (See *SPIRIT.*) Andes had previously played bass for Canned Heat. Curley Smith had been playing drums with Pumpkin.

After selecting their unusual name from a line in a vintage Chuck Berry song, the group began building a substantial reputation in Los Angeles-area clubs. They were eventually signed by Asylum Records, debuting in 1972 with an album titled *Jo Jo Gunne.* Following with a top twenty single, "Run, Run, Run," the group continued into the mid-seventies with several best-selling LP's, including *Bite Down Hard* and *Jumping the Gunne.* They disbanded in 1975.

Today Jay Ferguson records for Asylum Records and has a hit in "Thunder Island."

Mar. 72 **RUN, RUN, RUN / Asylum**

Linda Jones

BORN: 1945
DIED: Mar. 14, 1972
HOMETOWN: Newark, New Jersey

Born into a musical family known as The Jones Singers, Linda received her first exposure to music in church. During her late teens, she was able to affiliate briefly with Atlantic Records, releasing one unsuccessful single on their subsidiary Atco label.

In 1967 Linda formed an association with George Kerr, a veteran of several 1950s New York "doo-wopp" groups and a burgeoning record producer. Obtaining a contract with Loma Records, an R & B affiliate of Warner Brothers, the team collaborated on "Hypnotized" and achieved both an R & B and a pop hit. Linda followed with an LP of the same name and two additional hit singles, before leaving Loma.

During the late sixties, Linda (together with George Kerr) spent brief periods with a number of record companies, including Cotique and Neptune. By 1971 Kerr had become a staff producer for Joe and Sylvia Robinson's All Platinum complex, and he arranged for Linda to be signed to their Turbo subsidiary. She scored with a national chart entry, "Your Precious Love," and recorded three albums: Portrait, Your Precious Love, and Let It Be Me.

Early in 1972, after a history of severe diabetes, Linda collapsed backstage after a performance at New York's Apollo Theater and died shortly thereafter.

June 67	*HYPNOTIZED* /**Loma**	
Sept. 67	*WHAT'VE I DONE?* /**Loma**	
Jan. 68	*GIVE MY LOVE A TRY* / **Loma**	
Feb. 72	*YOUR PRECIOUS LOVE* / **Turbo**	

Tom Jones

FULL NAME: Thomas Jones Woodward
BORN: June 7, 1940
HOMETOWN: Pontypridd, South Wales, England

Tom Jones showed an early interest in singing, beginning in Welsh church choirs as a child. During his teens he formed several groups, including The Squires, Tommy Scott & The Senators, and The Playboys. He also performed occasionally as a solo artist, using the stage name "Tiger Tom."

During the early sixties, one of The Playboys' performances was seen by manager-songwriter Gordon Mills. He assumed management of the group, changing its name to Tommy Scott— "The Twisting Vocalist"—And His Playboys. Eventually, Mills concentrated on building Tom's career as a solo artist, suggesting that he assume the name of Tom Jones to capitalize on the highly successful 1963 film of that name. After building a reputation on the London club circuit, he was offered a recording contract in 1964. His initial releases were unsuccessful, but he achieved a number one British hit in 1965 with Gordon Mills's composition of "It's Not Unusual." After this became a major American hit as well, Jones reached the top of the charts with the title song from the movie What's New Pussycat, following up during the next years with a series of Country-flavored Pop hits.

During the early seventies, Tom Jones achieved the pinnacle of success, hosting his own network television show and drawing sellout crowds wherever he appeared. Today he lives with his wife, Melinda, and their son, Mark, in Surrey, England.

Apr. 65 *IT'S NOT UNUSUAL* /**Parrot**

Tom Jones

Tom Jones

May 65	*LITTLE LONELY ONE* / Tower	**Mar. 68**	*DELILAH* / Parrot
June 65	*WHAT'S NEW PUSSYCAT* / Parrot	**Aug. 68**	*HELP YOURSELF* / Parrot
Aug. 65	*WITH THESE HANDS* / Parrot	**Dec. 68**	*A MINUTE OF YOUR TIME* / Parrot
Aug. 65	*THUNDERBALL* / Parrot	**May 69**	*LOVE ME TONIGHT* / Parrot
Feb. 66	*PROMISE HER ANYTHING* / Parrot	**July 69**	*I'LL NEVER FALL IN LOVE AGAIN* (rereleased)/ Parrot
June 66	*NOT RESPONSIBLE* / Parrot	**Dec. 69**	*WITHOUT LOVE* / Parrot
Dec. 66	*GREEN, GREEN GRASS OF HOME* / Parrot	**May 70**	*DAUGHTER OF DARKNESS* / Parrot
Mar. 67	*DETROIT CITY* / Parrot	**Aug. 70**	*I WHO HAVE NOTHING* / Parrot
May 67	*FUNNY, FAMILIAR, FORGOTTEN FEELINGS* / Parrot	**Nov. 70**	*CAN'T STOP LOVING YOU* / Parrot
Aug. 67	*SIXTEEN TONS* / Parrot	**Feb. 71**	*SHE'S A LADY* / Parrot
Sept. 67	*I'LL NEVER FALL IN LOVE AGAIN* / Parrot	**May 71**	*PUPPET MAN* / Parrot
		Oct. 71	*TILL* / Parrot
Dec. 67	*I'M COMING HOME* / Parrot	**Apr. 72**	*THE YOUNG NEW MEXICAN PUPPETEER* / Parrot

May 73 *LETTER TO LUCILLE* / **Parrot**
Dec. 76 *SAY YOU'LL STAY UNTIL TOMORROW* / **Epic**

The Joneses

MEMBERS:
Glenn Dorsey
Harold Taylor
Cy Brooks
Ernest Holt
HOMETOWN: Pittsburgh, Pennsylvania

This group formed originally during the late sixties, moving to New York City in 1971 to break into the music business. No one connected with the group was named Jones, but they selected the name because they hoped to develop into an act that others would have "to keep up with!"

After some recording experience with a small label, The Joneses were signed in 1973 by Mercury Records, where they scored with two soul hits and a pop hit titled "Sugar Pie Guy."

During a relatively brief career, the group has undergone a number of major personnel changes. Cy Brooks and Ernest Holt were the first to leave, to be replaced by brothers Reggie and Bubby Noble and their cousin, Sam White. (All three replacements came to The Joneses from another group, The Boys of Wonder.) After working as a quintet until early 1975, they changed their membership almost entirely. Today the group consists of original member Harold Taylor, Jim Richardson, Fred Rue, and David Evans, and they are a popular disco and concert attraction.

Oct. 74 *SUGAR PIE GUY* / **Mercury**

Janis Joplin

BORN: Jan. 19, 1943
Died: Oct. 3, 1970
HOMETOWN: Port Arthur, Texas

Affectionately known as "Pearl," Janis Joplin had only a brief career but was able, during that period, to rise to the absolute heights of rock superstardom.

Janis began singing during her early teen years, patterning herself after the vintage recordings of such blues figures as Bessie Smith and Huddie (Leadbelly) Ledbetter. During the mid-sixties she traveled about, briefly entering a number of colleges and singing for little or no money in countless bars and clubs. She eventually settled in San Francisco, becoming close friends there with Chet Helms, a fellow she had previously known in her home state of Texas. Helms brought her together with Big Brother & The Holding Company, which led to her legendary appearance at the 1967 Monterey Pop Festival, her management offer from Albert Grossman (who also handled the likes of Bob Dylan and Peter, Paul & Mary) and her meteoric rise to fame. (See *BIG BROTHER & THE HOLDING COMPANY.*)

After her last public appearance with Big Brother, on December 1, 1968, Janis embarked on a solo career and formed her own back-up group, The Full Tilt Boogie Band (containing Sam Andrew from Big Brother). Beginning with the release of her first solo album, *I Got Dem Ol' Kozmic Blues Again Mama,* she was to reign for the next two years as rock music's leading female vocalist. However, her career came to a tragic and abrupt end on October 1970, when her body was found at Hollywood's Landmark Motor Hotel. A victim of accidental drug overdose, Janis was cremated and her ashes scattered at sea near Stinson Beach in Marin County, California.

257

Janis Joplin

Early in 1971 Columbia Records released an album that had been completed just before Janis's death. Titled simply *Pearl,* it became an instant best seller and yielded the chart-topping single recording of Kris Kristofferson's "Me & Bobby McGee." The company continued to issue previously unreleased or repackaged material well into the mid-seventies.

A highly controversial figure, Janis Joplin has, since her passing, been the subject of a film, *Janis* (three years in the making and in which she appears singing eighteen songs), and of nearly half a dozen books.

Nov. 69	***KOZMIC BLUES /*** **Columbia**
Jan. 71	***ME & BOBBY MC GEE /*** **Columbia**
May 71	***CRY BABY /* Columbia**
Sept. 71	***GET IT WHILE YOU CAN /*** **Columbia**
July 72	***DOWN ON ME /* Columbia**

Kansas

MEMBERS:
Robby Steinhardt (violin, vocals)
Steve Walsh (keyboards, vocals)
Kerry Livgren (guitar)
Rich Williams (guitar)
Dave Hope (bass guitar)
Phil Ehart (drums)
HOMETOWN: Topeka, Kansas

The group met in 1971 and began playing many clubs throughout Kansas. After sending out dozens of demo tapes, rock entrepreneur Don Kirshner received one of the group's demos and decided to sign them to his label. After working diligently on new material and traveling around the country as an opening act for other rock groups, they finally made it on their own in 1977 with their first pop single on the charts, "Carry On Wayward Son." This is one of the few American groups that has a classical music background and incorporates it into the music.

Dec. 76	**CARRY ON WAYWARD SON /** **Kirshner**
Nov. 77	**POINT OF NO RETURN /** **Kirshner**
Jan. 78	**DUST IN THE WIND / Kirshner**

Kansas. Left to right: Kerry Livgren, Steve Walsh, Dave Hope, Robby Steinhardt, Phil Ehart, Rich Williams

The Kasenetz-Katz Singing Orchestral Circus

HOMETOWN: New York City

Jerry Kasenetz and Jeff Katz are a team of New York record producers who are best known as the primary creators of the "bubble gum" sound of the middle and late sixties. They were responsible for numerous multimillion sellers by groups such as The Ohio Express, The 1910 Fruitgum Company, and The Music Explosion.

Although most of these records were made by studio vocalists, touring groups were assembled to make public appearances. In 1968 many of these groups were combined into one large ensemble, containing several dozen members, to give a concert at Carnegie Hall. The concept was so well received that the producers began issuing records under the communal name of The Singing Orchestral Circus. One of these records, the single release of "Quick Joey Small," placed within the national top twenty.

Today Jerry Kasenetz and Jeff Katz operate a large recording studio in the Long Island suburbs of New York, while also continuing with their production work.

Oct. 68 *QUICK JOEY SMALL* / **Buddah**

K.C. & The Sunshine Band

MEMBERS:

K.C. (Harry Wayne Casey) (keyboards, lead vocals) / born: Jan. 31, 1951 / Miami, Florida

Richard "Rick" Finch (bass guitar) / born: Jan. 23, 1954 / Indianapolis, Indiana

Jerome "J" Smith (guitar) / born: June 18, 1953 / Miami, Florida

Fermin Goytisolo (congas) / born: Dec. 31, 1951 / Havana, Cuba

Ronnie Smith (trumpet) / born: 1952 / Hialeah, Florida

Denvil Liptrot (sax)

James Weaver (trumpet)

Charles Williams (trombone) / born: Nov. 18, 1954 / Rockingham, North Carolina

Robert "Shotgun" Johnson (drums) / born: Mar. 21, 1953 / Miami, Florida

H. W. Casey and Rick Finch met at the T. K. Studios in Miami in the early seventies and began working on tunes that the two of them had cowritten. One of their compositions, "Rock Your Baby," went on to become a number one national hit for George McCrae. At about this time they decided to form their own group, featuring a disco sound that was brass oriented. They called the group K.C. (Casey's last name) & The Sunshine Band (because they came from the "sunshine" state, Florida).

The group's first single, "Blow Your Whistle," had a mild R & B impact, but it wasn't until the summer of 1975 that their big break came, when Casey and Finch wrote the tune "Get Down Tonight," which went on to become a number one national hit. Today they are one of the hottest disco groups in the business.

July 75	*GET DOWN TONIGHT* / **T.K.**	
Oct. 75	*THAT'S THE WAY (I LIKE IT)* / **T.K.**	
Mar. 76	*QUEEN OF CLUBS* / **T.K.**	
July 76	*(SHAKE, SHAKE, SHAKE) SHAKE YOUR BOOTY* / **T.K.**	
Dec. 76	*I LIKE TO DO IT* / **T.K.**	
Feb. 77	*I'M YOUR BOOGIE MAN* / **T.K.**	
July 77	*KEEP IT COMIN' LOVE* / **T.K.**	
Dec. 77	*WRAP YOUR ARMS AROUND ME* / **T.K.**	
Feb. 78	*BOOGIE SHOES* / **T.K.**	
May 78	*IT'S THE SAME OLD SONG* / **T.K.**	

Keith

REAL NAME: James Barry Keefer
BORN: May 7, 1949
HOMETOWN: Philadelphia, Pennsylvania

James Keefer decided as a teenager to attempt singing as a career. Using his "one name" gimmick that had worked so well for Donovan, he began billing himself as "Keith" and eventually came to the attention of record producer Jerry Ross.

In 1966 Keith emerged on the Mercury label with a Top 40 hit, "Ain't Gonna Lie." He followed with his biggest success, the chart-topping "98.6" (on which he was backed by The Tokens), and a series of light Pop hits. His career was brought to an end shortly thereafter when he entered the military, only to be arrested and discharged for desertion!

Today Keith has left the music business and makes his home in Los Angeles.

Sept. 66 *AIN'T GONNA LIE* / **Mercury**
Dec. 66 *98.6* / **Mercury**
Mar. 67 *TELL ME TO MY FACE* / **Mercury**
June 67 *DAYLIGHT SAVING TIME* / **Mercury**

Eddie Kendricks

BORN: Dec. 17, 1940
HOMETOWN: Union Springs, Alabama

Eddie Kendricks grew up in Birmingham, Alabama, to which his family moved when he was one year old. During his teen years, he developed a relationship with another Birmingham resident, Paul Williams, and the two organized a vocal group called The Primes.

During the sixties The Primes evolved into The Temptations, one of the superstar groups of Rhythm &

Eddie Kendricks

Blues. (They also had a sister group, The Primettes, who were to become The Supremes.) Although he left the group for a brief period in 1968, Kendricks remained with them until 1971, having sung lead on many of their major hits. (See *THE TEMPTATIONS.*)

In May 1971, Kendricks launched his solo career with a Soul hit titled "It's So Hard for Me to Say Goodbye," which became a modest Pop chart entry as well. His subsequent releases became progressively more popular, culminating in a national number one record in 1973, "Keep on Truckin'."

Eddie Kendricks has continued into the mid-seventies with a number of best sellers and is today considered a star in his own right.

May 71 *IT'S SO HARD FOR ME TO SAY GOODBYE* / **Tamla**

June 72 *EDDIE'S LOVE* / Tamla
Oct. 72 *IF YOU LET ME* / Tamla
Feb. 73 *GIRL, YOU NEED A CHANGE OF MIND* / Tamla
July 73 *DARLING COME BACK HOME* / Tamla
Aug. 73 *KEEP ON TRUCKIN'* / Tamla
Jan. 74 *BOOGIE DOWN* / Tamla
May 74 *SON OF SAGITTARIUS* / Tamla
Aug. 74 *TELL HER LOVE HAS FELT THE NEED* / Tamla
Dec. 74 *ONE TEAR* / Tamla
Feb. 75 *SHOESHINE BOY* / Tamla
July 75 *GET THE CREAM OFF THE TOP* / Tamla
Oct. 75 *HAPPY* / Tamla
Feb. 76 *HE'S A FRIEND* / Tamla

Andy Kim

REAL NAME: Andrew Joachim
HOMETOWN: Montreal, Canada

Andy Kim began singing as a child, performing at parties and school functions. As he grew older, his interest began to turn toward songwriting, and he made regular trips to New York City to sell his songs. In this fashion, he eventually met writer-producer Jeff Barry, and that proved to be the turning point in his career.

In 1968 Barry formed his own Steed label, and Kim was signed to the artist roster. With a combination of Barry-Kim collaborations and remakes of earlier hits written by Barry, Andy was able to achieve nearly a dozen chart entries before temporarily fading from American popularity during the early seventies. He and Barry also scored with hits by other artists, including The Archies' multimillion-selling "Sugar Sugar."

In 1972 Kim affiliated with the MCA label, placing a few minor hits on the Canadian charts but meeting with no American success. In 1974 he and his brother Joe decided to form their own Ice record label, and the debut release was to have been his own production of "Rock Me Gently." A tape of the song was heard by executives of Capitol, who offered him a contract and rushed the record into release. "Rock Me Gently" firmly reestablished his career by reaching number one on the national charts.

Today Andy Kim is managed by his older brother, Joe, and makes his permanent home in Los Angeles.

May 68 *HOW'D WE EVER GET THIS WAY* / Steed
Sept. 68 *SHOOT 'EM UP BABY* / Steed
Dec. 68 *RAINBOW RIDE* / Steed
May 69 *BABY, I LOVE YOU* / Steed
Sept. 69 *SO GOOD TOGETHER* / Steed
Feb. 70 *A FRIEND IN THE CITY* / Steed
July 70 *IT'S YOUR LIFE* / Steed
Nov. 70 *BE MY BABY* / Steed
Mar. 71 *I WISH I WERE* / Steed
July 71 *I'VE BEEN MOVED* / Steed
June 74 *ROCK ME GENTLY* / Capitol
Oct. 74 *FIRE BABY, I'M ON FIRE* / Capitol

Jonathan King

BORN: Dec. 6, 1944
HOMETOWN: London, England

A leading British music entrepreneur of the seventies, Jonathan King began his career in 1965 while a student at Cambridge University. Through his activities with a group called The Bumblies, he became acquainted with Tony Hall of British Decca, who encouraged him to record some of his own songs.

King made an immediate impact with "Everyone's Gone to the Moon," which was also released in the United States on Parrot and became an international best seller. Although he continued to record, his interest rapidly turned to other areas, including production, management, and rock commentary. Beginning with "It's Good News Week" by Hedgehoppers Anonymous, King was responsible for a string of records by groups such as The Weathermen, Saccharine, The Piglets, Nemo, and Shag. He also hosted both radio and television programs, on which he offered strong and often highly unpopular opinions on issues of the day.

During the seventies King established his own U.K. record label, kicking off with the unusual arrangement of "Hooked on a Feeling" which was to become the basis for the later Blue Swede hit. The label became firmly established with the success during the mid-seventies of 10 cc, and King has become widely known via his regular columns in some of England's leading music publications.

Today U.K. is one of the most successful of the British independent record companies, while Jonathan King's own recordings are distributed in the United States on the Big Tree label.

Sept. 65 *EVERYONE'S GONE TO THE MOON* / **Parrot**
Jan. 66 *WHERE THE SUN HAS NEVER SHONE* / **Parrot**

King Harvest

MEMBERS:
Ed Tuleja (lead guitar)
Ron Altback (keyboards)
Rod Novak (sax)
Doc Robinson (keyboards, trombone)
Sherman Kelly (keyboards)
Tony Cahill (bass)
David Montgomery (drums)

King Harvest was formed in 1964 by several members of rival college bands. They spent the next several years working in clubs in both the United States and Europe.

During the early seventies, the group came to the attention of Terry Phillips,

owner of the small, independent Perception label. Signed to a contract, they achieved a top ten single with "Dancing in the Moonlight." After a moderately successful follow-up hit and an album, the group changed affiliation to the A & M label with Ed, Ron, Rod, and Doc still remaining in the group.

Oct. 72 *DANCING IN THE MOONLIGHT* / **Perception**
May 73 *A LITTLE BIT LIKE MAGIC* / **Perception**

The Kinks

MEMBERS:
Raymond Douglas Davies (lead guitar) / born: June 21, 1944 / Muswell Hill, London, England
David Davies (rhythm guitar) / born: Feb. 3, 1947 / Muswell Hill, London, England
Peter Quaife (bass) / born: Dec. 27, 1943 / Tavistock, Devonshire, England / replaced (1969) by John Dalton
Mick Avory (drums) / born: Feb. 15, 1944 / London, England
John Gosling (keyboards) / (added to group in 1970)
Laurie Brown (trumpet) / (added to group in mid-seventies)
Alan Holmes (sax, flute) / (added to group in mid-seventies)
John Beecham (trombone, tuba) / (added to group in mid-seventies)

This group was organized late in 1963 by brothers Ray and Dave Davies. Billing themselves at first as The Ramrods, they began building a following on the London-area club circuit. After adopting the British slang word *kink* as their name, the group's reputation grew to the point where they were offered a contract by Pye Records.

Early in 1964 The Kinks debuted with two modest British hits, Little Richard's "Long Tall Sally" and "You Still Want Me." These were released in the United States on Cameo, but with no

The Kinks. Left to right: Ray Davies, Dave Davies, John Gosling, Mick Avory

success. Later in the year, however, they achieved a major hit with "You Really Got Me," which also reached the American top ten when released by Reprise. With a sound that gradually evolved from basic "hard rock" to Pop-oriented social satire, The Kinks were able to remain on the singles charts through the beginning of the seventies. They also accrued a long list of best-selling LP's, including *The Kinks, Kinda Kinks, Kink Controversy, Live at Kelvin Hall, Something Else, Village Green Preservation Society, Arthur, Lola Versus Powerman,* and *Percy.*

In 1971 The Kinks changed affiliation to RCA and concentrated far less on hit singles and much more on "concept" albums. Their releases included *Muswell Hillbillies, Everybody's in Show Biz,* and *Preservation.* In addition, much of their earlier material was repackaged and it sold just as well.

Although leader Ray Davies announced that he would leave the group in 1973, he reconsidered and the original line-up was left intact. In fact, with the addition of a permanent horn section, The Kinks' membership today numbers eight. Today the group now records for Arista Records.

Sept. 64	*YOU REALLY GOT ME / Reprise*
Dec. 64	*ALL DAY AND ALL OF THE NIGHT / Reprise*
Mar. 65	*TIRED OF WAITING FOR YOU / Reprise*
June 65	*SET ME FREE / Reprise*
Aug. 65	*WHO'LL BE THE NEXT IN LINE / Reprise*
Dec. 65	*A WELL RESPECTED MAN / Reprise*
Mar. 66	*TILL THE END OF THE DAY / Reprise*
May 66	*DEDICATED FOLLOWER OF FASHION / Reprise*
Aug. 66	*SUNNY AFTERNOON / Reprise*
Jan. 67	*DEADEND STREET / Reprise*
July 67	*MR. PLEASANT / Reprise*

Kiss

MEMBERS:

Ace Frehley (lead guitar, vocals) / born: Apr. 27, 1951 / Bronx, New York

Paul Stanley (rhythm guitar) / born: Jan. 20, 1952 / New York City

Gene Simmons (bass) / born: Aug. 25, 1949 / Haifa, Israel

Peter Criss (drums) / born: Dec. 20, 1947 / Brooklyn, New York

An outgrowth of the seventies trend toward highly theatrical rock music, Kiss was formed on and grew out of the New York "hard rock" club circuit during the mid-seventies.

After building a wide reputation with their outrageous appearance and stage antics, the group was signed by Casablanca Records. Their first single, a reworked version of Bobby Rydell's hit of "Kissin' Time," became only a moderate hit. They broke through with their second release, "Rock & Roll All Nite," which reached the national top 20.

Today, after several best-selling LP's—*Hotter Than Hell, Dressed to Kill, Alive, Destroyer, Rock and Roll Over, Love Gun,* and *Alive II*—Kiss draws sellout crowds wherever they appear and are considered the leading exponent of "glitter-punk" rock.

Kiss. Left to right: Peter Criss, Ace Frehley, Gene Simmons, Paul Stanley

Mac & Katie Kissoon

Mac & Katie Kissoon

HOMETOWN: Port-of-Spain, Trinidad

These siblings began their careers in Great Britain shortly after their parents moved there during the late fifties. Mac was the first to start performing, touring England and the continent with an R & B band known as The Marionettes. Katie later joined an all-female group called The Rag Dolls.

During the late sixties, Mac & Katie Kissoon teamed up to form an act. Signing with Miki Dallon's Young Blood label, they achieved both an American and a European hit with "Chirpy Chirpy Cheep Cheep" but received very little recognition in their homeland. This trend continued as they scored with a number of additional hits on the Continent, including "Sing Along," "Beautiful World Out There," "Change It All," and "I've Found My Freedom."

Their major breakthrough with British audiences finally came during the mid-seventies, when they affiliated with the State label and achieved four best sellers: "Sugar Candy Kisses," "Don't Do It Baby," "Like A Butterfly," and "I'm Not Dreaming."

July 71 *CHIRPY CHIRPY CHEEP CHEEP* / ABC

The Knickerbockers

MEMBERS:
Buddy Randell (lead vocals, sax)
Beau Charles (guitar)
John Charles (bass)
James Walker (drums)
HOMETOWN: Bergenfield, New Jersey

This group formed in mid-1964, taking their name from a street in their home town of Bergenfield. All the members had previous experience in other bands—most notably Buddy Randell, who had played with The Royal Teens and had cowritten that group's biggest hit, "Short Shorts."

After establishing a reputation in upstate New York clubs, The Knickerbockers came to the attention of Jerry Fuller, songwriter and staff producer for Challenge Records. He arranged for the group to be signed and produced two unsuccessful singles and two albums for the group before they scored with their top 20 recording of "Lies." An out-and-out Beatles sound-alike, this record brought the group two follow-up hits and an extended series of appearances on TV's "Where the Action Is."

By the late sixties, however, The Knickerbockers had disbanded, leaving two of the members, Buddy Randell and Jimmy Walker, to continue recording as solo acts. Walker also went on to temporarily replace Bill Medley in The Righteous Brothers but returned to his solo career when Medley rejoined the act.

Dec. 65 *LIES* / Challenge
Mar. 66 *ONE TRACK MIND* / Challenge
July 66 *LIGHT ON LOVE* / Challenge

Jean Knight

HOMETOWN: New Orleans, Louisiana

Jean launched her career by singing with a number of bands around the New Orleans area. During the late sixties, she also recorded for a number of the region's small labels.

In 1971 Jean came to the attention of producer Wardell Quezerque, who assumed management of her career. He took her to the famed Malaco studio in Jackson, Mississippi, where he produced a record titled "Mr. Big Stuff" and arranged for its release by Stax Records. This reached the top of the national charts and was followed by a lesser hit, "You Think You're Hot Stuff."

Today Jean Knight continues as a leading New Orleans performer.

May 71 *MR. BIG STUFF* / Stax
Oct. 71 *YOU THINK YOU'RE HOT STUFF* / Stax

Robert Knight

BORN: Apr. 24, 1945
HOMETOWN: Franklin, Tennessee

Robert Knight began his career as a soprano in his high school choir, then later joined a group called The Paramounts.

In 1961 Knight began recording solo, achieving a minor regional hit with a record titled "Free Me." As the sixties progressed, he entered college and sang part time in clubs. During one of these performances, he was spotted by writer-producers Bobby Russell and Buzz Cason, who signed him to their Rising Sons label. Beginning with "Everlasting Love," which reached the top ten, Knight achieved a series of hits in association with Russell & Cason (his last was on another of the producers' labels, Elf). In 1974 Bobby Russell would produce a hit version of the same song by another artist, Carl Carlton.

Today Robert Knight continues his club work while recording for Private Stock.

Sept. 67 *EVERLASTING LOVE* / Rising Sons
Jan. 68 *BLESSED ARE THE LONELY* / Rising Sons
Oct. 68 *ISN'T IT LONELY TOGETHER?* / Elf

Terry Knight & The Pack

MEMBERS:
Terry Knight (Terry Knapp) / born: Apr. 9, 1943
Mark Farner (guitar) / born: Sept. 29, 1948
Don Brewer (drums) / born: Sept. 3, 1948
HOMETOWN: Flint, Michigan

Much more important because of who they became rather than who they were, this group was organized during the mid-sixties by Terry Knight, a Flint deejay who decided he would try his hand at singing. They were signed by the local Lucky Eleven label and immediately achieved a regional hit with "Better Man than I." They followed with "A Change Is on the Way," shortly after which national distribution of the label was assumed by Cameo Records. As a result their next release, "I Who Have Nothing," managed to place within the national top 40. Terry Knight and the group subsequently separated and all pursued separate

careers until Cameo eventually ceased operations during the late sixties.

By 1969 Capitol Records was actively signing many of the former Cameo-affiliated acts. This served to bring together Mark Farner and Don Brewer from The Pack, Mel Schacher from Question Mark & The Mysterians and Terry Knight, who had since turned manager. Under Knight's direction, the other three went on to form Grand Funk Railroad, the most successful seventies rock band of American origin. (See *GRAND FUNK RAILROAD*.)

Nov. 66 *I WHO HAVE NOTHING* / Lucky Eleven

Kool & The Gang

MEMBERS:
Robert "Kool" Bell (lead vocals, bass) / Youngstown, Ohio
Ronald Bell (tenor sax) / Youngstown, Ohio
Dennis "Dee Tee" Thomas (alto and tenor sax, flute) / Jersey City, New Jersey
Claydes "Clay" Smith (lead guitar) / Jersey City, New Jersey
Robert "Spike" Mickens (trumpet) / Jersey City, New Jersey
Rick "West" Westfield (keyboards) / Jersey City, New Jersey
George "Funky" Brown (drums) / Jersey City, New Jersey

One of the earliest exponents of the funky, jazz-oriented big-band sound that took hold in the seventies, this group was started during the mid-sixties by several Jersey City high-school friends. Beginning as The Jazziacs, they played local clubs and eventually were hired to back some of the leading R & B acts appearing in the area. As the R & B sound began increasingly to influence their music, they underwent name changes from The Soul Town Review to The New Dimensions to Kool & The Gang.

In 1969 one of the group's performances was seen by producer Gene Redd, Jr., who signed them to his Red Coach label. Following the release of their first record, which was named after the group, distribution of Red Coach was taken over by the larger De-Lite label. "Kool & The Gang" became the first of more than a dozen hits which the group had accumulated by the mid-seventies, the biggest of which was the chart-topping "Jungle Boogie."

Today Kool & The Gang operate their own recording studio and manage the interests of a subsidiary group known as the Kay-Gees.

Sept. 69	*KOOL & THE GANG* / De-Lite
Dec. 69	*THE GANG'S BACK AGAIN* / De-Lite
July 70	*LET THE MUSIC TAKE YOUR MIND* / De-Lite
Sept. 70	*FUNKY MAN* / De-Lite
Sept. 73	*FUNKY STUFF* / De-Lite
Dec. 73	*JUNGLE BOOGIE* / De-Lite
Apr. 74	*HOLLYWOOD SWINGING* / De-Lite
Sept. 74	*HIGHER PLANE* / De-Lite
Jan. 75	*RHYME TYME PEOPLE* / De-Lite
Apr. 75	*SPIRIT OF THE BOOGIE* / De-Lite
Nov. 75	*CARIBBEAN FESTIVAL* / De-Lite
Mar. 76	*LOVE AND UNDERSTANDING* / De-Lite
Nov. 76	*OPEN SESAME (PART 1)* / De-Lite

Billy J. Kramer & The Dakotas

MEMBERS:

Billy J. Kramer (William Ashton) (lead vocals) / born: Aug. 19, 1943 / Bootle, England

Michael Maxfield (lead guitar) / born: Feb. 23, 1944 / Manchester, England

Robin Macdonald (rhythm guitar) / born: July 18, 1943 / Nairn, Scotland / replaced (1964) by Michael Green

Ray Jones (bass) / born: Oct. 20, 1939 / Oldham, England / (left the group in 1964)

Tony Mansfield (drums) / born: May 28, 1943 / Salford, England

One of the "beat" groups that became known to American audiences via the "British invasion" of 1964, Billy J. Kramer & The Dakotas were actually a band put together by Beatles manager Brian Epstein.

Kramer had gotten experience as a member of several skiffle groups during the late fifties, later playing rhythm guitar in local rock 'n' roll bands. In 1963 he was employed by British Railways while performing part time with a group called The Coasters (no relation to the American R & B group of the fifties). One of their performances was caught by Epstein, who liked Kramer and signed only him to a management contract. Placing Kramer in front of The Dakotas, Manchester's leading band at the time, Epstein booked the group into the Star Club in Hamburg, Germany, where they received rave notices. Consequently, they were signed by Parlophone Records, the same label that had earlier acquired The Beatles.

Now sharing a manager, a record company, and a producer (George Martin) with The Beatles, The Dakotas went one step further and began recording Beatles songs. Debuting with such Lennon-McCartney songs as "Do You Want to Know a Secret" (which never became popular in the United States). "Bad to Me," "I Call Your Name," "From a Window," and "I'll Keep You Satisfied," The Dakotas achieved a string of British hits and were swept onto the American charts with the tide of Beatlemania. Their popularity was not so long lived as some of the other groups, however,

Kris Kristofferson

and they faded from the best-seller lists before the end of 1965.

Today Billy J. Kramer continues to perform on the British club circuit and occasionally also performs at "revival" type shows.

Apr. 64	***LITTLE CHILDREN* /Imperial**
May 64	***BAD TO ME* /Imperial**
July 64	***I'LL KEEP YOU SATISFIED* / Imperial**
Aug. 64	***FROM A WINDOW* /Imperial**
Feb. 65	***IT'S GOTTA LAST FOREVER* / Imperial**
June 65	***TRAINS AND BOATS AND PLANES* /Imperial**

Kris Kristofferson

BORN: June 22, 1936
HOMETOWN: Brownsville, Texas

The son of a military career man, Kristoffer Kristofferson moved with his family to San Mateo, California, during his high school years. While attending college, he began dabbling in the writing of short stories and songs.

During the late fifties, Kris moved to England to study literature at Oxford University, writing two (unpublished) novels and increasingly greater numbers of songs. His work came to the attention of Tommy Steele's manager, who signed him to a songwriting-and-recording contract and was, able to build somewhat of a reputation for him under the name Kris Carson.

After receiving his degree at Oxford, Kris entered the military with the intention of making it his career. While playing some of his songs at an NCO club one evening, one of his buddies suggested that he send his material to a relative, music publisher Marijohn Wilkin, in Nashville. As a result many of his songs were recorded by leading artists, some becoming instant contemporary standards: "Help Me Make It through the Night," "Me & Bobby McGee," "For the Good Times," "Sunday Mornin' Comin' Down," and "Why Me Lord."

With the encouragement of such leading Country-music figures as Johnny Cash and Roger Miller, Kris decided to become a performer as well, debuting in 1970 at L.A.'s Troubador. Amidst rave notices, he was signed to Fred Foster's Monument label and began recording a series of best-selling singles and albums.

During the seventies Kris also launched an acting career, gaining wide acclaim for his roles in films such as *The Last Movie, Cisco Pike, Blume In Love, Pat Garrett and Billy the Kid,* *The Sailor Who Fell from Grace with the Sea,* and the remake of *A Star Is Born.*

Today, Kris lives in Nashville with his wife, rock star Rita Coolidge. Since marrying late in 1973, they often have toured and occasionally have recorded together.

Kris Kristofferson

Aug. 71 *LOVING HER WAS EASIER /* **Monument**

Mar. 72 *JOSIE /* **Monument**

Dec. 72 *JESUS WAS A CAPRICORN /* **Monument**

Apr. 73 *WHY ME /* **Monument**

May 77 *WATCH CLOSELY NOW /* **Columbia**

Kris Kristofferson & Rita Coolidge

Nov. 73 *A SONG I'D LIKE TO SING /* **A & M**

Mar. 74 *LOVING ARMS /* **A & M**

LaBelle

MEMBERS:

Patti LaBelle (Patricia Holt)/born: May 24, 1944/Philadelphia, Pennsylvania

Sara Dash /born: August 18, 1945/Trenton, New Jersey

Nona Hendryx /born: October 4, 1944/Trenton, New Jersey

In 1961, vocalists Patti LaBelle and Cindy Birdsong were members of a Philadelphia group called the Ordetts, while schoolmates Sarah Dash and Nona Hendryx were in another group, The Dell Capris. By 1962 the two groups had disbanded, yielding a third called Patti LaBelle & the Blue Belles. This combination went on to have several hits during the early-middle sixties. (See *Patti LABELLE & THE BLUE BELLES, Rock On: The Solid Gold Years.*)

In 1967 Cindy Birdsong left to replace Florence Ballard in The Supremes, leaving The Blue Belles to continue as a trio. In 1970, during a trip to Britain, they came to the attention of manager Vicki Wickham, who agreed to handle the group and suggested the name change to "LaBelle." She also helped fashion the group into a harder rock-and-soul act.

In 1971 the "new" LaBelle debuted with a Warner Brothers album titled *Moonshadow* and backed Laura Nyro on her *Gonna Take a Miracle* package. After a label change to RCA, they followed with *Night Birds*. This record-

ing became a major success and yielded the number one single "Lady Marmalade."

Today both Patti LaBelle and Nona Hendryx record for Epic Records, each as a solo performer.

Jan. 75 *LADY MARMALADE* /Epic
May 75 *WHAT CAN I DO FOR YOU?* / Epic

Vicki Lawrence

BORN: May 26, 1949
HOMETOWN: Los Angeles, California

Vicki Lawrence began preparing for her show-business life as a child, studying ballet, modern and tap dancing, piano, guitar and a variety of other instruments. During her college years, she got her first singing experience as a member of two folk-oriented groups.

In 1964 Vicki launched her professional career by successfully auditioning for the Young Americans singing group. After she appeared with them in concerts, on television, and in a feature film, a newspaper writer wrote an article pointing out her resemblance to comedy star Carol Burnett. Highly flattered, Vicki sent Carol a clipping and was surprised to receive a phone call from Carol in return. At Carol's suggestion, Vicki tested for and got the role of Carol's "television sister," a part which she began playing regularly in l967.

During the filming of one of the

show's episodes in 1969, Vicki met songwriter Bobby Russell and eventually married him in 1972. Early the following year, Russell wrote "The Night the Lights Went Out in Georgia," a song that he had intended to record himself. Thinking it might be a better song for a female vocalist, he offered it to Cher but was turned down. Not to be outdone, he and producer Snuff Garrett (who was working with Cher at the time) had Vicki record the song and sold the master to Larry Utall's Bell label. The record reached number one on the charts, and was followed later in the year by a lesser hit.

Today Vicki Lawrence continues to be seen weekly on "The Carol Burnett Show."

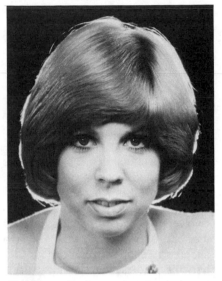

Vicki Lawrence

Feb. 73 *THE NIGHT THE LIGHTS WENT OUT IN GEORGIA* / **Bell**
June 73 *HE DID WITH ME* / **Bell**

The Leaves

MEMBERS:

William Rinehart (vocals) / Honolulu, Hawaii / replaced (1966) by Robert Arlin

John Beck (guitar)

Robert Lee Reiner (guitar) / born: 1946 / Hartford, Connecticut

James Pons (bass) / born: Mar. 14, 1942 / Santa Monica, California

Tom "Ambrose" Ray (drums) / Hollywood, California

Formed in the spring of 1965, this group was organized at San Fernando Valley State College by Jim Pons and Bill Rinehart. Starting out on a note of satire the group took its name from a conversation between two of the group's members: "What's happening?" asked one. "The leaves are happening," answered the other, as he watched the breeze shake some leaves off a nearby tree!

The Leaves began by playing small local clubs, eventually working their way into some of Hollywood's more substantial spots. At one of these performances, they were noticed by Pop singer Pat Boone, who employed them to back up his *Departures* album. Signed to the L.A.-based Mira label, they reached the twenties on the national charts with "Hey Joe," a record that is considered today to be among the classics of psychedelic "punk rock" (the same song was later recorded by such artists as Cher, Wilson Pickett, and Jimi Hendrix.)

In 1967 The Leaves were signed by the major Capitol label. However, they became disillusioned when they could not duplicate their prior success and disbanded soon thereafter. Bobby Arlin went on to join Hook, while Jim Pons became a member of the highly successful Turtles. He, along with Turtles Mark Volman and Howard Kaylan, ultimately joined Frank Zappa's Mothers of Invention.

May 66 *HEY JOE* / **Mira**

LeBlanc & Carr

MEMBERS:

Lenny LeBlanc (guitar)/born: June 17, 1951/
Daytona, Florida

Pete Carr (guitar)/born: Apr. 22, 1950/
Daytona, Florida

Lenny and Pete met in Daytona in 1968. A year later they commuted to Miami as session musicians, but the trip proved to be too much for LeBlanc who moved to Cincinnati.

Carr moved to Muscle Shoals, Alabama, to work as a producer and got involved with the group Sailcat and their hit "Motorcycle Mama." After a successful stint as a producer, Carr became lead guitarist for the Muscle Shoals Sound Rhythm Section.

In 1973, LeBlanc and Carr were reunited in Muscle Shoals and in a short time Carr was working as a studio bass guitarist.

In 1976 both LeBlanc and Carr released solo albums for Big Tree Records and felt that they would like to record together. The material they recorded produced a hit single in the summer of 1977 called "Something About You" which was also a big hit for The Four Tops in the fall of 1965.

Today they continue to travel as a duo, but spend a lot of time still working as studio musicians in Muscle Shoals.

LeBlanc & Carr
July 77 SOMETHING ABOUT YOU /Big Tree
Oct. 77 FALLING /Big Tree
Lenny LeBlanc
Sept. 77 HOUND DOG MAN /Big Tree

Led Zeppelin

MEMBERS:

James Page (lead guitar)/born: Jan. 9, 1945/
Heston, Middlesex, England

Robert Plant (lead vocals, harmonica)/born: Aug. 20, 1947/Birmingham, England

John Paul Jones (John Baldwin) (bass, keyboards)/born: Jan. 3, 1946/London, England

John "Bonzo" Bonham (drums)/born: May 31, 1947/Birmingham, England

One of the biggest of the seventies supergroups, Led Zeppelin was formed immediately after The Yardbirds disbanded in July, 1968. (See *THE YARDBIRDS.*)

Left with the ownership of the group's name and several concert obligations to fulfill, Jimmy Page assembled a new group known at first as The New Yardbirds. Beginning with John Paul Jones, a good friend and a leading British session musician, Page rounded out the line-up by recruiting Robert Plant and John Bonham from The Band Of Joy. Once assembled, the group changed its name to Led Zeppelin at the suggestion of Page's friend, Keith Moon of The Who.

Almost immediately the group traveled to the United States, touring the country, signing with Atlantic, and recording their first album, *Led Zeppelin I.* During the next three years, they followed with *Led Zeppelin II, III,* and *IV,* and also placed a number of singles on the charts. By this time their albums were selling in the millions within days of release, and they continued with *Houses of the Holy* and *Physical Graffiti.* The attendance figures for their personal appearances established and broke a number of records with some of their tours selling out well before they were formally announced!

Today the Led Zeppelin organization operates its own Swan Song record label, the artist roster of which includes Bad Company, The Pretty Things, Maggie Bell, and Roy Harper. The group has recently been the subject of a major feature film, *The Song*

Led Zeppelin. Left to right: John Bonham, Robert Plant, Jimmy Page, John Paul Jones

Remains the Same, which documents their 1973 American tour.

Mar. 69	***GOOD TIMES, BAD TIMES / Atlantic***
Nov. 69	***WHOLE LOTTA LOVE / Atlantic***
Mar. 70	***LIVING LOVING MAD / Atlantic***
Nov. 70	***THE IMMIGRANT SONG / Atlantic***
Dec. 71	***BLACK DOG / Atlantic***
Mar. 72	***ROCK & ROLL / Atlantic***
June 73	***OVER THE HILLS AND FAR AWAY / Atlantic***
Oct. 73	***D'YER MAK'ER / Atlantic***
Apr. 75	***TRAMPLED UNDERFOOT / Swan Song***

The Left Banke

MEMBERS:
Steven Martin (lead vocals)
Jeff Winfield (lead guitar) / replaced by Rick Brand
Michael Brown (keyboards)
Thomas Finn (bass)
George Cameron (drums)
HOMETOWN: New York City

The Left Banke was organized in 1966 by Mike Brown, whose father, Harry Lookofsky, had his own recording studio and a great deal of prior experience in the music business. Lookofsky acted as the group's manager, publisher, and producer, and arranged for a contract with Mercury Records' subsidiary Smash label.

The group launched its recording career with "Walk Away Renee," an unusual blending of rock music with the sound of the classics. A slow seller at first, the record became a major regional hit in Ohio and eventually reached the top five nationally. They

The Lemon Pipers

followed with "Pretty Ballerina," which became a top 15 hit after being played by Leonard Bernstein on the same television special that established the career of Janis Ian. In 1967 Mike Brown left the group and recorded two relatively unsucessful records, "And Suddenly" and "Ivy Ivy," under the Left Banke name. After a flurry of lawsuits, the original line-up regrouped to place one last entry on the charts, entitled "Desiree."

The Left Banke disbanded permanently early in 1968. Mike Brown went on to major success with the group Stories, subsequently leaving for a solo career. Today he records for the Sire label with yet another group, The Beckies.

Sept. 66 *WALK AWAY RENEE*/Smash
Jan. 67 *PRETTY BALLERINA*/Smash
Oct. 67 *DESIREE*/Smash

The Lemon Pipers

MEMBERS:
Ivan Browne (lead vocal, rhythm guitar)/born: 1947
William Bartlett (lead guitar)/born: 1946
R. G. Nave (keyboards, tambourine)/born: 1945
Steven Walmsley (bass)/born: 1949
William Albaugh (drums)/born: 1948
HOMETOWN: Cincinnati, Ohio

Known originally as Ivan & the Sabres, The Lemon Pipers emerged in 1967 with an unusual "goodtime" psychedelic sound.

Working in association with producer Paul Leka, the group launched its recording career on Buddah Records with Bill Bartlett's composition of "Turn Around, Take a Look." This failed to make the charts, but their next release, Paul Leka's "Green Tambourine," went straight to number one and remained on the best-seller lists for a quarter of a year.

The Lemon Pipers were able to follow with two additional hits before fading from popularity in 1968.

Dec. 67	***GREEN TAMBOURINE /*** **Buddah**
Mar. 68	***RICE IS NICE /*** **Buddah**
May 68	***JELLY JUNGLE /*** **Buddah**

John Lennon

John Lennon

BORN: Oct. 9, 1940
HOMETOWN: Liverpool, England
Yoko Ono
BORN: Feb. 18, 1933
HOMETOWN: Tokyo, Japan

Lennon was the most explosive and controversial member of The Beatles, and it was primarily his actions during

the late sixties that signaled to the world that the end of the group could not be far off. (See *THE BEATLES*.)

In 1968 Lennon became the first Beatle to record outside the group, issuing an album with his wife-to-be, Yoko Ono, titled *Two Virgins*. Next he organized the Plastic Ono Band, an informal and constantly changing group of musicians that would back him on most of his future solo recordings. In the beginning the band consisted of Yoko Ono, Eric Clapton, Alan White, and Klaus Voormann, and this combo made an album in 1969 titled *Live Peace at Toronto*. Yielding Lennon's first solo hit single, an antiwar anthem called "Give Peace a Chance," this was followed by two very personal and introspective releases, *Life with the Lions* and *Wedding Album*. A major news story in 1969 was the March 20 marriage of Lennon to Yoko.

The year 1970 brought the official break-up of The Beatles and Lennon's first "official" solo album, *Plastic Ono Band*. He continued into the mid-seventies with *Imagine, Sometime in New York City, Mind Games, Walls and Bridges*, and an "oldies" package titled *Rock & Roll*. He also made his dramatic acting debut during the seventies with his role in *How I Won the War*.

In recent years John Lennon has been in the news as much for his personal difficulties as for his professional life. These have included his break-up with Yoko Ono and their eventual reconciliation, the search for Yoko Ono's young child and the Lennons' battle with American immigration authorities for permission to remain in the country.

July 69	*GIVE PEACE A CHANCE / Apple*
Nov. 69	*COLD TURKEY / Apple*
Feb. 70	*INSTANT KARMA / Apple*
Jan. 71	*MOTHER / Apple*
Apr. 71	*POWER TO THE PEOPLE / Apple*
Oct. 71	*IMAGINE / Apple*
May 72	*WOMAN IS THE NIGGER OF THE WORLD / Apple*
Nov. 73	*MIND GAMES / Apple*
Sept. 74	*WHATEVER GETS YOU THRU THE NIGHT / Apple*
Dec. 74	*#9 DREAM / Apple*
Mar. 75	*STAND BY ME / Apple*

Gary Lewis & The Playboys

MEMBERS:

Gary Lewis (Gary Levitch) (drums) / born: July 31, 1946 / New York City

Al Ramsey (guitar) / born: July 27, 1943 / Danfield, New Jersey / replaced by Tom Tripplehorn / born: Feb. 2, 1944 / Tulsa, Oklahoma

John R. West (guitar) / born: July 31, 1939 / Uhrichsville, Ohio / replaced by James Karstein / Tulsa, Oklahoma

David Walker (keyboards) / born: May 12, 1943 / Montgomery, Alabama

David Costell (bass) / born: Mar. 15, 1944 / Pittsburgh, Pennsylvania / replaced by Carl Radle / Tulsa, Oklahoma

HOMETOWN: Los Angeles, California

The son of comedian Jerry Lewis, Gary was exposed to music from the beginning of his life. Given a set of drums as a gift on his fourteenth birthday, he decided to organize a group to play at private affairs.

After a few years' experience, The Playboys auditioned successfully for Disneyland in 1964 and became one of the park's resident bands. They also began appearing on the "Shindig" TV show, which eventually led to a contract offer from Liberty Records' A & R director Snuff Garrett.

Beginning with "This Diamond Ring" (written in part by Al Kooper) in 1965, The Playboys achieved a series of major best sellers that lasted into early

1967. Their recordings were arranged by future rock superstar Leon Russell, who also wrote many of the songs and recruited a number of the West Coast's leading studio musicians to help on the sessions.

Late in 1966 Gary Lewis began a two-year stint in the service while Liberty continued to issue records "from the can." Returning in 1968, he attempted to reorganize the group, but with very little commercial success. The Playboys disbanded soon thereafter, freeing the members to join other bands and to do session work. Of particular note was Carl Radle, who joined Delaney & Bonnie's Friends and later achieved international fame with Derek & The Dominoes.

Today, Gary Lewis lives in Los Angeles with his wife, dancer Kay Elaine.

Jan. 65	**THIS DIAMOND RING** /Liberty	
Apr. 65	**COUNT ME IN** /Liberty	
July 65	**SAVE YOUR HEART FOR ME** /Liberty	
Sept. 65	**EVERYBODY LOVES A CLOWN** /Liberty	
Dec. 65	**SHE'S JUST MY STYLE** /Liberty	
Mar. 66	**SURE GONNA MISS HER** /Liberty	
May 66	**GREEN GRASS** /Liberty	
July 66	**MY HEART'S SYMPHONY** /Liberty	
Oct. 66	**PAINT ME A PICTURE** /Liberty	
Dec. 66	**WHERE WILL THE WORDS COME FROM?** /Liberty	
Mar. 67	**THE LOSER** /Liberty	
May 67	**GIRLS IN LOVE** /Liberty	
Aug. 67	**JILL** /Liberty	
June 68	**SEALED WITH A KISS** /Liberty	
Apr. 69	**RHYTHM OF THE RAIN** /Liberty	

The Ramsey Lewis Trio

MEMBERS:
Ramsey E. Lewis, Jr. (piano)/born: May 27, 1935/Chicago, Illinois

Eldee Young (bass)/born: Jan. 7, 1936/ Chicago Illinois/replaced (1966) by Cleveland Eaton
Isaac "Red" Holt (drums)/born: May 16, 1932/Rosedale, Mississippi/replaced (1966) by Maurice White/replaced (1969) by Morris Jennings
HOMETOWN: Chicago, Illinois

This group was formed in 1956 by three boyhood friends, each of which had had experience in other bands before coming together as the jazz-oriented Ramsey Lewis Trio.

After gaining a reputation on the Chicago club circuit, the group was signed in 1958 by Chess's subsidiary Argo label (which later underwent a name change to Cadet). Debuting with *Gentlemen of Jazz,* they recorded nearly a dozen albums through the mid-sixties, all best sellers in the jazz market. They also achieved a modest hit single with Chris Kenner's "Something You Got."

In 1966 The Ramsey Lewis Trio recorded a "live" album during an engagement at the Bohemian Caverns in Washington, D.C. A cut from this LP, an instrumental version of Dobie Gray's "In Crowd," established the group with Pop audiences by nearly reaching the top of the charts. They continued through the sixties with similar versions of hit songs for other artists.

After the trio's national success, Eldee Young and Red Holt left to form their own group, Young-Holt Unlimited. They were replaced by Cleveland Eaton and Maurice White, with the latter leaving in 1969 to organize Earth, Wind & Fire, one of the most successful groups of the seventies.

Today Ramsey Lewis is billed as a solo artist and records for Columbia Records, occasionally in association with Earth, Wind & Fire.

Oct. 64	**SOMETHING YOU GOT** / Argo
July 65	**THE IN CROWD** / Argo
Nov. 65	**HANG ON SLOOPY** / Cadet
Jan. 66	**A HARD DAY'S NIGHT** / Cadet
Mar. 66	**HI HEEL SNEAKERS** / Cadet
July 66	**WADE IN THE WATER** / Cadet
Oct. 66	**UPTIGHT** / Cadet
Dec. 66	**DAY TRIPPER** / Cadet
Feb. 67	**ONE, TWO, THREE** / Cadet
Sept. 67	**DANCING IN THE STREET** / Cadet
Nov. 67	**SOUL MAN** / Cadet
Aug. 68	**SINCE YOU'VE BEEN GONE** / Cadet
Sept. 69	**JULIA** / Cadet
Mar. 73	**KUFANYA MAPENZIE** / Columbia

With Earth, Wind & Fire

Jan. 75	**HOT DAWGIT** / Columbia
Mar. 75	**SUN GODDESS** / Columbia
Jan. 76	**WHAT'S THE NAME OF THIS FUNK (SPIDER MAN)** / Columbia

Gordon Lightfoot

BORN: Nov. 17, 1938
HOMETOWN: Orillia, Ontario, Canada

Gordon Lightfoot began playing piano as a child, then joined a number of bands during his teen years. In 1958 he traveled to Los Angeles, entering Westlake College as a music major and breaking into the recording business as a session vocalist and arranger.

During the early sixties, Lightfoot became greatly influenced by the folk styles of Bob Gibson, Peter Seeger, and Canada's Ian & Sylvia. Returning home to Canada, he took up the guitar and began performing on the local club circuit. He was signed by United Artists in 1965, where his album releases, including *Lightfoot, Did She Mention My Name,* and *The Way I Feel,* gradually established him as Canada's leading folksinger. His songs began receiving recognition from American artists— "Early Morning Rain" (Judy Collins),

"For Loving Me" (Peter, Paul & Mary), and "Ribbon Of Darkness" (Marty Robbins)—and the release of his *Sunday Concert* album in 1969 firmly established him with American audiences.

In 1970 Lightfoot signed with Reprise Records, debuting with an album titled *Sit Down, Young Stranger.* By the end of the year, he was at the top of the singles charts with "If You Could Read My Mind," the first of a long series of hits. His albums have continued to be best sellers, including *Summer Side of Life, Don Quixote, Old Dan's Records, Sundown,* and *Summertime Dream.*

Today Lightfoot lives with his wife and two children in Toronto, Canada.

Dec. 70	**IF YOU COULD READ MY MIND** / Reprise
June 71	**TALKING IN YOUR SLEEP** / Reprise
Sept. 71	**THE SUMMER SIDE OF LIFE** / Reprise
May 72	**BEAUTIFUL** / Reprise
Apr. 74	**SUNDOWN** / Reprise
Aug. 74	**CAREFREE HIGHWAY** / Reprise
Mar. 75	**RAINY DAY PEOPLE** / Reprise
Sept. 76	**THE WRECK OF THE EDMUND FITZGERALD** / Reprise
Feb. 77	**RACE AMONG THE RUINS** / Reprise
Feb. 78	**THE CIRCLE IS SMALL** / Warner Bros.

Lighthouse

MEMBERS:
Robert McBride (lead vocals)
Ralph Cole (lead guitar)
Lawrence Smith (piano)
Paul Hoffert (keyboards)
John Naslen (trumpet)
Rick Stepton (trombone)
Dale Hillary (sax)
Donald Dinovo (violin)
Richard Armin (cello)

Gordon Lightfoot

Al Wilmot (bass)
Skip Prokop (drums)
HOMETOWN: Toronto, Canada

This group was organized during the late sixties by two leading figures on the Canadian music scene, Skip Prokop and Paul Hoffert. Prokop had led one of Canada's leading rock 'n' roll bands, The Paupers, while Hoffert was widely known as a composer of commercial jingles, films, and documentaries. The group's unusual name was selected by Prokop after he watched some tropical fish swimming in and out of a lighthouse at the bottom of an aquarium.

Attracting almost immediate attention with their large, big-band sound, the group was signed by RCA in New York. Three albums were released and a concert was held at Carnegie Hall, but none of these efforts met with success. Returning to Canada, the group formed their own management company and began to strengthen their reputation with a number of major concert appearances.

Lighthouse eventually achieved both Canadian and American success with "One Fine Morning," which reached the top 20 on the American charts. While enduring a number of personnel changes, they followed during the next years with a series of best-selling singles and albums, eventually disbanding late in 1974. Most of the group's members went on to pursue solo careers.

Sept. 71 *ONE FINE MORNING /* **Evolution**
Dec. 71 *TAKE IT SLOW /* **Evolution**
Apr. 72 *I JUST WANNA BE YOUR FRIEND /* **Evolution**
Oct. 72 *SUNNY DAYS /* **Evolution**
Nov. 73 *PRETTY LADY /* **Polydor**

Bob Lind

BORN: Nov. 25, 1944
HOMETOWN: Baltimore, Maryland

Robert Neale Lind grew up in Chicago, to which his family moved when he was only a few years old. A devout fan of Bob Dylan, he occasionally sang for fun in Dylan's style.

During the mid-sixties Lind was attending Western State University in Colorado when he entered a local hootenanny contest for original tunes. He won ten dollars as first prize, and this eventually led to a regular singing engagement at a club called The Analyst in Denver. After nearly two years at

The Analyst, a friend of Lind's recorded one of his performances and sent the tape to World Pacific Records, a division of Liberty. Lind was offered both a songwriting and an artist contract, and by early 1966 was near the top of the national charts with his composition of "Elusive Butterfly." Following with an album, *Don't Be Concerned,* and two additional hit singles, Lind's style paved the way for the emergence of such folk-oriented artists as Tim Buckley and Tim Hardin.

During the late sixties the complexities of life as a recording star prompted Bob Lind to retire to Santa Fe, New Mexico. He continues to live there today, performing only occasionally.

Jan. 66 *ELUSIVE BUTTERFLY /* **World Pacific**
Apr. 66 *REMEMBER THE RAIN /* **World Pacific**
May 66 *TRULY JULIE'S BLUES /* **World Pacific**

Mark Lindsay

BORN: Mar. 9, 1944
HOMETOWN: Eugene, Oregon

Mark Allen Lindsay rose to fame during the sixties and early seventies as the lead vocalist and sax player with Paul Revere & The Raiders. (See *Paul REVERE & THE RAIDERS, Rock On: The Solid Gold Years.*)

In 1969, while continuing to record with the group, Lindsay began pursuing a solo career on the side. He achieved a number of hits, the biggest of which was his top ten entry "Arizona."

Today Lindsay makes his home in Los Angeles and occasionally appears with The Raiders at revival shows.

July 69 *1ST HYMN FROM GRAND TERRACE /* **Columbia**
Dec. 69 *ARIZONA /* **Columbia**

Apr. 70 **MISS AMERICA** / Columbia
June 70 **SILVER BIRD** / Columbia
Sept. 70 **AND THE GRASS WON'T PAY
NO MIND** / Columbia
Jan. 71 **PROBLEM CHILD** / Columbia
June 71 **BEEN TOO LONG ON THE
ROAD** / Columbia
Oct. 71 **ARE YOU OLD ENOUGH?** /
Columbia

Little Milton

REAL NAME: Milton Campbell
BORN: Sept. 7, 1934
HOMETOWN: Inverness, Mississippi

Little Milton began singing in church as a child. He sent for a mail-order guitar at the age of eleven and taught himself to play by imitating such blues artists as T-Bone Walker, Roy Brown, Roy Milton, and Big Joe Turner.

During the late forties, Milton left home to join The Eddie Kusick Band. He made his first record in 1953, on Sam Phillips's Sun label, and was backed by a band led by his friend Ike Turner. For the remainder of the fifties, he recorded for a number of small blues labels, including Meteor and Bobbin.

In 1961 Milton was signed to the Chicago-based Checker label, where he achieved a number of R & B hits during the early sixties. He was also responsible for bringing a number of other artists to the label, including Fontella Bass and Albert King. His major breakthrough came in 1965, when his releases began appearing on the national best-seller lists.

During the early seventies, Milton affiliated with Stax Records, which, unfortunately, ceased operations shortly thereafter. Today he makes his home in Chicago, where he also operates a number of business enterprises, and records for T. K. Records in Florida.

Jan. 65 **BLIND MAN** / Checker
Mar. 65 **WE'RE GONNA MAKE IT** /
Checker
June 65 **WHO'S CHEATING WHO?** /
Checker
Feb. 66 **WE GOT THE WINNING
HAND** / Checker
Feb. 67 **FEEL SO BAD** / Checker
Feb. 69 **GRITS AIN'T GROCERIES** /
Checker
May 69 **JUST A LITTLE BIT** / Checker
Jan. 70 **IF WALLS COULD TALK** /
Checker
May 70 **BABY I LOVE YOU** / Checker
Feb. 72 **THAT'S WHAT LOVE WILL
MAKE YOU DO** / Checker

Little River Band

MEMBERS:
Glenn Shorrock (lead vocals) / born: June 30, 1944
David Briggs (lead guitar) / born: Jan. 26, 1951
Beeb Birtles (guitar and vocals) / born: Nov. 28, 1948
Graham Goble (rhythm guitar) / born: May 15, 1947
George McArdle (bass guitar) / born: Nov. 30, 1954
Derek Pellicci (drums) / born: Feb. 18, 1953
HOMETOWN: Sydney, Australia

Little River Band was formed in 1975 when the group Mississippi, of which Goble, Birtles, and Pellicci were members, broke up and joined studio musicians McArdle and Briggs and vocalist Shorrock, who just left the group Esperanto. They chose the name Little River Band from an Australian road sign. Glenn Wheatley, their manager and guiding force, helped them record their first album. To date, their biggest album is *Diamantina Cocktail,* which happens to be a potent Australian drink made of rum, cream, an amu's egg, ice, and a leaf from a gum tree.

Jan. 77 **I'LL ALWAYS CALL YOUR
NAME** / Harvest
Aug. 77 **HELP IS ON THE WAY** / Capitol

Little River Band. Left to right: George McArdle, Derek Pellicci, David Briggs, Glenn Shorrock, Beeb Birtles, Graham Goble

Little Sister

MEMBERS:
Vannetta Stewart
Elva Melton
Mary Rand

This was an all-female grouped structured by Sly Stone around his "little sister," Vannetta Stewart. During the late sixties, the group often appeared as part of the Sly & the Family Stone revue.

In 1970 Sly established his own Stoneflower label to issue recordings by Little Sister. The group achieved two hits with songs written and produced by Sly and suggesting social conscience—"You're the One" and "Somebody's Watching You."

Feb. 70 *YOU'RE THE ONE*/**Stoneflower**
Dec. 70 *SOMEBODY'S WATCHING YOU*/**Stoneflower**

Lobo

REAL NAME: Kent Lavoie
BORN: July 31, 1943
HOMETOWN: Tallahassee, Florida

Not a group, as commonly supposed, Lobo was actually a pseudonym adopted by singer-songwriter Kent Lavoie.

Lavoie grew up in Winter Haven, Florida, where he attended high school and began his career in a group called The Rumors. Playing part time with them while attending the University of South Florida, he eventually left both to join another group called The Sugar Beats. During this period he became acquainted with producer Phil Gernhard, who worked with the group to create a minor regional hit. Shortly thereafter, Lavoie left The Sugar Beats for a brief stint in the army, returning to spend the next years with a band known as Me & The Other Guys.

During the early seventies, Phil Gernhard emerged as an executive of Big Tree Records, and he signed Lavoie to the label. Beginning with "Me and You and a Dog Named Boo," Kent Lavoie, a/k/a Lobo, achieved an unbroken string of hits that lasted well into the mid-seventies. He also became active as a producer, scoring with several major hits by Jim Stafford ("Spiders & Snakes," etc.).

Today Kent Lavoie and his wife make their home in the St. Petersburg area of Florida while he records for Warner/Curb Records.

Apr. 71	**ME AND YOU AND A DOG NAMED BOO** /Big Tree
June 71	**SHE DIDN'T DO MAGIC** /Big Tree
Sept. 71	**THE CALIFORNIA KID & REEMO** /Big Tree
July 72	**A SIMPLE MAN** /Big Tree
Sept. 72	**I'D LOVE YOU TO WANT ME** / Big Tree
Dec. 72	**DON'T EXPECT ME TO BE YOUR FRIEND** /Big Tree
Apr. 73	**IT SURE TOOK A LONG LONG TIME** /Big Tree
June 73	**HOW CAN I TELL HER?** /Big Tree
Nov. 73	**THERE AIN'T NO WAY** /Big Tree
Apr. 74	**STANDING AT THE END OF THE LINE** /Big Tree
July 74	**RINGS** /Big Tree
Mar. 75	**DON'T TELL ME GOODNIGHT** / Big Tree

Dave Loggins

BORN: Nov. 10, 1947
HOMETOWN: Bristol, Tennessee

A distant relative of Kenny Loggins (of Loggins & Messina), Dave Loggins was introduced to music by his father, a country fiddler.

During the late sixties, Loggins composed half a dozen original songs and

Dave Loggins

traveled to New York City in search of a publishing deal. He was signed as a writer to MCA Music, and that soon led to a recording contract with Vanguard. He cut an album titled *Personal Belongings,* embarking shortly thereafter on a tour to promote sales. While playing at a club in Denver, Colorado, he performed a song from the album *Pieces of April.* It was heard by a member of the Three Dog Night organization, who brought the song to the group and suggested they record it. The Three Dog Night version reached the national top 20, thereby drawing a great deal of attention to Dave Loggins.

In 1974 Loggins was signed by the Epic label, debuting with an album titled *Apprentice in a Musical Workshop* and a top five single, "Please Come to Boston." Over a year in the making, his second album, *Country Suite,* was released early in 1976 and became an immediate best seller.

285

Loggins & Messina. Left to right: Jim Messina, Kenny Loggins

Today Dave Loggins makes his permanent home in Nashville, Tennessee.

June 74	***PLEASE COME TO BOSTON/*** Epic
Nov. 74	***SOMEDAY/*** Epic

Loggins & Messina

MEMBERS:

Kenneth Loggins (guitar, bass)/born: Jan. 7, 1948/Everett, Washington

James Messina (guitar, bass)/born: Dec. 5, 1947/Maywood, California

Loggins and Messina became a team in 1970 after each had enjoyed a period of individual success.

During the late sixties, Kenny Loggins had recorded with two groups, Second Helping and Gator Creek, and had achieved chart success as a songwriter with The Nitty Gritty Dirt Band's "House at Pooh Corner." Jim Messina was widely known as a member of Buffalo Springfield and as a charter member of Poco.

In 1971 Loggins was signed as an artist by Columbia Records, and A & R man Don Ellis began searching for someone to produce him. Jim Messina, who had just left Poco, accepted the assignment, but wound up as Loggins's partner instead. Their first album, *Sitting In,* brought them modest success, as did their first single releases. Their next LP, *Loggins & Messina,* became a best seller and yielded a major hit titled "Your Mama Don't Dance." They continued into the mid-seventies with a string of singles hits and albums such as *Full Sail, On Stage,* and *Motherlode.* Other artists began having hits with their material as well, including Anne Murray with Loggins's "Danny's Song" and "Love Song," and Lynn Anderson with Messina's "Listen to a Country Song."

In July, 1976, Loggins and Messina announced that they were separating to pursue individual careers once again.

Loggins & Messina
Apr. 72 *VAHEVALA* / **Columbia**
June 72 *NOBODY BUT YOU* / **Columbia**
Nov. 72 *YOUR MAMA DON'T DANCE* / **Columbia**
Mar. 73 *THINKING OF YOU* / **Columbia**
Nov. 73 *MY MUSIC* / **Columbia**
Mar. 74 *WATCHING THE RIVER RUN* / **Columbia**
Feb. 75 *CHANGES* / **Columbia**
Apr. 75 *GROWIN'* / **Columbia**
Aug. 75 *I LIKE IT LIKE THAT* / **Columbia**
Oct. 75 *A LOVER'S QUESTION* / **Columbia**

Kenny Loggins
July 77 *I BELIEVE IN LOVE* / **Columbia**

Shorty Long

REAL NAME: Frederick Long
BORN: May 20, 1940
DIED: June 29, 1969
HOMETOWN: Birmingham, Alabama

Shorty Long taught himself to sing as a child by listening to the recordings of Johnny Ace and Little Willie John. As he grew older, he began singing at parties and at Birmingham Baptist Church.

During the fifties Long became the resident singer at a leading Birmingham club, The Old Stable, and toured nationally for nearly two years with The Ink Spots. He also had a brief career in radio, hosting his own show in Alabama.

Signed by Motown during the mid-sixties, Long launched the subsidiary Soul label with his recording of "Devil with a Blue Dress." Although not a chart entry for him, it became the basis for Mitch Ryder's major hit just a few years later. With the release of "Func-tion at the Junction," Long emerged on the national charts, achieving his biggest hit in 1968 with the top ten recording of "Here Comes the Judge."

In 1969, just after completing an album titled *The Prime of Shorty Long,* Frederick Long died as the result of a boating accident.

Sept. 66 *FUNCTION AT THE JUNCTION* / **Soul**
Feb. 68 *NIGHT FO' LAST* / **Soul**
June 68 *HERE COMES THE JUDGE* / **Soul**

Looking Glass

MEMBERS:
Elliott Lurie (lead guitar, vocals) / born: Aug. 19, 1948 / Brooklyn, New York
Lawrence Gonsky (keyboards) / born: Oct. 20, 1949 / Paterson, New Jersey
Pieter Sweval (bass) / born: Apr. 13, 1948 / Toms River, New Jersey
Jeffrey Grob (drums) / born: Dec. 6, 1950 / Orange, New Jersey

Looking Glass was formed in 1969 by four students at Rutgers University. After getting their start by playing fraternity parties and dances in the vicinity of the college, they spent the months following graduation rehearsing and developing an act.

In 1971 they began circulating their material to record companies and were offered a contract by Epic. They began work on an album, *Looking Glass,* which was issued early in 1972. A single released from it, "Brandy (You're a Fine Girl)," was a slow seller at first, but eventually began to receive a lot of airplay in the Washington, D.C., area. From there the record took off nationally, soon reaching number one. After a lesser hit in 1973, Looking Glass disbanded and Elliott Lurie began recording for Epic as a solo artist.

Today, although they no longer record together, the members of Looking Glass own an 82-acre farm in Glen Gardner, New Jersey.

| June 72 | BRANDY (YOU'RE A FINE GIRL) / Epic |
| July 73 | JIMMY LOVES MARY ANNE / Epic |

Los Bravos
MEMBERS:
Michael Kogel (lead vocals)
Antonio Martinez (guitar)
Manuel Fernandez (keyboards)
Miguel Vicens Danus (bass)
Pablo Sanllehi (drums)

Los Bravos were the first Spanish rock group to achieve international success. With the exception of Mike Kogel, who came from Germany, all its members were natives of Spain.

During the early-middle sixties, the group accumulated several hit singles in Spain under the name Mike & The Runaways. Observing the number of successful groups emerging from Britain, the group moved there to try their fortunes and formed an association almost immediately with veteran music director Ivor Raymonde. With his help they were signed by the British Decca label and, changing their name to Los Bravos, launched their new career with a hit record titled "Black Is Black." Released in the United States on the Press label, the record nearly reached the top of the charts and was followed shortly by a lesser hit.

Although Los Bravos managed a modest American hit as late as 1968, the group's popularity had already begun to center largely in their home country of Spain.

Aug. 66	BLACK IS BLACK / Press
Dec. 66	GOING NOWHERE / Press
May 68	BRING A LITTLE LOVING / Parrot

Love Unlimited
MEMBERS:
Linda James
Glodean James
Diane Taylor
HOMETOWN: San Pedro, California

Sisters Glodean and Linda James began singing during their childhood in a local church choir. Later they joined a school choir and became acquainted with Diane Taylor.

A number of years later, after all three had pursued separate nonmusical careers, the trio was asked by a friend to help out at a recording session. Present at the session was producer Barry White, who was so taken with their sound that he took over management of their career. After an extended period of rehearsals, White produced "Walking in the Rain with the One I Love" (his deep voice is heard on the introductory "rap") and sold the master to Universal. Released early in 1972, it became a million seller and established the group's career.

In 1973, after Barry White had become established on the 20th Century label, Love Unlimited reemerged under his musical direction and compiled a number of pop and soul hits. (See Barry WHITE.)

Today Barry White and Glodean James are husband and wife.

Apr. 72	WALKING IN THE RAIN WITH THE ONE I LOVE / Universal
Dec. 73	IT MAY BE WINTER OUTSIDE / 20th Century
Mar. 74	UNDER THE INFLUENCE OF LOVE / 20th Century
Nov. 74	I BELONG TO YOU / 20th Century

Love Unlimited Orchestra

Dec. 73	LOVE'S THEME / 20th Century
Apr. 74	RHAPSODY IN WHITE / 20th Century
Feb. 75	SATIN SOUL / 20th Century

Love Unlimited. Left to right: Glodean James, Diane Taylor, Linda James

Sept. 76 *MY SWEET SUMMER SUITE /*
20th Century
Jan. 77 *THEME FROM KING KONG (Pt.*
1) /20th Century

The Lovin' Spoonful

MEMBERS:

John Benson Sebastian (lead vocals,
harmonica) / born: Mar. 17, 1944 / New York
City

Zalman Yanovsky (lead guitar) / born: Dec. 19,
1944 / Toronto, Canada / replaced (1967) by
Jerry Yester

John Stephen Boone (bass) / born: Sept. 23,
1943 / Camp Lejeune, North Carolina

Joseph Campbell Butler (drums) / born: Sept.
16, 1943 / Great Neck, New York

HOMETOWN: New York City

The inventors of "goodtime," jug-
band rock 'n' roll, The Lovin' Spoonful
was formed in 1965 by John Sebastian
(son of the famous classical harmonica player) and Zal Yanovsky. As was
outlined by The Mamas & Papas in
their autobiographical "Creeque Alley," John and Zal originally played together with Cass Elliott and Denny
Doherty in a group called The Mugwumps. After Cass and Denny left to
form The Mamas & Papas, John and
Zal organized the Spoonful, taking the
group's name from a song by blues-
man Mississippi John Hurt.

During the summer of 1965, The
Lovin' Spoonful began a legendary se-

ries of rehearsals in the basement of the Albert Hotel in New York's Greenwich Village. After accumulating a large following at the Nite Owl and other local clubs, the group was signed by Kama Sutra, where they debuted with an album titled *Do You Believe in Magic?* The title cut became the first of more than a dozen hits, and their subsequent albums included *Daydreams, Hums, Everything's Playing,* and *Revelation-Revolution.* The group also supplied the sound tracks for two major films, *What's Up Tiger Lily* and *You're a Big Boy Now.*

In 1967 Zal Yanovsky was forced by personal difficulties to leave the group and was replaced by Jerry Yester, a brother of The Association's Jim Yester. During the following year, John Sebastian left for a solo career, and that marked the end of the Lovin' Spoonful.

In 1976 Sebastian returned to the top of the charts with his recording of the theme from the popular TV series "Welcome Back Kotter."

Aug. 65	*DO YOU BELIEVE IN MAGIC /* Kama Sutra
Nov. 65	*YOU DIDN'T HAVE TO BE SO NICE /* Kama Sutra
Feb. 66	*DAYDREAM /* Kama Sutra
May 66	*DID YOU EVER HAVE TO MAKE UP YOUR MIND? /* Kama Sutra
July 66	*SUMMER IN THE CITY /* Kama Sutra
Oct. 66	*RAIN ON THE ROOF /* Kama Sutra
Dec. 66	*NASHVILLE CATS /* Kama Sutra
Jan. 67	*FULL MEASURE /* Kama Sutra
Feb. 67	*DARLING BE HOME SOON /* Kama Sutra
Apr. 67	*SIX O'CLOCK /* Kama Sutra
Oct. 67	*SHE'S STILL A MYSTERY /* Kama Sutra
Jan. 68	*MONEY /* Kama Sutra
July 68	*NEVER GOING BACK /* Kama Sutra
Feb. 69	*ME ABOUT YOU /* Kama Sutra

L.T.D.

MEMBERS:

Johnny McGhee (guitar) / Chicago, Illinois

Henry Davis (bass guitar) / Los Angeles, California

Arthur "Lorenzo" Carnegie (tenor sax) / Haines City, Florida

Jake Riley Jr. (trombone) / Miami, Florida

Carle Vickers (trumpet) / Washington, D. C.

Abraham Joseph "Onion" Miller Jr. (sax) / North Carolina

Jimmy "J. D." Davis (keyboards) / North Carolina

Melvin Webb (percussion) / Kansas City, Missouri

Bill Osborne (vocals, percussion) / Providence, Rhode Island

Jeff Osborne (lead vocals, drums) / Providence, Rhode Island

During the late sixties "Onion" Miller and "J. D." Davis left the popular soul duo Sam & Dave as back-up musicians and formed their own group. They, along with a few of their friends, left North Carolina—headed for New York City—in a battered '57 Chevy and decided to call themselves L.T.D., meaning Love, Togetherness and Devotion.

After a while Carle, Lorenzo, Jake, and Jeff joined the group and worked hard at trying to get a break in New York. With not much success they ventured to Los Angeles, where they added Jeff's older brother, Billy, and the group started to jell.

In 1974 they got a recording contract with A & M Records and have, in a short time, blossomed into one of pop music's most popular bands.

Oct. 76	*LOVE BALLAD /* A & M
Jan. 77	*LOVE TO THE WORLD /* A & M
Oct. 77	*BACK IN LOVE AGAIN /* A & M
Mar. 78	*NEVER GET ENOUGH OF YOUR LOVE /* A & M

L.T.D.

Lulu

REAL NAME: Marie McDonald McLaughlin
Lawrie
BORN: Nov. 3, 1948
HOMETOWN: Lennoxtown, Scotland

Marie Lawrie began singing at the age of three and was performing at concert parties in local pubs by the time she was nine. She acquired her stage name when someone in her audience described her as "a lulu of a singer."

After graduating from Glasgow's Whitehill Senior Secondary School, Lulu began a period of residency at Scotland's Lindella Club. She drew a great deal of attention, receiving offers from several backing groups and settling in with a band called The Luvvers. Lulu & The Luvvers were signed by the British Decca label, where they achieved a major hit with the standard "Shout." This was released in the United States on the Parrot label and introduced Lulu to American audiences.

In 1967 Lulu was on a British tour with The Beach Boys when she was seen by the producer of the movie *To Sir with Love* and offered a leading role. Her recording of the movie's theme reached number one and was her first in a string of pop hits that lasted into the early seventies.

Today Lulu is a major international club attraction. Although she was married for a time to Maurice Gibb of The Bee Gees, they are presently separated.

Aug. 64	*SHOUT* / Parrot	
Sept. 67	*TO SIR WITH LOVE* / Epic	
Dec. 67	*SHOUT* (rereleased) / Parrot	
Dec. 67	*THE BEST OF BOTH WORLDS* / Epic	
Mar. 68	*ME, THE PEACEFUL HEART* / Epic	
Aug. 68	*MORNING DEW* / Epic	

Lynyrd Skynyrd. Left to right: Ronnie Van Zant, Allen Collins, Gary Rossington, Artemus Pyle, Leon Wilkeson, Billy Powell

Dec. 69 *OH ME, OH MY, I'M A FOOL FOR YOU BABY* / Atco
Apr. 70 *HUM A SONG* / Atco

Lynyrd Skynyrd

MEMBERS:

Ronald Van Zant (lead vocals) / born: 1949 / died: Oct. 20, 1977

Ed King (lead, rhythm guitar) / (left group in 1975) / replaced by Steve Gaines / died: Oct. 20, 1977

Allen Collins (lead, rhythm guitar)

Gary Rossington (lead, rhythm guitar)

Leon Wilkeson (bass)

William Powell (keyboards)

Robert Burns (drums) / replaced (1975) by Artimus Pyle

HOMETOWN: Jacksonville, Florida

Lynyrd Skynyrd emerged during the seventies as one of the earliest and foremost exponents of the ''Dixie Rock'' sound. Gradually evolving from a band formed by several Jacksonville high-school friends, the group adapted its name from Leonard Skinner, a gym teacher who had barred them from class because of their long hair. All the members had had experience in other bands—most notably Ed King, who had achieved national success during the late sixties as lead guitarist for Strawberry Alarm Clock.

After a period on the southern rock-club circuit, Lynyrd Skynyrd was spotted at Funocchio's, a small club in Atlanta, Georgia, by veteran rock musician and producer Al Kooper. He signed them to his new Sounds of the South label and produced their first album, *Pronounced Leh-nerd Skin-nerd.* After touring with The Who late in 1973, the group became extremely popular as a concert attraction and the album placed high on the best-seller lists. In 1974 they began a series of hit singles with their top ten entry of "Sweet Home Alabama," following with an album titled *Nuthin' Fancy*.

On October 20, 1977, in the midst of a fifty-city tour, the group chartered a Convair 240 prop jet in Greenville, South Carolina, en route to Baton Rouge. The plane, reportedly low on fuel, nosedived into a swamp in Mississippi, killing Ronnie Van Zant; his guitarist Steve Gaines; Gaines's sister, Cassie, along with the two-man flight crew and the assistant road manager. There were twenty survivors who will continue to keep the group active.

July 74	***SWEET HOME ALABAMA / MCA/Sounds of the South***
Nov. 74	***FREE BIRD / MCA/Sounds of the South***
June 75	***SATURDAY NIGHT SPECIAL / MCA/Sounds of the South***
Mar. 76	***DOUBLE TROUBLE / MCA/Sounds of the South***
Dec. 76	***FREE BIRD* (rereleased)/ MCA/Sounds of the South**
Dec. 77	***WHAT'S YOUR NAME / MCA/Sounds of the South***
Apr. 78	***YOU GOT THAT RIGHT / MCA***

M

"Moms" Mabley

REAL NAME: Loretta Mary Aiken
BORN: Mar. 19, 1897
DIED: May 23, 1975
HOMETOWN: Bravard, North Carolina

"Moms" Mabley began her show business career at the age of 14. In 1921 she joined the dance team of Butter Beans and Susie and went on a tour of the larger northeastern cities. From that point on, she became a leading lady of vaudeville and later, through the medium of television, she became famous for her frank sense of humor, in much the same vein as Redd Foxx. Over the years, she toured with such acts as Duke Ellington, Count Basie, Cab Calloway, Slappy White, and more recently, Brook Benton.

Although she had several best-selling comedy albums throughout the years, her only successful single was, ironically enough, quite serious: a touching version of the classic "Abraham, Martin and John."

**June 69 ABRAHAM, MARTIN AND
JOHN / Mercury**

C. W. McCall

REAL NAME: William Fries
BORN: Nov. 15, 1928
HOMETOWN: Audubon, Iowa

Credited with sparking the citizens-band radio craze that swept the nation during the mid-seventies, Bill Fries began his musical career in the University of Iowa Concert Band. He later developed an interest in commercial art, temporarily giving up music to design sets for a television station.

During the early sixties, Fries assumed a position with the Bozell & Jacobs advertising agency and eventually became the firm's creative director. One of the agency's accounts, the Metz Baking Company of Iowa, asked him to come up with a new campaign to stimulate the sales of their bread. Fries responded by creating the characters of C. W. McCall, a truck driver for Old Home Bread, "Mavis," a gum-chewing waitress who has eyes for McCall, and a mythical place called "The Old Home Filler-up an Keep on-a-Truckin' Cafe." The campaign proved a tremendous success, and prompted Fries to issue a 45-rpm recording of the song as C. W. McCall.

In 1974, after the song had become an immense regional hit, MGM took over national distribution and offered Bill Fries, a.k.a. C. W. McCall, a recording contract. After one more release, "Wolfcreek Pass," Fries scored with the number one recording of "Convoy," which began to make CB slang terms instant household words.

Today Bill Fries records for Polydor Records while continuing his career in advertising. He lives with his wife, Rena, and their children in the Missouri Bluffs area of Omaha, Nebraska.

C. W. McCall

Paul McCartney & Wings

MEMBERS:

Paul McCartney (lead vocals, bass) / born: June 18, 1942 / Liverpool, England

Denny Laine (Brian Arthur Haynes) (guitar) / born: Oct. 29, 1944 / Birmingham, England

Linda McCartney (keyboards) / born: Sept. 24, 1942 / New York City

Henry McCollough (guitar) / (added to group in 1973) / replaced by Jimmy McCulloch / Scotland

Denny Seiwell (drums) / replaced by Jeff Britton / replaced by Joe English / Macon, Georgia

Paul McCartney was the first to officially leave The Beatles, marrying Linda on March 12, 1969, and beginning work on his first solo album in 1970.

His debut effort, *McCartney,* was pressed into release just before The Beatles' last album, *Let It Be,* appeared in 1971. (See *THE BEATLES.*)

Highly criticized but commercially successful, *McCartney* was followed by *Ram,* an album made with the help of Linda McCartney and a group of New York's leading session musicians. This record yielded two major singles, "Another Day" and "Uncle Albert/Admiral Halsey," which in turn were followed by the bizarre "Give Ireland Back to the Irish" and "Mary Had a Little Lamb."

In 1973 Paul and Linda formed a permanent working unit called Wings, beginning a long string of hits with "Hi, Hi, Hi." The original personnel included Denny Laine, formerly with The Moody Blues, Henry McCollough, a veteran of Joe Cocker's Grease Band, and Denny Seiwell, one of the New York studio musicians who had contributed to *Ram.*

Paul McCartney

Paul McCartney & Wings. Left to right: Jimmy McCulloch, Joe English, Linda McCartney, Paul McCartney, Denny Laine

In addition to their singles hits, Paul McCartney & Wings have also achieved a number of best-selling albums, including *Wild Life, Red Rose Speedway, Band on the Run, Venus & Mars, Rock Show,* and *Wings at the Speed of Sound.*

Today Paul and Linda McCartney maintain two permanent homes, one in London and one in Scotland. They have four children: Heather (Linda's daughter by a former marriage), Mary, Stella, and James Louis. Joe English and Jim McCulloch left Wings in late 1977 to pursue individual careers.

Mar. 71	*ANOTHER DAY* / Apple
Aug. 71	*UNCLE ALBERT/ADMIRAL HALSEY* / Apple
Mar. 72	*GIVE IRELAND BACK TO THE IRISH* / Apple
June 72	*MARY HAD A LITTLE LAMB* / Apple
Dec. 72	*HI, HI, HI* / Apple
Apr. 73	*MY LOVE* / Apple
July 73	*LIVE AND LET DIE* / Apple
Nov. 73	*HELEN WHEELS* / Apple
Feb. 74	*JET* / Apple
Apr. 74	*BAND ON THE RUN* / Apple
Nov. 74	*JUNIOR'S FARM* / Apple
Feb. 75	*SALLY G.* / Apple
May 75	*LISTEN TO WHAT THE MAN SAID* / Capitol
Oct. 75	*LETTING GO* / Capitol
Nov. 75	*VENUS & MARS ROCK SHOW* / Capitol
Apr. 76	*SILLY LOVE SONGS* / Capitol
July 76	*LET 'EM IN* / Capitol
Feb. 77	*MAYBE I'M AMAZED* / Capitol
Nov. 77	*GIRLS SCHOOL* / Mull of Kintyre / Capitol
Mar. 78	*WITH A LITTLE LUCK* / Capitol

Marilyn McCoo & Billy Davis, Jr.

MEMBERS:

Marilyn McCoo /born: Sept. 30, 1943/Jersey City, New Jersey

Billy Davis, Jr. /born: June 26, 1940/St. Louis, Missouri

After singing with the highly successful Fifth Dimension for over ten years, Marilyn and husband Billy left the group in early 1976 to pursue a new career as a singing duo. They signed with ABC Records and before the end of the year had their first number-one national hit, "You Don't Have to Be a Star (to Be in My Show)."

Today they are considered one of the hottest duos in the business.

Mar. 76	*I HOPE WE GET TO LOVE IN TIME* / ABC
Sept. 76	*YOU DON'T HAVE TO BE A STAR (TO BE IN MY SHOW)* / ABC
Mar. 77	*YOUR LOVE* / ABC
Aug. 77	*LOOK WHAT YOU'VE DONE TO MY HEART* / ABC

Van McCoy

HOMETOWN: Washington, D.C.

Beginning as a singer during the early sixties, Van McCoy subsequently became much better known as a producer and songwriter. Over the years, McCoy has produced hits for such artists as The Shirelles, Brenda & the Tabulations, Faith, Hope & Charity, Gladys Knight & the Pips, Peaches & Herb, The Presidents, Chris Bartley, and many others. His writer credits include "Baby I'm Yours" (Barbara Lewis), "When You're Young and in Love" (Ruby & The Romantics, The Marvelettes) and "Right on the Tip of My Tongue" (Brenda & The Tabulations). Additionally, he was a partner in a number of record companies, including Vando, Maxx, and Maxwell.

During the mid-seventies McCoy formed an association with Hugo & Luigi's Avco label, working with such groups as The Stylistics and recording disco instrumentals under his own name. In the latter capacity, he scored with his number one recording of "The Hustle," sparking one of the biggest dance crazes since the Twist days of the early sixties.

Today McCoy records for MCA and is more active than ever as an independent producer.

Apr. 75	*THE HUSTLE* / Avco
Oct. 75	*CHANGE WITH THE TIMES* / Avco
May 76	*NIGHT WALK* / H & L
Aug. 76	*PARTY* / H & L

The McCoys

MEMBERS:

Rick Zehringer (lead vocals, guitar) /born: Aug. 4, 1947/Celina, Ohio

Ronnie Brandon (keyboards) /born: Jan. 25, 1946/Greenville, Ohio/replaced by Randy Hobbs

Randy Hobbs (bass) /born: Mar. 22, 1948/Union City, Indiana

Randy Zehringer (drums) /born: Nov. 21, 1949/Celina, Ohio

Formed in 1963, this group first established a reputation on the midwestern club circuit under such names as Rick & The Raiders and The Rick Z. Combo. They eventually adopted their permanent name after selecting a Ventures' tune called "McCoy" as their theme song.

In 1965 The McCoys were booked for an appearance in Dayton, Ohio, as an opening group for The Strangeloves. After the show, The Strangeloves—who were in actuality the writing and production team of Feldman-Goldstein-Gottehrer (see *THE STRANGELOVES*)—invited them to New York for a recording session. Signing with Bert Berns's Bang label, the same company for which The Strangeloves recorded, The McCoys launched their recording career with their number one entry of "Hang on Sloopy" (an old Vibrations tune). They continued well into 1968 with a string of hits, after which they began to subside from popularity as a recording act.

In 1969 The McCoys became the house band at Steve Paul's Scene and eventually the backing band for Johnny Winter. Rick Zehringer became Rick Derringer and began a highly successful solo career. (See *Rick DERRINGER*.)

Aug. 65	***HANG ON SLOOPY***	**/Bang**
Nov. 65	***FEVER***	**/Bang**
Feb. 65	***UP AND DOWN***	**/Bang**
Apr. 66	***COME ON, LET'S GO***	**/Bang**
July 66	***SO GOOD***	**/Bang**
Oct. 66	***DON'T WORRY MOTHER***	**/Bang**
Jan. 67	***I GOT TO GO BACK***	**/Bang**
May 67	***BEAT THE CLOCK***	**/Bang**
Oct. 68	***JESSE BRADY***	**/Bang**

George & Gwen McCrae

MEMBERS:

George McCrae /born: Oct. 19, 1944/West Palm Beach, Florida

Gwen McCrae /born: Dec. 21, 1946/ Pensacola, Florida

Interested in music since his youth, George McCrae began his singing career in a high school group called The Jiving Jets. He temporarily disbanded the group, briefly studying law and entering the navy, but re-formed them at a later date. He also performed for a time with a group known as Atsugi Express.

George McCrae

During the late sixties, George met and married Gwen, and the two formed an act together. They signed with Henry Stone's Florida-based Alston label, but, after meeting with little initial success, split up as a professional act. Gwen switched to Columbia, where she recorded some eleven sides, while George managed her career and continued to record occasionally for Stone.

In 1974 George got the opportunity to record "Rock Your Baby" for Stone's T.K. label. An instant smash, the record reached number one and eventually became a multimillion seller. This prompted Gwen to return to Stone's family of labels, recording a hit called "Rockin' Chair" for the Cat division.

Today George and Gwen McCrae make their home in West Palm Beach, where they live with their two children.

George McCrae
June 74 ***ROCK YOUR BABY*** **/T.K.**

Oct. 74   *I CAN'T LEAVE YOU ALONE /*
    T.K.
Jan. 75   *I GET LIFTED /* **T.K.**
May 75   *CHANGE WITH THE TIMES /*
    T.K.
Jan. 76   *HONEY I /* **T.K.**

Gwen McCrae
May 75   *ROCKIN' CHAIR /* **Cat**

Maureen McGovern

BORN: July 27, 1949
HOMETOWN: Youngstown, Ohio

Maureen McGovern began her career as a folksinger, singing and playing guitar part-time while working as a doctor's secretary. During one of her engagements, she was heard by Pat Padula, head of a theatrical agency called Destiny, Inc. Padula assumed her management, working with her to record a demo and circulating it to record companies.

In 1972 Russ Regan, president of 20th Century Records, responded with a contract offer. Maureen made her first record, "The Morning After," which, despite being featured in the movie *The Poseidon Adventure,* met with very little success. That was rapidly to change, however, when the song received an Oscar as best movie song of the year. The record went to number one on the charts and became the first of several hits to follow.

Today Maureen McGovern is a popular club attraction and often appears on television variety programs.

June 73   *THE MORNING AFTER (THEME*
    FROM THE POSEIDON
    ADVENTURE) / **20th Century**
Oct. 73   *I WON'T LAST A DAY*
    WITHOUT YOU / **20th Century**
Oct. 74   *GIVE ME A REASON TO BE*
    GONE / **20th Century**
Jan. 75   *WE MAY NEVER LOVE LIKE*
    THIS AGAIN / **20th Century**

Byron MacGregor

HOMETOWN: Detroit, Michigan

In 1973 an editorial called "Americans" was issued by Gordon Sinclair, a Canadian writer and owner of radio station CFRB in Toronto. Proclaiming Americans as one of the world's most unjustly maligned peoples, the editorial was reprinted in many newspapers.

Somewhat later Byron MacGregor, news director of station CKLW in Detroit, read it on the air during a newscast. The station was swamped with over three thousand calls, prompting Armen Boladian, head of the Detroit-based Westbound label, to record MacGregor reading "Americans" with an instrumental backing of "America the Beautiful." The record became an instant smash, eventually reaching the national top five.

Jan. 74   *AMERICANS /* **Westbound**

Mary MacGregor

HOMETOWN: St. Paul, Minnesota

Mary began her musical career with classical piano training, voice training, and violin lessons in her hometown of St. Paul. In 1976 she was signed to a new label called Ariola America Records (in fact, she was only the third artist signed to the newly formed label.) As her debut song she recorded the Peter Yarrow (formerly of Peter, Paul & Mary) tune "Torn between Two Lovers." In just a short time the ballad became a number one national hit and established her as a new talent to watch.

Nov. 76   *TORN BETWEEN TWO*
    LOVERS / **Ariola America**
Apr. 77   *THIS GIRL (HAS TURNED INTO*
    A WOMAN) / **Ariola America**
Aug. 77   *FOR A WHILE /* **Ariola America**

Barry McGuire

BORN: Oct. 15, 1935

An Oklahoman by birth, Barry McGuire first became noted during the early sixties as the lead voice of The New Christy Minstrels. (See *THE NEW CHRISTY MINSTRELS, Rock On: The Solid Gold Years.*)

By 1965 McGuire had separated from The Minstrels and was recording solo for the Dunhill label. During the late summer, he made an astounding impact with P. F. Sloan's "Eve of Destruction," a record that went to number one and rapidly became one of the anthems of the mid-sixties protest movement.

After several additional releases, McGuire began to focus on an acting career. He made a number of television and film appearances, later joining the Broadway company of *Hair.* During the early seventies he became increasingly involved with religious pursuits, joining and touring the country with a spiritual group known as The Agape Force.

Today McGuire is based in Waco, Texas, and occasionally records for his own label. He has recently issued an album titled *Seeds* and a single called "David & Goliath."

Aug. 65	*EVE OF DESTRUCTION /* Dunhill
Nov. 65	*CHILD OF OUR TIMES /* Dunhill
May 66	*CLOUDY SUMMER AFTERNOON /* Dunhill

Scott McKenzie

BORN: Oct. 1, 1944
HOMETOWN: Arlington, Virginia

A self-taught musician, Scott McKenzie began his career by operating a bank computer while singing with various folk groups on weekends. During the early sixties, he joined John Phillips in a group known as The Smoothies, after which the two went on to form The Journeymen. Debuting at Gerde's Folk City in 1961, The Journeymen went on to record three albums for Capitol before disbanding. John Phillips, of course, was soon to become a founding member of The Mamas & Papas. (See *THE MAMAS & PAPAS.*)

In 1967, after The Mamas & Papas had become well established on Lou Adler's Dunhill label, Mckenzie was contacted by Adler and Phillips. Phillips provided a song, "San Francisco," which was released on Adler's Ode label and soon became one of that summer's biggest hits. In addition, it became a virtual theme song for the "flower-power" movement of the middle and late sixties.

During the early seventies, after several years' absence from recording, McKenzie resumed his activities with an album entitled *Stained Glass Morning.* Today his namesake, Mackenzie Phillips (John Phillips's daughter), is a leading film and television actress.

| May 67 | *SAN FRANCISCO (BE SURE TO WEAR FLOWERS IN YOUR HAIR) /* Ode |
| Oct. 67 | *LIKE AN OLD TIME MOVIE /* Ode |

Don McLean

BORN: Oct. 2, 1945
HOMETOWN: New Rochelle, New York

Deeply interested in music since the age of seven, Don McLean began learning technique by listening to such folk artists as Pete Seeger, Josh White, and Fred Hellerman. As he reached his teens, he became a regu-

Don McLean

lar feature on the northeastern coffee-house circuit.

During the mid-sixties McLean became a resident performer at Lena Spencer's Cafe Lena. Through Lena's connections, he was offered a job with the State of New York traveling and singing ecology songs under the name Hudson Valley Troubadour. This, in turn, led to an engagement with Pete Seeger on the *Clearwater,* a sloop that conducted cruises on behalf of various antipollution causes.

In 1970 McLean began actively to seek a recording contract. After having been turned down by nearly forty companies, he was signed by the small Mediarts label and recorded an album titled *Tapestry* (well before the Carole King LP of the same name). He was eventually picked up by United Artists, which brought him some attention and provided material that was later to become successful for other artists (most notable "And I Love You So," for Perry Como). Next came *American Pie,* the album and the single that would catapult him to worldwide fame. A chronicle of sixties rock history, this became one of the largest sellers of the seventies and indeed of all time. He followed with "Vincent," a song about Dutch painter Vincent van Gogh, and a series of highly poetic hit songs.

Today Don McLean records for Arista Records.

Nov. 71 *AMERICAN PIE* /United Artists
Mar. 72 *VINCENT* /United Artists
Dec. 72 *DREIDEL* /United Artists
Mar. 73 *IF WE TRY* /United Artists
June 75 *WONDERFUL BABY* /United Artists

Robin McNamara

Robin McNamara rose to fame during the late sixties as one of the original—and longest enduring—stars of *Hair.*

While continuing his work in the show, McNamara began working with producer Jeff Barry on an album titled *Lay a Little Lovin' on Me.* Recorded with the assistance of several of the show's cast members, the album was released on Barry's Steed label and yielded a top-ten single of the title cut. McNamara was able to achieve one more chart entry (also culled from the LP) before his brief recording career came to an end.

May 70 *LAY A LITTLE LOVIN' ON ME* /Steed
Oct. 70 *GOT TO BELIEVE IN LOVE* /Steed

The Magic Lanterns

MEMBERS:
"Bev" Beveridge (guitar)
Peter Garner (guitar)
James Bilsbury (keyboards)

Michael "Oz" Osborne (bass)
Harry Paul Wara (drums)
HOMETOWN: Warrington, Lancashire, England

During the mid-sixties this group became popular in Europe with an unusual stage show combining rock music with images produced by magic lanterns (primitive, turn-of-the-century projectors).

When they scored with a hit called "Shame Shame," two American companies, Atlantic and Big Tree, expressed interest in the American distribution rights. Amidst a dispute over who actually owned these rights, the record was simultaneously issued by both companies and reached the top thirty on the American charts. The group followed during the early seventies with two additional hits.

Oct. 68	*SHAME SHAME* / Big Tree and Atlantic
Jan. 71	*ONE NIGHT STAND* / Big Tree
July 72	*COUNTRY WOMAN* / Charisma

The Main Ingredient

MEMBERS:
Enrique Antonio Silvester / born: Oct. 7, 1941/ Colon, Panama / replaced (1974) by Carl Tompkins
Luther Simmons, Jr. / born: Sept. 9, 1942 / New York City
Donald McPherson / born: July 9, 1941 / died: July 4, 1971 / Indianapolis, Indiana / replaced by Cuba Gooding / born: Apr. 27, 1944 / New York City

This vocal group was organized during the mid-sixties in the Harlem area of New York City. Originally known as The Poets, they briefly recorded for the Red Bird label and later worked under the name of The Insiders. They finally settled on The Main Ingredient, after reading the words on a Coke bottle.

During the late sixties, the group signed with RCA and began working with the A & R director in the area of R & B, Buzzy Willis (a former member of the fifties Solitaires). They started appearing on the charts in 1970, and they achieved their major breakthrough in 1972 with a top-three hit called "Everybody Plays the Fool." In 1971 Donald died of leukemia and was replaced by Cuba Gooding.

In 1974 charter member Tony Silvester left the group to try his hand at record production. He became an important producer of the "disco" sound, working with such acts as Ben E. King, Sister Skedge, and Linda Lewis.

June 70	*YOU'VE BEEN MY INSPIRATION* / RCA
Oct. 70	*I'M BETTER OFF WITHOUT YOU* / RCA
Dec. 70	*I'M SO PROUD* / RCA
May 71	*SPINNING AROUND* / RCA
Sept. 71	*BLACK SEEDS KEEP ON GROWING* / RCA
July 72	*EVERYBODY PLAYS THE FOOL* / RCA
Dec. 72	*YOU'VE GOT TO TAKE IT* / RCA
Feb. 74	*JUST DON'T WANT TO BE LONELY* / RCA
June 74	*HAPPINESS IS JUST AROUND THE BEND* / RCA
Nov. 74	*CALIFORNIA MY WAY* / RCA
May 75	*ROLLING DOWN A MOUNTAINSIDE* / RCA

Malo

MEMBERS:
Arcelio Garcia (lead vocals) / born: May 7, 1946 / Manati, Puerto Rico
Jorge Santana (lead guitar) / born: June 13, 1954 / Jalisco, Mexico
Abel Zarate (lead guitar) / born: Dec. 2, 1952 / Manila, Philippines
Pablo Tellez (rhythm guitar) / born: July 2, 1951 / Granada, Nicaragua
Richard Kermode (keyboards) / born: Oct. 5, 1946 / Lovell, Wyoming

Luis Gasca (trumpet)/born: Mar. 23, 1940/
Houston, Texas

Forrest Buchtel (trumpet)

Hadley Caliman (sax, trumpet)/replaced by
Steve Sherard

Leo Rosales (percussion)/San Francisco, California

Raul Rekow (percussion)/born: June 10,
1944/San Francisco, California

Richard Spremick (drums)/born: July 2, 1951/
San Francisco, California

Formed in the San Francisco area during the early seventies, Malo was actually a conglomeration of several Latin and Latin-rock bands.

Jorge Santana (Carlos Santana's brother), Pablo Tellez, and Arcelio Garcia were in a group called The Malibus, while Abel Zarate and Rick Spremick came from Naked Lunch. Richard Kermode and Luis Gasca were veterans of Janis Joplin's Kozmic Blues Band. The rest of the members came from such varied bands as Soul Sauce and Soul Sacrifice.

Once organized, Malo formed an association with producer Dave Rubinson and signed with Warner Brothers. They soon achieved a top twenty single called "Suavecito," and scored with best-selling albums such as *Malo, Dos,* and *Evolution.*

Mar. 72 SUAVECITO /Warner Bros.

The Mamas & Papas

MEMBERS:

John Phillips /born: Aug. 30, 1945/Parris
Island, South Carolina

Dennis Doherty /born: Nov. 29, 1941/Halifax,
Nova Scotia

Holly Michelle Gilliam Phillips /born: Apr. 6,
1944/Long Beach, California

Cassandra Elliott (Ellen Naomi Cohen)/born:
Sept. 19, 1943/Baltimore, Maryland/died: July
29, 1974/London, England

The Mamas & Papas stood alongside The Lovin' Spoonful as a leading exponent of sixties "goodtime rock 'n' roll."

As chronicled in their autobiographical "Creeque Alley," three of the members previously had sung with other groups. John Phillips had started out in a group called The Smoothies, which also included his friend Scott McKenzie. He later joined a folk trio, The Journeymen, and married Michelle Gilliam in 1964. Cass Elliott had sung with Tim Rose and James Hendricks in The Big Three, later joining The Mugwumps with Denny Doherty (formerly of The Halifax Three) and Zal Yanovsky (soon to become a founding member of The Spoonful).

Once agreed on forming a group, the four Mamas & Papas headed for a vacation in the Caribbean "to get into each other's heads" and to accumulate material. Heading for Los Angeles upon their return, they formed an association with writer-producer Lou Adler and began recording for his newly-formed Dunhill label. Beginning with "California Dreaming," they racked up more than a dozen major hits before professional pressures began to pull the group apart in 1968. They also recorded a number of highly successful albums, including *If You Can Believe Your Eyes and Ears, Deliver, Cass, John, Michelle, Denny, The Papas and the Mamas,* and *People Like Us.*

Once separated, each of the group's members (including John and Michelle, whose marriage had disintegrated) began pursuing other interests. Cass achieved a number of hit singles and recorded an album with British rock star Dave Mason. Cass died in 1974 in her hotel room in London by choking on a sandwich. Denny Doherty and John Phillips also recorded solo, and John became more active as a producer and business person. Michelle became interested in acting, eventually costarring with Rudolf Nureyev in a film called *Valentino*. (John's daughter by an earlier marriage, Mackenzie Phillips, is also an actress, known for her roles in the movie *American Graffiti* and television's "One Day at a Time.")

The Mamas & Papas

Jan. 66	**CALIFORNIA DREAMING / Dunhill**
Apr. 66	**MONDAY, MONDAY / Dunhill**
July 66	**I SAW HER AGAIN / Dunhill**
Oct. 66	**LOOK THROUGH MY WINDOW / Dunhill**
Dec. 66	**WORDS OF LOVE / Dunhill**
Dec. 66	**DANCING IN THE STREET / Dunhill**
Feb. 67	**DEDICATED TO THE ONE I LOVE / Dunhill**
Apr. 67	**CREEQUE ALLEY / Dunhill**
Aug. 67	**TWELVE THIRTY / Dunhill**
Oct. 67	**GLAD TO BE UNHAPPY / Dunhill**
Dec. 67	**THE DANCING BEAR / Dunhill**
June 68	**SAFE IN MY GARDEN / Dunhill**
Sept. 68	**FOR THE LOVE OF IVY / Dunhill**
Nov. 68	**DO YOU WANNA DANCE / Dunhill**
Feb. 72	**STEP OUT / Dunhill**

"Mama" Cass Elliott

July 68	**DREAM A LITTLE DREAM OF ME / Dunhill**
Nov. 68	**CALIFORNIA EARTHQUAKE / Dunhill**
Mar. 69	**MOVE IN A LITTLE CLOSER, BABY / Dunhill**
June 69	**IT'S GETTING BETTER / Dunhill**
Oct. 69	**MAKE YOUR OWN KIND OF MUSIC / Dunhill**
Jan. 70	**A NEW WORLD COMING / Dunhill**
Aug. 70	**A SONG THAT NEVER COMES / Dunhill**

John Phillips

May 70	**MISSISSIPPI / Dunhill**

Melissa Manchester

BORN: Feb. 15, 1951
HOMETOWN: Bronx, New York

The product of a musical family, Melissa Manchester knew as a child that she would make music her career. Her father, David Manchester, is a long-established bassoonist with the Metropolitan Opera Orchestra, while both her mother and her older sister were singers at one time. (Today her mother, Ruth Manchester, is a leading fashion designer.)

As she grew older Melissa attended the High School for the Performing Arts and began singing on commercials. She also became one of only nine students accepted by Paul Simon for a songwriting/record-production course that he taught at New York University.

During the late sixties Melissa was working at a coffeehouse called The Focus (owned by her future husband, Larry Brezner) when an unknown named Bette Midler came in looking for a job. The two became fast friends, and Bette ultimately recruited Melissa for her back-up group, The Harlettes. After several months with the group, and a final concert on New Year's Eve, 1973, Melissa set out on her own.

After signing with Bell/Arista, Melissa recorded a series of highly acclaimed albums, including *Home to Myself, Bright Eyes, Melissa,* and *Better Days and Happy Endings*. The third of these yielded her first hit single, "Midnight Blue."

Today Melissa and her husband make their permanent home in Los Angeles.

May 75	**MIDNIGHT BLUE / Arista**
Feb. 76	**JUST YOU AND I / Arista**
May 76	**BETTER DAYS / Arista**
Aug. 76	**RESCUE ME / Arista**

Melissa Manchester

The Manhattans

MEMBERS:

Winfred "Blue" Lovett / born: Nov. 16, 1943

Edward "Sonny" Bivens / born: Jan. 15, 1942

Kenneth "Wally" Kelly / born: Jan. 9, 1943

Richard "Ricky" Taylor / (left group in 1976)

George Smith / died: 1970 / replaced by Gerald Alston / born: Nov. 8, 1942

HOMETOWN: Jersey City, New Jersey

The history of this vocal group began in the early sixties, when Sonny Bivens and Rick Taylor formed The Dulcets. After several personnel changes, the group arrived at the above line-up, deriving their new name from the fact that one of their members was living in Manhattan.

In 1962 The Manhattans decided to enter the "amateur night" competition at New York's Apollo Theater. Winning third prize, they came to the attention of Joe Evans, head of Carnival Records, who signed them to a contract.

The Manhattans. Left to right: Gerald Alston, Kenny Kelly, Blue Lovett, Sonny Bivens

After several releases, their records began appearing on the national charts in 1965.

In 1972, after brief affiliations with DeLuxe and Capitol, The Manhattans were signed by Mickey Eichner to Columbia Records. They continued their string of hits, achieving a number-one record in 1976 with "Kiss & Say Goodbye."

As of today, with only two exceptions, The Manhattans have maintained their original line-up. In 1970 lead singer George Smith became a fatal victim of brain damage and was replaced by Gerald Austin, a vocalist whom they had met during an appearance in Henderson, North Carolina. Rick Taylor left for a solo career in 1976, leaving The Manhattans to continue as a quartet.

Jan. 65	*I WANNA BE* / Carnival
Jan. 66	*FOLLOW YOUR HEART* / Carnival
Mar. 66	*BABY I NEED YOU* / Carnival
Dec. 67	*I CALL IT LOVE* / Carnival

The Manhattan Transfer. Left to right: Tim Hauser, Janis Siegel, Laurel Masse, Alan Paul

June 70	**IF MY HEART COULD SPEAK /** **DeLuxe**
June 73	**THERE'S NO ME WITHOUT** **YOU /Columbia**
Sept. 73	**YOU'D BETTER BELIEVE IT /** **Columbia**
Jan. 75	**DON'T TAKE YOUR LOVE** **FROM ME /Columbia**
May 75	**HURT /Columbia**
Apr. 76	**KISS & SAY GOODBYE /** **Columbia**
Oct. 76	**I KINDA MISS YOU /Columbia**
Mar. 77	**IT FEELS SO GOOD TO BE** **LOVED SO BAD /Columbia**
Oct. 77	**WE NEVER DANCED TO A** **LOVE SONG /Columbia**

Manhattan Transfer

MEMBERS:
Tim Hauser
Janis Siegel
Alan Paul
Laurel Masse
HOMETOWN: New York City

The group was formed by Tim Hauser in 1973 and became something of a cult attraction in New York, doing a variety of tunes dealing with nostalgia. Because of their popularity they were signed by Atlantic Records and shortly thereafter released their only chart single, "Operator."

The foursome has not only had success with recordings and live concert appearances but has also starred for four weeks on a summer replacement television show in 1975.

Sept. 75 OPERATOR /Atlantic

Barry Manilow

Barry Manilow

BORN: June 17, 1946
HOMETOWN: Brooklyn, New York

Barry Manilow took a childhood interest in music, learning the accordion at age eleven and the piano at age thirteen. He eventually attended the Juilliard School of Music at night, working in the CBS mailroom during the day to learn what he could about the music business.

During the late sixties, Manilow became established in the world of commercials. He recorded for such products as Kentucky Fried Chicken,

Spaghetti-O's, Pepsi-Cola, and Rheingold beer, but became best known for his singing on the "You Deserve a Break Today" jingle for McDonald's.

In 1970 Manilow was working as a house pianist for New York's famed Continental Baths when Bette Midler began making her celebrated series of appearances there. Manilow joined her entourage, becoming her resident producer-arranger and gaining a great deal of attention in the process. He signed with Bell/Arista in 1974, debuting with an album simply entitled *Barry Manilow*. This yielded a single called "Mandy" (a rewrite of Scott English's 1972 chart entry of "Brandy"), a record that went straight to number one and firmly established Manilow as a star.

Today Manilow tours with a trio of young women known as Lady Flash. (One of its members, Lorraine Mazzola, is a veteran of the sixties "girl-group" Reparata & the Delrons.)

Nov. 74	*MANDY* / Bell
Mar. 75	*IT'S A MIRACLE* / Arista
June 75	*COULD IT BE MAGIC* / Arista
Nov. 75	*I WRITE THE SONGS* / Arista
Mar. 76	*TRYIN' TO GET THE FEELING AGAIN* / Arista
Sept. 76	*THIS ONE'S FOR YOU* / Arista
Nov. 76	*WEEKEND IN NEW ENGLAND* / Arista
May 77	*LOOKS LIKE WE MADE IT* / Arista
Oct. 77	*DAYBREAK* / Arista
Feb. 78	*I CAN'T SMILE WITHOUT YOU* / Arista
May 78	*EVEN NOW* / Arista

Herbie Mann

REAL NAME: Herbert Jay Solomon
BORN: Apr. 16, 1930
HOMETOWN: Brooklyn, New York

Herbie Mann became known during the fifties and sixties as a leading jazz flutist and bandleader. He began appearing on the singles charts during the mid-sixties with jazz-flavored Pop songs and dance records.

In 1975 Mann achieved the biggest hit of his career with "Hijack," an energetic disco record that placed well within the top twenty.

Oct. 66	*PHILLY DOG* / Atlantic
Oct. 67	*TO SIR WITH LOVE* / Atlantic
Feb. 68	*UNCHAIN MY HEART* / A & M
May 69	*MEMPHIS UNDERGROUND* / Atlantic
Nov. 69	*IT'S A FUNKY THING* / Atlantic
Feb. 75	*HIJACK* / Atlantic

Manfred Mann

MEMBERS:
Paul Jones (Paul Pond) (lead vocals)/born: Feb. 24, 1944/Portsmouth, England/replaced by Michael D'Abo

Michael Vickers (guitar)/born: Apr. 18, 1942/ Southhampton, England/replaced by Jack Bruce/born: May 14, 1943/Glasgow, Scotland/ replaced by Klaus Voorman/ Germany

Manfred Mann (Michael Leibowitz) (keyboards)/born: Oct. 21, 1941/Johannesburg, South Africa

David Richmond (bass)/replaced by Tom McGuinness/born: Dec. 2, 1941/Wimbleton, London, England

Michael Huggs (drums)/born: Aug. 11, 1942/ Andover, Hampshire, England

Manfred Mann's Earth Band

MEMBERS:
Mick Rogers (lead vocals, guitar)
Manfred Mann (keyboards, synthesizer)
Colin Pattenden (bass)
Chris Slade (drums)

A major British group, and only the second after The Beatles to reach number one in the United States (The Animals were the first), this band start-

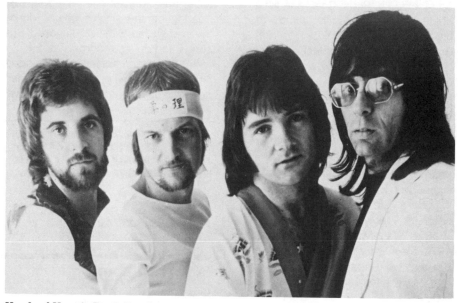

Manfred Mann's Earth Band

ed in 1963 as a trio called The Mann-Hugg Blues Brothers. With the addition of Dave Richmond and Paul Jones, the group assumed the name of its keyboard player and began recording for HMV.

After several releases, they made their impact with "Doo Wah Diddy Diddy," a song that had previously been a chart hit for an American R & B group called The Exciters. They followed with a piece of similar material, "Sha La La" (previously done by The Shirelles), and continued their string of hits into 1969. At that point, several of the members became anxious to pursue solo careers, and the group disbanded. Tom McGuinness went on to McGuinness-Flint, Jack Bruce and Klaus Voorman began evolving into superstars, and Paul Jones played the lead role in a film entitled *Privilege*.

Manfred Mann organized another band, Emanon ("no name," spelled backwards), but with very little suc-

cess. His next venture, along with Mike Hugg, was a jazz band called Chapter Three, but this proved similarly unsuccessful. During the early seventies, however, he returned to the charts with yet another new group, Manfred Mann's Earth Band.

Manfred Mann

Sept. 64 *DO WAH DIDDY DIDDY /* Ascot

Nov. 64 *SHA LA LA /* Ascot

Feb. 65 *COME TOMORROW /* Ascot

July 66 *PRETTY FLAMINGO /* United Artists

Mar. 68 *THE MIGHTY QUINN (QUINN THE ESKIMO) /* Mercury

Jan. 69 *FOX ON THE RUN /* Mercury

Manfred Mann's Earth Band

Feb. 72 *LIVING WITHOUT YOU /* Polydor

Apr. 76 *SPIRIT IN THE NIGHT /* Warner Bros.

Dec. 76 *BLINDED BY THE LIGHT /* Warner Bros.

Apr. 77 *SPIRIT IN THE NIGHT* (rereleased)/Warner Bros.

Bob Marley & The Wailers

REAL NAME: Robert Nesta Marley
BORN: Feb. 5, 1945
HOMETOWN: Kingston, Jamaica

Bob Marley formed his first group, called The Wailing Rudeboys, in 1964, when he began playing his Jamaican reggae music. In 1966 the group became more refined and their music began to be heard in other parts of the world.

A few years later American Pop star Johnny Nash came to Jamaica looking for new material and eventually met Marley. The result was a Nash recording of Marley's tune "Stir It Up," which became a big American hit in 1973. Another artist who had success with Marley's material was Eric Clapton, who recorded Marley's "I Shot the Sheriff."

In 1975 Marley toured the United States, where he was able to play his Jamaican Rastafarian music (a religious movement that spawned many reggae songs) for the first time. Today Marley is an artist of major importance, playing a form of music that is becoming very popular.

July 76 *ROOTS, ROCK, REGGAE /* Island

Marmalade

MEMBERS:

Dean Ford (lead vocals) / born: May 31, 1947 / Airdrie, Scotland

Junior Campbell (lead guitar) / born: July 24, 1946 / Glasgow, Scotland

Patrick Fairley (bass) / born: Apr. 14, 1946 / Glasgow, Scotland

Graham Knight (bass) / born: Dec. 8, 1946 / Glasgow, Scotland

Alan Whitehead (drums) / born: July 24, 1947 / Oswestry, Salop, England

Formed during the mid-sixties, Marmalade became extremely popular in Britain as a harmony-oriented "light rock" group. They achieved a number of British best sellers during the late sixties and early seventies, two of which appeared on the American charts as well. Although nearly six years passed before they were heard by American audiences again, they returned to the American charts in 1976 with "Falling Apart at the Seams."

May 70 *REFLECTIONS OF MY LIFE /* London

Aug. 70 *RAINBOW* / London

Mar. 76 *FALLING APART AT THE SEAMS* / Ariola America

The Marshall Tucker Band

MEMBERS:

Doug Gray (lead vocals, percussion)

Toy Caldwell (lead guitar)

George McCorkle (rhythm guitar)

Jerry Eubanks (sax, flute, percussion)

Tommy Caldwell (bass)

Paul Riddle (drums)

HOMETOWN: Spartanburg, South Carolina

Often compared with the Allman Brothers, this was one of several "Dixie rock" bands to emerge during the mid-seventies. Their name was taken from an old key found by Toy Caldwell in a warehouse.

The group actually began in 1970 as The Toy Factory but was broken up shortly thereafter by the draft. They reformed in 1972 under their new name, signing with the Capricorn label and debuting with an album called *The Marshall Tucker Band*. This became a best seller, and was followed successfully by *A New Life* and *Where We All Belong.*

Until 1975 The Marshall Tucker

Band was thought of entirely as an "album" group. In April of that year, however, their singles also began appearing on the charts.

Apr. 75 *THIS OL' COWBOY /*
Capricorn
Oct. 75 *FIRE ON THE MOUNTAIN /*
Capricorn
Mar. 77 *HEARD IT IN A LOVE SONG /*
Capricorn
Aug. 77 *CAN'T YOU SEE /* Capricorn

George Martin

BORN: Jan. 3, 1926
HOMETOWN: London, England

An A & R man for the British Parlophone label, George Martin rapidly rose to fame in 1962 after signing an unknown group called The Beatles. He subsequently became their producer, working with the group on all their early recordings.

In 1964 Martin himself briefly hit the charts with an instrumental from the film *A Hard Day's Night*.

Today George Martin is an independent producer, having recently attained major success in his work with the group America and Jeff Beck. In addition, he is a partner in London's famed AIR recording studio.

July 64 *RINGO'S THEME (THIS BOY) /*
United Artists

The Marvelows

MEMBERS:
Melvin Mason (lead)
Frank Paden (tenor)
Willie Stephenson (tenor)
Andrew Thomas (tenor)
John Paden (bass)
HOMETOWN: Chicago Heights, Illinois

Known originally as The Mighty Marvelows, this vocal group was organized during the early sixties at Bloom Township High School.

Melvin Mason had been a three-year veteran of The Populaires when the draft suddenly broke up the group. Having been the youngest member, he stayed behind and joined with brothers Frank and John Paden in forming The Marvelows.

After signing with the ABC-Paramount label, the group achieved a major hit with their recording of "I Do."

May 65 *I DO /* ABC-Paramount

Hugh Masekela

BORN: Apr. 4, 1939
HOMETOWN: Wilbank, South Africa

Introduced to music as a child, Hugh Masekela began studying piano at the age of seven. Later, after having been inspired by the film *Young Man with a Horn* (a biography of Bix Beiderbecke), he took up the trumpet instead.

After high school Masekela entered the Royal Academy Of Music in England and eventually came to the United States via a four-year scholarship at the Manhattan School of Music. He soon formed his own band, working extensively in clubs and affiliating briefly with the MGM Records organization.

In 1967 Masekela began recording for Uni, barely denting the charts with his first release of "Up, Up and Away." He followed with "Grazing in the Grass," a jazz-rock instrumental which went straight to number one and firmly established his career. (The same song, recorded later as a vocal by The Friends of Distinction, reached the top of the charts as well.)

Today Masekela records for his own Chisa label and is backed by a Ghanaian band known as Hedzoleh

Soundz. He is married to African singer Miriam Makeba.

Dec. 67 *UP, UP AND AWAY* /Uni
June 68 *GRAZING IN THE GRASS* /Uni
Sept. 68 *PUFFING ON DOWN THE TRACK* /Uni
Jan. 69 *RIOT* /Uni

Barbara Mason

BORN: Aug. 9, 1947
HOMETOWN: Philadelphia, Pennsylvania

Barbara Mason began her show-business career as a youngster by putting together local talent shows. She began playing piano during her early teens, becoming proficient by the time she reached fourteen.

During the mid-sixties Barbara organized a vocal group with some friends and auditioned for a small local club. Present in the audience was Arthur McDougal III (later promotion director for Motown), who strongly encouraged her to pursue a solo career. He introduced her to manager Jim Bishop, and her recording career was soon on its way.

In 1965 Barbara affiliated with the Philadelphia-based Arctic label and achieved a top-five hit with "Yes I'm Ready." She continued with a string of chart entries which lasted through the end of 1967.

After a brief hiatus in her recording activities, Barbara signed with Buddah in 1972 and began working with producer Curtis Mayfield. She has achieved a number of major hits, including "Give Me Your Love" from the sound track of the movie *Superfly*.

May 65 *YES I'M READY* /Arctic
Aug. 65 *SAD SAD GIRL* /Arctic
Nov. 65 *IF YOU DON'T* /Arctic
Jan. 66 *IS IT ME?* /Arctic
June 66 *I NEED LOVE* /Arctic

Dec. 67 *OH HOW IT HURTS* /Arctic
June 72 *BED AND BOARD* /Buddah
Jan. 73 *GIVE ME YOUR LOVE* /Buddah
Nov. 74 *FROM HIS WOMAN TO YOU* / Buddah
Apr. 75 *SHACKIN' UP* /Buddah

Dave Mason

BORN: May 10, 1946
HOMETOWN: Worcester, England

One of the outstanding guitarists in British rock, Dave Mason began his career in several bands in the Birmingham, England area. Starting out in The Jaguars, he moved over to The Hellians, which also contained drummer Jim Capaldi. Mason and Capaldi later formed Deep Feeling and ultimately became founding members of Traffic. (See *TRAFFIC*.)

In 1967 Mason separated from Traffic, and after a number of production

Dave Mason

projects moved his base of operation to Los Angeles. He debuted with a solo album, *Alone Together,* which yielded the hit single "Only You Know and I Know." (Delaney & Bonnie, with whom Mason often appeared during this period, had a hit with the same song in 1971.)

Today Dave Mason is affiliated with Columbia Records. His album releases, for which he has become best known over the years, have included *Dave Mason & Cass Elliott* (see *THE MAMAS & PAPAS*), *Headkeeper, Dave Mason Is Alive, It's Like You Never Left,* and *Split Coconut.*

Aug. 70	***ONLY YOU KNOW AND I KNOW*/Blue Thumb**
Dec. 70	***SATIN RED AND BLACK VELVET WOMEN*/Blue Thumb**
May 77	***SO HIGH (ROCK ME BABY AND ROLL ME AWAY)*/Columbia**
Sept. 77	***WE JUST DISAGREE*/Columbia**
Jan. 78	***LET IT GO, LET IT FLOW*/Columbia**

Matthews Southern Comfort

MEMBERS:

Ian Matthews (Ian McDonald) (lead vocals)/ Lincolnshire, England
Mark Griffiths (lead guitar)
Carl Barnwell (rhythm guitar)
Gordon Huntley (steel guitar)
Andrew Leigh (bass)
Ray Duffy (drums)

Ian Matthews first became noted during the mid-sixties as a member of a London band called The Pyramid. He later joined a highly successful band known as Fairport Convention, which he left in 1969 for a solo career.

In 1970, with the help of several members of Fairport Convention, Matthews recorded an album titled *Matthews Southern Comfort.* This proved so popular that he formed a new band under that name, featuring the above line-up. This group achieved several hit singles and best-selling albums, after which Matthews went solo once again. Southern Comfort continued for a time without him but eventually disbanded.

During the early seventies, Matthews made yet another attempt at forming a group, this one called Plainsong. This group broke up as well, and Matthews today has finally settled into a solo career.

Matthews Southern Comfort

Mar. 71	***WOODSTOCK*/Decca**
July 71	***MARE TAKE ME HOME*/Decca**
Oct. 71	***TELL ME WHY*/Decca**

Ian Matthews

Feb. 72	***DA DOO RON RON*/Vertigo**

Paul Mauriat

In 1967 Paul Mauriat, a French orchestra leader and arranger, made an album titled *Blooming Hits.* A collection of lush string arrangements of mid-sixties best sellers, the album included "Penny Lane," "This Is My Song," "Kind of Hush," "Something Stupid," "Puppet on a String," and an original composition entitled "L'Amour Est Bleu" ("Love is Blue").

Many months later, "Love Is Blue" began receiving a great deal of airplay and suddenly gained immense popularity. Rushed into release as a single by Philips, the record became an international smash and reached number one on the charts. This momentum brought success to a number of Mauriat's subsequent releases, but none did as well as the first.

Jan. 68 ***LOVE IS BLUE*/Philips**

May 68 *LOVE IN EVERY ROOM /*
Philips
Nov. 68 *CHITTY CHITTY BANG BANG /*
Philips

John Mayall

BORN: Nov. 29, 1933
HOMETOWN: MacClesfield, Cheshire, England

The undisputed "granddaddy" of British rock, John Mayall formed his first band, The Power House Four, in 1955.

In 1963, encouraged by the success of blues bandleader Alexis Korner at the famed Marquee Club, Mayall decided to form a blues band of his own called The Bluesbreakers. This became the breeding ground for literally dozens of rock's leading musicians, including John McVie, Hugh Flint, Eric Clapton, Mick Taylor, Peter Green, Jack Bruce, Mick Fleetwood, Harvey Mandel, and Jimmy McCulloch.

Not at all a "singles" artist (only one Mayall single ever appeared on the American charts), Mayall's prolific album output has included *John Mayall Plays John Mayall, Bluesbreakers, Blues Alone, A Hard Road, Crusade, Diary of a Band, Bare Wires, Blues from Laurel Canyon, Turning Point, Empty Rooms, USA Union, Memories, Back to the Roots, Jazz-Blues Fusion, Moving On, Ten Years Are Gone, Latest Edition, New Year, New Band, New company,* and *Notice to Appear.*

Today John Mayall has settled into a solo career.

Oct. 69 *DON'T WASTE MY TIME /*
London

Curtis Mayfield

BORN: June 3, 1942
HOMETOWN: Chicago, Illinois

Curtis Mayfield gained fame as a founding member of The Impressions, with whom he remained until 1970. He continued as their producer and principal songwriter, and as an owner of Curtom Records, the label for which they recorded. (See *THE IMPRESSIONS, Rock On: The Solid Gold Years.*)

As a solo artist, Mayfield has achieved a number of hit singles, as well as such best-selling albums as *Curtis, Curtis—Live, Roots, Back to My World, Sweet Exorcist, Got to Find a Way,* and *There's No Place Like America.* He has also distinguished himself in the area of motion pictures, appearing in *Superfly* and composing its sound track.

Nov. 70 *IF THERE'A HELL BELOW WE'RE ALL GOING TO GO /*
Curtom
Nov. 71 *GET DOWN /* Curtom
Aug. 72 *FREDDIE'S DEAD /* Curtom
Nov. 72 *SUPERFLY /* Curtom
July 73 *FUTURE SHOCK /* Curtom
Oct. 73 *IF I WERE ONLY A CHILD AGAIN /* Curtom
Dec. 73 *CAN'T SAY NOTHING /* Curtom
June 74 *KUNG FU /* Curtom
Sept. 75 *SO IN LOVE /* Curtom

Sister Janet Mead

BORN: 1938
HOMETOWN: Adelaide, Australia

Sister Janet Mead is a well-known Australian nun who draws audiences of over two thousand to her celebrated rock masses. In addition, she heads a band called Sister Janet Mead's Rock Band.

In 1974 Sister Mead recorded an editorial centering around the Lord's Prayer. After the record became an enormous success on Australia's Festival label, it was picked up for world-

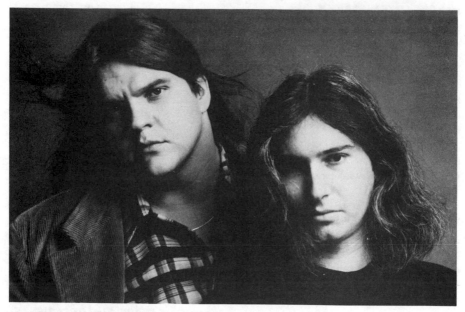

Meat Loaf. Left to right: Meat Loaf, Jim Steinman

wide distribution by A & M and became a major international hit. "The Lord's Prayer" reached the top five on the American best-seller lists and was to be Sister Mead's sole chart entry.

Feb. 74   *THE LORD'S PRAYER* / **A & M**

Meat Loaf

REAL NAME: Marvin Lee Aday
BORN: Sept. 27, 1947
HOMETOWN: Dallas, Texas

The son of a salesman and hymn-singing mother, Marvin chose the name Meat Loaf as a stage name to save his religious parents' embarrassment about his chosen profession. Meat Loaf, a 6'2", 260-pound singer, played in many local Texan bands during the mid-sixties, including a stretch as a vocalist with Ted Nugent's band, The Amboy Dukes.

After a bit part in the film *The Rocky Horror Picture Show,* he met a talented composer named Jim Steinman who began writing material for Meat Loaf's multioctave voice.

In early 1977 Steve Popovich of Epic Records joined forces with Stan Snyder and Sam Lederman of Columbia Records to form their own label called Cleveland International. Their first album release was Meat Loaf's *Bat Out of Hell,* for which Steinman wrote all the material. Popovich and Snyder agree that Meat Loaf will be one of the major forces of rock for a long time to come.

Mar. 78   *TWO OUT OF THREE AIN'T BAD* / **Cleveland International**

Meco

FULL NAME: Meco Monardo
BORN: Nov. 29, 1939
HOMETOWN: Johnsonberg, Pennsylvania

Meco is a man of many talents. After studying at New York's Eastman School of Music, he began working first as a studio musician playing the trombone and then as an arranger, putting together, in 1968, Tommy James's smash hit "Crimson and Clover." As a producer, in 1974, he worked with Gloria Gaynor and her hit "Never Can Say Goodbye" and Carol Douglas and her song "Doctor's Orders."

In 1977 he went to see the movie *Star Wars* and was so impressed by the film that he went back to see it several more times. He felt he could do something with the theme song and ended up doing a disco version of the sound track. The rest is history.

Aug. 77 **STAR WARS TITLE THEME /**
 Millennium
Jan. 78 **THEME FROM CLOSE**
 ENCOUNTERS /Millennium

Bill Medley

BORN: Sept. 19, 1940
HOMETOWN: Santa Ana, California

Bill Medley rose to fame during the early sixties as one half of The Righteous Brothers. (See *THE RIGHTEOUS BROTHERS, Rock On: The Solid Gold Years.*)

In 1968 The Righteous Brothers split up to pursue separate careers. Bobby Hatfield joined with Jimmy Walker, a former member of The Knickerbockers (see *THE KNICKERBOCKERS*), and continued to perform under The Righteous Brothers' name. Bill Medley went solo, signing with MGM and achieving a number of hits.

After a separation of nearly six years, the original Righteous Brothers reunited in 1974 and began recording for Lambert & Potter's Haven label. They have scored with several hits, including the chart-topping "Rock & Roll Heaven."

May 68 **I CAN'T MAKE IT ALONE /**
 MGM
Aug. 68 **BROWN EYED WOMAN / MGM**
Oct. 68 **PEACE BROTHER PEACE /**
 MGM

Mel & Tim

MEMBERS:
Melvin Harden
Timothy McPherson
HOMETOWN: St. Louis, Missouri

Mel and Tim had each sung in a group before meeting and pooling their talents as a duo. While in the service, Mel had joined a quartet called The Individuals, and Tim was a member of a group known as The Vandels.

Mel and Tim first met during the middle-to-late sixties, when both were employed as bus drivers by the same company. Although they originally talked of forming a larger group, they chose to try recording as a duet instead.

In 1969 Mel & Tim signed with the Chicago-based Bamboo label, debuting with a top ten record called "Backfield in Motion." After a successful follow-up, they affiliated with the Stax label, remaining with the company until it ceased operations during the mid-seventies.

Oct. 69 **BACKFIELD IN MOTION /**
 Bamboo
Feb. 70 **GOOD GUYS ONLY WIN IN THE**
 MOVIES / Bamboo
July 72 **STARTING ALL OVER AGAIN /**
 Stax

Melanie

BORN: Feb. 3, 1947
HOMETOWN: Astoria, Queens, New York

Melanie Safka Schekeryk became involved with music at a very early age, learning to play the ukelele at the age

Melanie

of four. She came from a musical family, her mother having been a jazz and blues singer and her uncle a folksinger. As she grew older, she taught herself guitar technique by listening to such artists as Bob Dylan and Pete Seeger.

During the late sixties, Melanie began performing on the northeastern bar-and-club circuit and studying drama for a potential acting career. While auditioning for a small part in a play, she accidentally came to the attention of music publisher Peter Schekeryk. He took over management of her career, becoming her producer and, ultimately, her husband.

In 1969 Schekeryk arranged for a contract with Buddah Records, and Melanie debuted with an album called *Born to Be*. She followed with *Affectionately Melanie* and *Candles in the Rain,* the latter of which featured backing tracks by The Edwin Hawkins Singers and yielded the first of her many hit singles. Her subsequent albums, all of which became best sellers, included *Leftover Wine, All the Right Noises, The Good Book, Gather Me, Carnegie Hall, Madrugada, As I See It Now,* and *Sunset & Other Beginnings.*

In 1972 Melanie and her husband formed their own Neighborhood label, for which she continued to record until 1975. Today she is affiliated with Atlantic Records.

Apr. 70	*LAY DOWN (CANDLES IN THE RAIN)* / **Buddah**
Aug. 70	*PEACE WILL COME* / **Buddah**
Dec. 70	*RUBY TUESDAY* / **Buddah**
Oct. 71	*BRAND NEW KEY* / **Neighborhood**
Jan. 72	*THE NICKEL SONG* / **Buddah**

Jan. 72	*RING THE LIVING BELL /* Neighborhood
Oct. 72	*TOGETHER ALONE /* Neighborhood
Feb. 73	*BITTER BAD /* Neighborhood
Dec. 73	*WILL YOU LOVE ME TOMORROW /* Neighborhood

Harold Melvin & The Bluenotes

For the earlier history of the group, see *Rock On: The Solid Gold Years, THE BLUENOTES.* In late 1976, lead vocalist Theodore Pendergrass left Harold Melvin's group to become a solo performer with Philadelphia International Records.

Apr. 74	*SATISFACTION GUARANTEED (OR TAKE YOUR LOVE BACK) /* Philadelphia International
Nov. 74	*WHERE ARE ALL MY FRIENDS /* Philadelphia International
Mar. 75	*BAD LUCK (PART 1) /* Philadelphia International
Nov. 75	*WAKE UP EVERYBODY /* Philadelphia International
Apr. 76	*TELL THE WORLD HOW I FEEL ABOUT 'CHA BABY /* Philadelphia International
Feb. 77	*REACHING FOR THE WORLD /* ABC

Sergio Mendes & Brasil '66

MEMBERS:

Sergio Mendes / born: Feb. 11, 1941 / Niteroi, Brazil

Lani Hall (lead vocals) / Ipanema, Brazil

Karen Phillipp (lead vocals) / Ipanema, Brazil

Sebastião Neto / Ipanema, Brazil

Dom Um Romão / Ipanema, Brazil

Rubens Bassini / Ipanema, Brazil

Sergio Mendes began playing piano as a child, and by the time he reached his teens, he was known in the Rio de Janeiro area as a leading jazz musi-cian. Before he reached twenty, he had formed his own group, known as Bossa Rio, and had joined the growing circle of musicians who were creating what came to be known as "bossa nova."

During the mid-sixties, Mendes came to the United States with a new group called Brasil '65. (He had made a previous American appearance, in 1962 with Bossa Rio, and had planned to return.) He toured extensively and made a number of records for Atlantic, but with only moderate success. The same group, with a few shifts in personnel, became Brasil '66 (with the above line-up) and signed with Herb Alperl's A & M label. Featuring a glowing endorsement from Alpert (who was then at the height of his popularity), their first album, *Sergio Mendes & Brasil '66,* became an instant success and yielded the first of many hit singles, "Mas Que Nada."

Today, Sergio Mendes makes his home in the San Fernando Valley area of Los Angeles. He records for the Arista label, and has formed a new band known as Brasil '77. In 1978 the group's name was changed to Brasil '88.

Sept. 66	*MAS QUE NADA /* A & M
Dec. 66	*CONSTANT RAIN /* A & M
Apr. 67	*FOR ME /* A & M
June 67	*NIGHT & DAY /* A & M
May 68	*THE LOOK OF LOVE /* A & M
Aug. 68	*THE FOOL ON THE HILL /* A & M
Nov. 68	*SCARBOROUGH FAIR /* A & M
May 69	*PRETTY WORLD /* A & M
June 69	*DOCK OF THE BAY /* A & M
Nov. 69	*WICHITA LINEMAN /* A & M

The Meters

MEMBERS:

Leo Nocentelli (guitar)

Art Neville (keyboards)

George Porter (bass)

Cyril Neville (percussion)
Joseph Modliste (drums)
HOMETOWN: New Orleans, Louisiana

Beginning as a back-up band for Fats Domino, this group evolved from an earlier aggregation known as The Hawketts. At one time the group contained Cyril and Art Neville's brother Aaron, who later achieved fame as a solo artist with "Tell It Like It Is."

During the late sixties, the band transformed into The Meters and formed an association with producers Allen Toussaint and Marshall Sehorn. Signed to the Josie label, they achieved a string of hits with "funk" instrumentals that soon made them one of the country's leading soul bands. In addition, they have been heard as the backing group on virtually every important record to come out of the New Orleans area during the last several years.

Today The Meters are affiliated with Warner Brothers/Reprise.

Feb. 69	**SOPHISTICATED CISSY / Josie**
Apr. 69	**CISSY STRUT / Josie**
July 69	**EASE BACK / Josie**
Dec. 69	**LOOK KA PY PY / Josie**
Apr. 70	**THE CHICKEN STRUT / Josie**
July 70	**THE HAND CLAPPING SONG / Josie**
Oct. 77	**BE MY LADY / Warner Bros.**

MFSB

HOMETOWN: Philadelphia, Pennsylvania

MFSB is not a working group, but rather a pool of more than thirty resident studio musicians based at Philadelphia's famed Sigma Sound Studios. The initials comprising their name stand for "Mother, Father, Sister, Brother."

Working closely over the years with producers Kenny Gamble and Leon Huff, and with arranger Thom Bell, these musicians have backed dozens of major hits by artists such as The Bluenotes, O'Jays, Stylistics, Spinners, Intruders, Three Degrees, Jerry Butler, Wilson Pickett, and Billy Paul.

In 1974 the musicians who comprise MFSB began recording, in various combinations, for the Philadelphia International label. Their first outing, "TSOP," reached number one and was most influential in establishing the "disco" sound. They have since followed with several additional hits.

Mar. 74	**TSOP (THE SOUND OF PHILADELPHIA) / Philadelphia International**
July 74	**LOVE IS THE MESSAGE / Philadelphia International**
June 75	**SEXY / Philadelphia International**
Nov. 75	**ZIP / Philadelphia International**

Lee Michaels

BORN: Nov. 24, 1945
HOMETOWN: Los Angeles, California

Famed for his work on the electric organ, Lee Michaels first began learning keyboard skills as a child. He later studied other instruments, becoming proficient on the trumpet and trombone as well.

During the mid-sixties Michaels played in a group called The Sentinels, whose drummer was Joe Barbata, later of Jefferson Starship. He and Barbata also played in the Joel Scott Hill group, shortly after which Michaels left to form his own band.

In 1968 Michaels was invited to audition for A & M and was signed to a contract. He debuted with an album called *Carnival of Life,* following with *Recital* (on which he played all the instruments), *Lee Michaels, Barrel* and

5th. The last album yielded "Do You Know What I Mean," a single that climbed into the top ten.

In 1972 Michaels's contract was bought out by Columbia Records. He debuted with a highly acclaimed album titled *Nice Day for Something,* followed by a package called *Tailface.* He continues today to be a highly popular concert attraction.

July 71	*DO YOU KNOW WHAT I MEAN* / A & M
Nov. 71	*CAN I GET A WITNESS* / A & M

Bette Midler

BORN: Dec. 1, 1945
HOMETOWN: Paterson, New Jersey

Bette Midler

Bette Midler was raised in Hawaii, where her parents had moved during her childhood. Named after Bette Davis by her mother, an avid movie fan, Bette had childhood aspirations of becoming an actress. As she grew older and completed her education, she began working at a series of odd jobs and looking for an acting part.

In 1965 Bette was hired as an extra in the film version of James Michener's novel *Hawaii.* This brought her to Los Angeles, where she was able to accumulate enough money for a trip to New York and a try at the theater. Offered a job in the chorus line of *Fiddler on the Roof,* she remained with the production for nearly three years and worked her way up to the lead role of Tzeitel.

After this initial period of success, Bette's major breakthrough was to come somewhat later when she was hired to entertain at New York's Continental Baths. She rapidly developed an enormous cult following, making her a sought-after guest on nighttime televi-sion talk shows and giving her a great deal of much-needed publicity.

In 1972 Bette was signed by Atlantic Records, debuting with an album called *The Divine Miss M* (the name she is affectionately known as). An eventual Grammy winner, this record solidly launched her career and was followed by *Bette Midler* and *Songs for the New Depression.* Although she succeeded with a number of hit singles as well, she became most popular for her outrageous concert appearances.

Today, a star of major proportions, Bette Midler recently starred in an extended Broadway revue called *Clams on the Half Shell,* had a successful two week-stint at New York's famed Copacabana, and performed the lead role in a film called *Rose.*

Dec. 72	*DO YOU WANT TO DANCE?* / Atlantic
May 73	*BOOGIE WOOGIE BUGLE BOY* / Atlantic
Sept. 73	*FRIENDS* / Atlantic
Jan. 74	*IN THE MOOD* / Atlantic
Apr. 77	*YOU'RE MOVIN' OUT TODAY* / Atlantic
Jan. 78	*STORYBOOK CHILDREN* / Atlantic

Buddy Miles

BORN: Sept. 5, 1946
HOMETOWN: Omaha, Nebraska

One of the leading drummers and bandleaders in the fields of rock and soul, Buddy Miles began learning the drums while still in grade school. He had his own group at fifteen, eventually going on the road with vintage R & B and R & R acts as part of the Dick Clark Caravan of Stars. He also did occasional session work, becoming well known for his unusual drum work in The Jaynettes' "Sally Go Round the Roses."

During the mid-sixties Miles became a featured drummer with the Wilson Pickett band and a founding member, with Mike Bloomfield, of The Electric Flag. After a highly acclaimed performance at the 1967 Monterey Pop Festival (which launched the careers of Janis Joplin, Jimi Hendrix, and Otis Redding), The Electric Flag disbanded and Miles went on to form a new group, The Buddy Miles Express. Next came The Band of Gypsies, which included Jimi Hendrix and Billy Cox, and finally a group known simply as The Buddy Miles Band. This group made a number of best-selling albums and beginning in 1969 achieved more than half a dozen entries on the singles charts.

During the early seventies Miles joined with Carlos Santana for a "concept" album, *Buddy Miles & Carlos Santana Live* (recorded in a Hawaiian volcano crater!), and played in a briefly re-formed Electric Flag group. Today, he records for Casablanca as a solo artist.

Aug. 69 *MEMPHIS TRAIN*/Mercury
May 70 *THEM CHANGES*/Mercury
July 70 *DOWN BY THE RIVER*/Mercury

Buddy Miles

Oct. 70 *DREAMS*/Mercury
Dec. 70 *WE GOT TO LIVE TOGETHER*/Mercury
May 71 *WHOLESALE LOVE*/Mercury
July 71 *THEM CHANGES* (rereleased)/Mercury
Sept. 75 *ROCKIN' & ROLLIN' ON THE STREETS OF HOLLYWOOD*/Casablanca

Jody Miller

BORN: Nov. 29, 1941
HOMETOWN: Phoenix, Arizona

Coming from a musical family, Jody Miller decided on a singing career at a very early age. With the encouragement of her four singing sisters and her father, a former country fiddler, Jody joined with two of her friends to form a group called The Melodies.

In 1962 Jody traveled to Los Angeles in search of a solo career. Shortly after arriving, however, she was involved in a serious auto accident that forced her to return home. Once recovered, Jody was making a local appearance when she was heard by actor Dale Robertson. He arranged an audition for Capitol Records, which resulted in a contract with the label. She achieved a long string of Country hits, several of which also placed on the Pop charts, and reached the national top ten with "Queen of the House" (an answer to Roger Miller's "King of the Road").

During the mid-sixties Jody became disenchanted with the recording business and retired for a time into private life. By 1970, however, she had reactivated her career, signing with Epic and forming an association with producer Billy Sherrill.

Today Jody Miller makes her home in Blanchard, Oklahoma, where she lives with her husband, Monty Brooks, and their daughter, Robin.

Feb. 64	**HE WALKS LIKE A MAN / Capitol**
Apr. 65	**QUEEN OF THE HOUSE / Capitol**
June 65	**SILVER THREADS & GOLDEN NEEDLES / Capitol**
Aug. 65	**HOME OF THE BRAVE / Capitol**
June 71	**HE'S SO FINE / Epic**
Oct. 71	**BABY, I'M YOURS / Epic**

Mrs. Miller

HOMETOWN: Claremont, California

The mid-sixties seem to have yielded a number of "camp" novelty acts, most notably Tiny Tim and The New Vaudeville Band. Another to fall into this category was Mrs. Elva Miller, whose semi-operatic, thirties-style versions of current pop songs became quite the rage during 1966.

Interested in music since childhood, Mrs. Miller had taken vocal lessons for more than seven years. As she grew older she began performing at various civic affairs, but her career was dis-

couraged by her family, who felt she was becoming too involved in public life. Frustrated, she began making private recordings for her own pleasure, an activity which eventually brought her to the attention of Capitol Records. The result was a widely publicized album, *Mrs. Miller's Greatest Hits,* a flurry of major television appearances, and two singles that appeared on the charts during the summer of 1966.

Today Mrs. Miller has once again retired into private life.

Apr. 66	**DOWNTOWN / Capitol**
May 66	**A LOVERS' CONCERTO / Capitol**

Roger Miller

BORN: Jan. 2, 1936
HOMETOWN: Fort Worth, Texas

Roger Miller emerged during the mid-sixties with a unique blend of Pop, country music, and comedy.

He grew up in Erick, Oklahoma, where his interest in music first developed. At seventeen he joined the army and was shipped to Korea as a jeep driver, eventually switching to Special Services and joining a hillbilly band. The audience response to his material encouraged him to consider music as a career, and he moved to Nashville during the late fifties.

Beginning as a songwriter, Miller achieved his first success when Ray Price recorded his composition of "Invitation to the Blues." He was hired as a writer by Faron Young, and eventually was offered a contract by the Tree Music publishing company. This led to an affiliation with Mercury's subsidiary Smash label and a top ten debut hit titled "Dang Me."

During the next several years, Miller scored with more than a dozen addi-

Steve Miller

Steve Miller

tional hits. He hosted his own network television program and established the King of the Road, a major hotel in Nashville.

Today Miller makes his home in Encino, California, and records for the Columbia label.

June 64	*DANG ME* / Smash
Sept. 64	*CHUG A LUG* / Smash
Nov. 64	*DO WACKA DO* / Smash
Jan. 65	*KING OF THE ROAD* / Smash
May 65	*ENGINE ENGINE #9* / Smash
July 65	*ONE DYIN' AND A BURYIN'* / Smash
Sept. 65	*KANSAS CITY STAR* / Smash
Nov. 65	*ENGLAND SWINGS* / Smash
Feb. 66	*HUSBANDS & WIVES* / Smash
June 66	*YOU CAN'T ROLLER SKATE IN A BUFFALO HERD* / Smash
Sept. 66	*MY UNCLE USED TO LOVE ME BUT SHE DIED* / Smash
Nov. 66	*HEARTBREAK HOTEL* / Smash
Mar. 67	*WALKING IN THE SUNSHINE* / Smash
Mar. 68	*LITTLE GREEN APPLES* / Smash
Dec. 68	*VANCE* / Smash

Steve Miller

BORN: Oct. 5, 1943
HOMETOWN: Dallas, Texas

One of the leading guitarists in rock, Steve Miller gained fame during the sixties and seventies as head of The Steve Miller Band. A constantly changing group of musicians, this band has, at one time or another, featured such rock luminaries as William ''Boz'' Scaggs and Nicky Hopkins.

Miller began his career at the age of twelve in a Texas-based group called

The Marksmen Combo. An avid blues buff, he later moved to Chicago where he played with such leading blues figures as T-Bone Walker, Muddy Waters, and Junior Wells.

During the mid-sixties, Miller relocated in San Francisco to form his band, at first known as The Steve Miller Blues Band. They made their recording debut by playing on the sound track of *Revolution,* later becoming noted for their backing work on Chuck Berry's *Live at the Fillmore* album. Offered a spot in the 1967 Monterey Pop Festival, they were so well received that Capitol Records offered a contract.

In spite of a few early singles, the group was known until early seventies as an album-and-concert act. In 1973, however, they began a series of major hit singles with their number-one recording of "The Joker." Over the years, their album releases have included *Children of the Future, Sailor, Brave New World, Your Saving Grace, Number Five, Rock Love, Recall from the Beginning, The Joker,* and *Fly like an Eagle.*

Today The Steve Miller Band's lineup consists of Miller (lead guitar), Dickie Thompson (keyboards), Gerald Johnson (bass), and John King (drums).

Nov. 68	*LIVING IN THE U.S.A.* / Capitol
Aug. 70	*GOING TO THE COUNTRY* / Capitol
Oct. 73	*THE JOKER* / Capitol
Mar. 74	*YOUR CASH AIN'T NOTHIN' BUT TRASH* / Capitol
May 74	*LIVING IN THE U.S.A. (rereleased)* / Capitol
May 76	*TAKE THE MONEY AND RUN* / Capitol
Aug. 76	*ROCK N' ME* / Capitol
Dec. 76	*FLY LIKE AN EAGLE* / Capitol
Apr. 77	*JET AIRLINER* / Capitol
Aug. 77	*JUNGLE LOVE* / Capitol
Oct. 77	*SWINGTOWN* / Capitol

Joni Mitchell

REAL NAME: Roberta Joan Anderson Mitchell
BORN: Nov. 7, 1943
HOMETOWN: McLeod, Alberta, Canada

Originally bent on a career in commercial art, Joni Mitchell enrolled at the Alberta College of Art in Calgary. Just to pass the time, she took along a ukulele but soon found that she could earn extra money by singing in local coffeehouses. Her first engagement, at a place called The Depression, went extremely well and encouraged her to begin favoring music as a career.

In 1964 Joni traveled to the Mariposa Folk Festival in Toronto, Ontario. Deciding not to return home, she found work in several of the area's coffeehouses, eventually meeting and marrying Chuck Mitchell and moving with him to Detroit. Although this was a short-lived marriage, she retained his name as a professional identity and continued performing in the Detroit area. This led to engagements in New York, where she was heard and signed by Andy Wickham of Warner/Reprise.

Joni's first album, *Songs to a Seagull,* was not an immediate best seller but did bring her a great deal of attention as a songwriter. Other artists began recording her material (including songs such as "Both Sides Now," "Chelsea Morning," "Circle Game," "Big Yellow Taxi," "Woodstock," and "Michael from Mountains") and by the early seventies, she had become firmly established as a star. Her album releases have included *Clouds, Ladies of the Canyon, Blue, For the Roses, Court and Spark, Miles of Aisles,* and *Hissing of Summer Lawns.*

Although primarily an album-and-concert artist, Joni has achieved a number of major hit singles as well.

Joni Mitchell

She has been recording since 1972 for the Asylum label, and today makes her permanent home in California.

July 70	*BIG YELLOW TAXI* / Reprise
Sept. 71	*CAREY* / Reprise
Nov. 72	*YOU TURN ME ON, I'M A RADIO* / Asylum
Dec. 73	*RAISED ON ROBBERY* / Asylum
Mar. 74	*HELP ME* / Asylum
July 74	*FREE MAN IN PARIS* / Asylum

Dec. 74	*BIG YELLOW TAXI (rereleased)* / Asylum
Feb. 76	*IN FRANCE THEY KISS ON MAIN STREET* / Asylum

Willie Mitchell

HOMETOWN: Memphis, Tennessee

Known today as the president and A & R director of Hi Records, Willie

Mitchell has been responsible for the discovery and development of such acts as Al Green, Ann Peebles, and Syl Johnson.

During the mid-sixties, Mitchell was an artist for the Hi label, fronting a large band of Memphis-based musicians and touring extensively. Beginning with "20-75" (the song title was the record's release number!), Mitchell achieved a series of hits with "funk" instrumentals, the biggest of which was King Curtis's "Soul Serenade." Upon the death of the label's president, Joe Cuoghi, Mitchell was increasingly pressed into administrative service, eventually assuming the presidency.

Aug. 64	*20-75* / Hi	
Dec. 64	*PERCOLATIN'* / Hi	
July 65	*BUSTER BROWN* / Hi	
May 66	*BAD EYE* / Hi	
July 67	*SLIPPIN' & SLIDIN'* / Hi	
Mar. 68	*SOUL SERENADE* / Hi	
July 68	*PRAYER MEETING* / Hi	
Oct. 68	*UP HARD* / Hi	
Feb. 69	*30-60-90* / Hi	

Mocedades

MEMBERS:

Amaya Uranga Amezaga (lead vocals) / born: Feb. 18, 1947 / Bilbao, Spain

Izaskum Uranga Amezaga (lead vocals) / born: Apr. 17, 1950 / Bilbao, Spain

Carlos Zubiaga Uribarri (guitar, keyboards) / born: Oct. 10, 1944 / Bilbao, Spain

José Ipina Urien (guitar) / born: Jan. 7, 1949 / Madrid, Spain

Roberto Uranga Amezaga (guitar) / born: Apr. 21, 1948 / Bilbao, Spain

Javier Garay Barrenechea (bass) / born: Dec. 16, 1946 / Bilbao, Spain

Formed during the early seventies in the mountain city of Bilbao, Spain, Mocedades began as a folk group in the vein of Peter, Paul & Mary. They later became known for their unique rock adaptations of hymns and for their stage show built around black American music.

In 1973 Mocedades hit the top of the Spanish best-seller lists with Juan Calderon's composition of "Eres Tu." Its success soon spread throughout most of Europe, and it was picked up by the Tara label for American distribution. "Eres Tu" placed well with the American top ten and became the group's only American chart entry. They have, however, continued with great success in Europe.

Jan. 74	*ERES TU (TOUCH THE WIND)* / Tara

The Moments

MEMBERS:

Al Goodman / born: Mar. 31, 1947 / Jackson, Mississippi

Harry Ray / born: 1948 / Hackensack, New Jersey

William Brown / born: June 30, 1946 / Perth Amboy, New Jersey

Originally known as The Vipers, this group was formed during the mid-sixties in the Hackensack area of New Jersey.

Once organized, the group approached Joe and Sylvia Robinson's New Jersey-based All Platinum label and was signed to a contract. With Sylvia as the group's producer, their records were released on the subsidiary Stang label and became Soul and minor Pop hits. They achieved a major breakthrough, however, when their release of "Love on a Two Way Street" reached the top of both the Soul and the Pop charts in 1970.

Dec. 68	*NOT ON THE OUTSIDE* / Stang
May 69	*SUNDAY* / Stang
Aug. 69	*I DO* / Stang
Apr. 70	*LOVE ON A TWO WAY STREET* / Stang

The Monkees. Left to right: Michael Nesmith, Mickey Dolenz, Peter Tork, Davy Jones

Aug. 70 **IF I DIDN'T CARE** / Stang
Nov. 70 **ALL I HAVE** / Stang
Aug. 71 **LUCKY ME** / Stang
Sept. 73 **GOTTA FIND A WAY** / Stang
Jan. 74 **SEXY MAMA** / Stang
July 75 **LOOK AT ME** / Stang

The Monkees

MEMBERS:
Mickey Dolenz (lead vocals, guitar, drums) /
born: Mar. 9, 1945 / Los Angeles, California
Peter Tork (guitar) / born: Feb. 13, 1944 /
Washington, D.C.
Michael Nesmith (bass) / born: Dec. 30, 1942 /
Dallas, Texas
Davy Jones (tambourine) / born: Dec. 30, 1946 /
Manchester, England

In 1966 Columbia Pictures decided to create a television series based on the concept of The Beatles' highly successful movie *A Hard Day's Night*. Placing advertisements in the tradepapers, they auditioned hundreds of actors and musicians (during which such people as Steve Stills, Danny Hutton, and John Sebastian were rejected) and finally assembled the above group. Dolenz and Jones had had some singing and acting experience (particularly Jones, who had starred in the Broadway production of *Oliver*), while only Nesmith and Tork had any credentials whatsoever as musicians.

With Don Kirshner at the helm as

music director, "The Monkees" went on the air in the fall of 1966 and became an overwhelming success. In addition, Kirshner drew upon some of Pop music's leading writers (including Boyce & Hart, John Stewart, Leiber & Stoller, and Neil Diamond) to provide material for the "group" to record. In actuality, however, the tracks were provided by studio musicians while The Monkees themselves furnished only the vocals. After creating an issue over this, the group was allowed to make its own records and enjoyed continued success.

By 1969 internal difficulties had begun to pull the group apart. Peter Tork was the first to leave, forming his own group called The Release. Although The Monkees continued for a while as a trio, Mike Nesmith soon left to organize The First National Band (see *Mike NESMITH*) and thus brought the group to an end.

In 1975 Dolenz and Jones joined with writers Tommy Boyce and Bobby Hart in a re-formed Monkees group, which has been touring extensively and has recently signed with Capitol Records.

Sept. 66	*LAST TRAIN TO CLARKS-VILLE*/Colgems
Dec. 66	*I'M A BELIEVER*/Colgems
Dec. 66	*STEPPING STONE*/Colgems
Mar. 67	*A LITTLE BIT ME, A LITTLE BIT YOU*/Colgems
Mar. 67	*THE GIRL I KNEW SOMEWHERE*/Colgems
July 67	*PLEASANT VALLEY SUNDAY*/Colgems
July 67	*WORDS*/Colgems
Nov. 67	*DAYDREAM BELIEVER*/Colgems
Mar. 68	*VALLERI*/Colgems
Mar. 68	*TAPIOCA TUNDRA*/Colgems
June 68	*D. W. WASHBURN*/Colgems
June 68	*IT'S NICE TO BE WITH YOU*/Colgems

Oct. 68	*THE PORPOISE SONG*/Colgems
Feb. 69	*TEAR DROP CITY*/Colgems
May 69	*SOMEDAY MAN*/Colgems
June 69	*LISTEN TO THE BAND*/Colgems
Sept. 69	*GOOD CLEAN FUN*/Colgems
June 70	*OH MY MY*/Colgems

The Moody Blues

MEMBERS:

Denny Laine (Brian Haynes) (lead vocals, guitar)/born: Oct. 29, 1944/Jersey Coast, England/replaced by Justin Hayward/born: Oct. 14, 1946/Swindon, Wiltshire, England

Ray Thomas (sax, flute)/born: Dec. 29, 1941/Stourport-on-Severn, England

Michael Pinder (keyboards)/born: Dec. 27, 1941/Birmingham, England

Clint Warwick (bass)/born: June 25, 1949/Birmingham, England/replaced by John Lodge/ born: July 20, 1945/Birmingham, England

Graeme Edge (drums)/born: Mar. 30, 1944/Rochester, Staffordshire, England

Launched as an R & B band in 1964, The Moody Blues was organized by four musicians playing the Birmingham, England, club circuit. Once organized and rehearsed, they debuted at the Marquee and were so well received that they were signed almost immediately to the British Decca label. Their first single, "Lose Your Money," was a moderate British success, but the follow-up, "Go Now" (a cover of the song done by Bessie Banks for Leiber & Stoller's Tiger label) became an international best seller. They also made an impact with the album *Moody Blues No. 1,* shortly after which Denny Laine and Clint Warwick left the group for other interests.

In 1967, after having acquired the Mellotron that characterized all their future recordings, The Moodies achieved major success with their second LP, titled *Days of Future Passed.*

The Moody Blues. Clockwise from far left: Justin Hayward, John Lodge, Graeme Edge, Michael Pinder, Ray Thomas

(This album contained "Nights in White Satin," which was reissued nearly five years later and became a major hit!) In spite of nearly a dozen hit singles over the following years, the group is most highly regarded for its albums, including *In Search of the Lost Chord, On the Threshold of a Dream, To Our Children's Children's Children, A Question of Balance, Every Good Boy Deserves Favor,* and *Seventh Sojourn.*

Although there has never been an official announcement of a split, The Moodies have not worked together since 1973 and each has pursued solo projects. Additionally, Justin Hayward and John Lodge have recorded together as The Blue Jays. To this day, however, The Moodies operate their own Threshold label, which they established in 1969, and a major record shop. These operations are headquartered in Cobham, a small village outside London.

Feb. 65	*GO NOW*/London
June 65	*FROM THE BOTTOM OF MY HEART*/London
Apr. 66	*STOP*/London
July 68	*TUESDAY AFTERNOON*/London
Oct. 68	*RIDE MY SEE SAW*/London
June 69	*NEVER COMES THE DAY*/London
May 70	*QUESTION*/Threshold
Aug. 71	*THE STORY IN YOUR EYES*/Threshold
Apr. 72	*ISN'T LIFE STRANGE*/Threshold
Aug. 72	*NIGHTS IN WHITE SATIN*/Deram
Feb. 73	*I'M JUST A SINGER IN A ROCK & ROLL BAND*/Threshold

Dorothy Moore

BORN: 1946
HOMETOWN: Jackson, Mississippi

About ten years ago, Dorothy began her career by singing lead with the female group The Poppies, who had one national hit in 1966 with "Lullabye of Love." She left the group and did some background vocals on records such as Jean Knight's "Mr. Big Stuff" and King Floyd's "Groove Me."

In early 1976 she recorded for Malaco the blues ballad "Misty Blue," which became a national top ten hit.

Mar. 76	*MISTY BLUE*/Malaco
July 76	*FUNNY HOW TIME SLIPS AWAY*/Malaco
Aug. 77	*I BELIEVE IN YOU*/Malaco

Van Morrison

BORN: Aug. 31, 1945
HOMETOWN: Belfast, Ireland

At the age of sixteen, Van Morrison began his career as a tenor sax player in an Irish R & B group called The Mon-archs. He toured with this group in England, Scotland, and Germany, eventually being cast for the role of a jazz musician in a German film. In 1964 Morrison opened the R & B Club in Belfast and subsequently formed his own group, Them. (See *THEM*.)

In 1967 Them began to collapse as a working unit and Morrison left to pursue a solo career. He traveled to New York to visit Bert Berns, owner of the Bang label and writer of one of Them's hits, "Here Comes the Night." Morrison was offered a contract, and his first release, "Brown Eyed Girl," reached the top ten. At the end of 1967, however, Berns suddenly died and Morrison was left in a state of limbo.

In 1970, after several years of struggling to support himself with club work, Morrison's contract was picked up by Warner Brothers. He debuted with a highly acclaimed album titled *Astral Weeks* and achieved the first of many hit singles with "Come Running." Primarily an album artist, however, his subsequent releases have included *Moondance, Van Morrison, Tupelo Honey, St. Dominic's Preview, Hard Nose to the Highway, It's Too Late to Stop Now,* and *Veedon Fleece.*

July 67	*BROWN EYED GIRL*/Bang
Apr. 70	*COME RUNNING*/Warner Bros.
Nov. 70	*DOMINO*/Warner Bros.
Feb. 71	*BLUE MONEY*/Warner Bros.
June 71	*CALL ME UP IN DREAMLAND*/Warner Bros.
Oct. 71	*WILD NIGHT*/Warner Bros.
Jan. 72	*TUPELO HONEY*/Warner Bros.
Aug. 72	*JACKIE WILSON SAID*/Warner Bros.
Oct. 72	*REDWOOD TREE*/Warner Bros.
Nov. 77	*MOON DANCE*/Warner Bros.

Van Morrison

Motherlode

MEMBERS:

Ken Marco (guitar)

Steve Kennedy (tenor sax, harmonica)

William "Smitty" Smith (keyboards)

Wayne "Stoney" Stone (drums)

A group of Canadian origin, Motherlode began during the mid-sixties as a club band playing current hits. Several of their members eventually developed into songwriters, however, and they began introducing original material into their act.

In 1969 Motherlode came to the attention of producer Mort Ross. He began working with the group, producing a Smith-Kennedy song entitled "When I Die" and placing it with the Canadian Revolver label. After this became a substantial hit, it was picked up by Buddah for American distribution and eventually reached the American top 20 as well.

Late in 1971 the entire Motherlode group (minus only "Smitty" Smith) became part of a seven-man band called Dr. Music and signed with Bell Records.

Aug. 69 *WHEN I DIE* / **Buddah**

Mott the Hoople. Left to right: Ray Major, Overend Watts, Morgan Fisher, Dale Griffin, Nigel Benjamin

Mott the Hoople

MEMBERS:

Ian Hunter (guitar, lead vocals)/born: June 3, 1946/Shrewsbury, Shropshire, England

Overend Watts (bass guitar)/born: May 13, 1949/Birmingham, England

Nigel Benjamin (lead vocals)

Morgan Fisher (keyboards)

Ray Major (guitar)

Dale Griffin (drums)/born: Oct. 24, 1948

In the late sixties, Overend Watts, Mick Ralphs, Verde Allen, and Terry Buffin first formed Mott The Hoople, eventually adding Ian Hunter, who became the lead vocalist and catalyst of the group.

Prior to signing with Columbia Records in 1972, the group had broken up but had been encouraged to re-form by friend David Bowie. With the re-forming of the group, Hunter became the new leader, which caused the departure of Verde Allen and Mick Ralphs. The group's first American hit single was "All the Young Dudes," a tune that was penned by Bowie.

In 1974 Hunter left the group to get together with Bowie guitarist Mick Ronson, and a new career began for both of them. Nigel Benjamin then became the new lead vocalist and the group began a brand-new career for Columbia.

Sept. 72 *ALL THE YOUNG DUDES* / Columbia
Jan. 73 *ONE OF THE BOYS* / Columbia
June 74 *THE GOLDEN AGE OF ROCK 'N' ROLL* / Columbia

Mouth & MacNeal

REAL NAMES:

Willem Duyn / born: 1942

Maggie MacNeal / born: 1951

HOMETOWN: Haarlem, The Netherlands

Mouth & MacNeal were actually two solo artists—each of whom had recorded for the Dutch Philips label—who were teamed up by producer Hans van Hempert.

Willem Duyn had started out as a drummer in The Holland Quartet, a well-known Dutch dance band. In 1967 he joined a vocal group called The Jay Jays and subsequently under the name of Mouth, made a solo recording of The Shangri-Las' classic "Walkin' in the Sand."

Maggie MacNeal had had three years of classical training. After abandoning classical music, she too sang in a Pop group, before going on to make a solo recording of "I Heard It through the Grapevine."

Once teamed up by van Hempert (who had produced both their solo efforts), Mouth & MacNeal achieved an instant Dutch smash with van Hempert's composition and production of "How Do You Do." The record was subsequently released in the United States as well, placing within the national top ten.

Although they achieved only one more American chart entry, Mouth & MacNeal continued to be successful in their native country.

Apr. 72 HOW DO YOU DO /Philips
Oct. 72 HEY, YOU LOVE /Philips

Maria Muldaur

BORN: Sept. 12, 1943
HOMETOWN: New York City

Maria Muldaur began her career during the late fifties in a high-school group called The Cashmeres. Although the group was offered a contract with George Goldner's Gone label and some background work with Jerry Butler, Maria's mother would not let her participate because she was still underage.

In 1961 Maria became a regular at the legendary Gerde's Folk City, where she played the fiddle and sang. During the following year she joined The Even Dozen Jug Band which at one time also contained Steve Katz (later of The Blues Project and Blood, Sweat & Tears) and John Sebastian. After this group broke up, Maria joined the Jim Kweskin Jug Band, eventually marrying the guitarist, Geoff Muldaur, and settling with him in Woodstock.

During the mid-seventies, the Muldaurs became legally and professionally separated, Geoff joining The Butterfield Blues Band and Maria embarking on a solo career. Maria was signed by Warner Brothers/Reprise and debuted with an album titled simply *Maria Muldaur*. A major success, this yielded her first single, "Midnight at the Oasis," and was followed by the highly acclaimed "Waitress in a Donut Shop" and "Sweet Harmony."

**Feb. 74 MIDNIGHT AT THE OASIS /
Reprise**
Dec. 74 I'M A WOMAN /Reprise

Mungo Jerry

MEMBERS:
Ray Dorset (lead vocals, guitar)
Colin Earl (keyboards)
Micheal Cole (bass)
Paul King (acoustic guitar)

MEMBERS(post-1972):
Ray Dorset (lead vocals, guitar)
John Cook (keyboards)
Robert Daisley (bass)
David Bidwell (drums)

Known originally as The Good Earth Rock & Roll Band, this group spent several years on the British pub circuit playing "goodtime" jug music. After some personnel changes, which saw them shift closer to rock, the group became Mungo Jerry and signed with the British Dawn label. Their first album, *Mungo Jerry,* was released in

1970 and yielded an unusual, reggae-oriented single titled "In the Summertime." A major British hit, it was released in the United States by Janus and very nearly reached the top of the charts.

Although this was the extent of their American chart activity, the group went on to record a half dozen British albums, as well as a number of singles. In 1972 Colin Earl and Paul King left the group for solo careers, which eventually prompted Ray Dorset to form an entirely reorganized band.

July 70 *IN THE SUMMERTIME* / Janus

Michael Murphey

HOMETOWN: Dallas, Texas

Although he had childhood ambitions of becoming a southern Baptist minister, Michael Murphey became involved with music at a fairly early age. He sang as part of a duet known as John & Mike, and later in a group called The Texas Twosome.

During the mid-sixties Murphey moved to Los Angeles to attend UCLA and began to think of music as a career. He joined the Lewis & Clarke Expedition, later accepting a job as staff writer for the Screen Gems music publishing company. Writing several hundred songs during the five years he was there, Murphey became well known in the music business and had his material cut by many leading artists.

In 1971 Murphey formed an association with producer Bob Johnston (known for his work with Bob Dylan) and signed with the A & M label. He recorded two albums, *Geronimo's Cadillac* and *Cosmic Cowboy Souvenir,* with the first yielding a modest hit single of the title cut. He switched in

1973 to the Epic label, where he made a highly acclaimed album titled simply *Michael Murphey.* This was followed by *Blue Sky Night Thunder,* a package that yielded the chart-topping single "Wildfire."

Today Michael Murphey and his wife, Caroline, make their permanent home in the Colorado mountains, near Denver. Murphey has a studio in his home, and he often records there.

Aug. 72 *GERONIMO'S CADILLAC* / A & M
Mar. 75 *WILDFIRE* / Epic
Aug. 75 *CAROLINA IN THE PINES* / Epic
Jan. 76 *RENEGADE* / Epic

Walter Murphy & The Big Apple Band

BORN: 1952
HOMETOWN: New York City

Walter began his career by studying classical and jazz piano at the Manhattan School of Music and eventually got into scoring and conducting television commercials, along with working on many recording sessions for various artists. In early 1976 he signed with Private Stock and decided to record a "disco"-style Beethoven symphony. The result was "A Fifth of Beethoven," which became a number one national hit. He is credited with familiarizing today's record buyers with many of the great classics of yesterday.

May 76 *A FIFTH OF BEETHOVEN* / Private Stock
Nov. 76 *FLIGHT 76* / Private Stock

Anne Murray

BORN: June 20, 1947
HOMETOWN: Springhill, Nova Scotia, Canada

The first Canadian woman to achieve a million-selling record in the

Anne Murray

Song,'' were written by Loggins & Messina.

Today Anne Murray is known as The Singing Sweetheart of Canada and tours with a large back-up band called Richard.

July 70	*SNOWBIRD* / **Capitol**
Dec. 70	*SING HIGH, SING LOW* / **Capitol**
Sept. 71	*TALK IT OVER IN THE MORNING* / **Capitol**
Apr. 72	*COTTON JENNY* / **Capitol**
Jan. 73	*DANNY'S SONG* / **Capitol**
May 73	*WHAT ABOUT ME?* / **Capitol**
Aug. 73	*SEND A LITTLE LOVE MY WAY* / **Capitol**
Dec. 73	*LOVE SONG* / **Capitol**
Apr. 74	*YOU WON'T SEE ME* / **Capitol**
Nov. 74	*JUST ONE LOOK* / **Capitol**
Dec. 74	*DAY TRIPPER* / **Capitol**
Nov. 75	*SUNDAY SUNRISE* / **Capitol**
Feb. 76	*THE CALL* / **Capitol**
Oct. 76	*THINGS* / **Capitol**

United States (Joni Mitchell was the second), Anne Murray originally harbored ambitions of becoming a physical education teacher in the Canadian school system. As she grew older, however, she began to favor performing as a career and auditioned for a spot on the "Sing Along Jubilee" television show. She appeared regularly for nearly two years, gaining a great deal of attention and making a record for the Canadian Arc label.

After she left the show, Anne was contacted by Brian Ahern, its producer, who offered to produce her as a solo artist on records. This resulted in a contract with Capitol of Canada and two best-selling albums. With the release of a single called "Snowbird," however, Anne achieved an American best seller and the first of a long string of hits. Two of her most popular releases, "Danny's Song" and "Love

The Music Explosion

MEMBERS:

James "Jamie" Lyons (lead vocals, percussion)/born: 1949

Donald Atkins (lead guitar)/born: 1949

Richard Nesta (rhythm guitar)/born: 1949

Burton Sahl (bass)/born: 1949

Robert Avery (drums)/born: 1947

Originally an Ohio valley club band, The Music Explosion came to prominence though the efforts of independent record producers Jeff Katz, Jerry Kasenetz, and Elliot Chiprut. This team produced the master of "Little Bit o' Soul," attempting to sell it to several record companies and finally succeeding at Laurie. Released during the early summer of 1967, the record reached the top of the charts and paved the way for Kasenetz and Katz to launch the "bubble gum" sound just a few months later.

Although The Music Explosion was able to follow with one additional hit, they soon faded from national popularity and disbanded. Jamie Lyons continued to record for Laurie, but with little success.

May 67 *LITTLE BIT O' SOUL* /**Laurie**
Sept. 67 *SUNSHINE GAMES* /**Laurie**

The Music Machine
MEMBERS:
Mark Landon (lead guitar)
Sean Bonniwell (rhythm guitar)
Doug Rhodes (keyboards)
Keith Olsen (bass)
Ron Edgar (drums)
HOMETOWN: Los Angeles, California

The Music Machine was a leading exponent of the mid-sixties West Coast psychedelic punk sound. Virtually all their original material was supplied by guitarist Sean Bonniwell, a prolific songwriter.

After building a reputation in Los Angeles-area clubs, the group was signed by Art Laboe's Original Sound label. Their initial release, "Talk Talk," reached the national top 15 and was followed by a lesser hit titled "The People in Me." After this success, the group continued in the Los Angeles area with an enormous regional following.

Nov. 66 *TALK TALK* /**Original Sound**
Jan. 67 *THE PEOPLE IN ME* /**Original Sound**

Graham Nash

See *CROSBY, STILLS, NASH & YOUNG*.

The Nashville Teens

MEMBERS:
Arthur Sharp (lead vocals)
Peter Shannon (guitar)
John Allen (guitar)
John Hawkens (keyboards)
Raymond Phillips (bass, harmonica)/born: Jan. 16, 1945
Barry Jenkins (drums)
HOMETOWN: Weybridge, Surrey, England

Formed originally in 1962, this group's name was drawn from a fascination with the American Country-rock sound of the late fifties and early sixties.

In 1963 The Nashville Teens spent several months backing "rockabilly" star Jerry Lee Lewis at Hamburg, Germany's legendary Star Club. Returning home late in the year, they went on a British tour with Bo Diddley and a band known as The Minutemen.

By 1964 The Teens had undergone a number of personnel changes, yielding the above line-up. One of The Minutemen, Mickie Most, had turned record producer and began working with the group, producing a version of John D. Loudermilk's "Tobacco Road" and selling the master to British Decca. It became a top ten hit, doing nearly as

well in the United States after being released by London.

Although they achieved only one additional American chart entry, The Nashville Teens continued recording in Britain well into the mid-seventies. The group has undergone countless changes in personnel, with many of the original members achieving fame in other groups over the years. Most notably, Arthur Jenkins joined The Animals in 1966, and John Hawkens became known during the seventies as a member of Renaissance.

Sept. 64 *TOBACCO ROAD* /London
Mar. 65 *FIND MY WAY BACK HOME* / London

Nazareth

MEMBERS:
Dan McCafferty (lead vocals)
Manny Charlton (guitar)
Peter Agnew (bass)
Daryl Sweet (drums)
HOMETOWN: Dunfermline, Scotland

Beginning in the early sixties as a semipro outfit called The Shadettes, this group became Nazareth after Manny Charlton joined the line-up in 1969.

After building a following in British clubs, the group was signed during the early seventies by the Pegasus label. Starting with the release of *Nazareth* in 1971, the group became well known during the seventies with albums such

Graham Nash

Nazareth

as *Exercises, Razamanaz,* and *Loud 'n' Proud.*

Nazareth broke through with American audiences late in 1975, when A & M issued their single recording of "Love Hurts." A top ten chart entry for the group, the same song had been recorded by The Everly Brothers during the early sixties and had been the "B" side of a major Roy Orbison hit, "Running Scared."

Nov. 75 *LOVE HURTS* / **A & M**

Nazz

MEMBERS:
Todd Rundgren (lead guitar) / born: June 22, 1948
Robert Antoni (lead vocals, keyboards)
Carson Von Osten (bass)
Thomas Mooney (drums)
HOMETOWN: Philadelphia, Pennsylvania

Nazz was formed in 1967, when guitarist Todd Rundgren left a Philadelphia band known as Woody's Truckstop to organize a new group.

After building a reputation on the northeastern teen-club circuit, Nazz was signed by the short-lived SGC label (a division of Screen Gems-Columbia that also had Neil Sedaka on its roster at the time), and in 1968 the group recorded its first album, *The Nazz,* which yielded a modest hit single titled "Hello It's Me." They followed with a second LP, *Nazz Nazz* and disbanded before the end of 1969.

In 1970 Todd Rundgren signed with the Ampex label and began his climb to fame as a solo artist. In the interim, SGC reissued "Hello It's Me" as a single, but with only slightly more success than previously. The same song, of course, ultimately became one of Rundgren's later solo hits. (See *Todd RUNDGREN.*)

Feb. 69 *HELLO IT'S ME /SGC*
Jan. 70 *HELLO IT'S ME* (rereleased)/ **SGC**

Sam Neely

BORN: Aug. 22, 1948
HOMETOWN: Cuero, Texas

Sam Neely began singing in small southern Texas clubs at the young age of eleven. He played in a number of local rock groups during the mid-sixties before settling in the city of Corpus Christi, Texas, to build a solo career.

While working in his father's construction business by day, Neely began to develop a substantial following by singing at night and on weekends. He eventually became a featured performer at Rogue's (the same club that launched the career of Tony Joe White) and was spotted there by re-

cord producer Rudy Durand. Signed shortly thereafter to the Capitol label, Neely scored with a top 30 national hit called "Loving You Just Crossed My Mind." After following with a somewhat lesser hit, "Rosalie," he changed affiliation to A & M and continued his series of chart entries with remakes of past R & R hits.

Today Sam Neely continues to live in Corpus Christi, where he is the resident performer at a club called The Electric Eel.

Sept. 72 *LOVING YOU JUST CROSSED MY MIND* /Capitol
Jan. 73 *ROSALIE* /Capitol
Sept. 74 *YOU CAN HAVE HER* /A & M
Feb. 75 *I FOUGHT THE LAW* /A & M

Neon Philharmonic

MEMBERS:
Tupper Saussy
Donald Gant
Robert McCluskey

Neon Philharmonic was a studio group made up of three leading session musicians from the Nashville area.

Signed to Warner Brothers during the late sixties, the "group" placed two records on the national charts, with "Morning Girl" nearly reaching the top ten.

Apr. 69 *MORNING GIRL* /Warner Bros.
May 70 *HEIGHDY HO PRINCESS* / **Warner Bros.**

Mike Nesmith & The First National Band

MEMBERS:
Michael Nesmith (guitar)/born: Dec. 30, 1943/ Dallas, Texas
"Red" Rhodes (steel guitar, dobro)/born: Dec. 30, 1930/Alston, Illinois
John London (John Kuehne) (bass)/born: Feb. 6, 1942/Bryan, Texas

John Ware / born: May 2, 1944 / Tulsa, Oklahoma

Mike Nesmith rose to international fame during the sixties as a member of The Monkees. (See *The MONKEES.*) When The Monkees disbanded in 1969, Nesmith was invited by Linda Ronstadt to join her back-up group, The Corvettes. Nesmith had written Linda's earlier hit, "A Different Drum," and they had known each other for some time.

After a brief stay with The Corvettes, Nesmith and two of the group's members, John London and John Ware, separated to organize their own group, The First National Band. Obtaining a contract with RCA, they debuted with an album titled *Magnetic South,* which yielded a top twenty single called "Joanne." They followed with two additional albums, *Loose Salute* and *Nevada Fighter,* as well as a number of singles.

Late in 1971 Nesmith dissolved the group and organized The Second National Band. A short-lived venture, this group soon disbanded as well, leaving Nesmith to record today as a solo artist.

Aug. 70 *JOANNE* / RCA
Nov. 70 *SILVER MOON* / RCA
Apr. 71 *NEVADA FIGHTER* / RCA

Aaron Neville

HOMETOWN: New Orleans, Louisiana

Aaron Neville is the brother of veteran musician Art Neville, who rose to fame during the late sixties as keyboard player for The Meters.

In 1954 both Art and Aaron Neville were members of an R & B group called The Hawketts. During the following years, the brothers pursued largely separate careers and became fixtures on the New Orleans music scene, Aaron achieving substantial regional success as an artist for the Minit label.

During the mid-sixties a former teacher named Warren Parker teamed up with two of the area's musicians, Red Tyler and George Davis, to form a record company called Parlo. Signing Aaron Neville as their first artist, they launched their company with Neville's recording of "Tell It like It Is," which became an overwhelming regional hit. Within a few weeks the record began receiving national airplay and eventually reached the top of the charts.

Neville was able to achieve only one more chart entry before Parlo ran into difficulties and ceased operations. Today he continues to perform around the New Orleans area and often works as a studio musician and vocalist.

Dec. 66 *TELL IT LIKE IT IS* / Parlo
Mar. 67 *SHE TOOK YOU FIR A RIDE* / Parlo

The Newbeats

MEMBERS:
Lawrence Henley (lead vocals) / born: June 30, 1941 / Arp, Texas

Marcus Mathis / born: Feb. 9, 1942 / Hahira, Georgia

Lewis "Dean" Mathis / born: Mar. 17, 1939 / Hahira, Georgia

Brothers Mark and Dean Mathis began performing as a duo during the late fifties and eventually expanded their act to an eight-man band. During one of their performances, Larry Henley came up from the audience and asked to join the group on stage. He was so well received that he remained with the group until it disbanded during the early sixties.

Several years later the Mathis brothers and Henley decided to form a trio and began circulating tapes to record companies. One of these came to the attention of Wesley Rose, head of Hickory Records, and he signed the group to that label. Beginning with "Bread & Butter," The Newbeats achieved a string of hits that lasted until the end of the sixties. During the early seventies, their records were re-issued in England, becoming immensely popular and, in some cases, bigger hits than they were originally!

In 1974 The Newbeats began recording for Playboy Records, debuting with a remake of Barbara George's "I Know."

Aug. 64	*BREAD & BUTTER* /Hickory
Oct. 64	*EVERYTHING'S ALRIGHT* /Hickory
Jan. 65	*BREAK AWAY* /Hickory
Apr. 65	*THE BIRDS ARE FOR THE BEES* /Hickory
Oct. 65	*RUN BABY RUN* /Hickory
Feb. 66	*SHAKE HANDS* /Hickory
Dec. 69	*GROOVIN'* /Hickory

New Birth

MEMBERS:
Charles Hearndon (lead guitar)
Leslie Wilson (mandolin)
James Baker (keyboards, trombone)
Robert Jackson (trumpet)
Austin Lander (baritone sax)
Anthony Churchill (tenor sax, percussion)
Londie Wiggins (percussion)
Melvin Wilson (bass)
Leroy Taylor (bass)
Robin Russell (drums)
HOMETOWN: Louisville, Kentucky

This large band evolved from an unusual concept originating in the early sixties—a touring company of five separate acts and seventeen people in all, who would perform individual sets and join together for a grand finale. After a number of years of touring and numerous personnel changes, this

eventually yielded two groups called New Birth and The Nite-liters. (See *THE NITE-LITERS*.)

In 1971 both groups affiliated with RCA, each achieving a number of best-selling singles and albums. New Birth changed affiliation to the Buddah label in 1975.

Oct. 71	*IT'S IMPOSSIBLE* /RCA
Mar. 73	*I CAN UNDERSTAND IT* /RCA
Aug. 73	*UNTIL IT'S TIME FOR YOU TO GO* /RCA
Feb. 74	*IT'S BEEN A LONG TIME* /RCA
May 74	*WILDFLOWER* /RCA
Oct. 74	*I WASH MY HANDS OF THE WHOLE DAMN DEAL* /RCA
May 75	*GRAND DADDY* /Buddah
July 75	*DREAM MERCHANT* /Buddah

The New Colony Six

MEMBERS:
Gerry Van Kollenberg (lead guitar)
Ronald Rice (rhythm guitar)
Charles Jobes (keyboards)
Patrick McBride (harmonica, percussion)
Les Kummel (bass)
William Herman (drums, percussion)
HOMETOWN: Chicago, Illinois

The New Colony Six emerged during the mid-sixties with a vocal style reminiscent of The Lettermen and The Four Freshmen.

After achieving a number of hits on the local Centaur label, the group was signed by the Chicago-based Mercury Record Company. Beginning with "I Will Always Think About You," they recorded a series of middle-of-the-road best sellers that lasted well into the seventies.

Feb. 66	*I CONFESS* /Centaur
Feb. 67	*LOVE YOU SO MUCH* /Centaur
Mar. 68	*I WILL ALWAYS THINK ABOUT YOU* /Mercury
June 68	*CAN'T YOU SEE ME CRY* /Mercury

Dec. 68 ***THE THINGS I'D LIKE TO SAY*** / Mercury
May 69 ***I COULD NEVER LIE TO YOU*** / Mercury
Aug. 69 ***I WANT YOU TO KNOW*** / Mercury
Jan. 70 ***BARBARA, I LOVE YOU*** / Mercury
Aug. 71 ***ROLL ON*** / Sunlight
Dec. 71 ***LONG TIME TO BE ALONE*** / Sunlight

Randy Newman

BORN: Nov. 28, 1943
HOMETOWN: New Orleans, Louisiana

Newman moved to California with his family at an early age and began playing the piano. Coming from a musical family—with three uncles, Alfred, Lionel, and Emil, respected conductors and film composers—it was no wonder he felt the urge to write songs.

At U.C.L.A. he began studying music theory and became fascinated in writing humorous lyrics. During the sixties he wrote many songs for other performers, including "Mama Told Me Not to Come" for Three Dog Night and "I Think It's Going to Rain Today" for Judy Collins.

He signed with Warner Brothers during the late sixties and since that time has turned out a few rather interesting albums. But it was his LP *Little Criminals,* recorded in late 1977, that got him the most notoriety. From that LP came the highly publicized "Short People," which created a wave of dissension with the undersized folk because of lyrics like "they don't deserve to live." Besides all the adverse publicity, Newman is a highly talented performer who writes tongue-in-cheek tunes that he feels compelled to write.

Nov. 77 ***SHORT PEOPLE*** / Warner Bros.

Randy Newman

The New Seekers

MEMBERS:
Eve Graham (Evelyn May Beatson) (lead vocals) / born: Apr. 19, 1943 / Perth, Scotland
Lyn Paul (Lynda Susan Belcher) / born: Feb. 16, 1949 / Manchester, England
Peter Doyle / born: July 28, 1949 / Melbourne, Australia / replaced (1973) by Peter Oliver
Marty Kristian (Martin Vanags) / born: May 27, 1947 / Leipzig, Germany
Paul Martin Layton / born: Aug. 4, 1947 / Beaconsfield, England

A direct descendant of The Seekers, this group was formed by Keith Potger, a member of the original group, after they disbanded in 1969. Potger sang with the new group as well, but he retired almost immediately from performing to handle management and production for The New Seekers. (See *THE SEEKERS*.)

After a period of rehearsal, The New

Seekers began to build an act by appearing extensively in theaters and clubs and on television. They were signed in 1970 by the British Philips label, debuting with a major hit recording of Melanie's "Look What They've Done to My Song." Released in the United States by Elektra, it became the first of many hits that the group would place on the American best-seller lists. By 1973, however, American distribution of their records was taken over by MGM's subsidiary Verve label.

The New Seekers disbanded during the mid-seventies, many of the members going on to solo recording careers.

Sept. 70	*LOOK WHAT THEY'VE DONE TO MY SONG, MA* / **Elektra**
Jan. 71	*BEAUTIFUL PEOPLE* / **Elektra**
Mar. 71	*THE NICKEL SONG* / **Elektra**
Dec. 71	*I'D LIKE TO TEACH THE WORLD TO SING* / **Elektra**
Apr. 72	*BEG, STEAL OR BORROW* / **Elektra**
July 72	*CIRCLES* / **Elektra**
Sept. 72	*DANCE, DANCE, DANCE* / **Elektra**
Jan. 73	*COME SOFTLY TO ME* / **Verve**
Feb. 73	*SEE ME, FEEL ME/PINBALL WIZARD* / **Verve**

Olivia Newton-John

BORN: Sept. 26, 1947
HOMETOWN: Cambridge, England

Olivia Newton-John grew up in Australia, where her family moved when she was five. Showing early musical inclinations, she began writing songs at the family piano and, at the age of fourteen, formed a singing group called The Sol Four.

During the mid-sixties Olivia began singing solo at her brother-in-law's coffeehouse. At the suggestion of a customer, she entered a talent contest held by Johnny O'Keefe, a popular Australian recording artist, and won first prize, a trip to London.

Arriving in England, she teamed up with Pat Carroll, another Australian singer, and began appearing regularly on television and in clubs. When Pat's visa ran out and forced her to return to Australia, Olivia continued on her own and began building a strong reputation. During this period she recorded a duet with British rock star Cliff Richard, starred in Harry Saltzman's film *Tomorrow* and sang in a group of the same name.

In 1971 Olivia was signed by the British Festival label and achieved her first hit with Bob Dylan's "If Not for You." Released in the United States by Universal, it became the first of a long string of hits which is as yet unbroken. She also co-starred with John Travolta in the hit movie *Grease*.

May 71	*IF NOT FOR YOU* / **Universal**
Oct. 71	*BANKS OF THE OHIO* / **Universal**
Nov. 73	*LET ME BE THERE* / **Universal**
Apr. 74	*IF YOU LOVE ME* / **MCA**
Aug. 74	*I HONESTLY LOVE YOU* / **MCA**
Jan. 75	*HAVE YOU NEVER BEEN MELLOW?* / **MCA**
June 75	*PLEASE MR. PLEASE* / **MCA**
Dec. 75	*LET IT SHINE* / **MCA**
Mar. 76	*COME ON OVER* / **MCA**
Aug. 76	*DON'T STOP BELIEVIN'* / **MCA**
Nov. 76	*EVERY FACE TELLS A STORY* / **MCA**
Jan. 77	*SAM* / **MCA**
June 77	*MAKING A GOOD THING BETTER* / **MCA**
Nov. 77	*I HONESTLY LOVE YOU (rereleased)* / **MCA**

John Travolta & Olivia Newton-John

Apr. 78	*YOU'RE THE ONE THAT I WANT* / **RSO**

Olivia Newton-John

The New Vaudeville Band

In 1966 British record producer Geoff Stephens assembled a group of session musicians to record an unusual novelty song he had written. Titled "Winchester Cathedral," the record featured a vocal sung through a megaphone in the style of Rudy Vallee and instrumental backing reminiscent of the vaudeville bands of the thirties. Purchased and released by Fontana, the record surprised everybody by becoming an international number one best seller and by generating literally dozens of vocal and instrumental "cover" versions. Its impact was so great that Vallee himself began appearing on television with his interpretation of the song.

In order to meet the demand, the record company hastily recruited a group of touring musicians to make public appearances. The New Vaudeville Band managed one more hit early in 1967, after which the fad disappeared as quickly as it had come.

Oct. 66 *WINCHESTER CATHEDRAL /*
Fontana
Feb. 67 *PEEK A BOO /* Fontana

New York City

MEMBERS:
Tim McQueen
John Brown
Edward Schell
Claude Johnson
HOMETOWN: New York City

This vocal quartet was made up of four high-school friends, each of whom

Paul Nicholas

had sung previously in church. In addition, Brown had sung for a time with two vintage R & B groups, The Cadillacs and The Five Satins.

In 1973 New York City came to the attention of independent record producer Thom Bell, who worked with the group to record a song called "I'm Doing Fine Now." Sold to Wes Farrell's Chelsea label, the record reached the national top 20 and was followed by two additional hits. By the mid-seventies, however, the group had faded from the charts.

Mar. 73 *I'M DOING FINE NOW /* Chelsea
Sept. 73 *MAKE ME TWICE THE MAN /*
Chelsea
Feb. 74 *QUICK, FAST, IN A HURRY /*
Chelsea

Paul Nicholas

HOMETOWN: Peterborough, England

Long before Paul Nicholas became an accomplished recording artist, he was a highly successful movie and theatrical star.

His first big acting break came in 1968 when, in London, he landed the role of Claude in the rock musical *Hair.* This was followed by theatrical roles in *Jesus Christ Superstar* (1972) and *Grease* (1974), and movie parts in *Stardust, Tommy,* and *Lisztomania.*

His career as a recording artist proved to be purely accidental. While auditioning in New York for the main role in the rock musical *Hamlet,* he was informed that he could not get the job because he was not a member of American Equity. He decided to turn to singing and recorded an album, *Paul Nicholas,* on which was the song "Heaven on the 7th Floor." Nicholas's good fortune continued as the song became a hit and he was signed to perform the role of Dougy Shears in the film *Sgt. Pepper's Lonely Hearts Club Band.*

Aug. 77 ***HEAVEN ON THE 7TH FLOOR /***
RSO

Maxine Nightingale

BORN: 1952
HOMETOWN: Wembley, England

Maxine began singing at the age of sixteen in a school band, after which she performed in local clubs. A few years later she signed with Pye Records and recorded a few unsuccessful songs.

After numerous roles in such stage shows as *Hair* (London production, 1970), *Jesus Christ Superstar, Godspell,* and a London comedy called *Savages,* she started to do some studio singing, whereupon she met writers Pierre Tubbs and Vince Edwards and recorded their song ''Right Back Where We Started From.''

Maxine Nightingale

Feb. 76 ***RIGHT BACK WHERE WE***
STARTED FROM /United
Artists
July 76 ***GOTTA BE THE ONE /United***
Artists

Nilsson

BORN: June 15, 1941
HOMETOWN: Brooklyn, New York

A native of the tough Bushwick section of Brooklyn, Harry Edward Nilsson III spent his teen years in California after moving there with his family during the early fifties. While completing his education, he won letters in several sports, began working as a theater usher, and eventually became a computer programmer for a bank. In his spare time he visited record- and music-publishing companies in an attempt to break into the business.

During the early sixties, Nilsson was signed by Mercury Records, for which he released an unsuccessful single, ''Donna,'' under the name of Johnny Niles. After switching to Capitol's subsidiary Tower label, he made a few more solo records and several releases as the lead singer of the New Salvation Singers. However, he soon began attracting attention as a writer and by 1967 his material had been recorded by such artists as The Ronettes, The Modern Folk Quartette, The Monkees, The Yardbirds, and Blood, Sweat & Tears. A contract from RCA soon followed, employing him both as an artist and a writer.

Nilsson's first album, *Pandemonium Shadow Show,* received rave notices and prompted The Beatles' John Lennon to describe him as his favorite American recording artist. In 1969 Nilsson achieved a major breakthrough when his recording of "Everybody's Talking" was selected as the theme for the film *Midnight Cowboy.* It became the first of his many hit singles, and his subsequent best-selling albums have included *Aerial Ballet, Harry, Nilsson Sings* [Randy] *Newman, The Point* (the soundtrack of an animated TV show that he helped create), *Schmilsson, Son of Schmilsson, Schmilsson in the Night,* and *Pussy Cat* (which was produced by John Lennon). In addition, he provided the scores for television's "Courtship of Eddie's Father," for the feature film *Skidoo,* and for *Son of Dracula,* in which he also appeared.

Today Harry Nilsson and his wife, Diane, live in the Los Angeles area with their family.

Aug. 69	**EVERYBODY'S TALKING / RCA**
Nov. 69	**I GUESS THE LORD MUST BE IN NEW YORK CITY /RCA**
Mar. 71	**ME & MY ARROW /RCA**
Dec. 71	**WITHOUT YOU /RCA**
Mar. 72	**JUMP INTO THE FIRE /RCA**
June 72	**COCONUT /RCA**
Sept. 72	**SPACEMAN /RCA**
Dec. 72	**REMEMBER /RCA**
Sept. 73	**AS TIME GOES BY /RCA**
Apr. 74	**DAYBREAK /RCA**

The 1910 Fruitgum Company

MEMBERS:

Chuck Travis (lead guitar) / born: 1946
"Mark" (rhythm guitar, keyboards) / born: 1948
Lawrence Ripley (bass, horns) / born: 1948
Bruce Shay (percussion) / born: 1948
Rusty Oppenheimer (drums) / born: 1948

During the late sixties, producers Jerry Kasenetz and Jeff Katz decided to make recordings specifically for the subteen youth market. Calling the product "bubble gum" music, they began their venture with a group called The 1910 Fruitgum Company, an idea taken from an old gum wrapper found by one of the producers. The actual recordings were made by session musicians and vocalists, featuring the lead voice of writer-producer Joey Levine.

As these records began selling in the millions, a touring group was organized, featuring the above line-up, to make personal appearances. This group was also part of The Kasenetz-Katz Singing Orchestral Circus, which appeared in 1968.

By the end of 1969, The 1910 Fruitgum Company had faded from popularity along with "bubble gum" music.

Jan. 68	**SIMON SAYS /Buddah**
Apr. 68	**MAY I TAKE A GIANT STEP / Buddah**
July 68	**1,2,3 RED LIGHT /Buddah**
Oct. 68	**GOODY GOODY GUMDROPS / Buddah**
Jan. 69	**INDIAN GIVER /Buddah**
May 69	**SPECIAL DELIVERY /Buddah**
Aug. 69	**THE TRAIN /Buddah**

The Nite-Liters

HOMETOWN: Louisville, Kentucky

The Nite-Liters evolved from the same large touring company that yielded New Birth during the early seventies. (See *NEW BIRTH*.)

Not nearly so successful as their brother group, The Nite-Liters managed to place two instrumentals on the charts before fading from national popularity. Their records were produced by Harvey Fugua, a veteran of the fifties Moonglows and an A & R director for RCA in 1971.

The Nitty Gritty Dirt Band. Left to right: Jeff Hanna, Jimmie Fadden, John McEwen, Jim Ibbotson

July 71 *K-GEE* /RCA
Feb. 72 *AFRO STRUT* /RCA

The Nitty Gritty
Dirt Band

MEMBERS:
Jeff Hanna (lead vocals, guitar, washboard, harmonica)/born: Aug. 11, 1947
Glen Grosclose (guitar)
Ralph Barr (guitar, banjo)
Les Thompson (guitar, banjo)
Bruce Kunkel (guitar, banjo, fiddle)
David Hanna (bass, drums, percussion)
HOMETOWN: Long Beach, California

This band was an outgrowth of The Long Beach Two, a duet formed in high school by Jeff Hanna and Bruce Kunkel. Gradually adding musicians, they evolved into the five-member Illegitimate Jug Band and eventually into The Nitty Gritty Dirt Band, featuring the above line-up.

During the mid-sixties the group developed a sizable reputation as a zany, rock-oriented jug band, often dabbling in Country and folk as well. Signed by Liberty Records (later purchased by United Artists), they achieved a hit almost immediately with "Buy for Me the Rain." They went on to achieve several additional hits during the seventies, the biggest of which was their top ten recording of "Mr. Bojangles." They became best known, however, for their many albums, including *Pure Dirt, Rare Junk, Alive, Dead & Alive, Uncle Charlie, All the Good Times,* and *Will the Circle Be Unbroken.* In addition, the group was featured in the film version of *Paint Your Wagon.*

Over the years The Nitty Gritty Dirt Band has undergone dozens of personnel changes, varying in size from four to six members. One of their early members was Jackson Browne, who has since gone on to solo stardom.

As of the mid-seventies, the group's line-up consisted of John McEuen, Jim Ibbotson, Jeff Hanna, and Jimmie Fadden.

Apr. 67	***BUY FOR ME THE RAIN/*** **Liberty**
Nov. 70	***MR. BOJANGLES/*****Liberty**
Apr. 71	***THE HOUSE AT POOH CORNER/*****United Artists**
Sept. 71	***SOME OF SHELLEY'S BLUES/*** **United Artists**
Apr. 72	***JAMBALAYA/*****United Artists**
Oct. 74	***THE BATTLE OF NEW ORLEANS/*****United Artists**

Kenny Nolan

HOMETOWN: Los Angeles, California

Kenny has long been a very successful songwriter, turning out hits for others. Among his many winners are "My Eyes Adored You" for Frankie Valli, "Lady Marmalade" for LaBelle, and "Get Dancin'" for Disco Tex & the Sex-O-Lettes.

In 1976 he signed with 20th Century as a recording artist and wrote and recorded a tune called "I Like Dreamin'," which went on to become a top-ten national hit.

Nov. 76	***I LIKE DREAMIN'/*****20th Century**
Apr. 77	***LOVE'S GROWN DEEP/*****20th Century**
Oct. 77	***MY EYES GET BLURRY/*****20th Century**

Ted Nugent

BORN: 1949
HOMETOWN: Detroit, Michigan

In 1963 Ted began his career by joining The Lourds, one of Detroit's most popular rock bands. Two years later he helped form the original Amboy Dukes ("Journey to the Center of the Mind") and for the next ten years

Ted Nugent

developed his unique style of high energy rock.

In 1975 he signed with Epic as a solo performer and since that time has had several platinum albums to his credit.

Aug. 77	***CAT SCRATCH FEVER/*****Epic**
Feb. 78	***HOMEBOUND/*****Epic**
Apr. 78	***YANK ME, CRANK ME/*****Epic**

Laura Nyro

REAL NAME: Laura Nigro
BORN: Oct. 18, 1947
HOMETOWN: Bronx, New York

Laura's first musical influence came from her father, a piano tuner by profession and a part-time trumpeter. In her teens she sang with a number of Bronx street groups, re-creating hits of the fifties and sixties.

During the mid-sixties Laura came to the attention of music publisher Paul Barry, who helped arrange for her signing with the Verve/Forecast label.

She recorded an album titled *More Than a New Discovery,* a very slow seller but the eventual key to her success. A single from the album, "Wedding Bell Blues," became a modest West Coast hit, but, more importantly, other artists began turning her songs into hits. Drawing upon this LP for material, The Fifth Dimension achieved best sellers with "Wedding Bell Blues" and "Blowin' Away," while Blood, Sweat & Tears hit the top of the charts with their version of "And When I Die." After gaining a great deal of attention, Laura was signed by Columbia Records and released a best-selling album called *Eli & the Thirteenth Confession.* From this LP The Fifth Dimension had hits with "Stoned Soul Picnic" and "Sweet Blindness," while Three Dog Night took "Eli's Coming" into the top ten. Barbra Streisand went on to have one of the biggest hits of her career with Laura's "Stoney End." Laura continued with a string of best-selling LP's, including *New York Tendaberry, Christmas and the Beads of Sweat, Gonna Take a Miracle* (on which the backgrounds were sung by LaBelle), and *Smile.*

Ironically, Laura Nyro herself has

Laura Nyro

had only one hit single, and not with her own material! Rather, she placed on the charts with a remake of The Drifters' "Up on the Roof."

Today after spending nearly three years in semiretirement as a resident of a Massachusetts fishing village, Laura Nyro once again makes New York her home.

Oct. 70   *UP ON THE ROOF* / Columbia

Ocean

MEMBERS:
Janice Morgan (lead vocals)
David Tamblyn (lead guitar)
Greg Brown (keyboards)
Jeff Jones (bass)
Charles Slater (drums)

HOMETOWN: London, Ontario, Canada

Formed during the early seventies, Ocean began as a club band in their home province of Ontario. Much of their material was drawn from other leading Canadian artists, including Ian & Sylvia, David Clayton-Thomas, Ronnie Hawkins & The Hawks (who later evolved into The Band), and singer-songwriter Gene MacLellan.

Ocean began recording in 1971 and almost immediately achieved a major international hit with MacLellan's composition of "Put Your Hand in the Hand." After a number of additional American chart entries, their popularity began to center mainly in Canada, where they made their home on a large farm in the city of Markham (just outside of Toronto).

Mar. 71 *PUT YOUR HAND IN THE HAND* / Kama Sutra
June 71 *DEEP ENOUGH FOR ME* / Kama Sutra
Aug. 71 *WE GOT A DREAM* / Kama Sutra
Sept. 72 *ONE MORE CHANCE* / Kama Sutra

Alan O'Day

BORN: Oct. 3, 1940
HOMETOWN: Hollywood, California

The son of a newspaper photographer, Alan formed a rock band while in high school and played the music of the rock stars of the fifties. It was during this time that he began writing tunes and getting seriously involved with music as a profession.

After working with many local groups in Los Angeles, Alan, in 1971, signed with Warner Brothers and began writing tunes for other performers. Throughout the seventies he has written many tunes, including "Angie Baby" for Helen Reddy and "Rock 'n' Roll Heaven" for The Righteous Brothers.

Early in 1977 a new label, Pacific Records, was to be started and O'Day was to have the distinction of being the new label's first artist. He recorded his debut album, *Appetizers,* whose song, "Undercover Angel" went on to become a number one national hit.

Apr. 77 *UNDERCOVER ANGEL* / **Pacific**
Oct. 77 *STARTED OUT DANCING, ENDED UP MAKING LOVE* / **Pacific**

Kenny O'Dell

REAL NAME: Kenneth Gist, Jr.

A native of Oklahoma, Kenny O'Dell grew up in a number of cities, eventually settling in the Los Angeles area. After graduating from high school, he formed the record company Mar-Kay (named after his parents) and released his own recording of "Old Time Love." It became a modest regional hit in southern California and prompted him to make the music business his career.

During the early sixties O'Dell played briefly with Duane Eddy's band, ultimately leaving to form his own group, called Guys & Dolls. He spent nearly five years traveling with the group, all the while writing songs and circulating demo tapes of his material. One of these, a song called "Beautiful People," was bought by the small Vegas label—which was based, naturally, in Las Vegas. Given to the White Whale label for national distribution, the record reached the Top 40 and generated a similarly successful cover version by Bobby Vee. At the same time, a group known as Rose Garden reached the top twenty with a Kenny O'Dell song titled "Next Plane to London." After one additional hit, Kenny O'Dell faded from national popularity and moved to Nashville to enter the Country music field.

After operating Bobby Goldsboro's publishing company for a number of years, O'Dell was signed as an artist by the Capricorn label. Today his songs are widely recorded by such leading artists as Charlie Rich, Dottie West, and Loretta Lynn.

Nov. 67 *BEAUTIFUL PEOPLE* /Vegas
Feb. 68 *SPRINGFIELD PLANE* /Vegas

Odyssey

MEMBERS:
Lillian Lopez (vocals)/born: Nov. 16, 1945
Louise Lopez (vocals)/born: Feb. 22, 1943
Tony Reynolds (bass guitar)

HOMETOWN: New York City

Lillian, along with sister Louise, moved from their country, the Virgin Islands, to Stamford, Connecticut, and toured in a show called *From Broadway to Stamford,* which starred Duke Ellington. Manila-born Reynolds came to New York and became a musician playing in many dance bands.

Early in 1977 they met and signed with Tommy Mottola, who manages Hall & Oates and Dr. Buzzard's Savannah Band.

Writers Sandy Linzer and Denny Randell wrote a tune about a person from the city they love best called "Native New Yorker," and presented the song to Odyssey. Arranger Charlie Calello took the trio into the studio to record the song and the result was a smash disco hit for their RCA debut.

Nov. 77 *NATIVE NEW YORKER* /RCA
May 78 *WEEKEND LOVER* /RCA

The Ohio Express

MEMBERS:
Dale Powers (lead guitar)
Douglas Grassel (rhythm guitar)
James Pfayler (keyboards)
Dean Kastran (bass)
Tim Corwin (drums)

This was one of several studio groups manufactured by producers Jerry Kasenetz and Jeff Katz. Their first recording, "Beg, Borrow & Steal," was an adaptation of "Louie Louie" and was released on the Attack label under the name of The Rare Breed. However, the same master was later released by The Ohio Express on Attack's parent label, Cameo Records. Reaching the twenties on the charts, it firmly established the group's name.

In 1968 one of the executives of

Cameo, Neil Bogart, became affiliated with the Buddah label. Taking the "Ohio Express" name and his association with the producers along, he began releasing records in the "bubble gum" vein that had worked so well for The 1910 Fruitgum Company. As the records became major best sellers, the above line-up of musicians was recruited to make personal appearances as The Ohio Express.

Along with most of the other "bubble gum" groups, The Ohio Express had faded from the charts by the end of 1969.

Oct. 67	BEG, BORROW & STEAL / Cameo
Feb. 68	TRY IT / Cameo
May 68	YUMMY, YUMMY, YUMMY / Buddah
Aug. 68	DOWN AT LULU'S / Buddah
Oct. 68	CHEWY, CHEWY / Buddah
Mar. 69	SWEETER THAN SUGAR / Buddah
Mar. 69	MERCY / Buddah
June 69	PINCH ME / Buddah
Sept. 69	SAUSALITO / Buddah

The Ohio Players

MEMBERS:

Leroy "Sugar" Bonner (lead guitar)

Bruce Napier (trumpet) / (left group in 1973)

Marvin "Merve" Pierce (flügelhorn)

Andrew Noland (alto sax, tenor sax) / replaced by Clarence "Satch" Satchell

Walter Morrison (keyboards) / replaced by William "Billy" Beck

Ralph Middlebrooks (trumpet)

Marshall "Rock" Jones (bass)

Greg Webster (drums) / replaced by James "Diamond" Williams

Clarence "Chet" Willis (rhythm guitar) / (added to group in 1975)

HOMETOWN: Dayton, Ohio

This group began during the early sixties as Greg Webster & The Ohio Untouchables. A well-known club band in the Northeast, they backed up Wilson Pickett on his recording of "I Found a Love." During the mid-sixties three members from another band joined the group, and they became The Ohio Players.

In 1967 The Players launched their recording career on the small Compass label and became active as a studio back-up band. At one particular session they recorded some of their own material during a break and, without their knowledge, a friend sent the tape to Capitol Records. The result was a contract with the label, and they cut their first album, titled Observation in Time. When this failed to become successful, the group switched their affiliation to the Detroit-based Westbound label, after which their releases began appearing on the national charts.

During 1974 The Ohio Players changed labels one again, this time to Mercury, and recorded an album called Skin Tight, which yielded two hit singles. Their next album Fire, produced a number one single of the same name.

Today The Ohio Players are a leading concert attraction, with one of the most visual stage presentations in the Soul field.

Dec. 71	PAIN / Westbound
Feb. 73	THE FUNKY WORM / Westbound
Aug. 73	ECSTASY / Westbound
June 74	THE JIVE TURKEY / Mercury
Sept. 74	SKIN TIGHT / Mercury
Dec. 74	FIRE / Mercury
May 75	I WANT TO BE FREE / Mercury
Sept. 75	SWEET STICKY THING / Mercury
Nov. 75	LOVE ROLLERCOASTER / Mercury
Feb. 76	RATTLESNAKE / Westbound
Feb. 76	FOPP / Mercury
June 76	WHO'D SHE COO / Mercury

The Ohio Players

Jan. 77 ***FEEL THE BEAT (EVERYBODY DISCO) / Mercury***
July 77 ***O-H-I-O / Mercury***

The O'Jays

MEMBERS:

Walter Williams / born: Aug. 25, 1942

Edward Levert / born: June 16, 1942

William Powell / died: May 26, 1977 / replaced (1976) by Sam Strain / born: Dec. 9, 1941

William Isles / (left group in 1965)

Robert Massey / (left group in 1972)

HOMETOWN: Canton, Ohio

Originally known as The Mascots, this group began in 1958 as a quintet at Canton, Ohio's McKinley High School. Early in their career, they made the acquaintance of (then) Cleveland disc jockey Eddie O'Jay, who was so helpful that they renamed their group in his honor.

In 1960 The O'Jays launched their recording career with a song titled "Miracles." Although the tune was originally released on the small Dayco label, the master was sold to Apollo and became a modest R & B hit. After a brief affiliation with another small company, Little Star, the group began working with producer H.B. Barnum at Imperial. They achieved a number of national hits before Imperial ceased operations during the mid-sixties and was absorbed by United Artists.

In 1969, after brief affiliations with Minit and Bell (and three chart entries on the latter label), The O'Jays signed

The O'Jays. Left to right: Walt Williams, Eddie Levert, Sam Strain

with Gamble & Huff's Neptune label. Kenny Gamble and Leon Huff eventually became proprietors of Philadelphia International, giving The O'Jays a vehicle for major success. Their release of "Back Stabbers" very nearly reached the top of the charts and has been followed by an unbroken string of Soul and Pop hits.

Today The O'Jays are reduced to three in number. Bill Isles left to pursue other interests in 1965, while Bobby Massey, who retired from performing in 1972, has remained as a musical consultant for the group. Sam Strain (formerly of Little Anthony & The Imperials) replaced William Powell in February 1976. William died in Canton a little over a year later.

Sept. 63	*THE LONELY DRIFTER* / Imperial
May 65	*LIPSTICK TRACES* /Imperial
Aug. 65	*I'VE CRIED MY LAST TEAR* / Imperial
Oct. 66	*STAND IN FOR LOVE* / Imperial
Nov. 67	*I'LL BE SWEETER TOMORROW* /Bell
June 68	*LOOK OVER YOUR SHOULDER* /Bell
Sept. 68	*THE CHOICE* /Bell

Aug. 69 *ONE NIGHT AFFAIR* / **Neptune**
Apr. 70 *DEEPER* / **Neptune**
Sept. 70 *LOOKY LOOKY* / **Neptune**
July 72 *BACK STABBERS* /
Philadelphia International
Nov. 72 *992 ARGUMENTS* /
Philadelphia International
Jan. 73 *LOVE TRAIN* / **Philadelphia International**
May 73 *TIME TO GET DOWN* /
Philadelphia International
Dec. 73 *PUT YOUR HANDS TOGETHER* / **Philadelphia International**
Apr. 74 *FOR LOVE OF MONEY* /
Philadelphia International
Dec. 74 *SUNSHINE* / **Philadelphia International**
May 75 *GIVE THE PEOPLE WHAT THEY WANT* / **Philadelphia International**
July 75 *LET ME MAKE LOVE TO YOU* /
Philadelphia International
Nov. 75 *I LOVE MUSIC* / **Philadelphia International**
Mar. 76 *LIVIN' FOR THE WEEKEND* /
Philadelphia International
Jan. 77 *DARLIN' DARLIN' BABY (SWEET TENDER LOVE)* /
Philadelphia International
Apr. 78 *USE TA BE MY GIRL* /
Philadelphia International

The O'Kasions

MEMBERS:
Donny Weaver (lead vocals, bass guitar) / born: 1946

Jimmy Hennant (guitar) / born: 1947

Wayne Pittman (lead guitar) / born: 1947

Jim Spidel (sax) / born: 1949

Bruce Joyner (drums) / born: 1946

Ron Turner (trumpet) / born: 1947

HOMETOWN: North Carolina

These six musicians first got together in the late sixties and were first known as The Kays. They began by playing spiritual music, but eventually moved toward rock.

In 1968 they recorded a song written by guitarist Wayne Pittman, "Girl Watcher," which went on to become a top ten national hit.

Aug 68 *GIRL WATCHER* / **ABC**
Nov. 68 *LOVE MACHINE* / **ABC**

Danny O'Keefe

HOMETOWN: Spokane, Washington

Danny O'Keefe began singing at a young age, teaching himself the guitar by imitating the Country music that he heard on the radio. After attending a military high school in St. Paul, Minnesota, he remained in that city for a period of time, working at a hospital and singing in the area's coffeehouses.

During the sixties, O'Keefe returned to his home state of Washington and eventually signed with the Seattle-based Jerden label. After some regional success, he traveled to Los Angeles in search of a bigger company and met Ahmet Ertegun of Atlantic. Signed to the label, O'Keefe recorded two albums during the early seventies, *Danny O'Keefe* and *O'Keefe*—the latter yielding a top ten single titled "Good Time Charlie's Got the Blues."

Today Danny O'Keefe is best known for his albums, including *Breezy Stories* and *So Long Harry Truman*. He records for Warner Brothers Records.

Sept. 72 *GOOD TIME CHARLIE'S GOT THE BLUES* / **Signpost-Atlantic**

Mike Oldfield

BORN: May 15, 1953
HOMETOWN: Reading, Essex, England

Mike Oldfield expressed an interest in music as a young child, launching his recording career at fourteen by teaming up with his sister under the name of Sallyangie. The duo made an album of acoustic folk songs for the Transatlantic label, after which Mike left to form a group called Barefeet. A short-lived group, Barefeet's agency was the same one that booked rock star Kevin Ayers, and this led to Oldfield's participation in Ayers's new band, The New World. During the early seventies, Oldfield achieved wide acclaim for his guitar work on two of the group's albums, *Shooting at the Moon* and *Whatevershebringswesing.*

In 1972 Oldfield left The New World to begin work on a massive symphonic-rock composition titled *Tubular Bells.* Nearly nine months in the making, this piece featured Oldfield playing literally dozens of different acoustic and electronic instruments and thousands of overdubs! No sooner was "Tubular Bells" released by the Virgin label than the producers of *The Exorcist* chose the piece for use in that film. As a result, the album became an international best seller and yielded a top ten single of the main theme.

Mike Oldfield has continued into the mid-seventies with two projects of similar scope: *Hergest Ridge* and *Omnadawn.*

Feb. 74 *TUBULAR BELLS* / Virgin

Oliver

REAL NAME: William Oliver Swofford
BORN: Feb. 22, 1945
HOMETOWN: Wilkesboro, North Carolina

Oliver began his singing career during the early sixties while a student at the University of North Carolina. Joining a bluegrass band called The Virginians, he toured the southern campus-and-coffeehouse circuit until the group broke up.

During the late sixties, Oliver helped organize a Country-rock band known as The Good Earth. Upon traveling to New York, the group became acquainted with writer-producer Bob Crewe, who began working with them. Before long, however, The Good Earth began slowly to disintegrate, eventually leaving Oliver to continue on a solo basis.

In 1968, just after the Broadway opening of *Hair,* Bob Crewe produced one of the show's songs, "Good Morning Starshine," with one of the artists signed to his label, Eddie Rambeau. This record achieved no success whatsoever, and Crewe decided to try again. Using the identical music track, he made a new recording of the song by substituting Oliver's voice for Rambeau's. Leased to the Jubilee label for national distribution, "Good Morning Starshine" became an instant best seller, soon reaching the top of the charts. Oliver followed with "Jean," the theme from the movie *The Prime of Miss Jean Brodie,* and two additional hits before fading from national popularity.

Today Oliver performs under his real name, Bill Swofford, and tours with a small folk-oriented back-up combo.

May 69 *GOOD MORNING STARSHINE* / Jubilee
Aug. 69 *JEAN* / Crewe
Nov. 69 *SUNDAY MORNING* / Crewe
Apr. 70 *ANGELICA* / Crewe

The Original Caste

MEMBERS:
Bruce Innes
Dixie Lee Innes
Graham Bruce
Joseph Cavender
Bliss Mackie

This folk-oriented group of native Canadians was formed during the mid-sixties by Bruce Innes, a veteran of several folk groups, including those led by Maury Wills and Josh White.

After building a reputation in clubs, The Original Caste was signed by Dot Records. The group achieved a number of best sellers in Canada, most notably a record titled "Can't Make It Anymore." Signing with the T.A. label in 1969, they placed high on the American charts with "One Tin Soldier," the same song that would later become widely known as "The Theme from *Billy Jack.*" (See *COVEN.*)

Although "One Tin Soldier" was their sole American chart entry, the group's subsequent releases became major hits in both Canada and Japan. One of their records, "Mr. Monday," actually reached number one on the Japanese charts!

Nov. 69 *ONE TIN SOLDIER* / T.A.

The Originals

MEMBERS:
Fred Gorman
Henry Dixon
Walter Gaines
Crathman Spencer / replaced by Ty Hunter
HOMETOWN: Detroit, Michigan

The Originals emerged during the mid-sixties with a sound reminiscent of the R & B "doo-wopp" groups of the fifties. The group was structured by Frank Gorman, a one-time solo artist for Detroit's Ric-Tic label and one of Motown's staff songwriter-producers.

Beginning in 1969 The Originals achieved four chart entries on Motown's subsidiary Soul label, eventually disbanding during the early seventies. However, they regrouped in 1975, with Ty Hunter replacing original member Crathman Spencer, and began recording for the parent label (Motown) under the production auspices of Lamont Dozier.

Sept. 69 *BABY, I'M FOR REAL* / Soul

Feb. 70 *THE BELLS* / Soul
Aug. 70 *WE CAN MAKE IT BABY* / Soul
Dec. 70 *GOD BLESS WHOEVER SENT YOU* / Soul

Tony Orlando & Dawn

See *DAWN.*

Orleans

MEMBERS:
John Hall (lead guitar, vocals) / born: 1948 / Baltimore, Maryland
Lawrence Hoppen (guitar, keyboards, lead vocals) / born: 1951 / Bayshore, Long Island, New York
Lance Hoppen (bass) / born: 1954 / Bayshore, Long Island, New York
Wells Kelly (vocals, organ)
Jerry Marotta (drums)
HOMETOWN: New York City

Orleans was organized in 1972 by John Hall, a New York theater composer and veteran East Coast session guitarist.

After building a strong following on the northeastern bar-and-club circuit, Orleans was signed during the mid-seventies by Asylum Records. Beginning with a moderate hit titled "Let There Be Music," the group went on to achieve two major best sellers that nearly reached the top of the charts— "Dance with Me" and "Still the One" (written by John and his wife, Johanna).

In June 1975, Orleans became the last band to play L.A.'s Troubador before the famed club went permanently dark.

In June 1977, John left the group to become a solo performer, after which the rest of the group disbanded.

Apr. 75 *LET THERE BE MUSIC* / Asylum
July 75 *DANCE WITH ME* / Asylum

Orleans. Left to right: Wells Kelly, Larry Hoppen, Jerry Marotta, Lance Hoppen, John Hall

July 76   *STILL THE ONE* / **Asylum**
Jan. 77   *REACH* / **Asylum**

Orpheus

MEMBERS:
Bruce Arnold (lead guitar)
Jack McKenes (rhythm guitar)
John Eric Gulliksen (bass)
Harry Sandler (drums)
HOMETOWN: Boston, Massachusetts

Along with Ultimate Spinach, Orpheus emerged during the late sixties as part of the "Boston sound" that was the subject of a massive promotion campaign by MGM Records. The group was organized by Bruce Arnold and Jack McKenes, two former members of a folk group known as The Villagers.

Although known primarily for their album work, Orpheus placed two singles on the national best-seller lists. One of these, "Can't Find the Time to Tell You," became a number one record in Hawaii.

After widespread interest in the "Boston sound" failed to materialize, Orpheus disbanded during the early seventies.

May 69   *BROWN ARMS IN HOUSTON* / **MGM**
Aug. 69   *CAN'T FIND THE TIME TO TELL YOU* / **MGM**

The Osmonds

MEMBERS:
Alan Osmond / born: June 22, 1949
Wayne Osmond / born: Aug. 28, 1951
Merrill Osmond / born: Apr. 30, 1953
Jay Osmond / born: Mar. 2, 1955
Donny Osmond / born: Dec. 9, 1957
Olive Marie Osmond / born: Oct. 13, 1959
Jimmy Osmond / born: Apr. 16, 1963

HOMETOWN: Ogden, Utah

The Osmonds emerged during the mid-sixties as one of the most popular musical families of the time.

Their career traces back to their local church where, during the early sixties, brothers Jay, Merrill, Wayne, and Alan performed regularly at social affairs as a "barbershop" quartet. They were so well received that they were invited to tour a number of churches in the West, a trip that resulted in a singing engagement at the Disneyland amusement park. Spotted by the father of singing star Andy Williams, the group was signed to appear regularly on Williams's television show and eventually was offered a contract by MGM Records.

By the time the group began recording, younger brother Donny had joined the act in the lead spot. Beginning with "One Bad Apple," a record first thought by many listeners to be by The Jackson Five, The Osmonds achieved a long series of best-selling singles and albums. In time sister Marie and younger brother Jimmy joined the act, after which the group began recording and making appearances in various combinations.

Today the family lives in Provo, Utah, where they have built an empire surrounding the weekly Donnie and Marie TV show, which is produced in their own studio. Additionally, they own Kolob Records, the label on which their releases now appear.

The Osmonds

Jan. 71 *ONE BAD APPLE* / **MGM**
May 71 *DOUBLE LOVING* / **MGM**
Sept. 71 *YO YO* / **MGM**
Jan. 72 *DOWN BY THE LAZY RIVER* / **MGM**
July 72 *HOLD HER TIGHT* / **MGM**
Oct. 72 *CRAZY HORSES* / **MGM**
June 73 *GOING HOME* / **MGM**

Sept. 73 *LET ME IN* / **MGM**
Aug. 74 *LOVE ME FOR A REASON* / **MGM**
July 75 *THE PROUD ONE* / **MGM**
Oct. 76 *I CAN'T LIVE A DREAM* / **Polydor**

Donny Osmond

Mar. 71 *SWEET & INNOCENT* / **MGM**
Aug. 71 *GO AWAY LITTLE GIRL* / **MGM**
Nov. 71 *HEY GIRL* / **MGM**
Feb. 72 *PUPPY LOVE* / **MGM**
June 72 *TOO YOUNG* / **MGM**
Aug. 72 *WHY* / **MGM**
Mar. 73 *THE TWELFTH OF NEVER* / **MGM**
July 73 *YOUNG LOVE* / **MGM**
Nov. 73 *ARE YOU LONESOME TONIGHT?* / **MGM**
Feb. 75 *I HAVE A DREAM* / **Kolob**
June 76 *C'MON MARIANNE* / **Kolob**

Marie Osmond

Sept. 73 *PAPER ROSES* / **MGM**
Mar. 75 *WHO'S SORRY NOW?* / **Kolob**
Apr. 77 *THIS IS THE WAY THAT I FEEL* / **Kolob**

Donny & Marie Osmond

July 74 *I'M LEAVING IT UP TO YOU* / **MGM**
Nov. 74 *THE MORNING SIDE OF THE MOUNTAIN* / **MGM**
June 75 *MAKE THE WORLD GO AWAY* / **Kolob**
Dec. 75 *DEEP PURPLE* / **Kolob**
Nov. 76 *AIN'T NOTHING LIKE THE REAL THING* / **Kolob**
Nov. 77 *YOU'RE MY SOUL AND INSPIRATION* / **Kolob**

"Little" Jimmy Osmond

Apr. 72 *LONG HAIRED LOVER FROM LIVERPOOL* / **MGM**
Jan. 73 *TWEEDLEE DEE* / **MGM**

Gilbert O'Sullivan

REAL NAME: Raymond Edward O'Sullivan
BORN: Dec. 1, 1946
HOMETOWN: Waterford, Republic of Ireland

Raymond O'Sullivan moved to England at the age of twelve, launching his musical career during his teens in such bands as The Doodles and The Prefects. He later borrowed his stage name from nineteenth-century operetta composers William Gilbert and Arthur Sullivan.

During the late sixties, O'Sullivan played in Rick's Blues (a group led by Rick Davis, later of Supertramp), eventually leaving for a solo career. After making a few unsuccessful'records for CBS and Major Minor, O'Sullivan came to the attention of Gordon Mills, manager of Tom Jones and Engelbert Humperdinck. Signed to Mills's MAM label, he achieved a major British hit single with "Nothing Rhymed" and a best-selling album titled *Himself.* His second album, *Back to Front,* yielded "Alone Again" and "Clair," two singles that reached number one on the American charts.

Today Gilbert O'Sullivan maintains a cottage in Surrey, England, where Tom Jones and Engelbert Humperdinck are his neighbors.

June 72	*ALONE AGAIN (NATURALLY)/* MAM
Oct. 72	*CLAIR/MAM*
Mar. 73	*OUT OF THE QUESTION/MAM*
June 73	*GET DOWN/MAM*
Oct. 73	*OOH BABY/MAM*
Mar. 74	*HAPPINESS IS ME & YOU/* MAM

Otis & Carla

MEMBERS:
Otis Redding / born: Sept. 9, 1941/died: Dec. 10, 1967/Macon, Georgia
Carla Thomas / born: 1947/ Memphis, Tennessee

Both Otis Redding and Carla Thomas rose to fame during the sixties as part of the "Memphis" R & B sound. (See *Otis REDDING* and *Carla THOMAS, Rock On: The Solid Gold Years.*)

In 1967, just prior to Redding's death, these two leading Stax-Volt artists teamed up for a series of record-ings as a duet. Their biggest hit was "Tramp," which reached the national top twenty.

May 67	*TRAMP/* Stax
Aug. 67	*KNOCK ON WOOD/* Stax
Feb. 68	*LOVEY DOVEY/* Stax

The Outsiders

MEMBERS:
Sonny Geraci (lead vocals)/born: 1947/ Cleveland, Ohio
William Bruno (lead guitar)/born: 1945/ Pittsburgh, Pennsylvania
Tom King (rhythm guitar)/born: 1943/ Cleveland, Ohio
Merdin Prince Gunnar "Mert" Madsen (bass, harmonica)/born: 1943/Denmark
Ricky Baker (drums)/born: 1948/Cleveland, Ohio

Known originally as The Starfires, this group was organized in 1965 by Tom King, a veteran of several Cleveland semipro bands. Beginning with "Mert" Madsen, he recruited the other members from the midwestern club circuit and built them into one of the area's leading attractions before the year's end.

Late in 1965 the group began circulating tapes of their material to record companies, meeting with a receptive ear and a contract offer from Capitol. Their initial release, "Time Won't Let Me," reached the top five and prompted the release of an album of the same name. They continued with a string of hits through the end of 1966, including a remake of The Isley Brother's "Respectable."

As their popularity faded, The Outsiders eventually disbanded during the late sixties. In 1972 Sonny Geraci, along with one of The Outsiders' backup musicians, Walter Nims, emerged in a new group called Climax. (See *CLIMAX.*)

Feb. 66	*TIME WON'T LET ME* / Capitol
May 66	*GIRL IN LOVE* / Capitol
Aug. 66	*RESPECTABLE* / Capitol
Oct. 66	*HELP ME GIRL* / Capitol

The Ozark Mountain Daredevils

MEMBERS:

Randle Chowning (lead guitar) / born: 1950

John Dillon (guitar, fiddle, mandolin) / born: 1947

Buddy Brayfield (keyboards) / born: 1951

Steven Cash (harmonica, percussion) / born: 1946

Michael "Supe" Granda (bass) / born: 1951

Lawrence Lee (drums) / born: 1947

HOMETOWN: Springfield, Missouri

This group began as an informal co-operative of musicians who "jammed" together in the Springfield area. As they gradually evolved into a permanent working unit, they were known under various names, such as Family Tree, The Emergency Band, Buffalo Chips & Burlap Socks, Rhythm of Joy, and Cosmic Corncob & His Amazing Mountain Daredevils!

In 1973 the group began recording demos of its material, eventually ending up with a tape of nearly two dozen songs. At the suggestion of their attorney, they sent a copy to David Anderle and Glyn Johns, a team of independent record producers. After arranging for a recording contract with A & M, Anderle and Johns began working with the group, producing a hit single called "If You Want to Get to Heaven." Although they have followed up with a number of additional hits, The Ozark Mountain Daredevils are best known for their albums, including *It'll Shine When It Shines* and *Car over the Lake*.

Today the group makes its home on a farm near Aldrich, Missouri.

Apr. 74	*IF YOU WANT TO GET TO HEAVEN* / A & M
Feb. 75	*JACKIE BLUE* / A & M
Jan. 76	*IF I ONLY KNEW* / A & M
Jan. 77	*YOU KNOW LIKE I KNOW* / A & M

P

Pablo Cruise

MEMBERS:
Cory Lerios (keyboards)
Dave Jenkins (guitar, vocals)
Bud Cockrell (bass guitar, vocals)
Steve Price (drums)
HOMETOWN: San Francisco, California

During the summer of 1973, these four musicians got together and chose the name Pablo Cruise, Pablo suggesting an everyman commonality, and Cruise suggesting a strong, fluid movement. They began playing around the Bay Area and started developing a large following of fans.

They eventually wound up with a recording contract and recorded a couple of albums, but it wasn't until early 1977 when they recorded the album *A Place in the Sun* that things started happening for the group. From that LP came the tune "Whatcha Gonna Do," which was the single that established them as a national sensation.

Apr. 77 *WHATCHA GONNA DO* / **A & M**
Sept. 77 *A PLACE IN THE SUN* / **A & M**
Jan. 78 *NEVER HAD A LOVE* / **A & M**

Pacific Gas & Electric

ORIGINAL MEMBERS:
Charles Allen (vocals)
Glenn Schwartz (lead guitar)
Thomas Marshall (rhythm guitar)
Brent Block (bass)
Frank Cook (drums)

One of the earliest exponents of what came to be known as "West Coast rock," Pacific Gas & Electric emerged in 1969 with a sound strongly influenced by gospel and jazz. Achieving modest success with their first album, *Get It On,* they added a vocal group called The Blackberries and recorded a best-selling album titled *Are You Ready.* An edited version of the title cut was released as a single and reached the top ten on the charts.

During the early seventies, the group underwent a number of major personnel changes, eventually increasing their membership to nine. At the same time, they shortened their name to simply P G & E.

Pacific Gas & Electric
May 70 *ARE YOU READY* / **Columbia**
Oct. 70 *FATHER COME ON HOME* / **Columbia**
P G & E
Mar. 72 *THANK GOD FOR YOU BABY* / **Columbia**

Paper Lace

MEMBERS:
Philip Wright (lead vocals, drums) / born: Apr. 9, 1948 / Nottingham, England
Michael Vaughn (lead guitar) / born: July 27, 1950 / Sheffield, Yorkshire, England
Chris Morris (guitar) / born: Nov. 1, 1954 / Nottingham, England
Carlo Santanna (rhythm guitar) / born: June 29, 1947 / Rome, Italy / (added: 1974)
Cliff Fish (bass) / born: Aug. 13, 1949 / Ripley, Derbyshire, England

Pablo Cruise. Left to right: Bruce Day, Steve Price, Dave Jenkins, Cory Lerios

Paper Lace was organized in 1969 by Philip Wright and Cliff Fish. The group's name was drawn from the fact that their city of origin, Nottingham, is known as "The Lace City."

Beginning as a quartet (Carlo Santanna—not to be confused with Carlos Santana of the American Latin-rock group—joined late in 1974), the group developed a reputation via club work and several television appearances. Eventually coming to the attention of veteran songwriter-producers Mitch Murray and Peter Callander, they were signed to the Bus Stop label and began recording in the early seventies.

In 1974 Paper Lace achieved a major British hit with Murray and Callander's "Billy, Don't Be a Hero," a tale of the American Civil War. Released in the United States by Mercury, it barely dented the charts but generated a cover version by Bo Donaldson & The Heywoods that reached number one. Soon thereafter, Paper Lace followed with a number one American chart entry of their own, titled "The Night Chicago Died."

Apr. 74	*BILLY, DON'T BE A HERO* / Mercury
June 74	*THE NIGHT CHICAGO DIED* / Mercury
Oct. 74	*THE BLACK-EYED BOYS* / Mercury

Robert Parker

BORN: Oct. 14, 1930
HOMETOWN: New Orleans, Louisiana

During the fifties and early sixties, Robert Parker was known as one of the New Orleans area's leading session musicians. He also achieved some regional success as a solo artist on the Ron and Imperial labels.

In 1964 Parker was signed by Nola Records, a new label just formed by producer Wardell Quezergue (and named by combining the initials of New Orleans with the abbreviation for Lou-

365

Paper Lace

isiana—*La.*). Early in 1966 he broke into the national top ten with a dance record titled "Barefootin'," following with a lesser hit called "Tip Toe."

Today Robert Parker continues to do session work and records for Chris Blackwell's Island Records.

Apr. 66 *BAREFOOTIN'* / **Nola**
Jan. 67 *TIP TOE* / **Nola**

Michael Parks

Michael Parks achieved recognition as an actor during the late fifties and early sixties with roles in such films as *The Man Who Came to Dinner, Night Must Fall, Wild Seed,* and *Back in Town.* His major breakthrough came in 1962, when he was offered a starring role in the "Channing" television series.

During the late sixties, Parks starred in another TV series, "Then Came Bronson," for which he also sang the opening theme. Released as a single by MGM, the song, "Long Lonesome Highway," took Michael Parks into the top 20 on the national best-seller lists. It was his only chart entry.

Feb. 70 *LONG LONESOME HIGHWAY* / **MGM**

The Parliaments

MEMBERS:
George Clinton / born: July 22, 1940
Charles Davis / replaced by Calvin Simon
Robert Clinton / replaced by Clarence "Fuzzy" Haskins
Robert Lambert / replaced by Grady Thomas
HOMETOWN: Detroit, Michigan

Formed in 1955, The Parliaments began as a "doo-wopp" group, appearing in clubs alongside such acts as The Heartbeats, The Crows, and the Nutmegs. Within a year they had attracted the attention of ABC-Para-

Parliament-Funkadelic

mount and made their first record, "Poor Willie." After very few sales developed, they signed with the local New label, meeting a similar fate with their second release, "Lonely Island."

In 1960 The Parliaments sent a demo to Detroit's then-infant Motown organization and were signed to a contract. They made a number of recordings during the next five years but, inexplicably, none was ever released. Their next stop was at a small Detroit company, Golden World (later absorbed by Motown), where they achieved a regional hit with a song titled "My Girl." Finally, after switching to yet another Motor City company, Revilot, The Parliaments broke through nationally with their top twenty recording of "(I Wanna) Testify."

During the late sixties, the group underwent a substantial change of personnel, eventually splitting into two groups called Parliament and Funkadelic. (See *FUNKADELIC*.) Today Parliament is a leading group in the Soul market and records for the Casablanca label.

The Parliaments

July 67 *(I WANNA) TESTIFY*/Revilot
Oct. 67 *ALL YOUR GOODIES ARE GONE*/Revilot

Parliament

Aug. 74 *UP FOR THE DOWN STROKE*/Casablanca
June 75 *CHOCOLATE CITY*/Casablanca
May 76 *TEAR THE ROOF OFF THE SUCKER*/Casablanca
Feb. 78 *FLASHLIGHT*/Casablanca

Dolly Parton

BORN: Jan. 19, 1946
HOMETOWN: Sevierville, Tennessee

Dolly was the fourth of a dozen children born in the foothills of the Smoky Mountains. Although times were rough for her as a youngster, she enjoyed writing songs and singing every chance she could, and by age seven could play a guitar proficiently.

At eighteen she left home for Nashville to pursue a singing career, and in a short while was signed by Monument Records. A few years later she met and married Carl Dean and also met

Dolly Parton

country star Porter Wagoner, who asked her to appear on his road show. She eventually went on to become Wagoner's singing partner until 1974 when she went on to become a solo performer.

Today Dolly is more diversified than ever, embracing both pop and country audiences. Her famously teased hair-do and skin-tight outfits have given her an image of uniqueness that has made her one of the hottest current female vocalists.

Jan. 74	*JOLENE* /RCA
June 77	*LIGHT OF A CLEAR BLUE MORNING* /RCA
Oct. 77	*HERE YOU COME AGAIN* / RCA
Mar. 78	*TWO DOORS DOWN* / RCA

The Partridge Family

MEMBERS:

David Bruce Cassidy / born: Apr. 12, 1950 / New York City

Shirley Jones / born: Mar. 31, 1934 / Smithton, Pennsylvania

"The Partridge Family" was a popular TV series during the early seventies. Aside from David Cassidy and his real-life stepmother, Shirley Jones, the "television" family included Daniel Bonaduce, Suzanne Crough, Brian Forster, Jeremy Russell Gelbwaks, Susan Dey, and Ricky Segall.

Beginning in 1970 a long string of hit recordings appeared under the Partridge Family name. However, only David Cassidy and Shirley Jones actually contributed to these records, since the others were primarily actors who were unable to sing. The additional voices heard on the records were provided by studio vocalists.

David Cassidy also achieved a number of hits as a solo artist during the same period. (See *David CASSIDY.*)

Oct. 70	*I THINK I LOVE YOU* / Bell
Feb. 71	*DOESN'T SOMEBODY WANT TO BE WANTED?* / Bell
May 71	*I'LL MEET YOU HALFWAY* / Bell
Aug. 71	*I WOKE UP IN LOVE THIS MORNING* / Bell
Dec. 71	*IT'S ONE OF THOSE NIGHTS* / Bell
Apr. 72	*AM I LOSING YOU* / Bell
July 72	*BREAKING UP IS HARD TO DO* / Bell
Dec. 72	*LOOKING THROUGH THE EYES OF LOVE* / Bell
Apr. 73	*A FRIEND & A LOVER* / Bell

Billy Paul

REAL NAME: Paul Williams
BORN: Dec. 1, 1934
HOMETOWN: Philadelphia, Pennsylvania

Billy Paul

Since his childhood, encouraged by his mother to sing, Billy Paul began working on his style by listening to early recordings by Nat Cole, Diana Churchill, and Sarah Vaughan. With the help of a neighborhood friend, an up-and-coming young comedian named Bill Cosby, Paul launched his professional career at the age of eleven by singing for a local radio station, WPEN. During the late fifties and early sixties, Paul sang with The Flamingos and The Blue Notes, eventually establishing his own Billy Paul Trio. He made a number of recordings for small Philadelphia companies and one for the nationally distributed Jubilee label.

Billy Paul began his climb to fame during the mid-sixties, when he met producers Kenny Gamble and Leon Huff. He recorded several regional hits on their Neptune and Gamble labels, but achieved his major breakthrough when they later emerged as proprietors of Philadelphia International. Beginning with the multimillion-selling recording of "Me & Mrs. Jones," Paul has accrued a series of best-selling singles and albums and has become a leading concert and club attraction.

Today, when not on the road, Billy Paul makes his home in Los Angeles, California.

Nov. 72	*ME & MRS. JONES /* Philadelphia International
Apr. 73	*AM I BLACK ENOUGH FOR YOU? /* Philadelphia International
Jan. 74	*THANKS FOR SAVING MY LIFE /* Philadelphia International
Apr. 76	*LET'S MAKE A BABY /* Philadelphia International

Freda Payne

BORN: Sept. 19, 1945
HOMETOWN: Detroit, Michigan

Interested in music since her childhood, Freda Payne took many years of piano lessons and received a greal deal of encouragement from her teacher to try singing as well. By the time she reached eighteen, she had won so many vocal contests and talent shows that she decided to travel to New York and make singing her career.

During the sixties Freda sang in the chorus of a Pearl Bailey show, toured Europe with Quincy Jones, and sang with the Duke Ellington Orchestra in Las Vegas. She also launched her recording career, making a number of jazz-oriented records for the MGM label.

In 1970 Freda changed musical direction by signing with Invictus, an R & B label owned by the Holland-Dozier-Holland writing-and-production team. Beginning with "Band of Gold," which came close to reaching the top of the national charts, she achieved a series of Pop and Soul hits that lasted well into the early seventies.

Today Freda Payne is a popular

Freda Payne

club attraction, with a style that strongly reflects her jazz origins, while recording for Capitol Records.

Apr. 70	*BAND OF GOLD /* Invictus
Sept. 70	*DEEPER AND DEEPER /* Invictus
Feb. 71	*CHERISH WHAT IS DEAR TO YOU /* Invictus
June 71	*BRING THE BOYS HOME /* Invictus
Oct. 71	*YOU BROUGHT THE JOY /* Invictus
Jan. 72	*THE ROAD WE DIDN'T TAKE /* Invictus

Peaches & Herb

MEMBERS:
Peaches (Francine Barker) / replaced (1968–1969) by Marlene Mack
Herb ("Fame") Feemster / born: 1943
HOMETOWN: Washington, D.C.

Although Peaches & Herb became known during the mid-sixties as The Sweethearts of Soul, they did not start their career as a team.

Francine Barker (nicknamed Peaches during her childhood) was with an all-female group, called The Sweet Things, that came to the attention of writer-producer Van McCoy. Working in association with Dave Kapralik, an A & R director for Columbia Records, McCoy produced a number of recordings for Columbia's subsidiary Date label. Herb Fame had previously come to the label in a similar fashion and had cut several sides as a solo artist.

In 1966 Herb Fame joined The Sweet Things on a tour to promote their individual recordings. While traveling on a train between appearances, Peaches and Herb began singing together and the reaction prompted their producers to team them up as a recording act. Their first release, "We're in This Thing Together," was a very slow seller, but the other side, a remake of the standard "Let's Fall in Love," later began receiving a great deal of airplay in New York. Eventually reaching the top 20 on the national charts, this became the first of nearly a dozen hits for the team, several of which had earlier been recorded by vintage R & B artists.

During the late sixties, Francine Barker briefly left the act for personal reasons, but eventually returned. Today Peaches & Herb operate their own BS record label, giving exposure to new talent in the Baltimore-Washington area. They have also signed with MCA Records.

Dec. 66	*LET'S FALL IN LOVE* /Date
Mar. 67	*CLOSE YOUR EYES* /Date
June 67	*FOR YOUR LOVE* /Date
Sept. 67	*LOVE IS STRANGE* /Date
Dec. 67	*TWO LITTLE KIDS* /Date
Feb. 68	*THE TEN COMMANDMENTS OF LOVE* /Date
May 68	*UNITED* /Date
Nov. 68	*LET'S MAKE A PROMISE* / Date
Mar. 69	*WHEN HE TOUCHES ME* /Date

Aug. 69	*LET ME BE THE ONE* /Date
June 71	*THE SOUNDS OF SILENCE* / Columbia

The People

MEMBERS:
Gene Mason (vocals)
Lawrence Norman (vocals)
Jeff Levin (lead guitar)
Albert Ribisi (keyboards)
Robb Levin (bass)
Dennis Fridkin (drums)
HOMETOWN: San Jose, California

This group was organized during the mid-sixties by Jeff Levin, a former member of a Country-rock band known as The Pine Valley Boys (another member of which was David Nelson, a key figure in the history of The Grateful Dead and The New Riders of the Purple Sage).

After developing a following on the northern California club circuit, The People were signed by Capitol Records and achieved a top 20 single with their recording of "I Love You." They were not heard from again until the early seventies, when they emerged on the Paramount label with an almost entirely new line-up and an album titled *There Are People.*

Apr. 68	*I LOVE YOU* /Capitol

Peter & Gordon

MEMBERS:
Peter Asher /born: June 22, 1944/London, England
Gordon Trueman Riviere Waller /born: June 4, 1945/Braemaer, Scotland

Peter Asher and Gordon Waller met and began performing at Westminster Boys School in London. Billing themselves at first as Gordon & Peter, they performed at school affairs and eventually branched out into nearby clubs.

In 1963 the duo began circulating demo tapes to record companies in the hope of obtaining a contract. Their cause was greatly aided by the fact that Peter's sister, actress Jane Asher, was dating Beatle Paul McCartney at the time, and they were signed early in 1964 by EMI. They launched their career with a Lennon-McCartney song, "World Without Love," which became a sizable British hit and reached the top of the American charts as released on the Capitol label. They followed with another Beatles' song, "Nobody I Know," and a dozen additional hits extending well into 1967. These included a Del Shannon tune, "I Go to Pieces," and "Woman," a song written by Paul McCartney under the pseudonym of Bernard Webb!

Peter & Gordon separated late in 1967, Gordon to perform as a solo artist and Peter to become a producer for Apple Records. One of Peter's first projects was to work with American folksinger James Taylor, and he eventually left Apple to manage Taylor and to build him into a major star. (See *James TAYLOR.*)

Today Peter Asher operates a talent agency and is an extremely successful independent record producer (Linda Ronstadt, etc.), while Gordon Waller has continued his career as a solo performer.

May 64	**A WORLD WITHOUT LOVE / Capitol**
June 64	**NOBODY I KNOW / Capitol**
Oct. 64	**I DON'T WANT TO SEE YOU AGAIN / Capitol**
Jan. 65	**I GO TO PIECES / Capitol**
Apr. 65	**TRUE LOVE WAYS / Capitol**
July 65	**TO KNOW YOU IS TO LOVE YOU / Capitol**
Nov. 65	**DON'T PITY ME / Capitol**
Feb. 66	**WOMAN / Capitol**
May 66	**THERE'S NO LIVING WITHOUT YOUR LOVING / Capitol**
July 66	**TO SHOW I LOVE YOU / Capitol**
Oct. 66	**LADY GODIVA / Capitol**
Dec. 66	**A KNIGHT IN RUSTY ARMOR / Capitol**
Mar. 67	**SUNDAY FOR TEA / Capitol**
June 67	**THE JOKERS / Capitol**

Pilot

MEMBERS:

William Lyall (keyboards) / born: Mar. 26, 1953 / Edinburgh, Scotland

David Paton (bass) / born: Oct. 29, 1951 / Edinburgh, Scotland

Stuart Tosh (drums) / born: Sep. 26, 1951 / Aberdeen, Scotland

Ian Bairnson (lead guitar) / (added to group in 1974) / born: Aug. 3, 1953 / Shetland Isles, Scotland

Pilot was organized in 1973 by three musicians at Edinburgh's Craighall Recording Studios. Bill Lyall was the head engineer, while Dave Paton and Stuart Tosh frequently played there as session musicians. After having decided to form a group, they created their name by forming a word from the initial letters of their last names.

Early in 1974 the group made a demonstration tape and traveled to London in search of a recording contract. They succeeded at EMI and began working almost immediately on their first album, *From the Album of the Same Name.* During these sessions, they were assisted on guitar by an old friend, Ian Bairnson, who was recruited as a permanent member when the group began making personal appearances in November, 1974.

After two British hits, including a number one record titled "January" (later released in the United States), their releases began receiving major American recognition as well. "Magic" reached the top five on the American best-seller lists, and they have contin-

Pink Floyd. Left to right: Dave Gilmour, Roger Waters, Nick Mason, Rick Wright

ued into the mid-seventies with a number of additional entries. Today they record for Arista Records.

Apr. 75 *MAGIC* /EMI
Oct. 75 *JUST A SMILE* /EMI
Jan. 76 *JANUARY* /EMI

Pink Floyd

MEMBERS:
Syd Barrett (lead guitar) / replaced (1968) by David Gilmour / born: Mar. 6, 1947
Rick Wright (keyboards) / born: July 28, 1945
Roger Waters (bass) / born: Sept. 6, 1947
Nick Mason (drums) / Jan. 27, 1945
HOMETOWN: London, England

Beginning in 1965 as an R & B band, Pink Floyd evolved into a highly innovative "underground" group in the vein of the mid-sixties "San Francisco sound." In 1967 they became the first British rock band to use a light show as part of their act and achieved wide acclaim in Britain with their album releases of *Piper at The Gates of Dawn* and *A Saucerful of Secrets.* During this period they also came to the attention of American audiences with the release of their *Pink Floyd* album on Capitol's subsidiary Tower label.

In 1969 Pink Floyd's albums began appearing on Capitol's affiliated Harvest label, including *Ummagumma, Atom Heart Mother, Relics, Meddle, Dark Side of the Moon*, and *A Nice Pair* (a repackaging of their first two releases). Although these records were best sellers, Pink Floyd became most widely known for the many films that utilized the group's music, including *Let's All Make Love in London, The*

Committee, The Valley, Zabriskie Point and *Pink Floyd*. Although not inclined to release many singles, the group's recording of "Money" (an original by Roger Waters—not the R & R standard by Barrett Strong) nearly reached the top ten.

Today Pink Floyd is one of the most visual acts in all of rock, continually presenting new special effects. Its touring equipment includes approximately eleven tons of sound and light devices. They currently record for Columbia Records.

May 73 *MONEY* / Harvest

The Pipkins

The Pipkins were a group of British studio musicians that featured the lead voice of noted session vocalist Tony Burrows.

The group was assembled by producer John Burges to record "Gimme Dat Ding," an unusual novelty song written by Albert Hammond ("It Never Rains in Southern California," etc.) and Mike Hazelwood for a children's television program titled "Oliver & the Underworld."

Released in the United States by Capitol, the record placed within the top ten on the national best-seller lists.

May 70 *GIMME DAT DING* / Capitol

Player

MEMBERS:
Peter Beckett (lead guitar, vocals) / Liverpool, England
Wayne Cook (keyboards, vocals) / Los Angeles, California
Ronn Moss (bass guitar, vocals) / Los Angeles, California
John Charles "J. C." Crowley (guitar) / Galveston Bay, Texas

John Friesen (drums) / Los Angeles, California

Each member of the group had played with various bands all around the country before uniting in Los Angeles. They decided that their own group would have a tight, "soulful" sound.

The group was spotted by veteran producers Dennis Lambert and Brian Potter who quickly signed them to their own label, Haven Records. Shortly thereafter Lambert and Potter negotiated a deal for them with Robert Stigwood's RSO Records whereby Lambert and Potter would remain as the group's producers.

They recorded their debut album called *Player,* from which came a tune Beckett and Crowley had written called "Baby Come Back."

Oct. 77 *BABY COME BACK* / RSO
Mar. 78 *THIS TIME I'M IN IT FOR LOVE* / RSO

Poco

MEMBERS:
James Messina (lead guitar) / born: Dec. 5, 1947 / Maywood, California
Richard Furay (rhythm guitar) / born: May 9, 1944 / Dayton, Ohio
Rusty Young (steel guitar) / born: Feb. 23, 1946 / Long Beach, California
Randy Meisner (bass) / born: Mar. 8, 1946 / Scottsbluff, Nebraska
George Grantham (drums) / born: Jan. 20, 1947 / Cordell, Oklahoma

Poco was organized in 1968 by Jim Messina and Richie Furay, two members of the short-lived Buffalo Springfield group. (See *BUFFALO SPRINGFIELD*.) Originally known as Pogo, they changed their name after becoming aware of the comic strip character of that name.

After several months of rehearsals and their debut performance at L.A.'s

Player. Left to right: Peter Beckett, Wayne Cook, John Friesen, Ronn Moss, J. C. Crowley

Troubador, Poco was signed by Epic Records and began work on their first LP, *Pickin' Up the Pieces*. Their next album *Poco,* became a best seller in 1970, and they placed two singles on the charts as well. They followed with a series of highly successful LPs, including *Deliverin', A Good Feelin' to Know, Crazy Eyes,* and *Poco Seven.*

In 1975 Poco changed affiliation to ABC, and, following a series of personnel changes, their line-up consisted of Paul Cotton (lead guitar), Rusty Young (steel guitar), Tim Schmidt (bass), and George Grantham (drums). Of the original line-up, Jim Messina went on to Loggins & Messina and Richie Furay to The Souther-Hillman-Furay Band. Randy Meisner, after brief subsequent affiliations with Rick Nelson and Linda Ronstadt, became a founding member of The Eagles.

Oct. 70 *YOU'D BETTER THINK TWICE* / Epic

Mar. 71 *C'MON* / Epic
Sept. 75 *KEEP ON TRYIN'* / ABC
Aug. 76 *ROSE OF CIMARRON* / ABC
Aug. 77 *INDIAN SUMMER* / ABC

The Pointer Sisters

MEMBERS:
Ruth Pointer / born: 1946
Anita Pointer / born: 1948
Bonnie Pointer / born: 1951
June Pointer / born: 1954 / (left group, 1974)
HOMETOWN: East Oakland, California

Born the daughters of two ministers (both their mother and their father were preachers at Oakland's Church of God), The Pointer Sisters naturally began singing in church. During their teens the three eldest sisters—Ruth, Anita, and Bonnie—decided on a performing career, developing an act while working at clerical jobs. June Pointer joined the act later, after they were somewhat established.

During the late sixties, the Pointers came to the attention of West Coast producer Dave Rubinson, who arranged for them to break into the recording field with session work. They sang backgrounds on recordings by such acts as Elvin Bishop, Taj Mahal, Little Esther, and Dr. Hook and began accompanying many of these acts on tours.

In 1973, after a brief and unproductive affiliation with Atlantic Records, The Pointer Sisters made their first appearance as a featured act at L.A.'s Troubador. Their rave notices led to a number of major television appearances, during which they established the "scat" style for which they are best known. They emerged late in 1973 on the Blue Thumb label with a top ten recording of Allen Toussaint's "Yes We Can Can," the first of many hits.

Often compared with The Andrews Sisters and other acts of the thirties and forties. The Pointer Sisters today are a major club and concert attraction. June Pointer retired from the act in 1974, and the others have continued as a trio.

Aug. 73	**YES WE CAN CAN /Blue Thumb**
Dec. 73	**THE WANG DANG DOODLE / Blue Thumb**
Oct. 74	**FAIRYTALE /Blue Thumb**
Mar. 75	**LIVE YOUR LIFE BEFORE YOU DIE /Blue Thumb**
July 75	**HOW LONG /Blue Thumb**
Nov. 75	**GOIN' DOWN SLOWLY /Blue Thumb**

The Poppies

MEMBERS:
Dorothy Moore (lead vocals)/born: 1946
Petsye McCune /born: 1946
Rosemary Taylor /born: 1946
HOMETOWN: Jackson, Mississippi

This all-female vocal trio was formed during the mid-sixties by three students at Jackson State College.

With the help of their manager, Bill McCree, The Poppies soon came to the attention of Billy Sherrill, producer for Epic Records. They achieved a substantial national hit early in 1966 with "Lullabye of Love."

In 1976 lead singer Dorothy Moore emerged on Jackson's Malaco label with one of the biggest Soul and Pop hits of the year: "Misty Blue."

Mar. 66 *LULLABYE OF LOVE /Epic*

The Poppy Family

MEMBERS:
Terry Jacks /Winnipeg, Manitoba, Canada
Susan Peklevits Jacks /Vancouver, British Columbia, Canada

Terry Jacks grew up in Vancouver, British Columbia, where his family moved during his childhood. Although he had planned originally on an architectural career, he became extremely interested in music and took the role of lead vocalist for a Vancouver band known as The Chessmen. He met Susan Peklevits during a television appearance, and the two soon married and began singing together professionally.

Under the name of The Poppy Family, Susan and Terry Jacks obtained a contract with London Records and achieved a number of international hits, including the number one recording of "Which Way You Going, Billy?" The continued their partnership until mid-1973, when they announced that both The Poppy Family and their marriage had come to an end.

Beginning late in 1973, Susan and Terry Jacks began pursuing separate careers. Terry achieved major success early in 1974 with his adaptation of "Seasons in the Sun," a Jacques Brel-Rod McKuen song which had previously been recorded by a number of leading rock figures. Susan broke through as a solo artist in 1975.

Today Terry Jacks maintains a large estate in Vancouver, which is the headquarters for his own recording studio and Goldfish record label (for which both Susan and Terry now record). Terry's records are released in the United States by Private Stock, and Susan's by Mercury.

The Poppy Family
Mar. 70 *WHICH WAY YOU GOING, BILLY?* / London
Aug. 70 *THAT'S WHERE I WENT WRONG* / London
Apr. 71 *I WAS WONDERING* / London
July 71 *WHERE EVIL GROWS* / London

Terry Jacks
Jan. 74 *SEASONS IN THE SUN* / Bell
June 74 *IF YOU GO AWAY* / Bell
Dec. 74 *ROCK & ROLL (I GAVE YOU THE BEST YEARS OF MY LIFE)* / Bell

Susan Jacks
Mar. 75 *YOU'RE A PART OF ME* / Mercury

Sandy Posey

BORN: 1947
HOMETOWN: Jasper, Alabama

Determined from her early teens to make music her career, Sandy Posey traveled to Memphis and Nashville to break into the recording field as a session vocalist. In this fashion she came to the attention of producer Chips Moman, who began working with her, and she obtained a contract with MGM Records.

Beginning with her top ten recording of "Born a Woman," Sandy achieved nearly half a dozen national chart hits with her Country-oriented style. Several of her records became major hits in Europe as well—particularly in England.

Today Sandy Posey records for Columbia Records and continues to maintain a large European following. She often tours there with such artists as Tom Jones and Engelbert Humperdinck.

July 66 *BORN A WOMAN* / MGM
Nov. 66 *A SINGLE GIRL* / MGM
Mar. 67 *WHAT A WOMAN IN LOVE WON'T DO* / MGM
June 67 *I TAKE IT BACK* / MGM
Oct. 67 *ARE YOU NEVER COMING HOME* / MGM

Mike Post

Mike Post first became known to rock audiences during the late sixties for his production work with such artists as Kenny Rogers & The First Edition, Mason Williams, and David Clayton Thomas. During the early seventies, he assembled a group of West Coast session musicians and recorded for Warner Brothers under the name of The Mike Post Coalition.

In 1975 Post was asked by Jimmy Bowen (see *Jimmy BOWEN, Rock On: The Solid Gold Years*), president of MGM Records, to record his (Post's) composition of the theme for television's "Rockford Files." The record became a top ten national hit, and was followed by a remake of Reg Owen's "Manhattan Spiritual."

May 75 *ROCKFORD FILES* / MGM
Sept. 75 *MANHATTAN SPIRITUAL* / MGM

Pratt & McClain

MEMBERS:
Truett Pratt / San Antonio, Texas
Jerry McClain / Pasadena, California

Truett, as a youngster, began singing in church choirs and later joined a rock band while in high school. Jerry, a minister's son, started singing in his father's weekly sermons, which were seen on a local TV station.

In 1966 Jerry met Michael Omartian and formed a band called The American Scene. Four years later Omartian brought Pratt and McClain together and they, along with a few other musicians, became Brotherlove. The group started out by doing studio session work and recording many commercials. In 1974 they signed with ABC-Dunhill Records. But it wasn't until Omartian and Steve Barri presented them with a theme song from a TV series that they made the charts—"Happy Days."

Apr. 76 HAPPY DAYS /Reprise
July 76 DEVIL WITH THE BLUE DRESS ON /Reprise

Prelude
MEMBERS:
Ian Vardy
Brian Hume
Irene Hume

This British folk group began during the late sixties as a duo composed of Ian Vardy and Brian Hume. In 1971 they were engaged in a home practice session when Brian's wife, Irene, joined in in a close harmony number and first produced the unusual sound for which the group became known. With Irene recruited as a permanent member, they took the name of Trilogy and began appearing at folk festivals and in local clubs.

In 1973 the group changed its name to Prelude and, after some inconsequential recording work, signed with the Island label. Prelude's first album,

How Long Is Forever, yielded an international hit single version of Neil Young's "After the Goldrush," a record that reached the American top twenty.

Today Prelude is a major British touring attraction with several additional (British) hits to their credit.

Oct. 74 AFTER THE GOLDRUSH /Island

The Premiers
MEMBERS:
Lawrence Perez (lead guitar)
George Delgado (rhythm guitar)
Phil Ruiz (tenor sax)
Joseph Urzua (baritone sax)
Frank Zuniga (bass)
John Perez (drums)
HOMETOWN: San Gabriel, California

One of the earliest exponents of Latin-rock, The Premiers joined such groups as The Midnighters and Cannibal & the Headhunters in paving the way for the later emergence of Santana.

After building a substantial reputation on the southern California club circuit, the group made a "live" recording in 1964 at a club called the Rhythm Room. Their material included "Farmer John," a fifties R & B hit by Don & Dewey, and this was released by the local Rampart label. After becoming a sizable regional hit, it was given over to Warner Brothers for national distribution, eventually becoming a top 20 best-seller.

June 64 FARMER JOHN /Warner Bros.

Elvis Presley
BORN: Jan. 8, 1935/Tupelo, Mississippi
DIED: Aug. 16, 1977/Memphis, Tennessee

Undoubtedly, Elvis was the "King of Rock 'n' Roll," a form of music he sin-

Elvis Presley

glehandedly gave the impetus it needed in the mid-fifties to make it popular with teen-agers.

He has sold more records (over 500 million), had more top ten hits (39), and had more gold records (127) than any other recording artist, and he was the biggest single exponent of rock in the world.

During his lifetime he made 33 films, all of which made money, but only a few TV appearances. Aside from his first television exposure in 1956, on the Dorsey Brothers show, Steve Allen's show, and Ed Sullivan's show, he only made three other TV appearances: on May 12, 1960 he appeared with Frank Sinatra on a show held in conjunction with his discharge from the army; in 1968 he starred in a Christmas special; and in April 1973 he appeared on a satellite broadcast from Hawaii that was seen worldwide by millions of people.

Elvis died of heart failure at his Graceland mansion in Memphis just two days after the anniversary of his mother's death on August 14, 1958 (she also died of heart failure at the age of forty-six).

In September 1977 CBS showed Elvis's last TV concert, which was taped a few months before his untimely death.

The King is dead, but his movies and music live on forever. (For prior career information see *Rock On: The Solid Gold Years*.)

Feb. 74	***I'VE GOT A THING ABOUT YOU BABY/TAKE GOOD CARE OF HER* /RCA**
June 74	***IF YOU TALK IN YOUR SLEEP* /RCA**
Oct. 74	***PROMISED LAND* /RCA**
Jan. 75	***MY BOY* /RCA**
May 75	***T-R-O-U-B-L-E* /RCA**
Oct. 75	***BRINGING IT BACK* /RCA**
Mar. 76	***HURT/FOR THE HEART* /RCA**
Dec. 76	***MOODY BLUE* /RCA**
June 77	***WAY DOWN* /RCA**
Nov. 77	***MY WAY* /RCA**

Billy Preston

BORN: Sept. 9, 1946
HOMETOWN: Houston, Texas

Raised primarily in Los Angeles, Billy Preston began playing piano at the age of three. At ten he played in church with James Cleveland and Mahalia Jackson and played the part of the young W. C. Handy in the film *St. Louis Blues*.

In 1962 Preston was introduced to rock 'n' roll by joining Sam Cooke and Little Richard on what was intended originally as a gospel tour! When they returned, Preston made an album for Cooke's Sar label, entitled "Sixteen-Year-Old-Soul."

During the mid-sixties Preston became the resident keyboard player for television's "Shindig," a situation which brought him to the attention of Ray Charles. They worked on an album together, *The Most Exciting Organ Ever,* and Preston made a series of singles for the Vee Jay label. As a further boost to his career, he toured in 1967 with the Ray Charles revue and began performing extensively in England. During a performance at London's Festival Hall, Preston was spotted by George Harrison, who invited him to the Abbey Road studios to meet The Beatles. He arrived just as they were recording "Get, Back" and was asked to sit in on the session, thus becoming the first American to receive label credit on a Beatles' recording. Additionally, he was recruited for the Apple roster of artists and began recording under the production auspices of George Harrison.

In 1971 Billy Preston signed with the A & M label and began a long series of best-selling singles and albums. Today he tours with a large group of musicians known as The God Squad.

Aug. 69	***THAT'S THE WAY GOD PLANNED IT* /Apple**
Feb. 71	***MY SWEET LORD* /Apple**
Jan. 72	***I WROTE A SIMPLE SONG* /A & M**
Apr. 72	***OUTA SPACE* /A & M**
July 72	***THAT'S THE WAY GOD PLANNED IT* (rereleased)/ Apple**
Sept. 72	***SLAUGHTER* /A & M**
Mar. 73	***WILL IT GO ROUND IN CIRCLES* /A & M**
Sept. 73	***SPACE RACE* /A & M**
Jan. 74	***YOU'RE SO UNIQUE* /A & M**
July 74	***NOTHING FROM NOTHING* / A & M**

Billy Preston

Dec. 74 *STRUTTIN'* / A & M
Oct. 75 *FANCY LADY* / A & M

"Country" Charley Pride

BORN: Mar. 18, 1938
HOMETOWN: Sledge, Mississippi

Charley Pride achieved worldwide fame during the late sixties as Country music's first black star.

Although he showed an early interest in music and bought his first guitar at the age of fourteen, Pride's primary interest was baseball. During his teens he joined the Negro American League

381

and played for the Memphis Red Sox. After a two-year stint in the army, he settled in Montana and played for the Birmingham Black Barons, then briefly played the outfield and pitched for the Los Angeles Angels in 1961.

Pride's musical career began in 1963, when he sang a song over a PA system between ball games. This led to a singing job at a club in Helena, Montana, where his act was caught by Country star Red Sovine. Sovine brought him to the attention of A & R man Chet Atkins, who signed him to a long-term contract with RCA. During the late sixties, Pride achieved a long string of Country hits and, by 1969, his releases were appearing on the national Pop lists as well.

Today Charley Pride and his wife, Roxanne, live in Dallas, Texas. They have three young children: Kraig, Dion, and Angela.

Aug. 69	***ALL I HAVE TO OFFER YOU / RCA***
Nov. 69	***AFRAID OF LOSING YOU AGAIN / RCA***
Mar. 70	***IS ANYONE GOIN' TO SAN ANTONE? / RCA***
July 70	***WONDER COULD I LIVE THERE ANYMORE / RCA***
Oct. 70	***I CAN'T BELIEVE THAT YOU'VE STOPPED LOVING ME / RCA***
Mar. 71	***I'D RATHER LOVE YOU / RCA***
Aug. 71	***I'M JUST ME / RCA***
Nov. 71	***KISS AN ANGEL GOOD MORNING / RCA***
Apr. 72	***ALL HIS CHILDREN / RCA***
Nov. 74	***MISSISSIPPI COTTON PICKIN' DELTA TOWN / RCA***

P. J. Proby

REAL NAME: James Marcus Smith
BORN: Nov. 6, 1938
HOMETOWN: Houston, Texas

Intent on making singing his career, Jim Smith studied it for three years before trying his talents in various Houston-area nightspots. During the late fifties, he traveled to Hollywood, changing his name to Jet Powers and making a number of R & B-oriented records. He also made several demos for Elvis Presley, to whom he was often later compared.

By the early-middle-sixties, Smith had adopted the name of P.J. Proby and was appearing regularly on television's "Shindig" show. Brought to England by the show's producer, Jack Good, he became a major success there in very much the same fashion as Presley did in America during the fifties. His performances featured tight pants (which often split on stage) and suggestive movements and lyrics and were always surrounded by a great deal of controversy. Although his American success never approached his British star status, he did achieve several hits, including the top twenty recording of "Niki Hoeky."

During the late sixties, Proby returned to the United States after a series of severe personal difficulties. He has now returned to England.

Sept. 64	***HOLD ME / London***
Feb. 65	***SOMEWHERE / Liberty***
Jan. 67	***NIKI HOEKY / Liberty***

Procol Harum

MEMBERS:
Ray Royer (lead guitar) / born: Mar. 9, 1945 / replaced by Robin Trower

Gary Brooker (keyboards) / born: May 29, 1949

Matthew Fisher (keyboards) / born: June 10, 1946

David Knights (bass) / born: June 28, 1945

Robert Harrison (drums) / born: Mar. 18, 1947 / replaced by Barry Wilson

Keith Reid (lyricist)/born: Oct. 19, 1945
HOMETOWN: London, England

During the early sixties Gary Brooker. was a member of The Paramounts, a British R & B band that also contained Robin Trower, Chris Copping, and B. J. Wilson. After achieving a number of best sellers with American fifties hits, they became a back-up band for singer Sandie Shaw and eventually disbanded.

In 1965 Brooker became acquainted with Keith Reid, a London lyricist, and the two collaborated on a number of songs. Deciding to record one of them, "A Whiter Shade of Pale," they assembled a group of musicians (the above line-up) under the name of Procol Harum (taken from a cat owned by a friend of Keith Reid's) and produced what was to become one of the largest-selling and most influential rock singles of the sixties. As the group began to tour, they underwent over the years a complex series of personnel changes that saw all the remaining Paramounts, as well as many other musicians, come aboard. Although they achieved several additional hit singles, they became best known for their albums, including *Procol Harum, Shine on Brightly, Salty Dog, Broken Barricades, Live in Concert, Grand Hotel,* and *Exotic Birds & Fruit.*

During the mid-seventies Procol Harum's membership included Mick Grabham (guitar), Gary Brooker (keyboards), Chris Copping (keyboards), Alan Cartwright (bass), and B. J. Wilson (drums). Keith Reid has continued to provide the lyrics.

June 67 *A WHITER SHADE OF PALE /* **Deram**
Oct. 67 *HOMBURG /* **A & M**
May 72 *CONQUISTADOR /* **A & M**

Gary Puckett & The Union Gap

MEMBERS:
Gary "General" Puckett (lead vocals, guitar)/born: Oct. 17, 1942/Hibbing, Minnesota
Dwight "Sergeant" Bement (sax)/born: Dec. 28, 1945/San Diego, California
Gary "Private" Withem (keyboards)/born: Aug. 22, 1946/San Diego, California
Kerry "Corporal" Chater (bass)/born: Aug. 7, 1945/Vancouver, Canada
Paul "Private" Wheatbread (drums)/born: Feb. 8, 1946/San Diego, California

Taking their name from the historic town of Union Gap, Washington, this group achieved fame by appearing in Civil War uniforms, each bearing a different rank:

The group was organized during the mid-sixties by Gary Puckett, a student at San Diego State College. After touring the northwestern club-and-bar circuit for most of 1967, they came to the attention of Jerry Fuller, a well-known songwriter and West Coast producer for Columbia Records. Beginning with "Woman, Woman" (an adaptation of a Glaser Brothers Country hit, "Girl, Girl"), The Union Gap achieved a string of major hit singles. These included two written by Fuller, "Young Girl" and "Lady Willpower."

In 1970 difficulties began to develop among the members of The Union Gap, and the group soon disbanded. Gary Puckett continued as a solo artist, achieving two modest hits before fading from popularity.

Gary Puckett & The Union Gap
Nov. 67 *WOMAN, WOMAN /* **Columbia**
Mar. 68 *YOUNG GIRL /* **Columbia**
June 68 *LADY WILLPOWER /* **Columbia**
Sept. 68 *OVER YOU /* **Columbia**
Mar. 69 *DON'T GIVE IN TO HIM /* **Columbia**
Aug. 69 *THIS GIRL IS A WOMAN NOW /* **Columbia**

Mar. 70 *LET'S GIVE ADAM & EVE ANOTHER CHANCE /* Columbia

Gary Puckett

Oct. 70 *I JUST DON'T KNOW WHAT TO DO WITH MYSELF /* Columbia

Feb. 71 *KEEP THE CUSTOMER SATISFIED /* Columbia

James & Bobby Purify

MEMBERS:

James Purify / born: May 12, 1944 / Pensacola, Florida

Robert Lee Dickey / born: Sept. 2, 1939 / Talahassee, Florida

During the mid-sixties James Purify and his good friend Robert Lee Dickey got together and decided to sing as a duo. They were presented a song writ-

ten by Lindon Oldham and Dan Penn called "I'm Your Puppet," a tune which Robert was to sing lead. Since Robert had trouble with the phrasing of the song, James sang lead. The song was released on Bell Records and became a top ten national hit.

Today James sings with Ben Moore under the name James & Bobby Purify and they record for Mercury Records.

Sept. 66 *I'M YOUR PUPPET /* Bell
Jan. 67 *WISH YOU DIDN'T HAVE TO GO /* Bell
Apr. 67 *SHAKE A TAIL FEATHER /* Bell
July 67 *I TAKE WHAT I WANT /* Bell
Sept. 67 *LET LOVE COME BETWEEN US /* Bell
Jan. 68 *DO UNTO ME /* Bell
Apr. 68 *I CAN REMEMBER /* Bell
Aug. 68 *HELP YOURSELF /* Bell

Queen

MEMBERS:

Fred Mercury (Frederick Bulsara) (lead vocals, keyboards)/born: Sept. 8, 1946/Zanzibar

Brian May (guitar)/born: July 19, 1947/ Hampton, Middlesex, England

John Deacon (bass)/born: Aug. 19, 1951/ Leicester, England

Roger Meadows Taylor (drums)/born: July 26, 1949/Kingslynn, Norfolk, England

One of Britain's leading glitter-rock bands, Queen was organized in 1971 by Brian May and Roger Taylor, two former members of Smile. After the latter band dissolved, they were anxious to begin a new project and first recruited vocalist Freddie Mercury (who suggested the name Queen for the new group). After nearly six months of auditions, they selected John Deacon as their bass player and began actively to rehearse.

In 1973 Queen began its search for a recording contract and succeeded almost immediately at EMI. The group's first album, *Queen,* became an excellent seller in Great Britain and did the same when released in the United States by Elektra. This was followed by *Queen II* and a British top ten single titled *"Seven Seas of Rhye."* Queen's

Queen. Left to right: Freddie Mercury, John Deacon, Brian May, Roger Taylor

major breakthrough with American audiences came with the 1975 release of the album *Sheer Heart Attack,* which became a best seller and yielded the group's first American hit, a top ten record called "Killer Queen." Surpassing this in 1976, Queen reached the top of the album charts with *A Night at the Opera* and achieved a major international hit with "Bohemian Rhapsody."

Feb. 75 *KILLER QUEEN* /Elektra
Jan. 76 *BOHEMIAN RHAPSODY* / Elektra
May 76 *YOU'RE MY BEST FRIEND* / Elektra
Nov. 76 *SOMEBODY TO LOVE* /Elektra
Mar. 77 *TIE YOUR MOTHER DOWN* / Elektra
Oct. 77 *WE ARE THE CHAMPIONS* / Elektra
May 78 *IT'S LATE* /Elektra

?(Question Mark) & The Mysterians

MEMBERS:
Question Mark (Rudy Martinez) (lead vocals)/ born: 1945
Robert Balderrama (lead guitar)/born: 1950
Frank Rodriguez (keyboards)/born: 1951
Frank Lugo (bass)/born: 1947
Edward Serrato (drums)/born: 1947

Of Mexican extraction, ?(Question Mark) & The Mysterians were a group of Texans who began their climb to national fame after relocating in the Saginaw valley region of Michigan. During the mid-sixties they developed a substantial following in the area's teen-age clubs, particularly with a classic punk-rock song called "96 Tears."

The Mysterians had made an amateur recording of the tune, giving it to the Texas-based Pa-Go-Go label for release. As demand began to build in Michigan, however, the group fur-

nished copies of the record to a local radio station in Flint. The song rapidly became one of the station's most requested numbers, and airplay soon spread to a major station in Detroit. This prompted the Cameo label to acquire it for general distribution which pushed it to number one on the national charts. The group was signed to Cameo and followed with a number of additional, although lesser, chart entries.

During the late sixties, The Mysterians emerged amidst the "bubble gum" trend on the Kasenetz-Katz Super-K label. They have since been affiliated with several record companies and, after numerous personnel changes, continue today with their club work.

Sept. 66 *96 TEARS* /Cameo
Nov. 66 *I NEED SOMEBODY* /Cameo
Mar. 67 *CAN'T GET ENOUGH OF YOU, BABY* /Cameo
June 67 *GIRL* /Cameo

Quicksilver Messenger Service

MEMBERS:
Dino Valenti (lead vocals)/born: Oct. 7, 1943/ New York City
John Cipollina (guitar)/born: Aug. 24, 1943/ Berkeley, California
Gary Duncan (guitar)/born: Sept. 4, 1946/San Diego, California
Nicky Hopkins (keyboards)/born: Feb. 24, 1944/London, England
David Freiberg (bass)/born: Aug. 24, 1938/ Boston, Massachusetts
Gregory Elmore (drums)/born: Sept. 4, 1946/ Coronado Naval Air Station, California

One of the original "San Francisco" bands, Quicksilver Messenger Service was organized in 1965 by guitarist David Freiberg. At first he recruited John Cipollina, Gary Duncan, and Greg Elmore, borrowing equipment from Jefferson Airplane and beginning rehearsals at The Matrix coffeehouse. Before long, vocalist Dino Valenti (who, under the name of Chester A. Powers, wrote the rock classic "Get Together") came aboard, as did Nicky Hopkins, the veteran British keyboards player.

Unlike most groups, Quicksilver Messenger Service did not rush to obtain a recording contract. Rather, they worked for nearly two years on their act, becoming regulars at the Haight-Ashbury community's free concerts and often appearing at such major rock showcases as the old Fillmore auditorium and the Avalon Ballroom. Eventually signed by Capitol in 1968, they recorded a series of best-selling albums, including *Quicksilver Messenger Service, Happy Trails, Quicksilver, Just for Love, What about Me,* and *Comin' Through.* They also achieved several entries on the singles charts.

During the early seventies, after a number of personnel changes, the group temporarily drifted apart. Today they are known simply as Quicksilver.

Aug. 69   *WHO DO YOU LOVE?* / **Capitol**
Oct. 70   *FRESH AIR* / **Capitol**
Mar. 71   *WHAT ABOUT ME?* / **Capitol**

Bonnie Raitt

BORN: Nov. 8, 1949
HOMETOWN: Los Angeles, California

Bonnie, whose father is Broadway singer John Raitt, began playing the guitar at the age of twelve and became very interested in country blues music. In 1967 she moved east to attend college in Cambridge, but all the while continued playing her guitar and performing wherever she could. After a few years of school she left to pursue a career as a singer working in clubs in Boston, Philadelphia, and New York. Her interest in the blues continued to grow and in a short while she was able to develop her own passionate blues sound.

In 1971 she signed with Warner Brothers and released her debut album, *Bonnie Raitt,* containing many traditional blues songs.

May 77 *RUNAWAY*/Warner Bros.

Eddie Rambeau

REAL NAME: Edward Cletus Flurie
BORN: June 30, 1943
HOMETOWN: Hazelton, Pennsylvania

Interested in a recording career since his teens, Eddie Rambeau traveled to Philadelphia during the late fifties to audition for the Swan label. He recorded briefly for Swan and made the acquaintance of one of its leading writer-producers at the time, Bob Crewe.

During the early sixties, Crewe established his own organization in New York and signed Rambeau as both a songwriter and an artist. Initially achieving success as the writer of Diane Renay's "Navy Blue," Rambeau later scored as an artist with his major hit recording of "Concrete & Clay." (The song was a hit at the same time for the British group Unit Four + 2.) For the next several years, he pursued an acting career, appearing on the Broadway stage in *Norman Is That You?,* *Heathen,* and *Jesus Christ Superstar.*

Eddie Rambeau reactivated his recording career in 1976 with a disco version of "The Big Hurt." He presently records for the Tom Cat label.

May 65 *CONCRETE & CLAY*/ Dyno-Voice

Rare Earth

MEMBERS:
Rob Richards (guitar)/replaced by Ray Monette
Kenneth James (keyboards)/replaced by Mark Olson
Gil Bridges (sax, flute, percussion)
John Persh (bass, trombone)/replaced by Michael Urso
Peter Rivera (drums)/replaced by Peter Hoorelbeke (lead vocals, percussion)
Edward Cuzman (percussion)
HOMETOWN: Detroit, Michigan

Originally known as The Sunliners (no relation to the Texas group), Rare

Bonnie Raitt

Earth began as a trio consisting of John Persh, Pete Rivera, and Gil Bridges. They spent most of the sixties playing Detroit area clubs and private affairs, eventually adding several members and adopting their new name.

During the late sixties, Rare Earth formed a brief association with Dennis Coffey, who worked with the group to produce a medley of former Motown hits ("Stop in the Name of Love"/"Where Did Our Love Go"). Released by Verve, this record paved the way for the group to be signed by Motown, on a new subsidiary bearing the group's own name! Continuing the pattern of recording earlier Motown hits, Rare Earth achieved major success with their first two releases, "Get Ready" and "I'm Losing You." They followed with a number of additional best sellers, several of which were of original composition.

In 1975 Rare Earth added a five-member back-up group and became a completely self-contained concert attraction.

Mar. 70	*GET READY* / Rare Earth
Aug. 70	*I'M LOSING YOU* / Rare Earth
Dec. 70	*BORN TO WANDER* / Rare Earth
July 71	*I JUST WANT TO CELE-BRATE* / Rare Earth
Nov. 71	*HEY, BIG BROTHER* / Rare Earth
Apr. 72	*WHAT'D I SAY* / Rare Earth
Nov. 72	*GOOD TIME SALLY* / Rare Earth
Jan. 73	*WE'RE GONNA HAVE A GOOD TIME* / Rare Earth
Apr. 78	*WARM RIDE* / Prodigal

The Rascals

MEMBERS:
Gene Cornish (guitar) / born: May 14, 1945 / Ottawa, Canada
Felix Cavaliere (keyboards) / born: Nov. 29, 1944 / Pelham, New York

Edward Brigati (percussion) / born: Oct, 22, 1946 / Garfield, New Jersey

Dino Danelli (drums) / born: July 23, 1945 / Jersey City, New Jersey

MEMBERS (1971):

Ann Sutton (vocals)

Buzzy Feiten (guitar)

Felix Cavaliere (keyboards)

Robert Popwell (bass)

Dino Danelli (drums)

Dec. 65	**I AIN'T GONNA EAT OUT MY HEART ANYMORE** / **Atlantic**
Mar. 66	**GOOD LOVING** / **Atlantic**
June 66	**YOU BETTER RUN** / **Atlantic**
Sept. 66	**COME ON UP** / **Atlantic**
Jan. 67	**I'VE BEEN LONELY TOO LONG** / **Atlantic**
Apr. 67	**GROOVIN'** / **Atlantic**
July 67	**A GIRL LIKE YOU** / **Atlantic**
Sept. 67	**HOW CAN I BE SURE** / **Atlantic**
Dec. 67	**IT'S WONDERFUL** / **Atlantic**
Apr. 68	**A BEAUTIFUL MORNING** / **Atlantic**
July 68	**PEOPLE GOT TO BE FREE** / **Atlantic**
Dec. 68	**A RAY OF HOPE** / **Atlantic**
Feb. 69	**HEAVEN** / **Atlantic**
May 69	**SEE** / **Atlantic**
Sept. 69	**CARRY ME BACK** / **Atlantic**
Jan. 70	**HOLD ON** / **Atlantic**
July 70	**GLORY, GLORY** / **Atlantic**
June 71	**LOVE ME** / **Columbia**

Known at first as The Young Rascals, this group emerged during the mid-sixties as one of the leading "blue-eyed Soul" bands. The Rascals were a spin-off from Joey Dee's back-up band, The Starlighters, of which Gene Cornish, Felix Cavaliere, and Eddie Brigati had been members.

Beginning as a dance band, The Rascals played a number of small clubs and eventually established residency at The Barge, a floating discotheque in the Long Island suburbs of New York City. They were spotted there by Sid Bernstein, who took over management of their career and obtained a recording contract with Atlantic. After a modest hit with "I Ain't Gonna Eat Out My Heart Anymore," the group achieved a number one chart entry with "Good Loving," following with a series of best sellers that lasted well into 1970.

In 1971 the original Rascals disbanded, giving rise to a new five-member group featuring a female lead singer. After two modestly successful albums on Columbia, *Peaceful World* and *Island of Real,* this group dissolved as well. Today Gene Cornish and Dino Danelli are on the Atlantic label in yet another new group, called Fotomaker, while Eddie Brigati records for Elektra Records and Felix does some producing for other artists.

The Raspberries

MEMBERS:

Eric Howard Carmen (lead vocals, guitar, bass) / born: Aug. 11, 1949 / Cleveland, Ohio

Wallace Carter Bryson (lead guitar) / born: July 18, 1949 / Gastonia, North Carolina

David Bruce Smalley (bass) / born: July 10, 1949 / Oil City, Pennsylvania / replaced by Scott McCarl (bass, keyboards, guitar)

James Alexander Bonfanti (drums) / born: Dec. 17, 1948 / Windber, Pennsylvania / replaced by Michael McBride

The Raspberries evolved from a Cleveland-based group called The Choir, known for their late-sixties hit "It's Cold Outside." (See *The CHOIR.*) After some initial success, The Choir began a series of personnel changes that eventually resulted in the addition to the group of Eric Carmen, a veteran of several Cleveland bands. Carmen suggested The Raspberries' name, and the new band began building an act in local clubs.

During the early seventies, the group began circulating demo tapes of their

The Raspberries. Left to right: James Bonfanti, Wally Bryson, Eric Carmen, Dave Smalley

material, one of which attracted the attention of independent record producer Jimmy Ienner. He began working with the group, obtaining a contract with Capitol and producing their first single, "Don't Want to Say Goodbye." By the summer of 1972, their first album, *Raspberries,* was becoming an excellent seller and their second single, "Go All the Way," very nearly did just that by reaching the top five on the charts. They followed with another LP, *Fresh Raspberries,* and a series of hit singles that lasted well into 1974.

In 1973 Jim Bonfanti and Dave Smalley separated from The Raspberries to form a new band called Dynamite. The Raspberries found replacements and continued until 1975, when Eric Carmen announced that he was leaving for a solo career.

May 72	*DON'T WANT TO SAY GOOD-BYE* / Capitol
July 72	*GO ALL THE WAY* / Capitol
Nov. 72	*I WANNA BE WITH YOU* / Capitol
Mar. 73	*LET'S PRETEND* / Capitol
Sept. 73	*TONIGHT* / Capitol
Dec. 73	*I'M A ROCKER* / Capitol
Sept. 74	*OVERNIGHT SENSATION* / Capitol

Lou Rawls

BORN: Dec. 1, 1936
HOMETOWN: Chicago, Illinois

Lou Rawls began singing in church at the age of seven, eventually joining several gospel groups during his teens. During the mid-fifties Rawls traveled to Los Angeles to sing with the well-known Pilgrim Travelers. This resulted in a national tour with Sam

Lou Rawls

Cooke, during which both he and Cooke were involved in a serious auto accident. After several days in a coma, Rawls recovered rapidly and returned to the road within a matter of weeks. (He and Cooke ultimately became good friends, and he is heard singing the "answers" on Cooke's 1962 hit "Bring It on Home to Me.")

The Pilgrim Travelers disbanded in 1959, leaving Rawls to pursue a solo career. The group had recorded briefly for Capitol, and this provided the "connection" he needed to obtain a contract for himself. Debuting during the early sixties with an album titled *Stormy Monday,* Rawls went on to achieve a series of more than 20 best-selling LP's—a string that has continued to the present day. By the mid-sixties, his "rap" singles also were appearing regularly on the charts.

During the early seventies, Lou Rawls switched to the MGM label and recorded Bobby Hebb's Grammy-winning composition of "A Natural Man." Today he continues to make his home in Los Angeles, where he often gives benefit concerts for underprivileged youth and records for Philadelphia International.

June 65	*3:00 IN THE MORNING /* Capitol
Sept. 66	*LOVE IS A HURTING THING /* Capitol
Nov. 66	*YOU CAN BRING ME ALL YOUR HEARTACHES /* Capitol
Jan. 67	*TROUBLE DOWN HERE BELOW /* Capitol
Mar. 67	*DEAD END STREET /* Capitol
July 67	*SHOW BUSINESS /* Capitol
Aug. 68	*DOWN HERE ON THE GROUND /* Capitol
July 69	*YOUR GOOD THING /* Capitol
Nov. 69	*I CAN'T MAKE IT ALONE /* Capitol
Mar. 70	*YOU'VE MADE ME SO VERY HAPPY /* Capitol
Aug. 70	*BRING IT ON HOME /* Capitol
Aug. 71	*A NATURAL MAN /* MGM
June 76	*YOU'LL NEVER FIND ANOTHER LOVE LIKE MINE /* Philadelphia International
Oct. 76	*GROOVY PEOPLE /* Philadelphia International
July 77	*SEE YOU WHEN I GET THERE /* Philadelphia International
Jan. 78	*LADY LOVE /* Philadelphia International

Redbone

MEMBERS:

Lolly Vegas (guitar) / Fresno, California
Anthony Bellamy (guitar) / Los Angeles, California
Pat Vegas (bass) / Fresno, California
Peter De Poe (Last Walking Bear) (drums) / Neah Bay Reservation, Washington / replaced (1974) by Butch Rillera

Formed in 1968 by four musicians of American Indian heritage (the word *redbone* is an Indian slang term for "half-breed"), this group became widely known during the early seventies with a sound called "swamp rock."

Brothers Pat and Lolly Vegas, who form the nucleus of Redbone, originally gained fame during the mid-sixties with their regular appearances on television's "Shindig." They also wrote a number of hit songs, most notably P. J. Proby's "Niki Hoeky," and became leading West Coast session musicians and vocalists. Tony Bellamy first played flamenco guitar at his family's restaurant, later switching to rock in order to play at local dances, while Pete De Poe began as a ceremonial drummer on the reservation where he was born.

After meeting and forming on the West Coast club circuit, Redbone built a reputation with their club and studio work and eventually signed with CBS's subsidiary Epic label. They achieved several single hits, including the chart-topping "Come and Get Your Love," and a number of best-selling albums, including *Redbone, Message From a Drum, Already Here, Wovoka,* and *Beaded Dreams through Turquoise Eyes.*

Today Redbone's music more strongly reflects their Indian heritage, and they are a leading club attraction.

Dec. 70 *MAGGIE*/Epic
July 71 *MAGGIE*(rereleased)/Epic
Nov. 71 *THE WITCH QUEEN OF NEW ORLEANS*/Epic
Jan. 74 *COME AND GET YOUR LOVE*/Epic

Helen Reddy

BORN: Oct. 24, 1941
HOMETOWN: Melbourne, Australia

A performer since infancy, Helen Reddy was born into a show-business family. Her father, Max Reddy (who died in September 1973), was a famed writer, producer, and comic actor while her mother, Stella Lamond (who also died in 1973), was a well-known musical comedienne. Her sister, Toni Lamond, also pursued a stage career, often appearing in Australian productions of Broadway musicals.

In 1966 Helen entered a "Bandstand International" contest sponsored by Mercury/Philips Records. Winning first prize, she traveled to the United States and recorded a single for the company titled "One Way Ticket." Although it gained her some attention, the record sold poorly and Helen spent the next months playing minor club engagements. In October 1966, on her twenty-fifth birthday, Helen was given a surprise party by several of her friends, and one of those to attend was Jeff Wald, an agent for the William Morris agency. Wald not only became her manager and the key to her success, but ultimately her husband as well. Through an old friend, Flip Wilson, Wald arranged for her to appear on the "Tonight Show," and, through another friend, A & R director Artie Mogull, he obtained a contract for her with Capitol Records.

Beginning with "I Don't Know How to Love Him," a song from *Jesus Christ Superstar,* Helen achieved a string of major hits that rendered her one of the leading recording stars of the seventies—including "I Am Woman," an original composition which has become the anthem for the women's liberation movement. Additionally, Helen appeared in the film *Airport '75* and became the regular host for television's "Midnight Special."

Today Jeff and Helen make their home in Brentwood, California. They

Helen Reddy

Helen Reddy

have two children, fifteen-year-old Traci (heard on Helen's recording of "You and Me Against the World") and five-year-old Jordan.

Feb. 71	*I DON'T KNOW HOW TO LOVE HIM* / Capitol
Aug. 71	*CRAZY LOVE* / Capitol
Dec. 71	*NO SAD SONG* / Capitol
June 72	*I AM WOMAN* / Capitol
Feb. 73	*PEACEFUL* / Capitol
Sept. 73	*DELTA DAWN* / Capitol
Nov. 73	*LEAVE ME ALONE* / Capitol
Mar. 74	*KEEP ON SINGING* / Capitol
June 74	*YOU AND ME AGAINST THE WORLD* / Capitol
Oct. 74	*ANGIE BABY* / Capitol
Feb. 75	*EMOTION* / Capitol
July 75	*BLUEBIRD* / Capitol
Aug. 75	*NO WAY TO TREAT A LADY* / Capitol
Dec. 75	*SOMEWHERE IN THE NIGHT* / Capitol
Aug. 76	*I CAN'T HEAR YOU NO MORE* / Capitol
Apr. 77	*YOU'RE MY WORLD* / Capitol
Oct. 77	*THE HAPPY GIRLS* / Capitol

Lou Reed

REAL NAME: Louis "Butch" Firbank
BORN: Mar. 2, 1944
HOMETOWN: Freeport, New York

Lou Reed began playing professionally during his early teens, leading such Long Island bands as Pasha & The Prophets, The Jades, and The Eldorados (not to be confused with the fifties R & B group). In 1965 he became a founding member of Velvet Underground, a highly acclaimed drug-oriented band organized by cult figure Andy Warhol.

When Velvet Underground disband-ed in 1970, Reed began recording solo for RCA and achieved a number of best-selling albums, including *Lou Reed, Transformer, Berlin, Rock & Roll Animal,* and *Sally Can't Dance.* In addition he scored with a top 20 single hit version of "Walk on the Wild Side."

Today Lou Reed makes his home on the Upper East Side of New York City. He continues to perform and is often referred to as "The King of Decadence" and "The Prince of Darkness."

Feb. 73 *WALK ON THE WILD SIDE / RCA*

Lou Reed

The Reflections

MEMBERS:

Anthony Micale (lead vocals)/born: Aug. 23, 1942/Bronx, New York

Phil Castrodale (first tenor)/born: Apr. 2, 1942/ Detroit, Michigan

Daniel Bennie (second tenor)/born: Mar. 13, 1940/Johnstone, Scotland

Raymond Steinberg (baritone)/born: Oct. 29, 1942/Washington, Pennsylvania

John Dean (bass)/Detroit, Michigan

This vocal group was formed in Detroit during the early sixties and began performing at hops sponsored by local deejays. Since they had no back-up band of their own, they were accompanied during their appearances by various house bands.

In 1963 The Reflections were signed by Ed Wingate's Detroit-based Golden World label and achieved an immediate regional hit with "Just like Romeo and Juliet." The success of the record soon spread to other markets, and it eventually placed within the top five on the national best-seller lists.

After two more national chart entries, Golden World ceased operations and The Reflections signed with ABC. However, they were not able to duplicate their initial success and their popularity continued to center mainly in the Detroit area.

Apr. 64	**JUST LIKE ROMEO & JULIET /** Golden World	
July 64	**LIKE COLUMBUS DID /** Golden World	
Mar. 65	**POOR MAN'S SON /** Golden World	

Diane Renay

REAL NAME: Renee Diane Kushner
HOMETOWN: Philadelphia, Pennsylvania

Diane Renay developed a serious interest in singing during her early teens.

Through her father, who was connected with the entertainment industry, Diane became acquainted with writer-producers Frank Slay and Bob Crewe, who were based largely in Philadelphia during the late fifties and early sixties.

Late in 1963 Crewe produced Diane's recording of "Navy Blue," a song written by Eddie Rambeau of "Concrete & Clay" fame. Released by 20th Century Fox, the record nearly reached the top of the charts and was followed successfully by a similar song, "Kiss Me Sailor."

Today, Diane is married and has retired to private life, while continuing to make her home in Philadelphia.

Jan. 64	**NAVY BLUE /20th Century Fox**
Apr. 64	**KISS ME SAILOR /20th Century Fox**

Reunion

MEMBERS:
Joey Levine (lead vocals)
Norman Dolph
Paul DiFranco
Marc Bellack
HOMETOWN: New York City

Not actually a working group, Reunion was the collective name assumed by several producers who cut a number of records for RCA. Their productions featured the lead voice of Joey Levine, who was also the studio voice of The Ohio Express, The 1910 Fruitgum Company, and numerous other groups.

Reunion reached the top ten late in 1974 with "Life Is a Rock," an unusual song whose lyrics were made up of song titles, names of performers, and assorted facts taken from rock 'n' roll history. Beginning with "Disco-Tekin" in 1975, the "group" changed direction and began making records to capitalize on the disco craze of the mid-seventies.

Sept. 74 *LIFE IS A ROCK (BUT THE RADIO ROLLED ME)* /RCA

Rhythm Heritage
MEMBERS:
Scott Edwards (bass guitar)
Ed Greene (drums)
Jay Graydon (lead guitar)
Victor Feldman (percussion)
Ernie Watts (horns)
Fred Seldon (horns)
Chuck Findley (horns)
Steve Madio (horns)
Oren Waters (vocals)
Luther Waters (vocals)
HOMETOWN: Los Angeles, California

In 1975, during the disco craze, Steve Barri and Michael Omartian assembled a group of studio musicians from Los Angeles and recorded disco-style the theme from a popular TV series. The result was the song "Theme from S.W.A.T.," which went on to become a number one national hit.

Nov. 75 *THEME FROM S.W.A.T.* /ABC
Apr. 76 *BARETTA'S THEME (KEEP YOUR EYE ON THE SPARROW)* /ABC
Feb. 77 *THEME FROM ROCKY (GONNA FLY NOW)* /ABC

Cliff Richard
REAL NAME: Harry Roger Webb
BORN: Oct. 14, 1940
HOMETOWN: Lucknow, India

In 1948 Richard's family left India for England, where he began to take an active interest in music. By 1959 he had a single called "Living Doll" that made the American charts, but it was the last one to achieve such transatlantic prominence for quite some time. Although he was extremely popular on radio, on TV, and with records in Great Britain throughout the fifties and sixties, he could never duplicate this success in the United States, although he had a few more releases on Epic Records in this country during that period. In early 1976 he signed with Rocket Records and recorded the album *I'm Nearly Famous,* from which came the top ten smash "Devil Woman." At last Richard had found the success in the United States that he had been searching for for almost eighteen years.

July 76 *DEVIL WOMAN* /Rocket
Dec. 76 *I CAN'T ASK FOR ANYMORE THAN YOU* /Rocket
June 77 *DON'T TURN THE LIGHT OUT* /Rocket

Jeannie C. Riley
BORN: Oct. 19, 1945
HOMETOWN: Anson, Texas

Interested in singing since her childhood, Jeannie traveled to Nashville during the mid-sixties to break into the country-music business. Between 1966 and 1968, she worked in several music-related fields, cutting demos for such Country stars as Johnny Paycheck and The Wilburn Brothers and doing secretarial chores for Jerry Chesnut's Passkey music publishing firm.

In 1968 one of Jeannie's demos was heard by producer Shelby Singleton, who thought her voice was perfect for a song that had been submitted to him by writer Tom T. Hall. "Harper Valley P.T.A." was released on Singleton's Plantation label, and, within only a few months, it became a multimillion seller and established the careers of both Jeannie C. Riley and Tom T. Hall.

Jeannie C. Riley

Jeannie has continued with a long string of Country hits, several of which have crossed over to the Pop charts as well.

Today Jeannie lives with her daughter in Brentwood, Tennessee, and tours with a large back-up band known as Homestead Symphony.

Aug. 68	***HARPER VALLEY P.T.A. /* Plantation**
Dec. 68	***THE GIRL MOST LIKELY /* Plantation**
Mar. 69	***THERE NEVER WAS A TIME /* Plantation**
Apr. 71	***OH SINGER /* Plantation**
July 71	***GOOD ENOUGH TO BE YOUR WIFE /* Plantation**

Minnie Riperton

BORN: Nov. 8, 1948
HOMETOWN: Chicago, Illinois

Minnie Riperton began singing in church as a child, launching her musical career at the age of ten by studying voice, opera, and ballet. She became a receptionist for the Chicago-based Chess label as a teen-ager, at the same time joining a vocal group called The Gems to back up several of the company's artists, including Fontella Bass, Etta James, The Dells, Ramsey Lewis, and Johnny Nash. Eventually signed to the label herself, Minnie made a number of albums as the lead singer of The Rotary Connection, recorded briefly under the name of Andrea Davis, and made a highly acclaimed solo album, under her own name, titled *Come to My Garden*.

During the early seventies, after her separation from Chess, Minnie often toured with such artists as Roberta Flack, Quincy Jones, and Freddie Hubbard while doing radio and television commercial work on the side. She signed with the Epic label in 1974, debuting with a highly successful album (produced by Stevie Wonder) titled *Perfect Angel*. This yielded the number one single recording "Lovin' You" and was followed successfully by an LP called *Adventures in Paradise*.

Today Minnie and her husband, Dicky Rudolph (with whom she cowrote "Lovin' You" and who presently plays rhythm guitar in her band), live with their two children in the Hollywood Hills section of California.

Jan. 75 *LOVIN' YOU* / **Epic**
Aug. 75 *INSIDE MY LOVE* / **Epic**

The Ritchie Family

MEMBERS:
Cassandra Ann Wooten
Cheryl Mason Jacks
Gwendolyn Oliver
HOMETOWN: Philadelphia, Pennsylvania

Philadelphia's Sigma Sound Studios is the home of some of the finest musicians in the country—people who have been used to back up such artists as Harold Melvin & the Bluenotes, The Spinners, Stylistics, Three Degrees, and Lou Rawls, to name a few.

Ritchie Rome assembled many of the great back-up musicians, along with vocalists Wooten, Jacks, and Oliver, to form a group called The Ritchie

Minnie Riperton

Family. They went on to record an old Xavier Cugat classic, "Brazil," which became a big disco hit.

Aug. 75 *BRAZIL* / **20th Century**
Dec. 75 *I WANT TO DANCE WITH YOU* / **20th Century**
Aug. 76 *THE BEST DISCO IN TOWN* / **Marlin**

Johnny Rivers

REAL NAME: John Ramistella
BORN: Nov. 7, 1942
HOMETOWN: New York City

At the age of three, Johnny Rivers moved with his family to Baton Rouge, Louisiana, where he began playing guitar and singing by imitating the area's blues singers. He launched his professional career in high school by forming his own group and, after graduation, spent a number of years in both New

Johnny Rivers

Johnny Rivers

York and Nashville writing songs and cutting demos. During one of his New York trips, he became acquainted with Alan Freed, who provided his stage name and helped him obtain a brief recording contract with George Goldner's Gone label.

In 1960 Rivers moved to Los Angeles to break into the business as a producer. At first continuing to support himself by writing songs and playing small clubs, he eventually became a resident headliner at the famed Whiskey A Go Go and began making "live" recordings of earlier R & R hits. Released by Imperial (which was later absorbed by United Artists), these records became major best sellers and did much to spark the discotheque craze of the mid-sixties. Once established as a recording artist, Rivers formed his own label, Soul City Records, to record other artists, and a publishing company, Johnny Rivers Music. Through these ventures, he was instrumental in developing the ca-

reers of such acts as The Fifth Dimension and Al Wilson, and of such major songwriters as Jimmy Webb and Laura Nyro. He also helped Glen Campbell by providing him with one of his first major hits, "By the Time I Get to Phoenix."

Aside from a long string of best-selling albums, Rivers has scored successfully in the seventies with hit revivals of vintage rock 'n' roll material. He signed with Epic Records in 1975, working with The Beach Boys' Brian Wilson on a remake of that group's classic "Help Me Rhonda." His 1965 recording of "Midnight Special" is presently being used as a theme by the network television show of the same name.

May 64	*MEMPHIS* / Imperial	
Aug. 64	*MAYBELLINE* / Imperial	
Oct. 64	*MOUNTAIN OF LOVE* / Imperial	
Feb. 65	*MIDNIGHT SPECIAL* / Imperial	
Feb. 65	*CUPID* / Imperial	
June 65	*THE SEVENTH SON* / Imperial	
Oct. 65	*WHERE HAVE ALL THE FLOWERS GONE?* / Imperial	
Dec. 65	*UNDER YOUR SPELL AGAIN* / Imperial	
Mar. 66	*SECRET AGENT MAN* / Imperial	
June 66	*MUDDY WATER* / Imperial	
Sept. 66	*THE POOR SIDE OF TOWN* / Imperial	
Feb. 67	*BABY, I NEED YOUR LOVING* / Imperial	
June 67	*THE TRACKS OF MY TEARS* / Imperial	
Nov. 67	*SUMMER RAIN* / Imperial	
Apr. 68	*LOOK TO YOUR SOUL* / Imperial	
Nov. 68	*RIGHTS RELATIONS* / Imperial	
Feb. 69	*THESE ARE NOT MY PEOPLE* / Imperial	
June 69	*MUDDY RIVER* / Imperial	
Oct. 69	*ONE WOMAN* / Imperial	
May 70	*INTO THE MYSTIC* / Imperial	
Sept. 70	*FIRE & RAIN* / Imperial	
May 71	*SEA CRUISE* / United Artists	
Aug. 71	*THINK HIS NAME* / United Artists	

Oct. 72 *ROCKIN' PNEUMONIA & THE BOOGIE WOOGIE FLU* / United Artists

Mar. 73 *BLUE SUEDE SHOES* / United Artists

July 75 *HELP ME RHONDA* / United Artists

Feb. 77 *ASHES & SAND* / Soul City

June 77 *SWAYIN' TO THE MUSIC (SLOW DANCIN')* / Big Tree

Dec. 77 *CURIOUS MIND* / Big Tree

Smokey Robinson

REAL NAME: William Robinson
BORN: Feb. 19, 1940
HOMETOWN: Detroit, Michigan

Once described by Bob Dylan as "the greatest living poet in America," Smokey Robinson was, of course, the lead singer of The Miracles since that group's formation in the mid-fifties. He was also their principal songwriter, providing virtually all the material they recorded. His wife, Claudette (sister of Bobby Rogers, another member of The Miracles), was with the group from the outset as well. (See *THE MIRACLES, Rock On: The Solid Gold Years*.)

In 1972, citing a desire to spend more time with his family (Claudette had long before ceased touring with the group, although she continued to record), Smokey announced that he would no longer travel with the group and that he would pursue a solo career. He also wished to devote more time to his writing and production activities, and to his duties as executive vice-president of the Motown Record Corporation.

Today Smokey and Claudette live in Los Angeles with their two children, Berry and Tamla.

July 73 *SWEET HARMONY* / Tamla
Nov. 73 *BABY COME HOME* / Tamla

Smokey Robinson

May 74 *IT'S HER TURN TO LIVE* / Tamla

Sept. 74 *VIRGIN MAN* / Tamla

Dec. 74 *I AM, I AM* / Tamla

Apr. 75 *BABY, THAT'S BACKATCHA* / Tamla

Sept. 75 *AGONY & THE ECSTASY* / Tamla

Jan. 76 *QUIET STORM* / Tamla

May 76 *OPEN* / Tamla

Feb. 77 *THERE WILL COME A DAY (I'M GONNA HAPPEN TO YOU)* / Tamla

Vicki Sue Robinson

BORN: 1955
HOMETOWN: Philadelphia, Pennsylvania

Vicki and her family moved to New York during the mid-sixties and shortly thereafter she became involved in the original Broadway productions of *Hair* and *Jesus Christ Superstar.*

She then appeared as a soloist at local clubs until 1975, when the disco sound hit New York. In a short time she had a recording contract with RCA and recorded the LP *Never Gonna Let You*

Go, from which came the smash disco hit "Turn the Beat Around," which became a top ten national hit.

Apr. 76	***TURN THE BEAT AROUND / RCA***
Oct. 76	***DAYLIGHT / RCA***
Aug. 77	***HOLD TIGHT / RCA***

Kenny Rogers & The First Edition

MEMBERS:

Kenneth Rogers / born: Aug. 21, 1941 / Houston, Texas

Mike Settle / born: Mar. 20, 1941 / Tulsa, Oklahoma / replaced by Kin Vassy / Carollton, Georgia

Terry Benson Williams / born: June 6, 1947 / Hollywood, California

Thelma Camacho / San Diego, California / replaced by Mary Arnold / Audubon, Iowa

Mickey Jones / Dallas, Texas

Formed during the mid-sixties, The First Edition was a group organized by several members of the highly successful New Christy Minstrels.

Each of the members had had an impressive musical background prior to joining the Minstrels. Kenny Rogers had played in a high-school band called The Scholars and had recorded a substantial regional hit, on the Carlton label, titled "That Crazy Feeling." After graduation he joined The Bobby Doyle Trio, a well-known jazz group, and often toured the country in tandem with The Kirby Stone Four. Mike Settle had been a member of The Cumberland Three (which also included John Stewart, later of The Kingston Trio), while Thelma Camacho had sung with the San Diego Opera. Terry Williams had been around the music business all his life, his father having been first trombonist for The Tommy Dorsey Orchestra, and his mother their vocalist. Mickey Jones, the only non-Minstrel re-

cruited for The First Edition, had backed Trini Lopez for nearly eight years and had played with such artists as Johnny Rivers, Ann-Margret, and Bob Dylan.

Once organized, The First Edition debuted in 1967 at Ledbetter's, an L.A. club owned by New Christy founder Randy Sparks. Their engagement brought them to the attention of Ken Kragen, manager of The Smothers Brothers, who began handling the Edition and arranged for an appearance on the brothers' network television show. This, in turn, led to a contract offer from Warner / Reprise, which resulted in a string of hits that lasted well into the seventies. The group also achieved a number of best-selling albums, including *The First Edition, 2nd, 69, Something's Burning, Tell It All Brother,* and *Ballad of Calice.* The pinnacle of their success came in 1972, when they hosted their own syndicated television series, "Rollin' on the River." Today Rogers records as a solo performer on United Artists Records.

Kenny Rogers & The First Edition

Feb. 68	***JUST DROPPED IN / Reprise***
Jan. 69	***BUT YOU KNOW I LOVE YOU / Reprise***
June 69	***RUBY, DON'T TAKE YOUR LOVE TO TOWN / Reprise***
Sept. 69	***RUBEN JAMES / Reprise***
Feb. 70	***SOMETHING'S BURNING / Reprise***
July 70	***TELL IT ALL BROTHER / Reprise***
Oct. 70	***HEED THE CALL / Reprise***
Mar. 71	***SOMEONE WHO CARES / Reprise***
June 71	***TAKE MY HAND / Reprise***
Apr. 72	***SCHOOL TEACHER / Reprise***

Kenny Rogers

Mar. 77	***LUCILLE / United Artists***
Aug. 77	***DAYTIME FRIENDS / United Artists***
Dec. 77	***SWEET MUSIC MAN / United Artists***

The Rolling Stones. Left to right: Charlie Watts, Mick Jagger, Ron Wood, Bill Wyman, Keith Richard

The Rolling Stones

MEMBERS:

Michael Philip Jagger (lead vocals)/born: July 26, 1943/Dartford, Kent, England

Keith Richard (lead guitar)/born: Dec. 18, 1943/ Dartford, Kent, England

Brian Jones (rhythm guitar)/born: Feb. 28, 1942/Cheltenham, Gloucestershire, England/ died: July 3, 1969/Hartford, England/ replaced by Mick Taylor/born: Jan. 17, 1948/Hertfordshire, England (left group in 1975)/replaced by Ron Wood/born: June 1, 1947/London, England

William Wyman (bass)/born: Oct. 24, 1941/ Siddenham, England

Charles Robert Watts (drums)/born: June 2, 1941/Islington, England

Thoroughly immersed in "raunchy" American blues and R & B, The Rolling Stones emerged during the mid-sixties as the complete antithesis to The Beatles and all other groups spearheading the "British invasion." Their irreverent approach to rock 'n' roll soon established them as the world's leading R & R band, a position that they are acknowledged by most to continue to occupy today.

The group's history traces back to the early sixties, when two primary-school friends, Keith Richard and Mick Jagger, began sitting in with a band called Alexis Korner's Blues Incorporated. The band's drummer was Charlie Watts, and the three eventually came together with Brian Jones and Bill Wyman as The Rolling Stones. After building a substantial cult following at such R & B clubs as the Marquee, the Flamingo, and the Crawdaddy, the group attracted the attention of an aspiring young manager named Andrew Loog Oldham. In partnership with Eric Easton, Oldham began handling The Stones and soon was able to obtain a recording contract with British Decca. Released in the United States on London (and later on their own Rolling Stones label), both their singles and their albums have been setting international sales records ever since. Over the years their album releases have included *The Rolling Stones, Now, Out of Our Heads, December's Children, Aftermath, Between the Buttons, Flowers, Their Satanic Majesties Request, Beggar's Banquet, Let It Bleed, Get Yer Ya-Yas Out, Sticky Fingers, Exile on Main Street, Goat's Head Soup* and *It's Only Rock & Roll.*

Apart from recording activities, the career of The Rolling Stones has been marked by a number of events. During the late sixties, the group suffered a number of drug-related arrests, a situation that led to the eventual departure of Brian Jones. Shortly after his resignation, he was found drowned in the swimming pool of his home. His replacement was Mick Taylor, who had been recruited from John Mayall's band and who remained with The Stones until 1975, when he left for The Jack Bruce Band. On December 6, 1969, The Stones were performing at California's Altamont Raceway when the infamous Hells Angels killing took place, an event gruesomely recorded in a feature film titled *Gimme Shelter.* The group was also the subject of a later film, *Ladies and Gentlemen . . . The Rolling Stones,* and Mick Jagger became known as a dramatic actor with his roles in *Ned Kelly* and *Performance.*

Today The Rolling Stones continue as a quintet, living once again in England after having briefly relocated in

France. Mick Jagger married Nicaraguan socialite Bianca Perez Moreno de Macias in a celebrated ceremony at St. Tropez in 1971. Their U.S. tour during the summer of 1978 is speculated as being the last tour for the group.

The Rolling Stones

May 64	*NOT FADE AWAY* / London
July 64	*TELL ME* / London
July 64	*IT'S ALL OVER NOW* / London
Oct. 64	*TIME IS ON MY SIDE* / London
Jan. 65	*HEART OF STONE* / London
Mar. 65	*THE LAST TIME* / London
May 65	*PLAY WITH FIRE* / London
June 65	*SATISFACTION* / London
Oct. 65	*GET OFF MY CLOUD* / London
Dec. 65	*AS TEARS GO BY* / London
Feb. 66	*19TH NERVOUS BREAKDOWN* / London
May 66	*PAINT IT BLACK* / London
July 66	*MOTHER'S LITTLE HELPER* / London
July 66	*LADY JANE* / London
Oct. 66	*HAVE YOU SEEN YOUR MOTHER, BABY, STANDING IN THE SHADOW* / London
Jan. 67	*RUBY TUESDAY* / London
Jan. 67	*LET'S SPEND THE NIGHT TOGETHER* / London
Sept. 67	*DANDELION* / London
Sept. 67	*WE LOVE YOU* / London
Dec. 67	*SHE'S A RAINBOW* / London
June 68	*JUMPIN' JACK FLASH* / London
Sept. 68	*STREET FIGHTING MAN* / London
July 69	*HONKY TONK WOMEN* / London
May 71	*BROWN SUGAR* / Rolling Stones
June 71	*WILD HORSES* / Rolling Stones
Apr. 72	*TUMBLING DICE* / Rolling Stones
July 72	*HAPPY* / Rolling Stones
Apr. 73	*YOU CAN'T ALWAYS GET WHAT YOU WANT* / London
Sept. 73	*ANGIE* / Rolling Stones
Jan. 74	*DOO DOO DOO DOO DOO (HEARTBREAKER)* / Rolling Stones
Aug. 74	*IT'S ONLY ROCK & ROLL* / Rolling Stones

Nov. 74 *AIN'T TOO PROUD TO BEG /*
Rolling Stones
June 75 *I DON'T KNOW WHY /* Abkco
Aug. 75 *OUT OF TIME /* Abkco
Apr. 76 *FOOL TO CRY /* Rolling Stones
June 76 *HOT STUFF /* Rolling Stones
May 78 *MISS YOU /* Rolling Stones
Bill Wyman
Dec. 67 *IN ANOTHER LAND /* London

Linda Ronstadt

BORN: July 15, 1946
HOMETOWN: Tucson, Arizona

Born into a family totally absorbed in music, Linda began singing and playing the guitar as a child. Her grandfather, father, sister, and brother were all musicians and, during high school, she was part of a family trio that made local television appearances and occasionally recorded.

In 1964 Linda traveled to Los Angeles in search of a recording contract. Joining with Bobby Kimmel and Kenny Edwards, she formed a trio called The Stone Poneys and began playing on the L.A. club circuit. This led to a contract with Capitol Records and the release of their debut album, *Stone Poneys,* in 1967. Only moderately successful, this album was followed by two others, ·*Evergreen* and *Stoney End,* and by a major single hit of Mike Nesmith's *Different Drum.* By the end of 1968, however, differences had developed among the group's members and the Poneys disbanded. (See *THE STONE PONEYS.*)

Linda assembled a back-up band (which at one time or another contained members of The Eagles) and continued to record for Capitol on a solo basis. Her albums included *Hand Sown, Home Grown, Linda Ronstadt,* and *Silk Purse,* and she scored with a number of moderate hit singles. In

Linda Ronstadt

1973 she changed affiliation to the Asylum label, forming an association with producer Peter Asher (formerly of Peter & Gordon) and debuting with a highly acclaimed album titled *Don't Cry Now.* Her career took a major upturn during the following year, when she recorded one last album for Capitol (which she owed to the company by virtue of her contract) titled *Heart like a Wheel.* This became a best seller, yielding two chart-topping singles ("You're No Good" and "When Will I Be Loved") and putting her in great demand for concert appearances.

With her 1975 release of an album called *Prisoner in Disguise,* Linda Ronstadt became firmly established as the leading female rock singer of the mid-seventies.

Aug. 70 *A LONG, LONG TIME /* Capitol
Jan. 71 *VERY LONELY WOMAN /*
Capitol

Mar. 72 *ROCK ME ON THE WATER /* **Capitol**

Dec. 73 *LOVE HAS NO PRIDE /* **Asylum**

Apr. 74 *SILVER THREADS & GOLDEN NEEDLES /* **Asylum**

Dec. 74 *YOU'RE NO GOOD /* **Capitol**

Apr. 75 *WHEN WILL I BE LOVED /* **Capitol**

July 75 *IT DOESN'T MATTER ANYMORE /* **Capitol**

Sept. 75 *HEAT WAVE /* **Asylum**

Dec. 75 *TRACKS OF MY TEARS /* **Asylum**

Aug. 76 *THAT'LL BE THE DAY /* **Asylum**

Dec. 76 *SOMEONE TO LAY DOWN BESIDE ME /* **Asylum**

June 77 *LOSE AGAIN /* **Asylum**

Sept. 77 *BLUE BAYOU /* **Asylum**

Oct. 77 *IT'S SO EASY /* **Asylum**

Jan. 78 *POOR POOR PITIFUL ME /* **Asylum**

Apr. 78 *TUMBLING DICE /* **Asylum**

The Rose Garden

MEMBERS:

Diana Di Rose (lead vocals, acoustic guitar)

John Noreen (lead guitar)

James Groshong (guitar)

William Fleming (bass)

Bruce Boudin (drums)

HOMETOWN: Parkersburg, West Virginia

Formed during the mid-sixties, The Rose Garden took their identity from the name of their lead vocalist, Diana Di Rose. Prior to joining the group, Diana had been a noted folksinger in her home state of West Virginia.

In 1967 The Rose Garden recorded an unusual song, written by Kenny O'Dell (of "Beautiful People" fame), titled "Next Plane to London." A commentary on the many young American girls who traveled to Britain to see The Beatles, this record reached the national top 20 and sent the group on an extensive tour. They followed with an album and a number of additional singles, but they disbanded before they were able to duplicate their initial success.

Today Diana Di Rose makes her home in Los Angeles and is planning to embark on a new recording career.

Oct. 67 *NEXT PLANE TO LONDON /* **Atco**

Rose Royce

MEMBERS:

Gwen "Rose" Dickey (lead vocals)

Michael Moore (sax)

Freddie Dunn (trumpet)

Kenji Chiba Brown (lead guitar)

Lequeint "Duke" Jobe (bass guitar)

Kenny "Captain Gold" Copeland (trumpet)

Mike Nash (keyboards)

Terral "Powerpack" Santiel (percussion)

Henry "Hammer" Garner (drums)

The eight male musicians started out as back-up musicians for many groups including The Temptations. It was at that time that their producer, Norman Whitfield, gave them the name Rose Royce and sent them on tour with other groups. He felt they needed a female voice and chose Gwen Dickey to belt out the group's numbers.

In 1976 Whitfield was chosen to write the music for a film called *Car Wash* and decided to use his group to do the sound track. It was their big break, for the title song went on to become a number one national hit.

Oct. 76 *CAR WASH /* **MCA**

Feb. 77 *I WANNA GET NEXT TO YOU /* **MCA**

June 77 *I'M GOING DOWN /* **MCA**

Sept. 77 *DO YOUR DANCE (PT. 1) /* **Whitfield**

Nov. 77 *OOH BOY /* **Whitfield**

Diana Ross

BORN: Mar. 26, 1944

HOMETOWN: Detroit, Michigan

Diana Ross was, of course, the original lead singer of the highly successful Supremes. She left the group for a solo career in 1970, making her final appearance with them, at the Frontier Hotel in Las Vegas, on January 15 of that year. (See *THE SUPREMES, Rock On: The Solid Gold Years.*)

Her first solo outing was "Reach Out and Touch," which reached the top twenty on the charts. Although she continued to produce hit singles (several in collaboration with Marvin Gaye), and a number of best-selling albums, her real breakthrough has been in the areas of television, nightclub work, and films. Her 1972 portrayal of Billy Holiday in *Lady Sings the Blues* won her an Oscar nomination for best actress (she lost to Liza Minnelli for *Cabaret*), and her first totally dramatic role, in *Mahogany,* was highly acclaimed. Additionally, her recording of the later film's theme reached number one on the charts and remained there for several weeks.

Today Diana is separated from her husband, Bob Silberstein, and lives in L.A. with their two children. As of this writing, she is filming the lead in *The Wiz.*

Diana Ross

Apr. 70 *REACH OUT AND TOUCH /* **Motown**
Aug. 70 *AIN'T NO MOUNTAIN HIGH ENOUGH /* **Motown**
Dec. 70 *REMEMBER ME /* **Motown**
May 71 *REACH OUT, I'LL BE THERE /* **Motown**
Aug. 71 *SURRENDER /* **Motown**
Nov. 71 *I'M STILL WAITING /* **Motown**
Jan. 74 *LAST TIME I SAW HIM /* **Motown**
May 74 *SLEEPIN' /* **Motown**
Nov. 75 *THEME FROM MAHOGANY /* **Motown**
Mar. 76 *I THOUGHT I TOOK A LITTLE TIME /* **Motown**

Apr. 76 *LOVE HANGOVER /* **Motown**
Aug. 76 *ONE LOVE IN MY LIFETIME /* **Motown**
Nov. 77 *GETTIN' READY FOR LOVE /* **Motown**
Mar. 78 *YOUR LOVE IS SO GOOD TO ME /* **Motown**
May 78 *YOU GOT IT /* **Motown**

Diana Ross & Marvin Gaye

Oct. 73 *YOU'RE A SPECIAL PART OF ME /* **Motown**
Feb. 74 *MY MISTAKE /* **Motown**
July 74 *DON'T KNOCK MY LOVE /* **Motown**

Billy Joe Royal

BORN: 1945
HOMETOWN: Valdosta, Georgia

Billy Joe Royal grew up in Marietta, Georgia, where his family moved when he was six. While attending high school there, he began taking up the guitar and eventually formed his own group, Billy Joe & The Corvettes.

After graduation Royal landed a two-year engagement at a leading Savannah Georgia night spot. During this period he met and became extremely friendly with Joe South, a leading Atlanta-based singer and songwriter. South introduced him to Bill Lowery, an influential figure in the southern music business, and this led to a contract with Columbia Records.

Beginning in 1965 Royal achieved a string of hits, all written by South and published by Lowery, which lasted well into the seventies. Touring with his back-up band, The Blue Royals, he also became a top club attraction and a featured performer at the Las Vegas hotels. By the mid-seventies, however, he had faded from national popularity.

Today he records for Private Stock Records.

July 65 *DOWN IN THE BOONDOCKS /* **Columbia**
Sept. 65 *I KNEW YOU WHEN /* **Columbia**

Billy Joe Royal

Dec. 65	*I'VE GOT TO BE SOMEBODY* / Columbia
May 66	*HEART'S DESIRE* / Columbia
Sept. 66	*CAMPFIRE GIRLS* / Columbia
Sept. 67	*HUSH* / Columbia
Oct. 69	*CHERRY HILL PARK* / Columbia
Feb. 71	*TULSA* / Columbia

The Royal Guardsmen

MEMBERS:

Chris Nunley (lead vocals)

Tom Richards (lead guitar)

Barry "Snoopy" Winslow (rhythm guitar)

William Balogh (bass)

William Taylor (keyboards)

John Burdette (drums)

HOMETOWN: Ocala, Florida

Best known for their songs based on the "Peanuts" cartoon strip, The Royal Guardsmen were among the most successful "novelty" acts of the sixties.

Discovered in Florida by independent record producer Phil Gernhard, the Guardsmen recorded for the Laurie label and reached the top of the charts with their first release, "Snoopy vs. the Red Baron." Subsequent releases in this vein included "Return of the Red Baron," "Snoopy's Christmas," "Snoopy for President," and "The Airplane Song" (written by Michael Murphy, later of "Wildfire" fame, and Boomer Castleman). By 1968 disagreements had developed among members of the group with respect to their future musical direction. Although they were able to succeed with such serious ballad material as "Baby Let's Wait," this friction caused the group eventually to disband.

Today there is talk among several original members of The Royal Guardsmen of an attempt to re-form the group.

Dec. 66	*SNOOPY VS. THE RED BARON* / Laurie
Feb. 67	*THE RETURN OF THE RED BARON* / Laurie
June 67	*THE AIRPLANE SONG* / Laurie
Sept. 67	*WEDNESDAY* / Laurie
Dec. 67	*SNOOPY'S CHRISTMAS* / Laurie
Feb. 68	*I SAY LOVE* / Laurie
July 68	*SNOOPY FOR PRESIDENT* / Laurie
Nov. 68	*BABY LET'S WAIT* / Laurie

The Royal Scots Dragoon Guards

In 1972, in one of those unpredictable events that characterize the record business, a recording of "Amazing Grace" made by The Royal Scots Dragoon Guards became one of the all-time best sellers in modern history. Released by RCA, the record's sales were rivaled only by The Archies' "Sugar Sugar," an earlier RCA release that racked up a worldwide total of over five million sales.

Led by a then twenty-five-year-old pipe major named Tony Crease, the band had made this recording in 1971 as part of an album commemorating the merger of two Scottish regiments, The Caribiniers and The Scots Greys. A modest seller at first, the album began receiving a great deal of attention after a British disc jockey played "Amazing Grace" on his late-night radio show. This prompted RCA to release it as a single, and the record was soon selling at the rate of 70,000 per day. Its success spread to the Continent, and also to the United States, where it reached the top ten on the charts.

Although a follow-up single was released, titled "The Day Is Ended," the Guards were not able to repeat their initial success and returned to their military duties.

May 72 *AMAZING GRACE* / **RCA**

David Ruffin

July 69 *I'VE LOST EVERYTHING I'VE EVER LOVED* / **Motown**
Dec. 69 *I'M SO GLAD I FELL FOR YOU* / **Motown**
Nov. 75 *WALK AWAY FROM LOVE* / **Motown**
Mar. 76 *HEAVY LOVE* / **Motown**
June 76 *EVERYTHING'S COMING UP LOVE* / **Motown**

David Ruffin

BORN: Jan. 18, 1941
HOMETOWN: Meridian, Mississippi

David was the lead voice of The Temptations from 1964 until his departure in 1968, during which time the group had countless hits and became one of the hottest acts ever to record for Motown Records. (See *THE TEMPTATIONS.*) In just a short time as a solo performer, Ruffin became a big star, turning out many hit records of his own.

Feb. 69 *MY WHOLE WORLD ENDED (THE MOMENT YOU LEFT ME)* / **Motown**

Jimmy Ruffin

BORN: May 7, 1939
HOMETOWN: Meridian, Mississippi

The son of a Baptist preacher, Jimmy is the brother of David Ruffin, the former lead singer of The Temptations and a leading solo performer.

With the help of his brother, who had become associated with the fledgling Motown organization during the early sixties, Jimmy began recording for Motown's subsidiary Miracle label in 1961. Success was not to come until several years later. Starting with "What Becomes of the Broken Hearted," which reached the national top ten, he achieved a string of Pop and Soul hits that was to last well into the early seventies.

Jimmy Ruffin
Aug. 66 **WHAT BECOMES OF THE BROKEN HEARTED** / Soul
Dec. 66 **I'VE PASSED THIS WAY BEFORE** / Soul
Mar. 67 **GONNA GIVE HER ALL THE LOVE I'VE GOT** / Soul
July 67 **DON'T YOU MISS ME A LITTLE BIT** / Soul
Mar. 68 **I'LL SAY FOREVER MY LOVE** / Soul
Feb. 71 **MARIA** / Soul

David & Jimmy Ruffin
Oct. 70 **STAND BY ME** / Soul

Rufus

MEMBERS:
Paulette McWilliams (lead vocals) / replaced by Chaka Kahn
Al Ciner (guitar) / replaced by Tony Maiden
Kevin Murphy (keyboards)
Ron Stockert (keyboards) / replaced by Nate Morgan / replaced by David "Hawk" Wolinski
Dennis Belfield (bass, strings, horns) / replaced by Bobby Watson
Andre Fischer (drums, percussion) / replaced by Richard "Moon" Calhoun
HOMETOWN: Chicago, Illinois

Originally known as Ask Rufus (a name borrowed from a column in *Mechanix Illustrated*), this group evolved, through a series of personnel changes, from a sixties rock 'n' roll band known as The American Breed. (See *THE AMERICAN BREED.*)

Once established as Rufus, the group was signed by ABC/Dunhill and began working on their debut album, titled simply *Rufus.* This was only moderately successful, and the group was at L.A.'s Record Plant, working on a follow-up *(Rags to Rufus)*, when Stevie Wonder happened into the studio and offered his help on the session. He contributed some material to the album, most notably "Tell Me Something Good," which was released as a single and which quickly rose to the top of the charts. The group has followed with a number of major hits and with best-selling albums such as *Rufusised* and *Rufus, Featuring Chaka Khan.*

Today Rufus is acknowledged as one of the leading acts in the soul field.

Rufus
June 74 **TELL ME SOMETHING GOOD** / ABC
Oct. 74 **YOU GOT THE LOVE** / ABC
Feb. 75 **ONCE YOU GET STARTED** / ABC
May 75 **PLEASE PARDON ME** / ABC
Jan. 76 **SWEET THING** / ABC
May 76 **DANCE WIT ME** / ABC
Feb. 77 **AT MIDNIGHT (MY LOVE WILL LIFT YOU UP)** / ABC
May 77 **HOLLYWOOD** / ABC

Rufus/Chaka Khan
Apr. 78 **STAY** / ABC

Todd Rundgren

BORN: June 22, 1948
HOMETOWN: Upper Darby, Pennsylvania

Todd Rundgren emerged during the early seventies as one of the leading multifaceted figures in rock.

His first professional experience, during the mid-sixties, was with a high-school group called Money. He later joined a group known as Woody's Truckstop, but achieved his first commercial success, between 1967 and 1969, with Nazz. (See *NAZZ.*)

In 1970 Rundgren produced an album for the Ampex label titled *Runt,* on which he sang all the parts, played all the instruments, and did all the sound engineering himself. This not only brought him a great deal of acclaim, but it prompted him to form a group called Runt. This aggregation reached

Rufus Featuring Chaka Khan. Back row, left to right: Bobby Watson, Tony Maiden, Kevin Murphy; middle row: Nate Morgan; front row, left to right: Andre Fischer, Chaka Khan

the top twenty with "We Gotta Get You a Woman" and provided Rundgren with his first major step to success.

During this period Rundgren also formed an association with Albert Grossman and was given several of Grossman's acts (including American Dream and The Band) to produce. When Grossman established his own Bearsville label, Rundgren not only became the company's resident producer, but he began recording for them as an artist as well. He also did outside independent productions, working with

such groups as Badfinger, Grand Funk, Fanny, Sparks, and The New York Dolls.

In the fall of 1973, Rundgren formed a permanent back-up band called Utopia, made up of Mark Klingman (keyboards), Ralph Shuckett (keyboards), M. Frog (synthesizer), John Siegler (bass), and Kevin Ellman (drums). Aside from a number of hit singles (including a remake of "Hello, It's Me," an earlier Nazz tune), Rundgren has achieved a series of best-selling albums, including *The Ballad of Todd*

Todd Rundgren & Utopia. Front, right: Todd Rundgren

Rundgren, Something/Anything, A Wizard, a True Star, Todd, Utopia, Initiation, Another Live, and *Faithful.* He now tours with the group Utopia.

Nov. 70	*WE GOTTA GET YOU A WOMAN* / Ampex
Apr. 71	*BE NICE TO ME* / Bearsville
Sept. 71	*A LONG TIME, A LONG WAY* / Bearsville
Apr. 72	*I SAW THE LIGHT* / Bearsville
July 72	*COULDN'T I JUST LOVE YOU* / Bearsville
Oct. 73	*HELLO, IT'S ME* / Bearsville
Apr. 74	*A DREAM GOES ON FOREVER* / Bearsville
Apr. 75	*REAL MAN* / Bearsville
June 76	*GOOD VIBRATIONS* / Bearsville
May 78	*CAN WE STILL BE FRIENDS* / Bearsville

Merilee Rush & The Turnabouts

HOMETOWN: Seattle, Washington

Interested in music since her childhood, Merilee Rush studied classical piano for nearly ten years. As she grew into her teens, her tastes turned more toward popular music and rock, and she formed a group called Merilee & The Turnabouts to play the northwestern club circuit.

During the mid-sixties one of the group's performances was noticed by Paul Revere & The Raiders, who invited them to come along on a tour. This eventually led to a production deal with the team of Tommy Cogbill and Chips Moman, and to a recording contract with Bell Records.

Their first outing, "Angel of the Morning," became a major hit and reached the top ten on the national charts. Although two other chart entries followed, neither approached the success of the initial hit.

| May 68 | *ANGEL OF THE MORNING* / Bell |
| Aug. 68 | *THAT KIND OF WOMAN* / Bell |

Dec. 68 *REACH OUT* / **AGP**
June 77 *SAVE ME* / **United Artists**

Leon Russell

REAL NAME: Hank Wilson
BORN: Apr. 2, 1941
HOMETOWN: Lawton, Oklahoma

Leon Russell grew up in Tulsa, where his family moved when he was a child. He began studying classical music at three, but soon became highly influenced by the Country and blues music of the South. He assembled his own band at the age of fourteen, lying about his age to land an engagement at a leading Tulsa night spot. This enabled him to play alongside such local "greats" as Ronnie Hawkins & The Hawks (later to evolve into The Band) and led to a national tour with Jerry Lee Lewis.

During the early sixties, Russell traveled to Los Angeles to break into the record business. At first supporting himself by playing and singing in small clubs along the Strip, he rapidly gained a reputation as a leading session musician and was employed as such by most of the prominent West Coast producers. As a result he worked in the studio with such acts as The Crystals, The Righteous Brothers, Glen Campbell, The Byrds, Gary Lewis & The Playboys, Bob Lind, Delaney & Bonnie, Herb Alpert, and Bob Lind.

As the sixties progressed, Russell worked briefly with the Viva label and spent nearly two years building a recording studio (which was later to produce a number of major hits) into his house. He also made one album for Mercury, *Asylum Choir,* before joining with British rock entrepreneur Denny Cordell in forming the new Shelter record label.

In 1970 Russell made his debut album for Shelter and helped organize the "Mad Dogs and Englishmen" tour that would propel him to stardom. Developing a strong image with his stovepipe hat and long, flowing hair, he became immensely popular as a concert attraction and was prominently featured at the famed Bangladesh benefit concert. He also became noted for his many albums and for the "superstars" (such as Ringo Starr, George Harrison, Charlie Watts, Bill Wyman, Steve Winwood, Delaney & Bonnie, and Joe Cocker) who would accompany him as session musicians. His albums have included *And the Shelter People, Carney, Live, Asylum Choir II* (recorded earlier for Mercury but never before released), *Hank Wilson's Back, Stop All That Jazz* and *Will o' the Wisp.*

In 1976 Leon Russell severed all connections with Shelter and formed his own Paradise label. He launched it with *The Wedding Album,* a recording celebrating his marriage to singer Mary McCreary (who had previously been a Shelter artist). Today Leon and Mary Russell tour as a husband-and-wife act.

Leon Russell
Aug. 72 *TIGHT ROPE* / **Shelter**
Sept. 73 *QUEEN OF THE ROLLER DERBY* / **Shelter**
Apr. 74 *IF I WERE A CARPENTER* / **Shelter**
Aug. 75 *LADY BLUE* / **Shelter**
Jan. 76 *BACK TO THE ISLAND* / **Shelter**
Hank Wilson
Oct. 73 *ROLL IN MY SWEET BABY'S ARMS* / **Shelter**

Mitch Ryder & The Detroit Wheels

MEMBERS:
Mitch Ryder (William S. Levise, Jr.) (lead vocals) / born: 1947

Mitch Ryder & The Detroit Wheels

James McCarty (lead guitar)/born: 1947
Joseph Kubert (rhythm guitar)/born: 1947
Earl Elliott (bass)/born: 1947/replaced by
James McCallister
"Little" John Badanjek (drums)/born: 1948
HOMETOWN: Detroit, Michigan

The Detroit Wheels emerged during the mid-sixties as one of the leading teen-age "blue-eyed soul" bands.

The group's central figure, Mitch Ryder, first broke into music with a high-school band known as The Tempest. His next group was called The Peps, but he soon left them to organize a new group, called Billy Lee & The Rivieras, with whom he gained a substantial reputation in the Detroit area. The group made several local recordings and managed to receive a great deal of regional airplay.

Early in 1965 Bob Prince, a disc jockey on Detroit's WXYZ, contacted New York producer Bob Crewe to bring the group to his attention. Crewe was impressed and signed them to his New Voice label. He also renamed the group, drawing "Mitch Ryder" from a phone book and substituting "Detroit Wheels" for "Rivieras" to avoid confusion with another Rivieras group. Their first outing, "Jenny Take a Ride" (a medley of two earlier R & B hits, Little Richard's "Jenny Jenny" and Chuck Willis's "C. C. Rider"), immediately established the group by reaching the top ten. After more than half a dozen hits with similar material, Mitch Ryder left the group for a solo career, debuting with his release of "Joy." His solo recordings, however, were never quite so successful as those made with the group.

During the early seventies, Ryder made somewhat of a comeback by organizing a new group (which also included John Badanjek), called Detroit. He also collaborated with Memphis writer-producer Steve Cropper on an album titled *The Detroit-Memphis Experiment.* In spite of high critical acclaim, these projects did not enable Ryder to duplicate his original success.

Mitch Ryder and The Detroit Wheels

Dec. 65 *JENNY TAKE A RIDE* /New Voice
Mar. 66 *LITTLE LATIN LUPE LU* /New Voice
May 66 *BREAK OUT* /New Voice
July 66 *TAKING ALL I CAN GET* /New Voice
Oct. 66 *DEVIL WITH A BLUE DRESS & GOOD GOLLY, MISS MOLLY* / New Voice
Feb. 67 *SOCK IT TO ME, BABY* /New Voice
Apr. 67 *TOO MANY FISH IN THE SEA & THREE LITTLE FISHES* /New Voice

Mitch Ryder

July 67 *JOY* /New Voice
Oct. 67 *YOU ARE MY SUNSHINE* /New Voice
Sept. 67 *WHAT NOW, MY LOVE* /Dyno Voice
Feb. 68 *PERSONALITY & CHANTILLY LACE* /Dyno Voice

Staff Sergeant Barry Sadler

BORN: 1941
HOMETOWN: Leadville, Colorado

In 1966, at the height of the conflict in Southeast Asia, Staff Sergeant Barry Sadler (a paratrooper stationed in Vietnam) suddenly gained fame with his unusual "Ballad of the Green Berets." A number one record and a major best seller, this went down in history as one of the fastest movers in the modern record business.

Although bent on a career in medicine as a teen-ager, Sadler was always interested in music and had learned the guitar at an early age. He began performing in Country & Western bars, eventually running out of money and enlisting in the armed forces. During the mid-sixties he was affiliated with the Green Berets and one of his buddies suggested that he write a song about the outfit. Originally recorded by the army for distribution to the troops, the record eventually came to the attention of RCA, which had Sadler record it with a full complement of studio musicians.

After a lesser follow-up hit, Sadler resumed his military career and later retired to civilian life. In 1973 he reactivated his recording career by forming his own Veteran label as a vehicle for his releases.

Today Sadler lives in Tucson, Arizona, with his wife, Levona, and their two children, Thor and Baron.

Feb. 66 *THE BALLAD OF THE GREEN BERETS* / RCA
Apr. 66 *THE "A" TEAM* / RCA

Crispian St. Peters

BORN: Apr. 5, 1944
HOMETOWN: Swanley, Kent, England

Interested in music since his early teens, Crispian St. Peters gained singing experience as a member of several local groups. He was taught to play guitar by the leader of a youth group to which he belonged, and, at one time, was considering a career as a session guitarist. He eventually decided, however, to pursue a performing career instead.

St. Peters began recording during the mid-sixties, but with very little initial success. His fourth release, a remake of We Five's "You Were on My Mind," brought him his first success by rising to the British top three. (It was also reissued in 1967 after his later American success.) His major breakthrough, however, came with the release of "Pied Piper," another earlier American hit. This nearly reached the top of the charts on both sides of the Atlantic, and became the first of his three American chart entries.

June 66 *THE PIED PIPER* / Jamie
Sept. 66 *CHANGES* / Jamie
July 67 *YOU WERE ON MY MIND* / Jamie

Buffy Sainte-Marie

BORN: Feb. 20, 1941
HOMETOWN: Saskatchewan, Canada

Born on an Indian reservation in Canada, Buffy Sainte-Marie (a full-blooded Cree Indian) was orphaned as a baby and was adopted by parents of Micmac Indian descent. While growing up in Maine, and later in Wakefield, Massachusetts, Buffy developed an interest in folk music and decided to make it a career.

During the mid-sixties Buffy signed with the Vanguard label and released a long string of folk- and protest-oriented albums. She became most widely known as a songwriter, however, as she composed such hits (for other artists) as "The Universal Soldier," "Until It's Time for You to Go," and "Piney Wood Hills." Her singles began appearing on the charts during the early seventies, when she achieved three hits of her own.

In 1975, after a brief affiliation with MCA, Buffy signed with the ABC label, for which she continues to record today.

Nov. 71 *I'M GONNA BE A COUNTRY GIRL AGAIN*/Vanguard
Apr. 72 *MISTER, CAN'T YOU SEE?*/Vanguard
Aug. 72 *HE'S AN INDIAN COWBOY IN THE RODEO*/Vanguard

The Salsoul Orchestra

One of the most talented producer-arrangers in the music business today is a Philadelphian named Vincent Montana, Jr. In 1975 he combined a group of Philadelphian musicians with vocalists Barb Ingram, Evette Benton, Carla Benson, Carl Helm, Ronni Tyson, and Phil Hurt and called the group The Salsoul Orchestra. In late 1975 the group debuted with the tune "Salsoul Hustle," which employed a Latin-flavored disco sound. The tune caught on and so did the group, which is now one of the hottest exponents of the disco sound.

Sept. 75 *SALSOUL HUSTLE*/Salsoul
Jan. 76 *TANGERINE*/Salsoul
May 76 *YOU'RE JUST THE RIGHT SIZE*/Salsoul
Sept. 76 *NICE 'N' NASTY*/Salsoul

Sam & Dave

MEMBERS:
Samuel David Moore/born: Oct. 12, 1935/Miami, Florida
David Prater/born: May 9, 1937/Ocilla, Georgia

Known during their heyday as "Double Dynamite," Sam & Dave were one of the leading Soul acts of the mid-sixties and a cornerstone of the "Stax-Volt sound."

Both Sam and Dave had started out as solo performers, each having first sung in church and having later toured the southern R & B club circuit. They met in the Miami, Florida area, forming an act and building a substantial reputation as a concert attraction.

In 1964 Sam & Dave were signed by Roulette Records. After three unsuccessful releases, they affiliated with the burgeoning Stax-Volt organization and began working with the writing and production team of Isaac Hayes and David Porter. Beginning with "You Don't Know Like I Know," the duo achieved a long string of hits with Hayes-Porter compositions, the biggest of which was their chart-topping release of "Soul Man." After switching to Atlantic in 1968, they continued for a time to place on the charts. By 1969, however, Isaac Hayes's developing solo career (which left him far less time

Sam & Dave

to write and produce) seemed to be taking its toll on the duo, and they eventually faded from popularity.

During the early seventies, after having disbanded for several years, Sam & Dave re-formed and began once again to tour. They signed with Contempo Records in early 1977.

Jan. 66	*YOU DON'T KNOW LIKE I KNOW* / Stax
Apr. 66	*HOLD ON, I'M COMING* / Stax
Sept. 66	*SAID I WASN'T GONNA TELL NOBODY* / Stax
Dec. 66	*YOU GOT ME HUMMIN'* / Stax
Feb. 67	*WHEN SOMETHING IS WRONG WITH MY BABY* / Stax
June 67	*SOOTHE ME* / Stax
Sept. 67	*SOUL MAN* / Stax
Jan. 68	*I THANK YOU* / Stax
May 68	*YOU DON'T KNOW WHAT YOU MEAN TO ME* / Atlantic
Aug. 68	*CAN'T YOU FIND ANOTHER WAY* / Atlantic
Nov. 68	*EVERYBODY GOT TO BELIEVE IN SOMEBODY* / Atlantic
Dec. 68	*SOUL SISTER, BROWN SUGAR* / Atlantic
Mar. 69	*BORN AGAIN* / Atlantic

Sam the Sham & The Pharaohs

MEMBERS:

Sam the Sham (Domingo Samudio) (lead vocals, keyboards) / Dallas, Texas

Ray Stinnet (lead guitar)

David Martin (bass)

Jerry Patterson (drums)

Butch Gibson (added in 1965) / (sax)

Formed during the early sixties by Domingo Samudio, this band became one of the leading domestic rock 'n' roll outfits of the "Beatles era." The lead singer's unusual identity was derived from his last name (Samudio) and the "shamming" (shuffling of the feet and twisting of the hips) that he often incorporated into his stage act.

In approximately 1960 Sam formed his first combo while attending Arlington State College in Texas. He later left for Louisiana to join a friend's band, a group that evolved into The Pharaohs and built a strong reputation on the southern club circuit. They recorded a number of regional hits for such labels as Tupelo, Dingo, and XL, which led to an affiliation with the MGM label in 1965. Starting with "Wooly Bully," which established the group by going straight to the top of the charts, Sam The Sham and company achieved a string of major novelty R & R hits lasting well into 1967. By the late sixties, however, the group had disbanded.

During the early seventies, Domingo Samudio emerged as a solo artist on the Atlantic label. His album release of *Sam, Hard & Heavy* was highly acclaimed and won him a Grammy award for the liner notes. Today he records for Fretone Records.

Apr. 65	***WOOLY BULLY* /MGM**
July 65	***JU JU HAND* /MGM**
Oct. 65	***RING DANG DOO* /MGM**
Feb. 66	***RED HOT* /MGM**
June 66	***LIL' RED RIDING HOOD* /MGM**
Oct. 66	***THE HAIR ON MY CHINNY CHIN CHIN* /MGM**
Dec. 66	***HOW DO YOU CATCH A GIRL* / MGM**
Mar. 67	***OH THAT'S GOOD, NO THAT'S BAD* /MGM**
June 67	***BLACK SHEEP* /MGM**

The Sandpipers

MEMBERS:

James Brady /born: Aug. 24, 1944/Los Angeles, California

Richard Shoff /born: Apr. 30, 1944/Seattle, Washington

Michael Piano /born: Oct. 26, 1944/Rochester, New York

Originally known as The Grads, this vocal group was made up of three young men who first met in the Los Angeles-based Mitchell Boys Choir. As they grew older, the trio left the choir in pursuit of a career as a pop singing group.

During the early sixties, the group succeeded in making an occasional record for several companies, including Valiant, MGM, and Mercury. None of these efforts was commercially successful, however, and they decided to audition for Herb Alpert's newly formed A & M label. Signed to a contract, the group made one record, "Everything in the Garden," before changing their name to The Sandpipers (a name borrowed from a small shore bird) and attaining major success with "Guantanamera." This became a top ten hit and was followed over the years by several additional chart entries.

The Sandpipers achieved their biggest success around 1969, when they were asked to record the theme for a Liza Minnelli film titled *The Sterile Cuckoo.* This song, "Come Saturday Morning," made the group well known among pop and middle-of-the-road audiences alike.

July 66	***GUANTANAMERA* /A & M**
Oct. 66	***LOUIE LOUIE* /A & M**
Dec. 69	***COME SATURDAY MORNING* / A & M**
Dec. 70	***FREE TO CARRY ON* / A & M**

Samantha Sang

BORN: Aug. 5, 1953

HOMETOWN: Melbourne, Victoria, Australia

Samantha, whose parents are Joan Clark and Reg Gray, two of Australia's most popular singers, began her career as a youngster on the radio singing under the name Cheryl Gray. As she grew older her voice developed to such a proportion that she became a favorite of three continents.

After a while she met Bill May, who became her manager and eventually got her an album deal with Private Stock Records. Her debut album for the label, *Emotion,* included a single, written by Barry and Robin Gibb of The Bee Gees, which became her first chart entry and an immediate hit.

Nov. 77 *EMOTION* / **Private Stock**
May 78 *YOU KEEP ME DANCING* / **Private Stock**

Santana

MEMBERS:

Devadip Carlos Santana (lead guitar, vocals) / born: July 20, 1947

Gregg Rolie (keyboards) / replaced (1973) by Tom Coster

José Chepito Areas (timbales, conga, percussion) / replaced by Armando Pereza

Michael Carabello (conga, percussion) / replaced by Greg Walker / (vocals)

David Brown (bass)

Michael Shrieve (drums) / replaced by Ndugu Leon Chancler

HOMETOWN: San Francisco, California

The leading exponent of Latin rock, Santana emerged as part of the vast San Francisco music explosion of the late sixties.

Carlos Santana, from whom the band had taken its name, was born the son of a Mariachi musician in Autlan, Mexico. His early years were spent playing in small Mexican clubs and bars, but he eventually moved to San Francisco and organized a band comprising some of the area's leading musicians. After building a strong reputation for their club work, the group was offered contracts by several companies and finally signed with Columbia. The release of their first album, *Santana,* was timed to coincide with their appearance at the Woodstock festival and was thereby rendered an immediate success. It also yielded two singles, "Jingo" and "Evil Ways," the latter of which reached the national top five.

In spite of a number of additional hit singles, Santana has been recognized primarily for their concert appearances and albums, including *Abraxas, Santana 3, Caravanserai, Welcome, Borboletta, Lotus,* and *Amigos.* The group has undergone literally dozens of personnel changes over the years, and is presently made up of eight members.

Although continuing to work with the group, Carlos Santana collaborates on occasional projects with other leading musicians. Since the early seventies, he has done albums with Buddy Miles, John McLaughlin, and Alice Coltrane.

Santana
Oct. 69 *JINGO* / **Columbia**
Jan. 70 *EVIL WAYS* / **Columbia**
Nov. 70 *BLACK MAGIC WOMAN* / **Columbia**
Feb. 71 *OYE COMO VA* / **Columbia**
Oct. 71 *EVERYBODY'S EVERYTHING* / **Columbia**
Feb. 72 *NO ONE TO DEPEND ON* / **Columbia**
May 76 *LET IT SHINE* / **Columbia**
Oct. 77 *SHE'S NOT THERE* / **Columbia**

Carlos Santana & Buddy Miles
Sept. 72 *EVIL WAYS/THEM CHANGES* / **Columbia**

Leo Sayer

REAL NAME: Gerard Sayer
BORN: May 21, 1948
HOMETOWN: Brighton-on-Sea, Sussex, England

Leo Sayer began his career working in various semipro bands and playing mouth organ behind such folk-blues figures as Michael Chapman, Mike Cooper, and Alexis Korner.

Leo Sayer

In 1972 Sayer was fronting a band called Patches when he responded to an ad placed by David Courtney, an associate of Pop star Adam Faith. Impressed by Sayer's demo tape, Faith and Courtney arranged for a contract with Warner Brothers, and a single titled "Living in America" was soon released. This achieved only minor commercial success, however, causing Patches to disband and leaving Sayer to continue on a solo basis.

Shortly thereafter, Sayer and Courtney formed a songwriting team, providing all the material for "Daltrey" (Roger Daltrey's premiere solo effort—see *THE WHO*)—and a hit single called "Giving It All Away." Sayer followed with a successful album of his own, *Silverbird,* which yielded his British hit single "The Show Must Go On" and a top five American cover version by Three Dog Night.

Leo Sayer's American breakthrough as an artist came in 1975, when he scored with his top ten recording of "Long Tall Glasses." His subsequent albums, *Just a Boy* and *Another Year,* have become best sellers in the United States.

Today Sayer works in partnership with Frank Farrell, a former member of his back-up band. David Courtney has gone on to pursue a solo career.

Feb. 75	*LONG TALL GLASSES /* **Warner Bros.**
June 75	*ONE MAN BAND /* **Warner Bros.**
Oct. 76	*YOU MAKE ME FEEL LIKE DANCING /* **Warner Bros.**
Feb. 77	*WHEN I NEED YOU /* **Warner Bros.**
July 77	*HOW MUCH LOVE /* **Warner Bros.**
Oct. 77	*THUNDER IN MY HEART /* **Warner Bros.**
Dec. 77	*EASY TO LOVE /* **Warner Bros.**

Boz Scaggs

REAL NAME: William Royce Scaggs
BORN: June 8, 1944
HOMETOWN: Dallas, Texas

Boz Scaggs

Boz Scaggs began his career in The Marksmen, an early-sixties group which also contained future rock star Steve Miller. (See *Steve MILLER.*) Later, while attending the University of Wisconsin, the two went on to form a group called The Ardells. Scaggs eventually returned to Texas, forming yet another band, The Wigs, and traveling with them to England for a try at success. After nothing substantial developed, Scaggs decided to pursue a solo career.

During the mid-sixties Scaggs moved to Europe, occupying himself as a roving folksinger and eventually settling in Stockholm, Sweden. He became affiliated with a Swedish label, Karusell Records, and cut a highly successful folk album titled *Boz.* At this point he was contacted by Steve Miller, who recruited him as a charter member of The Steve Miller Band. Scaggs remained with them for two albums, *Children of the Future* and *Sailor,* before going solo once again and signing with Atlantic.

After one Atlantic album, *Boz Scaggs,* Scaggs finally settled into a contract with Columbia. His singles began appearing on the charts, and his albums, including *Boz Scaggs and Band, My Time, Slow Dancer,* and *Silk Degrees,* began to sell very well. His biggest success came late in 1976 with the release of his chart-topping single "Lowdown."

Boz Scaggs's success today is due in part to the guidance of his manager, Irving Azoff, who operates Frontline Management, and also guides the careers of The Eagles, Dan Fogelberg, Steely Dan, Jimmy Buffett, and J. D. Souther.

Apr. 71	*WE WERE ALWAYS SWEET-HEARTS /* **Columbia**
July 71	*NEAR YOU /* **Columbia**
Sept. 72	*DINAH FLO /* **Columbia**
Apr. 76	*IT'S OVER /* **Columbia**
Aug. 76	*LOWDOWN /* **Columbia**
Nov. 76	*WHAT CAN I SAY /* **Columbia**

Seals & Crofts

Mar. 77	*LIDO SHUFFLE* / Columbia
Oct. 77	*HARD TIME* / Columbia
Feb. 78	*HOLLYWOOD* / Columbia

Seals & Crofts

MEMBERS:

James Seals / born: Oct. 17, 1941 / Sidney, Texas

Dash Crofts / born: Aug. 14, 1940 / Cisco, Texas

Both Dash Crofts and Jim Seals showed musical ability extremely early in life. Crofts began playing piano at the age of four, while Seals became a Texas state fiddle champion before he reached ten. The two first met during the early fifties at a Cisco jamboree, eventually playing together in a band called Dean Beard & The Crew Cats.

During the late fifties, Seals and Crofts got the opportunity to join The Champs, a group which had recently achieved a multimillion seller with "Te-

quila." On the strength of this hit, The Champs were able to remain active for nearly eight years, eventually disbanding during the mid-sixties. After Jim Seals made a few unsuccessful solo records, the duo's next stop was in a four-man band called The Mushrooms, but this was a short-lived venture. They soon joined a seven-member group called The Dawnbreakers, three of whose members were women (two of whom Seals and Crofts ultimately married); the group was managed by the women's mother, Marcia Day. Although The Dawnbreakers were only moderately successful, Mrs. Day provided a great deal of encouragement and paved the way for the duo's later success.

In 1970 Seals and Crofts emerged as a "soft rock" duo, rapidly building a reputation on the West Coast club circuit and affiliating with the TA label. After recording two albums, *Seals &*

Crofts and *Down Home,* they switched to Warner Brothers and achieved such best sellers as *Year of Sunday, Summer Breeze, Diamond Girl, Unborn Child,* and *I'll Play for You.* Their singles soon began appearing on the charts as well, and two—"Summer Breeze" and "Diamond Girl—became top ten hits.

Today Seals & Crofts are well known as leading exponents of the highly spiritual Baha'i faith.

Sept. 72	*SUMMER BREEZE* / Warner Bros.	
Jan. 73	*HUMMINGBIRD* / Warner Bros.	
May 73	*DIAMOND GIRL* / Warner Bros.	
Sept. 73	*WE MAY NEVER PASS THIS WAY AGAIN* / Warner Bros.	
Mar. 74	*UNBORN CHILD* / Warner Bros.	
May 74	*KING OF NOTHING* / Warner Bros.	
Apr. 75	*I'LL PLAY FOR YOU* / Warner Bros.	
Apr. 76	*GET CLOSER* / Warner Bros.	
Nov. 76	*BABY, I'LL GIVE IT TO YOU* / Warner Bros.	
Sept. 77	*MY FAIR SHARE* / Warner Bros.	
Apr. 78	*YOU'RE THE LOVE* / Warner Bros.	

The Searchers

MEMBERS:

Anthony Jackson (lead vocals, bass) / born: July 16, 1940 / Dingle, Liverpool, England / replaced (1965) by Frank Allen / born: Dec. 14, 1943 / Hayes, Middlesex, England

Michael Pendergast (lead guitar) / born: Mar. 3, 1942 / Kirkdale, Liverpool, England

John McNally (rhythm guitar) / born: Aug. 30, 1941 / Kirkdale, Liverpool, England

Chris Curtis (drums) / born: Aug. 26, 1942 / Oldham, Lancashire, England

Formed in 1960, The Searchers were organized by guitarist John McNally and took their name from the well-known John Ford movie western. After debuting at the Iron Door, the group began building a substantial reputation around Liverpool and later became one of the several Liverpool-area bands to appear regularly at Hamburg, Germany's, Star Club.

In 1963, after The Beatles' ascendancy to fame, the Liverpool-based Searchers had no problem in obtaining a recording contract. Signed by A & R director Tony Hatch to the British Pye label, they achieved a number of best sellers with former American hits, including "Sweets for My Sweet," "Sweet Nothin's," and "Sugar & Spice." Beginning with their fourth outing, "Needles & Pins" (written for singer Jackie DeShannon by a relative unknown named Sonny Bono), the group began a long series of American chart entries as well.

Today The Searchers continue to be a popular British cabaret attraction. Two of their members, John McNally and Mike Pendergast, are original Searchers, while the remaining two spots have been filled by a series of replacements. Tony Jackson left the group for a solo career, while Chris Curtis went on to form a group known as The Fix.

Mar. 64	*NEEDLES & PINS* / Kapp	
Apr. 64	*AIN'T THAT JUST LIKE ME* / Kapp	
May 64	*SUGAR & SPICE* / Liberty	
May 64	*DON'T THROW YOUR LOVE AWAY* / Kapp	
Aug. 64	*SOMEDAY WE'RE GONNA LOVE AGAIN* / Kapp	
Oct. 64	*WHEN YOU WALK IN THE ROOM* / Kapp	
Nov. 64	*LOVE POTION #9* / Kapp	
Mar. 65	*BUMBLE BEE* / Kapp	
Jan. 65	*WHAT HAVE THEY DONE TO THE RAIN?* / Kapp	
Apr. 65	*GOODBYE MY LOVER GOODBYE* / Kapp	
July 65	*HE'S GOT NO LOVE* / Kapp	
Jan. 66	*TAKE ME FOR WHAT I'M WORTH* / Kapp	

John Sebastian

Nov. 66 *HAVE YOU EVER LOVED SOMEBODY?*/**Kapp**
Sept. 71 *DESDEMONA*/**RCA**

John Sebastian

BORN: Mar. 17, 1944
HOMETOWN: New York City

Born into a musical family, John Sebastian was exposed to music from the beginning of his life. His father was a famed harmonica virtuoso, while his mother was employed for many years by New York City's Carnegie Hall.

During the early sixties, Sebastian was attending New York University in the Greenwich Village area when he became involved in the local folk-and-blues movements. He performed for a time with The Even Dozen Jug Band (using the name John Benson) and later joined Zal Yanovsky, Cass Elliott, and Denny Doherty in the legendary Mugwumps. By 1965, however, Sebastian and Yanovsky had gone on to form The Lovin' Spoonful while Doherty and Elliott had become founding members of The Mamas & Papas. (See *THE LOVIN' SPOONFUL* and *THE MAMAS & PAPAS*.)

After the break-up of The Spoonful, Sebastian's first solo project was to score a Broadway production titled *Jimmy Shine*, which starred Dustin Hoffman. He soon settled into a recording and performing career, achieving a moderate hit single and signing with Reprise for a series of albums. His releases have included *John B. Sebastian, The Real Live John Sebastian, The Four of Us, The Tarzana Kid*, and *Welcome Back*. This last album yielded a number one single of the title cut, which is still in use today as the theme for television's popular "Welcome Back Kotter."

At the present time, John Sebastian makes his permanent home in Los Angeles.

Jan. 69   *SHE'S A LADY* /Kama Sutra
Mar. 76   *WELCOME BACK* /Reprise

Neil Sedaka

BORN: Mar. 13, 1939
HOMETOWN: Brooklyn, New York

After "making it" in the sixties, Neil reached a recording hiatus during the early seventies. With help from his agent, Dick Fox, who would later guide Barry Manilow's career, Sedaka began plotting a comeback that began in England. By 1972, Fox had engineered this comeback so successfully that rock star Elton John signed Neil to his Rocket Records. Sedaka's first release, "Laughter in the Rain," was the song that catapulted him back to stardom on the music scene. His songs became hits for other performers as well—"Love Will Keep Us Together," by the Captain & Tennille and "Solitaire" by The Carpenters.

Today Neil records for Elektra Records and is kept busy traveling all over the country. His free time is spent with his wife, Leba, and their children. (For prior career information see *Rock On: The Solid Gold Years*.)

Oct. 74   *LAUGHTER IN THE RAIN* / Rocket
Feb. 75   *THE IMMIGRANT* /Rocket
June 75   *THAT'S WHEN THE MUSIC TAKES ME* /Rocket
Sept. 75   *BAD BLOOD* /Rocket
Dec. 75   *BREAKING UP IS HARD TO DO* /Rocket
Apr. 76   *LOVE IN THE SHADOWS* / Rocket
June 76   *STEPPIN' OUT* /Rocket
Sept. 76   *YOU GOTTA MAKE YOUR OWN SUNSHINE* /Rocket
May 77   *AMARILLO* /Elektra

The Seeds

MEMBERS:
Sky Saxon (Richard Marsh) (lead vocals)
Jan Savage (guitar)
Daryl Hopper (keyboards)
Rick Andridge (drums)
HOMETOWN: Los Angeles, California

Known originally as The Amoeba, this group emerged during the mid-sixties as one of the original and most powerful of the West Coast psychedelic rock bands. They ultimately became best known, however, as a "flower power" band.

The Seeds began their career in conventional fashion by playing small clubs along the Sunset Strip. After building a sizable cult following, they were signed by Gene Norman's Crescendo label and debuted with a major regional hit titled "Can't Seem to Make

Neil Sedaka

You Mine." Their next release, "Pushin' Too Hard," elevated them into the national top thirty and was followed by a number of additional chart entries. They also recorded a series of albums, including *The Seeds, Web of Sound, Future, A Full Spoon of Seedy Blues,* and *Raw & Alive.*

By the late sixties, the "flower power" movement had begun to disintegrate, and The Seeds along with it. After numerous personnel changes, the group recorded briefly for MGM during the early seventies but eventually disbanded. Sky Saxon, today known as "Sunstar," continues up to the present day on the fringes of what remains of the Los Angeles "underground" music scene.

Dec. 66	*PUSHING TOO HARD* / GNP Crescendo
Mar. 67	*MR. FARMER* / GNP Crescendo
Apr. 67	*CAN'T SEEM TO MAKE YOU MINE* / GNP Crescendo
July 67	*A THOUSAND SHADOWS* / GNP Crescendo

The Seekers

MEMBERS:
Judith Durham (lead vocals)
Keith Potger (guitar)
Bruce Woodley (Spanish guitar)
Athol Guy (string bass)

A vocal quartet of Australian origin, The Seekers originally gained popularity in Great Britain with a series of "hootenanny"-style singles. In 1965 they broke through in the United States as well with "I'll Never Find Another You," which reached the top five.

The Seekers reached the peak of their success in 1966, when they were asked to sing the theme for the British film *Georgy Girl*. Released as a single, this tune very nearly topped the charts and eventually generated an extremely popular soft drink commercial.

In 1968 The Seekers disbanded and its members pursued various other interests. Keith Potger went on to form The New Seekers, a very successful group he first sang for and later went on to produce. (See *THE NEW SEEKERS*.)

Mar. 65	**I'LL NEVER FIND ANOTHER YOU** / **Capitol**
May 65	**A WORLD OF OUR OWN** / **Capitol**
Dec. 66	**GEORGY GIRL** / **Capitol**
Feb. 67	**MORNINGTOWN RIDE** / **Capitol**

Bob Seger

BORN: May 6, 1945
HOMETOWN: Ann Arbor, Michigan

One of the leading exponents of Midwest rock 'n' roll, Bob Seger began his career during the early sixties in a number of Detroit-based bands. He first gained attention as an organist with Doug Brown & The Omens, later signing with the local Hideout label.

Bob Seger

After several releases Seger's contract was acquired by the Cameo label. They issued nearly half a dozen singles, one of which, titled "Heavy Music," became a major Midwest hit. By the middle-to-late sixties, however, Cameo had begun to crumble because of legal difficulties and Seger became one of several of the label's artists to affiliate with Capitol.

In 1968 Seger formed a band called The System, which included Dan Honaker (bass), Mike Erelwine (blues harp), Bob Schultz (keyboards), "Pep" Perrine (drums), and Seger on lead guitar. Beginning with "Ramblin' Gamblin' Man," which reached the national top twenty, The Bob Seger System placed three hits on the charts before Seger began once again to assume solo billing.

During the early seventies, Seger affiliated briefly with Palladium/Reprise, after which his releases began once again to appear on Capitol. He achieved the biggest hit of his career in 1976 with a haunting song titled "Night Moves," with his Silver Bullet band.

The Bob Seger System

Dec. 68 *RAMBLIN' GAMBLIN' MAN /* Capitol
May 69 *IVORY /* Capitol
Apr. 70 *LUCIFER /* Capitol

Bob Seger

Nov. 71 *LOOKING BACK /* Capitol
July 72 *IF I WERE A CARPENTER /* Palladium
July 74 *GET OUT OF DENVER /* Palladium
Aug. 75 *KATMANDU /* Capitol
June 76 *NUTBUSH CITY LIMITS /* Capitol
Dec. 76 *NIGHT MOVES /* Capitol
Apr. 77 *MAINSTREET /* Capitol
July 77 *ROCK AND ROLL NEVER FORGETS /* Capitol
May 78 *STILL THE SAME /* Capitol

Senator Bobby

In 1967 Bill Minkin assembled a group of studio musicians known as The Hardly Worthit Players in order to make political parody records. His primary targets were Senator Robert Kennedy and Senator Everett McKinley Dirksen, and he recorded The Troggs' "Wild Thing" in the styles of both politicians. Released back-to-back by the Parkway label, the "Senator Bobby" side became the more popular and eventually climbed into the national top 20. It was followed by a version of Donovan's "Mellow Yellow," which became a lesser hit and the last of the "group's" chart entries.

Jan. 67 *WILD THING /* Parkway
Mar. 67 *MELLOW YELLOW /* Parkway

The Serendipity Singers

MEMBERS:
Bryan Sennett / born: 1942 / Cleveland, Ohio
H. Brooks Hatch / born: 1942 / Los Angeles, California

Lynne Weintraub / born: 1944 / Dallas, Texas
John Madden / born: 1939 / Omaha, Nebraska
Jon Arbenz / born: 1942 / Los Angeles, California
Robert Young / born: 1941 / Denver, Colorado
Michael Brovsky / born: 1942 / Colorado Springs, Colorado
Dianne Decker / born: 1944 / Dallas, Texas
Thomas E. Tiemann / born: 1942 / Austin, Texas

A large folk group in the vein of The New Christy Minstrels, The Serendipities created a unique sound with the use of several guitars, banjos, bass fiddles, and drums. Virtually everyone in the group also sang.

Signed to the Philips label, the group reached the national top ten with "Don't Let the Rain Come Down (Crooked Little Man)," a song written by Ersel Hickey of "Bluebirds over the Mountain" fame. They followed with another major hit called "Beans in My Ears," after which they remained popular largely as a concert attraction.

Feb. 64 *DON'T LET THE RAIN COME DOWN (CROOKED LITTLE MAN) /* Philips
May 64 *BEANS IN MY EARS /* Philips

The Shadows of Knight

MEMBERS:
Sim Sohns (lead vocals, percussion)
Joseph Kelley (lead guitar, bass, blues harp)
Warren Rogers (lead guitar, bass)
Jerry McGeorge (rhythm guitar)
Thomas Schiffour (drums)
HOMETOWN: Chicago, Illinois

A product of Chicago's northwestern suburbs, The Shadows of Knight began as a "garage band" during the mid-sixties. They eventually graduated to the local club circuit, becoming well known for their appearances at such teen clubs as The Cellar in Arlington Heights, Illinois.

In 1966 the group's reputation resulted in a contract offer from the Chicago-based Dunwich label. Debuting with a remake of Van Morrison's "Gloria" (previously recorded by Morrison's group, Them, and the absolute standard among sixties garage bands), The Shadows reached the national top ten and followed with several additional hits. After a two-year hiatus, they emerged in 1968 on the Kasentz-Katz Team label and briefly became part of that year's "bubble gum" trend. They soon disbanded, however, for lack of national hit activity.

Today The Shadows of Knight have regrouped and are active once again in the Chicago area.

Mar. 66 *GLORIA* / Dunwich
June 66 *OH YEAH* / Dunwich
Sept. 66 *BAD LITTLE WOMAN* / Dunwich
Dec. 66 *I'M GONNA MAKE YOU MINE* / Dunwich
Oct. 68 *SHAKE* / Team

Sha Na Na

MEMBERS:
Frederick "Dennis" Greene / born: Jan. 11, 1949 / New York City
"Screamin'" Scott Simon / born: Dec. 9, 1948 / Boston, Massachusetts
John "Jocko" Marcellino / born: May 12, 1950 / Boston, Massachusetts
Donald York / born: Mar. 13, 1949 / Boise, Idaho
John "Bowser" Bauman / born: Sept. 14, 1947 / Queens, New York
Tony Santini / born: Aug. 13, 1948 / Dallas, Texas
Lenny Baker / born: Apr. 18, 1946 / Whitman, Massachusetts
Johnny Contardo / born: Dec. 23, 1951 / Boston, Massachusetts
Dave "Chico" Ryan / born: Apr. 9, 1948 / Arlington, Massachusetts
Dan McBride / born: Nov. 20, 1945 / Boston, Massachusetts

This group was organized at Columbia University in 1969 to perform at a fifties "nostalgia" dance. Taking their name from the recurring chant in The Silhouettes' 1958 recording of "Get a Job," the group was so well received that they decided to develop a professional act.

After rapidly building a reputation for their college and club appearances, Sha Na Na became one of the hits of the Woodstock festival in the summer of 1969. They were also featured at Richard Nader's first rock 'n' roll "revival" in October of that year, debuting soon thereafter with a Kama Sutra album titled *Rock & Roll Is Here to Stay* followed by *Sha Na Na; The Night Is Still Young; The Golden Age of Rock & Roll; From the Streets of New York; Hot Sox;* and *Sha Na Now.*

The group is best known by far for their hit TV show on NBC each week, along with their highly theatrical concert appearances.

Several of the original members have left over the years to pursue other interests—most notably Henry Gross, who had a major solo hit in 1976 with "Shannon." (See *Henry GROSS.*)

Aug. 71 *TOP 40 OF THE LORD* / Kama Sutra
Apr. 75 *JUST LIKE ROMEO & JULIET* / Kama Sutra

The Shangri-Las

MEMBERS:
Mary Weiss (lead vocals)
Betty Weiss
Mary Anne Ganser
Marge Ganser / (deceased)
HOMETOWN: New York City

Undoubtedly the "punkiest" of the mid-sixties "girl-groups," The Shangri-Las were formed by four young women

Sha Na Na. Back row, left to right: John "Bowser" Bowman, John "Jocko" Marcellino; center row, left to right: Dave Ryan, Lenny Baker, Don York, Dan McBride; front row, left to right: "Screamin'" Scott Powell, Denny Greene, John Contardo, Tony Santini

at Andrew Jackson High School in Queens, New York City. Comprising two pairs of sisters (the Ganser sisters were identical twins), the group gained local fame with their imitations of then-current hits.

In 1964 The Shangri-Las came to the attention of independent producer George "Shadow" Morton, who ar-

ranged for a contract with the newly formed Red Bird label. Morton wrote and produced "Remember (Walkin' in the Sand)," a record that quickly established the group by climbing to the national top five. He next employed the writing services of Jeff Barry and Ellie Greenwich (the husband-and-wife team that had earlier provided several

The Shangri-Las

"girl-group" hits for Phil Spector and Lesley Gore) to supply a follow-up. Their contribution was "Leader of the Pack," an instant classic that went straight to number one. In 1967, after several additional hits, the group's career was dealt a severe blow by Red Bird's faltering status, and both soon folded.

Today The Shangri-Las continue to perform and are occasionally seen as part of rock "revival" shows. Now three in number, they have been appearing as a trio ever since Marge Ganser became the fatal victim of an accidental drug overdose several years ago.

Aug. 64	***REMEMBER (WALKIN' IN THE SAND)*** /Red Bird
Oct. 64	***THE LEADER OF THE PACK*** / Red Bird
Dec. 64	***GIVE HIM A GREAT BIG KISS*** / Red Bird
Dec. 64	***MAYBE*** /Red Bird
Apr. 65	***OUT IN THE STREETS*** /Red Bird
May 65	***GIVE US YOUR BLESSING*** / Red Bird
Oct. 65	***RIGHT NOW, NOT LATER*** /Red Bird

Nov. 65	***I CAN NEVER GO HOME ANYMORE*** /**Red Bird**
Feb. 66	***LONG LIVE OUR LOVE*** /**Red Bird**
Apr. 66	***HE CRIED*** /**Red Bird**
June 66	***PAST, PRESENT AND FUTURE*** /**Red Bird**

Sandie Shaw

REAL NAME: Sandra Goodrich
BORN: Feb. 26, 1947
HOMETOWN: Dagenham, Essex, England

One of Great Britain's leading pop stars of the mid-sixties, Sandie Shaw was discovered by yet another pop idol, Adam Faith. Her management was assumed by Eve Taylor, who also handled Faith, and her songwriting and production were taken over by Chris Andrews, who had provided Faith with several major hits. (Andrews later recorded a 1966 hit of his own titled "Yesterday Man.")

In 1964 Sandie began recording for the Pye label and debuted with a rendition of Burt Bacharach and Hal David's "Always Something There to Remind Me." After reaching number one on the British charts, the record was released in the United States by Reprise and became a sizable American hit as well. Sandie followed with "Girl Don't Come," the song for which she became best known, and a number of additional British chart entries. Only one, however, gained popularity with American audiences.

Today Sandie continues her recording career in Great Britain and makes regular appearances on musical television programs. She is also a favorite on the cabaret circuit, often touring the Continent to highly enthusiastic audiences.

Nov. 64	***ALWAYS SOMETHING THERE TO REMIND ME*** /**Reprise**

Mar. 65	***GIRL DON'T COME*** /**Reprise**
June 65	***LONG LIVE LOVE*** /**Reprise**

Bobby Sherman

BORN: July 22, 1945
HOMETOWN: Santa Monica, California

One of the leading teen idols of the sixties, Bobby Sherman decided as a young boy to become a performer. He took up the trumpet at the age of eight, later learning to play such diverse instruments as the piano, French horn, tuba, drums, and guitar. He also gave serious consideration to a career in acting.

Sherman got his first break in the mid-sixties, when he was invited to a party attended by such leading film stars as Natalie Wood, Sal Mineo, and Roddy McDowall. This resulted in an introduction to Jack Good, creator of television's "Shindig," and to an extended engagement on that program. After "Shindig" left the air, he played the role of Jeremy Bolt on "Here Come the Brides" and later costarred in a situation comedy called "Getting Together."

In 1969, after a series of unsuccessful affiliations with such labels as Condor, Decca, and Parkway, Sherman signed with Metromedia and burst onto the charts with his top three recording of "Little Woman." He followed with a string of additional hits that lasted well into the early seventies.

Today Bobby Sherman lives in Los Angeles with his wife, Patty, and their son, Christopher Noel.

Aug. 69	***LITTLE WOMAN*** /**Metromedia**
Nov. 69	***LA LA LA*** /**Metromedia**
Feb. 70	***EASY COME, EASY GO*** /**Metromedia**
May 70	***HEY MR. SUN*** /**Metromedia**
Aug. 70	***JULIE, DO YOU LOVE ME?*** /**Metromedia**

Feb. 71 *CRIED LIKE A BABY /*
Metromedia
May 71 *THE DRUM /* **Metromedia**
Aug. 71 *WAITING AT THE BUS STOP /*
Metromedia
Oct. 71 *JENNIFER /* **Metromedia**
Feb. 72 *TOGETHER AGAIN /*
Metromedia

Shirley & Company

BORN: June 19, 1936
HOMETOWN: New Orleans, Louisiana

A veteran of the record business, Shirley Pixley Goodman began her career in the early fifties by recording a two-dollar demo at New Orleans's Cosmo studio. This was heard by Eddie Messner, head of Aladdin Records, who signed her and created the team of Shirley & Lee. The duo enjoyed a number of chart hits before eventually separating in the early sixties. (See *SHIRLEY & LEE, Rock On: The Solid Gold Years.*)

As the sixties progressed, Shirley occupied herself with session work and made an occasional record under her own name. She also toured for several years with Dr. John's band and periodically sang with Leonard Lee (who is now deceased) at rock "revival" shows.

During the mid-seventies Shirley signed with Sylvia Robinson's Vibration label (Sylvia is yet another veteran of the fifties. See *MICKEY & SYLVIA, Rock On: The Solid Gold Years*). Sylvia provided a song titled "Shame Shame Shame" and assembled a group of studio musicians to record as "Shirley & Company." The record very nearly reached the national top ten and was followed by a lesser hit called "Cry Cry Cry."

Jan. 75 *SHAME SHAME SHAME /*
Vibration
June 75 *CRY CRY CRY /* **Vibration**

The Shocking Blue

MEMBERS:
Mariska Veres (lead vocals)
Robby Van Leeuwen (lead guitar, sitar)
Klaaseje Van Der Wal (bass)
Cornelis Van Der Beek (drums)

The spearhead of the brief "Dutch invasion" of early 1970, this was the first of several Dutch groups that were brought to the attention of American audiences by producer Jerry Ross (See also *THE TEE SET* and *THE GEORGE BAKER SELECTION.*)

The Shocking Blue had been organized in 1967 by Robby Van Leeuwen, a veteran of a well-known Dutch rock band called The Motions. After some inconsequential recording work, they signed with the Pink Elephant label and swept Europe in 1969 with a major hit titled "Venus." This was released by Ross on his Colossus label, and it soon became a number one American hit as well.

Although The Shocking Blue achieved only two more American chart entries, they continued recording successfully at home well into the mid-seventies. Today, Robby Van Leeuwen has left the group, and their future appears to be somewhat in limbo.

Dec. 69 *VENUS /* **Colossus**
Mar. 70 *MIGHTY JOE /* **Colossus**
June 70 *LONG & LONESOME ROAD /*
Colossus

Bunny Sigler

HOMETOWN: Philadelphia, Pennsylvania

Bunny Sigler began his career by singing with various groups on Philadelphia street corners. He eventually decided to go solo, achieving some recognition on the local small-club circuit.

During the mid-sixties Sigler began recording for a number of local "Philly" labels, gaining success in 1967 with Parkway Records. Specializing in medleys of earlier R & B hits, he reached the top 20 with "Let the Good Times Roll & Feel So Good" and followed successfully with a similar piece of material. By the end of 1967, however, he had been brought into the Gamble-Huff fold and had begun concentrating his activities on songwriting. Over the following years, he provided material for such artists as The Three Degrees, Blue Magic, The Stylistics, The O'Jays, The Intruders, and Billy Paul.

In 1973 Sigler resumed his recording career by affiliating with Gamble & Huff's Philadelphia International label. He has continued this affiliation through the present day, and he often produces for that company as well.

June 67	*LET THE GOOD TIMES ROLL & FEEL SO GOOD* /Parkway
Oct. 67	*LOVEY DOVEY & YOU'RE SO FINE* /Parkway
Feb. 73	*TOSSIN' & TURNIN'* / Philadelphia International
Feb. 78	*LET ME PARTY WITH YOU* / Gold Mind

The Silkie

MEMBERS:
Silvia Tatler (lead vocals) /born: 1945 /Stoke-On-Trent, England
Michael Ramsden (guitar) /born: 1943 /Devon, England
Ivor Aylesbury (guitar) /born: 1943 /Surrey, England
John Kevyn Cunningham (bass) /born: 1940/ Liverpool, England

Silvia Tatler, Mike Ramsden, and Ivor Aylesbury first got together at Hull University during the summer of 1963. Originally a folk trio, they were joined by Kev Cunningham in October of that year and made their first appearance as a quartet at a student folk festival.

During the mid-sixties after building a reputation in clubs, The Silkie came to the attention of Beatles manager Brian Epstein. He began to handle the group, obtaining a contract with Fontana Records and arranging for their first release, "Blood Red River." Their second release, recorded on August 13, 1965, is somewhat historic in that it was one of very few outside projects pursued by The Beatles during this period. Titled "You've Got to Hide Your Love Away" (a song performed by The Beatles in the film *Help!*), this recording was produced by The Beatles and employed John, Paul, and George as session musicians. It became a major international hit and reached the American top ten.

Although this was The Silkie's only American chart entry, the group continued recording in England through the end of 1966. By the late sixties, however, the group had disbanded.

Oct. 65	*YOU'VE GOT TO HIDE YOUR LOVE AWAY* /Fontana

Silver Convention

MEMBERS:
Penny McLean
Ramona Wolf
Rhonda Heath
HOMETOWN: Munich, Germany

Just when the disco sound was catching on in this country around 1975, a group from Munich, Germany, formed by Michael Kunze and Silvester Levay, started getting a lot of play throughout Europe. The group, which consisted of six musicians and three female vocalists, recorded a tune written by Levay called "Fly, Robin, Fly,"

Carly Simon

which went on to become a number one national hit in the United States.

Oct. 75	***FLY, ROBIN, FLY*** /**Midland International**
Mar. 76	***GET UP AND BOOGIE*** / **Midland International**
Aug. 76	***NO, NO, JOE*** /**Midland International**

Carly Simon

BORN: June 25, 1945
HOMETOWN: New York City

The daughter of Richard Simon of the Simon & Schuster publishing company, Carly Simon was born into a rich musical environment. Both her parents were deeply interested in the classics, while her oldest sister pursued a career as an opera singer.

During the early sixties, Carly teamed up with another of her sisters, Lucy, to form The Simon Sisters. They performed regularly on the Greenwich Village folk circuit, eventually signing with Kapp Records and achieving a moderate hit entitled ''Winkin, Blinkin & Nod.'' The act broke up when Lucy got married, and Carly continued as a solo artist.

In 1966 Carly came to the attention of Albert Grossman, the famed manager of Bob Dylan, Peter, Paul & Mary, and later of The Band. He arranged a recording session for Columbia, which was supervised by Bob Johnston (Dylan's producer) and included material especially written by Dylan for the occasion. In addition, the session musicians included the likes of Al Kooper, Mike Bloomfield, Paul Griffin, Robbie Robertson, and Rick Danko. By the time the material was ready for release, however, severe differences had developed between Carly and Grossman, and the entire project was shelved.

After spending several years contemplating her next move, Carly signed with Elektra in 1970 and began work on her debut album, titled *Carly Simon.* Released in 1971, this established her career and yielded the first of her many hit singles, "That's the Way I've Always Heard It Should Be." Her subsequent albums have been continual best sellers, including *Anticipation, No Secrets, Hotcakes, Playing Possum,* and *Another Passenger.*

Today Carly Simon is married to rock star James Taylor, and they have two children.

The Simon Sisters
Apr. 64　**WINKIN, BLINKIN & NOD /
　　　　Kapp**
Carly Simon
Apr. 71　**THAT'S THE WAY I'VE
　　　　ALWAYS HEARD IT SHOULD
　　　　BE / Elektra**
Dec. 71　**ANTICIPATION / Elektra**
Mar. 72　**A LEGEND IN YOUR OWN
　　　　TIME / Elektra**
Dec. 72　**YOU'RE SO VAIN / Elektra**
Mar. 73　**THE RIGHT THING TO DO /
　　　　Elektra**
Feb. 74　**MOCKINGBIRD (with James
　　　　Taylor) / Elektra**
May 74　**HAVEN'T GOT TIME FOR THE
　　　　PAIN / Elektra**

May 75　**ATTITUDE DANCING / Elektra**
July 75　**WATERFALL / Elektra**
Oct. 75　**MORE & MORE / Elektra**
June 76　**IT KEEPS YOU RUNNIN' /
　　　　Elektra**
July 77　**NOBODY DOES IT BETTER /
　　　　Elektra**
Apr. 78　**YOU BELONG TO ME / Elektra**

Joe Simon

BORN: 1945
HOMETOWN: Shimmesport, Louisiana

Raised in a small town just outside New Orleans, Joe Simon was strongly influenced by the area's rhythm & blues, jazz, and gospel. When he was fifteen, his family relocated to Oakland, California—another musically rich area—where he began singing regularly in church.

In 1960 Simon began recording for such small labels as Hush and Gee-Bee. After nearly half a dozen releases, two were acquired by Vee Jay for national distribution and one, called "Let's Do It Over," became a substantial R & B hit in 1965. This led to a contract offer from John Richbourg, who signed him to his (Richbourg's) Sound Stage 7 label.

Beginning in 1966 Simon achieved a long string of hits for the company, including a top ten entry called "The Chokin' Kind." He switched in 1970 to Julie Rifkind's Spring label, where his string of successes remains unbroken up to the present day.

Today Joe Simon is a major soul star and a highly popular concert attraction.

June 66　**A TEENAGER'S PRAYER /
　　　　Sound Stage 7**
Feb. 67　**MY SPECIAL PRAYER / Sound
　　　　Stage 7**
Sept. 67　**NINE POUND STEEL / Sound
　　　　Stage 7**
Jan. 68　**NO SAD SONGS / Sound Stage7**

Apr. 68	*HANGIN' ON* / Sound Stage 7
Sept. 68	*A MESSAGE FROM MARIA* / Sound Stage 7
Nov. 68	*I WORRY ABOUT YOU* / Sound Stage 7
Dec. 68	*LOOKING BACK* / Sound Stage 7
Mar. 69	*THE CHOKIN' KIND* / Sound Stage 7
June 69	*BABY, DON'T BE LOOKING IN MY MIND* / Sound Stage 7
Sept. 69	*SAN FRANCISCO IS A LONELY TOWN* / Sound Stage 7
Oct. 69	*IT'S HARD TO GET ALONG* / Sound Stage 7
Jan. 70	*MOON WALK* / Sound Stage 7
Apr. 70	*FARTHER ON DOWN THE ROAD* / Sound Stage 7
Aug. 70	*YOUR LOVE* / Sound Stage 7
Oct. 70	*THAT'S THE WAY I WANT OUR LOVE* / Sound Stage 7
Dec. 70	*YOUR TIME TO CRY* / Spring
May 71	*HELP ME MAKE IT THROUGH THE NIGHT* / Spring
July 71	*YOU'RE THE ONE FOR ME* / Spring
Sept. 71	*ALL MY HARD TIMES* / Spring
Nov. 71	*DROWNING IN THE SEA OF LOVE* / Spring
Mar. 72	*THE POOL OF BAD LUCK* / Spring
July 72	*THE POWER OF LOVE* / Spring
Oct. 72	*MISTY BLUE* / Sound Stage 7
Nov. 72	*TROUBLE IN MY HOME* / Spring
Feb. 73	*STEP BY STEP* / Spring
July 73	*THEME FROM CLEOPATRA JONES* / Spring
Nov. 73	*THE RIVER* / Spring
Apr. 75	*GET DOWN, GET DOWN* / Spring
Aug. 75	*MUSIC IN MY BONES* / Spring

Simon & Garfunkel

MEMBERS:

Paul Frederick Simon / born: Nov. 5, 1941 / Newark, New Jersey

Arthur Garfunkel / born: Oct. 13, 1942 / Queens, New York

The absolute leading exponents of urban folkrock, Simon and Garfunkel emerged during the mid-sixties as one of the leading recording acts in the his-tory of the modern record business. Additionally, Paul Simon soon became established as one of the most important songwriter-poets of his generation.

Simon and Garfunkel first met during the early fifties in a school play at PS 164 in Queens, New York City. After the two had become friends and discovered a mutual interest in music, they eventually formed an act called Tom and Jerry and began making demo records. One of these, "Hey Schoolgirl," was heard in 1957 by Sid Prosen, who released it on his Big label and helped make it into a moderate national hit. (See *TOM & JERRY, Rock On: The Solid Gold Years*.) Although several additional releases were forthcoming, none was successful and the duo split up for a time to pursue individual interests.

During the early sixties, Art Garfunkel was relatively inactive in the music business (he recorded briefly for Warwick as Artie Garr) while Paul Simon was exactly the opposite. Simon teamed up with Carol King to make demo records for various companies, and, under the name of Jerry Landis, contributed to a number of records as a writer, producer, and artist. He also recorded with a group called Tico & The Triumphs, achieving a brief chart entry with a song called "Motorcycle." (See *TICO & THE TRIUMPHS, Rock On: The Solid Gold Years*.)

In 1964 Simon and Garfunkel rejoined forces and signed with Columbia Records. Their first project, under the production auspices of Tom Wilson, was an acoustic folk album titled *Wednesday Morning, 3 A.M.* When this failed to generate any interest, they traveled to England to work on a project called *The Paul Simon Songbook.*

Simon & Garfunkel. Art Garfunkel (left), Paul Simon

In the interim, Tom Wilson began to experiment with the album, dubbing electric guitar and rhythm onto one of the cuts, "Sounds of Silence," and releasing it as a single. This became an instant hit, eventually reaching number one, and was high on the charts by the time the surprised Simon and Garfunkel returned from Europe!

Their career solidly in motion, the duo followed with a long string of major hit singles and a series of multimillion-selling albums, including *Sounds of Silence, Parsley, Sage, Rosemary & Thyme, Bookends,* and *Bridge over Troubled Water.* Additionally, their music was used by Mike Nichols as the soundtrack for the movie *The Graduate,* and the resulting album ranked with the others as a major best seller.

In 1971 Simon & Garfunkel announced that they were separating to pursue individual careers. Art Garfunkel went on to high acclaim as an actor, eventually recording as a solo artist. (See *Art GARFUNKEL.*) Paul Simon continued with a string of hit singles, and with albums such as *Paul Simon, There goes Rhymin' Simon, Live Rhymin',* and *Still Crazy after All These Years.*

Late in 1975 the duo decided to record together once again, but only on an occasional basis. They began this arrangement with a major hit titled "My Little Town."

Simon & Garfunkel
Nov. 65 *THE SOUNDS OF SILENCE /* **Columbia**

Feb. 66	*HOMEWARD BOUND /* **Columbia**
May 66	*I AM A ROCK /* **Columbia**
Aug. 66	*THE DANGLING CONVER- SATION /* **Columbia**
Nov. 66	*A HAZY SHADE OF WINTER /* **Columbia**
Mar. 67	*AT THE ZOO /* **Columbia**
July 67	*FAKIN' IT /* **Columbia**
Mar. 68	*SCARBOROUGH FAIR/ CANTICLE /* **Columbia**
Apr. 68	*MRS. ROBINSON /* **Columbia**
Apr. 69	*THE BOXER /* **Columbia**
Feb. 70	*BRIDGE OVER TROUBLED WATER /* **Columbia**
Apr. 70	*CECELIA /* **Columbia**
Sept. 70	*EL CONDOR PASA /* **Columbia**
Sept. 72	*FOR EMILY, WHENEVER I MAY FIND HER /* **Columbia**
Nov. 72	*AMERICA /* **Columbia**
Oct. 75	*MY LITTLE TOWN /* **Columbia**

Paul Simon

Feb. 72	*MOTHER & CHILD REUNION /* **Columbia**
Apr. 72	*ME AND JULIO DOWN BY THE SCHOOLYARD /* **Columbia**
July 72	*DUNCAN /* **Columbia**
May 73	*KODACHROME /* **Columbia**
Aug. 73	*LOVES ME LIKE A ROCK /* **Columbia**
Dec. 73	*AN AMERICAN TUNE /* **Columbia**
Dec. 75	*50 WAYS TO LEAVE YOUR LOVER /* **Columbia**
May 76	*STILL CRAZY AFTER ALL THESE YEARS /* **Columbia**
Oct. 77	*SLIP SLIDIN' AWAY /* **Columbia**

Paul Simon & Phoebe Snow

Aug. 75	*GONE AT LAST /* **Columbia**

Nancy Sinatra

BORN: June 8, 1940
HOMETOWN: Jersey City, New Jersey

The eldest child of Frank Sinatra (and the subject of the song "Nancy with the Laughing Eyes"), Nancy had a great deal of preparation in the arts as a child. Her training included 11 years of piano, eight years of dance, five years of voice and singing lessons under Carlo Menotti, and five years of dramatic study. Her first major appearance came in 1960, when she joined Elvis Presley and her father for a television special.

In 1961 Nancy signed with Reprise Records (then owned by her father) and made a number of singles, including "Like I Do," "Tonight You Belong to Me," and "Think of Me." These reached the top of the charts in such far-flung countries as Italy, Japan, Holland, Belgium, and South Africa, but received very little attention at home. After forming an association with writer-producer Lee Hazlewood, however, she broke through in 1966 with her number one recording of "These Boots Are Made for Walkin'." This was followed by a long string of hits, some in collaboration with Hazlewood as an artist and one, "Somethin' Stupid," with her famous father.

Today Nancy lives in Los Angeles with her husband, TV producer Hugh Lambert (she was at one time married to singing star Tommy Sands), and their daughter, Angela Jennifer. She is affiliated with the Private Stock label and records in association with producer Snuff Garrett.

Nancy Sinatra

Oct. 65	*SO LONG, BABE /* **Reprise**
Jan. 66	*THESE BOOTS ARE MADE FOR WALKIN' /* **Reprise**
Apr. 66	*HOW DOES THAT GRAB YOU, DARLIN'? /* **Reprise**
July 66	*FRIDAY'S CHILD /* **Reprise**
Sept. 66	*IN OUR TIME /* **Reprise**
Nov. 66	*SUGAR TOWN /* **Reprise**
Mar. 67	*LOVE EYES /* **Reprise**
June 67	*YOU ONLY LIVE TWICE /* **Reprise**
Sept. 67	*LIGHTNING'S GIRL /* **Reprise**
Dec. 67	*TONY ROME /* **Reprise**
Mar. 68	*100 YEARS /* **Reprise**
July 68	*HAPPY /* **Reprise**
Nov. 68	*GOOD TIME GIRL /* **Reprise**
Mar. 69	*GOD KNOWS I LOVE YOU /* **Reprise**

May 69 *HERE WE GO AGAIN* / **Reprise**
Sept. 69 *DRUMMER MAN* / **Reprise**
Nancy & Frank Sinatra
Mar. 67 *SOMETHIN' STUPID* / **Reprise**
Nancy Sinatra & Lee Hazlewood
Mar. 67 *SUMMER WINE* / **Reprise**
June 67 *JACKSON* / **Reprise**
Oct. 67 *LADY BIRD* / **Reprise**
Jan. 68 *SOME VELVET MORNING* /
Reprise

Gordon Sinclair

BORN: June 3, 1900
HOMETOWN: Toronto, Canada

On June 5, 1973, Gordon Sinclair, a famed author and commentator, read an editorial called "The Americans" as part of his "Let's Be Personal" program on Toronto's radio station CFRB. Proclaiming Americans as one of the world's most unappreciated and unjustly maligned peoples, the editorial was widely reprinted and stirred a greal deal of controversy.

Later in the year, a Detroit newscaster named Byron MacGregor read it on the air and ultimately drew thousands of phone calls. This prompted the Detroit-based Westbound label to record MacGregor's rendering, which became a major best seller. (See *Byron MacGREGOR.*) Avco Records released a similar recording by Sinclair, the editorial's original author, and it, too, became a major hit.

Jan. 74 *THE AMERICANS* / **Avco**

The Sir Douglas Quintet

MEMBERS:
Sir Douglas (Douglas Saldana Sahm) (lead vocals & guitar) / born: Nov. 6, 1942
Augie Meyer (keyboards)
Jack Barber (bass)
Leon Beatty (percussion)
John Perez (drums)

HOMETOWN: San Antonio, Texas

One of the leading "Tex-Mex" rock 'n' roll bands, this group was organized by its leader and driving force, Doug Sahm.

Sahm had begun his career at the age of six, when he appeared as "Little Doug" on radio station KMAC in his hometown, San Antonio. He became fascinated with the blues as a teenager, often attending the performances of such artists as T. Bone Walker and Little Willie John and imitating their styles.

In 1957 Sahm began performing in local clubs, eventually forming a number of groups. Two of these, The Markays and The Spirits, recorded for such labels as Harlem, Swingin', Personality, and Renner and brought Sahm to the attention of Houston producer Huey P. Meaux. Signing with Meaux's Tribe label, Sahm assembled The Sir Douglas Quintet (a name he picked to give the impression that it was a British group!) and achieved a major worldwide hit with "She's about a Mover." He later switched to Mercury and scored with two hits on the subsidiary Smash label.

Today, after a series of continuous personnel changes, the group is known simply as Doug Sahm and Band. They are affiliated with the Atlantic label, and often assist other artists as session musicians.

Apr. 65 *SHE'S ABOUT A MOVER* /
Tribe
Jan. 66 *THE RAINS CAME* / **Tribe**
Jan. 69 *MENDOCINO* / **Smash**
Aug. 69 *DYNAMITE WOMAN* / **Tribe**

Skylark

MEMBERS:
Donny Gerrard (lead vocals)
Bonnie Jean Cook Foster (lead vocals)

Norman McPherson (lead guitar) / replaced by Allan Mix

David Foster (keyboards)

Steven Pugsley (bass)

Carl Graves (percussion)

Duris Maxwell (drums) / replaced by Brian Hilton

HOMETOWN: Vancouver, British Columbia

Skylark was organized during the early seventies by David Foster and B. J. Cook, two former members of Ronnie Hawkins's backing band. Once separated from Hawkins, they recruited the new group from the back-up bands of other leading artists.

After nearly six months of rehearsals, Skylark was signed by Capitol of Canada and began work on their first album in 1972. A single was culled from the album, but with very little success. In the meantime, however, another cut, titled "Wildflower," was receiving a great deal of airplay on Windsor's CKLW. Released as the group's next single, its success soon spread across the border to Detroit and eventually throughout the United States and Canada. "Wildflower" became a top ten hit, but, before the group could prepare a follow-up, internal difficulties caused them to disband.

Feb. 73 *WILDFLOWER* / Capitol

Percy Sledge

BORN: 1941
HOMETOWN: Leighton, Alabama

Interested in a singing career since his mid-teens, Percy Sledge began by performing at local parties and dances. At the age of twenty, he joined a group called The Esquires Combo and became well known around the Alabama-Mississippi area.

In 1965 one of Sledge's friends suggested that he pursue a solo career. He also recommended Quin Ivy, a well-known deejay and record producer, as a possible source of help. Sledge auditioned for Ivy, who immediately arranged for a recording session at his Norala Studio in Sheffield, Alabama. The result was "When a Man Loves a Woman," which was released by Atlantic and eventually climbed to number one on the charts. He followed with a long string of hits that lasted well into the late sixties.

During the mid-seventies Sledge signed with Phil Walden's Capricorn label and returned once again to the national best-seller lists.

Apr. 66	*WHEN A MAN LOVES A WOMAN* / Atlantic
July 66	*WARM & TENDER LOVE* / Atlantic
Oct. 66	*IT TEARS ME UP* / Atlantic
Feb. 67	*BABY, HELP ME* / Atlantic
Apr. 67	*OUT OF LEFT FIELD* / Atlantic
June 67	*LOVE ME TENDER* / Atlantic
July 67	*WHAT AM I LIVING FOR* / Atlantic
Sept. 67	*JUST OUT OF REACH* / Atlantic
Nov. 67	*COVER ME* / Atlantic
Mar. 68	*TAKE TIME TO KNOW HER* / Atlantic
Aug. 68	*SUDDEN STOP* / Atlantic
Feb. 69	*MY SPECIAL PRAYER* / Atlantic
Apr. 69	*ANY DAY NOW* / Atlantic
Nov. 74	*I'LL BE YOUR EVERYTHING* / Capricorn

Sly & The Family Stone

MEMBERS:

Sly Stone (Sylvester Stewart) (lead vocals, keyboards) / born: Mar. 15, 1944 / Dallas, Texas

Fred Stone (Fred Stewart) (guitar) / born: June 5, 1946 / Dallas, Texas

Cynthia Robinson (trumpet) / born: Jan. 12, 1946 / Sacramento, California

Jerry Martini (sax) / born: Oct. 1, 1943 / Boulder, Colorado

Rose Stone (Rose Stewart) (keyboards) / born: Mar. 21, 1945 / Vallejo, California

Sly Stone

Lawrence Graham, Jr. (bass)/born: Aug. 14, 1946/Beaumont, Texas

Gregg Errico (drums)/born: Sept. 1, 1946/San Francisco, California

One of the earliest of the "psyche-delic soul" bands and highly influential on many future groups, Sly & The Family Stone emerged from the San Francisco area during the mid-sixties.

The group's central figure, Sly Stone, began singing in a family gospel group when he was four. At sixteen he cut a song called "Long Time Away" for the G & P label and was able to achieve a moderate local hit. During the early sixties, Sly teamed up with his brother Fred to form a number of groups. They recorded for Ensign as The Stewart Brothers and achieved regional success in a group called The Viscanes. As the sixties progressed, Sly gained fame as a disc jockey on San Francisco's KDIA. He also became affiliated with the Autumn label, making several records while writing and producing for such acts as The Beau Brummels, Bobby Freeman, and The Mojo Men.

In 1966 Sly organized a band called The Stoners. Although this was an un-successful and relatively short-lived venture, it did bring him into contact with Cynthia Robinson, a trumpet play-er who would become one of the key figures in his next group, The Family Stone.

After becoming noted for their club appearances and for some recording work on the local Loadstone label, Sly & The Family Stone were signed in 1967 by Epic Records. They debuted with an album called *A Whole New Thing,* which yielded a major hit single titled "Dance to the Music." In addition to a long string of additional hits, the group achieved several best-selling al-bums, including *Dance to the Music, Stand!, There's a Riot Going On, Fresh, Small Talk,* and *High on You.* Additionally, they were one of the out-standing attractions at the Woodstock festival and were prominently featured in the film of that event.

Although the group continues offi-cially to exist, their future seems some-what cloudy. They have undergone nu-merous personnel changes (the most notable one involving Larry Graham, who went on to form Graham Central Station), and they seemingly have not yet overcome the stigma of Sly Stone's celebrated personal difficulties.

Feb. 68	*DANCE TO THE MUSIC*/Epic
July 68	*LIFE*/Epic
Aug. 68	*M'LADY*/Epic
Nov. 68	*EVERYDAY PEOPLE*/Epic
Mar. 69	*SING A SIMPLE SONG*/Epic
Apr. 69	*STAND!*/Epic
May 69	*I WANT TO TAKE YOU HIGHER*/Epic
Aug. 69	*HOT FUN IN THE SUMMERTIME*/Epic

Jan. 70 *THANK YOU* / **Epic**
Jan. 70 *EVERYBODY IS A STAR* / **Epic**
May 70 *I WANT TO TAKE YOU HIGHER*
(rereleased) / **Epic**
Nov. 71 *A FAMILY AFFAIR* / **Epic**
Feb. 72 *RUNNIN' AWAY* / **Epic**
Apr. 72 *SMILING* / **Epic**
June 73 *IF YOU WANT ME TO STAY* / **Epic**
Nov. 73 *FRISKY* / **Epic**
July 74 *TIME FOR LIVIN'* / **Epic**
Oct. 74 *LOOSE BOOTY* / **Epic**

Millie Small

REAL NAME: Millicent Smith
BORN: Oct. 6, 1946
HOMETOWN: Jamaica, West Indies

During the early sixties, Chris Blackwell, a British entrepreneur, helped to organize the Jamaican record business by consolidating a number of small labels under his Island banner.

In 1964 Millie Small became one of the first Island artists to achieve major international success. Reviving Barbie Gaye's earlier hit "My Boy Lollipop," she added a "ska" beat and contributed much to the popularization of this sound. After the record had become a best seller in Jamaica and England, it was distributed in the United States by Smash (a subsidiary of Mercury) and very nearly reached the top of the charts. Millie followed with a lesser hit called "Sweet William," after which her popularity centered mainly in her native Jamaica.

Today the "ska" has gradually evolved into what we now know as reggae.

May 64 *MY BOY LOLLIPOP* / **Smash**
Aug. 64 *SWEET WILLIAM* / **Smash**

The Small Faces

MEMBERS:
Steven Marriott (lead vocals, guitar) / born: Jan. 30, 1947

James Winston (keyboards) / replaced (1966) by Ian McLagen / born: May 12, 1946
Ronald Lane (bass) / born: Apr. 1, 1948
Kenneth Jones (drums) / born: Sept. 16, 1949

This band was organized during the mid-sixties by Steve Marriott, a former child actor who had played previously in such groups as The Moments and The Frantics. Marriott provided the group's unusual name ("small" denoting the members' relative lack of height and "face" having been a popular "mod" term for a person of importance) and they began by playing clubs in the Sheffield area of England.

The Small Faces were signed by British Decca in 1966, debuting with a major hit single titled "Sha La La La Lee." They followed with the chart-topping "All or Nothing" and with an album titled *The Small Faces*, after which they switched affiliation to the Immediate label. At this point, their singles began to appear on the American charts as well, while their subsequent albums included *Ogden's Nut Gone Flake* and *Autumn Stone*—both best-sellers.

In 1968 Steve Marriott announced that he was leaving the group to join Humble Pie. Although this was perceived at first to be a fatal blow, the group replaced him with Ron Wood and Rod Stewart (both formerly of The Jeff Beck Group) and achieved new heights of acclaim and commericial success as Faces. (See *FACES*.)

Nov. 67 *ITCHYCOO PARK* / **Immediate**
Mar. 68 *TIN SOLDIER* / **Immediate**

Smith

MEMBERS:
Gayle McCormick (lead vocals)
Alan Parker (guitar)
Judd Huss (bass)

Robert Evans (drums, percussion)

One of the very few sixties "hard rock" bands to feature a female lead singer (the most noted were, of course, Big Brother and Jefferson Airplane), Smith emerged in 1969 with the driving vocals of Gayle McCormick.

Signed to the Dunhill label, the group reached the national top five with a slowed-down revival of The Shirelles' "Baby It's You." They were able to follow with two lesser hits before disbanding in the early seventies. Gayle McCormick went on to pursue a solo career, and she records today for the Shady Brook label.

Sept. 69 *BABY IT'S YOU* /Dunhill
Feb. 70 *TAKE A LOOK AROUND* / Dunhill
June 70 *WHAT AM I GONNA DO* /Dunhill

Hurricane Smith

REAL NAME: Norman Smith
BORN: 1923

Born in north England, Norman Smith came from a musical family of gypsy ancestry. He began playing drums at the age of six, eventually becoming proficient on such other instruments as the trumpet, trombone, piano, bass, and vibes.

During the early sixties, Smith was employed by EMI's famed Abbey Road studios in London. He became well known for his production work with Pink Floyd and for the engineering work that he did for The Beatles (up through their *Rubber Soul* album). He was also extremely active as a session musician.

During the early seventies, Smith assumed the pseudonym of "Hurricane" (from the 1952 film *Hurricane Smith*) and launched his career as a recording artist. He achieved a British hit single with "Don't Let It Die," a poignant ecology song, and major international success with "Oh Babe, What Would You Say" (a top three chart entry).

Today Norman Smith continues his activities in England as a producer.

Dec. 72 *OH BABE, WHAT WOULD YOU SAY* /Capitol
Mar. 73 *WHO WAS IT?* /Capitol

Sammi Smith

BORN: Aug. 5, 1943
HOMETOWN: Orange, California

Sammi began her career during the early sixties by touring the southwestern club circuit. In 1967, while appearing in Oklahoma City, she met Johnny Cash and his band, who also were appearing there. She gave an audition tape to Marshall Grant, Cash's bass player, who in turn brought her to Cash's attention.

With the help of Cash and Grant, Sammi traveled to Nashville and signed with Columbia Records. Although this brought her very little success, she did meet a then-unknown named Kris Kristofferson, who was doing odd jobs around the Columbia studios at the time. When Sammi later signed with Mega, Kristofferson supplied his composition of "Help Me Make It through the Night," a record that ultimately became a multimillion seller.

Today Sammi Smith lives in Garland, Texas, and maintains an extremely active touring schedule.

Jan. 71 *HELP ME MAKE IT THROUGH THE NIGHT* /Mega
Aug. 72 *I'VE GOT TO HAVE YOU* / Mega

Phoebe Snow

REAL NAME: Phoebe Laub
BORN: July 17, 1952
HOMETOWN: New York City

Raised in Teaneck, New Jersey, Phoebe took piano lessons as a child and developed an early interest in the blues and jazz forms. As she grew older, however, she took up the guitar as her primary instrument.

During the early seventies, Phoebe attended Shimer College in Illinois but soon dropped out to perform in New York. She became a regular on the Greenwich Village club circuit and drew the attention of talent scouts and record producers during a performance at The Bitter End.

In 1974 Phoebe obtained a contract with the Shelter label, debuting with an album titled simply *Phoebe Snow*. This yielded the top five single "Poetry Man," a highly acclaimed record which firmly established her as an important new artist. Before she could prepare a follow-up, severe differences developed between Phoebe and Shelter, and she expressed the desire to affiliate with a new company. After protracted legal proceedings, she was allowed to sign with Columbia in 1975 and begin work on a second album.

Today Phoebe lives in Fort Lee, New Jersey, with her husband, Phil Kearns, and their daughter, Valerie Rose.

Jan. 75 *POETRY MAN*/**Shelter**
Jan. 77 *SHAKY GROUND*/**Columbia**

Sonny & Cher

MEMBERS:
Salvatore Phillip Bono /born: Feb. 16, 1935/ Detroit, Michigan
Cherilyn Sakisian LaPierre /born: May 20, 1946/El Centro, California

Sonny & Cher emerged during the mid-sixties as leading teen idols but eventually became favorites among adult audiences as well.

Sonny had begun his career during the fifties as an A & R man and producer for Specialty Records. He occasionally recorded for the label as Don Christy, and did some songwriting under the name of Sonny Christy. During the early sixties, he worked briefly for the Hi-Fi label and began to achieve some success as a songwriter. The Righteous Brothers recorded his composition of "Koko Joe," while Jackie DeShannon picked up his "Needles & Pins" (which later became a hit for The Searchers).

In 1964 Sonny was working as a session singer for Phil Spector when he met and married Cher, another of Spector's background vocalists. The two are heard on many of Spector's hits of the period, and Cher made one solo record, as Bonnie Jo Mason, titled "I Love You Ringo."

By 1965 the duo had separated from Spector and were performing as Caesar & Cleo. After assuming their real names, they recorded briefly for Reprise and subsequently signed with the Atco label. Beginning with the classic "I Got You Babe," they achieved a long string of hits (on various labels) that extended well into the seventies. Although Sonny did very little solo recording (he occupied himself mainly with songwriting and production), Cher also scored with a number of her own best sellers.

During the early seventies, Sonny & Cher added a new phase to their career by hosting their own network television program. This eventually split into two individual shows, both of which failed, and they rejoined forces in 1975. Although they have continued their professional association, Sonny and Cher were divorced in 1974. Cher subsequently married rock star Gregg Allman, but this relationship recently

Sonny & Cher

Sonny & Cher

ended as well. Cher's two children are
Chastity Bono and Elijah Blue Allman.

Sonny & Cher

July 65	*I GOT YOU BABE* / Atco
Aug. 65	*BABY DON'T GO* / Reprise
Oct. 65	*THE LETTER* / Atco
Aug. 65	*JUST YOU* / Atco
Oct. 65	*BUT YOU'RE MINE* / Atco
Jan. 66	*WHAT NOW, MY LOVE* / Atco
June 66	*HAVE I STAYED TOO LONG?* / Atco
Oct. 66	*LITTLE MAN* / Atco
Nov. 66	*LIVING FOR YOU* / Atco
Jan. 67	*THE BEAT GOES ON* / Atco
Apr. 67	*A BEAUTIFUL STORY* / Atco
June 67	*PLASTIC MAN* / Atco
Aug. 67	*IT'S THE LITTLE THINGS* / Atco
Dec. 67	*A GOOD COMBINATION* / Atco
Oct. 71	*ALL I EVER NEED IS YOU* / Kapp
Feb. 72	*A COWBOY'S WORK IS NEVER DONE* / Kapp
July 72	*WHEN YOU SAY LOVE* / Kapp
Mar. 73	*MAMA WAS A ROCK & ROLL SINGER* / Kapp

Sonny

Aug. 65	*LAUGH AT ME* / Atco
Nov. 65	*THE REVOLUTION KIND* / Atco

Cher

July 65	*ALL I REALLY WANT TO DO* / Imperial
Oct. 65	*WHERE DO YOU GO* / Imperial
Mar. 66	*BANG BANG* / Imperial
July 66	*ALFIE* / Imperial
Nov. 66	*BEHIND THE DOOR* / Imperial
Sept. 67	*HEY JOE* / Imperial
Oct. 67	*YOU BETTER SIT DOWN, KIDS* / Imperial
Sept. 71	*GYPSIES, TRAMPS & THIEVES* / Kapp
Jan. 72	*THE WAY OF LOVE* / Kapp

May 72 *LIVING IN A HOUSE DIVIDED*/Kapp
Sept. 72 *DON'T HIDE YOUR LOVE*/Kapp
Aug. 73 *HALF BREED*/MCA
Jan. 74 *DARK LADY*/MCA
May 74 *TRAIN OF THOUGHT*/MCA
Aug. 74 *I SAW A MAN AND HE DANCED WITH HIS WIFE*/MCA

Sopwith Camel

MEMBERS:
Peter Kraemer (lead vocals, sax)
Terry MacNeil (lead guitar)
William Sievers (guitar)
Martin Beard (bass)
Norman Mayell (drums)
HOMETOWN: San Francisco, California

Formed during the early-middle sixties, Sopwith Camel took their name from a famed World War I aircraft. They were among the leading protagonists of the "goodtime" sound but often played alongside such "heavy" San Francisco bands as The Grateful Dead and Jefferson Airplane.

In 1966 Sopwith Camel formed an association with producer Erik Jacobsen, known for his work with The Lovin' Spoonful. He produced "Hello Hello" and arranged for its release on the Kama Sutra label. It became a top 20 hit, but, after one follow-up, the group disbanded.

In 1973, after having occupied themselves as session musicians, four of the original members re-formed Sopwith Camel. William Sievers did not join the new group, but instead pursued a solo career under the name of William Truckaway. The "new" Camel signed with Warner Brothers and debuted with an album titled "The Miraculous Bump Returns from the Moon."

Dec. 66 *HELLO HELLO*/Kama Sutra

Apr. 67 *A POSTCARD FROM JAMAICA*/Kama Sutra

David Soul

HOMETOWN: Mexico City, Mexico

As a youngster David traveled all over the country because of his father's diplomatic career. It was while living in Mexico City that he learned to play the twelve-string guitar and made his first singing debut.

In 1966 he made an appearance on "The Merv Griffin Show" wearing a hood and sang a song as "the Covered Man." He was so successful that during the next year he made over twenty appearances on the show. When he finally made an appearance without the hood, he performed so well that Screen Gems signed him for a lead in their TV series "Here Comes the Bride."

After several other TV shows, he landed a key role in the series "Starsky and Hutch" and he became extremely popular.

In 1976 he signed with Private Stock Records and recorded the album David Soul, on which was the hit single "Don't Give up on Us" which launched his recording career.

Jan. 77 *DON'T GIVE UP ON US*/Private Stock
May 77 *GOING IN WITH MY EYES OPEN*/Private Stock
Sept. 77 *SILVER LADY*/Private Stock

The Soul Survivors

MEMBERS:
Richard Ingui (vocals)
Charles Ingui (vocals)
Michael Burke (guitar)
Paul Venturini (keyboards)
Joseph Forgione (drums)

One of the leading "blue-eyed soul" bands of the mid-sixties, The Soul Survivors were a conglomeration of musicians from New York City and Philadelphia.

Once organized, the group came to the attention of Kenny Gamble and Leon Huff, who wrote and produced their recording of "Expressway to Your Heart" for the Philadelphia-based Crimson label. This became a top five national hit and was followed by two lesser chart entries. The group spent several years on the northeastern club circuit, but the lack of hit activity caused them to disband.

In 1972 brothers Richard and Charles Ingui organized a new Soul Survivors group, made up of several musicians with whom they had become associated in the Woodstock area. The new group began recording for Gamble & Huff's TSOP label in 1973.

Sept. 67 *EXPRESSWAY TO YOUR HEART* / Crimson
Dec. 67 *EXPLOSION IN YOUR SOUL* / Crimson
Apr. 68 *THE IMPOSSIBLE MISSION* / Crimson

The Souther-Hillman-Furay Band

MEMBERS:
John David Souther (guitar)
Richie Furay (guitar)
Al Perkins (steel guitar)
Paul Harris (keyboards)
Chris Hillman (bass)
James Gordon (drums) / replaced by Ron Grinel
HOMETOWN: Los Angeles, California

A short-lived "supergroup," the Souther-Hillman-Furay Band was assembled through the negotiating talents of Asylum's David Geffin.

Each member had previously been an outstanding figure in the West Coast music business. Of the three principals, J. D. Souther had been a member of Longbranch Pennywhistle and had accrued an impressive list of writing and production credits, while Chris Hillman had played with The Byrds, The Flying Burrito Brothers, and Manassas. Richie Furay was best known for his roles in Buffalo Springfield and Poco, and the remaining members had all had comparable experience.

Recording in association with producer Richard Podolor (known for his work with Steppenwolf and Three Dog Night), the group debuted in 1974 with the album *The Souther-Hillman-Furay Band*. This yielded a top twenty single, "Fallin' in Love," and was followed by an LP titled *Trouble in Paradise*. A prophetic title indeed, for internal pressures soon caused the group to disband.

Aug. 74 *FALLIN' IN LOVE* / Asylum

Spanky & Our Gang

MEMBERS:
Elaine "Spanky" McFarlane (lead vocals) / born: June 19, 1942 / Peoria, Illinois
Lefty Baker (Eustace Britchforth) (guitar) / Roanoke, Virginia—now deceased
Malcolm Hale (guitar) / Butte, Montana—now deceased
Geoffrey Myers (bass) replaced by Kenneth Hodges / Jacksonville, Florida
John George Seiter (drums) / St. Louis, Missouri
Nigel Pickering (leader) / Pontiac, Michigan
Oz Bach (kazoo)

MEMBERS (post–1975):
Spanky McFarlane (lead vocals)
Nigel Pickering (lead guitar)
Marc McClure (steel guitar) / Los Angeles, California
William Plummer (bass) / Boulder, Colorado
James Moon (drums) / New York City

Spanky & Our Gang

Formed during the mid-sixties, Spanky & Our Gang was one of the most successful pop groups of that period.

The group's lead singer, Spanky McFarlane, had begun singing when she was three. During her teens she moved to Chicago, where she worked for an insurance company by day and sang in a small jazz club on Rush Street by night. She later turned to folk singing, briefly joining a group called The New Wine Singers (which contained Malcolm Hale, a future member of Our Gang) and later traveling around the country in search of a career. When nothing substantial developed, she re-turned to Chicago and began singing solo at the Mother Blues club in the Old Town section. She was eventually joined there by Nigel Pickering and Oz Bach, two musicians whom she had met previously on a trip to Florida, and Our Gang was organized soon thereafter.

In 1967 Spanky & Our Gang affili-ated with the Chicago-based Mercury label, debuting with their top ten re-cording of "Sunday Will Never Be the Same." They followed with a string of hits that lasted until 1969, when Spanky temporarily retired to tend to her family.

In 1975 Spanky and Nigel Pickering

(who had spent the interim traveling around the world) got together to form an entirely new group (two of the original members had died—Malcolm Hale of bronchial pneumonia, and Lefty Baker of an enlarged liver). This group signed with Epic and debuted with an album titled *Change.*

Today Spanky McFarlane lives in California with her husband, Charles Galvin (The Turtles' former road manager), and their two children.

May 67	*SUNDAY WILL NEVER BE THE SAME*/Mercury
Aug. 67	*MAKING EVERY MINUTE COUNT*/Mercury
Oct. 67	*LAZY DAY*/Mercury
Jan. 68	*SUNDAY MORNING*/Mercury
Apr. 68	*LIKE TO GET TO KNOW YOU*/Mercury
Aug. 68	*GIVE A DAMN*/Mercury
Dec. 68	*YESTERDAY'S RAIN*/Mercury
Feb. 69	*ANYTHING YOU CHOOSE*/Mercury
June 69	*AND SHE'S MINE*/Mercury

Spirit

MEMBERS:

Jay Ferguson (lead vocals)/born: May 10, 1947/Los Angeles, California

Randy California (lead guitar)/born: Feb. 20, 1946/Los Angeles, California

John Locke (keyboards)/born: Sept. 25, 1943/Los Angeles, California

Mark Christopher Andes (bass)/Philadelphia, Pennsylvania

Ed Cassidy (drums)/born: May 4, 1931/Chicago, Illinois

Formed in 1967, this band evolved from an electric folk-rock trio known as The Red Roosters. With the addition of John Locke and Ed Cassidy, the group became Spirit and began playing the West Coast club circuit. Each of the members, and particularly Cassidy, had had a great deal of experience in other groups or as session musicians,

and Spirit soon began attracting attention.

In 1968 Spirit was noticed by record company executive Lou Adler, who signed them to his Ode label. They recorded three highly acclaimed albums—*Spirit, The Family That Plays Together,* and *Clear*—and placed two singles on the charts. Their next move, to Epic, resulted in two more singles and two albums, titled *Twelve Dreams of Doctor Sardonicus* and *Feedback.* During this latter period, however, the group experienced a great deal of internal turmoil (which saw various members come and go) and soon disbanded. Jay Ferguson and Mark Andes went on to form Jo Jo Gunne. (See *JO JO GUNNE.*)

In 1975 Ed Cassidy and Randy California became principals in a new Spirit group, which was rounded out by bassist Barry Keene. This group affiliated with Mercury and recorded two LP's, *Spirit of 76* and *Son of Spirit.*

Jan. 69	*I GOT A LINE ON YOU*/Ode
Feb. 70	*1984*/Ode
Sept. 70	*ANIMAL ZOO*/Epic
Oct. 73	*MR. SKIN*/Epic

Dusty Springfield

REAL NAME: Mary Isobel Catherine O'Brien
BORN: Apr. 16, 1939
HOMETOWN: Hampstead, North London, England

Britain's leading female vocalist during the mid-sixties, Dusty Springfield was introduced to music by her brother Tom, a folksinger. Although he often encouraged her to sing along with his various groups, she briefly formed an all-female group of her own called The Lana Sisters.

In 1959 Dusty joined her brother and Tim Field in a folk trio called The

Dusty Springfield

Springfields (the origin of her stage name) and achieved several hits on the Philips label. (See *THE SPRING-FIELDS, Rock On: The Solid Gold Years.*) After The Springfields broke up in 1963, Dusty began recording solo, soon achieving a major international hit with "You Don't Have to Say You Love Me." She followed with a long string of best sellers and switched in 1968 to the Atlantic label. Her albums over the years have included *A Girl Called Dusty, Everything's Coming Up Dusty, Where Am I Going,* the highly acclaimed *Dusty in Memphis, A Brand New Me,* and *Cameo.*

Today Dusty Springfield makes her permanent home in the United States and records for United Artists. She is also extremely active as a session vocalist.

Jan. 64 *I ONLY WANT TO BE WITH YOU* / Philips
Mar. 64 *STAY AWHILE* / Philips

June 64 *WISHIN' & HOPIN'* / Philips
Sept. 64 *ALL CRIED OUT* / Philips
Mar. 65 *LOSING YOU* / Philips
May 66 *YOU DON'T HAVE TO SAY YOU LOVE ME* / Philips
Sept. 66 *ALL I SEE IS YOU* / Philips
Mar. 67 *I'LL TRY ANYTHING* / Philips
July 67 *GIVE ME TIME* / Philips
July 67 *THE LOOK OF LOVE* / Philips
Nov. 67 *WHAT'S IT GONNA BE?* / Philips
Nov. 68 *THE SON OF A PREACHER MAN* / Atlantic
Mar. 69 *DON'T FORGET ABOUT ME* / Atlantic
Apr. 69 *BREAKFAST IN BED* / Atlantic
May 69 *THE WINDMILLS OF YOUR MIND* / Atlantic
July 69 *WILLIE AND LAURA MAE JONES* / Atlantic
Nov. 69 *A BRAND NEW ME* / Atlantic
Feb. 70 *SILLY SILLY FOOL* / Atlantic

Rick Springfield

BORN: Aug. 23, 1949
HOMETOWN: Sydney, Australia

Rick Springfield first became seriously interested in music during his mid-teens. He taught himself the guitar, later took up the harmonica and the piano, and began playing regularly in high-school bands. After graduation he began sitting in with an assortment of groups, securing his first extended engagement as part of the house band at Melbourne's Whiskey A Go Go.

During the late sixties, after a brief affiliation with the MPD Band, Springfield joined a group called Zoot. Notorious for its extremely "heavy" rock sound and pink clothing, Zoot became Australia's leading band of the early seventies.

In 1972 Springfield went solo and debuted with a top twenty release called "Speak to the Sky." Although he has achieved only two other American chart entries, he has continued to be extremely popular in Australia. His

Bruce Springsteen

American releases today appear on the Chelsea label.

Aug. 72 *SPEAK TO THE SKY* / **Capitol**
Nov. 72 *WHAT WOULD THE CHILDREN THINK* / **Capitol**
July 74 *AMERICAN GIRLS* / **Columbia**
Aug. 76 *TAKE A HAND* / **Chelsea**

Bruce Springsteen

BORN: Sept. 23, 1949
HOMETOWN: Freehold, New Jersey

Springsteen first emerged on the national music scene in 1972, when he signed with Columbia Records and released his debut LP, *Greetings from Asbury Park, N.J.* For his second LP for the label he assembled his incredible back-up band, led by saxophonist Clarence Clemons, and called it the E-Street Band.

Nineteen seventy-five was the year of Bruce Springsteen: during one week of that year, his face was on the cover of *Time, Newsweek,* and *Record World* magazines. He also conquered

nightclubs such as The Bottom Line in New York City and The Roxy in L.A., where he played to capacity crowds during his engagements. His album *Born to Run* also was a smash. He became a rock superstar and one of the exciting new stars of the seventies.

On the other hand, 1976 was a bad year for Springsteen, who, because of some legal problems, was not able to record or release any other material. That problem has now been resolved and it looks as if he will be back bigger than ever.

Sept. 75 *BORN TO RUN* / **Columbia**
Jan. 76 *TENTH AVENUE FREEZE-OUT* / **Columbia**

Jim Stafford

BORN: 1944
HOMETOWN: Winter Haven, Florida

Jim Stafford began his career as a teen-ager when he joined a high-school band called The Legends. This group also contained Kent Lavoie, who later became known as Lobo, and Gram Parsons (now deceased), who was soon to gain fame as a member of The Byrds and The Flying Burrito Brothers.

During the mid-sixties Stafford sang and played guitar on the local club circuit and traveled to Nashville as a sideman for Bill Carlisle at the Grand Ole Opry. He also became increasingly prolific as a songwriter and by the early seventies, he had come up with a song that he thought had a real chance at success. He contacted his old friend Lobo (who had become an active record producer), and Lobo in turn brought in his partner, Phil Gernhard, to help produce the record. The result was "Swamp Witch," which was sold to MGM and became a sizable best

Jim Stafford

seller. Stafford followed with "Spiders & Snakes," which nearly topped the charts, and a series of "double entendre" Country-oriented hits.

In 1975 Stafford added a new dimension to his career by hosting his own national television program. He records today for the Polydor label.

May 73	*SWAMP WITCH* / MGM
Nov. 73	*SPIDERS & SNAKES* / MGM
Apr. 74	*MY GIRL BILL* / MGM
July 74	*WILDWOOD WEED* / MGM
Dec. 74	*YOUR BULLDOG DRINKS CHAMPAGNE* / MGM
Aug. 75	*I GOT STONED AND I MISSED IT* / MGM
Apr. 76	*JASPER* / Polydor

Terry Stafford

An ardent fan of Elvis Presley, Terry Stafford's main claim to fame was his ability to sound almost exactly like his idol. Signed to the Crusader label, he reached the national top three with "Suspicion," an early and fairly obscure recording by Presley. After one follow-up, however, Stafford rapidly faded from national popularity.

Feb. 64	*SUSPICION* / Crusader
May 64	*I'LL TOUCH A STAR* / Crusader

The Stampeders

MEMBERS:
Rich Dodson (lead guitar, bass)
Ronnie King (guitar, bass)
Kim Berly (guitar, drums)
HOMETOWN: Calgary, Alberta, Canada

Formed during the mid-sixties, this group took its name from a local rodeo called the Calgary Stampede. They began as a sextet, but original members Brent Little, Race Holliday, and Van Lewis retired from the band (and the music business) before they were able to achieve success.

During the late sixties, The Stampeders (now a trio) formed an association with manager and producer Mel Shaw. This resulted in a number of appearances at clubs and rock festivals, and eventually in a Canadian recording contract. The group achieved two Canadian hits, "Morning Magic" and "Carry Me," after which their releases began appearing in the United States on the Bell label. Their first outing under this arrangement, Rich Dodson's "Sweet City Woman," made a major impact on American audiences by reaching the top ten. After one more American chart entry, however, their popularity was limited primarily to their native Canada.

Aug. 71 *SWEET CITY WOMAN* /Bell
Dec. 71 *DEVIL YOU* /Bell
Feb. 76 *HIT THE ROAD JACK* /Quality

The Standells

MEMBERS:
Lawrence Tamblyn (lead guitar)
Dick Dodd (rhythm guitar)
Gary Lane (bass)
Tony Valentino (drums)
HOMETOWN: Los Angeles, California

Formed during the early-middle sixties, The Standells (a name they chose because they would often *stand* behind an agent's office, waiting for work) were one of the first and foremost "punk" groups of the period.

Their early history included a great deal of small-club work, a succession of record company affiliations (including MGM, Liberty, and Vee Jay), and several personnel changes (one of

their original members was Gary Leeds, later of The Walker Brothers). By the time they signed with Capitol's subsidiary Tower label in 1966, they had arrived at the above line-up (including Larry Tamblyn, brother of actor Russ, and Dick Dodd, an original Mouseketeer) and formed an association with writer-producer Ed Cobb. They debuted with the top ten classic "Dirty Water," following with several lesser hits. They also appeared in a series of West Coast films, including *Get Yourself a College Girl, Zebra in the Kitchen, When the Boys Meet the Girls,* and *Riot on Sunset Strip.*

After a number of personnel changes, following which the only surviving original member was Tony Valentino, The Standells continue through the present day to perform around the Los Angeles area.

Apr. 66 *DIRTY WATER* /Tower
Aug. 66 *SOMETIMES, GOOD GUYS DON'T WEAR WHITE* /Tower
Oct. 66 *WHY PICK ON ME?* /Tower
Nov. 67 *CAN'T HELP BUT LOVE YOU* /Tower

The Staple Singers

MEMBERS:
Roebuck "Pop" Staples
Cleo Staples
Mavis Staples
Yvonne Staples
Pervis Staples / (left group in 1971)
HOMETOWN: Drew, Mississippi

America's foremost gospel group The Staple Singers are made up of "Pop" Staples and several of his children.

"Pop" first organized the group after relocating his family to Chicago in the late forties. Their first recording affiliation was with the local United label, after which they were picked up by the larger, independent Vee Jay label in 1956. During the next decade, they made a number of gospel albums and became recognized as the leading group in the field.

By 1967 Vee Jay had ceased operations and The Staple Singers had affiliated with Epic. It was at this point that they began to achieve success with Pop material, particularly with Steve Stills's "For What It's Worth." Their next stop was at Stax-Volt, where they accrued a number of major hits and a number one record, "I'll Take You There."

The Staples remained with Stax until that company folded during the early seventies. They are presently signed to the Warner Brothers-distributed Curtom label. Pervis Staples left the group during the early seventies, and Mavis occasionally records solo while continuing her activities with the group.

The Staple Singers
June 67 *WHY* / Epic
Sept. 67 *FOR WHAT IT'S WORTH* / Epic
Feb. 71 *HEAVY MAKES YOU HAPPY* / Stax
July 71 *YOU'VE GOT TO EARN IT* / Stax
Oct. 71 *RESPECT YOURSELF* / Stax
Apr. 72 *I'LL TAKE YOU THERE* / Stax
Aug. 72 *THIS WORLD* / Stax
Mar. 73 *OH LA DE DAH* / Stax
June 73 *BE WHAT YOU ARE* / Stax
Oct. 73 *IF YOU'RE READY* / Stax
Feb. 74 *TOUCH A HAND, MAKE A FRIEND* / Stax
Aug. 74 *CITY IN THE SKY* / Stax
Dec. 74 *MY MAIN MAN* / Stax
Oct. 75 *LET'S DO IT AGAIN* / Curtom
Feb. 76 *NEW ORLEANS* / Curtom
Mavis Staples
Sept. 70 *I HAVE LEARNED TO DO IT WITHOUT YOU* / Volt

Starbuck

MEMBERS:
Bruce Blackman (lead vocals, keyboards)
Jimmy Cobb (vocals, bass guitar)
Sloan Hayes (vocals, keyboards)
Darryl Kutz (vocals, guitar)
David Shaver (vocals, keyboards)
Bo Wagner (percussion, vibes)
Ken Crysler (drums)
HOMETOWN: Atlanta, Georgia

Starbuck first got together in Atlanta in 1974 and began playing around the local area. A short while later they got a recording contract with Private Stock to record their first LP. Their first single release was a tune Bruce Blackman had written called "Moonlight Feels Right," which went on to become a top ten national hit.

Apr. 76 *MOONLIGHT FEELS RIGHT* / Private Stock
Sept. 76 *I GOT TO KNOW* / Private Stock
Dec. 76 *LUCKY MAN* / Private Stock
Apr. 77 *EVERYBODY BE DANCIN'* / Private Stock

Starland Vocal Band

MEMBERS:
Bill Danoff (vocals) / born: May 7, 1946 / Springfield, Massachusetts
Kathy "Taffy" Danoff (vocals) / born: Oct. 25, 1944 / Washington, D.C.
Margot Chapman (keyboards, vocals) / born: Sept. 7, 1957 / Honolulu, Hawaii
Jon Carroll (keyboards, guitar, vocals) / born: Mar. 1, 1957 / Washington, D.C.

Bill and Taffy worked a lot around the Washington area in the early seventies, performing in many coffeehouses. In early 1971 they became friends with singer John Denver and cowrote with Denver his first big hit for RCA, "Take Me Home, Country Roads," for which he was forever grateful.

A few years later Bill decided to form a quartet and got his wife, Taffy, and their two friends Jon and Margot to join

Starland Vocal Band. Left to right: Taffy Danoff, Bill Danoff, Margot Chapman, Jon Carroll

them. They worked for a full year on the sound that Danoff wanted.

In 1976 John Denver decided to launch his own label, Windsong Records, and wanted his old friends to be the first artists signed to the label and to release the first recordings. The result was the album *Starland Vocal Band* from which came the smash single "Afternoon Delight."

May 76	*AFTERNOON DELIGHT /*	**Windsong**
Oct. 76	*CALIFORNIA DAY /* **Windsong**	
Jan. 77	*HAIL! HAIL! ROCK AND ROLL /* **Windsong**	

Edwin Starr

REAL NAME: Charles Hatcher
BORN: Jan. 21, 1942
HOMETOWN: Nashville, Tennessee

Raised in Cleveland, Ohio, Edwin Starr early developed an interest in music. He started his singing career in high-school shows, later making his first professional engagement as a member of a group called The Futuretones.

During the mid-sixties Starr signed as a solo artist with the Detroit-based Golden World label. Several of his releases appeared on the subsidiary Ric Tic label, but the company eventually ceased operations and was absorbed by Motown. His subsequent releases, including the number one recording of "War," appeared on Motown's affiliated Gordy and Soul labels. He also collaborated briefly with another Motown artist, Sandra Williams—a young woman known professionally as "Blinky."

Today Starr records for the Granite label, a division of the British ATV group of companies.

Edwin Starr

Aug. 65	*AGENT DOUBLE-O-SOUL /* **Ric Tic**	
Dec. 65	*BACK STREET /* **Ric Tic**	
Feb. 66	*STOP HER ON SIGHT /* **Ric Tic**	
May 66	*HEADLINE NEWS /* **Ric Tic**	
Feb. 69	*TWENTY-FIVE MILES /* **Gordy**	

June 69	*I'M STILL A STRUGGLING MAN* / Gordy
July 70	*WAR* / Gordy
Dec. 70	*STOP THE WAR NOW* / Gordy
Apr. 71	*FUNKY MUSIC SHO NUFF TURNS ME ON* / Gordy
June 73	*THERE YOU GO* / Soul
Feb. 76	*ABYSSINIA JONES* / Granite

Edwin Starr & Blinky

| Aug. 69 | *OH HOW HAPPY* / Gordy |

Edwin Starr

Ringo Starr

REAL NAME: Richard Starkey
BORN: July 7, 1940
HOMETOWN: Liverpool, England

Of all the former members of The Beatles, Ringo's career has, since the group's break-up, been the least "eventful." He has recorded nearly a dozen best-selling singles, including two—"Photograph" and "You're Sixteen"—that reached number one. His albums, for the most part best sellers, have included *Sentimental Journey, Beaucoups of Blues, Ringo,* and *Goodnight Vienna.*

Ringo has also pursued, somewhat, a career in films. During the early seventies, he starred in *The Magic Christian, Blindman,* and *That'll Be the Day,* and he produced a documentary about Marc Bolan (of T. Rex) called *Born to Boogie.* More recently, he has collaborated with Harry Nilsson on *Son of Dracula* and *Ringo's Night Out.*

Today Ringo operates his own Ring' O record label, which is internationally distributed through Polydor, while recording for Portrait Records.

See *THE BEATLES.*

Ringo Starr

Nov. 70	*BEAUCOUPS OF BLUES* / Apple
May 71	*IT DON'T COME EASY* / Apple
Apr. 72	*BACK OFF BOOGALOO* / Apple
Oct. 73	*PHOTOGRAPH* / Apple
Dec. 73	*YOU'RE SIXTEEN* / Apple
Mar. 74	*OH MY MY* / Apple
Nov. 74	*ONLY YOU* / Apple
Feb. 75	*THE NO NO SONG / SNOOKEROO* / Apple
June 75	*IT'S ALL DOWN TO GOOD NIGHT VIENNA* / Apple
Oct. 76	*A DOSE OF ROCK AND ROLL* / Atlantic
Jan. 77	*HEY BABY* / Atlantic

Starz

Starz

MEMBERS:

Michael Lee Smith (lead vocals)/born: Oct. 9,1951

Brenden Harkin (guitar)/born: Dec. 10, 1948

Richie Ranno (guitar)/born: Jan. 21, 1950

Peter Sweval (bass guitar)/born: Apr. 13, 1948

Joe X. Dube (drums)/born: Dec. 6, 1950

HOMETOWN: New York City

In the fall of 1975 five musicians gathered in a loft in New York's Chinatown to form a new band. By December, after much writing and playing, they had created their own sound. A few months later they made an appearance at the Calderone in Long Island as an opening act for Roxy Music. Record companies were invited that evening to see the group. Out of the ones that showed up, Capitol presented the best offer and the group quickly signed with the label.

In June 1976 the group released their debut album called *Starz*.

Mar. 77 *CHERRY BABY* / **Capitol**
June 77 *SING IT, SHOUT IT* / **Capitol**
Mar. 78 *I'LL BE THERE* / **Capitol**
May 78 *HOLD ON TO THE NIGHT* / **Capitol**

The Statler Brothers

MEMBERS:

Lew C. DeWitt /born: Mar. 3, 1938/Roanoke County, Virginia

Don S. Reid /born: June 5, 1945/Staunton, Virginia

Harold W. Reid /born: Aug. 21, 1939/Augusta County, Virginia

Phillip E. Balsley /born: Aug. 8, 1939/Augusta County, Virginia

Originally known as The Kingsmen (not be confused with the group of "Louie Louie" fame), this group eventually borrowed a new identity from a box of Statler Tissues. Nobody in the

The Statler Brothers

group is named "Statler," and the only two brothers are Don and Harold Reid.

All four members met in elementary school and grew up as childhood friends. Harold, Lew, and Phil formed The Kingsmen in 1955 and waited nearly five years for the youngest member, Don, to get out of school. During the early sixties, they approached Johnny Cash for an audition and were hired (under their new name) as his opening act. The Statlers did this for nearly eight years, signing in the interim with Columbia (Cash's label) and achieving several Country hits of their own. One of these, Lew DeWitt's composition of "Flowers on the Wall," very nearly topped the Pop charts as well.

Today, after having been separated from Cash for several years, The

Statler Brothers record for Mercury and are an extremely successful country act.

Nov. 65	***FLOWERS ON THE WALL /* Columbia**
Jan. 71	***BED OF ROSE'S* / Mercury**

Candi Staton

HOMETOWN: Hanceville, Alabama

Candi Staton began singing in church at the age of five. During the late sixties, with the encouragement of her brother, she began singing at local Alabama clubs and considering a recording career. She eventually met and married singer Clarence Carter, who brought her to Rick Hall's Fame label in Muscle Shoals, Alabama.

In 1969 Candi debuted with "I'd Rather Be an Old Man's Sweetheart," a song she and her husband had written. This became a sizable hit—the first of many for the company.

Today Candi lives in Atlanta, Georgia, with her second husband, a mortician. She records for Warner Brothers Records.

June 69	*I'D RATHER BE AN OLD MAN'S SWEETHEART* / Fame
Jan. 70	*I'M JUST A PRISONER* / Fame
May 70	*SWEET FEELING* / Fame
Aug. 70	*STAND BY YOUR MAN* / Fame
Jan. 71	*HE CALLED ME BABY* / Fame
June 72	*IN THE GHETTO* / Fame
Nov. 72	*LOVIN' YOU, LOVIN' ME* / Fame
Feb. 73	*DO IT IN THE NAME OF LOVE* / Fame
Dec. 74	*AS LONG AS HE TAKES CARE OF HOME* / Warner Bros.
May 76	*YOUNG HEARTS RUN FREE* / Warner Bros.

The Status Quo

MEMBERS:
Francis "Mike" Rossi (lead guitar)
Rick Parfitt (rhythm guitar)
Roy Lynes (keyboards)
Alan Lancaster (bass)
John Coghlan (drums)
HOMETOWN: London, England

The history of this band can be traced back to 1962, when Francis Rossi and John Coghlan organized a semipro band to play around the London area. They eventually turned professional, assuming the name of The Spectres and backing visiting American rock 'n' roll acts. Toward the late sixties, they changed their name once again to Traffic Jam but encountered resistance from Steve Winwood's Traffic group. They finally decided on Status Quo.

In 1968 Status Quo signed with the British Pye label and debuted with an album titled *Picturesque Matchstikable Messages*. This yielded a single, "Pictures of Matchstick Men," which was released in the United States by Cadet and became a top ten hit. They have recorded a number of additional albums over the years, including *Status Quotation, Ma Kelly's Greasy Spoon, Dog of Two Head, Piledriver, Hello, Quo, On the Level,* and *Blue for You.*

Presently a four-man group (Ron Lynes is no longer with them), Status Quo records for the Vertigo label.

| May 68 | *PICTURES OF MATCHSTICK MEN* / Cadet Concept |
| Sept. 68 | *ICE IN THE SUN* / Cadet Concept |

Stealer's Wheel

MEMBERS:
Paul Pilnick (lead guitar)
Gerry Rafferty (guitar) / replaced by Luther Grosvenor
Tony Williams (bass) / replaced by De Lisle Harper
Rod Coombes (drums)
HOMETOWN: London, England

Formed during the late sixties, this group emerged from a band called The Humblebums. After a number of complex personnel changes, the group evolved into the above line-up and signed a contract with A & M Records. Working in association with the legendary team of Jerry Leiber and Mike Stoller, the group recorded its debut album, titled simply *Stealer's Wheel,* in 1972. This yielded two international hit singles, "Stuck in the Middle with You," and "Everyone's Agreed," and several tracks that became exclusively British single releases. By this time, however, the band was almost hopelessly plagued with internal problems and their future output became severely limited. Various

Steam. Back row, left to right: Mike Daniels, Bill Steer, Tom Zuke, Hank Schorz; Front row, left to right: Ray Corriea, Jay Babina.

members of the group managed to come up with two additional albums, *Ferguslie Park* and *Right or Wrong,* and another singles chart entry titled "Star."

Today, Gerry Rafferty and Joe Egan are the only two permanent members of Stealer's Wheel, and the future of the group appears somewhat nebulous.

Mar. 73	***STUCK IN THE MIDDLE WITH YOU* / A & M**
July 73	***EVERYONE'S AGREED* / A & M**
Jan. 74	***STAR* / A & M**

Steam

HOMETOWN: New York City

Not an actual working group, Steam was a group of session musicians assembled by producer Paul Leka to record his material. The vocal parts were sung by Garrett Scott, Tom Zuke, Hank Schorz, and Bill Steer.

Although "Na, Na, Hey, Hey, Kiss Him Goodbye" reached number one on the charts, it was not intended as the original "A" side! In fact, it was hastily composed in the studio, during the recording session, merely to fill up the "B" side. Released by Mercury's subsidiary Fontana label, "Na, Na" eventually received all the airplay and reached the top of the charts. Steam was able to follow with one more hit, released on the parent label.

Oct. 69	**NA, NA, HEY, HEY, KISS HIM GOODBYE**/Fontana
Jan. 70	**I'VE GOTTA MAKE YOU LOVE ME**/Mercury

Steely Dan

MEMBERS:

David Palmer (vocals)/Plainfield, New Jersey/ (left group in 1972)

Donald Fagen (lead vocals, keyboards)/New York

Denny Dias (guitar)/Hicksville, New York

Jeff Baxter (steel guitar, percussion)/Mexico City, Mexico

Walter Becker (bass)/New York

James Hodder (drums)/Boston, Massachusetts

Formed during the early seventies, Steely Dan's unusual name was taken from the famed dildo in William Burroughs's *Naked Lunch.*

The group was built around Walter Becker and Don Fagen, two musicians who met at New York's Bard College. They met Denny Dias during an early attempt to form a band, but this project was not to succeed.

During the late sixties, Becker and Fagen spent two years as members of the back-up band for Jay & The Americans. This brought them together with Gary Katz, a West Coast producer, who relocated them to Los Angeles as staff writers for ABC/Dunhill. Katz later suggested that they form a group as an outlet for their material, and they began actively to recruit members. The additions included Denny Dias, with whom they had worked before, and Jeff "Skunk" Baxter, a former member of Ultimate Spinach.

Steely Dan debuted in 1972 with a highly acclaimed album titled *Can't Buy a Thrill*. They also achieved a major hit single with "Do It Again," which was the first of many to follow. Their subsequent albums, all best sellers, have included *Countdown to Ecstasy, Pretzel Logic, Katy Lied, The Royal Scam* and *AJA.*

In 1974 Jeff Baxter left to join The Doobie Brothers, throwing Steely Dan into prolonged turmoil. The personnel changes since that point have been many, with the only three permanent members being Becker, Fagen, and Dias.

Nov. 72	**DO IT AGAIN**/ABC
Mar. 73	**REELING IN THE YEARS**/ABC
July 73	**SHOW BIZ KIDS**/ABC
Nov. 73	**MY OLD SCHOOL**/ABC
May 74	**RIKKI DON'T LOSE THAT NUMBER**/ABC
Oct. 74	**PRETZEL LOGIC**/ABC
May 75	**BLACK FRIDAY**/ABC
July 76	**KID CHARLEMAGNE**/ABC
Sept. 76	**THE FEZ**/ABC
Nov. 77	**PEG**/ABC
Apr. 78	**DEACON BLUES**/ABC

Steppenwolf

MEMBERS:

John Kay (Joachim Krauledat) (lead vocals, guitar)/born: Apr. 12, 1944/Tilsit, East Prussia, Germany

Michael Monarch (guitar)/born: June 5, 1946/ replaced (1969) by Larry Byrom/born: Dec. 27, 1948/replaced by Kent Henry

Goldy McJohn (keyboards)/born: May 2, 1945

Rushton Moreve (bass)/replaced by John Russell Morgan/replaced by Nick St. Nicholas/ born: Sept. 28, 1943/replaced by George Biondo/born: Sept. 3, 1945

Jerry Edmonton (drums)/born: Oct. 24, 1946

MEMBERS (post–1974):

John Kay (lead vocals, guitar)

Robert Cochran (guitar)

Wayne Cook (keyboards)

George Biondo (bass)

Jerry Edmonton (drums)

Known originally as The Sparrow (under which name the group recorded briefly for Columbia), Steppenwolf was formed by John Kay in the Toronto area of Canada. After a number of personnel changes, they arrived at the above line-up and took their new identity from the celebrated novel by Hermann Hesse.

The group's driving force, John Kay, had grown up in East Germany but had escaped to the West during the late fifties. He eventually settled in Canada, forming a number of blues bands and ultimately joining The Sparrow. The group formed an association with producer Gabriel Mekler, who suggested the name-change to Steppenwolf, and affiliated with the Dunhill label in 1968.

Steppenwolf's debut release, "The Ostrich," was not a success, but their second, "Born to Be Wild," immediately established the group by climbing to the top of the charts. Their follow-up, "Magic Carpet Ride," very nearly did the same, and the group went on to achieve nearly a dozen additional hits before disbanding in 1972. John Kay pursued a brief solo career, while Goldy McJohn and Jerry Edmonton formed a new group called Manbeast.

In 1974 Kay reactivated Steppenwolf with an almost entirely revamped line-up. The new group began recording for Mums and once again appeared on the charts.

Steppenwolf

July 68	***BORN TO BE WILD*** / Dunhill
Oct. 68	***MAGIC CARPET RIDE*** / Dunhill
Mar. 69	***ROCK ME*** / Dunhill
May 69	***IT'S NEVER TOO LATE*** / Dunhill
Aug. 69	***MOVE OVER*** / Dunhill
Dec. 69	***MONSTER*** / Dunhill
Apr. 70	***HEY LAWDY MAMA*** / Dunhill

Aug. 70	***SCREAMING NIGHT HOG*** / Dunhill
Nov. 70	***WHO NEEDS YOU*** / Dunhill
Mar. 71	***SNOW BLIND FRIEND*** / Dunhill
July 71	***RIDE WITH ME*** / Dunhill
Nov. 71	***FOR LADIES ONLY*** / Dunhill
Sept. 74	***STRAIGHT SHOOTIN' WOMAN*** / Mums

John Kay

Apr. 72	***I'M MOVIN' ON*** / Dunhill

Cat Stevens

REAL NAME: Stephen Demetri Georgiou
BORN: July 21, 1948
HOMETOWN: Hammersmith, London, England

Born to music-oriented parents of Greek ancestry, Cat Stevens, the youngest of three children, was exposed to music at a very early age. As he grew older, he became increasingly interested in rock 'n' roll, and, after taking up the guitar, began performing in local clubs. Soon thereafter he began circulating demo tapes of his material and was offered a contract by British Decca.

During the mid-sixties Decca began issuing Stevens's recordings on their subsidiary Deram label. He achieved British hits with "I Love My Dog" and "Matthew & Son," and, as a songwriter, provided other artists with such hits as "Here Comes My Baby" (The Tremeloes) and "The First Cut Is the Deepest" (P. P. Arnold, and, later, Keith Hampshire). Unfortunately, however, the pressures of success led to a serious and protracted illness, tuberculosis, and Stevens retired for nearly two years from the music business.

In 1970 Stevens reemerged on the Island label with an album titled *Mona Bone Jakon*. Released in the United States by A & M, this brought him international attention and was followed by the highly successful *Tea for the Tillerman*. By 1971 his singles were appear-

Cat Stevens

ing on the American charts as well, and he continued with such best-selling albums as *Teaser and the Firecat, Catch Bull at Four, Buddah and the Chocolate Box, Numbers,* and *Izitso.*

Today Cat Stevens makes his home in Rio de Janeiro and lives in a large house that he calls "Chateau Cat."

Feb. 71	*WILD WORLD* / A & M
June 71	*MOON SHADOW* / A & M
Sept. 71	*PEACE TRAIN* / A & M
Apr. 72	*MORNING HAS BROKEN* / A & M
Nov. 72	*SITTING* / A & M
July 73	*THE HURT* / A & M
Mar. 74	*OH VERY YOUNG* / A & M
Aug. 74	*ANOTHER SATURDAY NIGHT* / A & M

Dec. 74	*READY* / A & M
July 75	*TWO FINE PEOPLE* / A & M
Feb. 76	*BANAPPLE GAS* / A & M
June 77	*(REMEMBER THE DAYS OF THE) OLD SCHOOL YARD* / A & M
Nov. 77	*WAS A DOG A DOUGHNUT* / A & M

B. W. Stevenson

BORN: 1949
HOMETOWN: Austin, Texas

B. W. Stevenson began his career as a teen-ager in a number of rock 'n' roll bands. He eventually went solo and drifted around the country playing small clubs and bars.

In 1972 Stevenson was appearing in Dallas when he was seen by a local RCA promotion man, who contacted David Kershenbaum, a Chicago-based A & R man. Kershenbaum arranged for Stevenson to be signed to the RCA label, and Stevenson recorded two albums, *B. W. Stevenson* and *Lead Free,* but with only moderate regional success. He followed in 1973 with a single of Danny Moore's "Shambala," a record that almost immediately began to sell. Shortly thereafter, however, Three Dog Night released the same song, and their version eventually reached number one and totally eclipsed Stevenson's release.

During the summer of 1973, Stevenson achieved his major breakthrough with the top ten recording of "My Maria." This generated a best-selling album of the same name and was followed by another hit LP, *Calabasas.*

Today he records for Warner Brothers.

May 73   SHAMBALA/RCA
July 73   MY MARIA/RCA
Dec. 73   THE RIVER OF LOVE/RCA
Apr. 77   DOWN TO THE STATION/
Warner Bros.

Al Stewart

BORN: 1945
HOMETOWN: Glasgow, Scotland

During the mid-sixties Stewart left Scotland and went to London, where he at first began to work with R & B music, then gradually shifted toward folk material.

During the late sixties he signed with Columbia in England and released four reasonably successful LP's, in fact, the album *Love Chronicles* was voted Folk Album of the Year by the British music critics.

In 1973 he signed with his present label, Janus Records, and in late 1976 released the album *Year of the Cat,* from which came the top ten single of the same name.

Dec. 76   YEAR OF THE CAT/Janus
Apr. 77   ON THE BORDER/Janus

Rod Stewart

BORN: Jan. 10, 1945
HOMETOWN: North London, England

One of the cornerstones of British R & B and rock 'n' roll, Rod Stewart became widely known to popular-music audiences during the early seventies. By that time, however, he had already put the equivalent of an entire career behind him.

Stewart began singing as a teenager, traveling around Europe with British folksinger Wizz Jones. As he grew older, he became increasingly involved with blues and R & B, and his first professional engagement came with a Birmingham-based R & B band called Jimmy Powell & The Dimensions. His next stop was as a vocalist with The Hoochie Coochie Men, where he shared the lead chores with Long John Baldry. Next came an affiliation with the legendary Steampacket, followed by a stint with Shotgun Express. From there he went to The Jeff Beck Group, which he, along with Ron Wood, left to join Faces in 1968. (See *FACES.*)

Once established with Faces, Stewart began pursuing a parallel solo career in 1969. Signed to Vertigo/Mercury, he recorded two highly acclaimed albums, titled *An Old Raincoat Will Never Let You Down* and *Gasoline Alley.* But it was his third release, *Every Picture Tells A Story,* that provided his major international breakthrough by yielding a double-sided hit single,

Rod Stewart

Rod Stewart

"Reason to Believe"/"Maggie May." A number one best seller, this was followed by a long string of follow-up hits and the albums *Never a Dull Moment, Smiler, Atlantic Crossing,* and *A Night on the Town.*

Today Rod Stewart records solo for Warner Brothers, while The Faces appear to have come to a permanent end. Ron Wood has become a resident member of The Rolling Stones, and rumors persist that the original Small Faces (from which Faces evolved) might regroup.

July 71	*REASON TO BELIEVE/* Mercury
July 71	*MAGGIE MAY/Mercury*
Nov. 71	*I'M LOSING YOU/Mercury*

Feb. 72 **HANDBAGS AND GLADRAGS / Mercury**
Aug. 72 **YOU WEAR IT WELL / Mercury**
Nov. 72 **ANGEL / Mercury**
Aug. 73 **TWISTING THE NIGHT AWAY / Mercury**
Oct. 73 **OH NO, NOT MY BABY / Mercury**
Dec. 74 **MINE FOR ME / Mercury**
Oct. 75 **SAILING / Warner Bros.**
Jan. 76 **THIS OLD HEART OF MINE / Warner Bros.**
Sept. 76 **TONIGHT'S THE NIGHT (GONNA BE ALRIGHT) / Warner Bros.**
Feb. 77 **THE FIRST CUT IS THE DEEPEST / Warner Bros.**
June 77 **THE KILLING OF GEORGIE / Warner Bros.**
Oct. 77 **YOU'RE IN MY HEART / Warner Bros.**
Feb. 78 **HOT LEGS / Warner Bros.**
Apr. 78 **I WAS ONLY JOKING / Warner Bros.**

The Stone Poneys

MEMBERS:
Linda Ronstadt (lead vocals) / born: July 15, 1946 / Tucson, Arizona
Robert Kimmel (guitar) / Los Angeles, California
Ken Edwards (keyboards) / Los Angeles, California

Formed during the mid-sixties, The Stone Poneys were the first of several groups fronted by vocalist Linda Ronstadt. After coming to Los Angeles from Arizona, her home state, Linda met musicians Bobby Kimmel and Ken Edwards and joined with them to form a trio. They circulated demo tapes of their material to record companies, eventually receiving a contract offer from Capitol and achieving a top ten single with Mike Nesmith's "Different Drum." After only one more chart entry, The Stone Poneys disbanded in 1968 and Linda pursued her solo career.

Today Linda Ronstadt is one of rock music's leading female performers.

Ken Edwards has rejoined her and is presently a member of her back-up band. (See *Linda RONSTADT.*)

Nov. 67 **A DIFFERENT DRUM / Capitol**
Mar. 68 **UP TO MY NECK IN MUDDY WATER / Capitol**

Stories

MEMBERS:
Ian Lloyd (Ian Buonconciglio) (lead vocals, bass) / born: 1947 / Seattle, Washington
Michael Brown (keyboards) / born: Apr. 25, 1949 / New York City / replaced (1972) by Ken Aronson (bass) / Brooklyn, New York, and Ken Bichel (keyboards) / born: 1945 / Detroit, Michigan
Steven Love (guitar) / born: 1951 / New York City
Bryan Madey (drums) / born: 1951 / New York City

Stories was organized during the late sixties by Michael Brown and Ian Lloyd. They had been introduced by their fathers, two friends who had worked together for many years as session violinists. Prior to forming Stories, Michael Brown had been a founding member of The Left Banke, while Ian Lloyd had recorded briefly as Lloyd London. (See *THE LEFT BANKE.*)

During the early seventies, Stories assembled enough material for an album, *Stories,* and sold it to Kama Sutra for release. With the album a moderate success at best, the group was in the process of recording a follow-up when Michael Brown suddenly left the group. They auditioned for new members, hiring Ken Aronson and Ken Bichel, and continued working on the project, titled *About Us.* Almost as an afterthought, they recorded a cover version of Hot Chocolate's "Brother Louie" and added it to the album. Released as a single, this climbed to number one and ultimately became a multimillion seller.

Stories

In spite of their success, Stories soon became severely crippled by internal difficulties and ceased to record. Michael Brown now heads a band called The Beckies, while Ken Bichel recently became a permanent member of Peggy Lee's backing band. Ian Lloyd records as a solo with Polydor.

June 72 *I'M COMING HOME*/Kama
 Sutra
June 73 *BROTHER LOUIE*/Kama Sutra
Oct. 73 *MAMMY BLUE*/Kama Sutra

The Strangeloves

MEMBERS:
Robert Feldman
Jerry Goldstein
Richard Gottehrer
HOMETOWN: Brooklyn, New York

The Strangeloves were actually a team of New York-based writer-producers well known for their work with such artists as The Angels ("My Boyfriend's Back") and The McCoys ("Hang on Sloopy").

During the mid-sixties the trio signed with Bert Berns's Bang label and recorded a number of hits as The Strangeloves. They continued, at the same time, with their outside songwriting and production activities.

In 1970 Richard Gottehrer became a partner in the Sire label, on which several additional recordings by the group appeared under the name The Strange Brothers Show. None, however, duplicated the success of their original releases.

Today, although working individually, all three members continue to be active as independent record producers.

June 65 *I WANT CANDY*/Bang
Sept. 65 *CARA-LIN*/Bang
Jan. 66 *NIGHT TIME*/Bang
June 66 *HAND JIVE*/Bang

The Strawberry Alarm Clock

MEMBERS:

Edward King (lead guitar)

Lee Freeman (rhythm guitar, harmonica)

Mark Weitz (keyboards)

Gary Lovetro (bass)

George Bunnell (bass)

Randy Seol (drums)

HOMETOWN: Los Angeles, California

Formed during the mid-sixties, The Strawberry Alarm Clock were among the last of the West Coast "psychedelic" bands to achieve national popularity for any length of time.

Working in association with veteran producer Frank Slay, the group signed with Universal and debuted with their number one recording of "Incense & Peppermints." They followed with a number of additional hits, as well as the albums *Incense and Peppermints, Wake Up, It's Tomorrow* and *World in a Sea Shell.*

During the mid-seventies Ed King emerged as one of the lead guitarists with Lynyrd Skynyrd, but he has since left that group as well.

Sept. 67 *INCENSE & PEPPERMINTS /* **Universal**

Dec. 67 *TOMORROW /* **Universal**

Mar. 68 *SIT WITH THE GURU /* **Universal**

Aug. 68 *BAREFOOT IN BALTIMORE /* **Universal**

May 69 *GOOD MORNING STARSHINE /* **Universal**

Barbra Streisand

BORN: Apr. 24, 1942

HOMETOWN: Brooklyn, New York

Undoubtedly the leading singer-actress to emerge in recent times, Barbra (who dropped the second "a" from her name early in her career) had de-

Barbra Streisand

cided as a young child to pursue a career in show business. At fifteen she appeared in amateur productions of *Picnic* and *The Desk,* and later in an off-Broadway production titled *Another Evening with Harry Stoones.*

In 1962 Barbra became widely known for her role as Miss Marmelstein in the Broadway production of *I Can Get It for You Wholesale.* (This production also featured actor Elliott Gould, whom she later married and ultimately divorced.) Her major breakthrough came in 1964, however, when she was chosen to star in the Broadway production of *Funny Girl.* This, coupled with the success of her debut recording, "People," elevated her to the heights of stardom. Aside from her nearly two dozen hit singles, her best-selling albums have included *People, My Name Is Barbra I & II, Je M'appelle Barbra, Simply Streisand, What About Today, Barbra Joan Streisand, Stoney End,* and a number of movie soundtracks.

Barbra launched her film career in 1968 by duplicating her stage role in *Funny Girl.* Her subsequent films have

469

included *Hello Dolly, On a Clear Day, The Owl & The Pussycat, What's Up Doc, The Way We Were,* and *Funny Lady.*

During the mid-seventies Barbra added a new dimension to her career with the controversial remake of *A Star Is Born.* She not only starred in the film, but directed it and provided much of the original music as well.

Today Barbra makes her permanent home in the Malibu Mountains of California with boyfriend Jon Peters.

Apr. 64	*PEOPLE* / **Columbia**
Sept. 64	*FUNNY GIRL* / **Columbia**
Apr. 65	*WHY DID I CHOOSE YOU?* / **Columbia**
July 65	*MY MAN* / **Columbia**
Oct. 65	*HE TOUCHED ME* / **Columbia**
Dec. 65	*SECOND HAND ROSE* / **Columbia**
Feb. 66	*WHERE AM I GOING?* / **Columbia**
May 66	*SAM, YOU MADE THE PANTS TOO LONG* / **Columbia**
Oct. 66	*FREE AGAIN* / **Columbia**
Aug. 67	*STOUT HEARTED MEN* / **Columbia**
Oct. 70	*STONEY END* / **Columbia**
Mar. 71	*TIME AND LOVE* / **Columbia**
May 71	*THE FLIM FLAM MAN* / **Columbia**
July 71	*WHERE YOU LEAD* / **Columbia**
Oct. 71	*MOTHER* / **Columbia**
June 72	*SWEET INSPIRATION* / **Columbia**
Sept. 72	*SING A SONG* / **Columbia**
Dec. 72	*DIDN'T WE?* / **Columbia**
Nov. 73	*THE WAY WE WERE* / **Columbia**
Mar. 74	*ALL IN LOVE IS FAIR* / **Columbia**
Dec. 76	*LOVE THEME FROM "A STAR IS BORN" (EVERGREEN)* / **Columbia**
May 77	*MY HEART BELONGS TO ME* / **Columbia**

Jud Strunk

REAL NAME: Justin Roderick Strunk, Jr.
BORN: June 11, 1936
HOMETOWN: Jamestown, New York

Raised in the small town of Farmington, Maine, Jud Strunk decided as a young boy to become a performer. At the age of seven, he won an award for playing the spoons and tap dancing at a local Grange Hall talent contest.

As he grew older, Strunk pursued a performing career on a number of levels. He often sang and recited poems at local clubs, later traveling around the world as a "one-man show" for the armed forces. He also appeared in an off-Broadway production titled *Beautiful Dreamer.*

By the early seventies Strunk had moved permanently to California and had become established as a television performer. He was often a guest on variety shows and hosted a number of specials of his own.

In 1973 Strunk began a successful recording career with a major hit titled "A Daisy a Day." He has since achieved several additional hits for a variety of companies.

Feb. 73	*A DAISY A DAY* / **MGM**
Sept. 74	*MY COUNTRY* / **Capitol**
July 75	*THE BIGGEST PARAKEETS IN TOWN* / **Melodyland**

The Stylistics

MEMBERS:
Russell Tompkins, Jr. (lead vocals)
Herb Murrell
James Dunn
James Smith
Airrion Love
HOMETOWN: Philadelphia, Pennsylvania

Formed during the late sixties, The Stylistics resulted from a merger of two previously existing vocal groups, The Monarchs and The Percussions. Both had entered a Benjamin Franklin High School talent contest, in which they won first and second place, respectively, and decided afterward to pool their talents. From The Monarchs came Russell Tompkins, James Smith, and Airrion Love, and from The Percussions came James Dunn and Herb Murrell; The Stylistics were born.

After touring Pennsylvania with a backing band called Slim & The Boys, the group came to the attention of record-company owner Bill Perry. He had them record an original composition, "You're a Big Girl Now," which he released on his Sebring label and which became a minor regional hit. The record was eventually picked up by Hugo & Luigi at Avco Embassy, but it barely dented the national charts.

The Stylistics were subsequently signed by Avco, forming an association with producer-arranger Thom Bell and lyricist Linda Creed. Beginning with "Stop, Look & Listen," they have achieved a long string of hit singles which has continued up to the present day.

Jan. 71	*YOU'RE A BIG GIRL NOW* / Avco Embassy
June 71	*STOP, LOOK & LISTEN* / Avco Embassy
Nov. 71	*YOU ARE EVERYTHING* / Avco Embassy
Feb. 72	*BETCHA BY GOLLY, WOW* / Avco Embassy
June 72	*PEOPLE MAKE THE WORLD GO ROUND* / Avco Embassy
Oct. 72	*I'M STONE IN LOVE WITH YOU* / Avco Embassy
Feb. 73	*BREAK UP TO MAKE UP* / Avco Embassy
May 73	*YOU'LL NEVER GET TO HEAVEN* / Avco Embassy
Oct. 73	*ROCKIN' ROLL BABY* / Avco Embassy
Mar. 74	*YOU MAKE ME FEEL BRAND NEW* / Avco Embassy
July 74	*LET'S PUT IT ALL TOGETHER* / Avco Embassy
Oct. 74	*HEAVY FALLIN' OUT* / Avco Embassy
Jan. 75	*STAR ON A T.V. SHOW* / Avco Embassy
Apr. 75	*THANK YOU BABY* / Avco Embassy
July 75	*CAN'T GIVE YOU ANYTHING* / Avco Embassy
Dec. 75	*FUNKY WEEKEND* / Avco Embassy
Mar. 76	*YOU ARE BEAUTIFUL* / Avco Embassy

Styx

MEMBERS:
James Young (lead guitar, vocals)
John Curulewski (guitar, keyboards) / replaced (1976) by Tommy Shaw
Dennis De Young (keyboards)
Charles Panozzo (bass)
John Panozzo (drums, percussion)
HOMETOWN: Chicago, Illinois

The history of this group goes back to 1964, when twin brothers Chuck and John Panozzo joined with Denny De Young to form a trio called The Tradewinds. As other groups of that name began gaining national popularity, they added John Curulewski in 1968 and assumed the name of TW4. Jim Young finally joined in 1970, completing the line-up of what is now known as Styx.

After developing a reputation on the local club circuit, Styx came to the attention of Chicago's well-known record producer and executive Bill Traut. Signed to his Wooden Nickel label, they debuted in 1972 with a moderate hit called "The Best Thing." Their major breakthrough came in 1974, however, when they reached the top ten with "Lady."

Today, Styx records for A & M.

Sept. 72	*THE BEST THING* / Wooden Nickel
Dec. 74	*LADY* / Wooden Nickel
May 75	*YOU NEED LOVE* / Wooden Nickel
Feb. 76	*LORELEI* / A & M
Nov. 76	*MADEMOISELLE* / A & M

Styx. Left to right: Dennis De Young, James Young, John Curulewski, Chuck Panozzo, John Panozzo

Sept. 77 *COME SAIL AWAY* /**A & M**
Feb. 78 *FOOLING YOURSELF* /**A & M**

Sugarloaf

MEMBERS:

Jerry Corbetta (lead vocals, keyboards)/born:
Sept. 23, 1947/Denver, Colorado

Robert Webber (lead guitar)/born: Oct. 7,
1945/ Ogden, Utah

Robert Raymond (bass)/born: Mar. 4, 1946/
Santa Ana, California

Robert MacVitte (drums)/born: May 12, 1946/
Chicago, Illinois/replaced by Myron Pollack

Robert Yezal (guitar)/born: Nov. 1, 1946/
Denver, Colorado/(added in 1970)

Robert Pickett (guitar, bass)/born: Dec. 11,
1945/Georgetown, Texas/(added in 1971)

Fascinated by music since infancy,
Jerry Corbetta began playing the
drums at the age of four. He later spent
several years traveling with his sister,
Nancy, who led a Swing band through
a series of U.S.O. tours.

During the late sixties, Corbetta was
attending the University of Denver
when he first gave thought to forming a
group. He eventually organized Sugarloaf, playing the western club circuit
and preparing demo tapes of the
group's material. This led to a contract
with Liberty Records (later absorbed
by United Artists), and they debuted
with a top three hit called "Green Eyed
Lady." They followed with several additional hits, after which they temporarily faded from popularity.

In 1974 the group reemerged as
Jerry Corbetta & Sugarloaf. Signed to
Frank Slay's Claridge label, they returned to the charts with a hit titled
"Don't Call Us, We'll Call You" (an
autobiographical song based on their
difficulty in getting a recording contract
after their initial hit period).

Aug. 70 *GREEN EYED LADY* /**Liberty**
Mar. 71 *TONGUE IN CHEEK* /**Liberty**
June 71 *MOTHER NATURE'S WINE* /
United Artists

Donna Summer

Donna Summer

REAL NAME: Donna Gaines
BORN: Dec. 31, 1948
HOMETOWN: Boston, Massachusetts

Donna grew up in Boston wanting to be a singer like Mahalia Jackson. Her big break came in the late sixties, when she moved to Europe and got a job as a cast member in the Munich, Germany, production of *Hair*. She stayed with the show for over a year and then traveled throughout Europe doing many other productions.

It was while doing some studio work in Munich that she met producers Giorgio Moroder and Pete Bellotte, who owned a small label called Oasis. They liked her voice, signed her to their label, and had her record two songs that became European hits.

They then came across a French lovemaking song called "Je t'aime" which inspired the three of them to cowrite a tune called "Love to Love You Baby." When the song was first

473

released, there was much controversy engendered by Summer's sensual approach to the tune. Her "sex rock" finally found its way to discos in New York and soon the entire 16-minute, 50-second version was being played. The song was shortened for radio play and in a short while became a top ten national smash.

Donna, who is currently the reigning disco queen and star of the film *T.G.I.F.* (Thank God It's Friday), lives in Beverly Hills with her Austrian husband, actor Helmut Sommer, and their 5-year-old daughter.

Dec. 75	*LOVE TO LOVE YOU BABY* / Oasis
May 76	*COULD IT BE MAGIC* / Oasis
July 76	*TRY ME I KNOW WE CAN MAKE IT* / Oasis
Dec. 76	*SPRING AFFAIR* / Casablanca
Feb. 77	*WINTER MELODY* / Casablanca
Aug. 77	*I FEEL LOVE* / Casablanca
Dec. 77	*I LOVE YOU* / Casablanca
Mar. 78	*RUMOR HAS IT* / Casablanca
May 78	*LAST DANCE* / Casablanca

Billy Swan

BORN: May 12, 1944
HOMETOWN: Cape Girardeau, Missouri

As the sixties progressed, Swan played the Southwestern club circuit and busied himself with a number of diverse activities. He was employed to guard the gate at Graceland, Elvis Presley's mansion, and he acted as road manager for various Country acts. He also emptied ashtrays at the Columbia Records Nashville studio, a job that he eventually gave over to another unknown, Kris Kristofferson. During the late sixties, Swan began producing such acts as Kristofferson and Tony Joe White, and he briefly joined Kinky Friedman's celebrated Texas Jewboys.

Swan's major breakthrough came in 1974, when he began recording as an artist for Monument. His first outing, "I Can Help," went straight to number one and became a worldwide bestseller. He followed with "I'm Her Fool" and two highly acclaimed albums, titled *I Can Help* and *Rock & Roll Moon*.

Today Billy Swan often tours with his old friend, Kris Kristofferson, and the latter's wife, singer Rita Coolidge.

| Sept. 74 | *I CAN HELP* / Monument |
| Mar. 75 | *I'M HER FOOL* / Monument |

Sweet

MEMBERS:
Brian Connolly (lead vocals) / born: Oct. 5, 1948 / Middlesex, England
Frank Torpy (lead guitar) / replaced by Andrew Scott / born: June 30, 1949 / Wrexham, North Wales
Steven Priest (bass) / born: Feb. 23, 1950 / Middlesex, England
Mick Tucker (drums) / born: July 17, 1948 / Middlesex, England

Sweet was formed in 1968 by Brian Connolly and Mick Tucker, two musicians who had previously played together in a Soul band called Wainwright's Gentlemen. This group had also contained Ian Gillian and Roger Glover, both of whom went to fame soon thereafter as members of Deep Purple.

After one unsuccessful single for Fontana and three for EMI, Sweet signed in 1970 with the management-and-songwriting team of Mike Chapman and Nicky Chinn. After obtaining a contract with British RCA, the duo provided the group with their first hit, titled "Funny Funny." They followed with "Co Co," which was released in the United States by Bell and became a minor American hit as well. Their American breakthrough came early in 1973,

Sweet. Left to right: Steve Priest, Andy Scott, Brian Connolly, Mick Tucker

when their release of "Little Willie" very nearly reached the top of the charts.

In 1975 Sweet left the Chapman-Chinn stable and switched affiliation to Capitol. They soon scored with two of the biggest hits of their career, "Ballroom Blitz" and "Fox on the Run."

Oct. 71	*CO CO* /Bell	
Jan. 73	*LITTLE WILLIE* /Bell	
June 73	*BLOCKBUSTER* /Bell	
June 75	*BALLROOM BLITZ* /Capitol	
Nov. 75	*FOX ON THE RUN* /Capitol	
Feb. 76	*ACTION* /Capitol	
Aug. 77	*FUNK IT UP (DAVID'S SONG)/* Capitol	
Feb. 78	*LOVE IS LIKE OXYGEN* /Capitol	

The Sweet Inspirations

MEMBERS:

Emily "Cissy" Drinkard Houston

Myrna Smith

Sylvia Shamwell

Estelle Brown

Formed during the early sixties, this group began as one of the leading studio vocal groups in the field of Soul. In this capacity, they have been heard over the years on literally hundreds of records, particularly those by Aretha Franklin and other Soul artists in the Atlantic stable.

All the members came from gospel-music backgrounds, having sung with such outstanding groups as The Drinkard Singers and The Gospelaires. (In fact, Cissy Houston, Sylvia Shamwell and such stars as Dionne and DeeDee Warwicke and Judy Clay were all in The Drinkard Singers together!)

Once established as session vocalists, the group broke out during the late sixties with several hit recordings under their own name. Cissy Houston left the group during the early seventies for a solo career, and the remaining three members have continued as a trio. All, including Houston, continue to be active with session work.

The Sweet Inspirations
June 67 *WHY* / **Atlantic**
July 67 *LET IT BE ME* / **Atlantic**
Mar. 68 *SWEET INSPIRATION* / **Atlantic**
July 68 *TO LOVE SOMEBODY* / **Atlantic**
Aug. 68 *UNCHAINED MELODY* / **Atlantic**

Cissy Houston
Apr. 71 *BE MY BABY* / **Janus**

The Swingin' Bluejeans

MEMBERS:
Ray Ennis (lead guitar) / born: May 26, 1942
Ralph Ellis (rhythm guitar) / born: Mar. 8, 1942
Les Braid (bass) / born: Sept. 15, 1941
Norman Kuhlke (drums) / born: June 17, 1942
HOMETOWN: Liverpool, England

Known originally as The Bluegenes, this group was formed in 1959 by Ray Ennis and Norman Kuhlke, two musicians who had previously played together in a skiffle group. They spent the early sixties on the Liverpool club circuit and appeared occasionally at Hamburg, Germany's, legendary Star Club.

In 1963, after the British breakthrough led by The Beatles, The Swingin' Bluejeans were offered a contract by the HMV label. After two moderate hit singles had been released, the group achieved major international success with Chan Romero's "Hippy Hippy Shake." Although this reached the twenties on the national charts, the group was able to score with only two additional American chart entries (including "You're No Good," a hit for Betty Everett and more recently for Linda Ronstadt).

Today, after a great number of personnel changes (which saw Terry Sylvester, now of The Hollies, briefly affiliate with the group), The Swingin' Bluejeans continue to record and make personal appearances in England.

Mar. 64 *THE HIPPY HIPPY SHAKE* / **Imperial**
May 64 *GOOD GOLLY MISS MOLLY* / **Imperial**
Aug. 64 *YOU'RE NO GOOD* / **Imperial**

The Swingin' Medallions

MEMBERS:
Jimbo Doares (lead guitar)
John McElrath (keyboards)
Carroll Bledsoe (trumpet)
Charles Webber (trumpet)
Brent Forston (keyboards, sax, flute)
Steven Caldwell (sax)
James Perkins (bass)
Joseph Morris (drums)

All natives of South Carolina, the eight members of this group became known as a leading rock 'n' roll band in Birmingham, Alabama. Their repertoire consisted mostly of current hits of the mid-sixties.

The Swingin' Medallions began recording in 1966, achieving a number one regional hit with an original titled "Double Shot of My Baby's Love." This eventually spread in popularity to the national top 20 and was followed successfully by one more hit. By the end of 1966, however, the group had vanished from the charts.

Apr. 66 *DOUBLE SHOT OF MY BABY'S LOVE* / **Smash**
Aug. 66 *SHE DRIVES ME OUT OF MY MIND* / **Smash**

The Sylvers

MEMBERS:
Olympia-Ann Sylvers / born: Oct. 13, 1951
Leon Frank Sylvers III / born: Mar. 7, 1953

The Sylvers. Back row, left to right: Leon, Ricky; front row, left to right: James, Angie, Foster, Pat, Edmund

Charmaine Elaine Sylvers / born: Mar. 9, 1954
James Jonathan Sylvers / born: June 8, 1955
Edmund Theodore Sylvers / born: Jan. 25, 1957
Joseph Richard Sylvers / born: Oct. 13, 1958
Foster Emerson Sylvers / born: Feb. 25, 1962

HOMETOWN: Memphis, Tennessee

Encouraged by their mother, a former opera singer, the Sylvers children all began singing virtually as infants. As they grew older, they formed an act called The Little Angels and entered a number of amateur shows. They also made several television appearances and soon began building a reputation.

In 1972, the group assumed the family name and began recording for the Pride label. They achieved several moderate hits, and youngest brother Foster reached the top 20 with his solo rendering of "Misdemeanor." Their major breakthrough came in 1976, however, when they signed with the Capitol label. They debuted with "Boogie Fever," a record that quickly climbed to the top of the best-seller lists and firmly established them as a leading Soul act.

Today The Sylvers make their home in Encino, California.

The Sylvers
Sep. 72 *A FOOL'S PARADISE* /Pride
Feb. 73 *WISH I COULD TALK TO YOU* / Pride
Aug. 73 *STAY AWAY FROM ME* /Pride
Feb. 76 *BOOGIE FEVER* /Capitol
June 76 *COTTON CANDY* /Capitol
Oct. 76 *HOTLINE* /Capitol
Apr. 77 *HIGH SCHOOL DANCE* /Capitol
Nov. 77 *ANYWAY YOU WANT ME* / Capitol

Foster Sylvers
June 73 *MISDEMEANOR* /Pride
Oct. 73 *HEY LITTLE GIRL* /Pride

Sylvia

BORN: May 6, 1936
HOMETOWN: New York City

Sylvia Vanderpool Robinson first became known during the mid-fifties as one half of Mickey & Sylvia. (See *MICKEY & SYLVIA, Rock On: The Solid Gold Years.*)

During the sixties Sylvia became an accomplished songwriter, producer, and engineer and was responsible for hit records by several artists.

In 1973 Sylvia decided to revive her own recording career, achieving a top three hit with her own composition of "Pillow Talk." (She had originally written the song for Soul star Al Green, who turned it down as too "effeminate.") In addition, Sylvia has recorded occasionally in collaboration with other artists on her label.

Sylvia
Mar. 73 *PILLOW TALK* /Vibration
July 73 *DIDN'T I* /Vibration

Sylvia & Ralfi Pagan
Sept. 73 *SOUL JE T'AIME* /Vibration

Sylvia & The Moments:
June 74 *SHO' NUFF BOOGIE* /All Platinum

The Syndicate of Sound

MEMBERS:
Donald Baskin (lead vocals, sax)
James "Bo" Sawyers (lead guitar)
John Sharkey (rhythm guitar, keyboards)
Robert Gonzales (bass)
John Duckworth (drums)
HOMETOWN: San José, California

A classic "punk"-oriented garage band, The Syndicate of Sound began during the mid-sixties by playing small clubs around the San José area. They soon got the opportunity to work with the local Scarlet label, and recorded an original composition titled "Little Girl." This gained such rapid popularity that its distribution was taken over by the larger Hush label (which had previously launched the career of Soul star Joe Simon), but this company eventually found it difficult to keep up with the increasing demand. The record was finally picked up by Bell, after which it quickly rose into the national top ten.

After this success, and a follow-up chart·entry, The Syndicate of Sound continued as one of northern California's leading rock 'n' roll bands. They briefly returned to the national bestseller lists in 1970, on the Buddah label.

June 66 *LITTLE GIRL* /Bell
Aug. 66 *RUMORS* /Bell
Mar. 70 *BROWN PAPER BAG* /Buddah

Tavares

MEMBERS:

Antone "Chubby" Tavares (lead vocals)/born: June 2, 1950

Feliciano "Butch" Tavares/born: May 18, 1953

Ralph Vierra Tavares/born: Dec. 10, 1948

Perry Lee "Tiny" Tavares/born: Oct. 24, 1954

Arthur "Pooch" Tavares/born: Nov. 12, 1949

Vic Tavares/(left the group in the early seventies)

HOMETOWN: New Bedford, Massachusetts

These brothers started out as an act during the fifties, when they performed with their father in small Massachusetts clubs. During the early sixties, they formed an act of their own, calling themselves Chubby & The Turnpikes and gaining a substantial reputation throughout New England. They also became a frequent attraction in such resort areas as Bermuda, the Bahamas, and Puerto Rico.

The group's "break" came several

Tavares. Clockwise from top left: Ralph, Pooch, Chubby, Butch, Tiny

years later, when they came to the attention of Brian Pinnella, then a Boston-area promotion man for Capitol Records. He became their manager and later succeeded in getting them a contract with the label, even though he himself had left Capitol. The group, now renamed Tavares, began receiving a great deal of promotion, since Capitol was anxious to break into the Soul field. Beginning with "Check It Out," which reached the national top 30, Tavares achieved a string of major best sellers and soon became a leading concert attraction.

Today Tavares functions as a five-man group. Vic Tavares left for a solo career during the early seventies and began recording for Warner Brothers.

Sept. 73	*CHECK IT OUT* / Capitol
Feb. 74	*ROCK & ROLL HOOCHIE KOO* / Capitol
June 74	*TOO LATE* / Capitol
Oct. 74	*SHE'S GONE* / Capitol
Apr. 75	*REMEMBER WHAT I TOLD YOU TO FORGET* / Capitol
July 75	*IT ONLY TAKES A MINUTE* / Capitol
Dec. 75	*FREE RIDE* / Capitol
June 76	*HEAVEN MUST BE MISSING AN ANGEL* / Capitol
Oct. 76	*DON'T TAKE AWAY THE MUSIC* / Capitol
Mar. 77	*WHO DUN IT* / Capitol
Nov. 77	*MORE THAN A WOMAN* / Capitol
Feb. 78	*MORE THAN A WOMAN (rereleased)* / Capitol

Bobby Taylor & The Vancouvers

MEMBERS:
Robert Taylor (lead vocals)
Thomas Chong (guitar)
Edward Patterson (guitar)
Robbie King (keyboards)
Wes Henderson (bass)
Ted Lewis (drums)

HOMETOWN: Vancouver, Canada

Largely made up of American members, this group settled in Canada and built a substantial following on the Vancouver club circuit during the mid-sixties. During one of their performances at a club called The Elegant Parlor, they were seen by Diana Ross (who was appearing in Vancouver with The Supremes) and brought to the attention of Motown Records President Berry Gordy, Jr. Signed to the subsidiary Gordy label, the group reached the American top 20 with "Does Your Mama Know about Me," a controversial song dealing with interracial love. They also appeared in a feature film, made in San Francisco, titled *Once A Thief.*

After several additional releases, Bobby Taylor & The Vancouvers began to drift apart. A number of the members joined other groups, and Thomas Chong went on to worldwide fame as one half of the rock-comedy team of Cheech & Chong. (See *CHEECH & CHONG.*)

Apr. 68	*DOES YOUR MAMA KNOW ABOUT ME* / Gordy
Aug. 68	*I AM YOUR MAN* / Gordy
Dec. 68	*MELINDA* / Gordy

James Taylor

BORN: March 12, 1948
HOMETOWN: Boston, Massachusetts

James Taylor is one of several famed singing brothers and sisters, including Alex, Kate, and Livingston Taylor.

James first got into music as a child by learning to play guitar and cello. Later, while attending boarding school in North Carolina, he and his brother Alex formed a group known as The Fabulous Corsairs. At seventeen he

James Taylor

developed severe personal difficulties and entered a mental institution for a period of recovery.

In 1966 Taylor moved to New York and joined with a childhood friend, Danny Kortchmar, in forming the now legendary Flying Machine (not to be confused with the later British group). This group became a regular feature on the Greenwich Village club circuit, but lasted only until 1967, when Taylor decided to try his luck in England. One of his demo tapes fell into the hands of producer Peter Asher (formerly of Peter and Gordon), who assumed his management and arranged for a recording contract with The Beatles' new Apple label. One album was released, but with only moderate success.

By 1969 Taylor had returned to the United States for a second stay in a mental institution. Upon his release, Asher (who had since relocated to the United States) negotiated a contract with Warner Brothers, and work was begun on a new album, titled *Sweet Baby James.* This became an instant success, yielding the chart-topping single "Fire & Rain" and establishing Taylor as a star. He has since achieved a number of hit singles, including one issued by Apple after his breakthrough, but he is most highly regarded for his albums, including *Mud Slide Slim, One Man Dog,* and *Walking Man.*

Today James Taylor lives in New York City with his wife, rock star Carly Simon (whom he married in 1972), and their two children, while recording for Columbia Records.

Sept. 70 *FIRE & RAIN* / Warner Bros.
Nov. 70 *CAROLINA IN MY MIND* / Apple
Feb. 71 *COUNTRY ROAD* / Warner Bros.
June 71 *YOU'VE GOT A FRIEND* / Warner Bros.
Oct. 71 *LONG AGO & FAR AWAY* / Warner Bros.
Dec. 72 *DON'T LET ME BE LONELY TONIGHT* / Warner Bros.
Mar. 73 *ONE MAN PARADE* / Warner Bros.
June 75 *HOW SWEET IT IS* / Warner Bros.
Oct. 75 *MEXICO* / Warner Bros.
July 76 *SHOWER THE PEOPLE* / Warner Bros.
June 77 *HANDY MAN* / Columbia
Oct. 77 *YOUR SMILING FACE* / Columbia
Feb. 78 *HONEY, DON'T LEAVE L.A.* / Columbia

Kate Taylor

BORN: August 15, 1949
HOMETOWN: Boston, Massachusetts

Kate, the younger sister of James Taylor, became interested in rock as a youngster growing up in the fifties. Although she enjoyed music very much, her personal life began to grow complicated and by 1967 she entered McLean Hospital in Belmont, Massachusetts, for psychiatric treatment. Ironically, a few years earlier her brothers James and Livingston had had to do the same thing.

At the hospital music became therapy for her and she practiced quite diligently. After one year in the hospital and another in a foster home, she joined her brother James on a trip to England where she met Peter Asher of Peter and Gordon fame. This meeting eventually led to a recording deal in 1970 with Cotillion Records and a debut LP called *Sister Kate* which Asher produced. This album, along with a massive tour, established her as a singer to watch in the years to come.

During the fall of 1977 she had her biggest single with an old Betty Everett tune from 1964 called "It's in His Kiss."

Sept. 77 *IT'S IN HIS KISS* / Columbia

KoKo Taylor

HOMETOWN: Chicago, Illinois

KoKo Taylor became known during the early sixties as one of Chicago's leading female blues performers.

Until 1963 KoKo was most widely known for her guest appearances with such artists as Buddy Guy and Junior Wells. During that year, she began singing with the legendary J. B. Lenoir band, making "Honkey Tonkey" her first recording, with them. Although this was not a hit, it did serve to bring her to the attention of blues writer-producer Willie Dixon. Under Dixon's direction, KoKo made a string of recordings for the Chess/Checker label and took Dixon's composition of "Wang Dang Doodle" onto the national best-seller lists in 1966.

Today KoKo Taylor is the only Chicago blueswoman leading her own band, and she records for the Alligator label.

Apr. 66 *WANG DANG DOODLE/* **Checker**

R. Dean Taylor

HOMETOWN: Toronto, Canada

A Canadian by birth, R. Dean Taylor began his career as a Country singer and was able to gain some success as a recording artist in his home country.

During the mid-sixties Taylor received a contract offer from Detroit's Motown label, largely as a writer and producer. He was associated with a number of hits in this capacity, most notably "Love Child," which he wrote for The Supremes and which reached number one late in 1968.

In 1970 Taylor began recording as an artist for Motown's subsidiary Rare Earth label. His release of "Indiana Wants Me" also reached number one, making him the first white artist in the history of Motown to achieve this distinction. After several lesser hits, he announced his separation from the Motown organization in September 1973, and formed his own Jane record company. This was a short-lived venture, however, and Taylor signed in 1974 with Polydor Records.

Sept. 70 *INDIANA WANTS ME/* **Rare Earth**

Feb. 71 *AIN'T IT A SAD THING/* **Rare Earth**
Apr. 71 *GOTTA SEE JANE/* **Rare Earth**
Apr. 72 *TAOS, NEW MEXICO/* **Rare Earth**

The Tee Set

MEMBERS:
Peter Tetteroo (lead vocals)
Dill Bennink (lead guitar)
Hans Van Eijck (keyboards, lead guitar)
Franklin Madjid (bass)
Joop Blom (drums)

This Dutch group was one of the major components of the brief "Dutch invasion" of the early seventies. Through the efforts of producer Jerry Ross, who released several Dutch rock records on his Colossus label, this group reached the American top five with their unusual multilingual recording of "Ma Belle Amie." After one more American chart entry, the popularity of the group centered once again in their native Holland. Additionally, lead singer Peter Tetteroo achieved a number of Dutch solo hits, although he continued to perform and record with the group.

Jan. 70 *MA BELLE AMIE/* **Colossus**
May 70 *IF YOU BELIEVE IN LOVE/* **Colossus**

The Temptations

MEMBERS:
Otis Williams (Otis Miles)/born: Oct. 30, 1949/Texarkana, Texas
Melvin Franklin (David English)/born: Oct. 12, 1942/Montgomery, Alabama
Edward James Kendricks /born: Dec. 17, 1939/Birmingham, Alabama/replaced (1971) by Damon Otis Harris/born: July 3, 1950/Baltimore, Maryland/replaced (1975) by Glenn Leonard
Paul Williams /born: July 2, 1939/died: Aug. 17, 1973/Birmingham, Alabama/replaced

The Temptations. Standing, left to right: Dennis Edwards, Glenn Leonard; stooping, left to right: Otis Williams, Melvin Franklin, Richard Street

(1971) by Richard Street/born: Oct. 5, 1942/ Detroit, Michigan

David Ruffin /born: Jan. 18, 1941/Meridian, Mississippi/replaced (1968) by Dennis Edwards/born: Feb. 3, 1943/Birmingham, Alabama/replaced by Louis Price

The Temptations emerged during the mid-sixties as one of the leading and most durable vocal groups of the Soul era. Their sound and stage fi- nesse became a model for countless groups that followed them.

The group's origins can be traced back to the late fifties, when their origi- nal members were in such groups as The Distants and The Primes (whose sister group was The Primettes, later known as The Supremes). By 1960 Otis Williams, Mel Franklin, Eddie Ken- dricks, and Paul Williams were calling

themselves The Elgins and had succeeded in obtaining a contract with the
fledgling Motown organization. David
Ruffin joined shortly thereafter, and the
five-man group, renamed as The
Temptations, began recording for the
Gordy label.

Early in 1964 The "Temps" reached
the national top ten with a Smokey
Robinson song titled "The Way You
Do the Things You Do." Their major
breakthrough came in 1965, however,
when another of Robinson's compositions, "My Girl," took them to number
one. Since that time they have rarely, if
ever, been absent from the best-seller
lists.

The Temptations' history has been
one of constant change, both in sound
and in personnel. After having been
one of the cornerstones of the unique
mid-sixties "Motown" sound, they
changed direction totally with their release of "Cloud 9" and helped initiate
the era of "psychedelic Soul." This
helped change the entire face of modern Rhythm & Blues music and laid the
groundwork for the "disco" sound of
the seventies. Their most important
personnel changes have involved David Ruffin and Eddie Kendricks, both of
whom were lead vocalists with the
group but left to establish solo careers.
Paul Williams left in 1971 for reasons
of health and eventually committed sui-
cide two years later.

Today The Temptations remain one
of the leading group concert attractions in the field of popular music, while
recording for their new label, Atlantic
Records.

Feb. 64	*THE WAY YOU DO THE THINGS YOU DO* / Gordy
May 64	*I'LL BE IN TROUBLE* / Gordy
Sept. 64	*GIRL (WHY YOU WANNA MAKE ME BLUE)* / Gordy
Jan. 65	*MY GIRL* / Gordy
Apr. 65	*IT'S GROWING* / Gordy
July 65	*SINCE I LOST MY BABY* / Gordy
Oct. 65	*MY BABY* / Gordy
Dec. 65	*DON'T LOOK BACK* / Gordy
Feb. 66	*GET READY* / Gordy
May 66	*AIN'T TOO PROUD TOO BEG* / Gordy
Aug. 66	*BEAUTY'S ONLY SKIN DEEP* / Gordy
Nov. 66	*I'M LOSING YOU* / Gordy
Apr. 67	*ALL I NEED* / Gordy
July 67	*YOU'RE MY EVERYTHING* / Gordy
Oct. 67	*IT'S YOU THAT I NEED* / Gordy
Jan. 68	*I WISH THAT IT WOULD RAIN* / Gordy
May 68	*I COULD NEVER LOVE ANOTHER* / Gordy
Aug. 68	*PLEASE RETURN YOUR LOVE TO ME* / Gordy
Nov. 68	*CLOUD 9* / Gordy
Feb. 69	*RUNAWAY CHILD, RUNNING WILD* / Gordy
May 69	*DON'T LET THE JONESES GET YOU DOWN* / Gordy
Aug. 69	*I CAN'T GET NEXT TO YOU* / Gordy
Jan. 70	*PSYCHEDELIC SHACK* / Gordy
May 70	*BALL OF CONFUSION* / Gordy
Oct. 70	*UNGENA ZA ULIMWENGU (UNITE THE WORLD)* / Gordy
Feb. 71	*JUST MY IMAGINATION* / Gordy
July 71	*IT'S SUMMER* / Gordy
Nov. 71	*SUPERSTAR* / Gordy
Mar. 72	*TAKE A LOOK AROUND* / Gordy
July 72	*MOTHER NATURE* / Gordy
Oct. 72	*PAPA WAS A ROLLING STONE* / Gordy
Feb. 73	*MASTERPIECE* / Gordy
June 73	*THE PLASTIC MAN* / Gordy
Aug. 73	*HEY GIRL* / Gordy
Dec. 73	*LET YOUR HAIR DOWN* / Gordy
Mar. 74	*HEAVENLY* / Gordy
June 74	*YOU'VE GOT MY SOUL ON FIRE* / Gordy
Dec. 74	*HAPPY PEOPLE* / Gordy
Mar. 75	*SHAKEY GROUND* / Gordy
July 75	*GLASS HOUSE* / Gordy
Feb. 76	*KEEP HOLDING ON* / Gordy
July 76	*UP THE CREEK (WITHOUT A PADDLE)* / Gordy

10 cc. Left to right: Graham Gouldman, Kevin Godley, Eric Stewart, Lol Creme

10 cc

MEMBERS:

Lol Creme (lead vocals, guitar)/born: Sept. 17, 1947/(left group in 1977)

Eric Stewart (lead guitar)/born: Jan. 20, 1945

Graham Gouldman (bass)/born: May 10, 1946

Kevin Godley (drums)/born: Oct. 7, 1945/replaced by Paul Burgess in 1977

HOMETOWN: Manchester, England

This group evolved during the early seventies from a three-man group called Hotlegs. (See: *HOTLEGS.*) With the addition of Graham Gouldman, the group became known as 10 cc (a name given them by their producer, rock satirist Jonathan King, and signifying the amount of semen ejaculated by the average male!).

In 1973, 10 cc began recording for King's U.K. label and had a British best seller with their first album, titled simply *10 cc.* Several singles were released from this package and became British hits, and one of these, titled "Rubber Bullets," barely dented the American charts. Their follow-up album was called *Sheet Music,* and it, too, sold well in England.

In 1975, 10 cc changed affiliation to Mercury/Phonogram, debuting with an LP titled *The Original Soundtrack.* This became a major success on both sides of the Atlantic, yielding the American-chart-topping single "I'm Not in Love."

Today 10 cc is acknowledged as one of Britain's outstanding rock bands. In addition, Eric Stewart and Graham Gouldman operate the famed

Strawberry Studio in a suburb of Manchester, where such rock luminaries as Paul McCartney and Neil Sedaka often record. Lol Creme and Kevin Godley record as a duo for Mercury while Eric and Graham continue to record as 10 cc.

Sept. 73	**RUBBER BULLETS** /UK
May 75	**I'M NOT IN LOVE** /Mercury
Nov. 75	**ART FOR ART'S SAKE** / **Mercury**
Apr. 76	**I'M MANDY, FLY ME** /Mercury
Dec. 76	**THE THINGS WE DO FOR LOVE** /Mercury
May 77	**PEOPLE IN LOVE** /Mercury
Aug. 77	**GOOD MORNING JUDGE** / **Mercury**

Tammi Terrell

REAL NAME: Tammi Montgomery
DIED: March 16, 1970
HOMETOWN: Philadelphia, Pennsylvania

Tammi Terrell first learned to sing as a child, and one of her first vocal coaches was Joe Cook, known as "Little Joe" in a fifties group called The Thrillers.

After several unsuccessful recording ventures with minor companies, Tammi signed with the Motown organization during the mid-sixties. Although she achieved some success as a solo artist, her real breakthrough came via a series of nearly a dozen duets recorded with Motown's Marvin Gaye. Several of these, including "Your Precious Love," "Ain't Nothing Like the Real Thing," and "You're All I Need to Get By," reached the top ten.

In 1967, while the two were performing at a college concert in Virginia, Tammi collapsed on stage and was rushed to the hospital. A victim of brain damage, she underwent a long series of operations, during which time the company continued to release pre-

viously recorded material. She eventually succumbed, however, passing away in the early part of 1970.

Tammi Terrell

Jan. 66	**I CAN'T BELIEVE YOU LOVE ME** /Motown
May 66	**COME ON AND SEE ME** / **Motown**
Jan. 69	**THIS OLD HEART OF MINE** / **Motown**

Marvin Gaye & Tammi Terrell

May 67	**AIN'T NO MOUNTAIN HIGH ENOUGH** /Tamla
Sept. 67	**YOUR PRECIOUS LOVE** / **Tamla**
Dec. 67	**IF I COULD BUILD MY WHOLE WORLD AROUND YOU** / **Tamla**
Mar. 68	**IF THIS WORLD WERE MINE** / **Tamla**
Apr. 68	**AIN'T NOTHING LIKE THE REAL THING** /Tamla
July 68	**YOU'RE ALL I NEED TO GET BY** /Tamla
Oct. 68	**KEEP ON LOVIN' ME HONEY** / **Tamla**
Feb. 68	**GOOD LOVIN' AIN'T EASY TO COME BY** /Tamla
Nov. 69	**WHAT YOU GAVE ME** /Tamla
Apr. 70	**ONION SONG/CALIFORNIA SOUL** /Tamla

Joe Tex

REAL NAME: Joseph Arrington, Jr.
BORN: Aug. 8, 1933
HOMETOWN: Rogers, Texas

A major Soul star of the sixties (much in the same vein as James Brown), Joe Tex had been recording for nearly a decade before recognition finally came his way.

Tex began his career during the mid-fifties by entering a talent contest in Baytown, Texas, to which his family had moved during his childhood. Winning first prize, he was given a trip to New York and a chance to perform at Harlem's Apollo Theater. This led to an extended engagement there, and eventually to a recording contract with the King label. After approximately half a dozen releases, he began a series of affiliations with various labels, including Ace, Anna (an early Motown label), Parrot, Checker, and Jalynne—but all with modest success at best.

In 1964 Tex signed with Buddy Killen's Nashville-based Dial label. Beginning with "Hold on to What You've Got," he began placing a long list of Country-Soul and novelty hits on both the Pop and R & B charts. This continued until 1972, when he retired from the music business on religious grounds and announced that he would be assuming the name of Joseph X.

As of this writing, Joe Tex has come out of retirement and has resumed his recording activities once again. Today he makes his permanent home in Montgomery, Alabama.

Dec. 64	HOLD ON TO WHAT YOU'VE GOT / Dial
Feb. 65	YOU BETTER GET IT / Dial
Feb. 65	YOU GOT WHAT IT TAKES / Dial
Apr. 65	A WOMAN CAN CHANGE A MAN / Dial
Apr. 65	DON'T LET YOUR LEFT HAND KNOW / Dial
June 65	ONE MONKEY DON'T STOP NO SHOW / Dial
Aug. 65	I WANT TO / Dial
Dec. 65	A SWEET LITTLE WOMAN LIKE YOU / Dial
Mar. 66	THE LOVE YOU SAVE / Dial
May 66	THE LETTER SONG (S.Y.S.L.J.F.M.) / Dial
July 66	I BELIEVE I'M GONNA MAKE IT / Dial
Oct. 66	I'VE GOT TO DO JUST A LITTLE BIT BETTER / Dial
Dec. 66	PAPA WAS TOO / Dial
Mar. 67	SHOW ME / Dial
June 67	A WOMAN LIKE THAT / Dial
Aug. 67	A WOMAN'S HANDS / Dial
Oct. 67	SKINNY LEGS AND ALL / Dial
Feb. 68	MEN ARE GETTING SCARCE / Dial
May 68	I'LL NEVER DO YOU WRONG / Dial
Aug. 68	KEEP THE ONE YOU GOT / Dial
Oct. 68	YOU NEED ME BABY / Dial
Jan. 69	THAT'S YOUR BABY / Dial
Apr. 69	BUYING A BOOK / Dial
July 69	THAT'S THE WAY / Dial
Jan. 72	I GOTCHA / Dial
May 72	YOU SAID A BAD WORD / Dial
Apr. 77	AIN'T GONNA BUMP NO MORE (WITH NO BIG FAT WOMAN) / Epic

Them

MEMBERS:

Van Morrison (lead vocals) / replaced by Keith McDowell

William Harrison (guitar) / replaced by Jim Armstrong

Jackie McAuley (keyboards) / replaced by Ray Elliot

Alan Henderson (bass)

Patrick McAuley (drums) / replaced by David Harvey

HOMETOWN: Belfast, Northern Ireland

This group was organized by Van Morrison, who began his career in a Country and Western group called Deanie Sands & The Javelins. He spent the early sixties in a group called The Monarchs, eventually leaving to form Them in 1963.

After gaining a reputation in clubs, Them was signed in 1964 by the British Decca label. Their first release, "Don't Start Crying Now," brought them some attention, and the follow-up, "Baby Please Don't Go," garnered a great deal of British airplay. Their subsequent releases began appearing in the United States on Parrot, and one of these, "Gloria," barely dented the American charts. (This record was later rereleased and was also the subject of a top ten cover record by The Shadows of Knight, an American group, in 1966.) After a number of additional releases, internal difficulties caused the group to disband.

In the summer of 1967, Van Morrison emerged as a successful solo performer and reached the American top ten with "Brown Eyed Girl." (See *Van MORRISON*.)

May 65	**GLORIA /Parrot**
May 65	**HERE COMES THE NIGHT / Parrot**
Oct. 65	**MYSTIC EYES /Parrot**
Apr. 66	**GLORIA (rereleased)/Parrot**

Think

HOMETOWN: New York City

Late in 1971 an unusual record called "Once You Understand" reached the top twenty on the charts. Highly controversial, it dealt with difficult problems between teen-agers and parents and was widely banned from airplay.

The idea was conceived by producers Lou Stallman and Bob Susser, who recorded segments of an "Encounter" session conducted by four teen-agers and three parents. After some creative editing and the inclusion of a backing track made by studio singers, the master was given to Laurie Records and released under the name of Think.

In 1974 the identical master was reissued by Big Tree Records and made a second appearance on the national charts. Between both releases the record had a chart life of more than four months!

Dec. 71	**ONCE YOU UNDERSTAND / Laurie**
Mar. 74	**ONCE YOU UNDERSTAND (rereleased)/Big Tree**

Thin Lizzy

MEMBERS:
Phil Lynott (vocals, bass guitar)
Brian Robertson (guitar)
Scott Gorham (lead guitar)
Brian Downey (drums)

Lynott and Downey first formed the group with Eric Bell in Ireland in 1970 and eventually moved to London, where they began performing. Four years later the group was re-formed, with Lynott and Downey adding the Scotsman Robertson and the American Gorham.

They recorded for a while with Vertigo Records before signing with Mercury in 1976. Their first smash single, "The Boys Are Back in Town" (from their debut LP *Jailbreak*), got them much exposure in the United States during the summer of 1976.

May 76	**THE BOYS ARE BACK IN TOWN /Mercury**
Sept. 76	**COWBOY SONG /Mercury**

B. J. Thomas

BORN: Aug. 7, 1942
HOMETOWN: Houston, Texas

Billy Joe Thomas began his singing career by joining his local church choir and later becoming the leader of his high-school choral group. While still in high school, he joined a group called The Triumphs and often played in small local clubs. This led to a brief affiliation with the Hickory label and a number of southwestern regional hits. (One of these, "Billy & Sue," was reissued after his later success and appeared on the national charts.)

On Independence Day, 1965, Thomas was playing in a Houston state park when he was heard by Charles Booth, head of the Pacemaker label. Booth offered him a contract, and the first record released was a version of Hank Williams's "I'm So Lonesome I Could Cry." After this became a major regional hit, Scepter Records purchased

Thin Lizzy. Left to right: Scott Gorham, Brian Robertson, Brian Downey, Phil Lynott

the master and eventually signed Thomas as an artist.

During the next three years, Thomas achieved several entries on the best-seller lists, with a few in the top ten. His biggest success came in 1969, however, when he was offered the title song from the movie *Butch Cassidy and the Sundance Kid,* "Raindrops Keep Falling on My Head." (This song had originally been offered to Bob Dylan, who turned it down!) "Raindrops" reached number one, and Thomas followed with a string of hits that lasted well into the early seventies.

In 1975 Thomas affiliated with the ABC label and returned to the top of the charts with "Another Somebody Done Somebody Wrong Song." Today, he tours with his own band, Beverteeth (which includes several for-mer members of The Candymen), and is considered a major figure in the Country market. He is now recording for MCA records.

Feb. 66	*I'M SO LONESOME I COULD CRY* / Scepter
May 66	*MAMA* / Scepter
June 66	*BILLY & SUE* / Hickory
July 66	*BRING BACK THE TIME* / Scepter
Sept. 66	*TOMORROW NEVER COMES* / Scepter
May 67	*I CAN'T HELP IT* / Scepter
June 68	*THE EYES OF A NEW YORK WOMAN* / Scepter
Nov. 68	*HOOKED ON A FEELING* / Scepter
May 69	*IT'S ONLY LOVE* / Scepter
July 69	*PASS THE APPLE, EVE* / Scepter
Nov. 69	*RAINDROPS KEEP FALLING ON MY HEAD* / Scepter
Mar. 70	*EVERYBODY'S OUT OF TOWN* / Scepter

B. J. Thomas

June 70	*I JUST CAN'T HELP BELIEV-ING* /Scepter
Nov. 70	*MOST OF ALL* /Scepter
Feb. 71	*NO LOVE AT ALL* /Scepter
July 71	*MIGHTY CLOUDS OF JOY* /Scepter
Nov. 71	*LONG AGO TOMORROW* /Scepter
Feb. 72	*ROCK & ROLL LULLABYE* /Scepter
July 72	*THAT'S WHAT FRIENDS ARE FOR* /Scepter
Oct. 72	*HAPPIER THAN THE MORNING SUN* /Scepter
Feb. 75	*ANOTHER SOMEBODY DONE SOMEBODY WRONG SONG* /ABC
Sept. 75	*HELP ME MAKE IT* /ABC
July 77	*DON'T WORRY BABY* /MCA
Nov. 77	*STILL THE LOVIN' IS FUN* /MCA
Jan. 78	*EVERYBODY LOVES A RAIN SONG* /MCA

Irma Thomas

HOMETOWN: New Orleans, Louisiana

Irma Thomas emerged during the early-middle sixties as one of the lead-

491

ing Soul singers from the New Orleans area.

She was discovered during the early sixties by Tommy Ridgley, a noted figure in the New Orleans music business. Irma was working as a club waitress when she noticed Ridgley in the audience. After obtaining permission to go on stage, she performed several numbers and so impressed Ridgley that he arranged for her immediate affiliation with Joe Ruffino's Ron label. She also recorded for Minit, another New Orleans-based company, and, after achieving a number of regional hits, signed with the nationally distributed Imperial label. This resulted in several chart entries, including her top 20 recording of "Wish Someone Would Care." (One of her most important records, although not a chart entry, was "Time is on My Side," which was picked up by The Rolling Stones and made into their first major American hit.)

Today Irma Thomas records for the Fungus label, in association with producer Jerry Williams.

Mar. 64	*WISH SOMEONE WOULD CARE* / Imperial
July 64	*ANYONE WHO KNOWS WHAT LOVE IS* / Imperial
Nov. 64	*TIMES HAVE CHANGED* / Imperial
Dec. 64	*HE'S MY GUY* / Imperial

Timmy Thomas

BORN: Nov. 13, 1944
HOMETOWN: Evansville, Indiana

Timmy Thomas is one of twelve children, all of whom are musically inclined. He played piano in church at the age of ten and later formed a five-man combo while attending high school.

During the mid-sixties Thomas enrolled at Tennessee's Lane College to pursue a degree in music education. While there, he traveled to Memphis to cut his first record, titled "Have Some Boogaloo," and was able to achieve a local hit.

Upon graduation Thomas accepted a number of teaching positions, eventually moving permanently to Miami and taking a job at Florida Memorial College. He opened a club in Miami Beach, and often provided entertainment by performing there himself. This led to an affiliation with the Florida-based Glades label, and to his top three hit "Why Can't We Live Together," a song he wrote while the Viet Nam War was raging.

Today Timmy Thomas continues to operate his lounge and occasionally records.

| Nov. 72 | *WHY CAN'T WE LIVE TOGETHER* / Glades |
| Apr. 73 | *PEOPLE ARE CHANGING* / Glades |

The Three Degrees

MEMBERS:
Fayette Pinkney
Linda Turner / replaced by Sheila Ferguson
Shirley Porter / replaced by Valerie Holiday
HOMETOWN: Philadelphia, Pennsylvania

Formed during the mid-sixties, The Three Degrees began their career by doing local engagements around the Philadelphia area. One evening, at a social occasion, they met writer-producer Richard Barrett, who took over the group's management. Barrett was then working in A & R at Swan Records, and he arranged for the group to be signed.

After Swan ceased operations, Barrett affiliated the group first with Warner Brothers and later with Metromedia, but with little success. After

The Three Degrees. Left to right: Sheila Ferguson, Fayette Pinkney, Valerie Holiday

making one record for Neptune (a label owned by Kenny Gamble and Leon Huff, a connection that would later prove invaluable), the group's next stop was Roulette Records. Barrett's production of "Maybe" (a song he had first produced for The Chantels during the late fifties) firmly established them by reaching the national top twenty.

In 1974 the Three Degrees resumed their affiliation with Gamble & Huff by signing with the team's new Philadelphia International label. Their first project was to back MFSB on their number one single, "TSOP," and, before year's end, they had scored with their own number one single, titled "When Will I See You Again." This became a worldwide smash (it was Britain's biggest-selling record for the year 1974) and put the group in constant demand for concert appearances.

Today The Three Degrees are considered the most popular female group in the Soul field.

Mar. 65	*GEE BABY* / Swan
Jan. 66	*LOOK IN MY EYES* / Swan
June 70	*MAYBE* / Roulette
Sept. 70	*I DO TAKE YOU* / Roulette
Jan. 71	*YOU'RE THE ONE* / Roulette
May 71	*THERE'S SO MUCH LOVE* / Roulette
Sept. 74	*WHEN WILL I SEE YOU AGAIN?* / Philadelphia International

Three Dog Night

MEMBERS:

Charles William Negron (lead vocals) / born: June 8, 1942 / Bronx, New York City

Daniel Anthony Hutton (lead vocals) / born: Sept. 10, 1942 / Buncrana, Ireland

Cory Julius Wells (lead vocals) / born: Feb. 5, 1942 / Buffalo, New York

Three Dog Night. Left to right, front row: Danny Hutton, Cory Wells, Chuck Negron

Michael Rand Allsup (lead guitar) / born: Mar. 8, 1947 / Modesto, California / replaced (1975) by James "Smitty" Smith

James Boyd Greenspoon (keyboards) / born: Feb. 7, 1948 / Los Angeles, California

Skip Konte (added to group in 1974) (keyboards) / Canyon City, Colorado

Joseph Schermie (bass) / born: Feb. 12, 1948 / Madison, Wisconsin / replaced (1973) by Jack Ryland / born: June 7, 1949 / replaced (1975) by Dennis Belfield

Floyd Chester Sneed (drums, percussion) / born: Nov. 22, 1943 / Calgary, Alberta, Canada / replaced (1975) by Mickey McMeel

Formed in Los Angeles in 1968, Three Dog Night developed into one of the most commercially successful American rock bands of the seventies. Their unusual name stems from the Australian aboriginal custom of sleeping with one's dogs when the temperature dips—a one-dog night is fairly chilly, a two-dog night is colder still, and a three-dog night is about as cold as it gets!

The group was started by Danny Hutton, who had previously been involved, as an artist or producer, with nearly a dozen record companies of all sizes. Cory Wells was recruited from

The Enemies, a group Hutton had produced for MGM, while Chuck Negron came from the ranks of the background singers who worked on Hutton's sessions. With their vocal section intact, the trio organized a four-man backing band made up of various available musicians on the L.A. scene.

After rapidly building a reputation on the club circuit, Three Dog Night was offered a long-term engagement at the Whiskey A Go Go and a recording contract by ABC/Dunhill. Their first album, titled simply *Three Dog Night*, brought the group a great deal of attention and yielded three singles: "Nobody" became a regional L.A. hit, "Try a Little Tenderness" reached the national top 20, and "One" (written by Harry Nilsson) became their first million seller. From that point on, they were virtually never absent from the charts and continued their string of hits well into the mid-seventies. They also achieved a number of best-selling albums, including *Suitable for Framing, Captured Live at the Forum, It Ain't Easy, Naturally, Seven Separate Fools, Around the World, Cyan, Hard Labor, Dog Style, Coming Down*, and *American Pastime*.

Although their original line-up remained intact for nearly five years, Three Dog Night's later history has been spotted with personnel changes. The most important shift involved Floyd Sneed, Jack Ryland, and Mike Allsup, all of whom left to form a new band called S.S. Fools. Three Dog Night has been an eight-man group since 1974, when Skip Konte was recruited from the now-defunct Blues Image. Cory Wells now records solo for A & M while the rest of the group has disbanded to pursue individual interests.

Feb. 69	*TRY A LITTLE TENDERNESS* / Dunhill
May 69	*ONE* / Dunhill
Aug. 69	*EASY TO BE HARD* / Dunhill
Oct. 69	*ELI'S COMING* / Dunhill
Feb. 70	*CELEBRATE* / Dunhill
May 70	*MAMA TOLD ME NOT TO COME* / Dunhill
Aug. 70	*OUT IN THE COUNTRY* / Dunhill
Nov. 70	*ONE MAN BAND* / Dunhill
Mar. 71	*JOY TO THE WORLD* / Dunhill
July 71	*LIAR* / Dunhill
Nov. 71	*AN OLD FASHIONED LOVE SONG* / Dunhill
Dec. 71	*NEVER BEEN TO SPAIN* / Dunhill
Mar. 72	*THE FAMILY OF MAN* / Dunhill
Aug. 72	*BLACK AND WHITE* / Dunhill
Nov. 72	*PIECES OF APRIL* / Dunhill
May 73	*SHAMBALA* / Dunhill
Oct. 73	*LET ME SERENADE YOU* / Dunhill
Mar. 74	*THE SHOW MUST GO ON* / Dunhill
June 74	*SURE AS I'M SITTING HERE* / Dunhill
Sept. 74	*PLAY SOMETHING SWEET* / Dunhill
July 75	*TILL THE WORLD ENDS* / ABC

Thunderclap Newman

MEMBERS:
John "Speedy" Keen (vocals)
James McCulloch (lead guitar)
Andy Newman (keyboards, sax)
Jim Pitman-Avery (bass)
Jack McCulloch (drums)

This bizarre British band came practically from out of nowhere in 1969 with a strange song titled "Something in the Air." Produced by Pete Townshend of The Who, the record rapidly climbed to number one on the British charts and made the group an instant sensation. Although the record became a substantial hit in the United States as well (Top 40), it probably would have received a great deal more airplay had it not announced that a "revolution" was in the works. They followed with another single, "Accidents," and a highly acclaimed album, but internal pressure caused the group to disband before its potential could be realized.

Speedy Keen and Andy Newman each continued to record on a solo basis. Jimmy McCulloch, after a subsequent period with Stone The Crows, emerged during the seventies as the lead guitarist with Paul McCartney & Wings.

Sept. 69 *SOMETHING IN THE AIR* / Track

Tin Tin

MEMBERS:
Steve Kipner
Fred Goodman
John Vallins / (added to the group in 1971)

Formed during the mid-sixties in Australia, this group began as a duet made up of Steve Kipner and Fred Goodman. Both had previously been affiliated with groups, but had left their respective organizations to form what was intended to be a songwriting partnership. The result was Tin Tin, a name they borrowed from a famed Belgian cartoon character.

By 1970 Kipner and Goodman had relocated to London and had begun making demos of their material. They approached fellow Australian Maurice Gibb (of The Bee Gees), who particularly liked one of their songs and arranged for them to record it. "Toast & Marmalade for Tea" soon became a major British hit and later reached the American top 20 as well. They followed successfully with another single and with an album titled "Astral Taxi." Although this was the extent of their American activity, they maintained their popularity in Great Britain and in their homeland of Australia. By the end of 1971, Tin Tin had expanded into a trio.

Apr. 71 *TOAST & MARMALADE FOR TEA* / Atco
Aug. 71 *IS THAT THE WAY?* / Atco

Tiny Tim

REAL NAME: Herbert Khaury
BORN: Apr. 12, 1933
HOMETOWN: New York City

Unquestionably the most successful novelty act of the sixties, Tiny Tim came crashing into the world's consciousness in the summer of 1968. He was far from an overnight success, however, since he had been doing the same act for many years under such diverse names as Larry Love, Derry Dover, The Human Canary, and Judas K. Foxglove. He was a regular fixture on the Greenwich Village club circuit and he often performed, literally for pennies, at various Times Square arcades.

In 1965 one of Tiny's Village performances was seen by producer Richard Perry, who decided to work with him. Drawing upon vintage "standard" material of years gone by, Perry produced a number of unsuccessful recordings for the Blue Cat label (in which his father-in-law, George Goldner, was a partner). Tiny's fortunes were soon to turn, however, when he wandered into Steve Paul's famed Scene one evening and wound up being booked as a resident act. These appearances caused his reputation to grow rapidly and prompted Richard Perry to begin work on a new album, titled *God Bless Tiny Tim*. Released by Warner / Reprise, this became an instant best seller and yielded the hit with

Tiny Tim

which he became most closely identified, "Tip Toe Thru the Tulips." His fame reached new heights when on December 18, 1969, he married "Miss Vicki" on the Johnny Carson television show and drew one of the largest audiences in TV history.

Today, after several years of "hard luck" (which have also seen his celebrated marriage disintegrate), Tiny Tim is hoping once again to record.

May 68	**TIP TOE THRU THE TULIPS / Reprise**
Aug. 68	**BRING BACK THOSE ROCKABYE BABY DAYS / Reprise**
Feb. 69	**GREAT BALLS OF FIRE / Reprise**

Gary Toms Empire

MEMBERS:

Gary Toms (keyboards, synthesizer) / born: Apr. 15, 1942 / Shelby, North Carolina

Helen Jacobs (lead vocals) / born: Jan. 1, 1942 / Ft. Worth, Texas

Rick Kenny (guitar) / born: Apr. 9, 1952 / Queens, New York

Eric Oliver (trumpet) / born: Aug. 12, 1952 / New York City

Les Rose (sax, flute) / born: Sept. 7, 1952 / Far Rockaway, New York

John Freeman (bass) / born: June 12, 1952 / Queens, New York

Warren Tesoro (percussion, whistle) / born: Mar. 8, 1946 / Bronx, New York

Ric Murray (drums) / born: Oct. 30, 1944 / Bronx, New York

One of the earliest groups to succeed as a result of the disco craze of the mid-seventies, the Gary Toms Empire was organized in New York City in 1973.

The group's central figure, Gary Toms, had begun his career in a number of fifties and sixties vocal groups. Although he briefly studied medicine, the lure of the music business proved irresistible and he began working with organist Jimmy Smith. He later moved to Miami, hiring talent for a club and backing them with his band. After spending several additional years on the road backing other artists, he eventually settled in New York City to form his own group.

In 1975, the Gary Toms Empire came to the attention of independent producers Rick Bleiweiss and Bill Stahl. They recorded "7-6-5-4-3-2-1" and began circulating test pressings among New York City-area discotheques. The record became an instant success, helping the Empire to obtain a contract with the P.I.P. label.

Today the group continues to be a popular attraction on the disco circuit.

| June 75 | 7-6-5-4-3-2-1 (BLOW YOUR WHISTLE) / P.I.P. |
| Nov. 75 | DRIVE MY CAR / P.I.P. |

The Tower of Power

MEMBERS:

Lenny Williams (lead vocals) / replaced (1975) by Hubert Tubbs

Bruce Conte (guitar)

Chester Thompson (keyboards)

Frank "Rocco" Prestnia (bass)

Brent Byars (drums)

MEMBERS, HORN SECTION:

Emilio Castillo (tenor sax)

Steve Kupka (baritone sax)

Lenny Pickett (tenor sax, flute, clarinet)

Greg Adams (trumpet, flügelhorn)

Mic Gillette (trumpet, trombone)

HOMETOWN: Oakland, California

The Tower of Power was one of the first, and ultimately one of the most successful of the "funk" bands.

Organized in 1968 by Emilio Castillo, the group was originally called The Motowns. After becoming known as The Tower of Power, they gained a reputation on the East Bay club circuit and came to the attention of promotor Bill Graham. He signed them to his Fillmore label, producing their debut album (today a sought-after collectors' item), titled "East Bay Grease."

In 1972, after a period of legal difficulties with Graham, The "Towers" switched affiliation to Warner Brothers. Their first album for that label, Bump City, became a best seller and yielded a hit single titled "You're Still a Young Man." Although they have had several additional hits, they are best known for their albums, including *Tower of Power, Back to Oakland, Urban Renewal, In the Slot,* and *Live and in Living Color.* Additionally, the entire five-man horn section is often employed by other artists as a studio band.

In 1975 original lead singer Lenny Williams left for a solo contract with Motown Records. His immediate replacement was Hubert Tubbs.

July 72	YOU'RE STILL A YOUNG MAN / Warner Bros.
Oct. 72	WHEN I GROW TOO OLD TO DREAM / Warner Bros.
May 73	SO VERY HARD TO GO / Warner Bros.
Sept. 73	THIS TIME IT'S REAL / Warner Bros.
Feb. 74	WHAT IS HIP? / Warner Bros.
Apr. 74	TIME WILL TELL / Warner Bros.
July 74	DON'T CHANGE HORSES / Warner Bros.
Oct. 76	YOU OUGHT TO BE HAVIN' FUN / Columbia

Tower of Power

The Toys

MEMBERS:

Barbara Harris (lead vocals)/born: Aug. 18, 1945/Elizabeth, New Jersey

Barbara Parritt /born: Oct. 1, 1944/Wilmington, North Carolina

June Monteiro /born: July 1, 1946/Jamaica, New York

The three members of The Toys first met and began singing together at New York City's Woodrow Wilson High School. After graduation they decided to continue working together and to pursue music as a career.

During the mid-sixties The Toys formed an association with manager Vince Marc. He broke them into the record business with studio background work and arranged for an audition with Bob Crewe's Dyno Voice label. Signed to a contract, the group began working with two of the company's staff writers and producers, Sandy Linzer and Denny Randell, who worked up an adaptation of a Bach piano exercise as their first release. Titled "A Lovers Concerto," the record went straight to number one and ultimately became one of the biggest sellers of 1965.

After several additional chart entries, the group began to fade from popularity. They continued to do occasional session work, on an individual basis.

Sept. 65 *A LOVERS CONCERTO* /Dyno Voice
Dec. 65 *ATTACK* /Dyno Voice

Apr. 66 *MAY MY HEART BE CAST*
INTO STONE /Dyno Voice
Sept. 66 *BABY TOYS* /Dyno Voice

The Trade Winds

MEMBERS:

Pete Anders (Peter Andreoli) /born: Apr. 28, 1941

Vincent Poncia /born: Apr. 29, 1942

HOMETOWN: Providence, Rhode Island

"The Trade Winds" was a fictitious name assigned to recordings made by the writing and production team of Pete Anders and Vinnie Poncia. In addition to releases as Anders 'n' Poncia, the team also made records as The Innocence ("Mairzy Doats") and were heard in an early sixties group called The Videls ("Mr. Lonely").

During the mid-sixties they scored as The Trade Winds with two substantial hits. The first, "New York's A Lonely Town," was a Beach Boys-type surf lament, while the second, "Mind Excursion," touched on the subject of psychedelic drugs.

Today Vinnie Poncia is a leading independent producer, having attained major success in his work with Melissa Manchester.

Feb. 65 *NEW YORK'S A LONELY*
TOWN /Red Bird
Sept. 66 *MIND EXCURSION* /Red Bird

Traffic

MEMBERS:

Steve Winwood (guitar, keyboards) /born: May 12, 1948 /Birmingham, England

Chris Wood (sax, flute) /born: June 24, 1944 / Birmingham, England

Dave Mason (guitar) /born: May 10, 1946 / Worchestershire, England

Jim Capaldi (drums) /born: Aug. 24, 1944 / Evesham, Worcestershire, England

Formed in 1967, Traffic was organized by Steve Winwood shortly after his departure from the Spencer Davis group. He had, in the interim, played briefly in a studio band called Powerhouse (which also contained Eric Clapton), but he recruited the above line-up in order to form a permanent working unit. They rehearsed for several months in the Berkshire section of England, emerging before summer's end to begin recording for Chris Blackwell's Island label.

Traffic's first album, *Mr. Fantasy* released in the United States by United Artists, immediately established the group, as did a "flower power" single titled "Paper Sun." Although they achieved several additional hit singles over the years, they are known almost entirely for their albums, including *Traffic, Last Exit, John Barleycorn Must Die, Welcome to the Canteen, Low Spark, Shoot-Out at the Fantasy Factory, On the Road,* and *When the Eagle Flies.*

The group's history has been characterized from the beginning by a series of complex personnel changes and periods of dormancy. Original members left and returned, new members were constantly recruited and interchanged, and the group periodically varied in size. Although all the principal members have recorded solo on the side while continuing to work with the group, only Dave Mason has concentrated entirely on his solo career. As of this writing, however, it appears as if Traffic is planning to disband permanently.

Sept. 67 *PAPER SUN* /United Artists
Sept. 70 *EMPTY PAGES* /United Artists
Oct. 71 *GIMME SOME LOVIN'* /United
Artists
Jan. 72 *ROCK & ROLL STEW* / Island

The Trammps

MEMBERS:

James Ellis (lead vocals)

Dennis Harris (lead guitar)

Harold "Doc" Wade (guitar)

Ron Kersey (keyboards)

John Hart (keyboards)

John Davis (sax)

Fred Jointer (trombone)

Roger Stevens (trumpet)

Stan Wade (bass)

Michael Thompson (drums)

Earl Young (drums)

HOMETOWN: Philadelphia, Pennsylvania

One of the earliest of the "disco" bands, The Trammps are actually a conglomeration of various vocal groups of the fifties and sixties. At one time or another, various members of The Trammps sang with such Philadelphia-based groups as The Exceptions, The Cordels, The Whirlwinds, and The Volcanos.

During the early seventies, The Trammps signed with the Buddah label and recorded a number of disco-oriented sides. They also achieved a single hit with their Coasters-style arrangement of "Zing Went the Strings of My Heart" while they changed the spelling of their name from Tramps to Trammps. As the seventies progressed and they became an increasingly more popular club attraction, the group formed its own Golden Fleece label (distributed by the Gamble-Huff organization) and scored with such Soul hits as "Love Epidemic" and "Where Do We Go from Here."

In August of 1975, The Trammps signed with the Atlantic label while retaining Golden Fleece as a publishing and production company. This led to the Group's biggest hit to date, "That's Where the Happy People Go."

The *Saturday Night Fever* movie has caused their "Disco Inferno" recording to be one of the biggest disco hits of 1978.

July 72	**ZING WENT THE STRINGS /** Buddah
Jan. 76	**HOLD BACK THE NIGHT /** Buddah
Apr. 76	**THAT'S WHERE THE HAPPY PEOPLE GO /** Atlantic
Mar. 77	**DISCO INFERNO /** Atlantic
Feb. 78	**DISCO INFERNO** (rereleased)/ Atlantic

John Travolta

BORN: February 18, 1954

HOMETOWN: Englewood, New Jersey

Travolta began his show-business career as a teen-ager by appearing in summer-stock productions of plays

John Travolta

such as *Bye Bye Birdie* and *The Boy-friend* before winding up on Broadway in *Grease* and *Over There.*

When Gabe Kaplan began a new series for ABC-TV in 1975, Travolta was cast as Vinnie Barbarino, one of Kaplan's "sweathogs." His popularity on the show moved Midland International Records to sign him as a recording artist in 1976 and the result was a top ten single called "Let Her In." A romance with actress Diana Hyland ended when the 41-year-old actress died in 1976.

Work in all areas of entertaining has kept Travolta busy. Films such as *Carrie, Saturday Night Fever,* and *Grease,* along with TV-movies such as *The Boy in the Plastic Bubble* have kept him very active.

This teen-age idol is a performer who excels in every area he enters and today is one of Hollywood's hottest stars.

John Travolta
May 76 *LET HER IN* / Midland International
Oct. 76 *WHENEVER I'M AWAY FROM YOU* / Midland International
Feb. 77 *ALL STRUNG OUT ON YOU* / Midland International

John Travolta & Olivia Newton-John
Apr. 78 *YOU'RE THE ONE THAT I WANT* / RSO

The Tremeloes

MEMBERS:
Brian Poole (lead vocals) / born: Nov. 3, 1941 / (left group in 1966)
Ricky West (lead guitar) / born: May 7, 1943
Alan Blakely (rhythm guitar) / born: Apr. 1, 1942
Alan Howard (bass) / replaced (1966) by Len "Chip" Hawkes / born: Nov. 2, 1946
David Munden (drums) / born: Dec. 2, 1943
HOMETOWN: Dagenham, Essex, England

Formed in 1959 by Brian Poole, a butcher's son, The Tremeloes began building a reputation in clubs during the early sixties. In 1961 they were featured on BBC Radio's "Saturday Club," and the resulting exposure led to a contract with the British Decca label. Although they achieved a number of hits with remakes of American R & B material ("Twist & Shout," "Do You Love Me," etc.), their biggest success was yet to come.

As the Merseybeat sound began to sweep Britain in 1963, The Tremeloes (not really a "beat" group but widely perceived as such) racked up half a dozen hits that reached the British top 20. They were dealt a severe, although temporary blow when Brian Poole left for a solo career in 1966. By the next year, however, they were signed to CBS and were back on the charts. Issued in the United States by Epic, several of these releases became American hits as well, including "Here Comes My Baby" (a Cat Stevens composition) and "Silence Is Golden" (an earlier and fairly obscure Four Seasons song).

Today The Tremeloes continue to appear regularly in British clubs and they have signed with DJM Records. Brian Poole, whose solo career never really took shape, works at his father's butcher shop in London's East End.

Apr. 67 *HERE COMES MY BABY* / Epic
June 67 *SILENCE IS GOLDEN* / Epic
Sept. 67 *EVEN THE BAD TIMES ARE GOOD* / Epic
Feb. 68 *SUDDENLY, YOU LOVE ME* / Epic

T. Rex

MEMBERS:
Marc Bolan (Marc Feld) (lead vocals, guitar) / born: Sept. 30, 1948 / Hackney, East London, England
Steven Peregrine Took (vocals) / born: July 28,

1949/replaced (1969) by Mickey Finn (percussion, vocals)
Jack Green (guitar)
Steven Currie (bass)
Bill Legend (drums)

Formed in 1967, this group began as an acoustic duo called Tyranosaurus Rex. The group's driving force, Marc Bolan, had previously recorded as a solo artist and had achieved two moderate British hits as part of a band known as John's Children. He left this group to form his own band but ran into difficulties and formed the duet instead.

Tyranosaurus Rex began recording in 1968, debuting with an album titled *My People Were Fair and Had Sky in Their Hair.* This brought the group a great deal of acclaim and was successfully followed by *Prophets, Seers and Sages, Unicorn,* and *Beard of Stars.* During this period Steve Took retired from the group and was replaced by Mickey Finn.

Around 1970 the group began expanding into a full-fledged electric band billed simply as T. Rex. They reached the height of their popularity during the early seventies, when they recorded several international hit singles and generated the kind of hysterical crowd response more usually associated with the earlier days of The Beatles. Since evolving into T. Rex, their album releases have included *T. Rex, Electric Warrior, Slider, Tanx, Zinc Alloy, Zip Gun Boogie,* and *Futuristic Dragon.*

Today, although the group officially continues to exist, it is somewhat in a state of limbo. Marc Bolan has relocated to the United States because of tax difficulties, and he occasionally makes personal appearances with singer Gloria Jones.

Jan. 71	***RIDE A WHITE SWAN*/Blue Thumb**
May 71	***HOT LOVE*/Reprise**
Jan. 72	***BANG A GONG*/Reprise**
Apr. 72	***TELEGRAM SAM*/Reprise**

The Troggs

MEMBERS:
Reg Presley (lead vocals)/born: June 16, 1944/Andover, Hampshire, England
Chris Britton (lead guitar)/born: Jan. 21, 1945/Watford, England/replaced by Richard Moore
Peter Staples (bass)/born: May 3, 1944/Andover, Hampshire, England/replaced by Tony Murray
Ronnie Bond (drums)/born: May 4, 1942/Andover, Hampshire, England

Originally known as The Troglodytes, this group emerged during the mid-sixties as one of the leading exponents of British "punk" rock.

In the course of their early club work, they were "discovered" by writer-producer Larry Page. He became their manager, obtaining a contract with Fontana Records and later signing them to his own Page One label. (Their American releases appeared on both Atco and Fontana, since there was some dispute as to which company had the American distribution rights.)

In 1966 The Troggs went straight to the top with their worldwide number one recording of "Wild Thing." Although their subsequent releases were successful, several—most notably "I Can't Control Myself"—were widely banned from airplay because of "suggestive" lyrics.

During the following years, the group underwent two personnel changes but remained intact. After several comeback attempts, they signed in 1975 with the Pye label.

June 66 ***WILD THING*/Atco & Fontana**

The Troggs. Back row: Reg Presley; front row, left to right: Tony Murray, Ronnie Bond, Colin Fletcher

Aug. 66	**WITH A GIRL LIKE YOU** / Atco & Fontana
Oct. 66	**I CAN'T CONTROL MYSELF** / Atco & Fontana
Feb. 68	**LOVE IS ALL AROUND** / Fontana

Andrea True Connection

HOMETOWN: Nashville, Tennessee

Growing up in Nashville, Andrea studied piano and drama and at fifteen hosted a television show on WLAC-TV. She later went on to college, attaining a B.S. degree in music. In 1968 she moved to New York City where she studied at the Herbert Berghof Studio while writing commercials. At this time she also designed clothing, mod-eled, and began a career in films. In fact, in 1972, she appeared in the X-rated *Illusions of a Lady.*

During the summer of 1974 she got her big break as a singer when she performed at the Riverboat in the Empire State Building. A year later she signed with Buddah Records and early in 1976 recorded a song written by Gregg Diamond called "More, More, More," which became an instant disco hit and established her as a recording star.

Andrea, and her back-up musicians called the Connection, are international stars and play to capacity crowds everywhere they go.

Mar. 76	**MORE, MORE, MORE (PART 1)** / Buddah

Andrea True

Aug. 76 *PARTY LINE* /Buddah
Feb. 77 *N.Y., YOU GOT ME DANCING* /
Buddah
Nov. 77 *WHAT'S YOUR NAME,
WHAT'S YOUR NUMBER* /
Buddah

Tanya Tucker
BORN: Oct. 10, 1958
HOMETOWN: Seminole, Texas

The daughter of a migrant construction worker, Tanya Tucker grew up in various cities around the country. By the time she was nine, she was determined to be a Country singer and her father spent the next several years circulating demo tapes in order to help her succeed.

In 1971 the family was living near Las Vegas when they became acquainted with an agent named Dolores Fuller. She contacted Billy Sherrill, Co-lumbia Records's A & R director in Nashville, and Sherrill flew to Las Vegas to hear Tanya sing. Sherrill signed her on the spot, began working with her in the studio, and soon came up with her first release, "Delta Dawn." Just before Tanya's fourteenth birthday, this record hit number one on the Country charts and "crossed over" as a Pop hit as well. She followed with a number of additional hits, switching affiliation in 1975 to the MCA label.

Today Tanya Tucker is a major Country star. She is managed by her parents, while her older brother functions as her road manager.

July 72 *DELTA DAWN* /Columbia
May 73 *WHAT'S YOUR MAMA'S
NAME?* /Columbia
Aug. 73 *BLOOD RED AND GOING
DOWN* /Columbia
Feb. 74 *WOULD YOU LAY WITH ME?* /
Columbia
Aug. 74 *THE MAN THAT TURNED
MAMA ON* /Columbia
May 75 *LIZZIE & THE RAINMAN* /MCA
Oct. 76 *HERE'S SOME LOVE* /MCA

Spyder Turner
REAL NAME: Dwight D. Turner
HOMETOWN: Beckley, West Virginia

As a youngster Dwight Turner moved a great deal with his family but finally settled in Detroit. He began singing there in a local glee club, eventually forming his own group called The Nonchalants. It was during this period that he picked up the nickname Spyder from his fellow group members.

After the group disbanded, Turner continued on a solo basis and, through an acquaintance, got an audition with MGM. Signed to the label, he scored with a top ten version of Ben E. King's "Stand by Me," and with a less successful follow-up.

Today Turner tours with his own band, The Spyder Turner Revue, and records for Warner Brothers.

Dec. 66 *STAND BY ME*/MGM
Mar. 67 *I CAN'T MAKE IT ANYMORE*/MGM

The Turtles

MEMBERS:

Howard Kaylan (Howard Lawrence Kaplan) (lead vocals)/born: June 22, 1947/New York City

Mark Volman (vocals)/born: Apr. 19, 1947/Los Angeles, California

G. Allan Nichol (lead guitar)/born: Mar. 31, 1946/Winston-Salem, North Carolina

James Ray Tucker (rhythm guitar)/born: Oct. 17, 1946

Charles M. Portz (bass)/born: Mar. 28, 1945/replaced by Jim Pons/Santa Monica, California

Donald Ray Murray (drums)/born: Nov. 8, 1945/replaced by John Barbata/Passaic, New Jersey/replaced by John Seiter.

This group's history goes back to 1963, when Howard Kaylan, Al Nichol, Jim Tucker, and Chuck Portz were in a Los Angeles-based surf band called The Nightriders. With the addition of Mark Volman on sax, they became known as The Crossfires and appeared extensively with the area's leading surf acts.

In 1965 the group became acquainted with Reb Foster, KRLA deejay and owner of the Revelaire Club in Redondo Beach. After booking them into the club, Foster assumed their management and suggested that they change their name to The Tyrtles (after The Byrds—the group, however, chose to adopt the conventional spelling). He

also contacted Ted Feigen, a former promotion man for Liberty Records who had just become a partner in a new label called White Whale. Signed to that label, The Turtles debuted with Bob Dylan's "It Ain't Me, Babe," a record that reached the top ten and firmly established the group. They followed with a long string of hits, which lasted until internal difficulties caused them to drift apart in 1970.

Mark Volman, Howard Kaylan, and Jim Pons subsequently joined Frank Zappa's Mothers of Invention, with Volman and Kaylan later emerging as Fluorescent, Leech & Eddie and now as Flo & Eddie. John Barbata went on to join Jefferson Airplane.

Aug. 65 *IT AIN'T ME, BABE*/White Whale
Oct. 65 *LET ME BE*/White Whale
Feb. 66 *YOU BABY*/White Whale
June 66 *GRIM REAPER OF LOVE*/White Whale
Oct. 66 *CAN I GET TO KNOW YOU BETTER?*/White Whale
Feb. 67 *HAPPY TOGETHER*/White Whale
May 67 *SHE'D RATHER BE WITH ME*/White Whale
Aug. 67 *YOU KNOW WHAT I MEAN*/White Whale
Nov. 67 *SHE'S MY GIRL*/White Whale
Mar. 68 *SOUND ASLEEP*/White Whale
June 68 *THE STORY OF ROCK & ROLL*/White Whale
Sept. 68 *ELENORE*/White Whale
Jan. 69 *YOU SHOWED ME*/White Whale
June 69 *YOU DON'T HAVE TO WALK IN THE RAIN*/White Whale
Oct. 69 *LOVE IN THE CITY*/White Whale
June 70 *THE EVE OF DESTRUCTION*/White Whale

The Undisputed Truth

MEMBERS:
Billie Calvin
Brenda Evans
Joe Harris

In 1971 Motown producer Norman Whitfield was at the height of success with The Temptations and their re-vamped "psychedelic Soul" sound. Seeking a new project to work on, he brought The Undisputed Truth into the Motown fold.

Their first effort, an album titled simply *Undisputed Truth,* was highly ac-claimed and yielded a top three single titled "Smiling Faces Sometimes." They returned to the charts several times during the next years, once with the original version of "Papa Was a Rolling Stone," which Whitfield later produced as a number one record for The Temps.

Today The Undisputed Truth is affili-ated with their producer's Whitfield la-bel and consists of Taka Boom, Joe Harris, Tyrone "Lil Ty" Barkley, and Calvin "Dhaakk" Stephenson.

June 71	**SMILING FACES SOMETIMES /** **Gordy**
Dec. 71	**YOU MAKE YOUR OWN** **HEAVEN / Gordy**
Feb. 72	**WHAT IT IS / Gordy**
June 72	**PAPA WAS A ROLLING** **STONE / Gordy**
Apr. 74	**HELP YOURSELF / Gordy**
Feb. 77	**YOU + ME = LOVE / LET'S GO** **DOWN TO THE DISCO /** **Whitfield**

Unit 4 + 2

MEMBERS:
Peter "The Count" Moules (lead vocals)
David "Buster" Meikle (guitar)
Howard "Lem" Lubin (guitar)
Thomas "Sweat" Moeller (keyboards)
Rod "Humble" Garwood (bass)
Hugh "Pigmy" Halliday (drums)
HOMETOWN: Hertfordshire, England

Formed in 1963, this band evolved from a folk-oriented group to a four-man rock band composed of Moules, Meikle, Lubin, and Moeller, called Unit 4. With the subsequent addition of Garwood and Halliday, they became Unit 4 + 2.

Signed by the British Decca label, the group debuted in 1965 with an un-usual song called "Concrete & Clay." It became a British hit, while battling in the United States with a cover version released by Eddie Rambeau. Both ver-sions eventually did about equally well, reaching the low twenties on the charts.

Although Unit 4 + 2 had only one more American chart entry, they con-tinued recording in Britain through the end of 1967. Their later history was marked by a number of personnel changes, one of which saw future Ar-gent members Bob Henrit and Russ Ballard spend a brief period with the group.

May 65	**CONCRETE & CLAY / London**
July 66	**YOU'VE NEVER BEEN IN LOVE** **LIKE THIS BEFORE / London**

Uriah Heep

MEMBERS:

David Byron (lead vocals)/born: Jan. 29, 1947/
Epping, Essex, England

Mick Box (lead guitar)/born: June 8, 1947/
Waltamstow, London, England

Ken Hensley (keyboards)/born: Aug. 24, 1945/
Stevenagem, England

Paul Newton (bass)/replaced by Mark Clarke/
born: July 25, 1950/Liverpool, England/
replaced by Gary Thain/died: Mar. 19, 1976/
replaced by John Wetton/Bournemouth,
England

Al Napier (drums)/replaced by Keith Baker/
replaced by Lee Kerslake

This group's history can be tracked back to the late sixties, when Mick Box and David Byron first played together in a British group called The Stalkers. They eventually left to form a group called Spice, which in 1970 borrowed from Charles Dickens and changed its name to Uriah Heep (after the character in *David Copperfield*).

Uriah Heep began recording soon thereafter, but their first two albums, *Very 'eavy, Very 'umble* and *Salisbury*, were not well received. They did, however, achieve a breakthrough with their third release, titled *Look at Yourself*. Although they subsequently achieved a number of hit singles, they are best known for their albums, including *Demons & Wizards, Magician's Birthday, Live, Sweet Freedom, Wonderworld*, and *Return to Fantasy*.

Today, after several major personnel changes and severe internal difficulties, Uriah Heep's future is somewhat in limbo.

July 72	*EASY LIVIN'* / Mercury	
Jan. 73	*SWEET LORRAINE* / Mercury	
Oct. 73	*STEALIN'* / Warner Bros.	

Frankie Valli

REAL NAME: Frank Castelluccio
BORN: May 3, 1937
HOMETOWN: Newark, New Jersey

Frankie has been the main voice of The Four Seasons since they began in 1962. (See *THE FOUR SEASONS, Rock On: The Solid Gold Years.*)

Today Frankie records as a solo performer with Private Stock while residing in Los Angeles with his wife, Marianne.

Nov. 74	***MY EYES ADORED YOU* / Private Stock**
May 75	***SWEARIN' TO GOD* / Private Stock**
Oct. 75	***OUR DAY WILL COME* / Private Stock**
Apr. 76	***FALLIN' ANGEL* / Private Stock**
Aug. 76	***WE'RE ALL ALONE* / Private Stock**
Oct. 76	***BOOMERANG* / Private Stock**
May 78	***GREASE* / RSO**

Vanilla Fudge

MEMBERS:
Tim Bogert (guitar, bass) / born: Aug. 27, 1944 / Richfield, New Jersey

Mark Stein (keyboards) / born: Mar. 11, 1947 / Bayonne, New Jersey

Vincent Martell (guitar, bass) / born: Nov. 11, 1945 / Bronx, New York City

Carmine Appice (drums) / born: Dec. 15, 1946 / Brooklyn, New York City

Formed in the New York City area in 1966, this band was originally known as The Pigeons. With the addition of Vince Martell, they became Vanilla Fudge and rapidly gained a reputation for their heavy, slowed-down versions of then-current hits and for their psychedelic light shows.

After a highly acclaimed performance at the Village Theater (soon to become the legendary Fillmore East), Vanilla Fudge was signed by Atlantic and began recording for the subsidiary Atco label. Their first release, "You Keep Me Hanging On," became only a modest American hit but an instant best seller in England. It was reissued during the following year, however, and very nearly reached the top of the American charts. They followed with several additional chart entries and with a best-selling album, *Vanilla Fudge.* By the early seventies, internal pressure caused the group to disband.

Tim Bogert and Carmine Appice went on to become founding members of Cactus and later joined with Jeff Beck to form Beck, Bogert & Appice.

July 67	***YOU KEEP ME HANGING ON* / Atco**
Feb. 68	***WHERE IS MY MIND?* / Atco**
July 68	***YOU KEEP ME HANGING ON* (rereleased) / Atco**
Oct. 68	***TAKE ME FOR A LITTLE WHILE* / Atco**
Dec. 68	***SEASON OF THE WITCH* / Atco**
Mar. 69	***SHOTGUN* / Atco**

Vanity Fare

MEMBERS:
Richard Allix
Anthony Jarret
Anthony Goulen
Trevor Brice
Barry Landeman
HOMETOWN: Kent, England

During the "hard rock" era of the late sixties, this British group emerged with an uncharacteristic light Pop sound. Signed by producer Larry Page to his Page One label, they achieved several international hits and two American top ten entries, "Early in the Morning" and "Hitchin' a Ride."

Nov. 69 *EARLY IN THE MORNING /* **Page One**
Mar. 70 *HITCHIN' A RIDE /* **Page One**
Aug. 70 *SUMMER MORNING /* **Page One**

Billy Vera & Judy Clay

MEMBERS:
Billy Vera (William McCord, Jr.) / born: May 28, 1944 / Riverside, California
Judy Clay / Fayetteville, North Carolina

During childhood Billy Vera moved around the country with his parents, both of whom were in show business. His father, William McCord, was (and still is) a radio personality, while his mother, Ann Ryan, sang on various radio and television shows.

As rock 'n' roll began to make its impact during the fifties, Vera decided that he would like to be part of it. Teaching himself the guitar and piano, he eventually joined a group called The Knight-Riders (also known as The Contrasts) and recorded for such labels as Rust (a subsidiary of Laurie) and Cameo. He also gained some success as a songwriter, composing

Billy Vera

"Mean Old World" for Ricky Nelson and "Make Me Belong to You" for Barbara Lewis.

In 1967 Vera signed with Atlantic Records and was teamed by the label with Judy Clay. (Judy was well connected in the music business—her sister, Sylvia Shamwell, was in The Sweet Inspirations, and that group's founder, Cissy Houston, is her aunt. Judy is also a cousin of Dionne Warwicke's.) This association resulted in two hit singles, after which Vera began recording solo.

During the mid-seventies Vera was signed by the Midland International label, debuting with the album *Out of the Darkness* and a single, "Private Clown." Judy Clay has not been active in the music business for the last several years.

Billy Vera & Judy Clay
Dec. 67 *STORYBOOK CHILDREN /* **Atlantic**
Feb. 68 *COUNTRY GIRL—CITY MAN /* **Atlantic**
Billy Vera
June 68 *WITH PEN IN HAND /* **Atlantic**

The Vogues. Standing, left to right: Don Miller, Hugh Geyer, Bill Burkette; kneeling: Chuck Blasko

The Vogues

MEMBERS:
William Burkette (lead vocals)/born: 1943
Hugh Geyer (first tenor)/born: 1943
Charles Blasko (second tenor)/born: 1943
Don Miller (baritone)/born: 1943
HOMETOWN: Turtle Creek, Pennsylvania

The four members of The Vogues grew up as childhood friends in a small town near Pittsburgh. During the early sixties, they formed a rock 'n' roll "teen-age" band, eventually recording an old Petula Clark song titled "You're the One" for the small Blue Star label. After becoming a regional hit, it was picked up by Herb Cohen and Nick Cenci's Pittsburgh-based Co & Ce label and soon reached the top five on the charts. Subsequently signed to Co & Ce, The Vogues continued for more than a year with a string of hits for the company.

In 1968 The Vogues signed with Reprise and totally changed musicial direction. Beginning with an old Glen Campbell song, "Turn Around, Look at Me," they recorded a series of syrupy Pop records which became major middle-of-the-road hits.

In 1971 they changed label affiliation once again, this time to Bell Records.

Sept. 65	*YOU'RE THE ONE*	/Co & Ce
Nov. 65	*FIVE O'CLOCK WORLD*	/Co & Ce
Feb. 66	*MAGIC TOWN*	/Co & Ce
June 66	*THE LAND OF MILK & HONEY*	/Co & Ce
Sept. 66	*PLEASE, MR. SUN*	/Co & Ce
Dec. 66	*THAT'S THE TUNE*	/Co & Ce
June 68	*TURN AROUND, LOOK AT ME*	/Reprise
Sept. 68	*MY SPECIAL ANGEL*	/Reprise
Nov. 68	*TILL*	/Reprise
Feb. 69	*WOMAN HELPING MAN*	/Reprise
Mar. 69	*NO NOT MUCH*	/Reprise
Apr. 69	*EARTH ANGEL*	/Reprise
June 69	*MOMENTS TO REMEMBER*	/Reprise
Aug. 69	*GREENFIELDS*	/Reprise

Loudon Wainright III

BORN: Sept. 5, 1946
HOMETOWN: Bedford, New York

A direct descendant of Peter Stuyvesant, the renowned one-legged governor of colonial New York, Loudon Wainright III is (naturally!) the son of Loudon Wainright II, the famed reporter and writer.

During the late sixties Wainright III established a reputation in his own right with his extreme antiestablishment views. He signed with Atlantic during the early seventies, recording two albums (*Album I* and *Album II*) of bitter, satirical material. In 1973 he changed affiliation to Columbia and recorded *Album III,* a turn toward slightly more conventional humor. This album yielded a major hit single, the top twenty recording of "Dead Skunk," and was followed by yet another album, titled *Attempted Moustache.*

Jan. 73 *DEAD SKUNK /*
    Columbia

Jerry Jeff Walker

REAL NAME: Ronald Crosby
BORN: Mar. 16, 1942
HOMETOWN: Catskill, New York

Raised in the Catskill Mountains area of New York, Jerry Jeff Walker took an early interest in such legendary folk performers as Woodie Guthrie and Pete Seeger. As he reached his late teens, he began touring the national coffeehouse circuit as a folk-oriented singer.

During the mid-sixties Walker met a musician named Bob Bruno on one of his tours. They formed a folk-rock band called Circus Maximus, traveling to New York in search of a recording contract. They succeeded at Vanguard, a traditional folk label, and recorded their first album, *Circus Maximus,* in 1967.

In 1968 Walker made an appearance on WBAI-FM, New York's "underground" station, and performed a song he had written called "Mr. Bojangles." This song (about an old minstrel-show dancer Walker had once met in jail) became an instant classic, prompting Atlantic Records to offer a contract and the chance to record it. Surprisingly, it became only a modest hit, but it generated a top ten version by The Nitty Gritty Dirt Band nearly two years later.

In 1973 Jerry Jeff Walker signed with MCA and developed into one of the Country-rock musicians known as "the outlaws." Today he is a leading concert attraction and heads his own Lost Gonzo Band.

July 68 *MR. BOJANGLES /*
    Atco
July 73 *L.A. FREEWAY /*
    MCA

Junior Walker & The All Stars

MEMBERS:

Junior Walker (Autrey DeWalt, Jr.) (sax, piano)/
born: 1942/Blytheville, Arkansas

Willie Woods (guitar)

Vic Thomas (keyboards)

James Graves (drums)

Interested in music since his childhood, Junior Walker first started playing sax while attending high school in South Bend, Indiana. He joined a band called The Jumping Jacks, which later merged with another band to become The Stix Nix.

During the early sixties, Walker played as a sideman for several midwestern bands. He eventually settled in Battle Creek, Michigan (where he lives to this day), forming his own All Stars band and touring with them. On one of his trips, he met Harvey Fuqua—former lead of The Moonglows and proprietor of the Harvey label—who signed them to a contract. After only a few releases, Harvey was absorbed by its parent company, Motown Records, and The All Stars soon began recording for another Motown-affiliated label, Soul.

Beginning with "Shotgun" in 1965, Junior Walker & The All Stars achieved a long string of hits and became Motown's undisputed leading instrumental group. Today Walker's son, Autrey DeWalt III, often plays drums with the band.

Feb. 65	*SHOTGUN* /Soul
June 65	*DO THE BOOMERANG* /Soul
July 65	*SHAKE & FINGERPOP* /Soul
Oct. 65	*CLEO'S BACK* /Soul
Jan. 66	*CLEO'S MOOD* /Soul
Apr. 66	*ROAD RUNNER* /Soul
July 66	*HOW SWEET IT IS* /Soul
Nov. 66	*MONEY* /Soul
Feb. 67	*PUCKER UP, BUTTERCUP* / Soul
July 67	*SHOOT YOUR SHOT* /Soul
Nov. 67	*COME SEE ABOUT ME* /Soul
Aug. 68	*HIP CITY* /Soul
Jan. 69	*HOME COOKING* /Soul
May 69	*WHAT DOES IT TAKE?* /Soul
Oct. 69	*THESE EYES* /Soul
July 70	*GOT TO HOLD ON TO THIS FEELING* /Soul
July 70	*DO YOU SEE MY LOVE FOR YOU GROWING?* /Soul
Dec. 70	*HOLLY HOLY* /Soul
Aug. 71	*TAKE ME GIRL, I'M READY* / Soul
Dec. 71	*WAY BACK HOME* /Soul
Apr. 72	*WALK IN THE NIGHT* /Soul

The Walker Brothers

MEMBERS:

John Maus (guitar)/born: Nov. 12, 1943/New York City

Scott Engel (bass)/born: Jan. 9, 1944/ Hamilton, Ohio

Gary Leeds (drums)/born: Sept. 3, 1944/ Glendale, California

Often thought of as a British "beat" group, The Walker Brothers were neither brothers nor British! The group was actually formed by three Americans in Los Angeles and gained some level of fame with their regular appearances on "Hollywood A Go-Go."

In 1965 The Walker Brothers traveled to London in search of wider fame than they were seemingly able to obtain at home. They soon succeeded, drawing frenzied crowds wherever they appeared and recording a series of best sellers in the British market. Surprisingly, very few of these became American hits, but two—"Make It Easy on Yourself" (the earlier Jerry Butler song) and "The Sun Ain't Gonna Shine Anymore"—did manage to reach the American top ten.

By 1967 internal pressures were pulling the group apart and all three members eventually embarked on solo careers. Although none became successful in the United States, each managed to place at least one record on the British charts.

Today John Maus is married to Kathy Young, known for her 1960 recording of "A Thousand Stars."

Oct. 65	***MAKE IT EASY ON YOUR-SELF* /Smash**
Jan. 66	***MY SHIP IS COMING IN* / Smash**
Apr. 66	***THE SUN AIN'T GONNA SHINE ANYMORE* /Smash**

Joe Walsh

HOMETOWN: Cleveland, Ohio

Joe Walsh gained fame during the early seventies as the lead guitarist of The James Gang (See *THE JAMES GANG.*)

After his separation from The James Gang, Walsh formed a group called Barnstorm with Rocke Grace (keyboards), Ken Passarelli (bass), and Joe Vitale (drums). This lasted until late 1973, when Walsh began recording solo.

Today Joe Walsh is an active record producer and session musician and records as a member of The Eagles.

Aug. 73	***ROCKY MOUNTAIN WAY* / Dunhill**
Jan. 74	***MEADOWS* /Dunhill**
Mar. 75	***TURN TO STONE* /Dunhill**

War

MEMBERS:

Howard E. Scott (lead guitar) / born: Mar. 15, 1946 / San Pedro, California

Lee Oskar (harmonica) / born: Mar. 24, 1946 / Copenhagen, Denmark

Charles William Miller (sax, flute) / born: June 2, 1939 / Olathe, Kansas

Lonnie Leroy Jordan (keyboards) / born: Nov. 21, 1948 / San Diego, California

Peter Rosen (bass) / died: 1969 / replaced by Morris DeWayne "B.B." Dickerson / born: Aug. 3, 1949 / Torrance, California

Thomas Sylvester "Papa Dee" Allen (percussion) / born: July 18, 1931 / Wilmington, Delaware

Harold Ray Brown (drums) / born: Mar. 17, 1946 / Long Beach, California

The history of this group dates back to 1959, when Harold Brown, Charles Miller, Howard Scott, Peter Rosen, B.B. Dickerson, and Lonnie Jordan first decided to play together. Working in clubs in the San Pedro area of California, they slowly built a reputation as one of the best club and back-up bands around. They eventually added Papa Dee Allen, evolving into a group known as The Night Shift and serving as the back-up band for football star David "Deacon" Jones.

In the interim the group had befriended Jerry Goldstein, a leading writer-producer in the Los Angeles area. When Goldstein became aware that Eric Burdon, formerly of The Animals, was seeking a new group, he immediately mentioned The Night Shift and suggested to Burdon that he catch their act. Burdon was accompanied by Lee Oskar, a harmonica player who happened to be staying with him at the time, and the evening ended with everybody "jamming" together and determined to form a group. Thus evolved Eric Burdon & War, an aggregation which placed two hits on the national charts in 1970.

In 1971 War broke away from Burdon and began recording for United Artists. After a string of major hits, the group today is considered one of the leading acts in the field of Soul while recording for MCA Records.

Eric Burdon & War

May 70 ***SPILL THE WINE* /MGM**

War

Dec. 70	***THEY CAN'T TAKE AWAY OUR MUSIC*/MGM**
War	
Aug. 71	***ALL DAY MUSIC*/United Artists**
Jan. 72	***SLIPPING INTO DARKNESS*/United Artists**
Nov. 72	***THE WORLD IS A GHETTO*/United Artists**
Mar. 73	***THE CISCO KID*/United Artists**
July 73	***GYPSY MAN*/United Artists**
Nov. 73	***ME & BABY BROTHER*/United Artists**
June 74	***BALLERO*/United Artists**
May 75	***WHY CAN'T WE BE FRIENDS?*/United Artists**
Sept. 75	***LOW RIDER*/United Artists**
July 76	***SUMMER*/United Artists**
July 77	***L.A. SUNSHINE*/Blue Note**
Jan. 78	***GALAXY*/MCA**

Jennifer Warnes

HOMETOWN: Los Angeles, California

It was while in high school that Jennifer knew she wanted to pursue a career as a singer. In fact, she would spend her after-school hours watching other performers in coffeehouses.

Her big break came when she was cast as the female lead in the Los Angeles production of *Hair*. Her performance, along with her strong reviews, enabled her to get some nightclub engagements, along with some network television shows.

In 1976 she signed a recording contract with Arista Records and later that year recorded the song "Right Time of the Night."

Jan. 77	***RIGHT TIME OF THE NIGHT*/Arista**
July 77	***I'M DREAMING*/Arista**

The Watts 103rd St. Rhythm Band

MEMBERS:

Charles Wright (guitar, keyboards)/born: 1942

Al McKay (guitar)

William Cannon (tenor sax)/born: 1939
"Big" John Rayford (tenor sax)/born: 1943
Gabriel Flemings (trumpet)/born: 1943
Joseph Banks (trumpet)
Ray Jackson (trombone, percussion)
Melvin Dunlap (bass)/born: 1946
James Gadson (drums)
HOMETOWN: Los Angeles, California

As its name implies, this large band was formed in the Watts section of Los Angeles. Their leader, Charles Wright, had once been a member of a fifties group called The Shields ("You Cheated") and had later played guitar for Bob B. Soxx & The Bluejeans.

Once organized, The Watts Band began playing the Los Angeles club circuit and was offered a contract with the local Keymen label. Although this resulted in a minor hit, their breakthrough was not to come until somewhat later, when comedian Bill Cosby decided to help the group. He not only offered advice and encouragement, but he arranged for the group to be signed to Warner Brothers. Beginning in 1969 they achieved a number of major hits and became one of the leading Soul bands of the early seventies.

In 1971 The Watts Band began to drift apart. Mel Dunlap, Jim Gadson, and Ray Jackson went on to become part of Bill Withers's band, while Al McKay became a member of Earth, Wind & Fire. Charles Wright began recording solo for ABC.

Sept. 67 **SPREADING HONEY**/Keymen
Feb. 69 **DO YOUR THING**/Warner Bros.
July 69 **TILL YOU GET ENOUGH**/Warner Bros.
Apr. 70 **LOVE LAND**/Warner Bros.
Aug. 70 **EXPRESS YOURSELF**/Warner Bros.
Jan. 71 **SOLUTION FOR POLLUTION**/Warner Bros.
May 71 **YOUR LOVE**/Warner Bros.

We Five

MEMBERS:
Beverly Bivens (lead vocals)/Santa Ana, California
Peter Fullerton (tenor)/Claremont, California
Jerry Burgan (tenor)/Kansas City, Kansas
Robert Jones (tenor, baritone)/Honolulu, Hawaii
Michael Stewart (baritone, bass)/Riverside, California

This group was organized in 1965 by five students at California's Mt. San Antonio College.

One of the group's members was Mike Stewart, younger brother of The Kingston Trio's John Stewart, so it was only natural that they be heard by Frank Werber, the famed trio's manager and producer. Through Werber's efforts, the group was signed and began recording for A & M Records.

In the summer of 1965, We Five very nearly reached the top of the charts with their first outing, "You Were on My Mind." Their follow-up efforts were nowhere near as successful, however, and the group soon faded from national popularity.

July 65 **YOU WERE ON MY MIND**/A & M
Nov. 65 **LET'S GET TOGETHER**/A & M

Bob Welch

BORN: July 31, 1946
HOMETOWN: Los Angeles, California

Bob Welch, an accomplished guitarist for many years, got his big break in 1971 when he replaced Jeremy Spencer as guitarist for Fleetwood Mac. Welch became the first non-Englishman to play with this famous band. After a few years with the group Welch left to pursue a career as a solo performer. In 1977 he was signed by Cap-

Wet Willie. Back row, left to right: T. K. Lively, Larry Berwald, Marshall Smith; front row, left to right: Michael Duke, Jack Hall, Jimmy Hall

itol Records and recorded his debut album called *French Kiss,* which was produced by Fleetwood Mac members Christine McVie and Lindsey Buckingham. The debut single from the album was a song Welch wrote called "Sentimental Lady" which established him as a national solo artist.

Oct. 77	*SENTIMENTAL LADY* / **Capitol**	
Jan. 78	*EBONY EYES* / **Capitol**	

Wet Willie

MEMBERS:
James Hall (lead vocals)
Rick Hirsch (lead guitar)
John Anthony (keyboards)
Jack Hall (bass)
Lewis Ross (drums)
Donna Hall (vocals) / added to the group in 1973
Ella Avery (vocals) / added to the group in 1973
HOMETOWN: Mobile, Alabama

The five original members of this "Dixie rock" group first played together in high school. After graduation they temporarily scattered into local groups such as The Devil's Disciples, The Blue Denims, and The Squires, eventually coming together again in a Mobile-based group called Fox.

In 1970 Fox traveled to Macon,

Georgia, for an audition with Phil Walden's Capricorn label. Signed on the spot, they changed their name to Wet Willie (after the children's "trick" of putting one's index finger in one's mouth and then in a companion's ear!) and began work on their first album, *Wet Willie*. They followed with *Wet Willie II,* but it was only with the release of their third album, *Drippin' Wet* (recorded live with The Allman Brothers at The Warehouse in New Orleans), that they achieved their major breakthrough. Their next LP, *Keep on Smilin'* was a major success, and it yielded the first of several hit singles for the group.

Today, accompanied by "The Williettes" (Donna Hall and Ella Avery), Wet Willie is a major concert attraction.

May 74	*KEEP ON SMILIN'* /Capricorn
Oct. 74	*THE COUNTRY SIDE OF LIFE* / Capricorn
Mar. 75	*LEONA* /Capricorn
May 75	*DIXIE ROCK* /Capricorn
May 76	*EVERYTHING THAT 'CHA DO* / Capricorn
Dec. 77	*STREET CORNER SERENADE* /Epic
Apr. 78	*MAKE YOU FEEL LOVE AGAIN* / Epic

Ian Whitcomb

BORN: July 10, 1941
HOMETOWN: Woking, Surrey, England

Interested in music since childhood, Ian Whitcomb began playing the accordion at twelve. He soon progressed to the ukulele, kazoo, tub bass, and jug and participated in a number of skiffle bands in his home area of Surrey.

During the mid-sixties Whitcomb was attending Trinity College in Dublin, Ireland, when he met a musician named Barry Richardson (later of Bees Make Honey). Together they formed a band called Bluesville Mfg, building a substantial following in local clubs and recording a number of "homemade" tapes.

In 1965 Whitcomb was vacationing in the United States when he met Northwestern producer Jerry Dennon (known for his work with The Kingsmen, Raiders, etc.). He played the tapes for Dennon, who decided to release one of the songs, "Soho," on his Jerden label. When this failed to catch on, Dennon agreed to release another song, titled "This Sporting Life," which proved considerably more successful. It was leased by Capitol for their subsidiary Tower label, just barely denting the charts, and was followed by the top ten release of "You Turn Me On." This enabled Whitcomb to appear widely on American television, and to gain yet another hit with "N-E-R-V-O-U-S."

During the late sixties, Whitcomb returned to England to work on a book titled "After the Ball, A History of Pop." It was published in 1972 to wide acclaim, and afterwards he resumed his writing, production, and recording activities. Today he lives in Los Angeles.

Mar. 65	*THIS SPORTING LIFE* /Tower
May 65	*YOU TURN ME ON* /Tower
Sept. 65	*N-E-R-V-O-U-S* /Tower

Barry White

BORN: Sept. 12, 1944
HOMETOWN: Galveston, Texas

Barry White grew up in Los Angeles, where he started singing in his church choir when he was eight. He made his professional debut just three years later, when he was paid $55 to play piano on Jesse Belvin's "Goodnight My Love."

In 1960 White joined an R & B group called The Upfronts, which played in

Barry White

small local clubs in the L.A. area. He broke into the record business during the mid-sixties, producing Bob & Earl's "Harlem Shuffle," working with Jackie Lee on "The Duck," and composing "I Feel Love Comin' On" for Felice Taylor.

During the early seventies, White organized the Love Unlimited group (see *LOVE UNLIMITED*) and sold his production of "Walking in the Rain with the One I Love" to MCA's Russ Regan. Shortly after this became a major hit, Regan became head of the 20th Century label and recruited White to its roster of artists.

Beginning with "I'm Gonna Love You Just a Little Bit More Baby," Barry "The Maestro" White accumulated a string of major hits during the early-middle seventies that rendered him the leading Soul star of the period. He also attained the heights of success with The Love Unlimited Orchestra, a large studio ensemble that he produced.

Today White lives in Sherman Oaks, California, with his wife, Glodean (a member of Love Unlimited whom he married, July 4, 1974), and their children: Kevin, Brigette, and Barry, Jr.

Apr. 73	**I'M GONNA LOVE YOU JUST A LITTLE BIT MORE BABY / 20th Century**
Aug. 73	**I'VE GOT SO MUCH TO GIVE / 20th Century**
Oct. 73	**NEVER, NEVER GONNA GIVE YOU UP / 20th Century**
Feb. 74	**HONEY PLEASE, CAN'T YOU SEE / 20th Century**
Aug. 74	**CAN'T GET ENOUGH OF YOUR LOVE / 20th Century**
Nov. 74	**YOU'RE THE FIRST, THE LAST, MY EVERYTHING / 20th Century**
Mar. 75	**WHAT AM I GONNA DO WITH YOU? / 20th Century**
May 75	**I'LL DO ANYTHING YOU WANT ME TO / 20th Century**
Dec. 75	**LET THE MUSIC PLAY / 20th Century**
July 76	**BABY, WE BETTER TRY TO GET IT / 20th Century**
Aug. 77	**IT'S ECSTASY WHEN YOU LAY DOWN / 20th Century**
Apr. 78	**OH WHAT A NIGHT FOR DANCING / 20th Century**

Tony Joe White

BORN: July 23, 1943
HOMETOWN: Oak Grove, Louisiana

A leading exponent of sixties "swamp rock," Tony Joe White was raised in the bayou country and began playing guitar during his early teens. He soon formed a band known as Tony & The Mojos, and later another called Tony & The Twilights. By the mid-sixties, however, he was no longer affiliated with any group and had settled in Corpus Christi, Texas, to concentrate on solo club work.

In 1965 White ventured to Nashville in an effort to place some songs he had written. He was signed as a writer to Fred Foster's Combine Music company and, later, as an artist to Foster's Monument label. After achieving re-

Wild Cherry. Left to right: Ron Beitle, Bryan Bassett, Marc Avsec, Bob Parissi

Wild Cherry

MEMBERS:
Bob Parissi (lead vocals, quitar)
Bryan Bassett (lead guitar)
Mark Avsec (keyboards)
Allen Wentz (bass)
Ron Beitle (drums)
HOMETOWN: Steubenville, Ohio

In the early seventies, while he was in the hospital Bob Parissi came up with the idea of forming the group and also with the name for the group, which he took from a box of cough drops in his room at the time.

The group played the Cleveland area and came to the attention of record producer Carl Maduri, who, along with his friend Mike Belkin, a local concert promoter, was in the midst of forming his own label. Thus the group was signed to and debuted on the new Sweet City label. The group's first release, a tune Parissi wrote called "Play That Funky Music," quickly became a number one national hit.

June 76	***PLAY THAT FUNKY MUSIC / Sweet City***
Jan. 77	***BABY DON'T YOU KNOW / Sweet City***
May 77	***HOT TO TROT / Sweet City***
Sept. 77	***HOLD ON / Sweet City***
Feb. 78	***I LOVE MY MUSIC / Epic***

Mason Williams

BORN: Aug. 24, 1938
HOMETOWN: Abilene, Texas

Mason Williams first began studying music while attending Oklahoma City University. During the following years, he continued to study music at a variety of other schools and in the navy.

Early in his career, Williams got a job in the Smothers Brothers' back-up band. He became close friends with Tommy Smothers, rooming with him in California, and was later hired as a principal writer for the Smothers Brothers' network television show.

During the late sixties, after recording briefly for Mercury (the label with which the Smothers were affiliated), Williams signed with the Warner Brothers label. He achieved a chart-topping single with "A Classical Gas," an unusual instrumental which combined the sound of chamber music with rock. He was able to follow with a number of additional chart entries in a similar vein.

Today Mason Williams is known primarily as an author, with more than half a dozen books to his credit.

June 68	***A CLASSICAL GAS*** / **Warner Bros.**
Oct. 68	***BAROQUE A NOVA*** / **Warner Bros.**
Feb. 69	***SATURDAY NIGHT AT THE WORLD*** / **Warner Bros.**
Apr. 69	***GREENSLEEVES*** / **Warner Bros.**

Paul Williams

BORN: 1940
HOMETOWN: Bennington, Nebraska

Paul Williams launched his show business career by writing material for comedian Mort Sahl. He began working as an actor during the mid-sixties, appearing in such films as *The Loved One* and *The Chase* and making his television debut in an ammonia commercial.

During the early seventies, Williams teamed up with Roger Nichols to compose a number of hit songs, including "We've Only Just Begun" and "Rainy Days & Mondays" for The Carpenters and "Out in the Country" for Three Dog Night. He also began a career as a recording artist, scoring with a hit single and making albums, including *Someday Man, Just an Old Fashioned Love Song,* and *Life Goes On.*

Paul Williams

Paul Williams's more recent successes have once again been associated with the world of film. During the mid-seventies he has starred in *Phantom of the Paradise* (for which he also composed the music) and collaborated with Barbra Streisand on the music for *A Star Is Born.* He records for Portrait Records.

Feb. 72	***WAKING UP ALONE*** / **A & M**

Al Wilson

BORN: June 19, 1939
HOMETOWN: Meridian, Mississippi

Al Wilson showed an early determination to make music his career. By the age of twelve, he had worked professionally as a country singer, formed his own spiritual quartet, and sang in a

Al Wilson

church choir. His first experience in the record business came during the late fifties, when he became a member of The Jewels (of "Hearts of Stone" fame). Next he joined The Rollers, and got his first taste of success when their "Continental Walk" became a national hit in 1960. After The Rollers broke up, Wilson formed his own instrumental quartet, known as The Souls.

In 1966 Wilson became acquainted with Marc Gordon, who became his personal manager and arranged for him to be signed to Johnny Rivers's Soul City label. This resulted in several hit singles, the biggest of which was a version of Oscar Brown, Jr.'s, "The Snake."

During the early seventies, Marc Gordon formed his own Rocky Road label and recruited Wilson to the roster. Working with producer Jerry Fuller, Wilson achieved a number one hit with "Show and Tell" and continued well into the mid-seventies with a series of best sellers.

Today Al Wilson records for Playboy Records and makes his home in San Bernardino, California.

Aug. 68	***THE SNAKE* / Soul City**
Jan. 69	***THE POOR SIDE OF TOWN* / Soul City**
Aug. 69	***LODI* / Soul City**
Oct. 73	***SHOW & TELL* / Rocky Road**
Mar. 74	***TOUCH & GO* / Rocky Road**
Oct. 74	***THE LA LA PEACE SONG* / Rocky Road**
Jan. 75	***I WON'T LAST A DAY WITHOUT YOU* / Rocky Road**
Mar. 76	***I'VE GOT A FEELING* / Playboy**

Hank Wilson

See *Leon RUSSELL.*

Wind

HOMETOWN: New York City

Wind was nothing more than a studio group assembled by producer Bo Gentry to record some of his material. What distinguished this "group," however, was that the lead was sung by Tony Orlando, soon to emerge as the central figure in Dawn. (See *DAWN;* also see *Tony ORLANDO* in *Rock On: The Solid Gold Years.*)

At this time Orlando still held down his position at Columbia's publishing house, April/Blackwood Music, singing for an occasional demo on the side and doing an occasional (anonymous) master session. Such was the case with Wind, whose recording of "Make Believe" rose to the top 30 on the charts.

Sept. 69 ***MAKE BELIEVE* / Life**

Wing and a Prayer Fife and Drum Corps

MEMBERS:
Linda November
Vivian Cherry
Arlene Martell
Helen Miles

In New York City in early 1975, just as the disco sound was booming, Stephen Scheaffer and Harold Wheeler decided to do an album of disco-arranged standards. They gathered together about twenty of New York's finest musicians, brought in Linda, Vivian, Arlene, and Helen to do the vocals, and recorded seven tunes. Of the seven, it was decided to release the disco-flavored "Baby Face" on their own Wing & a Prayer label. Consequently, they decided to call the assembled group Wing and a Prayer Fife and Drum Corps. The song became an instant smash at discotheques and a top chart record as well.

Nov. 75 ***BABY FACE* / Wing & a Prayer**

Wings

See *Paul McCARTNEY & WINGS.*

The Edgar Winter Group

MEMBERS:
Edgar Winter (guitar) / born: Dec. 28, 1946 / Beaumont, Texas
Ronnie Montrose (lead guitar) / replaced by Jerry Weems / replaced by Rick Derringer
Dan Hartman (bass) / Harrisburg, Pennsylvania
Chuck Ruff (drums) / Las Vegas, Nevada

Edgar Winter rose to fame during the early seventies along with his celebrated brother, Johnny Winter.

Once separated from Johnny's band, Edgar formed a group called White Trash, consisting of Floyd Radford (guitar), Jerry LaCroix (sax), Mike McLellan (trumpet), John Smith (sax), George Sheck (bass), and Bobby Ramirez (drums). This aggregation produced two albums, *White Trash* and *Road Work,* before breaking up.

Edgar formed a new group in 1973, recruiting Ronnie Montrose and Chuck Ruff, both formerly of Sawbuck, and Dan Hartman, a seven-year veteran of The Legends. This group achieved major commercial success, including a number one single titled "Frankenstein," and became an outstanding concert attraction.

Today Edgar Winter pursues a multi-faceted career. He continues to record with his own group, occasionally recording with his brother and working with Rick Derringer, on solo projects. Some of Edgar's best-selling albums over the years have been *They Only Come Out at Night, Shock Treatment, Jasmine Nightdreams,* and *The Edgar Winter Group with Rick Derringer.* (See *Rick DERRINGER.*)

Edgar Winter

Dec. 71	**KEEP PLAYING THAT ROCK & ROLL** /Epic
May 72	**I CAN'T TURN YOU LOOSE** / Epic
Mar. 73	**FRANKENSTEIN** /Epic
Aug. 73	**FREE RIDE** /Epic
Dec. 73	**HANGING AROUND** /Epic
July 74	**THE RIVER'S RISIN'** /Epic
Oct. 74	**EASY STREET** /Epic

Johnny Winter

BORN: Feb. 23, 1944
HOMETOWN: Leland, Mississippi

Johnny and Edgar Winter first began playing together during their early teens. During the late fifties and early sixties, the brothers were members of groups such as Johnny & The Jammers and Johnny Winter & The Black Plague. Also during the early sixties, Johnny became impassioned with the blues and began a period of several years as a sideman for various leading blues artists. In this capacity he developed a far-reaching reputation as an outstanding musician, which eventually brought him a write-up in *Rolling Stone.*

One of those to read the piece was Steve Paul, owner of New York's famed Scene. Highly intrigued, Paul flew to Texas to hear Johnny play, then booked him immediately and offered to become his manager. As Johnny began to play regularly to sell-out crowds, Paul obtained a contract with

Johnny Winter

Columbia Records and work on a debut album was begun. An informal group of musicians was recruited (including Edgar Winter), and *Johnny Winter* became an immediate success.

Although Johnny has achieved two hit singles, he is known almost entirely for his albums and for the ever-changing legion of musicians who accompany him. His releases include *First Winter, Second Winter, Johnny Winter And, Johnny Winter and Live, Still Alive & Well, Saints & Sinners, John Dawson Winter III,* and *Captured Live.*

Jan. 70	***JOHNNY B. GOODE*** / **Columbia**
May 71	***JUMPING JACK FLASH*** / **Columbia**

Bill Withers

BORN: July 4, 1938
HOMETOWN: Slab Fork, West Virginia

Although Bill Withers did some singing in church as a child, he did not give much thought to a singing career until he reached his middle twenties. In the interim, he had worked at a variety of odd jobs and spent nine years in the navy.

During the late sixties, Withers began spending his spare time making and circulating demo tapes of his material. Although he did not succeed at first, he eventually generated some interest from Clarence Avent, head of a new label called Sussex. Avent introduced him to Booker T. Jones (of the MG's), who assembled a group of leading session musicians and produced his first album, titled *Just As I Am.* This yielded "Ain't No Sunshine," a single that nearly reached the top of the charts and that eventually netted him a Grammy award. He followed with a long series of additional hits, evolving in the process into a leading Soul performer.

Today Bill Withers lives with his actress wife, Denise Nicholas in the San Fernando Valley area of California. He records for Columbia, and his backing group is composed of several former members of The Watts 103rd St. Rhythm Band.

July 71	**AIN'T NO SUNSHINE** / Sussex	
Oct. 71	**GRANDMA'S HANDS** / Sussex	
Apr. 72	**LEAN ON ME** / Sussex	
Aug. 72	**USE ME** / Sussex	
Dec. 72	**LET US LOVE** / Sussex	
Feb. 73	**KISSING MY LOVE** / Sussex	
July 73	**FRIEND OF MINE** / Sussex	
Apr. 74	**THE SAME LOVE THAT MADE ME LAUGH** / Sussex	
Dec. 74	**HEARTBREAK ROAD** / Sussex	
Dec. 77	**LOVELY DAY** / Columbia	

Bobby Womack

BORN: Mar. 4, 1944
HOMETOWN: Cleveland, Ohio

Bobby Womack began his career with The Valentinos, a group made up of his brothers that recorded for Sam Cooke's Sar label. (See *THE VALENTINOS, Rock On: The Solid Gold Years.*) Their recordings for the company included "It's All Over Now," which The Rolling Stones later picked up, and "Lookin' for a Love," a subsequent hit for The J. Geils Band (as well as for Womack himself).

Upon Sam Cooke's death in the summer of 1964, Womack left The Va-

Bobby Womack

lentinos for a solo career. Beginning as a songwriter and session musician, he composed "I'm in Love" and "Midnight Mover" for Wilson Pickett and played on sessions with Janis Joplin and Aretha Franklin. He also served for a time as the leader of Wilson Pickett's band.

In 1968 Womack signed with the New Orleans-based Minit label. He recorded two albums and a number of singles, several of which hit the charts, before moving to the company's parent label, United Artists. He achieved a long string of hits during the seventies, becoming known as a major Soul performer.

Today there are plans for Womack to star in a film based on the life of Sam Cooke. Chief among his film credits is *Across 110th St.,* for which he composed the sound track.

Aug. 68	**FLY ME TO THE MOON** / Minit	
Dec. 68	**CALIFORNIA DREAMING** / Minit	
Dec. 69	**HOW I MISS YOU, BABY** / Minit	
Apr. 70	**MORE THAN I CAN STAND** / Minit	

Dec. 71	**THAT'S THE WAY I FEEL ABOUT YOU**/United Artists
May 72	**A WOMAN'S GOT TO HAVE IT**/United Artists
Aug. 72	**SWEET CAROLINE**/United Artists
Dec. 72	**HARRY HIPPIE**/United Artists
Mar. 73	**ACROSS 110TH STREET**/United Artists
June 73	**NOBODY WANTS YOU WHEN YOU'RE DOWN AND OUT**/United Artists
Feb. 74	**LOOKIN' FOR A LOVE**/United Artists
July 74	**YOU'RE WELCOME, STOP ON BY**/United Artists
Apr. 75	**CHECK IT OUT**/United Artists

Stevie Wonder

Stevie Wonder

REAL NAME: Steveland Morris Hardaway
BORN: May 13, 1950
HOMETOWN: Detroit, Michigan

One of the real geniuses of pop music, Wonder has been a consistent hitmaker since 1963. After an almost two-year absence from the charts, he came back strong in October 1976, with the smash LP *Songs in the Key of Life.* (For prior career information see *Rock On: The Solid Gold Years.*)

Apr. 74	**DON'T YOU WORRY 'BOUT A THING**/Tamla
Aug. 74	**YOU HAVEN'T DONE NOTHING**/Tamla
Nov. 74	**BOOGIE ON REGGAE WOMAN**/Tamla
Dec. 76	**I WISH**/Tamla
Apr. 77	**SIR DUKE**/Tamla
Aug. 77	**ANOTHER STAR**/Tamla
Nov. 77	**AS**/Tamla

The Wonder Who

When The Wonder Who appeared on the charts in 1965, they didn't really leave many people wondering who they were. They were, of course, The Four Seasons, recording under a pseudonym to avoid conflict with their other hits of the period.

The concept of the high-pitched "warbling" and scat singing that characterized these records was introduced by Frankie Valli. An ardent fan of such forties artists as Nellie Lutcher and Rose Murphy (The Chee-Chee Girl), he began imitating them one day while recording what was intended to be an album of Bob Dylan songs. Although the album never came to be, the result was a top ten single of Dylan's "Don't Think Twice."

In 1966 The Four Seasons were able to score with two more "standards" before dropping The Wonder Who concept.

Nov. 65	**DON'T THINK TWICE**/Philips
July 66	**ON THE GOOD SHIP LOLLIPOP**/Philips
July 66	**YOU'RE NOBODY TILL SOMEBODY LOVES YOU**/Philips

Brenton Wood

BORN: July 26, 1941
HOMETOWN: Shreveport, Louisiana

After moving to California with his family at the age of two, Brenton Wood grew up in the San Pedro area and developed an early interest in sports. He became a track star in high school, making somewhat of a name for himself by running the 100-yard dash in just over nine seconds.

During the mid-sixties Wood's interests began to turn toward music. He became an accomplished pianist, making local appearances and hoping for a recording contract. He succeeded in 1967, signing with the L.A.-based Double Shot label and debuting with a novelty called "The Oogum Boogum Song." This became a substantial hit and was followed by his top ten recording of "Gimmie Little Sign."

By the end of 1967, Wood had become a star, touring widely with a back-up band called Kent & The Candidates. After several more releases, however, he began to fade from national popularity.

Apr. 67	THE OOGUM BOOGUM SONG / Double Shot
Aug. 67	GIMME LITTLE SIGN / Double Shot
Nov. 67	BABY, YOU GOT IT / Double Shot
Mar. 68	LOVEY DOVEY KIND OF LOVING / Double Shot

Betty Wright

BORN: Dec. 21, 1953
HOMETOWN: Miami, Florida

Betty Wright began her career at the age of three by joining her family's spiritual group, The Echoes of Joy. When they eventually broke up to branch out on their own, Betty became determined to make it as a solo performer. She entered a number of Miami talent shows, traveled to Caracas, Venezuela, for the Spanish Fiesta, and landed a spot on a South American television show.

During the late sixties, Betty was signed to Henry Stone's Florida-based Alston label. After two regional hits, she broke onto the national charts with "Girls Can't Do What the Guys Do" and followed with her top ten recording of "Clean Up Woman."

Today, with a number of hits under her belt, Betty Wright is a popular Soul performer and tours with her own band.

Aug. 68	GIRLS CAN'T DO WHAT THE GUYS DO / Alston
Nov. 71	CLEAN UP WOMAN / Alston
Oct. 72	BABY SITTER / Alston
Apr. 73	IT'S HARD TO STOP / Alston
Oct. 73	LET ME BE YOUR LOVEMAKER / Alston
July 74	SECRETARY / Alston
Apr. 75	WHERE IS THE LOVE / Alston

Gary Wright

BORN: Apr. 26, 1943
HOMETOWN: Englewood, New Jersey

Piano-playing Wright went to England in the late sixties and formed a rock band called Spooky Tooth, which had some hit LP's on Island Records. In 1970 he left the group to pursue a solo career, but when that did not seem to work, he reorganized Spooky Tooth. This lasted until 1974, when he left again to pursue a solo career. He went to Los Angeles, secured a recording contract with Warner Brothers, and began to write some new material for his debut LP, *Dream Weaver*. The title song from the LP was released as the first single and it quickly shot up the charts, becoming a top five national hit.

Jan. 76	***DREAM WEAVER*** /Warner Bros.
Apr. 76	***LOVE IS ALIVE*** /Warner Bros.
Sept. 76	***MADE TO LOVE YOU*** /Warner Bros.
Mar. 77	***PHANTOM WRITER*** /Warner Bros.
Jan. 78	***TOUCH & GONE*** /Warner Bros.

Tammy Wynette

REAL NAME: Wynette Pugh
BORN: May 4, 1942
HOMETOWN: Itawamba County, Mississippi

One of the true Country "superstars," Tammy Wynette launched her career during the mid-sixties on a local Alabama television show called "Country Boy Eddie." Her first major exposure came in 1966, when she was asked to perform at the Disc Jockey Convention in Nashville. She performed for a time with Porter Wagoner, eventually moving to Nashville to concentrate more on her career.

In 1967 Tammy became acquainted with Billy Sherrill, head of A & R for Columbia and Epic Records. Sherrill gave her a listen, signed her to the label, and began producing her records. After two regional hits with "Apartment 9" and "Your Good Girl's Gonna Go Bad," Tammy broke through nationally with "D-I-V-O-R-C-E." Her next record, "Stand By Your Man," went straight to number one on the Country charts and became the largest-selling single by a woman in the history of Country music.

Today known as The First Lady of Country Music, Tammy is married to another major star, singer George Jones. They have one daughter, Georgette.

June 68	***D-I-V-O-R-C-E*** /Epic
Nov. 68	***STAND BY YOUR MAN*** /Epic
Apr. 69	***SINGING MY SONG*** /Epic
Aug. 69	***THE WAYS TO LOVE A MAN*** /Epic
Jan. 70	***I'LL SEE THROUGH HIM*** /Epic
June 70	***HE LOVES ME ALL THE WAY*** /Epic
Oct. 70	***RUN WOMAN RUN*** /Epic
Jan. 72	***BEDTIME STORY*** /Epic
June 73	***KIDS SAY THE DARNDEST THINGS*** /Epic
May 76	***'TIL I CAN MAKE IT ON MY OWN*** /Epic

Y

Glenn Yarbrough

BORN: Jan. 12, 1930
HOMETOWN: Milwaukee, Wisconsin

Glenn Yarbrough began his career during the late fifties with a group called The Limeliters. (See *THE LIME-LITERS, Rock On: The Solid Gold Years.*)

After The Limeliters broke up in 1963, Yarbrough went solo and continued to record for the same label, RCA. He achieved major success in 1965, reaching the national top ten with the theme from the film *Baby, The Rain Must Fall.*

In 1973, exactly ten years after they disbanded, the original group reformed under the name of Glenn Yarbrough & The Limeliters. Today, their backing musicians include Mike Settle, formerly with The First Edition, and Tony Gottlieb, the son of original Limeliter Louis Gottlieb.

Mar. 65   ***BABY, THE RAIN MUST FALL / RCA***
July 65   ***IT'S GONNA BE FINE / RCA***

The Yardbirds

MEMBERS:
Keith Relf (lead vocals, harmonica) / born: Mar. 22, 1943 / Richmond, Surrey, England / died: 1976 / replaced by Robert Plant / born: Aug. 20, 1947 / Birmingham, England
Anthony "Top" Topham (lead guitar) / replaced by Eric Patrick Clapton / born: Mar. 30, 1945 / Ripley, Surrey, England / replaced by Jeff

Beck / born: June 24, 1944 / Surrey, England / replaced by James Patrick Page / born: Jan. 9, 1945 / Heston, Middlesex, England
Chris Dreja (rhythm guitar) / born: Nov. 11, 1945 / Surbiton, Surrey, England
Paul "Sam" Samwell-Smith (bass) / born: May 8, 1943 / London, England / replaced by John Paul Jones / born: Jan. 3, 1946 / London, England
James McCarty (drums) / born: July 25, 1943 / Liverpool, England / replaced by John Bonham / born: May 31, 1947 / Birmingham, England

The Yardbirds rank among the most important of the British bands, if only for the number of major rock figures who have emerged from the group over the years. In fact, the family tree of this group reads like a "Who's Who" of British rock.

Growing out of the London R & B scene of the early sixties, the group was originally known as The Metropolis Blues Quartette and consisted of Chris Dreja, "Sam" Samwell-Smith, Keith Relf, and Jim McCarty. With the addition of Top Topham, who was soon replaced by Eric Clapton, the group became The Yardbirds (a slang term for bums who survive by hitching trains) and rapidly gained a cult following at such leading R & B clubs as the Crawdaddy and the Marquee. They began recording in 1964 and, within a year, their releases began appearing on the American charts.

After a host of personnel changes, The Yardbirds split up in 1968. Relf, McCarty, and Samwell-Smith went on to form Renaissance, while Page, Bon-

The Yardbirds. Left to right: Jim McCarty, Jeff Beck, Paul Samwell-Smith, Chris Dreja, Keith Relf

ham, Plant, and Jones emerged as Led Zeppelin. Relf went on further to form Armageddon, but was electrocuted on stage during the summer of 1976. Eric Clapton and Jeff Beck are, of course, two of today's leading rock guitarists.

May 65	*FOR YOUR LOVE* / Epic
July 65	*A HEARTFUL OF SOUL* / Epic
Oct. 65	*I'M A MAN* / Epic
Mar. 66	*SHAPES OF THINGS* / Epic
June 66	*OVER, UNDER, SIDEWAYS, DOWN* / Epic
Nov. 66	*HAPPENINGS TEN YEARS TIME AGO* / Epic
Apr. 67	*LITTLE GAMES* / Epic
Aug. 67	*HA HA SAID THE CLOWN* / Epic
Nov. 67	*TEN LITTLE INDIANS* / Epic

Yes

MEMBERS:

Jon Anderson (lead vocals) / born: Oct. 25, 1944

Peter Banks (lead guitar) / replaced (1970) by Steve Howe / born: Apr. 8, 1947

Tony Kaye (keyboards) / replaced (1971) by Rick Wakeman / born: May 18, 1949 / replaced (1974) by Vangelis Papathanassiou / replaced (1974) by Patrick Moraz

Chris Squire (bass) / born: Mar. 4, 1948

William Bruford (drums) / born: May 17, 1950 / replaced (1972) by Alan White

HOMETOWN: Birmingham, England

Yes was formed in 1968 by members of various other bands. After establishing a reputation at the legendary Marquee Club, the group drew the attention of Ahmet Ertegun, who signed them directly to his Atlantic label.

Debuting with *Yes* in 1969, the group recorded a series of progressively more popular albums, including *Time and a Word, The Yes Album, Fragile, Close to the Edge, Tales from Topographic Oceans,* and *Relayer.* By 1971 their singles were appearing on the charts as well, and they achieved a top ten hit with "Roundabout." In 1975 they were the subject of a feature film called *Yessongs,* which also yielded a best-selling soundtrack album.

Yes. Left to right: Rick Wakeman, Jon Anderson, Alan White, Steve Howe, Chris Squire

Over the years Yes has successfully endured a number of major personnel changes. Two former members, Peter Banks and Rick Wakemen, have been able to establish lucrative solo careers. However, Wakeman returned to Yes during the summer of 1977.

Sept. 71 *YOUR MOVE* / **Atlantic**
Feb. 72 *ROUNDABOUT* / **Atlantic**
Aug. 72 *AMERICA* / **Atlantic**
Nov. 72 *AND YOU, AND I* / **Atlantic**

Dennis Yost & The Classics IV

MEMBERS:
Dennis Yost (lead vocals) / Detroit, Michigan
James Cobb (lead guitar) / Birmingham, Alabama / replaced by Auburn Burrell / Jacksonville, Florida
Wally Eaton (rhythm guitar) / Jacksonville, Florida

Joseph Wilson (bass) / Birmingham, Alabama / replaced by Dean Daughtry / Dothan, Alabama
Kim Venable (drums) / Tallahassee, Florida
MEMBERS (post-1972):
Dennis Yost (lead vocals)
Steve Pullias (guitar)
Sam Anderson (sax)
Daniel Ramos (keyboards)
William Gillmore (bass)
Michael Huey (drums)

This group was organized by Dennis Yost and Wally Eaton, two friends who had attended high school together in Jacksonville, Florida. Recruiting musicians from the southern club circuit, they formed a band and began sending demo tapes to record companies in the hope of obtaining a contract. They succeeded at Liberty/Imperial, signing in 1967 and scoring with an immediate top three hit called "Spooky." They followed with a number of additional hits, the biggest of which was "Traces," then temporarily faded from popularity in 1970.

In 1972 Dennis Yost re-emerged with a completely reorganized band. Signed to the MGM/South label, The Classic IV began once again to appear on the charts.

Dec. 67	*SPOOKY*/Imperial
May 68	*SOUL TRAIN*/Imperial
Oct. 68	*STORMY*/Imperial
Feb. 69	*TRACES*/Imperial
May 69	*EVERY DAY WITH YOU*/Imperial
Aug. 69	*CHANGE OF HEART*/Imperial
Nov. 69	*MIDNIGHT*/Imperial
Mar. 70	*THE FUNNIEST THING*/Imperial
Oct. 70	*WHERE DID ALL THE GOOD TIMES GO?*/Liberty
Oct. 72	*WHAT AM I CRYING FOR?*/MGM-South
Mar. 73	*ROSANNA*/MGM-South
Apr. 75	*MY FIRST DAY WITHOUT HER*/MGM-South

Neil Young

See *CROSBY, STILLS, NASH & YOUNG.*

The Youngbloods

MEMBERS:

Jesse Colin Young (Perry Miller) (lead vocals, bass)/born: Nov. 11, 1944/New York City

Jerry Corbitt (lead guitar, bass)

"Banana" (Lowell Levinger) (guitar, keyboards)/born: 1946/Cambridge, Massachusetts

Joseph Bauer (drums)/born: Sept. 26, 1941/Memphis, Tennessee

The nucleus of this group, Jesse Colin Young, began his career during the early sixties as a folksinger. While touring the northeastern coffeehouse circuit, he became acquainted with songwriter-producer Bobbie Scott, with whom he formed an association.

Neil Young

Scott produced two albums, *Soul of a City Boy* for Capitol and *Youngblood* for Mercury, but neither gained much attention.

In 1965 Young was working in Cambridge, Massachusetts, when he met a musician named Jerry Corbitt. The two decided to organize a band, and The Youngbloods came into being. After building a reputation with their club work, the group was signed by RCA and began work on their first album, *The Youngbloods*. This yielded a moderate hit single called "Grizzly Bear" and a less successful follow-up titled "Get Together." Two years later the latter song was picked as the theme for the National Council of Christians and Jews, and the resulting exposure sent it to the top of the charts.

After one more chart entry, Jerry Corbitt left the group in 1971 to try his hand at independent production. The group continued as a trio, forming their own Raccoon label and making an album. They eventually disbanded in 1972, however, with Jesse Colin Young pursuing a solo career and Lowell Levinger forming a group, with Joe Bauer, called Banana & the Bunch. Today Jesse records for Warner Brothers.

Dec. 66 *GRIZZLY BEAR* /RCA
Sept. 67 *GET TOGETHER* /RCA
June 69 *GET TOGETHER* (rereleased)/ RCA
May 70 *DARKNESS DARKNESS* /RCA

Young-Holt Unlimited

MEMBERS:
Eldee Young /born: Jan. 7, 1936/Chicago, Illinois

Isaac "Red" Holt /born: May 16, 1932/ Rosedale, Mississippi

Eldee Young and Isaac Holt were known for 13 years as two-thirds of The Ramsey Lewis Trio. (See *Ramsey LEWIS TRIO*.)

In 1966 Young and Holt left the trio to form their own group, Young-Holt Unlimited. They signed with Brunswick, achieving several hit singles and a chart-topping instrumental called "Soulful Strut." This partnership lasted until 1974, when Isaac Holt in turn left to form his own group, Red Holt Unlimited. This new group began recording for the Paula label.

Dec. 66 *WACK WACK* /Brunswick
Nov. 68 *SOULFUL STRUT* /Brunswick
Mar. 69 *WHO'S MAKING LOVE?* / Brunswick

Zager & Evans

MEMBERS:
Denny Zager /Wymore, Nebraska
Rick Evans /Lincoln, Nebraska

Zager and Evans first met in 1962 in a group called The Eccentrics. While Evans remained with the group until 1967, Zager left in 1965 to join another band, The Devilles. When their paths happened to cross again in 1968, they decided to pool their talents as a duo.

In the course of their club appearances, they often performed a song, which Evans had written in 1964, called "In the Year 2525." Sensing a demand among their audiences, they recorded the song and pressed several thousand copies on their own Truth label. They sold it wherever they performed and distributed copies to radio stations and record companies. Much to their amazement, the record became an enormous regional hit (11,000 orders in three weeks) and prompted RCA to offer a contract. Within just a few weeks, "2525" reached number one on the charts and passed the four-million mark in international sales!

Although several follow-up records were released, none became a hit. They signed with Vanguard in 1971, but this proved similarly unsuccessful.

Today Denny Zager performs with a trio around the Nebraska area, while Rick Evans deals in real estate and occasionally dabbles in music on the side. Perhaps he would like to see history repeat itself, for he has recently recorded a solo album in Nashville and has had it pressed up on his own label!

June 69 *IN THE YEAR 2525* /RCA

Frank Zappa

BORN: Dec. 21, 1940
HOMETOWN: Baltimore, Maryland

Frank was the oldest of four children, who moved with his family to Los Angeles while still in his teens. After graduation in June 1958, he began to develop an interest in music, especially rhythm and blues and rock. In fact, he began writing several songs at the time, one of them being recorded by a big group of the fifties, the Penguins (known for Earth Angel) they recorded Zappa's "Memories of El Monte."

In 1964 he formed the notorious Mothers of Invention, a group that gave him a vehicle for his many ideas. In the 1970s Zappa got involved with films, wanting to combine rock and classical material. The result of this involvement was the film *200 Motels,* which gained Zappa much publicity.

Today Zappa records for Warner Brothers as a solo performer.

Oct. 74 *DON'T EAT THE YELLOW SNOW* /DiscReet

Zager & Evans

The Zombies

MEMBERS:

Colin Edward Michael Blunstone (lead vocals, guitar) / born: June 24, 1945 / Lempsford, Herts, England

Paul Atkinson (guitar) / born: Mar. 19, 1946 / Cuffley, Herts, England

Rodney Terence Argent (keyboards) / born: June 14, 1945 / St. Albans, Herts, England

Christopher Taylor White (bass) / born: Mar. 7, 1943 / Barnet, Herts, England

Hugh Birch Grundy (drums) / born: Mar. 6, 1945 / Winchester, Herts, England

Formed in 1962 at St. Albans Public School, The Zombies began as a trio consisting of Rod Argent, Paul Atkinson, and Hugh Grundy. With the addition of Colin Blunstone and Chris White, they became a permanent working unit and began thinking about music as a career.

Frank Zappa & The Mothers. Center: Frank Zappa

In 1964 The Zombies entered a "beat" group contest sponsored by the *London Evening News*. Winning first prize, they received a great deal of publicity and the help they needed to obtain a recording contract. They were signed by the British Decca label and debuted with "She's Not There," a record that became a chart-topper on both sides of the Atlantic. After achieving several additional hits, the group affiliated briefly with CBS and disbanded shortly thereafter.

In 1969, long after the group had become defunct, CBS released "Time of the Season" on its subsidiary Date label. This reached number one, prompting a number of bogus groups to begin touring as The Zombies. The "real" Zombies, in the meantime, had embarked in other directions: Rod Argent had begun rehearsals with a new

ZZ Top. Left to right: Billy Gibbons, Dusty Hill, Frank Beard

group (Argent), Colin Blunstone had begun a solo career, and the remaining members had accepted positions in the music business. (See *ARGENT*.)

Oct. 64	*SHE'S NOT THERE* /**Parrot**	
Jan. 65	*TELL HER NO* /**Parrot**	
Apr. 65	*SHE'S COMING HOME* / **Parrot**	
June 65	*I WANT YOU BACK AGAIN* / **Parrot**	
Feb. 69	*TIME OF THE SEASON* /**Date**	

ZZ Top

MEMBERS:
William Gibbons (guitar)
Dusty Hill (bass)
Frank Beard (drums)
HOMETOWN: El Paso, Texas

This group was organized by Billy Gibbons, a well-known veteran of a psychedelic Texas band called Moving Sideways. In 1970 Gibbons approached Frank Beard with the idea of forming a band. The search for a third member began, and they eventually recruited Dusty Hill, with whom Beard had previously played in a group known as American Blues.

Early in 1971 ZZ Top debuted on London with an LP appropriately titled *The First Album*. While this was only moderately successful, their following albums, including *Rio Grande Mud, Tres Hombres*, and *Fandango*, be-

came major best sellers. In 1972 the group began placing an occasional entry on the singles charts as well.

Today ZZ Top is a major concert attraction, affectionately known as "that little ol' band from Texas."

May 72	*FRANCENE*/London
Mar. 74	*LA GRANGE*/London
July 75	*TUSH*/London
Sept. 76	*IT'S ONLY LOVE*/London
Mar. 77	*ARRESTED FOR DRIVING WHILE BLIND*/London

Appendix
These Too Made It

Ad Libs
Jan. 65   *THE BOY FROM NEW YORK CITY* / Blue Cat

Jewel Akens
Feb. 65   *THE BIRDS AND THE BEES* / Era
May 65   *GEORGIE PORGIE* / Era

Alive and Kicking
June 70   *TIGHTER AND TIGHTER* / Roulette
Sept. 70   *JUST LET IT COME* / Roulette

Assembled Multitude
July 70   *OVERTURE FROM TOMMY* / Atlantic
Oct. 70   *WOODSTOCK* / Atlantic

Beginning of the End
May 71   *FUNKY NASSAU (Pt. 1)* / Alston

Benny Bell
Mar. 75   *SHAVING CREAM* / Vanguard

Vincent Bell
Apr. 70   AIRPORT *LOVE THEME* / Decca

Bimbo Jet
May 75   *EL BIMBO* / Scepter

Jack Blanchard & Misty Morgan
Mar. 70   *TENNESSEE BIRD WALK* / Wayside
July 70   *HUMPHREY THE CAMEL* / Wayside

Blue Haze
Nov. 72   *SMOKE GETS IN YOUR EYES* / A & M

Blue Ridge Rangers
Dec. 72   *JAMBALAYA (ON THE BAYOO)* / Fantasy

Brass Ring
Mar. 66   *THE PHOENIX LOVE THEME* / Dunhill
Feb. 67   *THE DIS-ADVANTAGES OF YOU* / Dunhill

Beverly Bremers
Dec. 71   *DON'T SAY YOU DON'T REMEMBER* / Scepter
Apr. 72   *WE'RE FREE* / Scepter
Sept. 72   *I'LL MAKE YOU MUSIC* / Scepter

Brotherhood of Man
Apr. 70   *UNITED WE STAND* / Deram
Aug. 70   *WHERE ARE YOU GOING TO MY LOVE* / Deram
May 71   *REACH OUT YOUR HAND* / Deram

Candy & The Kisses
Nov. 64   *THE 81* / Cameo

Chakachas
Jan. 72   *JUNGLE FEVER* / Polydor

Tom Clay
July 71   *WHAT THE WORLD NEEDS NOW IS LOVE / ABRAHAM, MARTIN & JOHN* / Mowest

Clique
Sept. 69   *SUGAR ON SUNDAY* / White Whale

Dennis Coffey & The Detroit Guitar Band
Nov. 71   *SCORPIO* / Sussex
Feb. 72   *TAURUS* / Sussex
June 72   *GETTING IT ON* / Sussex

Bill Cosby
Sept. 67   *LITTLE OLE MAN (UPTIGHT EVERYTHING'S ALRIGHT)* / Warner Bros.
Dec. 67   *HOORAY FOR THE SALVATION ARMY BAND* / Warner Bros.
Feb. 68   *FUNKY NORTH PHILLY* / Warner Bros.
Apr. 70   *GROVER HENSON FEELS FORGOTTEN* / Warner Bros.
May 76   *YES, YES, YES* / Capitol

Les Crane
Oct. 71   *DESIDERATA* / Warner Bros.

Crazy Elephant
Mar. 69   *GIMME GIMME GOOD LOVIN'* / Bell

Crow
Oct. 69   *EVIL WOMAN DON'T PLAY YOUR GAMES WITH ME* / Amaret

Cymarron
June 71   *RINGS* / Entrance

Liz Damon's Orient Express
Dec. 70   *1900 YESTERDAY* / White Whale

Delegates
Oct. 72   *CONVENTION 72* / Mainstream

Senator Everett McKinley Dirksen
Dec. 66   *GALLANT MEN* / Capitol

Double Exposure
June 76   *TEN PERCENT* / Salsoul

8th Day
May 71   *SHE'S NOT JUST ANOTHER WOMAN* / Invictus

Electric Indian
Aug. 69   *KEEM-O-SABE* / United Artists
Dec. 69   *LAND OF 1,000 DANCES* / United Artists

Ernie (Jim Henson)
Aug. 70   *RUBBER DUCKIE* / Columbia

Esquires
Aug. 67   *GET ON UP* / Bunky
Nov. 67   *AND GET AWAY* / Bunky
Jan. 69   *YOU'VE GOT THE POWER* / Wand

Fantastic Johnny C
Oct. 67   *BOOGALOO DOWN BROADWAY* / Phil L.A. of Soul
Feb. 68   *GOT WHAT YOU NEED* / Phil L.A. of Soul
July 68   *HITCH IT TO THE HORSE* / Phil L.A. of Soul
Nov. 68   *(SHE'S) SOME KIND OF WONDERFUL* / Phil L.A. of Soul

Gene & Debbe
Oct. 67   *GO WITH ME* / TRX
Feb. 68   *PLAYBOY* / TRX
July 68   *LOVIN' SEASON* / TRX

Stan Getz / Astrud Gilberto
June 64   *THE GIRL FROM IPANEMA* / Verve

Godspell
May 72   *DAY BY DAY* / Bell

Charles Randolph Grean
June 69   *QUENTIN'S THEME* / Ranwood

Cyndi Greco
May 76   *MAKING OUR DREAMS COME TRUE* / Private Stock

Larry Groce
Jan. 76   *JUNK FOOD JUNKIE* / Warner Bros.

Noel Harrison
Dec. 65   *A YOUNG GIRL* / London
Oct. 67   *SUZANNE* / Reprise

Joey Heatherton
May 72   *GONE* / MGM
Nov. 72   *I'M SORRY* / MGM

Neal Hefti
Feb. 66   *BATMAN THEME* / RCA Victor

Hillside Singers
Nov. 71   *I'D LIKE TO TEACH THE WORLD TO SING* / Metromedia

Don Ho
Nov. 66   *TINY BUBBLES* / Reprise

Richard "Groove" Holmes
June 66   *MISTY* / Prestige
Oct. 66   *WHAT NOW MY LOVE* / Prestige

Hot Butter
July 72   *POPCORN* / Musicor

David Houston
July 66   *ALMOST PERSUADED* / Epic
Oct. 67   *YOU MEAN THE WORLD TO ME* / Epic

Hudson & Landry
Apr. 71   *AJAX LIQUOR STORE* / Dore
Jan. 72   *AJAX AIRLINES* / Dore

Human Beinz
Dec. 67   *NOBODY BUT ME* / Capitol
Mar. 68   *TURN ON YOUR LOVE LIGHT* / Capitol

Irish Rovers
Mar. 68   *THE UNICORN* / Decca
June 68   *WHISKEY ON A SUNDAY* / Decca
Sept. 68   *THE BIPLANE EVER MORE* / Decca

J. J. Jackson
Oct. 66   *BUT IT'S ALRIGHT* / Calla
Dec. 66   *I DIG GIRLS* / Calla

May 69   *BUT IT'S ALRIGHT* (rereleased) /
Warner Bros.

Horst Jankowski
May 65   *A WALK IN THE BLACK FOREST* /
Mercury

Sept. 65   *SIMPEL GIMPEL* / Mercury

Jefferson
Aug. 69   *THE COLOR OF MY LOVE* / Decca
Dec. 69   *BABY TAKE ME IN YOUR
ARMS* / Janus

Joe Jeffrey Group
June 69   *MY PLEDGE OF LOVE* / Wand

Jelly Beans
June 64   *I WANNA LOVE HIM SO BAD* / Red
Bird
Sept. 64   *BABY BE MINE* / Red Bird

Bob Kuban & The In-Men
Jan. 66   *THE CHEATER* / Musicland U.S.A.
Apr. 66   *THE TEASER* / Musicland U.S.A.
July 66   *DRIVE MY CAR* / Musicland U.S.A.

Jackie Lee
Nov. 65   *THE DUCK* / Mirwood

Leapy Lee
Oct. 68   *LITTLE ARROWS* / Decca

Michele Lee
Mar. 68   *L. DAVID SLOANE* / Columbia

Michel Legrand
Jan. 72   *BRIAN'S SONG* / Bell

Art Linkletter
Nov. 69   *WE LOVE YOU, CALL COLLECT* /
Capitol

Victor Lundberg
Nov. 67   *AN OPEN LETTER TO MY TEENAGE
SON* / Liberty

Cledus Maggard & The
Citizen's Band
Dec. 75   *THE WHITE KNIGHT* / Mercury
Apr. 76   *KENTUCKY MOONRUNNER* /
Mercury

Miriam Makeba
Oct. 67   *PATA PATA* / Reprise
Jan. 68   *MALAYISHA* / Reprise

Mandrill
June 71   *MANDRILL* / Polydor
Apr. 73   *FENCEWALK* / Polydor
Aug. 73   *HAND LOOSE* / Polydor

Bobbi Martin
Nov. 64   *DON'T FORGET I STILL LOVE
YOU* / Coral
Mar. 65   *I CAN'T STOP THINKING OF YOU* /
Coral
May 65   *I LOVE YOU SO* / Coral
Mar. 70   *FOR THE LOVE OF HIM* / United
Artists
July 70   *GIVE A WOMAN LOVE* / United
Artists

Robert Maxwell
Mar. 64   *SHANGRI-LA* / Decca
June 64   *PEG O' MY HEART* / Decca

Mercy
Apr. 69   *LOVE (CAN MAKE YOU HAPPY)* /
Sundi

Monarchs
Feb. 64   *LOOK HOMEWARD ANGEL* / Sound
Stage 7

Hugo Montenegro
Feb. 68   *THE GOOD, THE BAD AND THE
UGLY* / RCA Victor
June 68   *HANG 'EM HIGH* / RCA Victor

Napoleon XIV
July 66   *THEY'RE COMING TO TAKE ME
AWAY, HA-HA* / Warner Bros.

Neighborhood
June 70   *BIG YELLOW TAXI* / Big Tree

New Riders of the Purple Sage
June 72   *I DON'T NEED NO DOCTOR* /
Columbia

Cliff Nobles & Co
May 68   *THE HORSE* / Phil. L.A. of Soul
Sept. 68   *HORSE FEVER* / Phil. L.A. of Soul
Feb. 69   *SWITCH IT ON* / Phil. L.A. of Soul

Patty & the Emblems
June 64   *MIXED-UP, SHOOK-UP GIRL* / Herald

People's Choice
July 71   *I LIKES TO DO IT* / Phil L.A. of Soul
Aug. 75   *DO IT ANYWAY YOU WANNA* /
TSOP
Feb. 76   *NURSERY RHYMES (PART 1)* / TSOP

Peppermint Rainbow
Jan. 69   *WILL YOU BE STAYING AFTER
SUNDAY* / Decca
June 69   *DON'T WAKE ME UP IN THE
MORNING MICHAEL* / Decca

Pozo-Seco Singers

Feb. 66	*TIME* / Columbia
June 66	*I'LL BE GONE* / Columbia
Sept. 66	*I CAN MAKE IT WITH YOU* / Columbia
Dec. 66	*LOOK WHAT YOU'VE DONE* / Columbia
May 67	*I BELIEVE IT ALL* / Columbia
Sept. 67	*LOUISIANA MAN* / Columbia

Presidents

| Oct. 70 | *5-10-15-20 (25-30 YEARS OF LOVE)* / Sussex |

Arthur Prysock

| July 75 | *IT'S TOO LATE BABY TOO LATE* / Old Town |
| Dec. 76 | *WHEN LOVE IS NEW* / Old Town |

Rene & Rene

| July 64 | *ANGELITO* / Columbia |
| Nov. 68 | *LO MUCHO QUE TE QUIERO* / White Whale |

Reparata & The Delrons

| Jan. 65 | *WHENEVER A TEENAGER CRIES* / World Artists |
| May 65 | *TOMMY* / World Artists |

Miguel Rios

| June 70 | *A SONG OF JOY* / A & M |

Rivieras

Jan. 64	*CALIFORNIA SUN* / Riviera
May 64	*LITTLE DONNA* / Riviera
Sept. 64	*ROCKIN' ROBIN* / Riviera

Austin Roberts

| Oct. 72 | *SOMETHING'S WRONG WITH ME* / Chelsea |

Ronnie & The Daytonas

Aug. 64	*G.T.O.* / Mala
Nov. 64	*CALIFORNIA BOUND* / Mala
Dec. 64	*BUCKET T* / Mala

Jackie Ross

| Aug. 64 | *SELFISH ONE* / Chess |
| Nov. 64 | *I'VE GOT THE SKILL* / Chess |

Nino Rota

| Apr. 72 | *LOVE THEME FROM THE GODFATHER* / Paramount |

Royalettes

| July 65 | *IT'S GONNA TAKE A MIRACLE* / MGM |

Sailcat

| June 72 | *MOTORCYCLE MAMA* / Elektra |

San Remo Golden Strings

| Sept. 65 | *HUNGRY FOR LOVE* / Ric Tic |

Sapphires

| Jan. 64 | *WHO DO YOU LOVE* / Swan |

Lalo Schifrin

| Jan. 68 | *MISSION IMPOSSIBLE* / Dot |

Shades of Blue

| May 66 | *OH HOW HAPPY* / Impact |
| July 66 | *LONELY SUMMER* / Impact |

Jumpin' Gene Simmons

| Aug. 64 | *HAUNTED HOUSE* / Hi |

Sounds Orchestral

| Mar. 65 | *CAST YOUR FATE TO THE WIND* / Parkway |
| July 65 | *CANADIAN SUNSET* / Parkway |

Red Sovine

| July 76 | *TEDDY BEAR* / Starday |

Spiral Starecase

| Apr. 69 | *MORE TODAY THAN YESTERDAY* / Columbia |
| Aug. 69 | *NO ONE FOR ME TO TURN TO* / Columbia |

Street People

| Jan. 70 | *JENNIFER TOMKINS* / Musicor |

Sunshine Company

| July 67 | *HAPPY* / Imperial |
| Oct. 67 | *BACK ON THE STREET AGAIN* / Imperial |

Norma Tanega

| Feb. 66 | *WALKIN' MY CAT NAMED DOG* / New Voice |

T-Bones

| Dec. 65 | *NO MATTER WHAT SHAPE (YOUR STOMACH'S IN)* / Liberty |
| Mar. 66 | *SIPPIN' 'N' CHIPPIN'* / Liberty |

Teegarden & Van Winkle

| Sept. 70 | *GOD, LOVE AND ROCK n' ROLL* / Westbound |
| Dec. 70 | *EVERYTHING IS GOING TO BE ALRIGHT* / Westbound |

Tommy Tucker

| Feb. 64 | *HI-HEEL SNEAKERS* / Checker |
| May 64 | *LONG TALL SHORTY* / Checker |

Wadsworth Mansion

| Dec. 70 | *SWEET MARY* / Sussex |

Walter Wanderly

| Aug. 66 | *SUMMER SAMBA* / Verve |

White Plains

Apr. 70   *MY BABY LOVES LOVIN'* / Deram
Sept. 70   *LOVIN' YOU BABY* / Deram

Harlow Wilcox

Oct. 69   *GROOVY GRUBWORM* / Plantation

Danny Williams

Mar. 64   *WHITE ON WHITE* / United Artists
June 64   *A LITTLE TOY BALLOON* / United
Artists

John Williams

Aug. 75   *THEME FROM JAWS* / MCA

Jan. 78   *THEME FROM CLOSE
ENCOUNTERS OF THE THIRD
KIND* / Arista

J. Frank Wilson & The Cavaliers

Sept. 64   *LAST KISS* / Josie
Nov. 64   *HEY LITTLE ONE* / Josie
Dec. 73   *LAST KISS* (rereleased) / Virgo

Winstons

May 69   *COLOR HIM FATHER* / Metromedia
Sept. 69   *LOVE OF THE COMMON
PEOPLE* / Metromedia

Yellow Balloon

Apr. 67   *YELLOW BALLOON* / Canterbury

Barry Young

Nov. 65   *ONE HAS MY NAME* / Dot

Photo Credits

Page 1, Atlantic. **3,** Columbia. **5,** Capricorn. **6,** Warner/Reprise. **12,** Warner/Reprise. **14,** Kriegsmann. **15,** Atlantic. **16,** A & M. **17,** Chrysalis. **19,** Mercury. **21,** Portrait. **23,** Capitol. **25,** William Morris. **26,** United Artists. **27,** Arista. **28,** Apple. **29,** Apple. **32,** RSO. **37,** ABC/Michael Putland. **40,** Columbia. **44** (top), Mercury. **44** (bottom), Warner/Curb. **46,** Epic/Ron Pownall. **47,** RCA. **49,** Elektra. **53,** Kriegsmann. **54,** A & M. **55,** Asylum/Jim Shea. **57,** Columbia. **58,** Columbia. **60,** ABC. **61,** Columbia. **63,** United Artists. **65,** A & M. **67,** Arista. **69,** A & M. **72,** RCA. **73,** Warner/Curb. **76,** Elektra. **78,** William Morris. **79,** Columbia. **81,** Kriegsmann. **84,** Epic. **87,** A & M. **89,** Elektra. **91,** Kriegsmann. **93,** A & M. **95,** Warner/Reprise. **102,** Lifesong. **107,** Columbia. **109,** Columbia. **111,** Elektra. **113,** Kriegsmann. **117,** RCA. **123,** Columbia. **125,** Kriegsmann. **126,** RCA. **127,** Capitol/Tom Hill. **129,** Capitol. **130,** Epic. **132,** Warner/Reprise. **133,** Elektra. **134,** 20th Century. **135,** Epic. **138,** Columbia/Ken Regan. **141,** Kriegsmann. **143,** Columbia. **147,** United Artists. **149,** RSO. **150,** Atlantic. **151,** Columbia. **152,** Roadshow. **153,** Big Tree. **154,** CBS. **157,** Kriegsmann. **160,** RCA. **162,** ABC/Dot. **167,** Atlantic. **170** (top), Kriegsmann. **170** (bottom), Warner/Reprise. **172,** ABC. **174,** Kriegsmann. **177,** Atlantic. **179,** Warner/Curb. **181,** Kriegsmann. **182,** A & M. **184,** William Morris. **191,** Columbia. **193,** United Artists. **195,** Atlantic/David Gahr. **198,** RSO. **201,** Kriegsmann. **204,** Arista. **208,** RCA. **211,** Atlantic. **216,** Capitol. **217,** Atco. **218,** William Morris. **221,** Portrait. **222,** Reprise. **225,** Kriegsmann. **226,** Epic. **229,** Mercury. **231,** Big Tree. **234,** RCA. **235,** Epic. **237,** Columbia. **243,** RCA. **246,** Mercury. **247,** Grunt. **249,** RCA. **251,** Columbia. **252,** MCA. **256,** Epic. **258,** Columbia. **259,** Epic. **261,** Motown. **264,** Arista/David Gahr. **265,** Kriegsmann. **266,** William Morris. **270,** Columbia. **273,** William Morris. **275,** Swan Song. **276,** Kriegsmann. **277,** Capitol. **281,** Warner/Reprise. **284,** Harvest/Neil Zlozower/Mirage. **285,** Epic. **286,** Columbia. **289,** 20th Century. **291,** A & M. **292,** MCA.

295 (top), William Morris. **295** (bottom), Capitol. **296,** Capitol. **298,** William Morris. **301,** United Artists. **305,** Arista. **306,** Kriegsmann. **307,** Atlantic. **308,** Arista/Lee Gurst. **310,** Kriegsmann. **313,** Columbia. **316,** Cleveland International. **318,** William Morris. **321,** Atlantic. **322,** Columbia. **324,** Capitol. **326,** Asylum/Norman Seeff. **328,** William Morris. **330,** London. **332,** William Morris. **333,** CBS. **336,** Capitol. **339** (top), Atlantic. **339** (bottom), A & M. **343,** Warner Bros. **345,** MCA. **346,** RSO. **347,** United Artists. **349,** United Artists. **350,** Epic/Ron Pownall. **351,** William Morris. **355,** Mercury. **356,** Philadelphia International. **360,** Asylum. **365,** A & M. **366,** Mercury. **367,** Kriegsmann. **368,** RCA. **369,** William Morris. **370,** William Morris. **373,** Columbia. **375,** RSO. **379,** RCA. **381,** Kriegsmann. **385,** Elektra/Christopher Hopper. **389,** Warner/Reprise. **391,** Kriegsmann. **392,** Philadelphia International. **394,** Capitol. **395,** William Morris. **398,** Mercury. **399,** William Morris. **400,** Epic. **401,** Motown. **403,** Rolling Stones. **405,** Asylum. **408,** King. **409,** Motown. **411,** William Morris. **412,** Bearsville. **417,** United Artists. **420,** Warner/Reprise. **421,** Columbia. **422,** Warner Bros. **424,** Kriegsmann. **426,** MCA. **427,** Capitol. **430,** Kama Sutra. **431,** Kriegsmann. **435,** Elektra. **438,** Columbia. **442,** William Morris. **446,** Atlantic. **449,** Mercury. **451,** Atlantic. **452,** Columbia. **453,** William Morris. **456,** Windsong. **457** (top), Kriegsmann. **457** (bottom), Capitol. **458,** Capitol. **459,** Mercury. **461,** Kriegsmann. **464,** A & M. **466,** Warner Bros. **468,** Kama Sutra. **469,** Columbia. **472,** Kriegsmann. **473,** Casablanca. **475,** Capitol. **477,** Capitol. **479,** Capitol. **481,** Columbia. **484,** Motown. **486,** Mercury. **490,** Mercury. **491,** William Morris. **493,** Epic. **494,** Kriegsmann. **497,** Kriegsmann. **499,** Warner Bros. **501,** Midland International. **504,** Fontana. **505,** Buddah. **510,** Atlantic. **511,** Reprise. **516,** Kriegsmann. **518,** Epic. **520,** William Morris. **522,** MCA. **523,** Epic. **524,** William Morris. **525,** William Morris. **527,** Blue Sky. **528,** Columbia. **529,** United Artists. **530,** William Morris. **534,** Epic. **535,** Atlantic. **536,** Kriegsmann. **539,** RCA. **540,** Kriegsmann. **541,** Kriegsmann.

Index of Song Titles: "Top 100's"

Index of Song Titles

B

Index of Song Titles

C

Index of Song Titles

D

Index of Song Titles

Index of Song Titles

G

Index of Song Titles

H

Index of Song Titles

I

Index of Song Titles

Index of Song Titles

Index of Song Titles

L

Index of Song Titles

Index of Song Titles

N

Index of Song Titles

Index of Song Titles

Index of Song Titles

S

Index of Song Titles

Index of Song Titles

T

Index of Song Titles

U

V

Index of Song Titles